Export Control Law and Regulations Handbook

Global Trade Law Series

VOLUME 33

Series Editors

Prof. Ross P. Buckley, King & Wood Mallesons Professor of International Finance Law, Faculty of Law, University of New South Wales, Sydney, Australia
Prof. Andreas R. Ziegler, Faculty of Law, Criminal Sciences, and Public Administration, University of Lausanne, Switzerland

Introduction and Contents/Subjects

The *Global Trade Law Series* addresses key issues in international trade law. It covers a broad range of topics, including WTO dispute settlement, free trade agreements, investment law and arbitration, export control, and compliance with international trade obligations.

Objective & Readership

The volumes published in this series are aimed at offering high-quality analytical information and practical solutions, for practitioners, policy makers and academics.

Frequency of Publication

2-3 new volumes published each year.

The titles published in this series are listed at the end of this volume.

Export Control Law and Regulations Handbook

A Practical Guide to Military and Dual-Use Goods Trade Restrictions and Compliance

Third Edition

Edited by

Yann Aubin

Arnaud Idiart

Wolters Kluwer

Published by:
Kluwer Law International B.V.
PO Box 316
2400 AH Alphen aan den Rijn
The Netherlands
Website: www.wklawbusiness.com

Sold and distributed in North, Central and South America by:
Wolters Kluwer Legal & Regulatory U.S.
7201 McKinney Circle
Frederick, MD 21704
United States of America
Email: customer.service@wolterskluwer.com

Sold and distributed in all other countries by:
Turpin Distribution Services Ltd
Stratton Business Park
Pegasus Drive, Biggleswade
Bedfordshire SG18 8TQ
United Kingdom
Email: kluwerlaw@turpin-distribution.com

Printed on acid-free paper.

ISBN 978-90-411-5443-9

Cover design by Dominique Idiart

Printed in the United Kingdom.

FSC
MIX
FSC® C103993

List of Editors*

Yann Aubin

Yann Aubin is the Director of Compliance of Schlumberger. Prior to assuming his current role, Aubin served as the company's Director of Legal Operations, and, previously, held the position of General Counsel, Europe and Africa.

Aubin graduated from the Widener Law School in Delaware, United States of America where he received a Master's degree in law (LLM) and from the University of Paris X Nanterre, France where he received a PhD in law.

Aubin's recent publication include: International Bank and Other Guarantees Handbook, Africa and Middle East volume, Wolters Kluwer, lead editor.

Arnaud Idiart

Arnaud Idiart is the Head of Export Compliance for France for the Airbus Group. Prior to this role, Idiart held a variety of positions, over a twenty-eight years career, in the French military and more specifically within the French Ministry of Defense Export Control Department.

Idiart is the Chairman of the Committee of Foreign Export Control Regulations of the *Groupement des Industries Françaises Aéronautiques et Spatiales* (GIFAS).
Idiart also teaches at Paris I – La Sorbonne University and Paris XI – Sceaux University and regularly presents to vocational training seminars.

Idiart's recent publication include: *Droit de l'espace – télécommunications, observation, navigation, défense, exploration,* (co-author) Bruxelles, Larcier, 2009 (ouvrage collectif sous notre direction), 384 p. http://www.idest-paris.org/fr/parution-de-louvrage-droit-de-lespace-298.
'Pratiques Juridiques dans l'industrie aéronautique et spatiale' (co-author) 2014: http://www.pedone.info/715-Idest/Pratiques.html.

---

* The views or opinions expressed in the Export Control Laws and Regulations Handbook do not necessarily represent those of the Editors' respective employers.

List of Editors

List of Contributors

COMPLETE LIST OF CONTRIBUTORS TO THIS AND PREVIOUS EDITIONS

The list below contains the name and affiliations of each of the contributors to the Handbook since it was first published in 2007.

Name of Contributor	*Affiliation*	*Position*	*Chapter*	*Edition*
Lourdes Catrain	Hogan Lovells International LLP	Partner	Sanctions & Embargos	Third edition
Beth Peters	Hogan Lovells International LLP	Partner	Sanctions & Embargos	Third edition
Haley Boyette	Hogan Lovells International LLP	Partner	Sanctions & Embargos	Third edition
Christopher Lock	Hogan Lovells International LLP	Associate	Sanctions & Embargos	Third edition
Philippe Achilleas	Master on Space Activities and Telecommunications Law, University Paris Sud Sceaux, France	Director	International Regimes	First, Second and Third editions
Pedro Paulo Salles Cristofaro	Lobo & Ibeas	Partner	Brazil	Third edition
Daniela Bessone	Lobo & Ibeas	Partner	Brazil	Third edition
Daniel de Avila Vio	Lobo & Ibeas	Partner	Brazil	Third edition
Thiago Dias Oliva	Lobo & Ibeas	Associate	Brazil	Third edition

Name of Contributor	*Affiliation*	*Position*	*Chapter*	*Edition*
Marion Feurtey	Airbus Group	Business Strategy Analyst	China	Third edition
Jun Wei	Hogan Lovells International LLP	Partner	China	First edition
Steven Robinson	Hogan Lovells International LLP	Partner	China	First edition
Wen Jin	Paris Sud-11 University Law School Master on Space Activities and Telecommunications Law	Graduate	China	First edition
Marion Ringot	Stelia Aerospace, an Airbus Group subsidiary	Head of Export Compliance	The European Union and France	Third edition
Aude de Clercq	Paris Sud-11 University Law School Master on Space Activities and Telecommunications Law	Graduate	The European Union	First and second editions
Laurent Papiernik	Paris Sud-11 University Law School Master on Space Activities and Telecommunications Law	Graduate	The European Union	First and second editions
Virgile Delaboudinière	Paris Sud-11 University Law School Master on Space Activities and Telecommunications Law	Graduate	France	First edition
Henrik Brethauer	Airbus Group	Group Export Compliance Officer, Germany	Germany	Third edition
Wolfgang Sosic	Diehl BGT Defence GmbH	Head of Export Control	Germany	Second edition

Name of Contributor	*Affiliation*	*Position*	*Chapter*	*Edition*
Richard Hesse	Airbus Group (previously named EADS Deutschland)	Head of Export Control, Germany	Germany	First and second editions
Anand Prasad	Trilegal law firm	Partner	India	First, Second and Third editions
Samsuddha Majumder	Trilegal law firm	Partner	India	Third edition
Doron Hindin	Herzog Fox & Neeman	Consultant	Israel	Third edition
Stefano Tosi	Finmeccanica	Head of Trade Compliance and Export Control	Italy	Third edition
Anna Chiara Mazza	Finmeccanica	Trade Compliance and Export Control	Italy	Third edition
Massimo Viscogliosi	MBDA	Head of Export Control, Italy	Italy	First and second editions
Fabio Goj	Paris Sud-11 University Law School Master on Space Activities and Telecommunications Law	Graduate	Italy	First and second editions
Shinji Itoh	Hayabusa Asuka Law Offices	Partner	Japan	Third edition
Takehiro Fujita	Hayabusa Asuka Law Offices	Associate	Japan	Third edition
Yasufumi Shiroyama	Anderson Mori & Tomotsune	Partner	Japan	First edition
Mika Yamanka	Paris Sud-11 University Law School Master on Space Activities and Telecommunications Law	Graduate	Japan	First edition

Name of Contributor	*Affiliation*	*Position*	*Chapter*	*Edition*
Juliette Boutard	Airbus Group (previously named EADS/SMO)	Business Analyst, Japan	Japan	Second edition
Clémence Bastien	Airbus Helicopters	Chief of Staff for Executive VP Industry	Russia	First, Second and Third editions
Iliya Zotkin	King & Spalding LLC	Counsel	Russia	First, Second and Third editions
Ivan Davydov	King & Spalding LLC	Associate	Russia	First, Second and Third editions
Grégory Mardian	Paris Sud-11 University Law School Master on Space Activities and Telecommunications Law	Graduate	Russia	First edition
David de Terán	Airbus Defense and Space	Head of Export Compliance, Spain	Spain	Second and third editions
Isabela Ardalan	Paris Sud-11 University Law School Master on Space Activities and Telecommunications Law	Graduate	Spain	First edition
David Contreras	Airbus Group (previously named EADS Casa)	Head of Export Control Spain	Spain	First edition
Mattias Hedwall	Trade & Commerce practice group at Baker & McKenzie	Partner	Sweden	Third edition
David Lorello	Covington & Burling	Partner	United Kingdom	Third edition
Farouk Saeed	Thales UK	Head of Export Control Compliance and Regulations, United Kingdom	United Kingdom	First edition

Name of Contributor	*Affiliation*	*Position*	*Chapter*	*Edition*
Alexandre Gelbard	Paris Sud-11 University Law School Master on Space Activities and Telecommunications Law	Graduate	United Kingdom	First edition
Corinne Kaplan	Airbus Defense and Space	Vice-President, Trade Compliance, North America	US	Third edition
Candace M.J. Goforth	Goforth Trade Advisors, LLC	Managing Director	US	Third edition
Julia Mason	FD Associates	Senior Associate	US	Third edition
Dennis Burnett	Airbus Group (previously named EADS)	Head of Trade Compliance and Export Control for North America	US	First and second editions

The Editors would like to thank also the following contributors to this edition or to previous editions.

Khayala Rzazade is a Paris Sud-11 University Law School Master on Space Activities and Telecommunications Law Graduate, whose help was invaluable in putting together the expanded and reformatted third edition.

Haziz Ouattara is a Paris Sud-11 University Law School Master on Space Activities and Telecommunications Law Graduate, for the compilation of the annex documentation.

Amal Rakibi is a Paris Sud-11 University Law School Master on Space Activities and Telecommunications Law Graduate who has more specifically contributed to the US chapter of the first edition of the Handbook.

CONTRIBUTORS OF THIS EDITION

Philippe Achilleas is Professor, University Caen-Basse Normandie (CRDFEV), Director of the Master on Space Activities and Telecommunications Law and Director of the Institute of Space and Telecommunications Law (IDEST), University Paris Sud, Sceaux, France.

Daniel de Avila Vio is a practicing lawyer in Corporate Law, Capital Markets and Contracts in Brazil. Mr Vio is Master (2009) and Ph.D. (2014) in Commercial Law from the University of São Paulo Law School. Mr Vio also graduated in International Relations from the Catholic University of São Paulo.

Clémence Bastien currently is Chief of Staff of Airbus Helicopters' Executive-Vice President for Industry. She previously held positions in the Sales and Customer Relations Directory of Airbus Group, as Contracts Director and Key Account Managers for Airbus' customers in China and Airbus Helicopters' customers in Russia and Central Asia. She holds Master Degrees in Political Sciences from IEP Paris and in International Public Law from Paris XI University.

Daniela Bessone is a partner of Lobo & Ibeas. Mrs. Bessone has vast experience with Intellectual Property matters and also specializes in Mining, Contracts and Civil Litigation.

Haley Boyette is Corporate Counsel for Global Trade at Pfizer, a global pharmaceutical company. Prior to joining Pfizer, Ms Boyette practiced for over ten years in the Washington, D.C. office of Hogan Lovells US LLP, as an attorney in the International Trade and Investment Group. She holds a J.D. from Duke University School of Law and a B.A. from the University of Alabama.

Henrik Brethauer LL.M. (Canterbury) is member of the Group Export Compliance Office of Airbus Group in Germany.

Lourdes Catrain is a partner in the international law firm of Hogan Lovells and heads the firm's Trade and Investment Group in the EU. Recognized by Chambers and Legal 500, Ms Catrain has achieved milestone successes for clients on all areas of EU trade law and economic sanctions. She holds a law degree from Universidad Complutense (Madrid) and an LL.M. from the University of Michigan.

Pedro Paulo Salles Cristofaro is a partner of Lobo & Ibeas. Mr. Cristofaro. He specializes in Antitrust and Regulatory Law, Litigation, Contracts, Corporate Law and M&A Transactions. Mr. Cristofaro holds a Master of Law degree from University of Paris X, Nanterre (1994) and teaches Commercial Law and Antitrust Law at the Catholic University of Rio de Janeiro Law School.

Ivan Davydov is an associate in King & Spalding's Moscow office and a member of the Corporate Practice Group. Mr Davydov's practice includes advising clients on various aspects of international as well as domestic business transactions and corporate matters, including mergers and acquisitions, corporate reorganizations and corporate governance issues. Mr Davydov has vast experience advising clients on a wide range of Russian antitrust issues as well as on various issues of Russian law related to advertising, real estate, telecommunications, customs and export control-related issues.

Marion Feurtey is a strategy analyst with the Airbus Group. She holds a Master Degree in International Affairs (Chinese track) from the Institute of Political Sciences in Lyon, and an Advanced Master in strategy from ESSEC Business School.

Takehiro Fujita has developed expertise in finance and regulatory matters, advising local and foreign clients, and regularly handles general corporate, commercial and other transactions. He is a partner at Hayabusa Asuka Law Offices and holds an LL.B. from Keio University and an LL.M. from Boston University, School of Law.

Candace Goforth is Managing Director for Goforth Trade Advisors, LLC. In this capacity she provides strategic and advisory consulting services to US and non-US entities seeking successful compliance with US export/import laws and regulations. Previously she spent fifteen years at the Department of State where she served as the Director for Defense Trade Controls Policy.

Mattias Hedwall is a partner in the Trade & Commerce practice group at Baker & McKenzie's office in Stockholm. Mr Hedwall heads up Baker & McKenzie's EMEA Trade & Commerce group which has over 100 lawyers specializing in trade compliance and commercial agreements including but not limited to export control and trade sanctions.

Doron Hindin practices law in the US and Israel, advising local and foreign clients on regulatory and commercial matters related to international trade (including export controls and trade sanctions), anti-bribery compliance and a range of complex matters related to public international law and business and human rights. He is a consultant at Israel's premier international law firm, Herzog Fox and Neeman, and holds an LL.B. from Bar-Ilan University and an LL.M. from Columbia Law School.

Shinji Itoh has developed expertise in finance and real estate investment, advising local and foreign clients, and regularly handles international corporate, commercial and other transactions (including export controls and trade sanctions). He is a managing partner at Hayabusa Asuka Law Offices and holds an LL.B. from Waseda University and an LL.M. from Cornel Law School.

Corinne Kaplan is Vice-President Affiliate Trade Compliance at Airbus Defence and Space, Inc. In this capacity, she provides advocacy and guidance to Airbus's non-US affiliates on implementing compliance to US. Regulations and optimizing US licensing strategy in support of the execution of the programmes. Rudy Scott, also of Airbus Defence and Space, Inc., provided editing and proofreading support.

David Lorello is a partner in Covington & Burling's London office and serves as a vice chair of the firm's International Trade and Finance practice group. Mr Lorello advises clients concerning a range of international regulatory, white collar, and commercial matters under both European and US laws, with a particular focus on US and EU export controls and economic sanctions laws. Mr Lorello is a US lawyer but has worked in the European market for over a decade, and thus has equal fluency with regard to the US and EU trade controls regimes. He supports a broad range of international companies on these issues across industries, and is recognized in the leading peer review publications for his work on both compliance and investigations matters.

Christopher Lock is an associate in the international law firm Hogan Lovells and member of the firm's International Trade and Investment Group. Mr Lock specializes in helping clients understand EU export controls and economic sanctions, including coordinating EU trade investigations. He holds an undergraduate degree in law from Oxford University and a Masters in International Relations from the College of Europe, Bruges.

Samsuddha Majumder is partner of Trilegal, one of India's leading law firms, and is part of its tax practice. Samsuddha has been extensively involved in advising clients on direct and indirect tax matters specifically including foreign trade and export control related issues, Customs duty, Central and State Excise, VAT and Service tax; special tax-status units, corporate income taxation, international taxation and taxation aspects of M&A transactions. He advises clients in a wide range of industry sectors such as defence, aerospace and heavy engineering, manufacturing, retail, infrastructure and information technology. Samsuddha is an alumnus of National Law School, Bangalore and UCLA School of Law.

Julia Mason is a Sr. Associate at FD Associates and provides strategic planning, license, training, compliance plans and audit services to small and medium size US and non-US companies.

Beth Peters is a partner in the international law firm of Hogan Lovells US LLP and Co-Director of the firm's International Trade and Investment Group and has been in practice for over twenty-five years. Recognized by Chambers and Legal 500, Ms Peters advises clients on a variety of international trade matters, including export control laws, anti-money laundering and sanctions laws, and customs laws. She holds a J.D. from Columbia University and a B.A. from Duke University.

Anand Prasad is Partner at Trilegal, one of India's leading law firms, and is part of the corporate practice group of the firm. Anand specializes in investment structuring, establishing joint ventures, mergers and acquisitions, private equity deals and cross border and domestic financing. He has a significant experience in representing both international and domestic clients in a cross-section of sectors such as defence, aviation, security systems, telecoms, manufacturing and heavy industries. Anand has decades of experience in advising on the regulation and policy involved in doing business with government and public sector enterprises, including with relation to tender, procurement and licensing processes. Anand is an alumnus of the Symbiosis Society's Law College, Pune. He is a member of Supreme Court Bar Association, Delhi High Court Bar Association and Bar Council of Delhi. He is the Vice Chair of the Society of Indian Law Firms (SILF).

Marion Ringot has been the Head of Export Control, Risk Management and Internal Audit of Stelia Aerospace since January 2016. Prior to her current role, Ringot has held various Export Control related positions over a ten-year span within Airbus Group. Ringot regularly lectures on French, European or US export control regulations.

Anna Chiara Mazza works in Trade Compliance and export control in Finmeccanica Legal and Corporate Affairs and Compliance Directorate, Airborne and Space Systems, Land and Naval Defence Electronics and Security and Information Systems Divisions. She has been head of National Licensing Support of the Aircraft Division of Finmeccanica after a four-year-experience in the same function, supporting business on regulatory and commercial matters related to national trade compliance and keeping well-founded relations with the accountable bodies of the public administration. A new experience in the International Export Control is now starting off. She joined Finmeccanica Group in 2004 and the Defence Sector in 2007. She earned a Ph.D. in Political Science from the L.U.I.S.S. Guido Carli (the Guido Carli Free International University for Social Studies) in Rome, Italy.

Thiago Dias Oliva is an associate of Lobo & Ibeas. Mr. Oliva specializes in Corporate Law and Contracts. Mr. Oliva is Master in Human Rights from the University of São Paulo Law School (2015).

Stefano Tosi is the head of Trade Compliance and export control in Finmeccanica Legal and Corporate Affairs and Compliance Directorate, Airborne and Space Systems, Land and Naval Defence Electronics and Security and Information Systems Divisions. He took on this role following a three-year-experience in Finmeccanica Corporate and after several appointments in the Aircraft Division of Finmeccanica as Trade Compliance Coordinator and head of Import-Export Compliance, supporting business on regulatory and commercial matters related to national and international trade compliance and keeping well-founded relations with the accountable bodies of the public administration. He joined Finmeccanica Group and the Defence Sector in 2008 after having practiced the legal profession. He earned a Ph.D. in Law from the University of Rome La Sapienza (Università degli Studi di Roma La Sapienza), Italy.

Iliya Zotkin is a Counsel in King & Spalding's Moscow office and practices in the areas of corporate acquisitions, real estate, and general corporate and transactional advice.

His practice includes advice on mergers and acquisitions (including, *inter alia*, in respect of companies holding and developing substantial real estate), green-field projects in the areas of real estate and industry, real estate development projects as well as representation of clients in connection with various issues regarding commercial operation of real estate. Mr Zotkin represented clients in litigations in connection with a wide variety of disputes, including corporate and commercial dispute.

Summary of Contents

Table of Contents

Foreword

As Chairman of the Board of Directors of the Airbus Group, a global leader in aerospace and defence, I am proud to have been asked to provide a preface to the third edition of the Export Control Laws and Regulations Handbook.

The Board of Directors of the Airbus Group ensures specifically that the Airbus Group is committed to complying with all the laws of the countries in which it operates. Amongst the various laws and rules that are applicable to the activities of the Airbus Group, compliance with export controls requirements is very high on the agenda. Being able to ensure compliance with laws and regulations, particularly in the field of export controls, can reveal itself to be very complex. This is why we have welcomed the opportunity to work with a network of scholars and legal professionals around the world gathered through the Export Control Laws and Regulations Handbook project.

The Export Control Laws and Regulations Handbook is the result of a partnership between the Airbus Group (which then was called EADS) and the law school of Paris XI University. We very much support a model where industry practitioners and scholars work together to make available clear, concise and precise knowledge on a field of the law in constant evolution, where very little literature exist and which is key for the Group, its supply chain as well as all companies who want to trade internationally.

The partnership between the Airbus Group and Paris XI University began ten years ago. Such longevity is in itself a sign of success. However, success lies in the sustained efforts of the editors and contributors of the Export Control Laws and Regulations Handbook who have, edition after edition, continued to improve the content.

We are pleased to share the outcome of this unique enterprise with all.

Denis Ranque
Airbus Group
Chairman of the Board of Directors

The Wassenaar Arrangement works day in and day out to enhance an international order of security, peace and law. These efforts have contributed to greater stability, security and peace in many areas of the world. However, every year the forty-one Member States face new challenges.

One of these challenges is for the Wassenaar Arrangement to take into account the rapid development of technology, a constantly changing security environment and new market trends to create a strong common framework for the control of exports of Defence and Dual-Use products as well as related information and services. Adopted in 2013, the United Nations Arms Trade Treaty provides a new framework to those countries which have not yet adopted a fully comprehensive national export control system.

The European Union plays an important role in setting international standards for strategic trade control. By incorporating the control lists of all the export control regimes in the EU Dual-Use List and the Common Military List, the EU has created an international standard that more and more countries around the world strive to adopt. In addition, initiatives such as the adoption of the Common Rules for the exports of military goods have identified important criteria that need to be considered before a licence for export of a sensitive item is granted. More can be and should be achieved as mutual confidence among nations grows.

Ensuring that truly efficient rules exist and are enforced by the Wassenaar Arrangement partners constitutes one of the most important prerequisites for the success of a consistent streamlined European legislation with respect to export controls.

For all these reasons I warmly welcome the new edition of the Export Control Laws and Regulations Handbook. This is a joint initiative by industry practitioners, experts and university scholars and provides a gold mine of information in an area of law which is quite unknown, namely the laws and regulations which govern the trade in military or dual-use goods or services.

The Export Control Laws and Regulations Handbook, has been conceived to be practical in every respect. I am certain that it will be a valuable tool for companies involved in the commerce of controlled goods or services, particularly small or medium size enterprises for which the costs and time to understand how to comply with the related laws and regulations can be significant.

The Wassenaar Arrangement was set up to promote transparency and greater responsibility in transfers of conventional arms and dual-use goods and technologies and it has developed a number of best practice documents which are aimed at more responsible policy and a sound control of armaments and related technology. Indeed, the knowledge of laws and regulations, as well as the dissemination of good practices is an essential step towards achieving these goals.

Finally, I specifically like the Export Control Laws and Regulations Handbook because it gives an outstanding example of a private sector contribution to effective export controls, and is a very good example of how beneficial it is to bring the diversity of competences together through international cooperation.

Ambassador Sune Danielson
Former Head of Secretariat
Wassenaar Arrangement

Ambassador Sune Danielson is since June 2012 an independent consultant, expert of questions relating to non-proliferation and control of sensitive exports; adviser about items to be controlled and best practices for governments and industry. From June 2002 to June 2012, Ambassador Sune Danielson was the Head of Secretariat of the Wassenaar Arrangement an organisation for export control of conventional weapons and dual-use goods and technologies with forty-one Member States. He has been awarded the Grosses Goldenes Ehrenzeichen Mit Dem Stern für Verdienste um die Republik Österreich and the French Légion d'Honneur au grade de Chevalier.

Preface

Four years have passed by since the publication of the second edition the Export Control Laws and Regulations Handbook (the 'Handbook'). Very significant changes have taken place since 2011 in respect to export controls around the world. Out of all of the changes that have occurred, we would like to highlight three which we believe are transforming export controls globally.

The first change relate to the developments of the legal and regulatory regimes of a number of countries leading to a continued overall strengthening of the requirements applying to export controls regimes.

The second change has been the implementation of new sets of sanctions and embargos (e.g., Russia) while relaxing some of the existing ones (e.g., Myanmar, Cuba, Iran). The European Union, particularly for the sanctions against Russia in response to the Crimea annexation, has made its position evolve very significantly from that standpoint.

The third change is the drastic increase in the enforcement from governments around the world of trade control related laws and regulations.

We have amended the Handbook to reflect those evolutions. As a result, we have:

(1) Updated all the existing Handbook chapters to reflect relevant legal and regulatory evolutions;
(2) We have added three new country chapters (Brazil, Israel and Sweden) as we felt that those countries now play a significant role in the field of export controls; and
(3) We have also added a separate new chapter on sanctions and embargos and, in each country chapter, we have added a specific new section on sanctions and embargos.

In addition, we have updated the Handbook's annexes. Those annexes continue to contain a variety of practical documents (including standard export control compliance programme documents which companies may consider to use as a starting point to draft their own compliance programme). Where export control agency of countries covered in the Handbook simplified their processes through an internet based platform (in particular, to request export or import licences), we have provided the details of the same without appending a copy of the standard forms). Those annexes are too bulky to be part of the Handbook and are available on a dedicated URL: www.kluwer lawonline.com/eclrh-annexes.

The structure and organisation of the Handbook remain the same however. In particular, each country chapter remains built on an identical structure so that readers can find information more easily. We have finished the overall drafting and review of the Handbook in December 2015 and information contained in the Handbook is generally current up to that date. However, readers should know that the export controls laws and regulations evolve rapidly and constantly.

We hope that you will find as much interest reading the third edition of the Export Control Laws and Regulations Handbook than we had drafting it. This book is also yours. So if you have feedback, questions or comments, we would be delighted to get them. Should you wish to contact us, please send your comments to: contact. editors@gmail.com.

CHAPTER 1
Overall Introduction

Yann Aubin & Arnaud Idiart

Export control laws and regulations are an exception to free trade principles that govern international commercial exchanges.[1] Companies offering controlled goods or

1. See, e.g., the GATT (Article 20) or the Treaty of Rome (Article 296), both of which contain specific exclusions to ensure that the essential security interests of the parties to such agreements are

services need to comply with such rather complex and moving area of the law, wherever they are operating around the world.

The primary objective of the Export Control Laws and Regulations Handbook (hereinafter the 'Handbook') is to provide details to the readers on how certain countries around the world regulate, in particular, the manufacturing and exportation of products and technologies created under their jurisdiction. The scope of export control laws and regulations is now broader than the manufacturing and exportation of products and technologies (as it also touches the movement of people or financial streams). The Handbook does cover these aspects as well.

In this Overall Introduction, we will describe what the scope of the Handbook is (Section 1. Scope of the Handbook), what the terms and concepts used are (Section 2. Terminology and Concepts Used), what methodology has been followed in drafting each of the chapters (Section 3. Methodology Used), and provide an overview of the most salient features as well as current and future challenges of export control laws and regulations (Section 4. Current and Future Challenges). Finally, we have inserted some words of caution as to how the Handbook should be used in a notice section (Section 5. Notice).

SECTION 1 SCOPE OF THE HANDBOOK

The Handbook covers the legal and regulatory requirements on military and dual-use goods and services (Sub-Section 1) together with embargoes and related sanctions (Sub-Section 2). For the sake of clarity, we will expressly list the issues related or connected to export controls that are not covered by the Handbook (Sub-Section 3).

Sub-Section 1 A Particular Focus on Military and Dual-Use Goods and Services

Controls are also made on exports of nuclear, chemical, biological, military (which include weapons of mass destruction (WMD)) or dual-use goods,[2] technology (including software) or services. However, in reality, both from a quantity and a money value standpoint, an overwhelming proportion of the controlled exports relate only to military and dual-use goods, technology and services. The reason is that nuclear,

---

preserved. Such provisions are based on the founding and overarching principle contained in the United Nations Charter for the maintenance of international peace and security; its Article 51 which is as follows:

> *Nothing in the present Charter shall impair the inherent right of individual or collective self-defence if an armed attack occurs against a Member of the United Nations, until the Security Council has taken measures necessary to maintain international peace and security. Measures taken by Members in the exercise of this right of self-defence shall be immediately reported to the Security Council and shall not in any way affect the authority and responsibility of the Security Council under the present Charter to take at any time such action as it deems necessary in order to maintain or restore international peace and security.*

2. See *infra* definition of the term 'goods' in section Chapter 1, Section 2, Sub-Section 1.

chemical or biological weapons are hardly exported, and when they are exported, they are subject to specific laws and regulations.[3]

However, even though the Handbook country chapters' focus is military and dual-use goods, all major international treaties or programmes (including those which address nuclear, or biological or chemical weapons) are dealt with in the International Regime chapter of the Handbook. In addition, each country chapter of the Handbook provides a chart showing each country's participation to export control-related international treaties and programmes.

Sub-Section 2 Embargoes and Sanctions

The embargoes or related trade sanctions which are, from time to time, imposed by the international community, some groups of countries (e.g., the European Union) or individual countries have become an essential component of today's international relations and international trade. Embargoes and sanctions are one of the tools that states use to attempt to produce certain geopolitical outcomes.

The impact of embargoes and sanctions can be very drastic for the countries which are targeted but also for the industries and companies of the targeted country as well as companies from other countries doing business with that country. It is therefore critical for businesses to know whether their activities fall into the scope of any embargo or sanction related laws and regulations.

Sub-Section 3 Some Purposefully Excluded Elements

The Export Control Laws and Regulations Handbook does not aims at covering[4] laws and regulations dealing with related or connected subjects such as the following: (i) bribery in international commerce;[5] (ii) arms brokering; (iii) the participation in boycotts by other nations of third countries;[6] (iv) exchange control or currency regulation; (v) tax and custom duties; (vi) foreign investments; (vii) control of disclosure of classified information (i.e., information which, if they are disclosed to a foreign person, may endanger national security) or (viii) anti-trust.

All above-mentioned subjects are matters which are related to export controls in general but they are to be carefully looked at in the context of an export of military or

3. See the SIPRI Yearbook 2015 on Armaments, disarmaments and international security.
   In respect to dual-use products, evaluation of the exports volumes are difficult to make. They are in any event much more important than the export of military goods and services. In contrast, exports relating to weapons of mass destruction, nuclear, chemical or bacteriologic weapons have been significantly lower.
4. Chapters of the Export Control Laws and Regulations Handbook may, however, deal with such matters incidentally.
5. OECD Convention on Combating Bribery of Foreign Public Officials in International Business Transactions (http://www.oecd.org/document/20/0,2340,en_2649_34859_2017813_1_1_1_1,0 0.html) and the transposition of such convention into a number of domestic laws around the world.
6. Some references to boycotts can be found in the Export Control Handbook however (please further refer to the index for that purpose).

dual-use goods. In most cases, however, the issues linked to classified information and to foreign investments related laws and regulations will always have to be investigated since they are more directly connected to the control of exports of military or dual-use goods.

SECTION 2 TERMINOLOGY AND CONCEPTS USED[7]

Sub-Section 1 What Is an 'Export'?

Although the definition may vary according to the various applicable laws and regulations, export can be defined as an item that is sent from one country (the 'country of exportation') to a foreign country (the 'country of destination'). The term 'item' covers hardware, software or technology (which can include such things from clothing, building materials, circuit boards, automotive parts to blue prints, design plans, retail software packages or technical information). In the Export Control Handbook, except if the context in which they are used dictates otherwise, the terms 'goods', 'items' or 'equipment' shall cover hardware, software, technology and services. We will use, throughout the Export Control Handbook, as much as possible and unless the context dictates otherwise, the word 'goods' (in the singular form as the case may be) as a generic term to designate collectively hardware, software, technology and services.

As a general rule, regardless of the applicable laws or regulations, for export controls/licensing purposes, the means by which the hardware, the software or the technology is exported, does not really matter. Such means could be regular mail or hand-carried, but also fax (in the case of documents (such as schematics)), Internet sites (in the case of software downloads or uploads), or e-mail (technology transfer) or during a telephone conversation. Regardless of the method used for the good's transfer, it is considered an export for export control purposes in most of the countries studied in the Export Control Handbook.

An item is also considered an export even if it is temporarily leaving the country, if it is leaving the exporting country but is not for sale, (e.g., a gift) or if it is going to a wholly owned subsidiary in a foreign country. In some cases, even a foreign-origin item exported from the exporting country, transmitted or transshipped through the exporting country, or being returned from the exporting country to its foreign country of origin may be considered an export.

7. The information contained in this section has been found, in large proportion, on the US BIS internet site (http://www.bis.doc.gov/). Some similar information can be found on other governmental internet sites (e.g., for a site in English please refer to the UK DTI internet site (https://www.gov.uk/government/organisations/export-control-organisation).

Finally, release of information relating to controlled technology to a foreign national in the exporting country is 'deemed' to be an export to the home country of the foreign national.[8] This is the case under the laws of the United States of America (USA or US).

Sub-Section 2 What Are 'Export Controls'?

For security reasons mainly, but also for other reasons such as technology protection, States control the hardware, the software or the technology/data leaving their territory (or in case of a 'deemed export' as known under USA law, leaving the territory by being transferred to a foreign national even on USA soil). Such controls will be referred to generally in the Export Control Laws and Regulations Handbook as 'export controls'.

There are also controls by States on imports. However, these controls are comparatively much less important than those relating to exports because States are more interested in ensuring the control over their hardware, software and technology. Imports related requirements are also addressed in the Export Control Handbook. Accordingly, for practical reasons, when referring to 'export controls', we more broadly refer to, when the context does not dictate otherwise, 'import/export controls'.

As already discussed above, export controls (and the Export Control Handbook) do not cover the control of disclosure of classified information.

In any event, in world trade exchanges, a relatively small percentage of total exports and re-exports require a licence. In almost all jurisdictions covered by the Export Control Handbook, the licence requirements are dependent upon the good's technical characteristics, the destination, the end-user and the end-use, and it is up to the exporter to determine whether the contemplated export requires a licence.

- ***The technical characteristics of the goods***

A key element when determining whether an export licence is needed from the exporting countries authorities is whether the item which is intended to export is referenced by a specific legal or regulatory text. Usually, the laws or rules provide for lists of goods, technology or services comprising broad categories, and with further subdivision into product groups.

- ***Destination to which the goods are to be exported***

Restrictions vary from country to country. The most restricted destinations are the embargoed countries.[9]

- ***The person who takes delivery the exported items (end-user)***

Certain individuals and organizations are prohibited from receiving certain exporting countries exports and others may only receive goods if they have been licensed, even for items that do not normally require a licence.

8. This topic is more specifically addressed in this Handbook in each country chapters under the heading 'Persons/ Deemed export'.
9. See *supra* n. 6.

• ***What will the item be used for (end-use)***

Certain end-uses are prohibited and others may require a licence.

It should further be noted that, as a last general remark on the licensing process principles, even in instances where a licence is required, a licence exception (or a simplified procedure) are available in a large proportion of jurisdictions when the end-use or end-user is linked to governmental interests.

SECTION 3 METHODOLOGY USED

Sub-Section 1 Export Control Laws and Regulations Handbook Overall Content

The Handbook covers the export control laws and regulations of fourteen countries (or groups of countries) (Brazil, China, the European Union, France, Germany, India, Israel, Italy, Japan, the Russian Federation, Spain, Sweden, the United Kingdom (UK) and the USA).

In addition, a specific chapter is dedicated to the international regimes which purpose is to provide details of each regime covered (such chapter's reach extends beyond those of the country chapters limited to mainly military and dual-use equipment, technologies and services, to include WMD, nuclear, chemical and biological weapons). Another specific chapter is dedicated to embargoes and related sanctions.

The countries have been selected on the basis of their importance in respect of the commerce of defence and dual-use goods/services.

Sub-Section 2 Export Control Laws and Regulations Handbook Chapters Content

All the country chapters of the Handbook have been drafted on the same structure pattern. The reason is to allow the readers to find the same information always at the same place regardless of which country chapter they are consulting.

Such a structure also allows an easier comparison of the regimes scrutinized.

The logic adopted in each country chapters is to propose a structure that allows direct access to the questions that an importer/exporter would be confronted to when having to deal with an import or export of some military or dual-use equipment, technology or services.

Each country chapter invariably contains:

(i) an executive summary;
(ii) an introduction which provides the overall philosophy of the export control laws and regulations of the countries analysed (i.e., is there emphasis on security concerns rather than liberty of commerce concerns, what are the main features of the regime studies, etc.), some historical elements (context explaining what main the regime studied what it is) and the

participation of the country studied to international regimes (in the form of a chart which is consistent with and refers to the overall chapter on international regimes);

(iii) the description of the regime itself respect to military goods, technology and services, on the one hand, and dual-use goods, technology, and services on the other hand;

(iv) a part on the specificities (i.e., those provisions that are specific to the country studied and do not exist elsewhere);

(v) a section on any specificities of the export control requirements impacting the space related technologies;

(vi) a section on embargoes and related sanctions;

(vii) a list of acronyms (to ease the readers' reading); and

(viii) some practical references (applicable laws and regulations, useful documents and contact details of the governmental departments or agencies in charge of the export control procedure or the related enforcement).

For the sections dealing with the military and dual-use equipment, technology and services export control regimes, a distinction has been made between the 'construction phase' (i.e., when a company wishes to manufacture certain products which it may export at a later stage, and for which a licence may be required for the manufacturing) and the export stage (i.e., when the products are exported or may be exported). In both case, export as well as import considerations are taken into account for products (hardware, software and technology) as well as services.

In addition to the country chapters, the Handbook contains some annexes containing certain standard documents which are used in the import/export of military or dual-use goods procedures (e.g., standard licence application form, standard end-user certificate, etc.).

Of course, these documents are provided for information only. Thorough and tailored advice should in all cases be sought from recognized professionals in the field as to the appropriateness and exhaustiveness of the information and the documents contained in the Export Control Laws and Regulations Handbook in any given situation.

In addition to the general presentation in each of the regimes covered by the Export Control Handbook, a specific illustration is provided (when it exists in the laws and regulations covered) with outer space related activities and goods. Short developments are contained in all country chapters (in section 5) on such sector.

SECTION 4 CURRENT AND FUTURE CHALLENGES

Export controls laws and regulations are increasingly important for both regulatory and enforcement agencies as well as the industries concerned with their implementation (Sub-Section 2). They are also subject to a number of misconceptions (Sub-Section 1). They are complex and their implementation is difficult (Sub-Section 3).

Sub-Section 1 Some Misconceptions About What Export Controls Really Are

The first misconception (or rather a paradox) about export controls laws and regulations is that for such an important matter (since it has a great and direct impact on States and peoples security), it is rather unpublicized.

Very few publications exist describing what export controls are. It is very rarely taught in law schools and very few law firms have it as a practice or have significant experience in the field (except maybe in the USA).

This is rather surprising since export controls apply to a vast amount of goods and services amounting to vast sectors of the economy. In addition, export control laws and regulations are very complex and constantly evolving, requiring up-to-date and reliable knowledge.

In addition, there are growing concerns and demands regarding transparency on the part of governments but also, and that is new, of the corporate stakeholders (e.g., rating agencies, pension funds having an ethical inclination, non-governmental organizations, etc.) in respect to the commerce of arms and, more largely, of dual-use goods and services.

Today, given the state of development of technology, the immense possibilities for it to be disseminated speedily and anonymously (through internet for instance) and the rise of international terrorism, export controls have become extremely complex. Complex because of the way the rules are applied (they are applied with a high degree of political considerations together with numerous cases of extra-territorial applications from certain States) but also in the way controls are carried out (the administration in charge of the control have to master a constantly evolving technology with dissemination means which are more and more difficult to apprehend).

To add to the complexity of the existing laws and regulations, some 'soft laws' have come to play over the recent years in relation to which corporate 'stakeholders' attempt to directly or indirectly, impose, to companies certain conducts which sometimes go beyond the provisions of the applicable laws.[10]

Another frequent misconception about export controls is that they apply only to war materials and pieces of equipment of the like. In fact, they apply to a whole array of goods, technology, software and services that sometimes are only indirectly related to military purposes. For example, civil planes may be subject to export control regulations because they may be used ultimately for military missions or because they may contain some equipment or technology which may also have a military use.

Given the in-depth reach of export control legislations but also because of the possibilities offered by communications technologies, the control applies to a very large number of situations. One example is the sharing of information through electronic means (e.g., out of computer servers or collaboration electronic rooms (i.e., software which allows collaboration work from distant locations out of internet or

10. *Ibid.*

intranet technologies)) which can involve controlled data and be accessible from persons located in foreign countries or foreign persons. In such case, a licence for the export of the data may be required.

The bottom line is that breaches of export control laws and regulations can happen without the companies actually knowing if they do not pay sufficient attention to the issue. Such breaches are heavily sanctioned (including criminal sanctions and the resulting fall out (e.g., degraded corporate image)).

A further misconception is that, given the nature of the controls (international by nature), the laws and regulations that apply are primarily international. In fact, they are not. Due to the heavy sovereign nature of the commerce of arms, the related laws and regulations are, accordingly, also created and maintained by States. In fact, even in the domestic legislations, there are, in most cases, no general rules applicable to the commerce of weapons. The laws and regulations that exist are fundamentally industry by industry based (nuclear, chemicals, biological, military, dual-use, etc.).

Although the use of weapons may be banned by certain texts, exports of weapons are less rarely forbidden in a general way in international treaties. Such is the case, for instance, in the United Nations Charter that prohibits the recourse to force[11] but does not address, per se, the issue of the commerce of weapons.[12]

Although export control laws and regulations can be traced back to distant times, at least on a domestic level (e.g., 1775 US Congress decision to ban the export of goods to Great Britain[13]), international regulations only appeared during the twentieth century, and in a rather limited way as indicated above.

In spite of numerous attempts, the control of the commerce of weapons has never found a true base in the international arena through international or regional treaties.[14] The controls of export – at least those relating to weapons – have always been the reserved matters of the States, since such controls are one of the attributes of their sovereignty.

Sub-Section 2 The Increasing Importance of Export Controls

Par. 1 The Reasons

Given the rapid evolution of technology (which can be widespread in more and more intangible forms and, as a consequence, in a faster and easier way), the increasing threats (and in particular that resulting from terrorism), and the internationalization of trade, export controls are more and more important for governments to ensure world

11. United Nations Charter, Article 2, par. 4.
12. See Jean-Claude Martinez, 'Le droit international et le commerce des armes', *in* Société française pour le droit international, 'Le droit international et les armes', Editions A. Pedone, 1983, p. 115 (The same was true in the Nations Society Pact (which was the organization prevailing prior to the United Nations)).
13. For more information, see US Department of State, Office of the Historian at https://history.state.gov/milestones/1750-1775/parliamentary-taxation.
14. See *supra* n. 12, p. 143.

stability and peace. It is therefore crucial for the day-to-day business for exporting companies to ensure that they are compliant and that the entire chain of suppliers that they use is compliant as well.

The damages for non-compliant companies can be very serious. In addition to the fines or imprisonment sanctions[15] – which are traditional criminal sanctions – the damages to the corporate image can be significant. In that respect, the actions of 'stakeholders', beyond the governments or more traditional regulatory bodies themselves (e.g., rating agencies or so-called ethical investment funds), are increasingly important.

Par. 2 The Consequences

Companies' activities are affected by export control laws and regulations in an increasing number of situations. This is true for obvious situations when companies produce, market, sell their products or services but it is also true when they buy goods or services or when they invest in other businesses.

Companies will check compliance of suppliers to export control laws and regulations in order to ensure that the entire contracting chain is immune from any risks that would be harmful to their activities. In addition to the traditional scrutiny of governments (or governmental agencies) in their capacity of public client (through public procurement processes), the quality of the compliance and the means of compliance of a supplier (in general but more particularly in respect to export control laws and regulations) have become important selection criteria in a large number of companies. This will enable companies to make sure that they do not expose themselves to criminal sanctions but, more frequently and more realistically, that they are not delayed in their activities (which can lead them to be responsible for heavy (contractual) damages).

Particular attention will have to be paid to contractual provisions throughout the contractual chain (which can be very long and complex in an international context) in order for companies to be protected as much a possible vis-à-vis their suppliers but also their clients.

In investment situations also export control laws and regulations will have to be taken into account. This is the case in the acquisition of a company having some military or dual-use related activities. In such case, the buyer will want to determine the value of the company it is acquiring (and the potential liabilities). To do so, it will carry out some due diligence activities on the company to be purchased. In order to verify the value of the target company, the buyer will have to have access to the target company's licences in respect to military or dual-use goods (in particular to ensure that the target company has the right to deliver such controlled equipment in such country and, accordingly, be able to benefit from the revenues flowing from the related sale contract).

15. Please refer to the developments contained in the Par. 4 of all Sub-Sections 1 and 2 of the country chapters *infra*.

Sub-Section 3 The Increasing Complexity and Difficulty to Control/Comply

Export control laws are complex which leads to some difficulties for governments to implement the control and for companies to comply.

Par. 1 Complexity

Sub-Par. 1 Technology Evolution

Technology is constantly evolving and transfers are more and more difficult to control. The reasons due to the evolution of electronic work environments e.g., engineering offices located in several countries. The compliance with all the applicable export control laws and regulations will be difficult and careful assessment of the potential issues will have to be made. The questions to be answered will be the following: How is access to the environment controlled? How are the rights of the individuals who are to have access established? How is it ascertained that the person accessing the environment is actually the person who was given the right of access? How can the communication from the server to the user be protected against surreptitious interception? How can it be guaranteed that the content of a communication is unmodified?

Sub-Par. 2 Need for Governments to Control Outside of Their Jurisdiction

Due to the need to trace all items once they are exported to ensure that they are not exported in infringement of any laws or regulations, some governments - the USA and the UK - have developed an extensive notion of jurisdiction.

Such approach results from the idea that domestic jurisdiction should follow domestic items wherever they are located. It conflicts with other countries sovereignty and traditional rules of international public laws.

Of course the efficiency of such approach depends on the international economic and political weight of the country implementing it. This is probably why there are no other countries that have adopted such approach.

Par. 2 Difficulty to Control and to Comply

There are some elements that contribute to making the control of export of military and dual-use goods and services difficult that have already been mentioned in the preceding paragraph devoted to the complexity of export control laws and regulations (e.g., rapid technology evolution). There are other elements that need to be mentioned: (i) the lack of international harmonized rules; (ii) the complexity and variety of the applicable laws and regulations; and (iii) the lack of governmental resources to perform the control.

Sub-Par. 1 Lack of Internationally Harmonized Rules

One of the most important issues, both from the point of view of the governments carrying out the control and the companies which are being controlled, relates to the fact that no harmonized rules exist on an international level (even in Europe) in respect to export of military goods or services. More progress has been made in respect to dual-use goods and services but harmonization amounts, in most cases, to non-binding documents which interest is merely to provide common lists of controlled goods and services.

Even in Europe, where some harmonization has been achieved, there are still some enforcement discrepancies between the various Member States.[16]

This situation generates additional costs for companies which need to comply.

Sub-Par. 2 Complexity and Variety of the Applicable Laws and Regulations

I Complexity and Variety of the Export Control Laws and Regulations

The complexity for a company wishing to comply with the relevant applicable export control laws and regulations is important. Such exporting company will have into account: (i) its own laws (i.e., the laws of the country from which such company is operating/exporting); (ii) the laws of its suppliers/sub-contractors (the exporting company will not be the direct subject of the control but will need to ensure that the final product can be exported to the country of final destination); and (iii) the laws of the country of its client (when there are some import constraints).

Of course, in certain complex projects, there are applicable laws and regulations from other jurisdictions that need to be taken into account. This will be case when some tests need to be done on the equipment (to be eventually sold) during the development/manufacturing phases in countries that are different from the country of manufacturing or of final assembly. The cost of complying with all these various applicable laws and regulations is very significant and has become the subject of a debate in Europe for intra-community transfers.

Such complexity is increased by the fact that export control laws and regulations are evolving rapidly (in particular to take into account the evolution of technology but also to support States' international policies) and by the difficulty to know how texts are interpreted and implemented due to the relative lack of jurisprudence (there are very little court decisions or published administrative decisions on these matters). This leads to high compliance costs (for companies to be able to have internal or external experts being able to advice them) and to a discrepancy between the companies that can afford to pay for such compliance and those that cannot. This boils down to a question of competitiveness and it is frequent that some small firms that do not have the means to ensure tight compliance decide not to export in order not to be exposed to severe sanctions.

---

16. See further the European Union Chapter.

In addition, and as already noted above, the sanctions have increased drastically over the recent years. Another important element of complexity to highlight is the far reaching enforcement of the US laws and regulations. Given the reach of US export control laws and regulations and the weight of US economy in today's world, exporters will be well advised to ensure compliance (as well as that of their suppliers or sub-contractors) with US laws and regulations.

II The Need to Take into Account Other Laws and Regulations

As already indicated, foreign investment laws and regulations do not enter into the scope of the Export Control Laws and Regulations Handbook. However, it is important to mention the close relationship between the two subjects.

In respect to foreign investment laws and regulations, when investing in a foreign country (for instance, to incorporate a subsidiary or to create a joint venture company with a local partner) in military or dual-use sectors, a company will have to understand and deal with the constraints of the local jurisdiction in respect to export control issues. Prior to that, the investing company will have to understand and conform to any provisions of the local laws limiting, as the case may be, foreign investments in sectors related to military or dual-use goods.

All the countries which are studied in the Export Control Laws and Regulations Handbook have foreign investments laws and regulations which specifically address military and/or dual-use goods which need to be carefully understood before making any investment decisions.

Sub-Par. 3 Lack of Governmental Resources

The governmental resources dedicated to the control are limited. Some governments have started to develop some very detailed and, sometimes, interactive Internet sites. There are even some possibilities to do the licensing process directly through Internet.

However, this may not be enough to ensure efficient control. Governments need to master constant technology evolutions as well as the ever-faster transfer of technologies. There are some attempts from governments to 'partner' with industry to ensure a better control.

SECTION 5 NOTICE

The Export Control Laws and Regulations Handbook is merely an attempt to provide an introduction to the main issues which exporters face on a day-to-day basis in the covered countries or when they export military or dual-use goods, technology or services from such countries. As already indicated above, the Export Control Laws and Regulations Handbook does not intend to be a complete and detailed treatment of all export control regime which it covers, but rather to create an awareness of intent and scope of each export controls regimes covered.

In summary, for the sake of clarity, the information contained in the Export Control Laws and Regulations Handbook is:

- of a general nature only and is not intended to address the specific circumstances of any particular individual or entity;
- not necessarily comprehensive, complete or up to date;
- sometimes refers to internet sites over which the authors have no control and for which they assume no responsibility; and
- not professional or legal advice (if specific advice is needed, readers are invited to always consult a suitably qualified professional).

CHAPTER 2

Embargoes and Related Sanctions (European Union and United States Perspectives)

Lourdes Catrain, Beth Peters, Haley Boyette & Christopher Lock

SECTION 1 TABLE OF CONTENTS

SECTION 2 EXECUTIVE SUMMARY

Economic sanctions, otherwise known as restrictive measures or trade embargoes, are traditionally imposed by the United Nations (UN) Security Council with the aim of changing the behaviour of a targeted government, territory or certain parties, by non-military means. However the European Union (EU)[17] and the United States of America (US) have developed more autonomy in using sanctions to carry out foreign policy goals that go beyond the restrictions outlined in UN measures.[18] These 'semi-autonomous' (where based on an original UN regime) or 'autonomous' sanctions regimes have renewed breadth and depth: horizontally they can cover more sectors than UN sanctions, and vertically they can affect a deeper section of the target country than simply a government. Furthermore, the EU and the US have moved away from sanctions as a blanket ban on all trade relations, towards so-called smart or targeted sanctions. The latter seek to either target selected individuals or companies, or alternatively to disable specific sectors of a country's economy from which the target government or faction derives its main source of financing, while attempting to reduce the impact on the rest of the economy.

Sanctions are often imposed, and relaxed, in response to 'real time' foreign policy considerations. For example, in 2011, the international community demonstrated its ability to respond rapidly and jointly to Colonel Gaddafi's use of violence against Libyan civilians by imposing sanctions in February 2011,[19] expanding them in March

17. The EU's Treaty of Lisbon entered into force in 2009, amending the two constitutional treaties of the EU: the Treaty on the European Union (TEU), and the Treaty on the Functioning of the EU (TFEU). The Treaty of Lisbon added a new chapter to the TEU setting out General Provisions on the EU's External Action. This included clearer decision-making procedures for the European Council in Article 22 TEU. A second new chapter set out provisions on the EU's Common and Foreign and Security Policy in an attempt at bringing increased coherence to the EU's external action. New Article 215 TFEU provided an enhanced restrictive measures procedure.
18. Note that many other jurisdictions, such as Australia, Canada and Switzerland, also maintain separate sanctions rules that can impact operations of global companies.
19. UN Security Council Resolution 1970 of 26 Feb. 2011; Implemented in the EU by Council Decision 2011/137/CFSP of 28 Feb. 2011 concerning restrictive measures in view of the situation in Libya (OJ L 58, 3.3.2011) and Council Regulation (EU) No 204/2011 of 2 Mar. 2011 concerning restrictive measures in view of the situation in Libya (OJ L 58, 3.3.2011); US Executive Order 13566.

2011 as the conflict intensified,[20] and easing them in mid to late 2011,[21] following the death of Colonel Gaddafi and regime change.

The increased complexity and proliferation of sanctions regimes, and the continuous executive and legislative changes in this area, makes compliance with all applicable laws a particular challenge for global companies. Violations of sanctions regulations and restrictions may result in heavy fines for companies and individuals pursuant to both criminal and civil authorities, including potential imprisonment for individuals. Companies also risk reputational damage as well as causing simultaneous violations of other US federal and state laws, including but not limited to export control and anti-money laundering regulations. Certain activities involving sanctioned jurisdictions and parties trigger other notification and reporting requirements, including under US securities laws, government contracting regulations, and state and local procurement laws.

This chapter provides a practical overview, from the EU and US perspectives, of the various sanctions regimes currently in place.[22] This chapter does not seek to provide specific legal advice or advice regarding any particular factual scenario. In addition, this chapter does not focus primarily on export control regulations and policies of the EU and US, except in passing. Increasingly export controls overlap with and enhance the impact of economic sanctions (and vice versa), but primarily flow from separate authorities and policy considerations, and are dealt with in a separate chapter.

This chapter is divided into three sections. Section 3 gives an overview of international sanctions regimes. It provides the legal framework for EU and US sanctions regimes, including key institutions involved in the process. Section 4 describes the substantive aspects of EU and US sanctions regimes, identifying the anatomy of a sanctions regime, as well as setting out in detail the various regimes affecting key territories targeted by these measures. This section also highlights how increased litigation in the EU has impacted the way sanctions regimes are established. Section 5 explains practical aspects of compliance with sanctions regimes for companies, and identifies certain building blocks of a sanctions compliance strategy: companies need to be fully aware and up-to-date on sanctions issues, understand how sanctions affect their risk profiles and intersect with their business models, and implement appropriate monitoring tools and reporting lines to avoid unnecessary risks when doing business in sensitive geographic areas.

---

20. UN Security Council Resolution 1973 of 17 Mar. 2011; Implemented in the EU by Council Decision 2011/178/CFSP of 23 Mar. 2011 amending Decision 2011/137/CFSP concerning restrictive measures in view of the situation in Libya (OJ L 78, 24.3.2011) and Council Regulation (EU) No 296/2011 of 25 Mar. 2011 amending Regulation (EU) No 204/2011 concerning restrictive measures in view of the situation in Libya (OJ L 80, 26.3.2011).
21. UN Security Council Resolution 2009 of 16 Sep. 2011; Implemented in the EU by Council Decision 2011/625/CFSP of 22 Sep. 2011 amending Decision 2011/137/CFSP concerning restrictive measures in view of the situation in Libya (OJ L 246, 23.9.2011) and Council Regulation (EU) No 965/2011 of 28 Sep. 2011 amending Regulation (EU) No 204/2011 concerning restrictive measures in view of the situation in Libya (OJ L 253, 29.9.2011); US General License No 11 to Executive Order 13566 (dated 16 Dec. 2011).
22. The law is stated as at 15 Apr. 2016.

Today's world is still overshadowed by long military engagements in Iraq and Afghanistan. Furthermore, the international negotiations on Iran in 2015 appear to be, at least in part, attributable to the pressure wrought by international sanctions regimes against it. The relative ease with which sanctions can be imposed, as opposed to military action taken, and the increasing dexterity with which sanctions regimes are being deployed, indicates that these policies are an established part of the regulatory landscape. As such, robust sanctions compliance is an essential element to build into a company's trade compliance strategy.

SECTION 3 THE LEGAL FRAMEWORKS FOR EU AND US SANCTIONS REGIMES

Sub-Section 1 United Nations Law

The UN Charter[23] sets out the objectives and legal basis for UN actions. Chapter VII of the UN Charter prescribes what action the UN Security Council can call upon the UN Member States to take in the face of threats or breaches of peace or acts of aggression. Article 41 of Chapter VII of the UN Charter provides the legal basis for the adoption of sanctions regimes, that is, 'measures not involving the use of armed force'. These include, 'complete or partial interruption of economic relations and of rail, sea, air, postal, telegraphic, radio, and other means of communication, and the severance of diplomatic relations.'[24]

The UN Security Council adopts measures which interrupt partial or total economic relations, that is, sanctions, through a resolution. The adoption of a UN Security Council resolution imposing sanctions requires the support of a two-thirds majority of all UN Security Council members,[25] as well as the support of all five permanent members of the UN Security Council.[26]

A UN Security Council resolution creates an international law obligation on UN Member States: they are bound by their agreement in Article 25 of the UN Charter to accept and carry out the decisions of the UN Security Council.

Upon establishing a sanctions regime, the UN sets up a Sanctions Committee to monitor the implementation and observance of the particular sanctions regime. There are currently sixteen active Sanctions Committees.[27]

23. Charter of the United Nations, 1945 (UN Charter).
24. Article 41, UN Charter.
25. Article 27(3), UN Charter.
26. China, France, Russia, the United Kingdom, the US.
27. Somalia and Eritrea (Resolutions 751 (1992) and 1907 (2009)); Al-Qaida and associated individuals and entities (Resolutions 1267 (1999) and 1989 (2011)); Iraq and Kuwait (Resolution 1518 (2003)); Liberia (Resolution 1521 (2003)); Democratic Republic of the Congo (Resolution 1533 (2004)); Côte d'Ivoire (Resolution 1572 (2004)); Sudan (Resolution 1591 (2005)); Individuals suspected of involvement in the 14 Feb. 2005 terrorist bombing in Beirut, Lebanon (Resolution 1636 (2005)); North Korea (Resolution 1718 (2006)); Iran (Resolution 1737 (2006)); Libya (Resolution 1970 (2011)); designated individuals of the Taliban (Resolution 1988 (2011)); Guinea-Bissau (Resolution 2048 (2012)); Central African Republic (Resolution 2127 (2013)); Yemen (Resolution 2140 (2014)); South Sudan (Resolution 2206 (2015)).

Sub-Section 2 International Trade Law

Under World Trade Organization (WTO) agreements, member countries cannot normally discriminate between their trading partners. That is, they have to give them equally 'most-favored nation' status. In addition, WTO member countries cannot discriminate between their own domestic products, and foreign products, services or nationals – they have to give them 'national treatment'.[28] These are two core pillars of the WTO trading system.

Economic sanctions are arguably discriminatory barriers to trade that, when imposed on a WTO member, are contrary to WTO law. However, such actions may be justified under the security exception in Article XXI of the General Agreement on Tariffs and Trade (GATT), which permits:

> any action which [a contracting party] considers necessary for the protection of [its] essential security interests [...] in time of war or other emergency in international relations [or] in pursuance of [its] obligations under the UN Charter for the maintenance of international peace and security.[29]

Article XXI GATT does not contain any restrictions on its use, giving WTO members considerable latitude when defining their 'essential security interests'. Nevertheless, Article XXI GATT has been rarely used by WTO members to justify the implementation of economic sanctions against other members. For instance, in 1961 Ghana relied on Article XXI GATT to justify its boycott of Portuguese goods noting that '...under this Article each contracting party was the sole judge of what was necessary in its essential security interest.'[30] In another example, on May 1985, the US prohibited all imports of goods and services of Nicaraguan origin, all exports from the US of goods to or destined for Nicaragua (except those destined for the organized democratic resistance) and related transactions. Nicaragua objected to the measures stating that Article XXI GATT could not be applied in an arbitrary fashion and requested that a Panel be set up.[31] The Panel concluded that:

> as it was not authorized to examine the justification for the United States' invocation of a general exception to the obligations under the General Agreement, it could find the United States neither to be complying with its obligations under the General Agreement nor to be failing to carry out its obligations under that Agreement.[32]

In 1996 the EU requested consultations with the US concerning the Cuban Liberty and Democratic Solidarity (LIBERTAD) Act of 1996 (also known as the Helms-Burton Act)[33] and other legislation enacted by the US Congress regarding trade sanctions against Cuba. The EU asserted that US trade restrictions on goods of Cuban origin, as well as the possible refusal of visas and the exclusion of non-US nationals from US

28. Article I.1, General Agreement on Tariffs and Trade (GATT), 1994.
29. Article XIV*bis* of the General Agreement on Trade in Services provides for a similar exception.
30. Analytical Index of the GATT, 30 Sep. 2011, Part II, Article XXI, p. 600, available at https://www.wto.org/english/res_e/booksp_e/gatt_ai_e/art21_e.pdf (GATT Index).
31. GATT Index, p. 601.
32. GATT Index, p. 601.
33. 22 USC §§6021-6091.

territory, were inconsistent with US obligations under the WTO Agreement. Violations of various GATT Articles were alleged, and the EU alleged that even if these measures by the US were not be in violation of specific provisions of GATT, they nevertheless nullified or impaired its expected benefits and impeded the attainment of the objectives of GATT. At the EU's request, a panel was established to consider the matter in 1996 but, also at the request of the EU, the panel's work was suspended in 1997 (the panel's authority officially lapsed in 1998).

More recently, the EU and Russia imposed tit-for-tat economic sanctions regimes in response to the conflict in Eastern Ukraine.[34] Both Russia and the EU threatened to bring a case before the WTO accusing one another of violating their respective WTO obligations by the adoption of economic sanctions against each other.[35]

In reality, the compatibility of sanctions regimes and WTO law has not yet been fully explored. This is mainly due to the fact that international sanctions have been imposed largely on non-WTO members such as Belarus, Iran, North Korea, Syria and Sudan. In the absence of further precedent applying the security exception in Article XXI GATT to economic sanctions, the prevailing self-assessment of the existence of security interests provides significant leeway to the WTO members in the application of economic sanctions.

In its 2012 Guidelines on implementation and evaluation of restrictive measures in the framework of the Common Foreign and Security Policy, the EU specifically acknowledges that measures restricting trade have to meet the conditions laid down in Article XX, GATT or Article XIV GATS.[36] It further acknowledges that, in some cases restrictive measures could be incompatible with WTO rules.[37]

Sub-Section 3 EU Law

One of the objectives of the EU is to contribute to the strict observance and development of international law, including respect for the principles of the UN Charter.[38] Beyond this commitment to international law and the UN, the EU has its own authority for imposing autonomous sanctions regimes.[39]

The principal European institutions involved in establishing any sanctions regime are:

34. The sanctions regimes on Russia and Ukraine are described in detail below.
35. In his remarks at the 4th St Petersburg International Legal Forum on 20 Jun. 2014, Prime Minister Dmitry Medvedev stated that he had sent a communiqué to the WTO to protest at the imposition of Western sanctions: http://government.ru/en/news/13204/#dam; the EU has contested Russian measures on the importation of live pigs, pork and other pig products from the EU in WTO Dispute DS475, for which consultations were first requested on 8 Apr. 2014; the EU has also contested Russian measures against certain EU agricultural and manufacturing products in WTO Dispute DS485, for which consultations were first requested on 31 Oct. 2014.
36. *Guidelines on implementation and evaluation of restrictive measures (sanctions) in the framework of the EU Common Foreign and Security Policy* (EU Guidelines 2012), General Secretariat of the Council, 11205/12, Brussels, 15 Jun. 2012, paragraph 11.
37. EU Guidelines 2012, paragraph 11.
38. Article 3, TEU.
39. Article 22, TEU and Article 215, TFEU.

(a) The European Council – the intergovernmental group of Heads of State, sitting as the executive arm of the EU, that takes decisions on the strategic interests and objectives of the Union, including concerning relations of the EU with a specific country or region.[40]
(b) The Council of the EU (Council) – the intergovernmental meeting of ministers from all EU Member States that is the main legislative body in EU sanctions law (the Council meets as the Foreign Affairs Council (FAC) when the foreign affairs ministers of all EU Member States meet, and the FAC may make recommendations on external action to the European Council).[41]
(c) The European Commission – the European civil service, which may make legislative proposals in sanctions matters jointly with the European External Action Service (EEAS), and provides technical expertise to the FAC.
(d) The EEAS – the EU's diplomatic body, led by the High Representative on Common Foreign and Security Policy (High Representative), which may make legislative proposals in sanctions matters jointly with the European Commission (the EEAS has a key role in the preparation and review of sanctions regimes, as well as well as in the communication and outreach activities accompanying the sanctions, in close cooperation with EU Member States, relevant EU delegations[42] and the European Commission.[43]

Economic sanctions adopted against third countries form part of the EU's Common Foreign and Security Policy: the European Council sets the Union's strategy, while the Council is responsible for its definition and implementation.[44] Decisions in this field are adopted by unanimity in both the European Council and in the Council.[45] The European Parliament is only kept informed and takes no active role in the decision-making process.

Due to the different competences between the EU and its Member States, certain restrictive measures such as arms embargoes and travel bans, are implemented directly by EU Member States. Therefore, such measures only require a unanimous decision by the Council (Council Decisions).

Council Decisions can also contain other types of sanctions such as asset freezes or export bans, which do fall under the competence of the EU. This requires further implementation at the EU level, through legislative acts in the form of Council Regulations, adopted on the basis of Article 215 TFEU. By virtue of this provision, the Council adopts a measure by a qualified majority[46] on a joint proposal from the High Representative and the European Commission. These proposals are negotiated by the

40. Article 22, second paragraph, TEU.
41. Article 22, third paragraph, TEU.
42. EU delegations are the equivalent of embassies or missions, representing the EU in third countries and at international organizations.
43. *Recommendations for working methods for EU autonomous sanctions*, Foreign Relations Counsellors Working Party, Council of the EU, Note, 18920/11, Brussels, 21 Dec. 2011.
44. Article 26, TEU.
45. Article 31, TEU.
46. It must be pointed out that in practice the Council generally adopts acts by consensus regardless of the corresponding procedure.

EU Member State representations in Brussels in regular 'Relex – sanctions' meetings, chaired by the EEAS; as well as by the Committee of Permanent Representatives (COREPER II)[47] and Political and Security Committee (PSC).[48]

Often the Council Decision and the Council Regulation covering the same sanctions regime are adopted simultaneously, allowing for both legal acts to produce their effects at the same time.[49]

The following figure illustrates the decision-making process by which EU sanctions are adopted.

Figure 2.1 Decision-Making Process for EU Sanctions

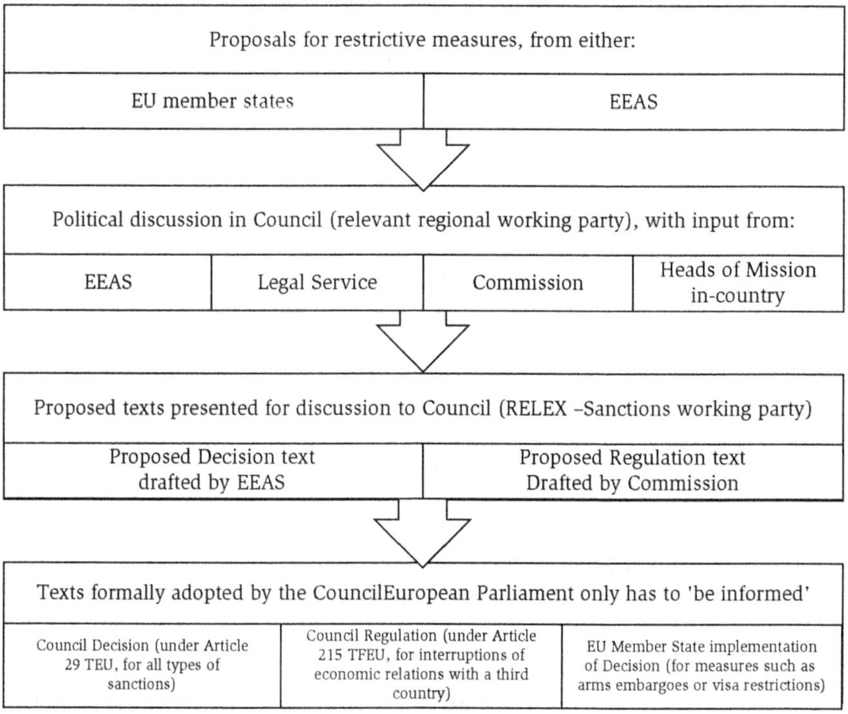

47. COREPER stands for the Committee of the Permanent Representatives of the Governments of the Member States to the European Union. It is the Council's main preparatory body, helping the Council to focus on the main points for negotiation. COREPER II is made up of each EU Member State's permanent representative and deals largely with political, financial and foreign policy issues.

48. *Establishment of a 'Sanctions' formation of the Foreign Relations Counsellors Working party (RELEX/Sanctions)*, Council of the EU, 5603/04, Brussels, 22 Jan. 2004. Note that 'Relex' is the abbreviation of the name of the committee subject-matter in French: *relations extérieures*.

49. *Adopting EU restrictive measures - 'sanctions' - An essential foreign policy tool*, available at http://www.consilium.europa.eu/en/policies/sanctions/.

Sub-Section 4 US Law

The US imposes economic sanctions against targeted countries, regimes, governments, entities and individuals, as well as on particular conduct or sectors of an economy. The primary US government agency tasked with promulgating economic sanctions regulations is the US Treasury Department's Office of Foreign Assets Control (OFAC). US sanctions regimes can restrict most activities and dealings with sanctions targets, whether directly or indirectly through third parties or third countries, or can be more limited in scope restricting only certain types of activities. US sanctions can apply to both US and non-US entities, and in the case of non-US entities may, in certain instances, apply even if the underlying transaction does not involve persons, goods, technology, software, currency or services subject to US jurisdiction (these extraterritorial measures are referred to as 'secondary' sanctions). Sanctions compliance continues to be a challenge for global companies, with potential criminal and civil penalties for non-compliance, for both individuals and companies.[50]

US economic sanctions also overlap with export controls administered by other US agencies, such as the US Commerce Department and US State Department. While a country may not be subject to comprehensive OFAC economic sanctions, that country may still be subject to stringent export controls that effectively limit the types of goods, software or technology that can be sent to the country. Export controls are discussed in more detail in a separate chapter.

Par. 1 Types of US Sanctions

Economic sanctions are foreign policy tools used by the US and other governments, as well as by international bodies such as the UN and EU, to prevent targeted nations, organizations, and individuals from benefitting or gaining access to capital, financial systems, goods, technology, or services. US sanctions can vary greatly in scope depending on the programme, and can include:

- Comprehensive territorial sanctions that target an entire country or territory, and/or the entire government of a country or territory.
- More limited 'list-based' sanctions targeting only specific persons, entities, industries, activities or sectors.
- Sanctions programmes can involve 'blocking' or 'freezing' of property, interests in property, funds and economic resources.
- Some persons or entities may be targeted under multiple sanctions programmes.
- Some exceptions and exclusions will apply, and in some cases licences permit otherwise prohibited activities.

50. By way of example, violation of the most common underlying US sanctions authority can result in civil administrative penalties of up to USD 250,000 per violation, or twice the value of the offending transaction, whichever is greater. OFAC's Enforcement Guidelines are available at http://www.treasury.gov/resource-center/sanctions/Documents/fr74_57593.pdf.

The US maintains comprehensive sanctions against the following territories and countries:

- the Crimea region
- Cuba
- Iran
- North Korea
- Sudan[51]
- Syria

More limited sanctions target the following territories and countries:

- Balkans[52]
- Belarus
- Burma (aka Myanmar)
- Burundi
- Central African Republic
- Democratic Republic of the Congo
- Iraq
- Ivory Coast
- Lebanon
- Libya
- Russia
- Somalia
- South Sudan
- Ukraine
- Venezuela
- Yemen
- Zimbabwe

A list of current OFAC sanctions programmes is available at http://www.treasury.gov/resource-center/sanctions/Programs/Pages/Programs.aspx. Not all of these country regimes target the entirety of these countries, but instead target individual persons, companies, entities, governments or groups.

OFAC also maintains a list of restricted parties called Specially Designated Nationals (SDNs). The list of SDNs includes individuals and entities from all over the world, including persons designated for their connections to sanctioned governments or parties, weapons proliferation activity, cybersecurity concerns, narcotics trafficking,

51. US comprehensive sanctions are maintained against the Republic of the Sudan, sometimes called 'North Sudan', the capital of which is Khartoum. The Republic of South Sudan, or 'South Sudan' is a separate country as of 2011, and its capital is Juba.
52. The current states that made up the former Socialist Federal Republic (SFR) of Yugoslavia include Bosnia and Herzegovina, Serbia, Croatia, Slovenia, the Former Yugoslav Republic of Macedonia, and Montenegro (Kosovo was formerly a province of the SFR Yugoslavia but its status as an independent state has not been formally recognized by the United Nations).

terrorism or other elicit activities. The SDN list contains thousands of names and changes frequently (sometimes multiple times a week). OFAC also implements sanctions programmes that target specific activities, industries or sectors, including trade in illegal goods such as uncertified rough diamonds, human rights violations, piracy, or undermining democratic processes, as well as restrictions that focus on the banking, energy, defence and oil sectors. Some of these other types of restrictions are promulgated via additions of names of restricted parties to OFAC's list of Foreign Sanctions Evaders (FSEs) and Sectoral Sanctions Identifications List (SSIL). A consolidated list of SDNs, FSEs and SSILs is available at http://www.treasury.gov/resource-center/sanctions/SDN-List/Pages/default.aspx.[53]

Par. 2 Legal Overview of US Sanctions

As noted above, the UN Security Council has responsibility for maintaining international peace and security, and economic sanctions are one of the tools it uses to prevent and stop aggression. Aside from UN actions, US economic sanctions principally derive from legislative acts issued by Congress, including both general legislation as well as acts targeted to a particular country or issue. Sources of broad legislative authority include the International Emergency Economic Powers Act (IEEPA),[54] the Trading with the Enemy Act (TWEA),[55] and the United Nations Participation Act (UNPA),[56] as well as other legislation targeting specific countries. Examples of specific legislation include the Cuban Democracy Act,[57] the Foreign Narcotics Kingpin Designation Act,[58] and the Iran Sanctions Act (ISA)[59] as amended in 2010 by the Comprehensive Iran Sanctions, Accountability, and Divestment Act (CISADA).[60]

Based on Congressional legislative acts and Constitutional authority, the US President can issue Executive Orders imposing sanctions and authorizing agencies to issue economic sanctions regulations. The US government has a decades-long history of using economic sanctions to achieve US foreign policy goals. Earlier use of sanctions tended to target entire countries (e.g., the broad, comprehensive sanctions against Cuba), while more recent sanctions actions tend to focus on specific groups, entities, persons, charities or sectors (e.g., the sanctions against Somalia, which target persons and entities identified by OFAC as having engaged in acts that threaten the peace, security, or stability of Somalia, to have obstructed the delivery of humanitarian assistance to or within Somalia, to have supplied arms or related materiel in violation of the UN arms embargo on Somalia, or to have provided support for any of these

53. There are also separate restricted parties lists maintain under US export control authorities, such as the Export Administration Regulations (EAR) and parties named to the Entity List, Denied Parties List and Unverified List maintained by the US Department of Commerce. 15 C.F.R. Parts 730-774.
54. 50 USC §§1701-1706.
55. 50 USC App. §§5, 16.
56. 22 USC §87c.
57. 22 USC §§6001-6010.
58. 21 USC §§1901-1908.
59. 50 USC § 1701 note.
60. PL 111-195.

activities; also the sanctions against Russia and Ukraine, which target persons on the SDN list and SSIL, as well as activities involving certain oil production and exploration projects).

As noted above, OFAC is the primary agency that implements, administers and enforces US economic sanctions based on US foreign policy and national security goals.[61] OFAC's website is available at http://www.treasury.gov/about/organizational-structure/offices/Pages/Office-of-Foreign-Assets-Control.aspx, and includes listings of the various sanctions regimes in place. Each OFAC sanctioned country webpage has a listing of the relevant legislation, executive orders, regulations and guidance for that particular country or programme. OFAC also lists certain frequently asked questions (FAQs) and responses on its website at http://www.treasury.gov/resource-center/faqs/Sanctions/Pages/ques_index.aspx. A graphical representation of the process, in basic terms, is provided below:

Figure 2.2 Implementation of US Sanctions

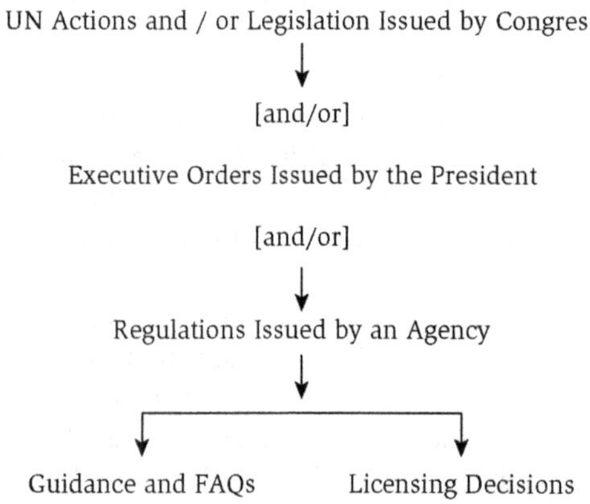

As an example, IEEPA is legislation enacted by Congress in 1977 that gives the President the power to issue orders to deal with 'any unusual and extraordinary threat, which has its source in whole or substantial part outside the United States, to the national security, foreign policy, or economy of the United States, if the President declares a national emergency with respect to such threat.' IEEPA is a primary legislative source in this example, but there is other relevant legislation. IEEPA specifically states that the legislation does not allow the President to regulate or prohibit the importation or exportation of information or informational materials, transactions ordinarily incidental to travel, or personal communications that do not involve a transfer of anything of value.[62]

61. OFAC and the US Commerce Department have overlapping jurisdiction for certain activities involving sanctioned countries and parties, such as exports and reexports of goods, technology and software subject to the US EAR. See 15 C.F.R. Parts 744 and 746.
62. See 50 USC § 1702.

Pursuant to IEEPA, the President issued, for example, Executive Order 12959 related to Iran, which states in part: 'By the authority vested in me...by the laws of the United States of America, including IEEPA...'. In this Executive Order, the President decided to 'take steps' to 'deal with the unusual and extraordinary threat to the national security, foreign policy and economy of the United States...'.[63] The Executive Order prohibits, among other things, exports of goods, technology and services to Iran, approval and facilitation of transactions, new investments, and other transactions. There have been several Executive Orders related to Iran. OFAC, for its part, issued the Iranian Transactions and Sanctions Regulations (ITSR). The ITSR regulations are found in the US Code of Federal Regulations (C.F.R.) at 31 C.F.R. §§560 et seq. There are other relevant regulations for Iran, but in terms of this example, the flow chart would read as follows:

Figure 2.3 Development and Implementation of the Iranian Transactions and Sanctions Regulations (ITSR)

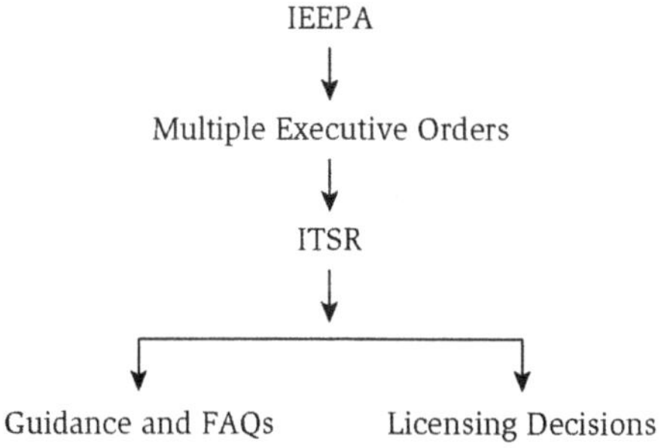

SECTION 4 THE SUBSTANTIVE ASPECTS OF EU AND US SANCTIONS REGIMES

Sub-Section 1 Overview

Economic sanctions were originally used as a blunt instrument attacking a target government's war financing and often in response to intractable intrastate conflicts. A revised approach became necessary following the widespread criticism of the effect of the UN's sanctions on the Iraqi population throughout the 1990s. In 1995, the UN Security Council permanent members recognized the need to minimize unintended adverse side-effects of sanctions on the most vulnerable segments of targeted countries.[64] This led to a series of key meetings to review the mechanics of sanctions

63. Executive Order 12959.
64. Letter dated 13 Apr. 1995 from the Permanent Representatives to the UN of China, France, the Russian Federation, the UK, the US, addressed to the President of the Security Council setting out a non-paper on the humanitarian impact of sanctions, Security Council Document 1995/300.

regimes: at Interlaken, on financial sanctions;[65] at Bonn and Berlin on arms embargoes and travel restriction measures;[66] and at Stockholm on procedures for implementation and monitoring.[67] These processes have informed a new, 'targeted' approach to modern sanctions regimes, the so-called smart sanctions. The most developed examples of targeted sanctions regimes have been the economic sanctions against Iran, and those against Russia. These regimes are described in more detail below.

Sub-Section 2 The Anatomy of an EU Sanctions Regime

EU sanctions regimes have the following aims:

- Political sanctions aim to make life unpleasant for the ruling elite of the target government, using tools such as asset freezes and visa restrictions.
- Military restrictions prohibit trade with the target country in the sector of arms and other tools of repression. This aims to restrict the government's ability to exercise its state monopoly on violence. This may be necessary in support of an opposition movement where the government has lost democratic backing, or where the government is using undue oppressive violence on its civilians.
- Economic restrictions are typically linked to a need for increased pressure on a target government, with restrictions across a variety of sectors of the economy. Economic restrictions aim to reduce the target government's ability to finance itself, and measures range from targeting high revenue sectors such as the oil and gas industries, to restricting access to Western capital markets in an attempt to force target governments to draw on their own capital reserves. Extreme economic restrictions include cutting off the country of the target government from the international finance system completely, by removing its access to financial messaging systems such as SWIFT.
- Retaliatory 'counter-measures' are sometimes imposed, both by the EU or against it, as a direct response to sanctions regimes. The principal examples in this category are the EU's legislative response to the US's boycott on Cuba,[68] and Russia's sanctions imposed on imports originating from the EU, US,

65. The Interlaken Process was first convened in March 1998 by the Swiss government to discuss targeted financial sanctions and concluded in March 1999.
66. The Bonn-Berlin Process was first convened in November 1999 by the German government and presented its findings to the UN Security Council on 22 Oct. 2001.
67. The Stockholm Process built on the findings of the earlier two policy meetings. It was first convened in April 2002 by the Swedish government and its report was presented to the UN Security Council on 25 Feb. 2003.
68. Joint Action 1996/668/CFSP of 22 Nov. 1996 adopted by the Council on the basis of Articles J.3 and K.3 of the TEU concerning measures protecting against the effects of the extraterritorial application of legislation adopted by a third country, and actions based thereon or resulting therefrom (OJ L 309, 29.11.1996); Council Regulation (EC) No 2271/1996 of 22 Nov. 1996 protecting against the effects of the extraterritorial application of legislation adopted by a third country, and actions based thereon or resulting therefrom (OJ L 309, 29.11.1996).

Canada, Australia and Norway of agricultural products, raw materials and foodstuffs in response to Western sanctions related to Russia.[69]

Within the various EU sanctions regimes, a basic anatomy can be identified. Five parts represent recurring features within modern sanctions regimes:

- Sectoral sanctions
- Arms embargoes
- Territorial sanctions
- Financial sanctions
- Asset freezes
- Visa restrictions.

Par. 1 Sectoral Sanctions

Sectoral sanctions restrict trade in specific sectors of the target country's economy. The sectors covered range from oil and gas, which generate high revenues for some of the target countries, to key technology and dual-use[70] goods.

EU policy-makers impose sanctions in the knowledge that not all jurisdictions may follow its lead and they could provide a 'backfill'. This is a situation where the vacuum created by the absence of EU products in the sanctioned economy allows products from non-EU Member States (and non-US origin) to prosper. The EU's sanctions restricting the provision of key products to Russia for use in certain oil exploration projects are a good example of the evolution of sectoral sanctions. Prohibiting provision of listed goods and technology used for oil exploration in particularly difficult environments - offshore in the Arctic Circle or in waters greater than 150 m deep, or in shale sands - specifically targets the advanced technology primarily available from EU and US companies, in an attempt to specifically impact the Russian economy in this sector. By targeting this technology, this reduces the risk that backfill will occur, meaning both that the restrictive measures will be more effective, and that the sanctions do not unduly hinder EU companies with respect to companies from other non-sanctioning jurisdictions.

Sectoral sanctions routinely cover the sale, supply, transfer or export or restricted goods and technology as well as related key services related to listed goods and technology, such as brokering services, and technical and financial assistance, as well as provision of insurance or reinsurance.

69. Resolution of the Government of the Russian Federation No 778 of 7 Aug. 2014, as amended by Resolution No 830 of 20 Aug. 2014.
70. Items that can be used for both commercial/civilian and military/defence related purposes.

Par. 2 Arms Embargoes

Arms embargoes are a traditional tool of sanctions regimes, used at an early stage in a regime's implementation. This is because of the favourable balance between the impact on the population's everyday needs, and the impact the target government's ability to exercise its state monopoly of violence, thereby weakening the government's capacity to suppress opposition. Arms embargoes are typically used against governments found to be committing human rights violations or otherwise harming its own people.

Par. 3 Territorial Sanctions

Territorial sanctions represent a blanket ban on trade relations with a particular country. This can be applied to a particular geographical territory within that country,[71] or to all the target country.[72]

Par. 4 Financial Sanctions

Financial sanctions have been developed in two separate categories. The first, more traditional, category can be seen as aiming to hinder the sanctioned government's economy from participating in international trade. There are degrees of restrictions in this category: prohibitions on providing financial assistance connected to other sanctioned trade; prohibitions on transfers of funds to persons or entities within the sanctioned government's country; prohibitions on access to international financial messaging systems, such as SWIFT. The latter is regarded as an extreme option, having the effect of cutting the sanctioned economy from jurisdictions other than that imposing the sanctions to the extent that SWIFT is used to transfer money between those jurisdictions.

In the recent Russia/Ukraine sanctions, a second, more innovative category of financial sanctions has been developed. This targets Russian capital reserves, by reducing access of key Russian banks and companies to the EU capital markets. This is aimed at forcing them to turn inwards for funding, depleting domestic capital.

---

71. For example, the EU's sanctions on Crimea and Sevastopol (Council Decision 2014/386/CFSP of 23 Jun. 2014 concerning restrictions on goods originating in Crimea or Sevastopol, in response to the illegal annexation of Crimea and Sevastopol (OJ L 183, 24.6.2014); Council Regulation (EU) 692/2014 of 23 Jun. 2014 concerning restrictions on the import into the Union of goods originating in Crimea or Sevastopol, in response to the illegal annexation of Crimea and Sevastopol (OJ L 183, 24.6.2014)).
72. For example, the EU's sanctions on North Korea (Council Decision 2013/183/CFSP of 22 Apr. 2013 concerning restrictive measures against the Democratic People's Republic of Korea and repealing Decision 2010/800/CFSP (OJ L 111, 23.4.2013); Council Regulation (EC) No 329/2007 of 27 Mar. 2007 concerning restrictive measures against the Democratic People's Republic of Korea (OJ L 88, 29.03.2007)).

Par. 5 Asset Freezing

Asset freezing measures target listed persons or entities in two principal ways:

- Prohibiting dealing with funds or economic resources belonging to, owned, held or controlled by listed persons or entities.
- Prohibiting making funds or economic resources available, directly or indirectly, to or for the benefit of the listed persons or entities.

Asset freezing measures punish listed persons or entities by creating offences for EU persons to deal with them and their assets. It is also an offence to participate, knowingly and intentionally, in activities the object or effect of which is to circumvent the two principal prohibitions.

Under EU sanctions law 'funds', 'economic resources' and 'dealing with' are all very widely defined. 'Funds' means 'financial assets and benefits of every kind', including cash, cheques, debt obligations, securities, bonds, notes, debentures, derivatives contracts, income from assets, rights of set-off, performance bonds, guarantees, letters of credit, bills of sale, documents showing evidence of an interest in funds or financial resources. 'Economic resources' means assets of every kind (tangible or intangible, movable or immovable), which are not funds but may be used to obtain funds, goods or services. Essentially, any asset of any kind is likely to fall within the definition of 'funds' or the definition of 'economic resources'. 'Dealing with' funds and economic resources covers everything from transferring funds to portfolio management and dealing with 'economic resources' means exchanging them, or using them in exchange, for funds, goods or services. 'Making available' has been interpreted widely by the European Courts.[73] This wide meaning encompasses all acts necessary under national laws for a person to obtain full power of disposal in relation to the relevant economic resources.[74] By way of an example of how extensive the European Courts sees this language, the formal registration of a property purchased prior to the listing of one of the buyers under the EU's Iran sanctions was prohibited because it constituted making economic resources available to a listed entity.[75]

In March 2015, the Council published best practice guidelines consolidating and summarizing all exemption grounds for asset freezes.[76] On these grounds a listed person or entity may apply for an authorization to the competent authorities in the EU Member States to receive payments, access funds or other actions prohibited under the asset freeze. These limited grounds are based on the fundamental rights of listed persons and entities as well as international humanitarian and diplomatic laws.

73. The term European Courts includes both the European Court of Justice and the General Court of the EU.
74. Foreign Relations Counsellors Working Party, *Update of the EU Best Practices for the effective implementation of restrictive measures*, Council, 7383/1/15, Brussels, 24 Mar. 2015 (EU Best Practices 2015), p. 22.
75. Case C-117/06 *Gerda Möllendorf and Christiane Möllendorf-Niehuus*.
76. EU Best Practices 2015, p. 27.

Par. 6 Visa Restrictions

Visa restrictions are often used alongside asset freezes to target individual members of a sanctioned government. Affecting the political elite's ability to travel to the jurisdiction imposing the sanctions is a limited economic tool, and often used to give strong political disapproval.

Visa restrictions fall within the competence of the EU Member States to implement individually. For this reason, visa restrictions are set out in Council Decisions, but not in Council Regulations.

Sub-Section 3 EU Sanctions Regimes on Iran

The EU has two separate sanctions regimes in place against Iran: measures stemming from a 2006 UN Security Council resolution targeting Iran's nuclear weapons programme,[77] and an autonomously-imposed regime responding to the Iran government's violent repression of its own people and other human rights violations in 2011.[78] The international negotiations with Iran related exclusively to nuclear-related sanctions, as described further below.

Par. 1 EU Iran Nuclear-Related Sanctions

In 2006, in response to the persistent non-cooperation of Iran with the international community's attempts to verify its nuclear weapons activity, the UN Security Council called for a sanctions regime on the country.[79] This regime was bolstered by subsequent UN Security Council Resolutions, notably in 2010 following the reports of the International Atomic Energy Agency (IAEA) that Iran had refused to take agreed non-proliferation steps.[80]

The EU initially implemented UN Security Council Resolution 1737 through Council Common Position 2007/140/CFSP and Council Regulation 423/2007.[81]

77. Council Decision 2010/413/CFSP of 26 Jul 2010 concerning restrictive measures against Iran and repealing Common Position 2007/140/CFSP (OJ L 195, 27.7.2010) and Council Regulation (EU) No 961/2010 of 25 Oct. 2010 on restrictive measures against Iran and repealing Regulation (EC) No 423/2007 (OJ L 281, 27.10.2010).
78. Council Decision 2011/235/CFSP of 12 Apr. 2011 concerning restrictive measures directed against certain persons and entities in view of the situation in Iran (OJ L 100, 14.4.2011) and Council Regulation (EU) No 359/2011 of 12 Apr. 2011 concerning restrictive measures directed against certain persons, entities and bodies in view of the situation in Iran (OJ L 100, 14.4.2011).
79. UN Security Council Resolution 1737 of 23 Dec. 2006.
80. UN Security Council Resolution 1929 of 9 Jun. 2010.
81. Council Common Position 2007/140/CFSP of 27 Feb. 2007 concerning restrictive measures against Iran (OJ L 61, 28.2.2007) and Council Regulation 423/2007 of 19 Apr. 2007 concerning restrictive measures against Iran (OJ L 103, 20.4.2007), followed in 2010 by Council Decision 2010/413/CFSP of 26 Jul 2010 concerning restrictive measures against Iran and repealing Common Position 2007/140/CFSP (OJ L 195, 27.7.2010) and Council Regulation (EU) No 961/2010 of 25 Oct. 2010 on restrictive measures against Iran and repealing Regulation (EC) No 423/2007 (OJ L 281, 27.10.2010).

However, in December 2011, amid a worsening in EU-Iran relations after attacks on the United Kingdom (UK) Embassy in Tehran, the Council agreed:

> to broaden existing sanctions by examining, in close coordination with international partners, additional measures including measures aimed at severely affecting the Iranian financial system, in the transport sector, in the energy sector, measures against the Iranian Revolutionary Guard Corps (IRGC), as well as in other areas.[82]

The IRGC is primarily a military and security organization formed to support the Iranian Supreme Leader, Ayatollah Khamenei, in the national security crisis following the 1979 Iranian revolution. One of the few organizations with the manpower to take on major construction contracts after the revolution, the IRGC became heavily involved in Iran's economy and is now the country's largest economic actor, through a network of subsidiary companies. Two industries, software and metals, are specifically targeted due to the monopoly over them held by the IRGC. Furthermore, the large number of entities listed under this particular regime is as a result of the IRGC's subsidiary-driven method of business.

A heavily-extended new sanctions regime was developed in further legislation in 2012.[83] A thawing of relations between 2013 and 2015 led to EU nuclear-related sanctions being all but removed.

A number of EU Member States have indicated that the enforcement of the EU Iran sanctions will continue. Infringements discovered following the lifting of the EU Iran sanctions may still be prosecuted by EU Member State authorities. For example, the UK Department for Business, Innovation and Skills has stated that 'while sanctions remain in place they will continue to be enforced robustly'.[84] For this reason, the following sub-paragraphs set out the detail of the historic regime, before discussing the remaining sanctions in force.

Sub-Par. 1 Previous EU Iran Regime: Sectoral Sanctions

The EU-Iran nuclear-related sanctions used to cover several sectoral areas. An overview of these is set out below.

In the nuclear industry, prohibitions were set out on the sale, supply, transfer or export of goods and technology contributing to Iran's enrichment-related, reprocessing or heavy-water-related activities, to the development of nuclear weapon delivery

82. Council of the EU, Foreign Affairs Council, 17720/11, Press release, Brussels, 30 Nov. and 1 Dec. 2011, p.9.
83. Council Decision 2012/35/CFSP (OJ L 19, 24.1.2012) and Council Regulation (EU) No 267/2012 of 23 Mar. 2012 concerning restrictive measures against Iran and repealing Regulation (EU) No 961/2010 (OJ L 88, 24.3.2012).
84. Export Control Organisation, *Iran Nuclear Deal – information for business,* Notice to Exporters 2015/20, 15 Jul. 2015.

systems, or to the pursuit of activities related to other topics about which the IAEA expressed concerns or identified as outstanding.[85]

In the oil, gas and petrochemical sector, prohibitions were set out on the sale, supply, transfer or export of key equipment and technology for the exploration and production of oil and natural gas, refining, liquefaction of natural gas as well as for the petrochemical industry.[86]

There were also restrictions on the purchasing of crude oil, petroleum products and natural gas products exported from Iran.[87]

In the maritime sector, there were prohibitions on the sale, supply, transfer or export of key naval equipment or technology, as well as on certain services in respect of Iranian oil tankers and cargo vessels: classification services, participation the design and production of ships and inspection and testing.[88]

In the IT sector, prohibitions were in place on software for integrating industrial processes relevant to Iran's nuclear, military or ballistic missile programme. This included Enterprise Resource Planning (ERP) software designed specifically for use in the nuclear, military, gas, oil, navy, aviation, financial and construction industries.[89]

In the mining and metals sector, there were prohibitions on the sale, supply, transfer or export of graphite and raw or semi-finished metals.[90] Restrictions were also in place for the sale, supply, transfer or export of diamonds to the Iranian government, or connected entity.[91] It was also prohibited to sell, supply, transfer or export to the Central Bank of Iran newly printed or unissued Iranian denominated banknotes and minted coinage.

The above prohibitions covered the sale, transfer or export to any Iranian person, or for use in Iran. Many prohibitions also extended to the provision of technical assistance, brokering services, financing or financial assistance in the context of these restrictions.

Sub-Par. 2 Previous EU Iran Regime: Financial Sanctions

The most severe economic restrictions imposed on Iran were in the financial sanctions category. These essentially stopped all trade between the EU and Iran. Restrictions on transfers of funds to and from Iran, as well as on Iranian access to international financial messaging systems, cut off the Iranian economy from the international economy. EU banks were required to notify or obtain prior authorization for transfers to and from any Iranian person of funds above EUR 10,000, though different

85. Council Regulation (EU) No 267/2012 of 23 Mar. 2012 concerning restrictive measures against Iran and repealing Regulation (EU) No 961/2010 (OJ L 88, 24.3.2012), as last amended by Council Regulation (EU) 2015/1328 (OJ L 206, 1.8.2015) on 1 Aug. 2015 (EU Iran Nuclear Sanctions), Annex IA, IB, II.
86. EU Iran Nuclear Sanctions, Annexes VI and VIA.
87. EU Iran Nuclear Sanctions, Annexes IVA, V and XI.
88. EU Iran Nuclear Sanctions, Annex VIB.
89. EU Iran Nuclear Sanctions, Annex VIIA.
90. EU Iran Nuclear Sanctions, Annex VIIB.
91. EU Iran Nuclear Sanctions, Annex VII.

thresholds. Certain exemptions were available for personal, humanitarian transfers, or transfers linked to specific non-sanctioned trade. These authorizations were issued by the competent authorities of the EU Member States.

Prohibitions were in place on financing enterprises engaged in: the manufacture of military goods, or listed dual-use items; the exploration of crude oil and natural gas, the refining or fuels or the liquefaction of natural gas; or in the petrochemical industry. Further investment restrictions were in place on the Iranian nuclear sector, including the uranium industry.

Sub-Par. 3 Previous EU Iran regime: Asset Freeze and Visa Restrictions

Large numbers of Iranian persons and entities were listed under the nuclear-related legislation, 120 persons and 424 entities.[92] Many of those listed were public companies, including commercial entities of the Iranian government.

Par. 2 International Negotiations with Iran

Sub-Par. 1 History of Negotiations with Iran

In August 2013 a more moderate President, Hassan Rouhani, replaced Mahmoud Ahmadinejad, who had been broadly distrusted by the international community. On 24 November 2013, the international community provided some limited sanctions relief as a gesture of goodwill through an interim Joint Plan of Action (JPOA). Under the JPOA the EU agreed to: pause efforts to reduce Iran's oil sales, as well as suspend EU sanctions on insurance and transportation services linked to those sales; suspend EU sanctions on Iran's petrochemical exports, as well as sanctions on associated services; establish a financial channel to facilitate humanitarian trade for Iran's domestic needs using Iranian oil revenues held abroad; suspend EU sanctions on gold and precious metals, as well as sanctions on associated services; increase tenfold the authorization thresholds for transactions for non-sanctioned trade.[93]

Since the JPOA, Iran has engaged with the permanent members of the UN Security Council plus Germany, and the EU who chaired the negotiations (the P5 + 1, or E3/EU + 3) to agree non-proliferation measures, combined with a lifting of international sanctions. On 14 July 2015, after months of negotiations, this culminated in the Joint Comprehensive Plan of Action (JCPOA).[94]

92. EU Iran Nuclear Sanctions, Annexes VIII and IX.
93. http://eeas.europa.eu/statements/docs/2013/131124_03_en.pdf.
94. The full JCPOA with Annexes is available at http://eeas.europa.eu/statements-eeas/2015/150714_01_en.htm.

Sub-Par. 2 EU Implementation of the JCPOA

On 18 October 2015, in accordance with the JCPOA, the EU adopted legal acts which provide for the termination of all EU nuclear-related economic and financial restrictive measures simultaneously with the IARA-verified implementation by Iran of the agreed nuclear-related measures.[95]

The JCPOA did not have an immediate impact on the EU Iran Sanctions. It was not until Implementation Day – the day that the IAEA verified that Iran had implemented key nuclear-related measures described in the JCPOA, which took place on 16 January 2016 – that most EU Iran sanctions were lifted.

On Implementation Day, the EU adopted a Council Decision[96] bringing into force regulations providing for sanctions relief that were previously issued pursuant to the EU's Adoption Day commitments.[97] By virtue of these legislative acts, the EU has lifted with immediate effect most of its nuclear-related sanctions, as described in the JCPOA.

The sanctions that were lifted cover a number of sectors, including banking, insurance, energy, transport, precious metals, and software. With respect to financial and banking activities, the broad restrictions on financial transfers to or from Iran and Iranian persons or entities have been lifted and, as a result, the previous reporting and authorization requirements for certain financial transactions with Iran no longer apply. Some Iranian banks have been delisted (such as Bank Mellat, Bank Melli Iran, Bank Tejarat and the Central Bank of Iran), but four Iranian banks remain listed: Ansar Bank, Bank Saderat Iran, Bank Saderat plc, and Mehr Bank.[98] Delisted Iranian banks were permitted to reconnect to SWIFT automatically, once SWIFT's normal connection processes were completed. Banking activities, such as the establishment of new correspondent banking relationships and the opening of branches, subsidiaries or representative offices of non-listed Iranian banks in EU Member States, are now permitted.

The following restrictions remain in place including:

(i) an arms embargo covering all goods on the EU Common Military List;
(ii) sanctions on dual-use items covering:
   - goods, technology and software on the Nuclear Suppliers Group list;
   - goods and technology that could contribute to reprocessing-related, enrichment-related, heavy water-related or other activities inconsistent with the JCPOA; and

95. Council Decision (CFSP) 2015/1863 of 18 Oct. 2015 amending Decision 2010/413/CFSP concerning restrictive measures against Iran (OJ L 274, 18.10.2015); Council Regulation (EU) 2015/1861 of 18 Oct. 2015 amending Regulation (EU) No 267/2012 concerning restrictive measures against Iran (OJ L 274, 18.10.2015); Council Implementing Regulation (EU) 2015/1862 of 18 Oct. 2015 implementing Regulation (EU) No 267/2012 concerning restrictive measures against Iran (OJ L 274, 18.10.2015).
96. Council Decision 2016/37; *see also* Information Notice OJ C15 1/1 (2016).
97. Council Regulation (EU) 2015/1861; Council Implementing Regulation (EU) 2015/1862; Council Decision 2015/1863.
98. On 23 Jan. 2016, the EU delisted Bank Sepah and Bank Sepah International separately from delistings as part of Implementation Day. *See* Council Implementing Decision 2016/78 and Council Implementing Regulation (EU) No. 2016/74.

- goods and technology set forth on the Missile Technology Control Regime List.

(iii) A prior authorization is required to export goods related to industries dominated by the IRGC:
  - graphite, raw or semi-finished metals such as aluminium and steel;
  - software for integrating industrial processes.

(iv) The provision of bunkering or ship supply services, or any other servicing of vessels, to vessels, or the provision of engineering and maintenance services to cargo aircraft, where those vessels, or those cargo aircraft are owned or controlled, directly or indirectly, by an Iranian person, entity or body, is prohibited where the providers of the service have information that provides reasonable grounds to determine that the vessels carry goods covered by the Common Military List or goods whose supply, sale, transfer or export is prohibited under the EU Iran Sanctions.

(v) The four Iranian banks which continue to be listed remain subject to asset-freezing measures and prohibitions on the provision of specialized financial messaging services (*i.e.*, SWIFT).

(vi) A significant number of Iranian individuals and entities also remain listed and continue to be subject to asset freezing measures.

(vii) Finally, the JCPOA does not affect EU sanctions related to Iran's human rights violations, as well as EU export control regimes for certain dual-use items.

EU sanctions remaining in place following Implementation Day are scheduled to be lifted in October 2023.

Where Iran is found to be breaching the terms of JCPOA following implementation, a dispute resolution mechanism is set out in the JCPOA: in the event of proven non-compliance by Iran, sanctions will be reimposed; this has been referred to as the 'snap back' of sanctions. It is unclear at this stage whether grandfathering would apply to contracts concluded with Iranian companies in the period between lifting of the sanctions and any snap back.[99]

Par. 3 EU Iran Sanctions Relating to Human Rights Violations

In 2011, the EU imposed specific sanctions on Iran related to human rights violations, with the aim of encouraging Iran to release all political prisoners and halt executions.[100] These sanctions remain in force following the JCPOA described above, and were not on the table for discussion during these talks.

99. Paragraph 37 of the JCPOA states that snap back provisions will not apply with retroactive effect. However, this has yet to be confirmed in EU implementing legislation.
100. Council Decision 2011/235/CFSP of 12 Apr. 2011 concerning restrictive measures directed against certain persons and entities in view of the situation in Iran (OJ L 100, 14.4.2011) and Council Regulation (EU) No 359/2011 of 12 Apr. 2011 concerning restrictive measures directed against certain persons, entities and bodies in view of the situation in Iran (OJ L 100, 14.4.2011) (the EU Iran Human Rights Sanctions).

The principal thematic areas of these sanctions are: equipment used for internal repression; equipment, technology or software used for monitoring or interception of communications by Iran's government or linked public bodies;[101] and an asset freeze and visa restrictions for listed individuals (eighty-six) and entities (one) responsible for serious human rights violations in Iran.[102]

Sub-Section 4 EU Sanctions Regimes Related to Russia, Ukraine, Crimea and Sevastopol

Throughout 2014, in response to Russia's actions with respect to Ukraine, the EU imposed a series of autonomous sanctions which escalated in severity as the situation developed. As a permanent member of the UN Security Council, Russia would have had a veto over the imposition of any UN sanctions regime. Therefore the EU Member States did not attempt to propose any measures within the UN framework.

Instead, the EU adopted the following measures:

(a) On 6 March 2014, asset freezing measures and visa restrictions for persons connected to violations in Ukraine and/or misappropriation of state funds in Ukraine.[103]
(b) On 17 March 2014, asset freezing measures and visa restrictions on key persons and entities responsible for threatening the territorial integrity, independence or sovereignty of Ukraine.[104]
(c) On 24 June 2014, restrictive measures on financing, trade in key sectors and investment in Crimea and Sevastopol.[105]
(d) On 31 July 2014, sectoral and financial sanctions on Russia itself, in response to Russia's complicity in the downing of Malaysian Airlines Flight MH17, and its failure to comply with requests for assistance with investigating and

101. EU Iran Human Rights Sanctions, Annex IV.
102. EU Iran Human Rights Sanctions, Annex I.
103. Council Decision 2014/119/CFSP of 5 Mar. 2014 concerning restrictive measures directed against certain persons, entities and bodies in view of the situation in Ukraine (OJ L 66, 6.3.2014); Council Regulation (EU) No 208/2014 of 5 Mar. 2014 concerning restrictive measures directed against certain persons, entities and bodies in view of the situation in Ukraine (OJ L 66, 6.3.2014).
104. Council Decision 2014/145/CFSP concerning restrictive measures in respect of actions undermining or threatening the territorial integrity, sovereignty and independence of Ukraine (OJ L 78, 17.3.2014); Council Regulation (EU) No 269/2014 of 17 Mar. 2014 concerning restrictive measures in respect of actions undermining or threatening the territorial integrity, sovereignty and independence of Ukraine (OJ L 78, 17.3.2014).
105. Council Decision 2014/386/CFSP of 23 Jun. 2014 concerning restrictions on goods originating in Crimea or Sevastopol, in response to the illegal annexation of Crimea and Sevastopol (OJ L 183, 24.6.2014); Council Regulation (EU) 692/2014 of 23 Jun. 2014 concerning restrictions on the import into the Union of goods originating in Crimea or Sevastopol, in response to the illegal annexation of Crimea and Sevastopol (OJ L 183, 24.6.2014).

to withdraw troops from the vicinity of the conflict zone.[106] This regime was extended in September 2014[107] and again with the most recent consolidation in December 2014.[108]

The continuation of these sanctions was linked to the Minsk peace agreement of 11 February 2015, in which Russia was given until the end of 2015 to comply with its obligations in the agreement.[109]

Par. 1 Sectoral Sanctions

There is a ban on the sale, supply, transfer or export, to any Russian person or entity for use in Russia of listed goods and technology suited to oil exploration or production in deep-water, Arctic and shale projects.[110] It is worth noting that the listed goods and technology are diverse, and may be used in a wide range of projects other than those specifically prohibited (i.e., oil exploration or production in deep-water, Arctic and shale projects). Licences for these products are available, but only where the items are not for use in the specifically prohibited projects. Technical assistance, brokering services, financing or financial assistance in relation to the above goods is also prohibited.

There are prohibitions to sell, supply, transfer, export, directly or indirectly, of dual-use goods and technology,[111] if intended for military use or for a military end-user, or to the following defence sector entities: JSC Sirius, OJSC Stankoinstrument, OAO JSC Chemcomposite, JSC Kalashnikov, JSC Tula Arms Plant, NPK Technologii Maschinostrojenija, OAO Wysokototschnye Kompleksi, OAO Almaz Antey, OAO NPO Bazalt.[112]

106. Council Decision 2014/512/CFSP of 31 Jul 2014 concerning restrictive measures in view of Russia's actions destabilizing the situation in Ukraine (OJ L 229, 31.7.2014); Council Regulation (EU) No 833/2014 of 31 Jul 2014 concerning restrictive measures in view of Russia's actions destabilizing the situation in Ukraine (OJ L 229, 31.7.2014)).
107. Council Decision 2014/659/CFSP of 8 Sep. 2014 amending Decision 2014/512/CFSP concerning restrictive measures in view of Russia's actions destabilizing the situation in Ukraine (OJ L 271, 12.9.2014); Council Regulation (EU) No 960/2014 of 8 Sep. 2014 amending Regulation (EU) No 833/2014 concerning restrictive measures in view of Russia's actions destabilizing the situation in Ukraine (OJ L 271, 12.9.2014).
108. Council Decision 2014/872/CFSP of 4 Dec. 2014 amending Decision 2014/512/CFSP concerning restrictive measures in view of Russia's actions destabilizing the situation in Ukraine, and Decision 2014/659/CFSP amending Decision 2014/512/CFSP (OJ L 349, 5.12.2014); Council Regulation (EU) No 1290/2014 of 4 Dec. 2014 amending Regulation (EU) No 833/2014 concerning restrictive measures in view of Russia's actions destabilizing the situation in Ukraine, and amending Regulation (EU) No 960/2014 amending Regulation (EU) No 833/2014 (OJ L 349, 5.12.2014).
109. European Council Conclusions on external relations, press release, 19 Mar. 2015.
110. Annex II, Council Regulation (EU) No 833/2014 of 31 Jul 2014 concerning restrictive measures in view of Russia's actions destabilizing the situation in Ukraine (OJ L 229, 31.7.2014).
111. As listed in Annex I of the EU's dual-use regulation: Council Regulation (EC) No 428/2009 of 5 May 2009 setting up a Community regime for the control of exports, transfer, brokering and transit of dual-use items (OJ L 134, 29.5.2009).
112. Annex IV to Council Regulation (EC) No 833/2014 of 31 Jul 2014 concerning restrictive measures in view of Russia's actions destabilizing the situation in Ukraine (OJ L 229, 31.7.2014).

It is also prohibited to provide related technical assistance, brokering services, financing or financial assistance. A carve out exists for the trade in dual-use goods and technology intended for the aeronautics and space industry for non-military use, and the maintenance and safety of existing civil nuclear capabilities within the EU for non-military use.

Par. 2 Financial Sanctions

The financial measures aim to restrict the access of state-owned Russian banks and key companies to EU capital markets. In particular, these measures prohibit five listed banks – Sberbank, VTB Bank, Gazprombank, VEB and Rosselkhozbank[113] – from the following activities:

- The sale or purchase of or dealing with transferable securities and money-market instruments with a maturity of over thirty days which have been issued by any listed bank after 12 September 2014 (or over ninety days if issued after 1 August 2014). Related investment services and assistance with such issues is also prohibited.
- Making or being part of any arrangement to extend new loans or credit with a maturity exceeding thirty days to any listed bank after 12 September 2014.

The restrictions also apply to any legal entity established outside the EU which is more than 50% owned by one of the listed banks; and any legal entity acting on behalf of or at the direction of any of the sanctioned entities.

Six other Russian companies are also subject to debt and equity restrictions: OPK Oboronprom, United Aircraft Corporation, Uralvagonzavod, Rosneft, Transneft and Gazprom Neft.[114] The measures also affect non-EU entities which are more than 50% owned by a listed entity, or entities acting on behalf of or at the direction of sanctioned entities. These restrictions on Russian companies mirror the restrictions on banks except that the companies' restrictions only apply to transferable securities and money-market instruments issued after 12 September 2014 or loans made after this date, in all cases where the maturity is over thirty days.

The following activities are carved out of these financial restrictions on making loans, if the purpose of that loan is specific and documented:

- Financing related to exports or imports in relation to non-restricted trade between the EU and Russia.
- Emergency funding to enable majority-owned EU-based subsidiaries of the listed banks to meet solvency and liquidity requirements.

113. List of institutions referred to in Article 5(a), Annex III to Council Regulation (EU) No. 833/2014 of 31 Jul 2014 concerning restrictive measures in view of Russia's actions destabilising the situation in Ukraine. OJ L 27, 12.9.2014.

114. Annexes V and VI to Council Regulation (EC) No 833/2014 of 31 Jul 2014 concerning restrictive measures in view of Russia's actions destabilizing the situation in Ukraine (OJ L 229, 31.7.2014).

Par. 3 Asset Freezing Measures

The EU has imposed asset freezing measures against eighteen persons subject to criminal proceedings by the Ukrainian authorities for the misappropriation of public funds.[115] It has also imposed asset freezing measures against a further 145 persons and thirty-seven entities, targeting persons responsible for Russia's military involvement in Crimea and Sevastopol, pro-Russian politicians and militia leaders in Eastern Ukraine.[116]

Par. 4 Territorial Sanctions on Trade with Crimea and Sevastopol

Territorial sanctions exist on the import into the EU of goods originating in Crimea and Sevastopol, as well as the provision, directly or indirectly financing or financial assistance as well as insurance and reinsurance related to those goods. Financial loans or credits or participation in companies is also prohibited where those companies are involved in the following sectors:

- The creation, acquisition or development of infrastructure in the areas of transport, telecommunications or energy in Crimea or Sevastopol.
- Exploitation of oil, gas or mineral resources in Crimea or Sevastopol.

The provision, directly or indirectly, of technical assistance, brokering services related to these investment activities is also prohibited.

Territorial prohibitions are also in place on the sale, supply, transfer, export, directly or indirectly, of listed equipment and technology relating to transport, telecommunications, energy, oil and gas to companies incorporated in Crimea or Sevastopol, or for use in that region.[117]

It is worth noting that the list of restricted equipment and technology[118] for Crimea and Sevastopol is significantly larger than the restricted list for the Russian sanctions.

115. Annex, Council Decision 2014/119/CFSP of 5 Mar. 2014 concerning restrictive measures directed against certain persons, entities and bodies in view of the situation in Ukraine (OJ L 66, 6.3.2014); Annex I, Council Regulation (EU) No 208/2014 of 5 Mar. 2014 concerning restrictive measures directed against certain persons, entities and bodies in view of the situation in Ukraine (OJ L 66, 6.3.2014).
116. Annex, Council Decision 2014/145/CFSP concerning restrictive measures in respect of actions undermining or threatening the territorial integrity, sovereignty and independence of Ukraine (OJ L 78, 17.3.2014); Annex I, Council Regulation (EU) No 269/2014 of 17 Mar. 2014 concerning restrictive measures in respect of actions undermining or threatening the territorial integrity, sovereignty and independence of Ukraine (OJ L 78, 17.3.2014).
117. Annex II, Council Regulation (EU) 692/2014 of 23 Jun. 2014 concerning restrictions on the import into the Union of goods originating in Crimea or Sevastopol, in response to the illegal annexation of Crimea and Sevastopol (OJ L 183, 24.6.2014).
118. Annex II, Council Regulation (EU) 692/2014 of 23 Jun. 2014 concerning restrictions on the import into the Union of goods originating in Crimea or Sevastopol, in response to the illegal annexation of Crimea and Sevastopol (OJ L 183, 24.6.2014).

Sub-Section 5 The Implementation of EU Sanctions Regimes Across the EU Member States

EU sanctions regimes apply to EU individuals and entities and to the activities of non-EU individuals and entities within the EU (including EU Member State flagged vessels or aircraft); and outside the EU, to EU nationals (being both EU individuals and entities incorporated in an EU Member State).[119] The EU has expressly stated that it 'will refrain from adopting legislative instruments having extraterritorial application in breach of international law.'[120]

On the administrative level, sanctions are applied and enforced at national level by the economic and finance ministry (or treasury), and the ministry for commerce. The treasury department will focus on financial sanctions, including asset freezing and management of lists of designated persons; the business department will apply sanctions to the extent they overlap with standard export control policy.

The competent authorities of EU Member States[121] are responsible for the following sanctions-related activities:

- Advice to prosecuting authorities regarding the determination of penalties for violations of the restrictive measures.[122]
- The granting of authorizations to perform certain activities. In certain cases, certain activities can be authorized despite existing sanctions legislation. In these cases, these departments are responsible for providing those licences.
- Receiving information from, and cooperating with, economic operators (including financial and credit institutions).
- Reporting upon the implementation of sanctions to the European Commission.
- For UN sanctions, liaison with UN Security Council sanctions committees, if required, in respect of specific exemption and de-listing requests.[123]

As implementation is effected at the national level, there is a possibility that Member State authorities adopt different interpretations as to the scope of application. The likely interpretation of the relevant national authority should be taken into account when seeking to understand how a particular sanctions provision will apply to a specific scenario.

Below is an illustrative description of the enforcement of sanctions by certain EU Member States.

119. EU Guidelines 2012, paragraph 88.
120. EU Guidelines 2012, paragraph 52.
121. A list of websites for competent EU Member State authorities is included in Section 7.3.
122. Penalties for breach of sanctions legislation may considered criminal, civil or regulatory and offences typically require actual knowledge or suspicion of breach of sanctions.
123. *Sanctions or restrictive measures: Frequently Asked Questions*, European Commission, Spring 2008, p.8.

Par. 1 France

In France, the *Direction Générale du Trésor* deals with asset freezing and other financial sanctions.[124] The *Service des Biens à Double Usage* within the *Direction Générale des Entreprises* deals with export control issues.[125]

Under the French *Code des douanes*, violations or attempted violations of international restrictive measures or embargoes, whether enacted by French laws and regulations or set out by EU Regulations, can give rise to criminal sanctions.[126]

Natural persons are subject to imprisonment of up to five years and a fine (proportional to the amount of the offence, up to twice the amount).[127] This fine is multiplied by five in the case of legal entities held liable for the offence.[128] Furthermore, when the object subject to confiscation cannot be seized, the criminal court can order that the offender (whether natural or legal person) pays a sum equal to the value of the object.[129]

The French financial and monetary code provides that senior managers or employees of financial institutions who breach asset freezing or prohibition measures shall incur the same penalties as under the French *Code des douanes*.

A three-year time limitation for prosecution applies to offences (*délits*).[130] This limit may begin on discovery of the offence, rather than from the date of the offence itself.

Par. 2 Germany

In Germany, the Public Prosecutor's office and Customs Prosecution Service are the competent authorities that enforce EU sanctions and export control legislation.

Under German law, breaches of EU sanctions and export controls can incur both criminal and administrative penalties. As regards criminal penalties, these come in the form of prison sentences and/or fines. The length of the former can vary between three months and fifteen years depending of the offence and possible aggravating circumstances. Fines can amount to 365 daily rates. The daily rate is calculated based on the income of the convicted. As regards administrative penalties, administrative fines can come up to EUR 500 000, and further up to EUR 10 million in special cases.

A five-year time limitation for prosecution applies to violations of imports and exports licensing requirements, as well as to breaches of EU sanctions regulations.[131]

---

124. http://www.tresor.economie.gouv.fr/sanctions-financieres-internationales.
125. http://www.entreprises.gouv.fr/biens-double-usage/accueil.
126. Article 459, French *Code des douanes*.
127. Article 459.1, French *Code des douanes*.
128. Legal entities might also incur additional penalties, such as dissolution, publication of all or part of the judicial decision, etc., Article 131-39 of the French *Code penal*.
129. Articles 459-1 and 459-2 of the French *Code des douanes* and Article 131-39 of the French *Code penal*.
130. Article 8, French Criminal Procedural Code.
131. Section 18(1), *Außenwirtschaftsgesetz* (German Federal Act on Foreign Trade).

Nonetheless, limitation periods can go up to twenty years in special cases depending of the criminal offence. The time limitation is reduced to three years for administrative violations.[132]

German export control laws and the criminal sanctions were revised in 2013.[133] Consequently, there have been few cases reported before the German courts.

Par. 3 United Kingdom

In the UK, HM Treasury's Asset Freezing Unit is responsible for the implementation and enforcement of financial sanctions, and the Export Control Organisation (ECO), within the Department for Business Innovation and Skills (BIS), is responsible for economic sanctions, and dual-use and military goods. Her Majesty's Revenue and Customs (HMRC) is responsible for investigating breaches of sanctions legislation linked to licensing and duty payments. In the event of a breach being discovered, its prosecution is led by the Crown Prosecution Service (CPS). The Financial Conduct Authority leads on the regulatory aspects of sanctions enforcement in the regulated financial sectors for which it has supervisory responsibility.

On 8 July 2015, the UK government announced the creation of a new Office of Financial Sanctions Implementation within HM Treasury, effective from April 2016.[134] This office will 'work closely with law enforcement to help ensure that financial sanctions are properly understood, implemented and enforced.' At the same time, new UK legislation was promised, increasing the penalties for non-compliance with financial sanctions, and giving new powers, akin to those held by the Office of Foreign Assets Control in the US, to the UK's HM Treasury to impose monetary penalties and reach 'deferred prosecution agreements' with offenders in return for payments of fines and/or reforms to their business practices.[135] This marks a declaration of intent by the UK government to increase its focus on this area, and potentially create a more aggressive enforcement regime.

In a recent case before the UK courts, the applicant, a sanctioned Russian company, OJSC Rosneft Oil Company, brought an action against all three of the UK government authorities responsible for implementation of sanctions: Her Majesty's Treasury, the Secretary of State for Business, Innovation & Skills, and the Financial Conduct Authority. Rosneft invoked a violation of the principles of legal certainty and a failure to clearly describe criminal charges to which the sanctions were a response. Rosneft also claimed that the measures contravene the duty to give reasons, infringe the right to a fair hearing and infringe the right to effective judicial protection.[136]

132. Section 31(2) *Ordnungswidrigkeitsgesetz*.
133. New versions of the *Außenwirtschaftsgesetz* and the *Außenwirtschaftsverordnung* (German Foreign Trade Ordinance) became effective on 1 Sep. 2013.
134. https://www.gov.uk/government/publications/summer-budget-2015/summer-budget-2015.
135. Part 8 of the Policing and Crime Bill (HC Bill 158).
136. *OJSC Rosneft Oil Company v. Her Majesty's Treasury*, [2015] EWHC 248 (Admin).

Rosneft was denied interim relief in the UK courts, but permitted an expedited hearing, at which the case was referred to the European Court of Justice.[137]

Criminal penalties for breaches of UK or EU sanctions prohibitions are currently provided for by secondary legislation.[138] This legislation takes the form of UK regulations implementing the relevant EU sanctions regime. Breach of sanctions is a criminal offence under UK domestic law, punishable by imprisonment and/or an unlimited fine. In February 2011, two Mabey & Johnson directors were convicted of breaching Iraqi sanctions and given custodial sentences.[139]

Failure to comply with UK sanctions legislation where this includes breach of the terms of a licence can result in the suspension or revocation of the licence and/or criminal prosecution. Where there have been minor infringements of the legislation or licence requirements, for example, discovered during a compliance inspection audit, ECO will issue a warning letter to the exporters in breach asking the matter to be addressed within a period of time. In more serious breach of licensing cases, the matter will be taken up by HMRC. In this event, HMRC has the power to seize goods, issue a fine, or a compound penalty fine in recognition of an agreement to settle, or refer the case to the CPS for prosecution.[140]

Where the UK's Crown Prosecution Service (CPS) decides to prosecute the offence under export control laws, there are two principal offences under which the CPS may choose to proceed: a strict liability offence of non-compliance, or the more serious offence of intent to evade export controls.[141] A defendant convicted on indictment of the 'intent to evade' offence can face an unlimited fine and a prison sentence of up to ten years.[142] A defendant convicted of a strict liability offence can face a maximum fine of up to three times the retail value of the goods, and/or to imprisonment for a term of up to six months, although in practice the fines imposed are less than GBP 1,000.[143]

The information on penalties in the UK is limited by the fact that only cases that go to trial (and are not settled) are publicly available. BIS provides a list of compound penalties per year.[144] A compound penalty is the means by which HMRC can offer to settle out of court a case where they would normally prosecute to save both the tax payer and the company time and resources. There were six compound penalties

137. Case C-72/15 Reference for a preliminary ruling from High Court of Justice (England & Wales), Queen's Bench Division (Divisional Court) (United Kingdom) made on 18 Feb. 2015 - *OJSC Rosneft Oil Company v. Her Majesty's Treasury*, Secretary of State for Business, Innovation and Skills, The Financial Conduct Authority.
138. For example, UK penalties applying to breaches of financial sanctions under the EU's nuclear-related Iran sanctions regime (Council Regulation 267/2012) are set out in Article 21 of the Iran (European Union Financial Sanctions) Regulations 2012; UK penalties applying to breaches of the EU's Russia sanctions regime (Council Regulation 833/2014) are set out in Article 11 of the Export Control (Russia, Crimea and Sevastopol Sanctions) Order 2014.
139. *R. v. Forsyth; R. v. Mabey*, [2010] EWCA Crim 2437.
140. Sections 68 and 152, Customs and Excise Management Act 1979.
141. Section 68(1) and (2), Customs and Excise Management Act 1979.
142. Section 68(3) and (4A), Customs and Excise Management Act 1979.
143. Section 68, Customs and Excise Management Act 1979.
144. Notices to Exporters, Compound Penalty Cases, 6 Jun. 2012, updated to Calendar year ending 2014.

imposed in 2014 which amounted to a total of GBP 257,906. The details released are limited but it is worth noting the duration of the alleged infringement which ranged from seven months to five years.

There is also a risk of regulatory action: enforcement is squarely on the Financial Conduct Authority's agenda in the financial sector following its thematic reviews in 2009 and 2013.[145] In 2010, the Royal Bank of Scotland was fined GBP 5.6 million by the (then) Financial Services Authority (FSA) for systems and controls breaches with respect to financial sanctions. In 2013, after a settlement reducing the total penalty, Guaranty Bank was fined GBP 0.5 million by the (by now) Financial Conduct Authority for poor systems and controls in relation to money laundering and sanctions.[146]

Sub-Section 6 EU Case Law on Its Sanctions Regimes

With the proliferation of sanctions regimes, sanctions cases have become a highly litigated field of law before European courts.[147] Cases brought directly against the EU to challenge persons' and entities' listings in Council Decisions or Regulations are heard in the General Court of the EU (General Court), or in the European Court of Justice (Court of Justice) if they have been referred by the national courts of the EU Member States.[148]

The majority of these rulings concern what is referred to as '*de-listing cases*', in which designated parties bring actions for annulment to have their names removed from lists subjecting them to asset freezing regimes. Applicants usually rely on one of the following two arguments.

The first is the right to effective judicial protection, and related defence and due process rights. In this area the Kadi saga[149] stands out in particular, imposing higher standards of proof to the European authorities, obliging them to provide adequate reasons which are 'individual, specific and concrete' in order to add a person on an EU sanctions list.[150] Both the General Court and the Court of Justice place great emphasis on the importance for applicants of submitting evidence refuting reasons for their designation, and are willing to assure full judicial review to assure the respect of these fundamental rights.

The second line of argument used in these cases concerns the ownership and control of third persons or entities by listed persons or entities. In *Persia International*

145. UK Financial Conduct Authority, *Banks' control of financial crime risks in trade finance*, TR13/3, 1 Jul 2013.
146. FCA Final Notice 2013: Guaranty Trust Bank (UK) Limited, 8 Aug. 2013.
147. 183 closed cases so far, out of which sixty-eight were handed down in 2014.
148. Previously the Court of First Instance.
149. Case T-315/01, *Kadi v. Council and Commission* [2005] ECR 2005 II-03649; Cases C-402/05 P and C-415/05 P, *Kadi and Al Barakaat International Foundation v. Council and Commission* [2008] ECR 2008 I-06351; Case T-85/09, *Kadi v. Commission* [2010] ECR 2010 II-05177; Joined Cases C-584/10 P, C-593/10 P and C-595/10 P, *Commission and Others v. Kadi* [2013] ECR 2013-00000.
150. Cases C-584/10 P, C-593/10 P and C-595/10 P, *Commission and Others v. Kadi* [2013] *ibid.*, *supra*, paragraph 116.

Bank,[151] the General Court held that 'the fact that the listed bank owned 60% of the applicant's share capital did not, by itself, justify the adoption and maintenance of the restrictive measures concerning the applicant.' The General Court noted that although the listed entity, Bank Mellat, owned 60% of the applicant's share capital, and could appoint four of the seven members of the board of directors, one of the four members was an independent non-executive director, and the three remaining were appointed by other shareholders. Therefore, Bank Mellat could only really exert its influence over three of the seven members of the board at most. Moreover, the General Court observed that the appointment of any new director was subject to approval by the FSA, thus, limiting Bank Mellat's position to freely alter the number or nature of the applicant's directors. With this in mind, the General Court reached the conclusion that although the designated entity was capable of exerting influence over the applicant, the ownership test had not been met, and consequently annulled the act adopted by the Council.

In its March 2015 guidelines, the Council of the EU endorsed the Court's interpretation of ownership and control in the light of *Persia International* and clarified the two concepts:[152]

(a) *Ownership*: Ownership is defined by the possession of more than 50% of the proprietary rights of an entity or having majority interest in it.
(b) *Control*: Assessing whether a legal person or entity is controlled by another person or entity is more complicated and the following criteria are given in the Best Practices document by way of illustration:
   - having the right or exercising the power to appoint or remove a majority of the members of the administrative, management or supervisory bodies;
   - having the right to exercise a dominant influence over a legal person or entity, pursuant to an agreement entered into with that legal person or entity, or to a provision in its Memorandum or Articles of Association;
   - having appointed solely as a result of the exercise of one's voting rights a majority of the members of the administrative, management or supervisory bodies of a legal person or entity who have held office during the present and previous financial year;
   - controlling alone, pursuant to an agreement with other shareholders in or members of a legal person or entity, a majority of shareholders' or members' voting rights in that legal person or entity;
   - having the power to exercise the right to exercise a dominant influence referred to above, without being the holder of that right;
   - having the right to use all or part of the assets of a legal person or entity;
   - managing the business of a legal person or entity on a unified basis, while publishing consolidated accounts;

151. Case T-493/10, *Persia International Bank plc* [2013] ECLI:EU:T:2013:398.
152. EU Best Practices 2015.

- sharing jointly and severally the financial liabilities of a legal person or entity, or guaranteeing them.

In May 2015, the General Court annulled (as far it concerned one of the applicants) EU restrictive measures against a joint venture, Petropars Resources Engineering Kish Co, a co-applicant.[153] The General Court ruled that the Council failed to demonstrate that a subsidiary of a listed entity, National Iranian Oil Company, a minority shareholder of Petropars, was in a position analogous to single ownership, especially where other shareholders have no interest in assisting that minority shareholder in circumventing sanctions through the subsidiaries. It is worth pointing that the General Court stated that in order to meet the listing criterion, an entity does not have to provide support for the Iranian government itself if the entity it is controlled by does provide that support.[154] In addition, a long chain of companies does not affect the application of the rebuttable presumption that a parent company exercises decisive influence over the conduct of a subsidiary. Furthermore, the General Court indicated that the criterion is met if a controlling or owning entity holds all or virtually all capital in a subsidiary, or holds a position analogous to being a single company in possession of the full share capital.[155]

It should be noted that the Court of Justice ruled in the *Melli Bank* case[156] that the controlled entity does not need to be actually involved in the unlawful activities that got the controlling party listed in the first place as long as the ownership and belonging test is satisfied.

As EU case law demonstrates, the ownership and control test is not limited to an assessment of whether the designated person has a majority of the share capital of the 'controlled' entity, but to whether the designated party actually can exert its control over the concerned entity.

Finally, it should be noted that EU sanctions have had deeper effects in the EU judiciary going beyond solely matters of interpretation. The new rules of procedure of the General Court, which entered into force in July 2015, incorporate new provisions regarding the treatment of information provided by national security agencies used by the Council in sanctions cases.[157] This has been a point of contention as the General Court has to conciliate, on the one hand, the respect of the fundamental right to due process of a person subject to sanctions,[158] and on the other hand, the practical needs

153. Case T-433/13, *Petropars Iran and Others v. Council.*
154. Case T-433/13, *Petropars Iran and Others v. Council,* Judgment of the General Court, paragraph 47.
155. Case T-433/13, *Petropars Iran and Others v. Council,* Judgment of the General Court, paragraph 73.
156. Case C-548/09, *Bank Melli Iran v. Council* [2011] ECR 2011-00000.
157. These are set forth in Article 105 of the Rules of procedure of the General Court, 23 Apr. 2015, OJ L 105, vol. 58.
158. It must be pointed out that in Kadi II (C-584/10 P, C-593/10 P and C-595/10 P, *European Commission v. Kadi* [2013] EU:C:2013:518.) the Court had explicitly stated that it would conduct a full judicial review on sanctions cases, and that the respect of fundamental rights requires that the person concerned must be able to ascertain the reasons upon which the decision taken in relation to him is based.

of Member States trying to avoid compromising national security by revealing confidential information. The new procedural rules try to strike a fair balance between the needs of both sides and sets forth a procedure which can be used by the main party relying on secret information, usually the Council. This way the General Court can assess whether there is sufficient evidence to support a listing decision, while minimizing the risk of leaking sensible confidential information to the general public.

Sub-Section 7 The Anatomy of a US Sanctions Regime

Most OFAC sanctions regulations are found in title 31 to the C.F.R. For example, the Sudanese Sanctions Regulations (SSR) are found at 31 C.F.R. §§538 et Seq. Typically the 200 series of OFAC's regulations will set forth the prohibitions of the programme, and possible exemptions. For example, under the SSR, 31 C.F.R. §538.205 provides for a prohibition on exportations and reexportations of goods, services and technology to Sudan, and 31 C.F.R. §538.212(a) allows an exemption for personal communications. The 300 series in the regulations will contain definitions. The 400 series will typically contain interpretations offered by OFAC, and the 500 series will contain information about licences (or permits) that may be available. In some cases, OFAC will publish interpretations or general licences on its website, and it may be some time before these get published into the regulations.

The remainder of this sub-section will address several 'key concepts' that are essential to understanding the applicability and scope of US economic sanctions regulations.

Par. 1 Jurisdiction

OFAC's sanctions regulations will apply to the activities of US Persons or activities in the US. 'US Persons' include:

- US citizens and permanent resident aliens ('green card' holders) wherever located, including when living and working abroad for a non-US company.
- Foreign (non-US) nationals present in the US, including transients or persons in the US only temporarily.
- Companies and other entities organized under the laws of the US, including their foreign branches.
- US branches and US subsidiaries of non-US companies.

For the Cuba and Iran sanctions programmes, all of the above are covered, plus non-US entities owned or controlled by US entities, including non-US subsidiaries of a US company.

Jurisdiction can also attach to transactions that involve US goods, software or technology, or non-US products derived therefrom. In addition, US dollar denominated financial transactions and/or transactions that clear through the US financial system will trigger OFAC jurisdiction as an export/import of a service within the meaning of the regulations. So, for example, any US banks involved in processing a US dollar wire payment from a French company to a company in Germany are required to comply with OFAC regulations (so, if the underlying transaction relates to a sale of Sudanese origin goods, the US bank may not be able to process the transaction without authorization from OFAC).[159]

Note that in some cases there are also extraterritorial 'secondary' sanctions rules that can apply even without a US nexus, person, parent, item or currency. For example, the US maintains secondary sanctions authorities involving Iran and Syria that have been the subject of particular attention and focus.[160] Certain US rules relating to Iran allow for imposition of penalties on non-US entities engaging in certain transactions with Iran's petroleum and other sectors, or with certain types of designated parties. These sanctions can deny access to certain US services to designated non-US Persons/ entities engaging in sanctionable activities (these extraterritorial sanctions have particular impact on foreign financial institutions and parties dealing with Iran's petroleum and petrochemical industries and companies, as well as parties involved in human rights abuses in Iran and Syria).[161]

Par. 2 50% Rule

OFAC takes the position that any entity 50% or more owned by an SDN or by an SSIL must, itself, be treated as an SDN or SSIL, even if that entity is not itself named on the SDN or SSIL list. This concept is sometimes referred to as the 'shadow' SDN/SSIL rule. OFAC has specifically written this requirement into some of its sanctions regulations, but in other cases relies upon published guidance with respect to this interpretation.[162]

OFAC applies the 50% rule on both an aggregating and a cascading basis. For example: If Company A, which is not a named SDN, is 30% owned by Company B which is a named SDN, and 30% owned by Company C which is a named SDN, then Company A must be treated like an SDN by virtue of its aggregate total of 60% SDN ownership. Similarly: If Company A, which is not a named SDN, is 50% owned by Company B, which is not a named SDN but which is itself 50% owned by Company C, and Company C is a named SDN, then both Company B and Company A must be treated as SDNs (OFAC cascades the ownership down from Company C, and does not dilute the share percentages through levels of ownership). Note that OFAC does not commingle SDN and SSIL interests – so if Company A, which is not a named SDN or

159. For example, OFAC has proceeded with enforcement actions in cases where non-US entities have originated electronic funds transfers that were processed through US financial institutions for the benefit of persons in Iran, as a violation of the prohibition against the exportation of services, directly or indirectly, from the United States to Iran, where the non-US entity prevented US financial institutions from assessing the permissibility of the transactions by omitting references to Iran in the payment messages. See http://www.treasury.gov/resource-center/sanctions/CivPen/Documents/20131021_alma.pdf.
160. See for example, the Iran Threat Reduction and Syria Human Rights Act of 2012 (PL 112-158).
161. See Sub-section 8, Sub-par. 3, below, for additional details regarding 'secondary' sanctions authorities.
162. See OFAC's guidance dated 13 Aug. 2014, available at http://www.treasury.gov/resource-center/sanctions/Documents/licensing_guidance.pdf.

SSIL, is owned 30% by named SDN Company B, and 30% by named SSIL Company C, then Company A is neither an SDN nor an SSIL (although US Persons would be remiss if they were not to exercise extreme caution when engaging in transactions or dealings with such an entity, should they be designated by OFAC in the future).

Although the 50% rule does not, per se, require that non-named entities be treated like restricted parties if the SDN/SSIL simply 'controls' the non-named entity but does not own 50% or more, indicia of control by restricted parties should be considered a red flag for US parties, and could result in future designations by OFAC. Moreover, an OFAC FAQ clarifies the agency's position that, although a country's government ministry is not blocked solely because the minister heading it is an SDN, US Persons should be cautious in dealings with the ministry to ensure that they are not providing funds, goods, or services to the SDN, and that US Persons should not enter into any contracts that are signed by an SDN.[163]

Par. 3 Blocking and Rejecting Transactions

Depending on the sanctions programme involved, US Persons may be required to 'block' (or 'freeze') a transaction, property or interest in property. In other cases, the US Person is simply required to 'reject' the transaction, property or interest in property.

All property and interests in property of SDNs in the US or in the possession or control of US Persons must be blocked. Blocking provisions also apply to some country governments, including all property and interests in property of the Governments of Cuba, Iran, Sudan and Syria. When property or interests in property become 'blocked' they have to be segregated and separately held. Funds, for example, must be placed in a separate, interest bearing account in the US, and reports to OFAC are required. Failure to block is an ongoing violation of the relevant underlying regulations (e.g., there is no statute of limitations for this violation). Property only becomes 'unblocked' upon receipt of OFAC authorization.

In some cases, US or non-US Persons must simply 'reject' transactions, rather than blocking them, where a sanctions target is involved, but where 'blocking' is not required. For example, a US bank could not generally process a payment where the remitter of the payment is in Syria. If the government of Syria or an SDN were the remitter, the payment would be blocked. However, if the remitter were someone in Syria other than the government or Syria or an SDN, the US bank would simply reject the payment. In addition, a bank may reject transactions where, although there are no SDNs involved and the payment is (or arguably may be) legally permitted, the payment relates to a transaction that does not align with the bank's policy. This is an increasing trend in economic sanctions compliance that both US and non-US banks are increasingly tending to decline transactions related to sanctions targets, even if technically they could legally process the transaction. Note that rejected transactions also have to be reported to OFAC.

---

163. See OFAC FAQ 285 available at http://www.treasury.gov/resource-center/faqs/Sanctions/Pages/faq_other.aspx#burma.

Par. 4 Property / Interest in Property

The concept of 'property' or an 'interest in property' under OFAC's regulations is a very broad definition. It includes but is not limited to: money, checks, drafts, bullion, bank deposits, savings accounts, debits, indebtedness, obligations, notes, guarantees, debentures, stocks, bonds, coupons, any other financial instruments, bankers acceptances, mortgages, pledges, liens or other rights in the nature of security, warehouse receipts, bills of lading, trust receipts, bills of sale, any other evidences of title, ownership or indebtedness, letters of credit and documents relating to any rights or obligations thereunder, powers of attorney, goods, wares, merchandise, chattels, stocks on hand, ships, goods on ships, real estate mortgages, deeds of trust, vendors' sales agreements, land contracts, leaseholds, ground rents, real estate and any other interest therein, options, negotiable instruments, trade acceptances, royalties, book accounts, accounts payable, judgments, patents, trademarks or copyrights, insurance policies, safe deposit boxes and their contents, annuities, pooling agreements, services of any nature whatsoever, contracts of any nature whatsoever, and any other property, real, personal, or mixed, tangible or intangible, or interest or interests therein, present, future or contingent.[164]

Par. 5 Direct and Indirect Transactions

Most economic sanctions regulations prohibit activity, dealings or transactions that are done either directly or indirectly. So, if a US company cannot export goods to Sudan directly, it cannot export goods to Eritrea first, for onward transfer to Sudan. Similarly, if a US bank cannot process a payment coming from Syria to the UK, it cannot process a payment that originates in Syria, goes through a bank in the United Arab Emirates, for forward transfer on to the UK.

Par. 6 Facilitation and Evasion

Closely related to the 'direct and indirect' concept is the OFAC concept of 'facilitation.' A US Person, wherever located, cannot approve or facilitate any transaction by a non-US Person if the US Person would be prohibited from undertaking the transaction in the US. Facilitation is a very broad concept, as interpreted by OFAC, and it is 'read into' all sanctions programmes, not just those that specifically reference this term.[165]

---

164. See e.g., 31 C.F.R. §538.310.
165. The SSR, for example, contain a provision called 'prohibited facilitation' that reads as follows:

> Except as otherwise authorized, the facilitation by a United States person, including but not limited to brokering activities, of the exportation or reexportation of goods, technology or services from Sudan to any destination, or to Sudan from any location, is prohibited.

31 C.F.R. §538.206.

For example, US companies cannot refer contracts involving sanctioned countries to their foreign affiliates. In addition, US companies cannot provide any approval, financial assistance, advice, consulting services, goods, or any other support to their affiliates in connection with prohibited transactions. US companies also cannot alter their operating policies or procedures, or even in some cases those of a foreign affiliate, in order to permit a foreign affiliate to engage in transactions involving a sanctioned country that otherwise were prohibited or required the approval or participation of the US company.[166]

For US Persons living and working outside the US, examples of prohibited activities with respect to transactions with, in, or involving a sanctioned country include: conducting negotiations; voting as a member of the board of directors in favour of a transaction; providing advice or recommendations; making decisions, or otherwise exercising discretionary authority. Recusal by US Persons from proceedings may be an option in certain cases.

Evasions of the sanctions regulations, or attempts to evade the regulations, are also prohibited.[167]

Par. 7 Exemptions

Certain types of transactions may be exempt from OFAC's sanctions prohibitions, including:

- Certain travel related transactions.
- Transactions involving personal communications.
- Certain humanitarian donations.
- Transactions involving information or informational materials.

Not all exemptions apply equally to all programmes. In addition, exemptions generally are narrowly construed by OFAC. For example, the sale and export of books is generally not prohibited by most sanctions programmes, because such books are 'informational materials'; however having a person in Iran undertake a marketing campaign or provide customized consulting services is likely outside the scope of the informational materials exemption unless specifically authorized in another provision of the regulations or authorized in a specific licence from OFAC.

Par. 8 Licences

A licence is essentially a permit from OFAC allowing an individual, entity or several parties to engage in activities that are otherwise prohibited by the regulations. There are two types of licences: general, and specific.

166. See e.g., 31 C.F.R. §560.417.
167. See e.g., 31 C.F.R. §560.203.

General licences are usually applicable to any individual or entity who satisfies the terms and conditions of the general licence. A listing of relevant general licences will be found in the 500 series of OFAC's sanctions regulations (in some cases general licences are posted on OFAC's website and take some time to appear in the text of the regulations). So, for example, 31 C.F.R. §538.528 contains the SSR's general licence allowing certain non-commercial, personal remittances to or from Sudan. Other types of general licences include general licences to send food to Iran and Sudan, general licences to send medicine to Iran, general licences for certain publishing activities for some countries, and general licences for certain UN activities in some cases.

Specific licences are documents issued on an application basis to a specific company, individual or group authorizing certain specific activities. OFAC typically generally authorizes transactions that are 'incident to a licensed transaction and necessary to give effect thereto' (there are some exceptions). So, for example, if a company obtains a specific licence to ship supplies to Sudan, receiving payment for the supplies and obtaining marine cargo insurance coverage for the shipment would be incident and necessary to the licensed export, and therefore also authorized so long as no persons, entities or banks designated under other programmes (e.g., a bank in Sudan which is designated as a weapons proliferation concern) are involved.

Note that both general and specific licences have terms and conditions which must be complied with, including in some cases reporting obligations and expiration dates. Even if there is no formal reporting requirement, licensees must keep records for five years.

Par. 9 Compliance

Compliance with OFAC's regulations is a 'strict liability' standard. That is, you do not have to 'know' that your behaviour was wrong to be penalized (although absence of knowledge can be a mitigating factor when OFAC is assessing a potential penalty for violations of its regulations).[168]

OFAC does not require any specific compliance procedures or programmes, but endorses a 'risk-based' approach for compliance.[169] OFAC expects that companies will consider:

(1) Your organization's risk that violations may occur:
   - For example, are you an international bank with offices all over the world, or are you a local vendor who, once or twice year, exports products outside the US?

(2) What are appropriate steps to mitigate your risk?

(3) If your risks are very high, the steps appropriate to mitigate your risks will be more complicated and onerous.

168. See OFAC's Enforcement Guidelines, available at http://www.treasury.gov/resource-center/sanctions/Documents/fr74_57593.pdf and in 31 C.F.R. Part 501, Appendix A.
169. See e.g., OFAC's FAQ 25, available at http://www.treasury.gov/resource-center/faqs/Sanctions/Pages/faq_compliance.aspx#start.

OFAC can glean compliance information regarding a company from a number of sources, including:

- Voluntary self-disclosures (VSDs) filed by the company, or by other companies that name your organization.
- Reports from other US government agencies (Commerce Department, State Department, Defence Department, Department of Homeland Security, etc.).
- Referrals from other Treasury Department divisions (e.g., for banks, from the Financial Crimes Enforcement Network, or 'FinCEN').
- US financial institutions (based on rejected or blocked transaction reports).
- 'Tip offs' from competitors.
- Public news stories.
- Websites.
- Anonymous tips/hotline calls.
- Securities and Exchange Commission (SEC) filings and disclosures.

OFAC personnel will regularly utilize these tools.

Sub-Section 8 US Sanctions Regimes

US sanctions can target specific countries, regimes, governments, entities, individuals, activities and/or sectors. Although there are variations amongst programmes, the sanctions can generally be divided into two types of broad categories: (1) comprehensive sanctions; and (2) targeted sanctions.

Par. 1 Comprehensive Sanctions

OFAC's comprehensive sanctions programmes target entire countries/territories or governments thereof, and restrict most types of activities (trade, exports, imports, investment, financing, etc.) with some exceptions. OFAC maintains comprehensive sanctions with respect to five countries, and one territory: the Crimea region; Cuba; Iran; North Korea; Sudan; and Syria. Iran, Sudan and Syria are also designated as state sponsors of terrorism by the US State Department.[170]

170. See http://www.state.gov/j/ct/rls/crt/2011/195547.htm for additional information regarding State Department designations. In the past, other countries such as Libya and Iraq have been similarly designated by the State Department. North Korea technically was delisted as a state sponsor of terrorism but broad restrictions remain so we have grouped this country along with Iran, Sudan and Syria. Similarly, Cuba was delisted as a state sponsor of terrorism in 2015, but we have retained Cuba in the list of comprehensive OFAC sanctions programmes given the broad restrictions that remain in place.

Sub-Par. 1 Crimea

Starting in December 2014, the US imposed comprehensive sanctions restrictions against the territory of Crimea, in response to the ongoing situation and territory disputes between Ukraine and Russia.[171]

These sanctions prohibit new investment in the Crimea region by a US Person, wherever located. The Crimea sanctions also prohibit the importation into the US, directly or indirectly, of any goods, services, or technology from the Crimea region, as well as the exportation, reexportation, sale or supply, directly or indirectly, from the US, or by a US person, wherever located, of any goods, services, or technology to the Crimea region.

OFAC has issued a general licence under the Crimea sanctions programme which authorizes the exportation or reexportation by US Persons of certain agricultural goods, medicine, medical supplies, and replacement parts to Crimea, or to persons in third countries purchasing specifically for resale to the Crimea, without a specific licence from OFAC if the terms and conditions of the general licence are met. The conduct of related transactions also is authorized, including the making of shipping and cargo inspection arrangements, the obtaining of insurance, the arrangement of financing and payment, shipping of goods, receipt of payment, and the entry into contracts (including executory contracts).

Sub-Par. 2 Cuba

The OFAC sanctions against Cuba are arguably historically the most restrictive, and are based on statutory instruments that are unique and distinct from other current sanctions programmes. OFAC's sanctions against Cuba are primarily found in the Cuban Assets Control Regulations (CACR), which were originally issued in the 1960s.[172] The primary statutory underpinning for the CACR is TWEA, as opposed to other sanctions programmes where the primary statutory instrument underlying the OFAC regulations is IEEPA. In addition, for the Cuba regime other relevant legislation includes the Antiterrorism and Effective Death Penalty Act of 1996,[173] the Cuban Democracy Act of 1992,[174] and LIBERTAD (also known as the Helms-Burton Act).

OFAC's sanctions against Cuba apply to persons subject to US jurisdiction, which includes US Persons, as well as to entities owned or controlled by US Persons, including foreign incorporated subsidiaries of US companies. Along with the Iran sanctions, this applicability to entities owned or controlled by US Persons is unique amongst territorial sanctions programmes administered by OFAC.[175] (For other programmes, non-US

171. Executive Order 13685.
172. 31 C.F.R. Part 515.
173. 18 USC §2332d.
174. 22 USC §§6001-6010.
175. Unlike OFAC's Iran sanctions regulations, 'owned or controlled' are not defined within the CACR. However, OFAC recognizes US ownership of a foreign entity where US Persons own 100% of the stock of the entity, and 'control' is presumed if US Persons own between 50% and 100% of the stock of the entity, although this presumption can be rebutted. OFAC views

entities may effectively be restricted due to approval or facilitation by a US parent company or the involvement of US Persons or US financial institutions, even though the non-US entity itself is not technically a US Person.)

The CACR prohibit persons subject to US jurisdiction from dealing in any property in which Cuba or a Cuban national has any interest of any nature whatsoever. This effectively prohibits all transactions with Cuba, including exports and imports of goods, services and technology, without authorization.[176]

In addition, the CACR are unique among existing US sanctions regulations in that they block the assets not only of the Cuban government, but also of all Cuban nationals (defined to include citizens and permanent residents of Cuba, persons domiciled in Cuba, and entities organized under the laws of Cuba, wherever they are located). There are exemptions and licences that mitigate the impact of this broad restriction on Cuban nationals wherever located.

The CACR also prohibit persons subject to US jurisdiction from engaging in transactions relating to travel to, from or within Cuba except as authorized by OFAC. As noted above, unlike the IEEPA-based sanctions programmes where a travel exemption is generally available, the CACR were promulgated pursuant to other legislation such as TWEA. There are several general licences in the CACR that will authorize certain types of travel without specific authorization from OFAC, such as travel related to visits to close relatives in Cuba, certain journalistic activity in Cuba, and certain professional research and educational activities.

Although certain other OFAC sanctions programmes, such as those against Iran, Sudan and Syria, are generally aligned with policies of other nations, such as the EU members states which also maintain sanctions against these countries, the Cuba sanctions are unique to the US. In fact, some other nations such as the EU use so-called blocking statutes to specifically prohibit EU companies from complying with the sanctions laws of other countries regarding Cuba. For companies subject to both US

ownership or control broadly as concepts, and may designate entities as 'persons subject to U.S. jurisdiction,' even where US Persons own less than 50% of the shares of the entity. In situations where US ownership is less than 50%, OFAC will evaluate whether US ownership or control exists on a case-by-case basis, taking into consideration a number of indicia of ownership or control. While these indicia are not explicitly identified in the CACR, OFAC may consider the following factors: (1) the distribution of stock ownership in the foreign entity, particularly the relative percentages of stockholders from the United States and other countries (there is not a bright line level of stock ownership under this factor); (2) a US entity or individual has the authority to appoint the majority of the members of the board of directors of the foreign entity; (3) there are voting agreements, supermajority requirements, veto authority or negative control provisions in the corporate charter or by-laws that have the effect of giving US Persons operational control over the foreign entity; (4) a US Person exercises control over the day-to-day management of the foreign entity (e.g., where the foreign entity is operated by a US Person pursuant to the provisions of an exclusive management contract); or (5) the majority of the members of the board of directors of the foreign entity also are members of the comparable governing body of the US entity. This is not necessarily an exclusive list of relevant factors, and OFAC may consider other factors in a particular case indicating that a foreign entity is in fact owned or controlled by US Persons, such as situations where the foreign entity receives a significant proportion of its funding from a US entity.

176. Depending on the facts associated with a particular transaction, authorization may be required from OFAC, or the US Commerce Department, as both have jurisdiction over certain types of Cuba-related transactions.

and EU rules (e.g., EU incorporated subsidiaries of US companies) this can raise particularly difficult, and conflicting, compliance obligations.

Note that, starting in 2015, the US published new regulations that represent a historic shift in US relations with Cuba.[177] While the statutory embargo and extensive sanctions remain in place, these changes are significant and provide a number of opportunities for US companies to pursue commercial business opportunities in Cuba in certain sectors, including telecommunications infrastructure and services, consumer communications devices, agriculture, environmental protection, travel services, banking, and insurance. The new rules:

- Loosen restrictions on certain activities undertaken in the banking, finance, and insurance sectors.
- Facilitate twelve categories of authorized travel pursuant to general licences.
- Remove barriers to scheduled air carrier service between US and Cuba.
- Ease restrictions on remittances and donations for certain purposes.
- Permit limited imports of goods from Cuba.
- Authorize non-US subsidiaries to conduct transactions with certain Cuban nationals located in other countries.

More specifically, the recent changes to the CACR generally allow the following types of activities, including:

(1) US banks are permitted to open and maintain correspondent accounts at Cuban financial institutions to facilitate the processing of authorized transactions, such as those incident to authorized travel, remittances, or certain sales of authorized goods. US financial institutions will also be allowed to enrol merchants and process credit and debit card transactions for transactions incident to authorized travel in Cuba.
(2) US insurers are now authorized to offer global health, life, or travel insurance policies for third country nationals travelling to Cuba, so long as the person is ordinarily resident outside of Cuba. This general licence authorizes US companies and their non-US subsidiaries to service those global policies and pay claims arising from events that occurred while the individual was travelling in, to, or from Cuba. US insurers are also authorized to provide health, life, or travel insurance to US Persons on authorized travel to Cuba, including making payments related to the receipt of emergency medical services.
(3) OFAC has expanded existing general licences to authorize a broader range of telecommunications-related transactions and services.
(4) The US government continues to prohibit tourist travel to Cuba. However, OFAC expanded the types of persons and activities that now qualify for travel to Cuba under general licences. Travel-related transactions are permitted by

177. See 80 Fed. Reg. 2291-15 (16 Jan. 2015), 80 Fed. Reg. 56915-26 (21 Sep. 2015), 81 Fed. Reg. 4583-86 (27 Jan. 2016), and 81 Fed. Reg. 13989-94 (16 Mar. 2016).

general licence for certain travel related to the following activities, subject to criteria and conditions in each general licence:

- Family visits.
- Official business of the US government, foreign governments, and certain intergovernmental organizations.
- Journalistic activity.
- Professional research and professional meetings.
- Religious activities.
- Public performances, clinics, workshops, athletics, other competitions, and exhibitions.
- Support for the Cuban people.
- Humanitarian projects.
- Activities of private foundations or research or educational institutes.
- Exportation, importation, or transmission of information or information materials.
- Certain authorized export transactions that are consistent with BIS licensing policy.

(5) Authorized US travellers to Cuba are allowed to import up to USD 400 worth of goods acquired in Cuba for personal use. This includes no more than USD 100 worth of alcohol or tobacco products.

(6) Commercial imports of certain independent Cuban entrepreneur-produced goods and services, as determined by the State Department, are also authorized.

(7) The new regulations now authorize a number of categories of US entities to engage in transactions necessary to establish and maintain a physical presence in Cuba:

- News bureaus.
- Exporters of goods that are licensed or otherwise authorized under the OFAC and BIS regulations (such as certain telecommunications equipment, consumers communications devices, building materials, medical products, and agricultural products).
- Entities providing mail, parcel, or cargo transportation services authorized by OFAC.
- Providers of telecommunications services.
- Entities organizing or conducting certain educational activities.
- Religious organizations engaging in certain religious activities.
- Providers of travel and carrier services.
- Providers of certain internet-based services.

These changes to the CACR represent a historic shift in the US's sanctions posture towards Cuba, and raise potential new opportunities for US companies and travellers.

Sub-Par. 3 Iran

The US sanctions against Iran have been in place since the 1970s and have historically been comprehensive in scope, although changes over the past several years have increased the complexity and reach of the sanctions, including various extraterritorial measures that impact non-US entities. The primary statutory underpinning for OFAC's sanctions against Iran is IEEPA, although other statutes are worth noting as outlined more fully below.

OFAC's primary sanctions regime regarding Iran is the ITSR.[178] The ITSR are a comprehensive sanctions regime prohibiting most transactions and dealings with Iran and the government of Iran. Virtually all trade or other dealings with Iran and the government of Iran (including exports, reexports, imports, and services) are prohibited.

The ITSR apply to US Persons. Pursuant to a law enacted in August 2012 (the Iran Threat Reduction and Syria Human Rights Act of 2012 (ITRSHRA)),[179] the ITSR now also apply to entities owned or controlled by US Persons, including foreign incorporated subsidiaries of US companies.[180] This jurisdictional 'hook' is similar to the scope of the Cuba regime outlined above, and was a significant development in Iranian sanctions that affects the non-US operations of US companies.

In addition to the ITSR, there are numerous extraterritorial US sanctions against Iran that can apply to activities of non-US Persons. There are several legal authorities involved, including the following:

- ISA, as amended by CISADA and ITRSHRA.
- Executive Order 13590 from 21 November 2011.
- Iran sanctions legislation enacted on 31 December 2011 called the National Defense Authorization Act for Fiscal Year 2012 (NDAA).[181]
- Iranian Financial Sanctions Regulations (IFSR).[182]
- Executive Order 13608 from 1 May 2012.
- Executive Order 13622 from 31 July 2012.
- Executive Order 13628 from 9 October 2012.
- Iran Freedom and Counter-Proliferation Act of 2012 (IFCA).[183]
- Executive Order 13645 from 1 July 2013.

178. 31 C.F.R. Part 560. Prior to 22 Oct. 2012 the ITSR were known as the Iranian Transactions Regulations (ITR). OFAC made significant changes to the ITR on 22 Oct. 2012, and as a result renamed them and reissued them in their entirety.
179. PL 112-158.
180. The ITSR state that an entity is 'owned or controlled' by a US Person if the US Persons: (1) hold a 50% or greater equity interest by vote or value in the entity; (2) hold a majority of seats on the board of directors of the entity; or (3) otherwise control the actions, policies, or personnel decisions of the entity. 31 C.F.R. §560.215(b).
181. PL 112-81.
182. 31 C.F.R. Part 561.
183. PL 112-239.

These extraterritorial measures and authorities are complex, but are primarily aimed at curtailing the activities of non-US entities, even where a transaction otherwise has no US nexus (e.g., no entities owned or controlled by US Persons, no US Person approval or facilitation, no US goods or technology, and no US funds). The intent behind these measures is to dissuade non-US entities and financial institutions from engaging in or processing certain Iran-related transactions that are inconsistent with the foreign policy goals of the US. These measures are sometimes referred to as 'secondary' sanctions, to distinguish them from the 'primary' US Iran sanctions in the ITSR which apply to US Persons including, as of 2012, non-US entities owned or controlled by US Persons. These secondary sanctions measures target certain activities in the oil/gas, petroleum and petrochemical, shipping and shipbuilding, automotive and energy sectors, as well as certain activities of foreign (non-US) financial institutions. The restrictions include certain measures that specifically target the Iranian financial system, including the Central Bank of Iran, as well as other types of designated parties, restrictions related to certain parties who have engaged in deceptive practices or transactions related to US sanctions, and restrictions related to parties engaging in human rights and other abuses in Iran. In some cases, the secondary sanctions measures have value thresholds or include language that requires offending transactions to be significant or material in some way, in the discretion of the US government, in order to be sanctionable. Certain aspects of the restrictions are administered by OFAC, while others are administered by the US State Department.

As noted above, on 14 July 2015, the US and Iran (and other parties) agreed to the JCPOA to ensure that Iran's nuclear programme will be exclusively peaceful. As part of this process, the US has agreed to roll back certain secondary sanctions targeting Iran after Iran undergoes agreed upon steps and international checks, including via certain waivers to statutory sanctions provisions. On 18 October 2015 the JCPOA was adopted (Adoption Day) and became effective. As such, the President has issued guidance directing relevant US agencies, including the Treasury Department, to take all appropriate preparatory measures to ensure the prompt and effective implementation of the US commitments set forth in the JCPOA upon Iran's fulfilment of the requisite conditions. In particular, the President directed the agencies to take steps to give effect to the US commitments with respect to sanctions described in the JCPOA beginning on Implementation Day, which would occur when the IAEA verified that Iran had implemented key nuclear-related measures described in the JCPOA. Prior to Implementation Day, the only changes to the Iran-related sanctions were those provided for in the JPOA of 24 November 2013, as extended.[184] On Implementation Day, which occurred on January 16, 2016, the US lifted nuclear-related secondary sanctions as agreed under the JCPOA, but the primary sanctions targeting Iran largely remain in place – that is, US Persons continue to be broadly prohibited from engaging in transactions or dealings involving Iran, including the government of Iran, with the exception of a few specific categories of transactions that OFAC has licensed.

184. See OFAC's website at http://www.treasury.gov/resource-center/sanctions/Programs/Pages/jpoa_archive.aspx for an archive of JPOA materials.

Sub-Par. 4 North Korea

Prior to 2008, OFAC's North Korea sanctions were imposed primarily pursuant to TWEA. However in 2008 the President terminated the application of TWEA authorities with respect to North Korea, and instead imposed a series of executive orders that blocks the property of a number of North Korean persons and prohibits certain types of activities. North Korea technically was delisted as a state sponsor of terrorism in October 2008, but broad restrictions remained.[185] In February of 2016, the US enacted the North Korea Sanctions and Policy Enhancement Act of 2016[186] imposing new sanctions against North Korea in response to North Korea's nuclear weapons and missile testing activities. This legislation expanded the scope of US primary sanctions targeting North Korea's nuclear and missile programs and human rights violations, and also authorized secondary sanctions. On 2 March 2016, the United Nations Security Council adopted a sanctions resolution against North Korea and the US imposed sanctions on additional designated certain North Korean government officials and entities related to nuclear and missile testing programs. On 15 March 2016, President Obama issued a new executive order with additional sanctions on the North Korean government and other North Korean entities.[187]

Specifically, the US sanctions against North Korea include a prohibition on the importation of most services, goods and technology from North Korea and on dealing with North Korean designated parties. Under US export control rules, there is also a ban on most exports and reexports of US items to North Korea without US government authorization. US persons are also prohibited from registering vessels in North Korea, obtaining authorization for a vessel to fly the North Korean flag, or owning, leasing, operating, or insuring any vessel flagged by North Korea. The most recently issued sanctions against North Korea target North Korean government officials and entities tied to North Korean missile and nuclear programs, and block the assets of such designated persons and entities. In addition, the new sanctions expand the extraterritorial reach of US sanctions through authorization of secondary sanctions which could impact companies doing business in other countries that trade with North Korea (such as China).

Sub-Par. 5 Sudan

OFAC's sanctions against Sudan are primarily found in the SSR.[188] OFAC's sanctions against Sudan prohibit virtually all trade or other dealings with Sudan (including exports, reexports, imports, and services). The entire government of Sudan, wherever located, is blocked and subject to sanctions.

The SSR apply to US Persons, which as noted above includes foreign branches of US entities. Unlike the Cuba and Iran sanctions, however, the SSR will not necessarily

185. See 31 C.F.R. Part 510.
186. See North Korea Sanctions and Policy Enhancement Act of 2016, Pub. L. No. 114-122, (2016).
187. See 81 Fed. Reg. 14943-46 (18 Mar. 2016).
188. 31 C.F.R. Part 538.

apply to activities of a subsidiary of a US company incorporated outside the US, provided no US Persons, dollars, goods, services or technology are involved in the transaction.

The SSR contain a carve out from the prohibitions for so-called 'Specified Areas of Sudan.' These Specified Areas are: Southern Kordofan/Nuba Mountains State, Blue Nile State, Abyei, Darfur and four marginalized areas in and around Khartoum for internally displaced persons as follows: Mayo, El Salaam, Wad El Bashir, and Soba. The prohibitions of the SSR do not apply to these areas. Note though, that exports to the Specified Areas, and imports from the Specified Areas, are no longer exempt if the goods, technology or services pass through non-Specified Areas of Sudan on their way to or from the Specified Areas (unless the goods or services involved are intended for humanitarian purposes, and then they can pass through Sudan).

Note also that South Sudan was formed on 9 July 2011 following its separation from Sudan. South Sudan is not subject to OFAC sanctions. In addition, unlike with the Specified Areas of Sudan, for South Sudan OFAC has issued a general licence (in 31 C.F.R. §538.537) for transshipment of goods, technology and services to or from South Sudan that pass through Sudan on their way to or from South Sudan.

Sub-Par. 6 Syria

OFAC's sanctions against Syria are slightly different and distinct from, for example, the Iran and Sudan sanctions. Between 2004 and August 2011, the OFAC sanctions against Syria primarily prohibited transactions involving SDNs of Syria, and are found in the Syrian Sanctions Regulations (SySR).[189] These sanctions were overlaid by a general Commerce Department prohibition on most exports and reexports of goods, software and technology to Syria (this export/reexport ban remains in place).

Then, in August 2011, in light of the increased violence in Syria, the President issued an executive order expanding the Syrian sanctions regime to block the entire government of Syria, as well as prohibiting virtually all services and other transactions involving Syria, certain imports from Syria into the US, and transactions involving Syria's petroleum industry.

Both the SySR and the executive order apply to US Persons, which as noted above includes foreign branches of US entities. Unlike the Cuba and Iran sanctions, however, the Syria measures will not necessarily apply to activities of a subsidiary of a US company incorporated outside the US, provided that no US Persons, dollars, goods, services or technology are involved in the transaction, and that no US Persons are ordinarily required to approve or facilitate the transaction.

Prior to the August 2011 change, for example, a non-US branch of a US insurance company (which would be considered a 'US Person') could provide cargo coverage insurance for a shipment of non-US goods to Syria, so long as no SDNs were involved. However, after the August 2011 order this would be considered a prohibited exportation of services to Syria, and would not be authorized without a licence from OFAC.

189. 31 C.F.R. Part 542.

Similarly, US financial institutions are no longer allowed to process payments relating to Syria, as these would be viewed as an exportation of financial services to Syria.

On 22 April 2012, the President issued Executive Order 13606 that blocked the property of, and suspended entry into the US of, certain persons designated as being connected to grave human rights abuses by the government of Syria via information technology means (note that this order also applied to activities by the government of Iran as well). The order results in designated persons being treated like SDNs, and designations can result from activities such as directing operations of information and communications technology that facilitates computer or network disruption, monitoring, or tracking that could assist in or enable serious human rights abuses by or on behalf of the government of Syria.

Note also that on 1 May 2012, the President signed Executive Order 13608 imposing sanctions targeting foreign entities that: (1) have violated, attempted to violate, conspired to violate, or caused a violation of US sanctions against Syria; (2) have facilitated deceptive transactions for persons subject to US sanctions concerning Syria; or (3) are owned or controlled or are acting or purporting to act on behalf of an entity described in (1) or (2). The Secretary of the Treasury, in consultation with the Secretary of State, is authorized to designate entities under the order. The purpose of the executive order is to expand the Department of the Treasury's ability to address the conduct of foreign entities engaged in the activities described above, where the exercise of US jurisdiction is constrained due to the foreign entities' lack of physical, financial, or other presence in the US. The Department of the Treasury may exercise this authority where the foreign entity may otherwise fail to meet criteria for designation under existing executive orders or regulations. Under the order, the Secretary of the Treasury may prohibit all transactions with designated entities relating to goods, services, or technology intended for the US or US Persons, wherever located. The order also prohibits providing anything of benefit to, or receiving anything from, a designated entity. The effect of these prohibitions is to generally bar access of designated entities to the US financial and commercial systems and to cut off access to the US marketplace.

Par. 2 Targeted Sanctions

OFAC's targeted sanctions programmes do not target entire countries. Rather, the targeted sanctions hone-in on specific industries, persons, entities, government actors or activities. So, for example, while OFAC maintains restrictions against persons designated as having contributed to the political and social unrest in Côte d'Ivoire (the Ivory Coast), the entire nation of the Ivory Coast and its government are not sanctioned.

Sub-Par. 1 Burma

The Burma programme[190] historically was a broad sanctions programme, but now most activities, while regulated, are authorized through a series of general licences. Historically, the regulations prohibited new investments in Burma, importations from Burma, and exports of financial services to Burma (not all services, just financial services).

However, in 2012 in response to various political reforms by Burma's government, OFAC issued general licences that suspend many of the restrictions that had been in place. One of the general licences broadly authorizes the exportation of US financial services to Burma, which include but are not limited to banking/investment services, processing of payments, provision of insurance, loans or guarantees. However, given human rights considerations, the general licence does not authorize the exportation of such services, in connection with the provision of security services, to the Burmese Ministry of Defence, state or non-state armed groups (which includes the military), or entities owned by these organizations. Nor does the general licence authorize the exportation of financial services to any SDN.

A second general licence permits new investment in Burma, subject to certain extensive reporting requirements. However, this general licence also does not authorize new investment resulting from an agreement with the Burmese Ministry of Defence, state or non-state armed groups (which includes the military), entities owned by these organizations, or any dealings with an SDN of Burma.

In addition, OFAC issued a general licence that significantly eased the US ban on imports of Burmese-origin goods into the US. Specifically, most Burmese-origin goods can now be imported into the US provided that no SDN is involved in the transaction. However, this general licence does not apply to jadeite or rubies mined or extracted from Burma, or any articles of jewellery containing such jadeite or rubies.

Sub-Par. 2 Libya

The Libya measures taken by OFAC in 2011[191] provide a good example of how OFAC can use targeted sanctions to swiftly and effectively address a particular foreign policy issue.

Historically, OFAC's Libya sanctions were comprehensive. Then, in 2004 the President terminated the national emergency designation with respect to Libya, effectively removing most economic sanctions against the country.

Then, in February 2011 in light of the Arab Spring uprisings and consequent government response, the President issued an executive order that read as follows:

- I find that 'Colonel Muammar Qadhafi, his government, and close associates have taken extreme measures against the people of Libya, including by using weapons of war, mercenaries, and wanton violence against unarmed civilians.

190. 31 C.F.R. Part 537.
191. See e.g., Executive Order 13566, of 25 Feb. 2011.

> I further find that there is a serious risk that Libyan state assets will be misappropriated by Qadhafi, members of his government, members of his family, or his close associates if those assets are not protected. The foregoing circumstances, the prolonged attacks, and the increased numbers of Libyans seeking refuge in other countries from the attacks, have caused a deterioration in the security of Libya and pose a serious risk to its stability, thereby constituting an unusual and extraordinary threat to the national security and foreign policy of the United States, and I hereby declare a national emergency to deal with that threat.'[192]

The order blocked the entire government of Libya and designated Libyan individuals and entities, including many Qadhafi family members. The EU followed suit with its own measures. The result was a huge impact on many businesses that, prior to the new measures, had been engaging in perfectly legal activity with the government of Libya, which included huge reserves of sovereign wealth funds and investments.

Then, as the Qadhafi regime began to crumble and the transitional authority took over more of the country, the OFAC restrictions on the government of Libya (which had been intended to mean the Qadhafi government) became particularly burdensome, with the lines between what was the 'government' or not being increasingly blurred. OFAC issued a series of general licences to ease the situation and allow for the transition to a new, non-Qadhafi government, culminating in December 2011 with a general licence that essentially unblocks the government of Libya, with some remaining, limited exceptions. So, activities, while still regulated, are authorized under a series of general licences. Certain Libyan government property in the US or in the possession of US Persons, however, remains blocked unless authorized by OFAC under a licence.

Sub-Par. 3 Ukraine / Russia Sanctions

Pursuant to Executive Orders 13660 and 13661, OFAC designated a number of persons and entities in and connected to Ukraine and Russia as SDNs due to the US government's determination regarding their role in contributing to the crisis in Ukraine. US Persons cannot engage in any transactions or dealings with SDNs and property and interests in property of SDNs that are in the possession or control of US Persons or in the US must be blocked (or 'frozen') and reported to OFAC.

Pursuant to Executive Order 13662, on 16 July 2014 OFAC created a new sanctions list called the SSIL, which has been updated since that time by the addition of new entities and restrictions resulting from amendments to the scope of the prohibitions (i.e., the reduction of new debt maturity trigger from ninety to thirty days for certain entities on the SSIL). The SSIL restrictions are not as broad as the SDN restrictions described above. Instead, they target certain named parties in or connected to Russia via four 'directives', including but not limited to the following. Vnesheconombank; Gazprombank; Bank of Moscow; Russian Agricultural Bank; VTB Bank; Sberbank; Novatek; Rosneft; Transneft; Gazprom Neft; Rostec; Gazprom OAO; Lukoil;

192. Executive Order 13566.

and Surgutneftegas. The restrictions on these entities differ depending on which directive they were designated pursuant to (and in some cases, entities are designated pursuant to multiple directives). The details of each directive are as follows:

- Directive 1 primarily targets banking/financial related parties. The following transactions by US Persons or within the US involving these parties are prohibited by Directive 1: 'all transactions in, provision of financing for, and other dealings in new debt of longer than 30 days maturity or new equity of [these] persons..., their property, or their interests in property...' All other transactions with these persons or involving any property in which one or more of these persons has an interest are permitted, provided such transactions do not otherwise involve property or interests in property of a person blocked pursuant to Executive Orders 13660, 13661 or 13662, or any other sanctions programmes implemented by OFAC.
- Directive 2 primarily targets energy related parties. With respect to these parties, the following transactions are prohibited: 'all transactions in, provision of financing for, and other dealings in new debt of longer than 90 days maturity of [these] persons..., their property, or their interests in property...' All other transactions with these persons or involving any property in which one or more of these persons has an interest are permitted, provided such transactions do not otherwise involve property or interests in property of a person blocked pursuant to Executive Order 13660, 13661, or 13662, or any other sanctions programmes implemented by OFAC. Unlike Directive 1, Directive 2 does not place restrictions on transacting in, providing financing for, or otherwise dealing in new equity of the entities listed pursuant to Directive 2.
- Directive three primarily targets defence related parties. With respect to these parties, the following transactions are prohibited: 'all transactions in, provision of financing for, and other dealings in new debt of longer than 30 days maturity of [these] persons..., their property, or their interests in property...' All other transactions with these persons or involving any property in which one or more of these persons has an interest are permitted, provided such transactions do not otherwise involve property or interests in property of a person blocked pursuant to Executive Order 13660, 13661, or 13662, or any other sanctions programmes implemented by OFAC. Unlike Directive 1, Directive 3 does not place restrictions on transacting in, providing financing for, or otherwise dealing in new equity of the entities listed pursuant to Directive 3.
- Directive 4 also primarily targets energy related parties. With respect to these parties, and their property and interests in property, the following transactions are prohibited by a US Person or within the US:

  > the provision, exportation, or reexportation, directly or indirectly, of goods, services (except for financial services), or technology in support of exploration or production for deep-water [more than 500 feet], Arctic offshore, or

> shale projects that have the potential to produce oil in the Russian Federation, or in maritime area claimed by the Russian Federation and extending from its territory.

The SSIL entities are not SDNs. Only specific types of activities listed in the directives are prohibited if engaged in by US Persons or within the US. As noted above, the SDN and SSIL restrictions apply to entities that are 50% or more owned by SDN or SSIL designees, even if the entity is not identified on the SDN list or SSIL.[193] The directives imposing SSIL restrictions also contain broad prohibitions on evasion or conspiracies to violate the rules.

Sub-Par. 4 Other List-Based Regimes

OFAC also maintains sanctions against specifically listed individuals and entities in the targeted regions/countries listed below:[194]

- Balkans
- Belarus
- Burundi
- Central African Republic
- Democratic Republic of the Congo
- Iraq
- Ivory Coast
- Lebanon
- Somalia
- South Sudan
- Venezuela
- Yemen
- Zimbabwe

193. Given the breadth of the holdings of some of the Russian parties named on the SDN list and the SSIL in response to the situation in Ukraine, and the broad scope of OFAC's 50% rule, compliance issues related to identification of 'shadow' SDNs and SSILs are a particularly burdensome area for global companies. Adding to this compliance burden is the fact that many of the Russia/Ukraine-related SDNs and SSIL entities were also added to US export control-related restricted parties lists.

194. While there are SDNs in many other countries, OFAC has not specifically targeted those countries in the same manner. In some limited cases, these sanctions regimes may go beyond just SDN list designations. For example the Iraq sanctions also prohibit trade in looted Iraqi cultural property illegally taken from various Iraqi museums and libraries. See 31 C.F.R. §576.208. On 25 Nov. 2015, the United States issued an Executive Order related to Burundi, see 80 Fed. Reg. 73633-36 (25 Nov. 2015). On 12 Nov. 2015, the United States revoked the Executive Order related to Liberia, see 80 Fed. Reg. 71679-80 (12 Nov. 2015).

For the most part, these sanctions only target individuals and entities that are specifically designated by OFAC and added to the SDN list. US Persons are prohibited from engaging in transactions or dealings with SDNs, regardless of what regime or country they are associated with.

In addition, OFAC adds to the SDN list names of persons and entities associated with conduct contrary to US national security and foreign policy interests, such as narcotics trafficking, cybersecurity concerns, terrorism, weapons proliferation/ weapons of mass destruction, and transnational criminal organization concerns. OFAC also maintains restrictions against trade in rough diamonds not controlled through the Kimberly Process Certification Scheme (e.g., a prohibition on trade in so-called 'blood diamonds').[195] Certain of these programmes also include the threat of imposition of sanctions on parties providing material assistance to such SDNs.[196]

The SDN list is available at http://www.treasury.gov/resource-center/sanctions /SDN-List/Pages/default.aspx, changes frequently (sometimes multiple times a week), and includes thousands of names. Changes to the SDN list are posted on OFAC's website and/or listed in the daily Federal Register. The page noted above allows one to sign up for notifications from OFAC on additions to the SDN list and other matters of note. The specific entries on the SDN list will include a 'tag' marker in brackets at the end of the entry, and this 'tag' indicates under which regime that particular person or entity is sanctioned. Multiple sanctions regimes may apply to one entry. The entries also list common AKAs and other identifying information where available (e.g., address, passport number, date of birth, etc.). It is important to understand which sanctions programme applies to a designation, especially if more than one programme applies. A general licence applicable to, for example, a Syria designation, might not apply if that entity is designated under the nuclear weapons proliferation programme. For example, the Commercial Bank of Syria is an SDN, but it is not designated under the Syria programme. Rather, its tag is '[NPWMD]' indicating that it is designated as a nuclear proliferation and weapons of mass destruction concern, so only the limited exemptions and licences applicable to NPWMD regime will be relevant.

Par. 3 Other Relevant US Government Agencies

As noted briefly above, there are other US government agencies that may have overlapping, or concurrent jurisdiction with OFAC that allows those agencies to impose measures that are similar to, or tantamount to, sanctions in their own right (albeit the nomenclature is different).

195. See e.g., Executive Orders 12947, 12938, 12978, 13094, 13099, 13224, 13268, 13312, 13372, 13382, 13581, 13608, 13694.
196. For example, Executive Order 13667 imposing sanctions upon certain parties related to the Central African Republic states that, in addition to blocking (freezing) the assets of persons named in the Annex to the order, the President can block any persons determined:

> to have materially assisted, sponsored, or provided financial, material, logistical, or technological support for, or goods or services in support of (i) any of the activities described in [specific sections of the order] or (ii) any person whose property and interests in property are blocked pursuant to [the] order.

Sub-Par. 1 State Department

For example, the State Department's Directorate of Defense Trade Controls (DDTC) administers the International Traffic in Arms Regulations (ITAR).[197] The ITAR regulate the transfer of defence articles, defence services, and related technical data. A specific licence permit from DDTC is required for most transactions involving defence articles, services and technical data, and exporters, manufacturers and brokers of such items must typically be registered with DDTC. Under the ITAR, certain countries are subject to an arms embargo, whereby ITAR controlled items are restricted. These arms embargoed countries currently include:

- Afghanistan
- Belarus
- Burma
- Central African Republic
- China (PR)
- Cuba
- Cyprus
- Ivory Coast
- Democratic Republic of the Congo
- Eritrea
- Haiti
- Iran
- Iraq
- Kyrgyzstan
- Lebanon
- Liberia
- Libya
- North Korea
- Russia
- Somalia
- Sri Lanka
- Sudan
- Syria
- Venezuela
- Vietnam
- Zimbabwe

The current list is available on DDTC's website.[198] These DDTC restrictions are separate and distinct from OFAC's sanctions programmes.

197. 22 C.F.R. Parts 120-130.
198. See https://www.pmddtc.state.gov/embargoed_countries/index.html, which also includes information on relevant authorities for these arms embargoes.

In addition, the State Department's Bureau of International Security and Nonproliferation may designate persons or entities under various non-proliferation legal authorities, such as the Iran and Syria Nonproliferation Act (see http://www.state.gov/t/isn/c15231.htm). Announcements of such designations are made in the Federal Register. Many of these individuals/entities are also listed on OFAC's SDN list. For individuals/entities not also listed as SDNs, the State Department measures can include restrictions such as a ban on certain US government procurement opportunities, and denial of export licence applications. Many of the secondary Iran sanctions have measures that the State Department administers (e.g., denial of export licences for defence articles).

In addition, applications submitted to OFAC for adjudication are subject to an inter-agency review process, including seeking foreign policy guidance from the State Department.

Sub-Par. 2 Commerce Department

For commercial items and 'dual use' items (e.g., items that have both military and commercial applicability), exports and reexports of such items (including goods, equipment, software, materials and technology) are regulated by the Commerce Department's Bureau of Industry and Security (BIS) under the Export Administration Regulations (EAR).[199] BIS-controlled items in some cases are highly controlled for export or reexport and may, for example, require a licence for export to all destinations except Canada, and in other cases, the controls are minimal (the lowest level of control for items subject to the EAR is called EAR99, and such items are controlled only for sanctioned countries, restricted parties[200] and restricted end-uses such as proliferation or other nefarious activities). With some limited exceptions, most exports and reexports of US items to Iran, North Korea, Sudan and Syria, and also the Crimea region and Cuba, require a BIS licence. Restrictions also apply to non-US made items that incorporate greater than *de minimis* (10% for certain countries, 25% for others) controlled-US content. The definition of what content is controlled differs depending on the country.

In terms of licensing jurisdiction, in some cases OFAC or BIS will defer to the other agency. For example, for exports of commercial items from the US to Cuba, the CACR state that such exports are authorized provided that 'the exportation...is licensed

199. As noted above, this is the 'Export Administration Regulations', found in 15 C.F.R. Parts 730-774.
200. In addition to the OFAC restricted parties lists, the US government maintains other lists of restricted parties, including as noted above the Entity List, Denied Parties List and Unverified List maintained by the US Department of Commerce. The Entity List identifies non-US parties that are prohibited from receiving some or all items subject to the EAR unless the exporter secures a licence. The Denied Parties List is a list of individuals and entities that have been denied export privileges. The Unverified List is a list of parties whose bona fides BIS has been unable to verify.

or otherwise authorized by the Department of Commerce…'.[201] Similarly for Iran, BIS concedes licensing jurisdiction to OFAC in most cases:

> To avoid duplication, exporters or reexporters are not required to seek separate authorization from BIS for an export or reexport subject to both the EAR and to [the ITSR]…Therefore, if OFAC authorizes an export or reexport, such authorization is considered authorization for purposes of the EAR as well.[202]

These efforts are designed to avoid potential 'double licensing' scenarios where both OFAC and BIS authorization is required. In some cases though, the 'double licensing' conundrum remains. The primary example is for exports of items controlled beyond just the lowest level to Sudan, which requires a licence from both OFAC and BIS.

Sub-Par. 3 SEC

Occasionally the SEC's Office of Global Security Risk will send requests for information to companies that file reports with the SEC, asking about the company's interactions with sanctioned countries and whether and how such transactions might potentially materially impact an investor's stance on the company given, for example, the various state and other divestment rules related to countries like Iran and Sudan. The requests and the company's response are typically publicly posted on the SEC website, but often with redacted proprietary or sensitive information.

In addition, ITRSHRA (enacted in August 2012 as noted above) requires that issuers who are required to file annual and quarterly reports with the SEC after February 2013 disclose certain Iran and SDN-related business of the company and of its affiliates (this is referred to as 'section 219' reporting, as the requirement to report flows from section 219 of ITRSHRA).[203] The reporting requirement reads specifically as follows:

- Each issuer required to file an annual or quarterly report under subsection (a) shall disclose in that report the information required by paragraph (2) if, during the period covered by the report, the issuer or any affiliate of the issuer—

  (A) knowingly engaged in an activity described in subsection (a) or (b) of section 5 of the Iran Sanctions Act of 1996 (Public Law 104–172; 50 U.S.C. 1701 note);
  (B) knowingly engaged in an activity described in subsection (c)(2) of section 104 of the Comprehensive Iran Sanctions, Accountability, and Divestment Act of 2010 (22 U.S.C. 8513) or a transaction described in subsection (d)(1) of that section;
  I knowingly engaged in an activity described in section 105A(b)(2) of that Act; or

201. See 31 C.F.R. 515.533.
202. See 15 C.F.R. 746.7(a)(2).
203. PL 112-158.

(D) knowingly conducted any transaction or dealing with—

(i) any person the property and interests in property of which are blocked pursuant to Executive Order No. 13224 (66 Fed. Reg. 49079; relating to blocking property and prohibiting transactions with persons who commit, threaten to commit, or support terrorism);

(ii) any person the property and interests in property of which are blocked pursuant to Executive Order No. 13382 (70 Fed. Reg. 38567; relating to blocking of property of weapons of mass destruction proliferators and their supporters); or

(iii) any person or entity identified under section 560.304 of title 31, Code of Federal Regulations (relating to the definition of the Government of Iran) without the specific authorization of a Federal department or agency.[204]

Reporting to the SEC would be required in certain cases, even if the activity was lawful.

Sub-Section 9 Other Multilateral Sanctions Regimes

In addition to the EU, other regional organizations have imposed multilateral sanctions regimes. For example, one of the longest-running arms embargo in place is that imposed by the Organization for Security and Co-operation in Europe (OSCE) on Nagorno-Karabakh, a break-away region in Azerbaijan. Initially imposed in response to hostilities in the territory in February 1992, the embargo continues to be observed by OSCE participating states.

The Economic Community of West African States (ECOWAS) has historically been active in imposing sanctions on trade with hostile states, namely Togo in 2005 and Guinea in 2009. The sanctions were lifted in 2005 and 2011 respectively.

Another regional sanctions regime currently in force is that of the League of Arab States (LAS) on arms trade with Syria. Established by a statement by the Ministerial Committee of the LAS on 3 December 2011 in reaction to the violent suppression of protests in Syria on 27 November 2011, the embargo restricts LAS members from supplying arms to Syria.

SECTION 5 COMPLIANCE WITH SANCTIONS REGIMES

Sub-Section 1 Practical Measures within Companies

The heart of any sanctions compliance programme is to know what the legal risks are and how to manage them within the applicable laws. As an example, OFAC's FAQs note the following: 'There is no single compliance programme suitable for every [type of] institution...What constitutes an adequate compliance programme depends in large

204. *Ibid.* at section 219.

part on who your customers are and what kinds of business you do…'.[205] If a company engages in routine international transactions and has a global footprint in an number of countries, its risk of sanctions compliance related issues is higher than an entity that engages only in domestic transactions in the US and/or in Europe.

Depending on an entity's particular risk profile, a compliance programme could include a sanctions compliance manual, work instructions, policy or procedures, as well as regular training and compliance auditing. It is important to keep in mind that, although most EU sanctions require some kind of knowing or willing behaviour in order to give rise to an offence, OFAC's sanctions are a 'strict liability' regime – meaning companies can be found guilty of violating US sanctions even where that was not their intention, or where the relevant parties were not aware that a particular activity violated sanctions. As such, it is imperative that companies assess their risk profile and act according.

Par. 1 Question 1: Does the Transaction Involve a Territory or Country Subject to Sanctions?

Territories and countries can be split into three categories of increasing risk:

- In the 'highest risk' category fall territories subject to EU or US territorial sanctions: Crimea and Sevastopol, Cuba, Iran, North Korea, Sudan and Syria. In this highest risk category, many, if not most, transactions or dealings with these territories/countries, their governments, and persons located in these territories/countries, are prohibited. Any potential involvement in a highest risk jurisdiction should be immediately flagged to the compliance team. The highest risk category also includes any transactions or dealings with many types of restricted parties (e.g., parties subject to an EU asset freeze, SDNs or FSEs), regardless of what territory/country is at issue (SDNs, for example, can be present in any country in the world, including in the US). Companies often have to employ screening software solutions to monitor transactions for restricted parties.
- In the 'increased risk' category fall territories and countries which are subject to more EU or US limited economic sanctions: Balkans, Belarus, Burma (Myanmar), Burundi, Central African Republic, Ivory Coast, Democratic Republic of Congo, Eritrea, Egypt, Iraq, Lebanon, Libya, Russia, Somalia, South Sudan, Tunisia, Ukraine, Venezuela, Yemen, Zimbabwe. Subject to the nature of the exports or others types of transactions (e.g., banking or insurance related business) of the company implementing the compliance process, transactions or dealings with these territories/countries may not need authorization to proceed, but may still need to be alerted to the compliance team so that proper consideration can be given to any applicable legal requirements.

205. See http://www.treasury.gov/resource-center/faqs/Sanctions/Pages/faq_compliance.aspx #start.

This increased risk category also includes any transactions or dealings with SSILs or parties subject to EU sectoral sanctions, wherever located.

- In the 'normal risk' category fall all other territories and countries which do not in themselves trigger sanctions issues. It should be noted that there are a number of SDNs and other restricted parties in such countries, and there may still be export control related restrictions or requirements for these other territories and countries, even if no sanctioned locations or parties are involved.

Par. 2 Question 2: Does the Transaction Involve Any Listed Parties or 'Shadow' SDNs/SSILs?

As noted above, screening for restricted parties (EU asset freeze parties, SDNs, FSEs, SSILs, and any other parties on EU or US restricted parties lists) is an important pillar for any successful sanctions compliance programme. Many third party vendors provide software screening solutions that can be implemented to screen transactions (e.g., payments, orders, contracts, shipments, etc.) for restricted parties.

However, given the 50% rule articulated and enforced by OFAC, companies cannot rely only on screening solutions to identify problematic parties, and instead are also expected to 'know their customers' and identify connections to 'shadow' SDNs and SSILs who are 50% or more owned by restricted parties. The ability to identify these 'shadow' parties, who are not themselves named on any restricted party lists published by OFAC and other authorities, is an ongoing and increasing challenge for global companies.

In addition, the timing of restricted party screening can cause compliance challenges for companies. For example, a company may screen for the involvement of restricted parties upon receiving an order from a party in the Middle East, and again when goods are due to be shipped. But if a 'sell to' party for the order becomes designated on a restricted party list after the goods have shipped, but before payment is due, and then tries to remit a payment, this will cause issues for the exporting company and the funds may have to be blocked ('frozen').

Par. 3 Question 3: Does the Transaction Involve 'Red Flags'?

A further element of counterparty checks concerns reviewing whether there is any information that a particular transaction may be diverted to improper locations or parties. Some examples of red flags are set out below:

- A customer or its address is similar to one of the parties found on the restricted parties lists.
- A customer or purchasing agent is reluctant to offer information about the end-use of the item or service being provided.
- A freight forwarding firm is listed as a product's final destination.

- When questioned, a buyer is evasive and especially unclear about whether the purchased product is for domestic use, for export, or for reexport.
- A product's capabilities do not fit the project for which the buyer claims the product is for.
- A customer is willing to pay cash for a very expensive item when the terms of sale would normally call for financing.
- Routine installation, training, or maintenance services are declined by a customer.
- Delivery dates are vague, or deliveries are planned for out of the way destinations.
- The shipping route is abnormal for a product and destination.
- Packaging is inconsistent with the stated method of shipment or destination.
- Payment for a product comes from a third party rather than the buyer.

Par. 4 Question 5: Can the Transaction Be Authorized under Certain Conditions?

Where an activity is prohibited under sanctions, it may be the case that there is a general licence or other exemption that applies to authorize the activity in certain cases. Careful review of relevant regulations and authorities is required to confirm this point.

Moreover, even if no general licence or exemption applies, it may still be possible to request an authorization from the relevant authorities. In particular, where the key interests of an EU Member State or the US is concerned, governments may consider granting authorization.

One example of this is the UK government's innovative approach to the Rhum gas field in the North Sea. This drilling concession is joint-owned by BP and the Iranian Oil Company's UK entity (the latter a listed entity under the EU's Iran sanctions regime). In 2010, production from the field was stopped entirely, in direct response to the UK's implementation of the EU's Iran sanctions. Stopping production had a significant detrimental effect on the UK's gas production, as well as requiring costly upkeep of the dormant facility to avoid any adverse environmental damage. By way of a solution, the UK government stepped in to co-manage the field with BP, placing any profits into a frozen bank account in the listed entity's name.[206]

A second example, from France in 2014, involved the cancelling of the sale of two Mistral-class warships to Russia. After initial reluctance to cancel the sale of the ships agreed in 2011, France postponed delivery of the first ship in November 2014.[207]

206. This action was permitted by the Hydrocarbons (Temporary Management Scheme) Regulations 2013.
207. http://www.elysee.fr/communiques-de-presse/article/la-livraison-du-premier-bpc-repoussee-jusqu-a-nouvel-ordre/.

Presidents Hollande and Putin announced in August 2015 that the sale would be cancelled, with France to repay the prepayment.[208]

Sub-Section 2 Contractual Issues

Par. 1 Pre-negotiations

Care should be taken in the lead up to a contract in an area which may be sanctioned. Even where a licence is sought or the regime likely to be lifted in the near future, the US and some EU Member States deem that even contracts conditional on the lifting of a sanctions regime to be in itself a breach of sanctions.[209] Advice should be taken according to the specific facts of the negotiation.

Par. 2 Contract Drafting

Where parties rely on the actions of others in verifying the end-use, or end-user, of a product or service, adequate representations and warranties should be obtained to ensure that the contracting party has taken or will take suitable steps to comply with international sanctions regimes for the purposes of the contract.

Where further protection is required, and depending on the nature of the potential loss at stake, an indemnity should be sought from the counterparty in the event of non-compliance with sanctions. This provides a wider guarantee for losses occasioned by the non-compliance, rather than simply foreseeable losses flowing directly from the breach of a representation or warranty.

Par. 3 Grandfathering and Wind-Downs

In certain, but not all, cases, sanctions regimes will permit existing contracts to continue to operate despite a sanctions regime – a so-called grandfathered contract – or a wind-down period may be put in place that allows parties until a specified date to un-wind pre-existing work. US sanctions laws generally only allow a wind-down period if authorized by a general or specific licence.

Par. 4 'Snap Back' of Iran Sanctions

In the context of the JCPOA for Iran outlined above, both EU and US authorities have stated that, should Iran fail to live up to its commitments, that relieved sanctions can 'snap back' into place, and that in general there will be no wind-down period for companies to remove themselves from the Iranian market should this 'snap back' take

208. http://www.elysee.fr/communiques-de-presse/article/entretien-telephonique-avec-m-vladimir-poutine-accords-sur-les-bpc/.
209. See e.g., OFAC FAQs published on 18 Oct. 2015, available at http://www.treasury.gov/resource-center/sanctions/Programs/Documents/jcpoa_adoption_faqs_20151018.pdf.

place. The following suggestions highlight boiler plate clauses which may provide opportunities to build flexibility and safeguards into a contract to the parties to react to changing events within the scope of the agreement, without renegotiating or unnecessarily terminating the contract. This business continuity is important, given the trend to permit grandfathering under EU sanctions.

Sub-Par. 1 Force Majeure

The thresholds for relying on a force majeure clause to terminate a contract due to the adoption of economic sanctions are very high. For example, under English law, a party must show that he has taken all reasonable steps to avoid relying upon it, or has attempted to mitigate its results. For this reason, expressly considering alternative contractual mechanisms to avoid frustration (see next sub-paragraph) may support reliance on a force majeure clause if those alternatives become no longer available.

Sub-Par. 2 Frustration of the Contract

Under English law, a contract can be terminated on grounds of frustration when an unforeseen event renders contractual obligations impossible. However, this concept cannot be invoked lightly, and it has been held that imposition of sanctions does not necessarily render a contract frustrated.[210]

Sub-Par. 3 Severance

It is possible to strike out contractual provisions in certain situations, allowing the remainder of the contract to continue as intended. Where contractual provisions may be contentious due to sanctions, these should be drafted as free-standing within the context of the contract.

Par. 5 Contract Drafting – Disputes

EU regulations contain non-liability clauses, meaning that broadly speaking, a party cannot be held liable under EU law for the consequences of complying with EU sanctions.[211] This clause would only be relevant for contracts subject to EU law; the choice of governing law and competent tribunal within a contract is therefore important to consider. Many US companies also broadly make use of sanctions compliance

210. *Melli Bank Plc v. Holbud Limited* [2013] EWHC [1506] (Comm).
211. For example: in the EU Iran nuclear-related regime, Article 42, Council Regulation (EU) No 267/2012 of 23 Mar. 2012 concerning restrictive measures against Iran and repealing Regulation (EU) No 961/2010 (OJ L 88, 24.2.2012); in the EU Russia regime, Article 10, Council Regulation (EU) No 833/2014 of 31 Jul 2014 concerning restrictive measures in view of Russia's actions destabilizing the situation in Ukraine (OJ L 229, 31.7.2014).

clauses in commercial contracts, including requirements to certify that parties are not restricted and that activities will not involve sanctioned countries, parties or transactions.

Companies may want to consider arbitration rather than litigation as several jurisdictions subject to EU sanctions are also parties to the New York Convention on the Recognition and Enforcement of Foreign Arbitral Awards and have adopted domestic legislation supporting international arbitration proceedings along the lines of the *Model Law on International Commercial Arbitration* of the UN Committee on International Trade Law (UNCITRAL).[212]

SECTION 6 LIST OF ACRONYMS

BIS	Bureau of Industry and Security
CACR	Cuban Assets Control Regulations
CISADA	Comprehensive Iran Sanctions, Accountability, and Divestment Act
C.F.R.	Code of Federal Regulations
COREPER II	Committee of Permanent Representatives
CPS	Crown Prosecution Service
DDTC	Directorate of Defense Trade Controls
EAR	Export Administration Regulations
ECOWAS	Economic Community of West African States
EEAS	European External Action Service
ERP	Enterprise Resource Planning
EU	European Union
FAC	Foreign Affairs Council
FinCEN	Financial Crimes Enforcement Network
FSA	Financial Services Authority
FSE	Foreign Sanctions Evader
GATT	General Agreement on Tariffs and Trade
HMRC	Her Majesty's Revenue and Customs
IAEA	International Atomic Energy Agency
IEEPA	International Emergency Economic Powers Act
IFCA	Iran Freedom and Counter-Proliferation Act of 2012

212. Belarus, Iran, Russia, Syria and Ukraine have all acceded to the New York Convention; domestic legislation based on the UNCITRAL Model Law has been adopted in Belarus, Iran, Russia and Ukraine. It should be noted in respect of Iran that the benefit of this domestic favouring of arbitration is only likely to be felt in commercial contracts where there is no involvement by an Iranian government body or public company. Foreign enforcement proceedings regarding a public body or company require the approval of the Iranian parliament.

IFSR	Iranian Financial Sanctions Regulations
IRGC	Iranian Revolutionary Guard Corps
ISA	Iran Sanctions Act
ITAR	International Traffic in Arms Regulations
ITR	Iranian Transactions Regulations
ITRSHRA	Iran Threat Reduction and Syria Human Rights Act of 2012
ITR	Iranian Transaction Regulations
ITSR	Iranian Transactions and Sanctions Regulations
JCPOA	Joint Comprehensive Plan of Action, 14 July 2015
JPOA	Joint Plan of Action, 24 November 2013
LAS	League of Arab States
LIBERTAD	Cuban Liberty and Democratic Solidarity Act of 1996
NDAA	National Defense Authorization Act for Fiscal Year 2012
OFAC	Office of Foreign Assets Control
OSCE	Organization for Security and Co-operation in Europe
PSC	Political and Security Committee
SDN	Specially Designated National
SEC	Securities and Exchange Commission
SSIL	Sectoral Sanctions Identifications List
SFR	Socialist Federal Republic
SSR	Sudanese Sanctions Regulations
SySR	Syrian Sanctions Regulations
TEU	Treaty on the European Union
TFEU	Treaty on the Functioning of the EU
TWEA	Trading with the Enemy Act
UK	United Kingdom
UN	United Nations
UNCITRAL	UN Committee on International Trade Law
UNPA	United Nations Participation Act
US	United States of America
VSD	Voluntary Self-Disclosure
WTO	World Trade Organization

SECTION 7 REFERENCES

Sub-Section 1 Principal EU Sanctions Regimes

Target Country (Sanctions Regime)	*Principal Council Decision**	*Principal Council Regulation**
Belarus	Council Decision 2012/642/CFSP of 15 October 2012 concerning restrictive measures against Belarus (OJ L 285, 17.10.2012) Last amended by Council Decision (CFSP) 2016/280 of 25 February 2016 amending Decision 2012/642/CFSP concerning restrictive measures against Belarus (OJ L 52, 27.2.2016)	Council Regulation (EC) No 765/2006 of 18 May 2006 concerning restrictive measures against President Lukashenko and certain officials of Belarus (OJ L 134, 20.5.2006) Last amended by Council Regulation (EU) 2016/277 of 25 February 2016 amending Regulation (EC) No 765/2006 concerning restrictive measures in respect of Belarus (OJ L 52, 27.2.2016)
Iran (Human rights-related sanctions)	Council Decision 2011/235/CFSP of 12 April 2011 concerning restrictive measures directed against certain persons and entities in view of the situation in Iran (OJ L 100, 14.4.2011) Last amended by Council Decision (CFSP) 2016/565 of 11 April 2016 amending Decision 2011/235/CFSP concerning restrictive measures directed against certain persons and entities in view of the situation in Iran (OJ L 96, 12.4.2016)	Council Regulation (EU) No 359/2011 of 12 April 2011 concerning restrictive measures directed against certain persons, entities and bodies in view of the situation in Iran (OJ L 100, 14.4.2011) Last amended by Council Implementing Regulation (EU) 2016/556 of 11 April 2016 implementing Regulation (EU) No 359/2011 concerning restrictive measures directed against certain persons, entities and bodies in view of the situation in Iran (OJ L 96, 12.4.2016)

Target Country (Sanctions Regime)	*Principal Council Decision*	*Principal Council Regulation*
Iran (Nuclear-related sanctions)	Council Decision 2010/413/CFSP of 26 July 2010 concerning restrictive measures against Iran and repealing Common Position 2007/140/CFSP (OJ L 195, 27.7.2010) Last amended by Council Implementing Decision (CFSP) 2016/78 of 22 January 2016 implementing Decision 2010/413/CFSP concerning restrictive measures against Iran (OJ L 16, 23.1.2016)	Council Regulation (EU) No 267/2012 of 23 March 2012 concerning restrictive measures against Iran and repealing Regulation (EU) No 961/2010 (OJ L 88, 24.2.2012) Last amended by Council Implementing Regulation (EU) 2016/74 of 22 January 2016 implementing Regulation (EU) No 267/2012 concerning restrictive measures against Iran (OJ L 16, 23.1.2016)
Libya	Council Decision (CFSP) 2015/1333 of 31 July 2015 concerning restrictive measures in view of the situation in Libya, and repealing Decision 2011/137/CFSP (OJ L 206, 1.8.2015)	Council Regulation (EU) 2016/44 of 18 January 2016 concerning restrictive measures in view of the situation in Libya and repealing Regulation (EU) No 204/2011 (OJ L 12, 19.1.2016)
North Korea	Council Decision 2013/183/CFSP of 22 April 2013 concerning restrictive measures against the Democratic People's Republic of Korea and repealing Decision 2010/800/CFSP (OJ L 111, 23.4.2013) Last amended by Council Decision (CFSP) 2016/319 of 4 March 2016 amending Decision 2013/183/CFSP concerning restrictive measures against the Democratic People's Republic of Korea (OJ L 60, 5.3.2016)	Council Regulation (EC) No 329/2007 of 27 March 2007 concerning restrictive measures against the Democratic People's Republic of Korea (OJ L 88, 29.3.2007) Last amended by Commission Implementing Regulation (EU) 2016/315 of 4 March 2016 amending Council Regulation (EC) No 329/2007 concerning restrictive measures against the Democratic People's Republic of Korea (OJ L 60, 5.3.2016)

Target Country (Sanctions Regime)	*Principal Council Decision*	*Principal Council Regulation*
Russia (Sectoral and financial sanctions)	Council Decision 2014/512/CFSP of 31 July 2014 concerning restrictive measures in view of Russia's actions destabilizing the situation in Ukraine (OJ L 229, 31.7.2014) Last amended and consolidated by Council Decision (CFSP) 2015/971 of 22 June 2015 amending Decision 2014/512/CFSP concerning restrictive measures in view of Russia's actions destabilizing the situation in Ukraine (OJ L 157, 23.6.2015)	Council Regulation (EU) No 833/2014 of 31 July 2014 concerning restrictive measures in view of Russia's actions destabilizing the situation in Ukraine (OJ L 229, 31.7.2014) Last amended and consolidated by Council Regulation (EU) 2015/1797 of 7 October 2015 amending Regulation (EU) No 833/2014 concerning restrictive measures in view of Russia's actions destabilizing the situation in Ukraine (OJ L 263, 8.10.2015)
Crimea/ Sevastopol (Sectoral, financial and territorial sanctions)	Council Decision 2014/386/CFSP of 23 June 2014 concerning restrictions on goods originating in Crimea or Sevastopol, in response to the illegal annexation of Crimea and Sevastopol (OJ L 183, 24.6.2014) Last amended and consolidated by Council Decision (CFSP) 2015/959 of 19 June 2015 amending Decision 2014/386/CFSP concerning restrictive measures in response to the illegal annexation of Crimea and Sevastopol (OJ L 156, 20.6.2015)	Council Regulation (EU) 692/2014 of 23 June 2014 concerning restrictions on the import into the Union of goods originating in Crimea or Sevastopol, in response to the illegal annexation of Crimea and Sevastopol (OJ L 183, 24.6.2014) Last amended and consolidated by Council Regulation (EU) No 1351/2014 of 18 December 2014 amending Regulation (EU) No 692/2014 concerning restrictive measures in response to the illegal annexation of Crimea and Sevastopol (OJ L 365, 19.12.2014)

Target Country (Sanctions Regime)	*Principal Council Decision*	*Principal Council Regulation*
Ukraine (asset freeze due to threat to sovereignty of Ukraine)	Council Decision 2014/145/CFSP concerning restrictive measures in respect of actions undermining or threatening the territorial integrity, sovereignty and independence of Ukraine (OJ L 78, 17.3.2014) Last amended by Council Decision (CFSP) 2016/359 of 10 March 2016 amending Decision 2014/145/CFSP concerning restrictive measures in respect of actions undermining or threatening the territorial integrity, sovereignty and independence of Ukraine (OJ L 67, 12.3.2016)	Council Regulation (EU) No 269/2014 of 17 March 2014 concerning restrictive measures in respect of actions undermining or threatening the territorial integrity, sovereignty and independence of Ukraine (OJ L 78, 17.3.2014) Last amended and consolidated by Council Implementing Regulation (EU) 2015/1514 of 14 September 2015 implementing Regulation (EU) No 269/2014 concerning restrictive measures in respect of actions undermining or threatening the territorial integrity, sovereignty and independence of Ukraine (OJ L 239, 15.9.2015)
Ukraine (asset freeze due to human rights violations)	Council Decision 2014/119/CFSP of 5 March 2014 concerning restrictive measures directed against certain persons, entities and bodies in view of the situation in Ukraine (OJ L 66, 6.3.2014) Last amended by Council Decision (CFSP) 2016/318 of 4 March 2016 amending Decision 2014/119/CFSP concerning restrictive measures directed against certain persons, entities and bodies in view of the situation in Ukraine (OJ L 60, 5.3.2016)	Council Regulation (EU) No 208/2014 of 5 March 2014 concerning restrictive measures directed against certain persons, entities and bodies in view of the situation in Ukraine (OJ L 66, 6.3.2014) Last amended by Council Implementing Regulation (EU) 2016/311 of 4 March 2016 implementing Regulation (EU) No 208/2014 concerning restrictive measures directed against certain persons, entities and bodies in view of the situation in Ukraine (OJ L 60, 5.3.2016)

Target Country (Sanctions Regime)	*Principal Council Decision*	*Principal Council Regulation*
Syria	Council Decision 2013/255/CFSP of 31 May 2013 concerning restrictive measures against Syria (OJ L 147, 1.6.2013) Last amended by Council Implementing Decision (CFSP) 2015/2359 of 16 December 2015 implementing Decision 2013/255/CFSP concerning restrictive measures against Syria (OJ L 331, 17.12.2015)	Council Regulation (EU) No 36/2012 of 18 January 2012 concerning restrictive measures in view of the situation in Syria and repealing Regulation (EU) No 442/2011 (OJ L 16, 19.1.2012) Last amended by Council Implementing Regulation (EU) 2015/2350 of 16 December 2015 implementing Regulation (EU) No 36/2012 concerning restrictive measures in view of the situation in Syria (OJ L 331, 17.12.2015)

* In each case, the legislation establishing the most recent sanctions regime is listed as well as the most recent amending acts up to 1 November 2015. Please check the latest amendments to this legislation at http://eur-lex.europa.eu/homepage.html.

Sub-Section 2 Further EU Sanctions Regimes Resources

EU law: http://eur-lex.europa.eu/homepage.html

EU sanctions in force: http://eeas.europa.eu/cfsp/sanctions/docs/measures_en .pdf

Consolidated list of persons, groups and entities subject to EU financial sanctions: http://eeas.europa.eu/cfsp/sanctions/consol-list/index_en.htm

Sub-Section 3 EU Member State Competent Authorities

EU sanctions legislation lists the following websites for EU Member State competent authorities

EU Member State	*Competent Authorities for Sanctions*
Austria	http://www.bmeia.gv.at/view.php3?f_id = 12750&LNG = en&version =
Belgium	http://www.diplomatie.be/eusanctions
Bulgaria	http://www.mfa.bg/en/pages/135/index.html
Croatia	http://www.mvep.hr/sankcije
Cyprus	http://www.mfa.gov.cy/sanctions

EU Member State	*Competent Authorities for Sanctions*
Czech Republic	http://www.mfcr.cz/mezinarodnisankce
Denmark	https://danishbusinessauthority.dk/contact
Estonia	http://vm.ee/et/estonian-competent-authorities-implementation-eu-restrictive-measures
Finland	http://formin.finland.fi/kvyhteistyo/pakotteet
France	http://www.tresor.economie.gouv.fr/sanctions-financieres-internationales
Germany	http://www.bmwi.de/DE/Themen/Aussenwirtschaft/aussenwirtschaftsrecht,did = 404888.htm
Greece	http://www.mfa.gr/en/foreign-policy/global-issues/international-sanctions.html
Hungary	http://2010-2014.kormany.hu/download/b/3b/70000/ENSZBT-ET-szankcios-tajekoztato.pdf
Ireland	http://www.dfa.ie/home/index.aspx?id = 28519
Italy	http://www.esteri.it/MAE/IT/Politica_Europea/Deroghe.htm
Latvia	http://www.mfa.gov.lv/en/security/4539
Lithuania	http://www.urm.lt/sanctions
Luxembourg	http://www.mae.lu/sanctions
Malta	https://www.gov.mt/en/Government/Government%20of%20Malta/Ministries%20and%20Entities/Officially%20Appointed%20Bodies/Pages/Boards/Sanctions-Monitoring-Board-.aspx
Netherlands	www.rijksoverheid.nl/onderwerpen/internationale-vrede-en-veiligheid/sancties
Poland	http://www.msz.gov.pl
Portugal	http://www.portugal.gov.pt/pt/os-ministerios/ministerio-dos-negocios-estrangeiros/quero-saber-mais/sobre-o-ministerio/medidas-restritivas/medidas-restritivas.aspx
Romania	http://www.mae.ro/node/1548
Slovakia	http://www.mzv.sk/sk/europske_zalezitosti/europske_politiky-sankcie_eu
Slovenia	http://www.mzz.gov.si/si/zunanja_politika_in_mednarodno_pravo/zunanja_politika/mednarodna_varnost/omejevalni_ ukrepi/
Spain	http://www.exteriores.gob.es/Portal/es/PoliticaExteriorCooperacion/GlobalizacionOportunidadesRiesgos/Documents/ORGANISMOS%20COMPETENTES%20SANCIONES%20INTERNACIONALES.pdf
Sweden	http://www.ud.se/sanktioner
United Kingdom	https://www.gov.uk/sanctions-embargoes-and-restrictions

Sub-Section 4 Principal US Sanctions Regimes

Sanctions Regime	*Principal Regulatory Source(S)*[213]
Balkans	Executive Orders 13304 and 13219; 31 C.F.R. Part 588 (Western Balkans Stabilization Regulations)
Belarus	Executive Order 13405; 31 C.F.R. Part 548 (Belarus Sanctions Regulations)
Burma (aka Myanmar)	Executive Orders 13651, 13619, 13464, 13448, 13310 and 13047; 31 C.F.R. Part 537 (Burmese Sanctions Regulations)
Burundi	Executive Order 13712, 31 C.F.R. Part 554 (Burundi Sanctions Regulations)
Central African Republic	Executive Order 13667; 31 C.F.R. Part 553 (Central African Republic Sanctions Regulations)
Cuba	Executive Order 12854; 31 C.F.R. Part 515 (Cuban Assets Control Regulations)
Democratic Republic of the Congo	Executive Orders 13671 and 13413; 31 C.F.R. Part 547 (Democratic Republic of the Congo Sanctions Regulations)
Iran	Executive Orders 13599, 13606, 13608, 13622, 13628, and 13645; 31 C.F.R. Parts 535 (Iranian Assets Control Regulations), 560 (Iranian Transactions and Sanctions Regulations), 561 (Iranian Financial Sanctions Regulations, and 562 (Iranian Human Rights Abuses Sanctions Regulations)
Iraq	Executive Orders 13668, 13438, 13364, 13350, 13315, 13303, 13290, 12817, 12724 and 12722; 31 C.F.R. Part 576 (Iraq Stabilization and Insurgency Sanctions Regulations)
Ivory Coast	Executive Order 13396; 31 C.F.R. Part 543 (Côte d'Ivoire Sanctions Regulations)
Lebanon	Executive Order 13441; 31 C.F.R. Part 549 (Lebanon Sanctions Regulations)
Libya	Executive Order 13566; 31 C.F.R. Part 570 (Libyan Sanctions Regulations)
North Korea	Executive Orders 13466, 13551, 13570, 13687, 13722; 31 C.F.R. Part 510 (North Korea Sanctions Regulations)
Somalia	Executive Orders 13620 and 13536; 31 C.F.R. Part 551 (Somalia Sanctions Regulations)
South Sudan	Executive Order 13664; 31 C.F.R. Part 558 (South Sudan Sanctions Regulations)

213. See OFAC's website at http://www.treasury.gov/resource-center/sanctions/Programs/Pages/Programs.aspx. In some cases OFAC general licences for a particular sanctions regime may not yet be reflected in the text of the relevant C.F.R. regulations, but instead only on OFAC's website page for that particular sanctions regime.

Sanctions Regime	*Principal Regulatory Source(S)*
Sudan	Executive Orders 13067, 13400, and 13412; 31 C.F.R. Part 538 (Sudanese Sanctions Regulations)
Syria	Executive Orders 13338, 13399, 13460, 13572, 13573, 13582, 13606, and 13608; 31 C.F.R. Part 542 (Syrian Sanctions Regulations)
Ukraine/Russia related	Executive Orders 13660, 13661, 13661 and 13685; 31 C.F.R. Part 589 (Ukraine-Related Sanctions Regulations)
Venezuela	Executive Order 13692; 31 C.F.R. Part 591 (Venezuela Sanctions Regulations)
Yemen	Executive Orders 13611; 31 C.F.R. Part 552 (Yemen Sanctions Regulations)
Zimbabwe	Executive Orders 13469, 13391 and 13288; 31 C.F.R. Part 541 (Zimbabwe Sanctions Regulations)
Counter narcotics restricted parties	There are two potentially relevant sets of OFAC regulations for these parties – the Narcotics Trafficking Sanctions Regulations (31 C.F.R. part 536) where persons and entities will be included on restricted parties lists with a '[SDNT]' tag, and the Foreign Narcotics Kingpin Sanctions Regulations (31 C.F.R. part 598) where persons and entities will be included on restricted parties lists with the a '[SDNTK]' tag.
Counter terrorism restricted parties	There are four potentially relevant sets of OFAC regulations for these parties – the Global Terrorism Sanctions Regulations (31 C.F.R. part 594) where persons and entities will be included on the restricted parties lists with a '[SDGT]' tag, the Terrorism Sanctions Regulations (31 C.F.R. part 595) where persons and entities will be included on the restricted parties lists with a '[SDT]' tag, and the Foreign Terrorist Organizations Sanctions Regulations (31 C.F.R. part 597) where persons and entities will be included on the restricted parties lists with a '[FTO]' tag.
Cybersecurity	Executive Order 13694; No regulations issued to date.
Non-proliferation related parties	Executive Orders 13608, 13382, 13094, 12938; 31 C.F.R. Part 539 (Weapons of Mass Destruction Trade Control Regulations) and 31 C.F.R. Part 544 (Weapons of Mass Destruction Proliferators Sanctions Regulations)
Rough diamond trade related	Executive Order 13312; 31 C.F.R. Part 592 (Rough Diamonds Control Regulations)
Transnational criminal organizations	Executive Order 13581; 31 C.F.R. Part 590 (Transnational Criminal Organizations Sanctions Regulations)

Sub-Section 5 US Competent Authorities

Agency	*Website*
Commerce Department	https://www.bis.doc.gov/
State Department	https://www.pmddtc.state.gov/index.html and http://www.state.gov/e/eb/tfs/spi/index.htm
Treasury Department	http://www.treasury.gov/about/organizational-structure/offices/Pages/Office-of-Foreign-Assets-Control.aspx

CHAPTER 3
International Regime

Philippe Achilleas

SECTION 1 INTRODUCTION

The devastating effects on the armed forces of the First World War led governments to establish intergovernmental mechanisms and initiatives to avoid further armed conflicts between countries. Whilst war was outlawed in 1928 by the Kellogg-Briand Pact, the League of Nations did not have the legal or the political means to prevent the outbreak of the Second World War. Once the war was over, the international community made even greater efforts to further international cooperation in order to maintain peace and international security, and in doing so, tried to avoid the mistakes of the past. These new international relations were built around this central purpose, with the United Nations (UN) forming the cornerstone of the initiative. The vision of an ideal world where peace between countries would be guaranteed through diplomacy was to be quickly overshadowed by the policies of the two superpowers of the post-war years: the United States of America (US) and the former USSR. The rivalry between Washington and Moscow not only generated a series of indirect regional conflicts, but also blocked any significant action by the UN in pursuing its principal mission. Apart from some significant progress in nuclear non-proliferation, it was not until the end of the Cold War and the continuous conflicts between the superpowers that the international community were finally able to cooperate in order to work towards international peace and stability. The dialogue between countries therefore resumed at this stage although the context of discussions had changed since the end of the cold war. On the one hand, the policies of 'rogue' countries such as North Korea and Iran and the emergence of terrorism represent new threats to peace and international security. From another viewpoint, with the globalization of trade, the expansion of the international market in sensitive goods and technologies has become a major worry as their potential to be used for non-peaceful ends has become a risk to security. The difficulty is linked to the need to establish a balance between various principles recognized by international public law, namely, on the one hand, the protection of peace and international security and, on the other hand, the right to legitimate self-defence, the right to development and economic freedom.

The protection of international security is based on three complementary techniques. First, the disarmament aims at eliminating one category of weapon. Second, arms control, aims at reducing the risk of war, making it less destructive when a war starts, and reducing defence costs through the signing of agreements between countries. The objective of these agreements is based on the reduction, the limitation or the regulation of use of certain weapons. Finally, non-proliferation aims at preventing the development and the sale of particular weapons.

Since 1945, the institutional framework relating to disarmament, arms control and to non-proliferation has become complex. If the UN continues to be the most important organization in the field of international security (the General Assembly adopted its first resolution on disarmament and international security in 1946), other organizations were created to deal with more specialized issues. For example, the International Atomic Energy Agency (IAEA) was established to promote the peaceful use of nuclear energy. The international community has also established parallel forums to discuss general questions relating to disarmament (like the Disarmament Conference) or to allow a strengthened cooperation between interested countries (like the Club of Nuclear Suppliers). Alongside these initiatives, the many countries have also strengthened their levels of regional cooperation.

International initiatives in this sphere differ from one another in accordance with their nature and their scope. States may decide to adopt a treaty, of which the provisions are binding on the participating countries, or they could choose to sign a 'gentlemen's agreement'. Such agreements are not recognized as a source of international law, but are entered into and adhered to on a voluntary basis by signatory countries. Gentlemen's Agreements are entered into some way to complete conventional mechanisms or as a preparation for the adoption of an international convention.

The documents which are signed by the States have different objectives. Some texts do not specifically establish disarmament, arms control and non-proliferation regimes but include provisions which create or refer to the need for such regimes. Other texts have been adopted for the purpose of creating disarmament, an arms control or a non-proliferation regime, or set of principles. The material scope of each text depends on which category of weapons, items and/or technology the text deals with. Some texts only State which category of technology they apply to without further defining that category. Others go into greater detail, defining the items the text applies to, and the circumstances in which the text is to apply. Others specify the exact scope of application, by annexing a list of the items to which the text applies, and defining the circumstances in which the control is to apply. On a geographical level, the universal rules stated by certain documents are implemented in specific regimes dealing with special regions or international zones.

The effectiveness of these regimes relies on the introduction of certain mechanisms. The implementation methods, the resolution of disputes, verification and sanctions in cases of non-adherence are particularly important. Implementation methods, when they are foreseen, go from the adoption of national measures to the creation of international structures, which can take the form of international organizations. If the peaceful settlement of disputes is an international obligation, it does not mean that interstate justice is obligatory. States involved in a dispute have first to accept the jurisdiction of the International Court of Justice. Although international law traditionally remains cautious of sanctions, some documents do establish such methods, and in particular, an action by the Security Council. Efficient verification and control methods, which rely on reports, technology (like satellite observations) and inspections undoubtedly remain central to this issue and strengthen the efficiency of the overall regime.

The various international initiatives relating to disarmament, arms control and non-proliferation can be grouped into two categories, both of which merit discussion: regimes concerning goods and technologies (Section 2) and regimes relating to international or regional zones (Section 3).

SECTION 2 REGIMES CONCERNING GOODS AND TECHNOLOGIES

International law is charged with the task of controlling the international movement of goods and technologies of a military or sensitive nature, and, in certain cases, related know-how through the adoption of laws and regulations specific to particular and identifiable domains. Originally, the international community sought only to combat the proliferation of weapons of mass destruction (WMD), of their constituents and other closely related matters, as these have for many years presented the main threat to international peace and security (Sub-Section 1). However, it quickly became necessary to pursue this particular aim in accordance with rules that corresponded to the scale of the WMD in question, such as missiles (Sub- Section 2). A strengthening of controls over conventional weapons and dual-use goods has also become necessary. This is due to the scale of the traffic of such weapons between countries during recent years and the destabilizing effect that this trade now has on international, regional and national security. This is also due to the possible use of such goods by terrorist groups (Sub-Section 3).

Sub-Section 1 Weapons of Mass Destruction

WMD are without doubt the deadliest of all weapons as they are designed to kill on a massive scale, and are aimed at civilians as well as military personnel. The expression 'weapons of mass destruction' first appeared in 1937 with the air-strike against the Basque village of Guernica in Spain, and its civilian population. The objective of the attack was to evaluate the potential for the Nazi army to completely destroy a town. Although no legal definition exists, WMD are often regrouped under the acronym NBC: Nuclear, Biological and Chemical weapons. It is useful to distinguish nuclear activities (paragraph 1) from biological and chemical activities (paragraph 2) which are often treated in an almost identical fashion.

Par. 1 Nuclear

Nuclear weapons are derived from atomic energy. They are produced in one of two ways. The first method involves the splitting of heavy atoms, such as uranium and plutonium, as it is the case in the A Bomb. The second method relates to the fusion of light atoms, such as hydrogen, and is the case for the H Bomb. The nuclear bomb was first developed in the US, during the Second World War. Entitled Project Manhattan, the plans came about following a letter sent by Albert Einstein to President Roosevelt stating that the Germans were working on a similar weapon which was capable of destroying an entire town. The first atomic explosion took place on 16 July 1945, at the military airbase of Alamogordo in New Mexico. With the aim of forcing the Japanese to surrender, the US later launched two atomic bombs. The first bomb hit Hiroshima on 6 August 1945 and the second hit Nagasaki on 9 August 1945. The first bomb killed over 200,000 people, while the second bomb was to kill 75,000 people. After the Second World War, the proliferation of the atomic bomb allowed other countries to acquire similar technology: Russia (1949), Great Britain (1952), France (1960), China (1964), India (1974), Israel (almost certainly since 1979) and Pakistan in 1998. However, since the 1950s, the international community, through the UN, has been aware of the risks associated with the increase in nuclear arms. There has therefore been a drive ever since to fight nuclear weapons on two fronts: (Sub-Par. 1) the banning of nuclear testing and (Sub-Par. 2) the non-proliferation of such weapons.

Sub-Par. 1 Nuclear Test Prohibition

The first treaty to ban nuclear explosions was concluded in 1963 (I). However, the treaty imposed only a partial ban. It is for this reason that the international community later adopted a second law to prohibit all explosions (II).

I Limited Test Ban Treaty (LTBT)

A. Status

- Official name: Treaty Banning Nuclear Weapon Tests in the Atmosphere, in Outer Space and Under Water.
- Reference: 480 *UNTS* 43.
- Nature: Multilateral treaty which is opened to all States.
- Opened for signature: 5 August 1963.
- Entered into force: 10 October 1963.
- Parties: 126.

B. Object and Purpose

During the 1950s, the general public became increasingly concerned about radioactive fall-out from atmospheric nuclear tests and the escalating arms race. The LTBT was negotiated by the USA, the USSR, and the UK in order to prohibit tests of nuclear devices in the atmosphere, in outer space, and under water.

C. Scope

The Treaty applies to any nuclear explosion on the Earth's surface, atmosphere and in outer space. The regime deals with underground explosions in certain circumstances. It does not provide any definition of 'nuclear explosion' or 'nuclear weapon'.

D. Legal Principles

Partial nuclear test ban. Parties agree to prohibit, to prevent, and not to carry out any nuclear explosion (including nuclear weapons tests) at any place under their jurisdiction and control, in the atmosphere, in outer space and under water (Article 1, 1, (a)).

Limitation of underground tests. Underground tests are prohibited if the explosion will cause radioactive debris to be present outside the territorial limits of the State under which jurisdiction or control such explosion is conducted (Article 1, 1, (b)).

No assistance to other States. Parties must not cause, encourage or participate in the carrying out of any explosion in violation of the Treaty (Article 1, 2).

E. Implementation Provisions

None.

F. Verification

None.

G. Measures in the Event of Non-compliance

None.

H. Settlement of Disputes Procedure

None.

I. Remarks

- In spite of the binding nature of the LTBT, the absence of a verification process and specific provisions in the event of non-compliance of its provisions weakens the effects of the treaty. However, in case of the violation of the LTBT, the general principles of international public law on settlement of disputes apply.
- Neither China nor France - both Nuclear Weapons States has signed the Treaty.
- LTBT was the first step towards the negotiation of a treaty prohibiting explosions in all locations, including underground ones.

II Comprehensive Test-Ban Treaty (CTBT)

A. Status

- Official name: Comprehensive Nuclear-Test-Ban Treaty.
- Reference: United Nations General Assembly (UNGA), resolution 50/245.
- Nature: Multilateral treaty which is opened to all States.
- Opened for signature: 24 September 1996.
- Entered into force: Not yet.
- Ratifications: 163.

B. Object and Purpose

CTBT supplements LTBT. It bans all nuclear explosions, including the underground ones.

C. Scope

The text deals with nuclear explosions anywhere on earth and in outer space. It does not contain any definition of 'nuclear weapon' or of 'nuclear explosive device'.

D. Legal Principles

Parties undertake not to carry out any nuclear explosion, including nuclear weapon tests. They shall prohibit and prevent such an explosion at any place under their jurisdiction or control. Parties also agree to refrain from causing, encouraging, or in any way participating in the carrying out of any nuclear explosion (Article I).

E. Implementation

CTBTO. The Comprehensive Nuclear-Test-Ban Treaty Organization (CTBTO) was established to ensure treaty implementation and verification. CTBTO is opened to all Parties and is located in Vienna, Austria. CTBTO organs are the Conference of the State Parties, the Executive Council and the Technical Secretariat, which includes the International Data Centre (Article II).

National measures. Parties have to take measures to prohibit their nationals from violating the Treaty on their territory or anywhere under their jurisdiction or their control. They must also designate or set up a national authority to be the national focal point linked with CTBTO and with other Parties (Article III).

F. Verification

When completed, the CTBTO verification regime will be the most intrusive monitoring system ever developed. First, the International Monitoring System (IMS) shall be composed of a network of 321 monitoring stations and sixteen radionuclide laboratories monitoring the Earth for evidence of nuclear explosions in all environments using the most modern technology available. The IMS will be supported by the International Data Centre, created to provide products and services necessary for effective global monitoring (Article 4, B). Second, the Treaty sets out a detailed procedure of consultation and clarification (Article 4, C). Third, on-site inspection measures may be undertaken if necessary to clarify whether a violation of the Treaty has occurred and to gather facts for the identification of any possible Treaty violator (Article 4, D). Finally, States have to provide information on a voluntary basis related to the implementation of the Treaty in order to build confidence among parties (Article 4, E).

G. Measures in the Event of Non-compliance

The Conference or the Executive Council will advise any infringing State Party to abide by the Treaty. If it does not rectify the situation, the Conference may decide to restrict or suspend the infringing State Party from the exercise of its rights and privileges under the Treaty and may recommend to States Parties, collective measures which are in conformity with international law, such as counter-measures or embargo. The Conference or the Executive Council may also bring the issue to the attention of the UN (Article 5). In no event shall the infringing State be deprived of its membership to CTBTO (Article 2).

H. Settlement of Disputes

The Executive Council may contribute to the settlement of a dispute and the Conference may establish or entrust organs with tasks related to the settlement of a dispute. The Conference and the Executive Council may, subject to authorization from the General Assembly of the UN, request the International Court of Justice to give an advisory opinion on any legal question arising within the scope of the activities of the CTBTO (Article VI).

I. Remarks

- To enter into force, all States listed in Annex 2 to the Treaty have to deposit the instruments of ratification. Conferences on facilitating the entry into force of the Treaty are organized on a regular basis (1999, 2003, 2005 and 2009).
- Review conferences may be held every ten years after the entry into force of the Treaty. These conferences may consider the possibility of permitting the conduct of underground nuclear explosions for peaceful purposes.

- The Preparatory Commission for the CTBTO is an international organization established by the States Signatories to the Treaty on 19 November 1996 in order to prepare the effective implementation of the Treaty.
- In 1998, while only partially operational, the IMS detected and identified the Indian and Pakistani nuclear tests explosions.

Sub-Par. 2 Nuclear Non-proliferation

On 8 December 1953, President Eisenhower put forward a plan to the General Assembly of the UN, proposing the implementation of an international agency charged with the promotion of nuclear energy for civil ends. However, Eisenhower also assured the international community that cooperation with the plan would not then entail efforts being turned towards military ends. The law founding the IAEA was approved on 23 October 1956. The conclusion of the non-proliferation treaty (NPT) fell within the framework of this policy (I). The IAEA is charged with monitoring the application of the treaty, notably its systems of guarantees (II). States which supply or potentially supply nuclear material and technologies (grouped into two cooperative structures), have established two arrangements which challenge this initiative: the trigger list of the Zangger Committee (III) and the guidelines of the Nuclear Suppliers' Group (IV).

I Nuclear Non-proliferation Treaty

A. Status

- Official name: Treaty on the Non-Proliferation of Nuclear Weapons.
- Reference: 729 *UNTS* 161.
- Nature: Multilateral treaty which is opened to all States.
- Opened for signature: 1 July 1968.
- Entered into force: 5 March 1970.
- Parties: 189.

B. Object and Purpose

The NPT represents a bargain between the Non-Nuclear-Weapon States (NNWS) and the Nuclear-Weapon States (NWS)[214] in order to prevent the spread of nuclear weapons and weapons technology and to promote cooperation in the peaceful uses of nuclear energy. The Treaty furthers the goal of achieving nuclear disarmament as well as general and complete disarmament.

C. Scope

The Treaty applies to nuclear weapons and any other nuclear explosive devices. The text does not provide any definition of 'nuclear weapon' or of 'nuclear explosive device'.

214. NWS are the following: China, France, Russia, the United Kingdom and the United States.

D. Legal Principles

Non-proliferation. The NWS agree not to transfer nuclear weapons technology or other nuclear explosive devices to NNWS and not to assist, encourage, or induce any NNWS to manufacture or acquire nuclear weapons or other nuclear explosive devices (Article I). NNWS accept not to manufacture or acquire nuclear weapons or other nuclear explosive devices and not to seek or receive any assistance in the manufacture of nuclear weapons or other nuclear explosive devices (Article II).

Right to peacefully use nuclear energy. All Parties have the inalienable right to develop the research, production and use of nuclear energy for peaceful purposes without discrimination. To this end, Contracting States undertake to facilitate, and have the right to participate in exchange of equipment, materials and scientific information for the peaceful uses of nuclear energy (Article IV). Moreover, each Party shall take appropriate measures to ensure that potential benefits from any peaceful applications of nuclear explosions will be made available to NNWS Party to the Treaty on a non-discriminatory basis at the lowest possible charge (Article V).

Disarmament. All States' Parties have to pursue negotiations in good faith on effective measures relating to the ending of the nuclear arms race and to nuclear disarmament (Article VI).

E. Implementation/Verification

Each NNWS accepts safeguards, as set forth in an agreement to be concluded with the IAEA, for the purpose of verification of the fulfilment of its obligations assumed under the Treaty. Its purpose is to prevent the diversion of nuclear energy from peaceful uses to nuclear explosive devices (Article III, par. 1). Moreover, the provision to an NNWS, for peaceful purposes, of a source or of special fissionable material, or equipment or material especially designed or prepared for the processing, use or production of special fissionable material is subject to IAEA safeguards (Article III, par. 2).[215]

F. Measures in the Event of Non-compliance

None.

G. Settlement of Disputes

None.

H. Remarks

- Five States are considered to be 'Nuclear-Weapon States' (NWS) under the terms of the NPT: in order of acquisition of nuclear weapons these are: the USA, the Russian Federation (successor State to the USSR), the United Kingdom, France, and China. All of them have ratified in the field of disarmament.
- India, Israel North Korea and Pakistan, which possess nuclear weapons, are the only non-States' Parties to the NPT together with South Sudan.

215. The Zangger committee was set up to implement Article III par. 2.

- In 2003, the Democratic Popular Republic of North Korea was the first country to announce its unilateral withdrawal from the NPT after having benefited from its membership by acquiring nuclear material, technology and equipment. This development underlines a weakness of the Treaty system.
- Conferences of Parties to the Treaty are organized every five years to review the implementation of the Treaty (Article 8).
- The amendment of the Treaty to add measures to take in the event of non-compliance could strengthen the NPT.

II IAEA Comprehensive Safeguards Agreement and Model Additional Protocol

A. Status

- Official name: Agreement Between the Agency and States Required in Connection with the Treaty on the Non-Proliferation of Nuclear Weapons (NPT) / Model Protocol Additional to the Agreement(s) between State(s) and the Agency for the Application of Safeguards.
- Reference: INFCIRC/153 (Corrected) / INFCIRC/540(Corrected).
- Nature: Bilateral agreements concluded between States and IAEA.
- Opened for signature: variable according to each agreement.
- Entered into force: variable according to each agreement.
- Parties: The IAEA has NPT safeguards agreements in force with 182 States and Model Additional Protocol in force with 128 States and Euratom.

B. Object and Purpose

The IAEA was created in 1957 in response to the fears and expectations resulting from the use of nuclear energy. One of the major functions of the Agency is establish and administer safeguards designed to ensure that special fissionable and other materials, services, equipment, facilities and information made available by the Agency or at its request or under its supervision or control are not used in such a way as to further any military purpose (Statute of the IAEA, Article III A, par. 5[216]). The safeguards system comprises sets of technical measures by which the IAEA Secretariat independently verifies the correctness and the completeness of the States' declarations on their nuclear material and activities. The objective is the timely detection of the diversion of significant quantities of nuclear material from peaceful uses to the manufacture of nuclear weapons or other explosive devices or for purposes unknown as well as the deterrence of such diversion by the risk of early detection.

C. Scope

The comprehensive safeguards agreements represent the most important ones. They are concluded by NNWS pursuant to the NPT and deal with all source or special

216. 276 *UNTS* 3.

fissionable material[217] in peaceful nuclear activities in a State. Some of them are also concluded pursuant to other bilateral[218] or regional[219] agreements which have the same scope. Measures under comprehensive safeguards agreements cover declared activities. Traditional safeguard measures deal with the verification of material and activities declared by States. The disclosure in 1991 of the clandestine military nuclear programme of Iraq and the difficulties of cooperation with North Korea in 1992 highlighted IAEA's inability to act in relation to material and activities which were not declared. For this reason, in 1997, States have been invited to ratify an additional protocol based on a model approved by the IAEA Board of Governors, usually referred to as the 1997 IAEA Model Additional Protocol to extend the IAEA safeguards to undeclared activities.

D. Legal Principles

National system of accounting. States shall establish and maintain a system of accounting for and control of all nuclear material subject to the safeguards agreement, in such a manner as to enable the Agency to verify that there has been no diversion of nuclear material (Comprehensive Safeguards Agreement Structure, par. 7).

Declarations of States. States have to provide to the Agency a minimum amount of information concerning nuclear material subject to safeguards under the Agreement and the features of facilities relevant to safeguarding such material (Comprehensive Safeguards Agreement Structure, paragraph 8). Among others, the State has to provide to the Agency, within thirty days after the agreement enters into force, an initial report on all nuclear material which is to be subject to safeguards thereunder (Comprehensive Safeguards Agreement Structure, par. 62). Only for States parties to a comprehensive safeguards agreement, the declarations are limited to nuclear material accounting reports and facility design information. States party to an additional protocol have to provide much more information about their nuclear activities (Model Additional Protocol, Articles 2 and 3).

Inspections. The verification procedure remains one of the key elements of each comprehensive safeguard agreement which provide that the Agency should organize various on-site inspections (Comprehensive Safeguards Agreement Structure, par. 70-89). Ad hoc inspections are carried out to verify a State's initial report of nuclear material or reports on changes of the initial situation. They are also made to verify

217. According to Article XX par. 1 of the AIEA Statute:

> The term 'special fissionable material' means plutonium-239; uranium- 233; uranium enriched in the isotopes 235 or 233; any material containing one or more of the foregoing; and such other fissionable material as the Board of Governors shall from time to time deter mine; but the term 'special fissionable material' does not include source material.

218. 1995 Agreement between the Republic of Argentina and the Federative Republic of Brazil for the Exclusively Peaceful Use of Nuclear Energy (INFCIRC/395).

219. 1967 Treaty for the Prohibition of Nuclear Weapons in Latin America and the Caribbean (Tlatelolco Treaty), 1985 South Pacific Nuclear Free Zone Treaty (Rarotonga Treaty), 1995 Treaty on the Southeast Asia Nuclear Weapon-Free Zone (Bangkok Treaty), 1996 African Nuclear-Weapon-Free Zone Treaty (Pelindaba Treaty). These treaties will be analysed *infra* Chapter 3, Section 3, Sub-Section 2.

nuclear material involved in international transfers. Routine inspections are made to locations within a nuclear facility or other strategic locations containing nuclear material or through which nuclear material is expected to flow. Special inspections are carried out when the Agency considers that information and explanations made available by the State, including those obtained from routine inspections, is not adequate for the Agency to fulfil its responsibilities under the Safeguard agreement. Under additional protocols, inspectors have access to all parts of a State's nuclear fuel-cycle and to any other location where nuclear material is or may be present. In addition, inspectors may have a complementary access to verify the absence of undeclared activities (Model Additional Protocol, Articles 4-10).

International transfers. Each safeguard agreement should include rules of procedure for control of international transfers of nuclear materials, which have to be applied under the responsibility of the State (Comprehensive Safeguards Agreement Structure, par. 91-97).

E. Implementation

Cooperation. Each comprehensive safeguard agreement should provide that the Agency and the State shall cooperate to facilitate the implementation of the safeguards provided for therein (Comprehensive Safeguards Agreement Structure, par. 3).

Measures in relation to verification of non-diversion. Each comprehensive safeguard agreement should provide that if the Board, upon report of the Director General, decides that an action by the State is essential and urgent in order to ensure verification that nuclear material is not diverted to nuclear weapons or other nuclear explosive devices, the Board shall be able to call upon the State to take the required action without delay. The Agreement should also provide that the Board may make a report or take actions if it finds that the Agency is not able to verify that there has been no diversion of *nuclear material* required to be safeguarded (Comprehensive Safeguards Agreement Structure, par. 18-19).

F. Verification

None.

G. Measures in the Event of Non-compliance/Settlement of Disputes

Each comprehensive safeguard agreement should provide that the parties shall, at the request of either of them, consult about any question dealing with its application. Such agreement should also provide that the State shall have the right to request that the Board considers the issue. The agreement should further provide that any dispute arising out of its interpretation or application (except a dispute resulting from a finding by the Board or an action taken by the Board pursuant to measures in relation to verification of non-diversion) which is not settled by negotiation or any other means agreed to by the parties should, upon the request of either party, be submitted to an arbitral tribunal composed according to the provisions of the Agreement (Comprehensive Safeguards Agreement Structure, par. 20-22).

H. Remarks

- For each country, the IAEA Secretariat evaluates the results of safeguards implementation on an annual basis and presents its conclusions to IAEA Board of Governors. When the States complies with its international obligations of non-proliferation, the Secretariat concludes to the non-diversions of nuclear material and non-misuse of specified items.
- In the event of non-compliance with any safeguard agreement, the inspectors shall report to the Director General who shall thereupon transmit the report to the Board of Governors. The Board shall call upon the recipient State or States to remedy forthwith any non-compliance which it finds to have occurred and shall report the non-compliance to all members and to the Security Council and General Assembly of the UN. In the event of failure of the recipient State or States to take fully corrective action within a reasonable time, the Board may decide the direct curtailment or the suspension of assistance being provided by the Agency or by a member, and may call for the return of materials and equipment made available to the recipient member or group of members. The Agency may also suspend any non-complying member from the exercise of the privileges and rights of membership (IAEA Statute, Article XX, C). In no event can a member be excluded from the organization.

III Zangger Trigger List

A. Status

- Official name: List of Items of equipment or material especially designed or prepared for the processing, use or production of special fissionable material.
- Reference: INFCIRC/209/Rev.2.
- Nature: Political document which contains a list which is applicable on a national basis. States have formally accepted the Trigger List in an exchange of letters among themselves and have written identical letters to the Director General of IAEA to inform him of their intention to control the items of the list.
- Adoption: 14 August 1974/published as an IAEA document on 3 September 1974.
- Participants: Thirty-nine States. The European Union (EU) has the status of Permanent Observer.

B. Object and Purpose

The Zangger[220] Committee is composed of suppliers or potential suppliers of nuclear material and equipment. It was established in 1971 following the coming into force of the NPT, in order to interpret and implement its Article III, par. 2. To this end, the Committee adopted basic understandings contained in two documents (Memorandum A and Memorandum B). Each of them defines the materials and equipment described

220. Prof. Claude Zangger was the first Chairman of the Committee.

in Article III, par. 2 and provides for procedures for their export. The memoranda are known as the 'trigger list' since the export of listed items 'triggers' IAEA safeguards.

C. Scope

The Zangger List provides details of what is envisaged by Article III, par. 2 of the NPT. Memorandum A deals with source and special fissionable material (Article III, par. 2, (a)). Memorandum B deals with equipment and material especially designed or prepared for the processing, use or production of special fissionable material (Article III, par. 2, (b)). Memorandum A gives the definition of source material and special fissionable material (Article 2). Memorandum B contains a list of controlled items completed by an Annex attached to the memoranda clarifying or defining the equipment and material of Memorandum B.

D. Commitments

The Trigger List establishes three conditions for supplying items to an NNWS not party to the NPT:

- *Non-explosive use assurance.* The Recipient State makes assurances to the supplying State that the item will not be diverted for use in nuclear weapons or other nuclear explosive devices (Article 3 par. a of Memoranda A and B).
- *IAEA safeguards.* Exports shall be subject to safeguards under an agreement concluded with IAEA (Articles 3 (par. a) and 4 of Memoranda A and B).
- *Re-export.* The Recipient State makes assurances to the supplying State that the item will not be re-exported to an NNWS not party to NPT unless the Recipient State has accepted IAEA safeguards on the re-export item (Article 5).

E. Implementation

National measures. Participating States have agreed to give effect to the Zangger list through their national export control legislation.

Exchange of information. Every year, participating members exchange information on exports and the issue of licences.

F. Verification

None.

G. Measures in the Event of Non-compliance

None.

H. Settlement of Disputes

None.

I. Remarks

- The Zangger Committee participates actively in the NPT review conferences.
- The Annex clarifying or defining the equipment and material of Memorandum B is revised on a regular basis to take into account technology developments.

IV Nuclear Suppliers Group Guidelines

A. Status

- Official name: Guidelines for Nuclear Transfers/Guidelines for Transfers of Nuclear-Related Dual-Use Equipment, Materials, Software and Related Technology.
- Reference: INFCIRC/254/Rev.7/Part 1 and INFCIRC/254/Rev.6/Part 2.
- Nature: Political document. The Guidelines are applicable on a national basis. States formally accepted them through an exchange of letters among themselves, and each sent an individual communication to the Director General of IAEA to inform him of their intention to respect the Guidelines.
- Adoption: Nuclear transfer guidelines: 1974 – published as an IAEA document in 1978; Dual-use guidelines: 1992 – published as an IAEA document in 1992.
- Participants: Forty-six States. The EU is a Permanent Observer.

B. Object and Purpose

Following the explosion in 1974 of a nuclear device by India, NNWS States decided to create the Nuclear Suppliers Group (NSG) to ensure that nuclear trade for peaceful purposes will not contribute to the proliferation of nuclear explosive devices. Taking into account the work achieved by the Zangger Committee, the NSG has published guidelines including a trigger list. The disclosure, in 1991, of the Iraqi secret nuclear weapons programme based on dual-use items not listed in the NSG Guidelines led to the adoption of guidelines for transfers of nuclear-related dual-use items. The first set of guidelines is known as 'Part I' and the second set of guidelines is known as 'Part II'.

C. Scope

Part I concerns the export of items and technology that are especially designed or prepared for nuclear use. Part II governs the export of nuclear-related dual-use items and technologies. Both parts provide detailed lists of controlled items.

D. Commitments

Conditions for transfers of listed nuclear items and related technology. Suppliers should authorize transfers only after they have received assurance from the recipients that the intended use will not result in the creation of any nuclear explosive device (Part I, par. 2). All nuclear items should be placed under effective physical protection to prevent unauthorized use and handling (Part I, par. 3). Suppliers should transfer items to an

NNWS only when the Receiving State has brought into force a safeguards agreement with the IAEA (Part I, par. 4). Stronger controls are exercised on sensitive exports and on the export of enrichment facilities, equipment and technology (Part I, par. 6 and 7). Suppliers should transfer items or related technology only if the recipient provides assurances that a potential retransfer will respect the Guidelines (Part I, par. 9). At least, according to the general principle of non-proliferation, suppliers should authorize a transfer only when there is neither a risk of proliferation of nuclear explosive devices nor a risk of contribution to nuclear terrorism (Part I, par. 10).

Conditions for transfer of nuclear-related dual-use items and related technology. Suppliers should not authorize transfers in the following three situations: (1) when the listed items will be used in an NNWS in a nuclear explosive activity or an unsafeguarded nuclear fuel-cycle activity; (2) when there is a general unacceptable risk that the items will be diverted for use in a prohibited activity, or an activity incompatible with the objective of non-proliferation; and (3) when there is an unacceptable risk that the items will be diverted for acts of nuclear terrorism (Part II, par. 2). To this end, the supplier should obtain, before authorizing the transfer, a statement from the end-user specifying the uses and end-use locations of the proposed transfers and an assurance stating that the proposed transfer or any replica thereof will not be used in any nuclear explosive activity or unsafeguarded nuclear fuel-cycle activity (Part II, par. 6). Before authorizing the transfer to a State which has not committed itself to the Guidelines, suppliers should also obtain assurances that their consent will be secured prior to any retransfer to a third-party State (Part II. par. 7).

E. Implementation

National measures. Each participant has to adopt legal measures to ensure the effective implementation of the Guidelines, including export licence regulations, enforcement measures and penalties in the event of violation (Part I, par. 11 and Part II, par. 4 and 5). Part II, par. 4 provides a list of relevant factors to take into account when authorizing the transfers.

Consultations and information. Suppliers should maintain contact with each other and consult each other on matters connected with the implementation of the Guidelines (Part I, par. 15 (a)). They should also consult other governments on specific sensitive cases (Part I, par. 15 (b)). Furthermore, NSG participants should exchange information which relates to the Guidelines during regular meetings (Part II, par. 9). The Consultative Group is a working body established to hold consultations on issues associated with the Guidelines on nuclear supply and the technical annexes. The Information Exchange Meeting is organized prior to each NSG Plenary to allow Participating Governments to share information on the NSG Guidelines.

F. Verification

None.

G. Measures in the Event of Non-compliance

When one or more suppliers believe that there has been a violation of the Guidelines, suppliers should consult each other promptly through diplomatic channels in order to determine and assess the reality and extent of the alleged violation. States should agree on a proportionate response, which could involve the termination of the nuclear transfers to the Recipient State (Part I, par. 15(c)).

H. Settlement of Disputes

None.

I. Remarks

- The NSG Guidelines are consistent, not only with the NTP, but also with all the Nuclear Weapons Free Zones (NWFZ) treaties.
- There are major differences between the NSG and the Zangger Committee. First, the scope of the trigger list of the Zangger Committee is restricted to items falling under Article III, par. 2 of the NPT,[221] whereas the NSG guidelines are applicable to all nuclear transfers for peaceful purposes. NSG Guidelines also include technology and dual-use items and technologies both not in the scope of the Zangger Trigger List. Second, the NSG Guidelines contain a non-proliferation clause. However, the two regimes have the same objective and the two institutions cooperate with each other.

Par. 2 Biological and Chemical Weapons

Biological weapons use biological agents designed to cause death or illness in humans, animals and plants. They can be toxins, such as botulinum toxin or ricin, bacteria, such as anthrax or Yersinia pestis, viruses, such as smallpox, or rickettsiae, such as Q-fever. Biological warfare has always existed and consisted, in its most basic form, of throwing human or animal carcasses into enemy territory. Since then, the international community has developed more sophisticated techniques, especially during the Second World War, and today it is terrorist groups who are most likely to use such weapons. Chemical weapons use a chemical product, or mixtures of chemical products which are poisonous for humans, and for all living species in general. Deadly weapons are usually differentiated from neutralizing weapons. Chemical agents are classified according to their effect on human beings. Amongst others, these include nerve agents, such as Sarin, blood agent or cyanogen agent, such as cyanogen chloride, blister agent, such as mustard gas and pulmonary agent such as chlorine. The first chemical weapon was used on 22 April 1915 by the German army during the First World War. After the war, global public opinion condemned use of chemical weapons, along with the potential use of biological weapons. The Geneva Protocol therefore represented the first significant step in the fight against such weapons (Sub-Par. 1). Both the Biological Weapons Convention (Sub-Par. 2) and the Chemical Weapons Convention (Sub-Par. 3) completed the process. These conventions are the basis of initiatives to prohibit the use and development of these types of weapons, but at the same time allowing countries to

221. That is to say source and special fissionable material or equipment and material especially designed or prepared for the processing, use or production of special fissionable material.

pursue biological and chemical research for peaceful ends. These initiatives establish a non-proliferation regime for the States which actively participate in the international markets of chemical and biological activity, and together form the 'Australia Group' (Sub-Par. 4).

Sub-Par. 1 Geneva Protocol

I Status

- Official name: Protocol for the Prohibition of the Use of Asphyxiating, Poisonous or Other Gases, and of Bacteriological Methods of Warfare.
- Reference: 94, *League of Nations Treaty Series*, n° 2138 (1929).
- Nature: Multilateral treaty, which is opened to all States.
- Opened for signature: 17 June 1925.
- Entry into force: For each signatory, the date of deposit of its ratification; accessions take effect on the date of the notification by the depositary Government.
- Parties: 138.

II Object and Purpose

Chemical and biological weapons have been used since the dark ages. Several treaties and conventions have been adopted to prohibit chemical weapons as an instrument of warfare, especially the 1907 Convention concerning the Laws and Customs of War.[222] In spite of that, 90,000 people died during the First World War from the use of chemical weapons. However, these effects were insignificant compared to Spanish influenza, which claimed 20 million lives - almost as much as the war itself although not a weapon. Public opinion realized the potential effects of a possible biological war, much higher than the effects of chemical weapons. States decided then to adopt the Geneva Protocol for banning the use of chemical and biological weapons.

III Scope

The Treaty applies to asphyxiating, poisonous or other gases, and to all analogous liquids materials or devices as well as to bacteriological weapons. The text provides neither specific definitions of the terms nor a list of prohibited products.

IV Legal Principles

Prohibition of chemical weapons use. States, so far as they are not already parties to treaties prohibiting the use of chemical weapons, accept such a prohibition (par. 1).

222. Schindler, D. & Toman J. *The Laws of Armed Conflicts.* Martinus Nihjoff Publisher, 1988, 69-93.

Prohibition of bacteriological weapons use. States agree to extend the prohibition to the use of bacteriological methods of warfare (par. 1).

V Implementation

None.

VI Verification

None.

VII Settlement of Disputes

None.

VIII Remarks

- In spite of the binding nature of the Protocol, the absence of verification process and specific provisions in the event of non-compliance of its provisions weakens the effects of the Geneva regime. However, in case of the violation of the Geneva Protocol, the general principles of international public law on settlement of dispute apply.
- The Protocol neither prohibits the development nor deployment of chemical or bacteriological weapons. It only prohibits the use of chemical and bacteriological weapons.
- Many of the signatories issued reservations permitting them to use chemical weapons against countries that have not joined the Protocol or to respond in kind if attacked with such weapons. Since the entry into force of the text, some States have dropped their reservations.

Sub-Par. 2 Biological and Toxin Weapons Convention

I Status

- Official name: Convention on the Prohibition of the Development, Production and Stockpiling of Bacteriological (Biological) and Toxin Weapons and on Their Destruction.
- Reference: 1015 *UNTS* 163.
- Nature: Multilateral treaty which opened to all States.
- Opened for signature: 10 April 1972.
- Entered into force: 26 March 1975.
- Parties: 110.

II Object and Purpose

In 1969, the unilateral decision of US to destroy their stockpile of biological weapons led to international negotiations for the adoption of a convention in order to supplement the Geneva Protocol in the field of biological weapons. The socialist States, as well as many neutral and non-aligned States opposed to a separate treatment of biological and chemical weapons. They accepted to negotiate a text on biological weapons only if it represented a first step towards the achievement of another agreement in the field of chemical weapons.

III Scope

The treaty is applicable to microbial or other biological agents, or toxins whatever their origin or method of production. The text does not define the prohibited items.

IV Legal Principles

Prohibitions. States Parties undertake to never develop, produce, stockpile, acquire or retain microbial or other biological agents or toxins for hostile purposes. These prohibitions also concern weapons, equipment or means of delivery designed to use such agents or toxins for hostile purposes or in armed conflict (Article I).

Destruction. Parties agree to destroy or to divert to peaceful purposes all agents, toxins, weapons, equipment and means of delivery prohibited by the Convention, which are in their possession or under their jurisdiction or control (Article II).

Non-proliferation. States' Parties accept not to transfer to any recipient whatsoever, directly or indirectly, and not to assist, encourage, or induce any State, group of States or international organizations to manufacture or otherwise acquire any of the agents, toxins, weapons, equipment or means of delivery prohibited by the Convention (Article III).

Peaceful activities. Parties have the right to participate in, to the fullest extent possible, the exchange of equipment, materials and scientific and technological information, for the use of biological agents and toxins for peaceful purposes especially for medical activities, protective purposes and scientific experimentation (Article X).

Assistance. Each State Party has to provide or support the provision of assistance to any Party which so requests it, in the event of exposure to danger as a result of a violation of the Convention (Article VII).

V Implementation

National measures. States Parties have to take any necessary measures to implement the Convention within their territory or a territory under their jurisdiction or control (Article IV). As a consequence, the national laws and regulations are adapted to take the provisions of the Convention into account.

Consultation and cooperation. States Parties undertake to consult one another and to cooperate in solving any problems which may arise in relation to the Convention (Article V).

Confidence-building measures. During the Review Conferences, Parties decided to adopt confidence-building measures to improve international cooperation in the field of peaceful biological activities. These voluntary measures include exchange of data on laboratories, national biological defence research programmes and outbreaks of infectious diseases and similar occurrences caused by toxins. States should also encourage the publication and use of results of biological research related to the Convention. Moreover, States should declare national measures adopted to implement the Convention, and any past activities in offensive and/or defensive biological research programmes, since 1946, as well as vaccine production facilities.

VI Verification

The Convention remains silent on verification. Therefore, in 1991, the third Review Conference established the Ad Hoc Group of Governmental Experts to Identify and Examine Potential Verification Measures from a Scientific and Technical Standpoint. The Group has identified off-site measures and on-site measures including exchange visits, inspections and continuous monitoring. The Convention has not yet been modified to include such measures.

VII Measures in the Event of Non-compliance

Any State Party which finds that any other Party is violating the provisions of the Convention may lodge a complaint with the Security Council of the UN. The complaint should include all possible evidence confirming its validity. Each State Party cooperates in carrying out any investigation which the Security Council may initiate. The Security Council shall inform the States' Parties of the results of the investigation (Article VI).

VIII Settlement of Disputes

None.

IX Remarks

- The Biological and Toxin Weapons Convention was the first universal treaty banning an entire category of weapons.
- The negotiations of the text were quite easy since biological weapons have a limited value in combat.
- Conferences are organized by the Parties on a regular basis to review the operation of the Convention.

- The Convention does not prohibit the use of biological and toxin weapons. Indeed, the 1925 Geneva Protocol, that prohibits the use of such weapons, remains in force (Article VIII). However, States are not obliged to withdraw their reservations to the Geneva Protocol according to which they can use biological weapons in certain circumstances.
- Declarations and information are transmitted on a voluntary basis.
- Very few States have the means to prove a violation of the Convention necessary for sending a complaint to the Security Council.
- Allegations of non-compliance with the provisions of the Convention have been made. For example, in 1980, the US accused the USSR of carrying out a biological weapons programme. The accusation was based on an outbreak of anthrax in the city of Sverdlovsk. In 1992, Russia admitted the breach of the Convention.

Sub-Par. 3 Chemical Weapons Convention

I Status

- Official name: Convention on the Prohibition of the Development, Production, Stockpiling and Use of Chemical Weapons and on their Destruction.
- Reference: Doc.CD/CW/WP.400/Rev.1.
- Nature: Multilateral treaty which is opened to all States.
- Opened for signature: 13 January 1993.
- Entered into force: 29 April 1997.
- Parties: 190.

II Object and Purpose

Despite the conclusion of international agreements prohibiting the use of chemical weapons, such weapons were used in several conflicts including the Second World War and the Iran-Iraq War of 1983-1988. After twenty years of negotiations, the Chemical Weapons Convention was adopted in order to ban chemical weapons and to ensure their elimination.

III Scope

The Chemical Weapons Convention applies to chemical weapons as defined in the text (Article II, 1).[223] The Annex on Chemicals lists toxic chemicals and their precursors relevant to the application of verification measures.

223. Article II, 1 reads as follows: 'any toxic chemical or its precursor that can cause death, injury, or temporary disabilities through its chemical action. Munitions or devices designed to deliver chemical weapons, whether filled or unfilled, are also considered weapons themselves'.

IV Legal Principles

Prohibitions. States Parties agree not to develop, produce, acquire, stockpile, retain chemical weapons or transfer chemical weapons to anyone. They also undertake not to use chemical weapons, not to engage in any military preparation to use chemical weapons and not to assist, encourage or induce anyone to engage in any activity prohibited under the Convention (Article I, 1).

Destruction. States undertake to destroy chemical weapons and chemical weapons facilities they own or possess, or that are located in any place under their jurisdiction or control, as well as all chemical weapons they abandoned on foreign territory (Article I, 2-Article I, 4).

Non-proliferation. Each State has the right, subject to the provisions of the Convention, to develop, produce, otherwise acquire, retain, transfer and use toxic chemicals and their precursors for peaceful uses. States have to ensure that toxic chemicals and their precursors are only developed, produced, otherwise acquired, retained, transferred, or used within their territory or in any other place under their jurisdiction or control for purposes not prohibited under the Convention (Article VI).

Economic and technological development. All States have the right, individually or collectively, to conduct research with, to develop, produce, acquire, retain, transfer, and use chemicals. They also have the right to participate in the fullest possible exchange of chemicals, equipment and scientific and technical information relating to the development and application of chemistry for purposes not prohibited under the Convention. Therefore, States must not restrict trade, development and promotion of scientific and technological knowledge in the field of chemistry for peaceful purposes (Article XI).

Protection and assistance. Each State Party commits itself to provide protection assistance in the event of chemical attack (Article X).

V Implementation

OPCW. The Organization for the Prohibition of Chemical Weapons (OPCW) is an international organization, which was established in 1997 at The Hague, The Netherlands, by the States' Parties in order to implement the obligations of the Convention at an international level, including those for verification of compliance with it, and to provide a forum for consultation and cooperation among States' Parties. The Conference of Parties, composed of all States, is the principal organ of the OPCW and makes major decisions about the Convention. The Executive Council, composed of representatives of forty-one Member States, takes all measures necessary to guide the OPCW's operations. The Technical Secretariat carries out the daily work of implementing the Convention, including conducting inspections (Article VIII).

National measures. Each State has to adapt its national criminal legislation, and to designate or establish a national authority to serve as the national focal point for effective liaison with the Organization and other States' Parties. States inform the OPCW of the measures taken to implement the Convention.

Declarations. Each State declares to the OPCW, within thirty days after the Convention enters into force for that particular State, its possession of chemical weapons and/or production facilities as well as its plans for destroying them. It also has to declare any other facilities designed for the development of chemical weapons, such as laboratories (Article III). Each State, in addition, submits annual declarations regarding the implementation of its plans for destruction of chemical weapons (Article IV, 7. b) and production facilities (Article V, 9. b), as well as the use of chemical weapons for non-prohibited purposes (Article VI, 8).

VI Verification

Verification represents a key element of the Convention. The Technical Secretariat verifies the destruction of chemical weapons stockpiles and production facilities, as well as the use of the scheduled chemicals for authorized purposes. The verification process is objective and transparent. All States are fairly treated, with due respect to national security and confidentiality concerns. Three types of inspections may be undertaken. First, routine inspections intended to verify the accuracy of information declared by States' Parties in their initial and annual declarations, as well as the extent to which the use of chemicals conforms to the provisions of the Convention. Second, 'challenge inspections' grant each State Party the right to request the Director General to undertake at short notice an inspection in order to clarify and resolve any questions of possible non-compliance. Third, an investigation of alleged use can be conducted by the OPCW at the request of a State Party, to confirm the actual use or threat of use of chemical weapons and/or to assess the need for assistance (Verification Annex).

VII Measures in the Event of Non-compliance

The Executive Council demands the State Party to take measures to rectify a situation raising problems. If the State Party fails to fulfil the demand within the specified time, the Conference may restrict or suspend the State Party's rights and privileges under the Convention until it conforms to its obligations under the Convention. In very serious cases, the Conference may also recommend collective measures, and bring the issue to the attention of the UNGA and the Security Council (Article XII). Under no circumstance shall a State be deprived from its membership of the OPCW (Article VIII, A. 2).

VIII Settlement of Disputes

The Executive Council and the Conference of Parties may contribute to the settlement of a dispute concerning the application or the interpretation of the Convention. They are separately empowered, subject to authorization from the General Assembly of the UN, to request the International Court of Justice to give an advisory opinion on any legal question arising within the scope of the activities of the Organization.

IX Remark

- The Chemical Weapons Convention represents the most detailed and complete disarmament convention.
- In 2013, the use of chemical weapons in the Syrian Civil War has been confirmed by the UN Mission to Investigate Allegations of the Use of Chemical Weapons in the Syrian Arab Republic during the civil war (UN Doc. A/67/997–S/2013/553, 16 September 2013). The mission was organized in cooperation with the OPCW. The UN Security Council Resolution 2118 was then adopted on 27 September 2013, in order to establish a framework for the elimination of Syrian chemical weapons. Two days later, the OPCW Executive Council also adopted a Decision on Destruction of Syrian chemical weapons on 27 September 2013 (EC-M-33/DEC.1). A joint OPCW-UN mission will supervise the destruction or removal of Syria's chemical arms. In 2014, operations were still ongoing. Syria also accepts to sign the Chemical Weapons Convention. The text entered into force for the Syrian Arab Republic on 14 October 2013.

Sub-Par. 4 Australia Group Guidelines

I Status

- Official name: Guidelines For Transfers of Sensitive Chemical or Biological Items.
- Reference: Not published.
- Nature: Political document; Guidelines are applicable on a national basis.
- Date of adoption: June 2002.
- Participants: Forty-two, including the EU.

II Object and Purpose

After the UN concluded, in 1984, that Iraq used chemical weapons during the Iran-Iraq War, States decided to adopt national licensing measures for the export of a number of chemical products. In April 1985, Australia proposed the organization of a meeting of the concerned States in order to harmonize their national licensing measures. Since 1985, this informal group of States, known as the Australia Group, has been meeting every year to enhance cooperation in the field of chemical and biological weapons prohibition. During the 2002 meeting, States decided to adopt formal guidelines to limit the risks of proliferation and terrorism involving chemical and biological weapons, by controlling transfers that could contribute to such activities consistent with international conventions and resolutions.

III Scope

The Guidelines apply to the transfer, to both governmental and non-governmental entities, of any item in the six common control lists established by the Australia Group. The six lists deals respectively with chemical weapons precursors, dual-use chemical manufacturing and equipment and related technology, dual-use biological equipment, biological agents as well as plants pathogens and animal pathogens. The Common Control Lists may be modified during each Australia Group Meeting.

IV Commitments

Transfer denial. Transfers are denied if a State knows or has reasons to believe that the controlled items are intended to be used in a chemical weapons or biological weapons programme, or for terrorism, or that a significant risk of diversion exists (par. 2). Participating States should use a non-exhaustive list of factors, stated in the Guidelines, to evaluate the risks of each transfer (par. 4).

Re-export. Each Participating State should, before authorizing a transfer of a controlled item, satisfy itself either that products are not intended for re-export or, if re-exported, that the goods will be controlled by the recipient government pursuant to the Guidelines. If not, the State should obtain satisfactory assurances that its consent will be secured prior to any retransfer to a third country (par. 5).

Non-listed items. National legislations shall include an authorization for non-listed items, when it is established that the items in question may be intended for use in connection with chemical or biological weapons activities (Second part, par. 1).

Components. Participating States should ensure that the objectives of the Guidelines are not defeated in the event of a transfer of any non-controlled item containing one or more controlled components, where the controlled component is the principal element of the item and can feasibly be removed or diverted for other purposes (par. 6).

Plants. Participating States should ensure that the objectives of the Guidelines are not defeated by the transfer of a whole plant that has been designed to produce any chemical or biological weapon agent or controlled precursor chemical (par. 6).

No undercut policy. An export licence identical to a licence denied by another participant will only be granted after consultations with that participant (Second part, par. 2).

V Implementation

Additional measures. Participating States may attach any additional conditions to a transfer that they consider necessary, or may apply the Guidelines to non-controlled items. They may apply also measures to restrict exports for other domestic public policy reasons (par. 7).

Exchange of information. The States exchange among themselves on the application of the Guidelines (par. 8).

VI Verification

During the 2005 Australia Group meeting, States decided to conduct a survey of participants' current application of the Guidelines.

VII Measures in the Event of Non-compliance

None.

VIII Settlement of Disputes

None.

Sub-Section 2 Missile Technology

The international regimes on the non-proliferation of WMD are only effective to the extent they also deal with the transfer of weapons delivery systems. These systems are either aircraft (with or without pilots), or missiles. Missiles which spend most of their trajectory in unpowered flight and which do not use aerodynamics to alter their course are known as ballistic missiles, because their motion is largely governed by the laws of ballistics, as opposed to cruise missiles, which spend most of their trajectory in powered flight. Both ballistic and cruise missiles, when they are equipped with nuclear, chemical or biological warheads, have a monumental destructive range and have the capacity to kill many people. The first missiles were the V2, developed by the Werner Von Braun's team for the Nazis to bomb London. This research led to the development of space launchers. When the USSR sent Sputnik 1 into orbit, the first artificial satellite launched from earth, the event marked the beginning of fierce competition between the two great power States dominant in this area to conquer space. At the same time, smaller missiles were beginning to appear. Guided by infrared, radar or Global Positioning Satellite (GPS), they were able to destroy planes, boats and even tanks. In the absence of an international treaty dealing with the non-proliferation of missiles, the international community cooperated in the political sphere, for example, the MTCR Guidelines (Par. 1) and The Hague International Code of Conduct (Par. 2).

Par. 1 MTCR Guidelines

Sub-Par. 1 Status

- Official name: Guidelines for Sensitive Missile-Relevant Transfers.
- Reference: 26 *ILM* 599 (1987).
- Nature: Political document; Guidelines are applicable on a national basis.

- Date of adoption: 16 April 1987.
- Participants: Thirty-four States.

Sub-Par. 2 Object and Purpose

In 1987, States decided to set up the Missile Technology Control Regime (MTCR), an informal agreement between participating States, which controls, in particular through the application of guidelines, transfers that could make a contribution to delivery systems other than manned aircraft for WMD. The MTCR guidelines are also aimed at limiting the risks of terrorist groups and malevolent individuals acquiring controlled items and associated technologies.

Sub-Par. 3 Scope

The Guidelines deal with missile-related equipment, materials, software or technology. The Equipment, Software and Technology Annex[224] lists the items controlled. The document includes a set of definitions associated to the control. The term 'missile' is interpreted in a broad sense. Category I of the Annex concerns certain complete rocket systems,[225] and complete unmanned aerial vehicle systems[226] capable of delivering at least a 500 kg payload to a range of at least 300 km. Category II of the Annex covers complete rocket systems and unmanned air vehicles not covered under Category I, but capable of a maximum range equal to or greater than 300 km, regardless of the payload weight. It also includes propulsion and propellant components launch and ground support equipment, as well as the materials required for missile construction. MTCR does not deal with manned aircraft in its principles or in its exceptions.

Sub-Par. 4 Commitments

Conditions for transfer authorization. Where the transfer of items listed in the Annex could contribute to a delivery system for WMD, the government will authorize the transfer only on receipt of appropriate assurances from the recipient State that the items will be used only for the purpose stated, and that the stated use will not be modified, and nor the items modified or replicated without the prior consent of the government. Furthermore, confirmation is required that the items, replicas and derivatives thereof will not be retransferred without the consent of the supplying government (par. 5).

Transfer denial presumption. There is a presumption to deny the transfer of any item in the Annex, or of any missiles, if the government considers that they are intended to be used in the delivery of WMD (par. 2).

224. MTCR/TEM/2005/ANNEX/002.
225. It includes ballistic missile systems, space launch vehicles, and sounding rockets.
226. It includes cruise missile systems, target drones and reconnaissance drones.

Evaluation criteria. In the evaluation of transfer applications for items listed in the Annex, six risk factors have to be taken into account (par. 3): (1) concerns about the proliferation of WMD; (2) capabilities and objectives of the missile and space programmes of the recipient State; (3) significance of the transfer in terms of the potential development of delivery systems (other than manned aircraft) for WMD; (4) assessment of the end-use of the transfers; (5) applicability of relevant multilateral agreements; (6) risk of controlled items falling into the hands of terrorist groups and individuals.

Design and production technology control. The transfer of design and production technology directly associated with any items listed in the Annex will be subject to an as strict scrutiny and control as the transfer of the products itself (par. 4).

Special regime for Category I products. Since Category I items are the most sensitive, there is a strong presumption of denial of the licence for their transfer. The transfer of Category I production facilities is prohibited. Moreover, if a Category I item is included in a system, that system will also be considered as Category I, except when the incorporated item cannot be separated, removed or duplicated. The transfer of other Category I items will be authorized on two conditions. First, the government has to obtain binding intergovernmental undertakings, which give assurances from the recipient government and recall the conditions for transfer authorization described in paragraph 5 of the Guidelines. Second, the government has to assume responsibility for taking all steps necessary to ensure that the item is put only to its stated end-use (par. 2).

Notifications. Notifications to all other participants of licences denied are mandatory for both Category I and II. Moreover, for Category I, it is compulsory to request the agreement of all other participants before issuing a licence and to notify them the agreement.

Undercut policy. Participants may allow export despite a previous licence denial within three year relating to the same product by another participant.

Non-listed items control. The government will provide that its national export controls require prior authorization for the transfer of non-listed items, if the exporter has been informed by the government that the items may be intended for use in connection with delivery systems for WMD. Moreover, any exporter aware that non-listed items are intended for use in such activities has to inform the government, which will decide whether or not it is appropriate to make the export concerned subject to authorization (par. 7).

Sub-Par. 5 Implementation

National measures. The government will implement the Guidelines in accordance with national legislation (par. 1).

End-user undertakings. MTCR partners agreed to obtain the following undertakings before the transfer of a controlled item: (1) a detailed statement from the end-user specifying the use and end-use location of the proposed transfer; (2) an assurance explicitly stating that the proposed transfers will not be used for any activities related to the development or production of delivery systems for WMD; and (3) where possible and if deemed necessary, an assurance that a post-shipment inspection may be made by the exporter or the exporting government. MTCR Partners should also obtain assurances that their consent will be secured prior to any retransfer to a third country of the equipment, material or related technology or any replica thereof.

Exchange of information. The governments have to exchange information on the application of the Guidelines (par. 6).

Sub-Par. 6 Verification

None.

Sub-Par. 7 Measures in the Event of Non-compliance

None.

Sub-Par. 8 Settlement of Disputes

None.

Sub-Par. 9 Remarks

- There is no international multilateral treaty on missile technology. A few bilateral agreements have been signed, such as START and ABM Treaties between the USA and Russian Federation.
- Countries possessing long-range missiles or space launch vehicles such as China, India, Israel, Japan and Saudi Arabia are not MTCR partners.

Par. 2 The Hague International Code of Conduct

Sub-Par. 1 Status

- Official name: The Hague Code of Conduct against Ballistic Missile Proliferation.
- Reference: Not published.
- Nature: Political document.
- Date of adoption: 25 November 2002.
- Subscribing States: 137.

Sub-Par. 2 Object and Purpose

Since 1998, the MTCR has been considering broader approaches to missile non-proliferation, including development of specific initiatives for confidence-building measures on missile activities and of dialogue with non-partners. The adoption of the International Code of Conduct represents the first attempt to establish for all States measures to prevent and curb the proliferation of ballistic missile systems capable of delivering WMD.

Sub-Par. 3 Scope

The Code is focused on ballistic missiles capable of delivering WMD. It also applies to all programmes and technologies that may conceal ballistic missile programmes, such as space launchers programmes.

Sub-Par. 4 Principles

Respect of principles. States agree to respect basic principles including: (1) strengthening and gaining wider adherence to norms and mechanisms for multilateral disarmament, non-proliferation and arms control; (2) peaceful uses of outer space in the interest of all States; (3) free use of outer space without contributing to the proliferation of ballistic missiles capable of delivering WMD; (4) no use of space launch vehicle programmes to conceal ballistic missile programmes; (5) necessity of appropriate transparency measures on ballistic missile programmes and space launch vehicle programmes (par. 2).

General measures implementation. States accept to adopt a set of measures including: (1) respect of relevant space law treaties; (2) curb and prevent the proliferation of ballistic missiles capable of delivering WMD; (3) exercise maximum possible restraint in the development, testing and deployment of ballistic missiles capable of delivering WMD; (4) exercise the necessary vigilance in the consideration of assistance to space launch vehicle programmes in any other country; (5) not to contribute to, support or assist any ballistic missile programme in countries which might be developing or acquiring WMD (par. 3).

Transparency and self-confidence. States agree to: (1) make an annual declaration providing an outline of their ballistic missile policies as well as of their space launch vehicle policies and launch sites; (2) provide annual information on the number and generic class of ballistic missiles and space launch vehicles launched during the preceding year; (3) consider, on a voluntary basis, inviting international observers to their launch sites. Furthermore, States agree to exchange pre-launch notifications on their ballistic missile and space launch vehicle launches and test flights (par. 4).

Sub-Par. 5 Implementation

Austria was appointed as the administrative central contact of the Code. Regular meetings among partners are also organized. During the second annual meeting held in 2003, it was decided to work on implementation issues.

Sub-Par. 6 Verification

None.

Sub-Par. 7 Measures in the Event of Non-compliance

None.

Sub-Par. 8 Settlement of Disputes

None.

Sub-Par. 9 Remark

States shall use the regular meetings to define, review and further develop the workings of the Code, particularly by establishing procedures regarding the exchange of notifications and other information in the framework of the Code and an appropriate mechanism for the voluntary resolution of questions arising from national declarations, and/or questions on the implementation of the Code.

Sub-Section 3 Conventional Arms and Dual-Use Goods and Technologies

A complete ban on weapons would be contrary to two fundamental principles of international law recognized by the UN Charter: a country's right of legitimate self-defence (Article 51 of the UN Charter) and the right of sovereignty (Article 2 of the UN Charter). These rights allow countries to maintain their independence on their own territory, and to allow them to pursue any economic activity whilst respecting their international obligations. Each country is therefore able to produce, sell or buy any weapons which are not prohibited by law, that is, conventional weapons. The proliferation of conventional weapons does however still represent a threat to society. Arms transfers, in all their aspects, represent three threats for the international order: (1) a potential effect in further destabilizing areas where tension and regional conflict threaten international and national security; (2) a potential negative effects on the progress of the peaceful social and economic development of all peoples; (3) a danger of increasing illicit and covert arms trafficking. Many economic activities rely on the use of technology and goods which are able to have both civil and military uses. The international community therefore committed itself to cooperate on the issues of the non-proliferation of conventional weapons and dual-use technologies dealt with in documents of a general nature (Par. 1) and documents focusing on specific weapons (Par. 2).

Par. 1 General Documents

Two approaches have been implemented to avoid that trade in conventional arms and dual-use technologies endangers international, regional or national security: transparency with the establishment of a UN register (Sub-Par. 1) and control of international transfers (Sub-Par. 2).

Sub-Par. 1 Transparency: UN Register on Conventional Arms

I Status

- Official name: Register on Conventional Arms.
- Reference: A/RES/46/36/L.
- Nature: Political document. The Register has been created by a recommendation of the General Assembly of UN.
- Date of adoption: 9 December 1991.
- Participating States: In each year of operation of the Register, over 173 States have submitted reports on international arms transfers.

II Object and Purpose

In 1924, the League of Nations decided to publish an Armaments Yearbook which contained data on the size and equipment of States' armed forces. The purpose of this transparency policy represented the first attempt to combat illegal arms trading activities. After the Second World War, some UN Member States requested the creation of arms registers. In the early 1990s, the end of the Cold War and the discovery of size of the Iraqi military arsenal, which had been made possible through conventional arms transfers, lead to the establishment of a register on conventional arms. It represents a key element of the international transparency in armaments and appears as a main confidence-building measure designed to improve security among States.

III Scope

The Register deals with the following categories of conventional arms: battle tanks; armoured combat vehicles; large-calibre artillery systems; manned and unmanned combat aircraft; attack helicopters; warships; missiles or missile systems.[227] The text provides definitions for each of these items. Some States suggested the amendment of

227. This Category does not include ground-air missiles. However, MANPADS have to be declared.

the list to add new categories of weapons such as small arms and light weapons (SALW), which have received a greater focus of attention in recent conflicts. Up to date, States do not succeed to agree on measures to expand the scope of the Register.

IV Principles

Responsibilities of the Secretary General. The Secretary General is requested to establish and maintain a universal and non-discriminatory Register of Conventional Arms, to include data on international arms transfers as well as information provided by Member States on military holdings, procurement through national production and relevant policies (par. 7).

Responsibilities of Member States. Member States are requested to address, on an annual basis, data for the Register to the Secretary General, on the number of items in each of the Register's categories of equipment imported into or exported from their territory. They shall also specify the supplying State (for imports), the recipient State (for exports) and the State of origin if not the exporting State (Annex, par. 2).

V Implementation

Technical procedures. The Secretary General, with the assistance of a panel of governmental technical experts, is requested to elaborate the technical procedures and adjustments to the Register (par. 8). The Panel met for the first time in 1992.

National, regional and global measures. States are invited to take measures to promote openness and transparency in armaments (par. 16) and to cooperate at a regional and sub-regional level (par. 17). Since then, the adoption of some regional documents is supporting the Register such as the 1999 Inter-American Convention on the Transparency in Conventional Weapons Acquisition.

VI Verification

None.

VII Measures in the Event of Non-compliance

None.

VIII Settlement of Disputes

None.

IX Remarks

- Only the declarations on complete military systems have to be made to the Register and not sub-systems, equipment, components or spare parts.
- The Register approach does not focus on technology but only on complete military systems. However, today, the measure of the military strength of the nations is deduced from their volume of military equipment but from their capacity to master technologies enabling the development of complex military systems.

Sub-Par. 2 Control of International Transfers

A decisive step was taken in 2013 with the signing of the Treaty on Arms Trade. This document is the first binding basis for national controls on international arms transfers (II). Until then, the control of international transfers of arms was established under the Wassenaar Arrangement 1996. This gentlemen's agreement also covers goods and dual-use technologies (I).

I Wassenaar Arrangement

A. Status

- Official name: Wassenaar Arrangement on Export Controls for Conventional Arms and Dual-Use Goods and Technologies.[228]
- Reference: Not published.
- Nature: Political document. The Arrangement is open on a global and non-discriminatory basis to States that comply with agreed criteria. To be admitted, a State must (1) be a producer/exporter of arms or industrial equipment respectively; (2) maintain non-proliferation policies and appropriate national policies, including adherence to relevant non-proliferation regimes and treaties; and (3) maintain fully effective export controls.
- Date of adoption: 19 December 1995.
- Participate: Forty-one States.

B. Object and Purposes

In 1950, some States decided to establish the Coordinating Committee for Multilateral Export Controls (COCOM), an informal organization in order to restrict the export of sensitive items that could be used to contribute to military potential and the proliferation of weapons systems. During the Cold War, the COCOM was, in fact, designed to impose an embargo on Western States' exports on Socialist Countries. At the end of Cold War, members of the COCOM recognized that East-West focus was no longer the appropriate basis for export controls and decided to adopt a new framework. COCOM

228. The basic document of the Wassenaar Arrangement called Initial Elements was adopted on 11-12 Jul. 1996.

ceased to exist in March 1994 and the Wassenaar Arrangement has been adopted in order to contribute to regional and international security and stability, by promoting transparency and greater responsibility in transfers of conventional arms and dual-use goods and technologies.

C. Scope

The Arrangement is applicable to conventional arms and dual-use goods and technologies set forth in the List of Dual-Use Goods and Technologies (Dual-Use List) and in the Munitions List. The Dual-Use List has two annexes: the sensitive items list (Sensitive List) and the very sensitive items list (Very Sensitive List). The documents contain the definitions of the terms used in the lists. The lists are reviewed on an annual basis to reflect technological developments and experience gained by Participating States.

D. Principles

Export control. States agree to control all items set forth in the lists with the objective of preventing unauthorized transfers or retransfers of those items (Initial elements, Section III). The decision to transfer or deny transfer of any item is under the sole responsibility of each Participating State (Initial elements, Section I, 3). States agree to exert extreme vigilance for items included in the Very Sensitive List by applying to those exports national conditions and criteria.

National policies co-ordination. States agree to exchange, on a voluntary basis, information in order to coordinate national control policies (Initial elements, Section II, 2).

Exchange of information on listed items. States agree to notify licences denied to non-participants with respect to items on the Dual-Use List (Initial elements, Section V). States also agree to exchange information on arms including matters such as emerging trends in weapons programmes and the accumulation of particular weapons systems, where they are of concern, for achieving the objectives of the Arrangement (Initial elements, Section VI). States agree to notify the licences issued relating to sensitive goods twice a year on an aggregate basis. Such notifications are made within thirty days and no more than sixty days on an individual basis if the denial relates to very sensitive goods. Notifications of licences granted are made twice a year.

On this point, the text of the Arrangement is as follows:

> *Notification of a denial will not impose an obligation on other Participating States to deny similar transfers. However, a Participating State will notify, preferably within 30 days, but no later than within 60 days, all other Participating States of an approval of a licence which has been denied by another Participating State for an essentially identical transaction during the last three years.*

Undercut policy. A Participating State may disregard a licence denial from another Participating State to authorize an export. In such cases, it must notify to the other Participating States such undercut decision within two months.

E. Implementation

Guidelines and procedures. States work on guidelines and procedures that take into account experience acquired (Initials elements, Section II, 5). States have adopted several documents.[229]

Meetings. States meet periodically to take decisions regarding the Wassenaar arrangement to consider ways of coordinating efforts to promote the development of effective export control systems. Plenary meetings are held at least once a year and chaired by a Participating State on the basis of annual rotation (Initial elements, Section VII).

Secretariat. The representatives agreed to locate the Secretariat of The Wassenaar Arrangement in Vienna, Austria.

F. Verification

None.

G. Measures in the Event of Non-compliance

None.

H. Settlement of Disputes

None.

I. Remarks

- The list of controlled equipment and services is contained in the Council Regulation (EC) n° 428/2009 of 5 May 2009 setting up a Community regime for the control of exports, transfer, brokering and transit of dual-use items.[230]
- Industries are associated to the updating of the lists by the States.
- The application of the Wassenaar Arrangement has led to the development of self-regulation by the industries, assessed, on a case-by-case basis, by the States.

II Arms Trade Treaty

A. Status

- Official name: Arms Trade Treaty.
- Reference: UNGA Resolution 67/234B of 2 April 2013.
- Nature: Multilateral treaty which is opened to all States.

229. The main documents are as follows: the 'Elements for Objective Analysis and Advice Concerning Potentially Destabilizing Accumulations of Conventional Weapons' (1998); the 'Statement of Understanding on Intangible Transfers of Software and Technology' (2001).
230. Council Regulation (EC) n° 428/2009, last modified by the 'Commission Delegated Regulation (EU) 2015/2420 of 12 October 2015 amending Council Regulation (EC) No 428/2009 setting up a Community regime for the control of exports, transfer, brokering and transit of dual use items'. (cf. Official Journal of the European Union L 340/1 of 24.12.2015) hereinafter the Regulation (EC) n° 428/2009, as modified.

- Date of adoption: 2 April 2013.
- Parties: seventy-nine States.

B. Object and Purposes

The treaty aims at preventing the security, social, economic and humanitarian dramatic consequences of the illicit and unregulated trade in conventional arms. The treaty has a dual object. The first object concerns the regulation of legitimate interstate commerce. The second is the prevention of illicit trafficking in conventional arms. To these ends, the text set up common international standards of transparency and control for the import, export and transfer of conventional weapons.

C. Scope

The treaty is applicable to all conventional arms within the following categories: (a) Battle tanks; (b) Armoured combat vehicles; (c) Large-calibre artillery systems; (d) Combat aircraft; (e) Attack helicopters; (f) Warships; (g) Missiles and missile launchers; and (h) SALW (Article 2, par. 1).[231] Ammunition, munitions, and parts and components for these conventional arms are also covered (Articles 3 and 4). The Treaty is applicable to 'activities of the international trade'. Such activities include export, import, transit, trans-shipment, and brokering (Article 2, par. 2).

D. Principles

Export control. The Treaty establishes two principles concerning international transfers of conventional arms, ammunition and parts and components. First transfers are prohibited if the transfer would violate relevant international obligations to which a State is a party, including the Charter of the UN. In addition, a State shall not authorize any transfer if it has knowledge at the time of authorization that the arms or items would be used in the commission of genocide, crimes against humanity, grave breaches of the Geneva Conventions, attacks directed against civilian objects or civilians, or other war crimes defined by international agreements to which the State is a party (Article 6). Second, where a transfer has not been prohibited pursuant to Article 6, each exporting State shall assess the potential that the arms or items would be detrimental to peace and security or could be used to commit or facilitate a serious violation of international humanitarian law, human rights law, international conventions against terrorism, or international conventions relating to transnational organized crime. If so, the State shall not authorize an export (Article 7).

Diversion. Each State involved in the transfer of conventional arms shall take measures to prevent their diversion (Article 11).

E. Implementation

National implementation. Each State shall establish and maintain a national control system, including a national control list. National definitions of any of the categories covered under the treaty shall not cover less than the descriptions used in the UN

231. Cf. categories of the UN list and Small Arms and Light Weapons (SALW).

Register of Conventional Arms at the time of entry into force of the Treaty. For the SALW category, national definitions shall not cover less than the descriptions used in relevant UN instruments at the time of entry into force of the Treaty. Each State shall designate competent national authorities in order to have an effective and transparent national control system regulating the transfer of conventional arms Each State shall also designate one or more national points of contact to exchange information on matters related to the implementation of the Treaty (Article 5).

Secretariat. States will establish a Secretariat to assist them in the effective implementation of the Treaty (Article 18).

Transparency. Each State shall maintain national records, pursuant to its national laws and regulations, of its issuance of export authorizations or its actual exports of the conventional arms (Article 12).

Conference of States Parties. A Conference of States Parties shall be convened on a regular basis. It shall review the implementation of the Treaty, including developments in the field of conventional arms (Article 17).

International cooperation. States Parties are encouraged to facilitate international cooperation, including exchange of information and consultations regarding the implementation and application of the Treaty (Article 15). In addition, in implementing the treaty, each Party may seek assistance including legal or legislative assistance, institutional capacity-building, and technical, material or financial assistance. Each Party in a position to do so shall provide such assistance, upon request (Article 16).

F. Verification

None.

G. Measures in the Event of Non-compliance

None.

H. Settlement of Disputes

Parties shall cooperate to pursue settlement of any dispute that may arise between them with regard to the interpretation or application of this Treaty including through negotiations, mediation, conciliation, judicial settlement or other peaceful means. In addition, they may pursue, by mutual consent, arbitration to settle any dispute (Article 19). The Conference of States Parties may also consider issues arising from the interpretation of the treaty (Article 17).

I. Remarks

- The Arms Trade Treaty is neither a disarmament treaty nor an arms control treaty. It does not place restrictions on the types or quantities of arms that may be bought, sold, or possessed by States. It also does not impact a State's domestic firearm regulations.
- The treaty establishes respect for humanitarian law and human rights law as one of the control criteria. The treaty thus recognizes an express link between export controls and compliance with these international principles.

Par. 2 Regimes Dedicated to Special Weapons

The proliferation of three specific weapons is of particular concern for the international community because they are able to endanger peace as well as international, regional and national security. These are: SALW (Sub-Par. 1), landmines (Sub-Par. 2) and cluster munitions (Sub-Par. 3).

Sub-Par. 1 Small Arms

The excessive accumulation and uncontrolled circulation of small arms, light weapons and their ammunition create a major threat to international peace and security. In all conflicts that have taken place since the end of the Cold War, it is the SALW which have mainly or exclusively been used. Such weapons represent the major source of casualties resulting from armed conflicts. Besides, there is a close link between terrorism, organized crime and trafficking in drugs and the illicit trade in SALW. At least, proliferation and easy acquisition of light weapons are destabilizing UN peace-keeping efforts as well as activities carried on by humanitarian non-governmental organizations. The UN has adopted a set of instruments in order to regulate the trade of such weapons within a comprehensive approach: a Protocol on firearms (I); a Programme of Action on SALW (II); and an International Tracing instrument (III)

I Protocol on Firearms to the Convention against Translational Organized Crime

A. Status

- Official name: Protocol against the Illicit Manufacturing of and Trafficking in Firearms, their Parts and Components and Ammunition, supplementing the UN Convention against Transnational Organized Crime.
- Reference: A/RES/55/225.
- Nature: Multilateral treaty which is opened to all States.
- Adoption: 31 May 2001.
- Entered into force: 3 July 2005.
- Parties: 110.

B. Object and Purpose

The Protocol has been adopted to supplement the 2001 UN Convention against Transnational Organized Crime[232] with an international instrument against the illicit manufacturing of and trafficking in firearms, their parts and components and ammunition will be useful in preventing and combating those crimes.

232. A/RES/55/25.

C. Scope

The text focuses on firearms,[233] their parts and components, that is to say, any element or replacement element specifically designed for a firearm and essential to its operation, and ammunition.[234] It shall not apply to State-to-State transactions or to State transfers in cases where the application of the Protocol would prejudice the right of a State Party to take action in the interest of national security consistent with the Charter of the UN (Article 4).

D. Legal Principles

Criminalization. States' Parties have to adopt legislative and other measures to establish as criminal offences, when committed intentionally, the illicit manufacturing and illicit trafficking of firearms, their parts and components and ammunition as well as the falsifying or illicitly obliterating, removing or altering the marking(s) on firearms required by the Protocol (Article 5).

Export/Import. States' Parties have to establish or maintain an effective system of export and import licensing or authorization, as well as of measures on international transit, for the transfer of firearms, their parts and components and ammunition. Before issuing export licences or authorizations for shipments of such items, each State Party shall verify (1) that the importing States have issued import licences or authorizations; (2) that the transit States have, at a minimum, given notice in writing, prior to shipment, that they have no objection to the transit. States' Parties may adopt simplified procedures for the temporary import and export and the transit of firearms, their parts and components and ammunition for verifiable lawful purposes such as hunting, sport shooting, evaluation, exhibitions or repairs (Article 10).

Other major obligations. States' Parties shall adopt within their domestic legal systems, measures to enable confiscation of firearms, their parts and components and ammunition that have been illicitly manufactured or trafficked (Article 6). In order to identify and track each firearm, States' Parties shall organize marking of firearms (Article 8).

E. Implementation

Cooperation. States' Parties have to encourage border controls, and of police and customs trans-border cooperation to increase the effectiveness of import, export and transit controls (Article 11 b)). They also have to cooperate at the bilateral, regional and international levels to reach the objectives of the Protocol (Article 13).

233. According to the Protocol, 'Firearm' shall mean 'any portable barrelled weapon that expels, is designed to expel or may be readily converted to expel a shot, bullet or projectile by the action of an explosive, excluding antique firearms or their replicas'. The text adds that 'Antique firearms and their replicas shall be defined in accordance with domestic law. In no case, however, shall antique firearms include firearms manufactured after 1899' (Article 3, par. a).

234. According to the Protocol, 'Ammunition' shall mean 'the complete round or its components, including cartridge cases, primers, propellant powder, bullets or projectiles, that are used in a firearm, provided that those components are themselves subject to authorization in the respective State Party' (Article 3, par. c).

Training and technical assistance. States' Parties may receive, upon request, the training and technical assistance necessary to implement the provisions of the Protocol (Article 14).

F. Verification

None.

G. Measures in the Event of Non-compliance

None.

H. Settlement of Disputes

Any dispute between two or more States' Parties concerning the interpretation or application of the Protocol that cannot be settled through negotiation within a reasonable time shall, at the request of one of those States' Parties, be submitted to arbitration. If, six months after the date of the request for arbitration, those States' Parties are unable to agree on the organization of the arbitration, any one of those States' Parties may refer the dispute to the International Court of Justice by request in accordance with the Statute of the Court (Article 16).

I. Remark

None.

II Programme of Action on SALW

A. Status

- Official name: Programme of Action to Prevent, Combat and Eradicate the Illicit Trade in Small Arms and Light Weapons in All Aspects.
- Reference: A/CONF.1992/15.
- Nature: Political document.
- Date of adoption: 20 July 2001.
- Participating States: UN Member States.

B. Object and Purpose

The UN Conference on the Illicit Trade in SALW in All Aspects has been organized in July 2001 to promote international efforts and cooperation in this field.

C. Principles

Measures to be taken at the national level. Among the set of measures adopted, States accepted to adopt or implement domestic law to exercise effective control over the production of SALW within their jurisdiction and over the export, import, transit or retransfer of such weapons, in order to prevent illegal manufacture of and illicit trafficking in SALW, or their diversion to unauthorized recipients (Part II; par. 2). States also agreed to establish as criminal offences under their domestic law, the illegal manufacture, possession, stockpiling and trade of SALW within their jurisdiction (Part

II; par. 3). Furthermore, States accepted to establish or designate a national point of contact dealing with to the implementation of the Programme of Action (Part II; par. 5).

Measures to be taken at regional level. Participating States decided to reinforce regional cooperation and to establish or designate regional points of contact for the application of the Programme of Action (Part II; par. 24-31).

Measures to be taken at global level. Participating States agree to support global cooperation in coordination with the UN, the International Criminal Police Organization (Interpol) and the World Customs Organization (Part II; par. 32-41).

D. Implementation

Participating States are encouraged to cooperate and to ensure coordination to deal with the illicit trade in SALW, including by providing technical and financial assistance and relevant information (Part III). States also meet on a biennial basis to consider the implementation of the Programme of Action (Part IV, par. 1).

E. Verification

States will provide to the UN, on a voluntary basis, national reports on implementation of the Programme of Action (Resolution, par. 33)

F. Measures in the Event of Non-compliance

None.

G. Settlement of Disputes

None.

H. Remarks

There is no harmonized filing process in the arms categories.

III International Tracing Instrument

A. Status

- Official name: International Instrument to Enable States to Identify and Trace, in a Timely and Reliable Manner, Illicit SALW.
- Reference: A/DEC/60/519.
- Nature: Political document.
- Date of adoption: 8 December 2005.
- Participating States: UN Member States.

B. Object and Purpose

The purpose of this instrument is to enable States to identify and trace, in a timely and reliable manner, illicit SALW. This instrument also aims at promoting and facilitating international cooperation in marking and tracing and to enhance the effectiveness of, and complement, existing international agreements to prevent, combat and eradicate the illicit trade in SALW in all its aspects. Within the scope of this regime, ‘tracing’ is 'the systematic tracking of illicit small arms and light weapons found or seized on the territory of a State from the point of manufacture or the point of importation through the lines of supply to the point at which they became illicit' (Resolution, par. 5). For the purposes of this instrument, SALW are 'illicit' if: (1) they are considered illicit under the law of the State within whose territorial jurisdiction the small arm or light weapon is found; (2) they are transferred in violation of arms embargoes decided by the Security Council in accordance with the Charter of the UN; (3) they are not marked in accordance with the provisions of this instrument; (4) they are manufactured or assembled without a licence or authorization from the competent authority of the State where the manufacture or assembly takes place; or (5) they are transferred without a licence or authorization by a competent national authority (Resolution, par. 6).

C. Principles

Marking. States will at the time of manufacture of each small arm or light weapon under their jurisdiction or control, either require unique marking providing the name of the manufacturer, the country of manufacture and the serial number, or maintain any alternative unique user-friendly marking permitting ready identification by all States of the country of manufacture. States will also and encourage the marking of such additional information as the year of manufacture, weapon type/model and calibre. Regarding international trade, States will require marking on each imported small arm or light weapon, permitting identification of the country of import and, where possible, the year of import and enabling the competent authorities of that country to trace the small arm or light weapon (Resolution, par. 8)

Illicit items. States will ensure that all illicit SALW that are found on their territory are uniquely marked and recorded, or destroyed, as soon as possible (Resolution, par. 8)

Record-Keeping. Records pertaining to marked SALW will, to the extent possible, be kept indefinitely, but in any case a State will ensure the maintenance of: (a) Manufacturing records for at least thirty years; and (b) All other records, including records of import and export, for at least twenty years (Resolution, par. 12).

Tracing request. A State may initiate a tracing request in relation to SALW found within its territorial jurisdiction that it considers to be illicit (Resolution, par. 16).

D. Implementation

National legislation. States will put in place, where they do not exist, the laws, regulations and administrative procedures needed to ensure the effective implementation of rules stated. They will also designate one or more national points of contact relating to the implementation of the instrument (Resolution, par. 24 and 25).

Cooperation. States will cooperate to support the effective implementation of the instrument including by rendering technical, financial and other assistance (Resolution, par. 26-29).

Transparency. States will provide the UN Secretary General with the following information: (a) Name and contact information for the national point(s) of contact; (b) National marking practices related to markings used to indicate country of manufacture and/or country of import as applicable (Resolution, par. 31)

Interpol. States, where appropriate, will cooperate with the International Criminal Police Organization (Interpol) to support the effective implementation of the instrument (Articles 33-35).

E. Verification

States will report on a biennial basis to the UN Secretary General on their implementation of the instrument including. They also will meet on a biennial basis to consider the reports mentioned (Resolution, par. 36 and 37).

F. Measures in the Event of Non-compliance

None.

G. Settlement of Disputes

None.

H. Remarks

While implementing the instrument, States are cooperating on the establishment of sub-regional or regional mechanisms with a view to prevent, combat and eradicating the illicit trade in SALW across borders.

Sub-Par. 2 Convention on Anti-personal Mines

I Status

- Official name: Convention on the Prohibition of the Use, Stockpiling, Production and Transfer of Anti-personal Mines and on their Destruction.
- Reference: 2056, *UNTS*, 211.
- Nature: Multilateral treaty which is opened to all States.
- Adoption: 18 September 1997.
- Entered into force: 1 March 1999.
- Parties: 162.

II Object and Purpose

More than sixty countries are affected by anti-personal landmines on their territory. Once mines have been laid, they are completely indiscriminate in their action which represents, among other things, a violation of humanitarian law.[235] Unless eliminated, they continue to have the potential to kill even after the conflict is over. Their presence creates a serious humanitarian problem, both because they kill or injure civilians, and

235. According to humanitarian law, parties to a conflict have to make a distinction between civilians and combatants since civilians must not be attacked. As a consequence they cannot use weapons that are inherently indiscriminate.

also prevent the economic development of the concerned countries. The Convention has been adopted to prevent future landmine problems and to solve the existing landmine problem.

III Scope

The Convention is applicable to anti-personal mines, that is to say, mines designed to kill or injure people, and excludes from its scope those designed to destroy tanks or vehicles, also referred as anti-vehicle mines or anti-tank mines (Article 2).[236] The text also concerns 'dual purpose' mines used both as anti-personal mines and anti-vehicle mines, although it is not expressly mentioned.

IV Legal Principles

Prohibited activities. States Parties undertake never under any circumstances to use, develop, produce, otherwise acquire, stockpile, retain or transfer to anyone, directly or indirectly, anti-personal mines. They also refrain from assisting, encouraging or inducing, in any way, anyone to engage in any activity prohibited to a State Party (Article, par. 1). The prohibition covers both peace and war times.

Anti-personal mines destruction and clearance. Each State has to destroy existing stocks within four years of the date on which the treaty enters into force for a given State (Article 4). One of the major provisions of the Convention is the obligation of destruction of anti-personal mines in mined areas (Article 5).

Transfer. A State must not, in any way or under any circumstances, transfer anti-personal mines either directly or indirectly. This obligation covers import and export as well as transfer of ownership of mines (Article 1, par. 1). However, States may transfer anti-personal mines for the purpose of destruction or training (Article 3).

V Implementation

International cooperation. Among others, States shall exchange equipment, material and scientific and technological information concerning the implementation of the Convention. State Party in a position to do so shall also provide assistance to other States Parties (Article 6).

National measures. State Parties shall take all appropriate measures, including the imposition of penal sanctions, to prevent and suppress any activity prohibited under the Convention undertaken by persons or on territory under its jurisdiction or control (Article 9).

236. According to Article 2 par. 1, 'Anti-personal mine' means 'a mine designed to be exploded by the presence, proximity or contact of a person and that will incapacitate, injure or kill one or more persons'. According to Article 2 par. 2, 'Mine' means 'a munition designed to be placed under, on or near the ground or other surface area and to be exploded by the presence, proximity or contact of a person or a vehicle'.

Meeting of the States. The States Parties shall meet regularly in order to consider any matter with regard to the application or implementation of the Convention (Article 11).

VI Verification

Transparency. In order to promote openness and confidence, each Party must provide the UN Secretary General an annual report concerning the action it has taken to comply with its provisions. The first report must be submitted but no later than 180 days after the date on which a State becomes a Party to the treaty (Article 7).

Resolving doubts about compliance. In the event that a State Party suspects another State Party of having failed to respect the provisions of the treaty, it may submit, through the Secretary General of the UN, a request for clarification of that matter to that State Party. If there is no response within a twenty-eight days time period, or if the response is deemed unsatisfactory, the issue may be presented to the next Meeting of States Parties. If, however, the issue is considered urgent, a Special Meeting of States Parties may be convened to consider the matter. The States attending the meeting will examine the information submitted and decide by a majority vote if further action is necessary. If additional information is required, a fact-finding mission may be sent to the State. The fact-finding mission shall report, through the Secretary General of the UN, to the (Special) Meeting of the States Parties the results of its findings (Article 8, par. 1-17).

VII Measures in the Event of Non-compliance

The (Special) Meeting of the States Parties may request a State Party to take measures to address the compliance issue within a specified period of time. The State Party shall report on all measures taken in response to this request. The Meeting of the States Parties may suggest to the States Parties concerned ways and means to further clarify or resolve the matter under consideration (Article 8, par. 18-19).

VIII Settlement of Disputes

The States Parties shall consult and cooperate with each other to settle any dispute that may arise with regard to the application or the interpretation of this Convention. Each State Party may bring any such dispute before the Meeting of the States Parties. The Meeting of the States Parties may contribute to the settlement of the dispute (Article 10).

IX Remark

None.

Sub-Par. 3 Convention on Cluster Munitions

I Status

- Official name: Convention on Cluster Munitions.
- Reference: 2688, *UNTS*, 39.
- Nature: Multilateral treaty which is opened to all States.
- Adoption: 30 May 2008.
- Entered into force: 1 August 2010.
- Parties: Eighty-eight.

II Object and Purpose

Cluster munitions were first used in the 1940s. They are generally delivered by air or fired from artillery, and disperse large numbers of explosive submunitions or bomblets over wide areas, potentially causing high civilian casualties especially when they are used in populated areas. Moreover, many of them often fail to explode as intended, causing a long-term threat to security. For these reason, Norway launched the 'Oslo Process' in February 2007 aimed at creating an international treaty to prohibit cluster munitions.

III Scope

The Convention is applicable to a 'conventional munition that is designed to disperse or release explosive submunitions each weighing less than 20 kg, and includes those explosive submunitions' (Article 2, par. 2). An explosive submunition means 'a conventional munition that in order to perform its task is dispersed or released by a cluster munition and is designed to function by detonating an explosive charge prior to, on or after impact' (Article 3 par. 3). The text is not applicable to mines (Article 1, par. 3).

IV Legal Principles

Prohibited activities. States accept to never use, develop, produce, acquire, stockpile, retain or transfer to anyone, directly or indirectly, cluster munitions. The also prohibit any assistance in any activity prohibited under the text (Article 1, par. 1).

Cluster munitions destruction and clearance. Each State accepts to destroy or ensure the destruction of all cluster munitions as soon as possible but not later than eight years after the entry into force of the Convention for that State Party (Article 3 par. 2). Furthermore, each State undertakes to clear and destroy, or ensure the clearance and destruction of, cluster munition remnants located in cluster munition contaminated areas under its jurisdiction or control (Article 4).

Transfer. The transfer of cluster munitions to another State Party for the purpose of destruction or for the purpose of development of and training in cluster munition and explosive submunition detection, clearance or destruction techniques, or for the development of counter-measures, is permitted (Article 3, par. 6 and 7).

V Implementation

International cooperation. In fulfilling its obligations under the Convention each State Party has the right to seek and receive international assistance (Article 6, par. 1).

National measures. States accept to take all appropriate legal, administrative and other measures to implement the Convention, including the imposition of penal sanctions (Article 12).

Meeting of States Parties. The States Parties shall meet regularly in order to consider any matter with regard to the application or implementation of the Convention (Article 11).

VI Verification

Transparency. Each State shall report to the Secretary General of the UN as soon as practicable, and in any event not later than 180 days after the entry into force of the Convention for that State Party, on the implementation of the convention. To this end, it shall send any technical and military relevant information (Article 7).

Resolving doubts about compliance. If one or more States Parties wish to clarify and seek to resolve questions relating to a matter of compliance with the provisions of the Convention by another State Party, it may submit, through the Secretary General of the UN, a Request for Clarification of that matter to that State Party. In the absence of response or if the response in unsatisfactory, the State may submit the matter to the next Meeting of States Parties (Article 8).

VII Measures in the Event of Non-compliance

None.

VIII Settlement of Disputes

States concerned by a dispute shall consult together with a view to the expeditious settlement of the dispute by negotiation or by other peaceful means of their choice, including recourse to the Meeting of States Parties (Article 10).

IX Remarks

None.

SECTION 3 REGIMES RELATING TO ZONES

Certain zones benefit from a specific regime characterized by the principles of complete or partial non-weaponization and/or peaceful use. In these zones, international rules have an effect on the presence of nuclear goods and technologies as well as on the conduct of military activities. We can distinguish between international zones (i.e., those which are not subject to national sovereignty (par. 1)) and regional areas were the States involved have concluded treaties to ban nuclear weapons (par. 2).

Sub-Section 1 International Zones

International zones are areas over which no State can claim a sovereign right. These are areas which are not located on national territory. National territories include dry land, the sea (up to a distance of 12 nmi from a country's coastline) and airspace above a State's land-based territory or sea. International zones are subject to special regimes in relation to international public law, and are characterized by principles of peaceful use and non-weaponization. These rules, which vary slightly, apply to both international zones (Par. 1) on earth and (Par. 2) to outer space.

Par. 1 Earth

Three treaties set out the rules of peaceful use and/or the denuclearization of international zones or *internationalised zones on earth:* the Antarctic Treaty (Sub-Par. 1), the Seabed Arms Control Treaty (Sub-Par. 2), and the Convention on the Law of the Sea (Sub-Par. 3).

Sub-Par. 1 Antarctic Treaty

I Status

- Official name: Antarctic Treaty.
- Reference: 402, *UNTS*, 71.
- Nature: Multilateral treaty which is opened to all States.[237]
- Opened for signature: 1 December 1959.
- Entered into force: 23 June 1961.
- Parties: Fifty.

237. The Treaty has been signed and ratified by a limited number of States which have a special interest in Antarctica and is opened to all States for accession.

II Object and Purposes

By late 1940s, permanent bases were established in Antarctica. The first substantial multilateral research programme was planned during the International Geophysical Year (IGY) in 1957-1958. In addition, since the Second World War, the increase of governments' interest in Antarctica has led to territorial claims. In 1959, the twelve States involved in the scientific exploration of Antarctica during the IGY decided to sign a Treaty in order to ensure that Antarctica will be used exclusively for peaceful purposes and shall not become the scene or object of international dispute.

III Scope

The provisions of the Treaty are applicable to the area south of 60° South Latitude, including all ice shelves (Article IV).

IV Legal Principles

Exclusive peaceful use of Antarctica. Any measure of a military nature is prohibited such as the establishment of military bases and fortifications, the carrying out of military manoeuvres, as well as the testing of any type of weapon (Article I). However, military personnel or equipment is authorized for scientific research or for any other peaceful purposes.

Non-nuclearization. Nuclear explosions are prohibited in Antarctica as well as the disposal there of radioactive waste material. In addition, any international agreement concerning the use of nuclear energy, including nuclear explosions, to which all of the Contracting States participating to the Treaty Consultative Meetings[238] are applicable in Antarctica (Article V).

V Implementation

Parties meet regularly in the Antarctic Treaty Consultative Meetings for the purposes of exchanging information and taking decisions on issues such as the use of Antarctica for peaceful purposes only and the facilitation of the exercise of the rights of inspection (Article IX). In 2003, States Parties decided to create an Antarctic Treaty Secretariat. It began its operations on 1 September 2004.[239]

VI Verification

The treaty organizes a strong observance mechanism. Each Contracting Party has the right to designate observers to carry out inspections of stations, installations and other

238. See *infra*.
239. The list of inspections conducted under Article VII of the Antarctic Treaty is available on the Internet address of the Antarctic Treaty Secretariat: www.ats.org.ar/index.htm.

facilities. Each observer has complete freedom of access at any time to any or all areas of Antarctica. To this end, all areas of Antarctica, including all stations, installations and equipment within those areas, and all ships and aircraft at points of discharging or embarking cargoes or personnel in Antarctica, are opened, at all times, to inspection by any observers. In addition, aerial observation may be carried out, at any time, over any or all areas of Antarctica by any of the Contracting Parties having the right to designate observers (Article VII).

VII Settlement of Disputes

States Parties shall consult among themselves with a view to having the dispute resolved by any peaceful means of their choice. If the dispute is not solved, States may refer the dispute to the International Court of Justice for settlement.

VIII Measures in the Event of Non-compliance

None.

IX Remarks

Claims to sovereignty over the Antarctic have just been suspended and have not been entirely banned by the Antarctic Treaty. The US considers the Antarctic to be an international zone, while other countries like France, regard it as an internationalized zone (while at the same time claiming sovereignty over a part of it).

Sub-Par. 2 Seabed Arms Control Treaty

I Status

- Official name: Treaty on the Prohibition of the Emplacement of Nuclear Weapons and other Weapons of Mass Destruction on the Seabed and the Ocean Floor and in the Subsoil Thereof.
- Reference: 955, *UNTS*, 115.
- Nature: Multilateral treaty which is opened to all States.
- Opened for signature: 11 February 1971.
- Entered into force: 18 May 1972.
- Participants: Ninety-four.

II Object and Purpose

At the beginning of the 1960s, the US and the USSR tried to use the seabed for the placement of fixed military installations capable of launching nuclear weapons. While these projects were abandoned for technical reasons, the USSR presented a draft treaty on exclusive peaceful use of the seabed and complete demilitarization of the zone including strategic missile submarines. The US only accepted to discuss the issue of the placement of WMD on the seabed. The treaty represents a compromise between the drafts of the then two superpowers.

III Scope

The delimitation of the seabed was a quite complicated issue during the negotiation phase. Although the Convention on the Territorial Sea and the Contiguous Zone, signed at Geneva on 29 April 1958[240] was fixing the limit at a distance of 12 nmi from the coastline, some countries were claiming an extension of their territorial sea up to 200 nmi. The drafters decided that the text is applicable beyond the outer limit of a seabed zone coterminous with the twelve-mile limit of the territorial sea referred to in the law of the sea conventions (Article II). In return, States Party agree not to use the Seabed Arms Control Treaty in order to support or prejudice the position of any State Party with respect to existing international conventions including conventions on the law of the sea (Article IV).

IV Legal Principles

States undertake not to place on the seabed, on the ocean floor or in the subsoil thereof, nuclear weapons or other WMD, as well as installations for launching, storing, testing or using such weapons (Article I).

V Implementation

None.

VI Verification

Observers from any party may verify the activities of any other party on the seabed to ensure compliance with the provisions of the Treaty. In case of doubt, parties shall consult and cooperate to remove such doubt by means of inspection and any other agreed procedures (Article III).

VII Measures in the Event of Non-compliance

If a serious question concerning fulfilment of the obligations under the Treaty still remains, a party may refer the matter to the UN Security Council, which may take action in accordance with the Charter (Article III).

240. 516, *UNTS*, 205.

VIII Settlement of Disputes

None.

IX Remark

The Treaty States that a review conference is held every five years. The 1977 Seabed Arms Control Treaty Review Conference concluded that the first five years in the life of the Treaty had demonstrated its effectiveness (Article VIII). Additional review conferences have been held and confirmed the Convention is complied with by the States.

Sub-Par. 3 Convention on the Law of the Sea

I Status

- Official name: Convention on the Law of the Sea.
- Reference: Doc. A/CONF.62/122 and Corr.1-11.
- Nature: Multilateral treaty which is opened to all States.
- Opened for signature: 10 December 1982.
- Entered into force: 16 November 1994.
- Participants: 166.

II Object and Purpose

The Convention represents both a codification and a progressive development of the law of the sea. It institutes a legal order for the seas and oceans, which aims at (1) facilitating international communication; (2) promoting the peaceful use of the seas and oceans; (3) promoting the equitable and efficient use of their resources as well as the conservation of their living resources; and (4) enhancing the protection and preservation of the marine environment.

III Scope

The Convention applies to all maritime zones except to landlocked seas. Among other things, the Convention recognizes two international zones: the high seas and the deep seabed, called 'The Area'. The high seas represent all those parts of the sea that are not included in the exclusive economic zone, in the territorial sea or in the internal waters of a State (Article 86). Usually, the high seas begin at a distance of 200 nmi from the coastline. The Area begins at the outer boundary of the Continental Shelf that is to say at a maximum distance of 350 nmi from the coastline.

IV Legal Principles

Peaceful use of the high seas. The high seas are subject to the freedom of the seas doctrine – a principle put forth in the seventeenth century by Grotius, in order to limit national rights and jurisdiction over the oceans (Articles 87 and 89). The high seas shall be reserved for peaceful purposes (Article 88), but military activities may be carried out for defensive purposes, and warships on the high seas have complete immunity from the jurisdiction of any State other than the flag State.

Exclusive peaceful use of 'The Area'. The Area and its resources are the common heritage of mankind (Article 136). As a direct consequence, the use of the deep seabed is reserved exclusively for peaceful purposes (Article 144).

Exclusive peaceful purposes of scientific research. Marine scientific research shall be conducted exclusively for peaceful purposes (Article 240). The same principle is applicable to scientific research in the Area (Article 143).

Definition of 'peaceful use'. A State Party makes peaceful use of the seas if it refrains from creating any threat or using force against the territorial integrity or political independence of any State, or acting in any other manner inconsistent with the principles of international law embodied in the Charter of the UN (Article 301).

V Verification

The Convention establishes The Authority, an international organization through which States Parties shall organize and control activities in the Area. This body is mainly responsible for the administration of the resources of the Area and has no clear mandate to control the peaceful use of the Area (Section 4 of Part XI).

VI Measures in the Event of Non-compliance

None.

VII Settlement of Disputes

The Convention sets out a detailed procedure in case of dispute concerning the interpretation or application of the Convention, including compulsory procedures entailing compulsory decisions (Part XV). The Convention also establishes the International Tribunal for the Law of the Sea.

VIII Remarks

The Convention on the law of the sea is the only treaty which contains a definition of the term 'peaceful use'.

Par. 2 Outer Space

Since man first conquered space, the superpowers have developed rules, which were at first customary and later codified in a treaty, to control the international community's use of outer space. For some, it was considered absolutely essential that mistakes on earth should not be repeated in space, and that the area should be used for exclusive peaceful ends. However, political realism led States to opt for less idealistic rules. The Outer Space Treaty represented a central element of the international laws dealing with space (Sub-Par. 1) and the Moon Agreement was adopted to give a legal framework to the exploration and exploitation of the celestial bodies of our solar system (Sub-Par. 2). These two initiatives introduce a partial regime of non-arsenalization.

Sub-Par. 1 Outer Space Treaty

I Status

- Official name: Treaty on Principles Governing the Activities of States in the Exploration and Use of Outer Space, including the Moon and Other Celestial Bodies.
- Reference: 610, *UNTS*, 205.
- Nature: Multilateral treaty, open to all States.
- Opened for signature: 27 January 1967.
- Entered into force: 10 October 1967.
- Parties: 102.

II Object and Purposes

With the advent of the race to the Moon in the 1960s, the US and the USSR decided to adopt a set of rules to regulate peaceful activities carried out in outer space and in particular to avoid sovereign claims over outer space or part of it. The Outer Space Treaty represents the space law's cornerstone.

III Scope

There is no legal written definition or delimitation of outer space in order not to restrict the freedom of the space faring nations. States consider, on a customary basis, that outer space begins at a distance ranging from 100 to 110 km above the level of the sea. Space law is applicable to activities intended to use space. It covers activities carried out by governmental, intergovernmental and private entities and is applicable to both scientific and commercial purposes. The Outer Space Treaty has been drafted by the UN Committee on Peaceful Uses of Outer Space (COPUOS), a subsidiary organ of the General Assembly whose mandate does not include military issues. Therefore, the text only deals with peaceful issues.

IV Legal Principles

Partial non-weaponization of Earth orbits. Earth orbits have a high strategic value since they represent the best location to see the world and to communicate with the Earth. Therefore, Space faring nations did not accept their complete non-weaponization. The Outer Space Treaty only prohibits the placement in orbit around the Earth of any kind of WMD (Article IV, §1). States can place in orbit around the Earth, weapons other than WMD, such as anti-satellites, which are satellites used to destroy or damage enemy space objects. They are also free to use space for the transit of WMD, including ballistic missiles.

Exclusive Peaceful use of celestial bodies including the Moon. Due to their lack of strategic value, celestial bodies benefit from a very restrictive regime. The establishment of military bases, installations and fortifications as well as the testing of any type of weapons and the conduct of military manoeuvres is forbidden. States have only the right to use military personnel, equipment or resources for peaceful purposes including scientific research (Article IV, §2).

Peaceful use of outer space. The concept of peaceful use is placed in the preamble of the Outer Space Treaty. Although the preamble of a treaty has no legal value, it represents a means of interpretation of its provisions. Thus, States can carry out only peaceful activities in space. According to the interpretation made by the US and the USSR, 'peaceful' means non-aggressive. Such interpretation has been subsequently accepted by the other nations. Therefore, States can carry out military programmes using space including telecommunications, remote sensing and positioning satellites.

Freedom to outer space. All States have the right to use outer space for peaceful purposes (Article I). Freedom to outer space also concerns private entities (Article VI) and international organizations (Article XIII).

Application of international law. Space activities have to comply with international law, including the Charter of the UN (Article III). Therefore, all disarmament and non-proliferation treaties are applicable to activities carried out in outer space.

V Implementation

In order to ensure that private entities will respect the treaty provisions, States have to authorize and supervise activities in outer space carried out by such entities (Article VI).

VI Verification

The treaty is organizing a weak on-site inspection mechanism according to which all installations, equipment and space vehicles on the Moon and other celestial bodies shall be opened to representatives of other States' Parties on a basis of reciprocity. Such representatives shall give reasonable advance notice of a projected visit, in order that appropriate consultations may be held and that maximum precautions may be taken to assure safety and to avoid interference with normal operations in the facility to be visited (Article XII). This article does not allow pre-launch inspections. The States Parties also shall consider on a basis of equality any requests by other States Parties to the Treaty to be afforded an opportunity to observe the flight of space objects launched by those States (Article X).

VII Measures in the Event of Non-compliance

In the event of violation of the treaty due to national activities in outer space, States bear international responsibility whether such activities are carried on by governmental or non-governmental entities (Article VI). When activities are carried on in outer space by an international organization, responsibility for compliance with the Treaty shall be borne both by the international organization and by the States' Parties to the Treaty participating in such organization (Article VI).

VIII Settlement of Disputes

None.

IX Remarks

- The 1975 Registration Convention[241] does not reinforce the prevention of an arms race in outer space. According to this treaty, States' only obligation is to send to the UN Secretary General information concerning objects launched in outer space in order to identify space objects responsible for damages caused as well as their launching State (Article III). Information provided is, therefore, not sufficient to verify the non-weaponization of outer space.
- The Conference on Disarmament, as the single multilateral disarmament negotiating forum, has the primary role in the negotiation of a multilateral agreement on the prevention of an arms race in outer space. Since 2008, the discussions are based on the Draft 'Treaty on Prevention of the Placement of Weapons in Outer Space and of the Threat or Use of Force against Outer Space Objects' (PPWT), introduced by the Russian Federation and China.[242] The US government, clearly against this initiative which might interfere with freedom of States in outer space, rejects any proposal on this point and has paralysed any further discussion. A new version of the draft treaty has been presented on 12 June 2014.[243]
- The Draft Code of Conduct for outer space activities, approved by the EU Council on 8-9 December 2008 is currently under discussion in parallel with the PPWT. The document was first presented by the EU during informal

241. Convention on Registration of Objects Launched into Outer Space, 1023 *UNTS*, 15, opened for signature on 14 Jan. 1975, entered into force on 15 Sep. 1976.
242. CD Doc. CD/1839.
243. CD Doc. CD/1985.

meetings. In 2014, it has been presented at the UN. Among others, the document call for nations: (1) to refrain from actions that would damage satellites or interfere with their communications; (2) to limit the creation of orbital debris, citing existing, non-binding guidelines for mitigating debris; (3) to notify others of launches, manoeuvres, and re-entries; and (4) to exchange of information on national space policies.

Sub-Par. 2 Moon Agreement

I Status

- Official Name: Agreement Governing the Activities of States on the Moon and Other Celestial Bodies.
- Reference: 1363, *UNTS*, 3.
- Nature: Multilateral treaty which is opened to all States.
- Opened for signature: 18 December 1979.
- Entered into force: 11 July 1984.
- Parties: Sixteen.

II Object and Purpose

The main object of the Treaty is to establish an international regime for the Moon and the other celestial bodies based on the common heritage of mankind principle especially in order to exploit their natural resources.

III Scope

The provisions of the Moon Agreement are applicable to the celestial bodies within the solar system, other than the Earth, including orbits around or other trajectories to or around them (Article 1).

IV Legal Principles

Complete weapons of mass destruction prohibition. States shall not place in orbit around or other trajectory, to or around a celestial body, objects carrying WMD, or place or use such weapons on or in a celestial body (Article 3.3).

Exclusive peaceful use. States must not create military bases, installations and fortifications and test any type of weapons on celestial bodies. The use of any military equipment or facility necessary for peaceful exploration and use of a celestial body is allowed (Article 3.4).

Application of international law. All activities on celestial bodies are carried out in accordance with international law, in particular the Charter of the UN and other treaties dealing with demilitarization and non-proliferation (Article 2).

V Implementation

In order to ensure that private entities comply with the Moon Agreement, States have to authorize and supervise activities carried out by such entities on celestial bodies (Article 14.1).

VI Verification

All space vehicles, equipments, facilities, stations and installations on the Moon shall be opened to other States' Parties. Such States' Parties shall give reasonable advance notice of a projected visit, in order that appropriate consultations may be held and that maximum precautions may be taken to assure safety and to avoid interference with normal operations in the facility to be visited (Article 15.1).

VII Measures in the Event of Non-compliance

Consultations. A State Party which has reason to believe that another State Party is not respecting the Moon Agreement may request consultations with that State Party. A State Party receiving such a request shall enter into consultations without delay. The Secretary General of the UN is informed of the results of the consultations and shall transmit the information received to all States' Parties concerned (Article 15.2).

Direct State responsibility. In case of violation of the Agreement, States Parties shall bear international responsibility for national activities on celestial bodies even if such activities are carried on by private entities.

VIII Settlement of Disputes

States' Parties in dispute have to find a mutually acceptable settlement by consultations or other peaceful means. States may seek the assistance of the Secretary General of the UN (Article 15.3).

IX Remarks

- Spacefaring nations have not ratified the text since they are opposed to the common heritage principle established by Article 11, which includes, among all an equitable sharing by all States Parties in the benefits derived from celestial bodies' resources exploitation.
- The review of the Moon Agreement should have taken place ten years after its entry into force (Article 18) that is to say in 1994. However, spacefaring nations have opposed to any discussion on such issue.

Sub-Section 2 Nuclear-Weapons-Free Zones

A 'nuclear-weapon-free zone' (NWFZ) is established by virtue of a treaty whereby:

> (a) The statute of total absence of nuclear weapons to which the zone shall be subject, including the procedure for the delimitation of the zone, is defined; and (b) an international system of verification and control is established to guarantee compliance with the obligations deriving from that statute.[244]

The exemption zones for nuclear arms are established by the States of a given region by way of a convention. All NWS shall undertake or reaffirm, in an additional protocol, their acceptance of the status of total absence of nuclear weapons the zone. There are five exemption zones for nuclear weapons in the world and these are the following: Latin America and the Caribbean (Par. 1), the South Pacific (Par. 2), Southeast Asia (Par. 3), Africa (Par. 4), and Central Asia (Par. 5).

Par. 1 Latin America and the Caribbean

Sub-Par. 1 Status

- Official name: Treaty for the Prohibition of Nuclear Weapons in Latin America and the Caribbean (Treaty of Tlatelolco).
- Reference: 634, *UNTS*, 326.
- Nature: Regional treaty opened to all Latin American States and other States situated in their entirety south of latitude 35° north in the western hemisphere; and all States when they have been admitted by the General Conference of the Convention. Non-regional parties may ratify additional protocols.
- Opened for signature: 14 February 1967.
- Entered into Force: 22 April 1968.
- Parties: Thirty-three (treaty) + four (Additional Protocol I) + five (Additional Protocol II).

Sub-Par. 2 Object and Purposes

The document has been negotiated few years after the Cuban crisis in order to create a nuclear weapons free zone in Latin America. In 1990, the treaty has been amended in order to be applicable to the Caribbean islands.

Sub-Par. 3 Scope

The zone of application of the Treat Nuclear: Energy territory of all States' Parties located in Central and Latin America (Article 4). The term 'territory' includes the

244. UNGA, Resolution 3472 (XXX) A adopted on 11 Dec. 1975, Comprehensive study of the question of nuclear-weapon-free zones in all its aspects.

territorial sea, air space and any other space over which a State exercises sovereignty in accordance with its own legislation (Article 3). The treaty deals with nuclear weapons defined as 'any device which is capable of releasing nuclear energy in an uncontrolled manner and which has a group of characteristics that are appropriate for use for warlike purposes'. The definition excluded any instrument that may be used for the transport or propulsion of the device if it is separable from the device and not an indivisible part thereof (Article 5).

Sub-Par. 4 Legal Principles

Prohibition of nuclear weapons. States Parties have to prohibit and prevent in their respective territories the testing, use, manufacture, production, acquisition, receipt, storage, installation, deployment and any form of possession of any nuclear weapons in any way by the Parties themselves, by anyone on their behalf (Article 2.1). States Parties also refrain from engaging in, encouraging or authorizing in any way participating in the testing, use, manufacture, production, possession or control of any nuclear weapon (Article 2.2). States may accept transit of nuclear weapons via their territories.

Exclusive peaceful use of nuclear material and facilities. States Parties undertake to use exclusively for peaceful purposes the nuclear material and facilities which are under their jurisdiction (Article 1.1). Moreover, they have right to use nuclear energy for peaceful purposes, in particular for their economic development and social progress (Article 17). States may also carry out explosions of nuclear devices for peaceful purposes. In such a case, they shall notify the OPANAL[245] and the IAEA of the date of the explosion and shall provide information (Article 18).

Sub-Par. 5 Implementation

OPANAL. In order to ensure compliance with the obligations of the Treaty, the States Parties have established an international organization known as the 'Agency for the Prohibition of Nuclear Weapons in Latin America and the Caribbean', referred to as 'OPANAL'. OPANAL organs are the General Conference, the Council and the Secretariat (Article 7). The seat of OPANAL is Mexico City, Mexico.

IAEA Safeguards. Each State Party shall negotiate multilateral or bilateral agreements with the IAEA for the application of IAEA safeguards to its nuclear activities (Article 13). OPANAL may conclude agreements with the IAEA to facilitate the efficient operation of the Control System established by the Treaty (Article 19).

245. OPANAL: Organismo para la Proscripción de las Armas Nucleares en la América Latina y el Caribe.

Sub-Par. 6 Verification

Control system. States Parties have to establish a Control System in order to be used, among other things, for the purpose of verifying the application of the Treaty (Article 12).

Reports and information. Contracting Parties have to submit to OPANAL and to the IAEA reports stating that no activity prohibited under the Treaty has occurred in their respective territories (Article 14). At the request of any of the Contracting Parties, a Contracting Party has to provide complementary or supplementary information (Article 15).

Inspections. The IAEA has the power of carrying out special inspections (Article 16).

Sub-Par. 7 Measures in the Event of Non-compliance

When a violation of the Treaty might endanger peace and security, the General Conference shall report thereon simultaneously to the UN Security Council and the General Assembly through the Secretary General of the UN, and to the Council of the Organization of American States. The General Conference shall likewise report to the IAEA (Article 21).

Sub-Par. 8 Settlement of Disputes

Any question or dispute concerning the interpretation or application of the Treaty which is not settled shall be referred to the International Court of Justice with the prior consent of the Parties to the dispute. Parties concerned may however agree on another mode of peaceful settlement (Article 25).

Sub-Par. 9 Remark

The Treaty of Tlatelolco is the first International Treaty which defines what a nuclear weapon is (Article 5).

Par. 2 Treaty of Rarotonga

Sub-Par. 1 Status

- Official name: South Pacific Nuclear Free Zone Treaty.
- Reference: 24, *ILM*, 1442.
- Nature: Regional treaty opened to any Member of the South Pacific Forum. Nuclear Weapon States and other States possessing territories under their responsibility in the Treaty application zone may ratify additional protocols.

- Opened to signature: 6 August 1985.
- Entered into force: 11 December 1986.
- Parties: Thirteen (Treaty); two (additional Protocol I); four (Protocol II); four (Protocol III).

Sub-Par. 2 Object and Purposes

South Pacific States, concerned with nuclear testing in their region and worried about the dumping of nuclear wastes at sea, decided to create a nuclear weapons free zone.

Sub-Par. 3 Scope

The Treaty concerns the South Pacific zone as described in Annex I (Article 1a). States have to apply the provisions of the Treaty to their 'territory', which includes internal waters, territorial sea and archipelagic waters, the seabed and subsoil beneath, the land territory as well as the airspace above them (Article 1b). The Treaty deals with nuclear explosive devices as defined by the text (Article 1c).

Sub-Par. 4 Legal Principles

Prohibition of nuclear explosive devices. First, States Parties undertake not to manufacture or acquire, possess or have control over any nuclear explosive device anywhere inside or outside the zone. States Parties shall not seek or receive any assistance in the manufacture or acquisition of any nuclear explosive device. They shall not take any action to assist or encourage the manufacture or acquisition of any nuclear explosive device by any State (Article 3). Second, each Party undertakes to prevent in its territory the stationing of any nuclear explosive device (Article 5). Third, each Party takes measures to prevent testing nuclear devices in its territory (Article 6). Nuclear-Weapon States undertake not to carry out nuclear tests within the zone (Protocol 3, Article 1), which is a new obligation in regard to the Treaty of Tlatelolco.

Peaceful nuclear activities. Parties undertake not to provide source or special fissionable material, or material or equipment designed or prepared for the processing, use or production of special fissionable material for peaceful purposes to any non-nuclear-weapon State unless subject to the safeguards required by the NPT, or the IAEA safeguards agreements (Article 4).

Prevention of dumping. Parties undertake not to dump radioactive wastes and other radioactive matter at sea anywhere within the South Pacific Nuclear Free Zone and to prevent the dumping of radioactive wastes and other radioactive matter by anyone in its territorial sea (Article 7).

Sub-Par. 5 Implementation

South Pacific Forum. The Director of the South Pacific Bureau for Economic Co-operation (now the South Pacific Forum) is responsible for the secretariat and the verification of the Treaty (Articles 9, 10, 11, 12, Annex 4).

Consultative Committee. The Treaty established a Consultative Committee (Annex 3) which is convened by the Director of the South Pacific Forum from time to time especially in matters of consultations and review (Articles 10) as well as complaints procedure (Annex 4(2)).

Reports and exchange of information. Each Party has to report to the Director of the South Pacific Forum any significant event within its jurisdiction affecting the implementation of the Treaty (Article 9).

Sub-Par. 6 Verification

IAEA Safeguards. States Parties agree to apply safeguards of IAEA to peaceful nuclear activities (Article 8(c) and Annex 2).

Inspections. Inspections may be organized in case of complaints (Annex 4).

Sub-Par. 7 Measures in the Event of Non-compliance

A Party which considers that another Party is in breach of its obligations may bring such a complaint to the Director of the South Pacific Forum. The Consultative Committee may decide a special inspection (Annex 4).

Sub-Par. 8 Settlement of Disputes

None.

Sub-Par. 9 Remarks

None.

Par. 3 South East Asia

Sub-Par. 1 Status

- Official name: South East Asia Nuclear-Weapon-Free Zone Treaty (Treaty of Bangkok).
- Reference: 35, *ILM*, 635.
- Nature: Regional limited to Association of Southeast Asian Nations (ASEAN) States treaty. Nuclear Weapon States may ratify additional protocol. There is

no protocol dealing with States possessing territories under their jurisdiction in the treaty application zone since such States do not exist.

- Opened for signature: 15 December 1995.
- Entered into force: 27 March 1997.
- Participants: Ten.

Sub-Par. 2 Object and Purposes

In November 1971, ASEAN States adopted the Zone of Peace, Freedom and Neutrality Declaration the major goal of which was the establishment of a nuclear-weapon-free zone in Southeast Asia. The project, postponed until the end of the Cold War, has been finalized thanks to the Bangkok Treaty.

Sub-Par. 3 Scope

The Treaty is applicable to the territories of all States in Southeast Asia (Article 1(a)).[246] The territory includes the land territory, internal waters, territorial sea, archipelagic waters, the seabed and the subsoil thereof and the airspace above them (Article 1(b)). Moreover, the treaty is applicable to the respective continental shelves and exclusive economic zones of these States (Article 1(a)) which is innovatory in regard to other NWFZ treaties. The text deals with nuclear weapons as defined by the treaty (Article 1(c)).

Sub-Par. 4 Legal Principles

Prohibition of nuclear weapons. Each State Party renounces to nuclear weapons development, use, acquisition, possession, transport, station and test anywhere inside or outside the Zone (Article 3.1). Each State Party also undertakes not to allow, in its territory, any other State to carry on such activities (Article 3.2).

Prohibition of dumping. States accept not to dump at sea or to discharge into atmosphere radioactive material or wastes anywhere within the zone (Article 3).

Use of nuclear energy for peaceful purposes. States have the right to use nuclear energy in particular for their economic development in accordance with international law and guidelines of the IAEA (Article 4).

Sub-Par. 5 Implementation

Commission. The Treaty is establishing the Commission for the Southeast Asia Nuclear Weapon-Free Zone (referred to as the 'Commission') to control its implementation and ensure compliance with its provisions. All States' Parties are members of the Commission (Article 8).

246. Such States are the following: Brunei Darussalam, Cambodia, Indonesia, Laos, Malaysia, Myanmar, Philippines, Singapore, Thailand and Vietnam.

Executive Committee. The Executive Committee is a subsidiary organ of the Commission responsible for verification measures. It is composed of all States Parties (Article 9).

IAEA Safeguards. All States Parties have to conclude an agreement with the IAEA for the application of full scope safeguards to their peaceful activities (Article 5).

Sub-Par. 6 Verification

Reports and exchange of information. States Parties submit reports to the Executive Committee on any significant event within their territory and areas under their jurisdiction and control affecting the implementation of the Treaty (Article 11).

Clarification. A State Party has the right to request another State Party for clarification concerning any situation which may be considered ambiguous or which may give rise to doubts about the compliance of that State Party with the Treaty. Each State Party also has the right to request the Executive committee to seek clarification from another State Party (Article 12) or to send a fact-finding mission to another State Party (Article 13 and Annex).

Sub-Par. 7 Measures in the Event of Non-compliance

In case the Executive Committee decides that there is a breach of the Treaty by a State Party, it can adopt remedial measures if the State Party does not comply with the Treaty (Article 14).

Sub-Par. 8 Settlement of Disputes

If, within one month, the parties to a dispute arising from the interpretation of the provisions of the Treaty are unable to achieve a peaceful settlement of the dispute, they may refer the dispute to arbitration or to the International Court of Justice.

Sub-Par. 9 Remarks

None.

Par. 4 Africa

Sub-Par. 1 Status

- Official name: African Nuclear Weapon-Free Zone Treaty (Treaty of Pelindaba).
- Reference: 35, *ILM*, 698.
- Nature: Regional treaty opened to African States. The five nuclear powers may ratify the first Protocol whereas States having territories under their

jurisdiction in the Treaty application area may ratify the third Protocol. The second Protocol prohibits nuclear tests in the application zone.

- Opened to signature: 11 April 1996.
- Entered into force: 15 July 2009.
- Ratifications: Thirty-seven (treaty), four (Protocol I), four (Protocol II), one (Protocol III).

Sub-Par. 2 Object and Purpose

In 1961, after the first French nuclear test in Sahara, the UN General Assembly adopted a resolution to recognize Africa as a non-nuclear zone. In 1964, the Conference of African Unity adopted a Declaration on the De-nuclearization of Africa (AHG/ Res. 11 (1)) recommending the adoption of an international treaty. Once again, negotiations could only start when the Cold War ended and the Treaty of Pelindaba had been adopted to create a NWFZ in Africa.

Sub-Par. 3 Scope

The treaty is applicable to the continent of Africa, the islands which are the States members of Organization of African Unity (OAU) and all islands considered by the OAU in its resolutions to be part of Africa (Article 1(a) and Annex I). Each State has to apply the obligations to its land territory, internal waters, territorial seas and archipelagic waters and the airspace above them as well as the sea bed and subsoil beneath (Article 1(b)). The text deals with nuclear explosive device, nuclear installations and nuclear material (as defined in Article 1(c), (e) and (f)).

Sub-Par. 4 Legal Principles

Prohibition of nuclear explosive devices. Parties undertake not to conduct research on, develop, manufacture, stockpile or acquire, possess or have control over any nuclear explosive device by any means anywhere (Article 3). Each State Party also prohibits, in its territory, the stationing of any nuclear explosive device (Article 4). Moreover, States shall not test nuclear explosive device and shall prohibit in their territories the testing of any nuclear explosive device (Article 5).

Prohibition of dumping of radioactive matters. States Parties have to implement or to use as guidelines the measures contained in the Bamako Convention on the Ban of the Import into Africa and Control of Trans boundary Movement and Management of Hazardous Wastes within Africa of 30 January 1991[247] in so far as it is relevant to radioactive waste. They also must not take any action to assist or encourage the dumping of radioactive wastes and other radioactive matter anywhere within the African NWFZ (Article 7).

247. 30, *ILM*, 773.

Exclusive peaceful Nuclear Activities. Parties may use nuclear energy for peaceful purposes including science and technology and shall cooperate in particular under the African Regional Cooperation Agreement for Research, Training and Development Related to Nuclear Science and Technology (Article 8). States may provide source or special fissionable material, or equipment or material especially designed or prepared for the processing, use or production of special fissionable material for peaceful purposes to any non-nuclear-weapon State in the respect of agreements concluded with IAEA (Article 9(c)).

Sub-Par. 5 Implementation

Declarations, dismantlement and destruction. Parties undertake to declare, dismantle, destroy or convert nuclear explosive devices and the facilities for their manufacture, under the supervision of the IAEA, existing before the entry into force of the Agreement (Article 6).

Non-proliferation measures. To conduct all activities for the peaceful use of nuclear energy Parties have to strictly apply non-proliferation measures (Article 9(a)).

Sub-Par. 6 Verification

IAEA safeguards. Parties have to conclude safeguards agreement with IAEA for the purpose of verifying compliance with the obligation of exclusive peaceful nuclear activities (Article 9(b), Annex II).

Commission. The African Commission on Nuclear Energy will be established (Article 12 and Annex III) to ensure verification and respect of treaty obligations. It shall be composed of twelve Members elected by Parties for a three-year period.

Information. States Parties have to submit an annual report to the Commission on their nuclear activities and on treaty implementation (Article 13).

Sub-Par. 7 Measures in the Event of Non-compliance/Settlement of Disputes

A Party may bring a complaint to the Commission which may decide to organize an inspection. If the Commission considers that there is a breach of the Convention, States Parties have to meet in extraordinary session to discuss the matter. The States Parties may make recommendations to the Party held to be in breach of its obligations and to the organization of OAU. The OAU may, if necessary, refer the matter to the UN Security Council.

Sub-Par. 8 Remarks

None.

Par. 5 Central Asia

Sub-Par. 1 Status

- Official name: Treaty on a Nuclear-Weapon-Free Zone in Central Asia (CANWFZ).
- Reference: not published.
- Nature: Regional closed treaty. The five nuclear powers may, by ratifying the Protocol, undertake not to use or threaten to use a nuclear weapon or other nuclear explosive device against any Party to the Treaty and not to contribute to any act that constitutes a violation of the Treaty or of this Protocol by Parties to them.
- Opened to signature: 8 September 2006.
- Entered into force: 21 March 2009.
- Ratifications: Five (Treaty); five (Protocol).

Sub-Par. 2 Object and Purpose

In 1992 Mongolia declared itself a NWFZ and called for a regional NWFZ in Central Asia. The first formal CANWFZ proposal was made by the Uzbek President at the 48th session of the UN General Assembly in 1993. Official negotiations were launched by the Almaty Declaration of 28 February 1997.

Sub-Par. 3 Scope

The treaty is applicable to a zone composed of Kazakhstan, Kyrgyzstan, Tajikistan, Turkmenistan and Uzbekistan (Article 1(a)). State territories concerned include the land territory, all waters (harbours, lakes, rivers and streams) and the air space above them (Article 2(a)). The text deals with nuclear weapon, nuclear explosive device, nuclear material, radioactive waste and nuclear facilities (as defined in Article 1(b), (d), (e) and (f)).

Sub-Par. 4 Legal Principles

Prohibition of nuclear explosive devices. The treaty forbids development, manufacture, stockpiling, acquisition, or possession of nuclear weapons or any nuclear explosive device within the zone (Article 3). States parties also undertake not to test nuclear weapons or other nuclear explosives (Article 5).

Environmental security. Each party accepts to participate to the environmental rehabilitation of territories contaminated as a result of past activities related to nuclear weapons or other nuclear explosive devices (Article 6).

Right to peaceful nuclear activities. Parties may use nuclear energy for peaceful purposes (Article 7).

Sub-Par. 5 Implementation

IAEA safeguards. The use of the nuclear material and facilities for exclusively peaceful purposes has to comply with IAEA safeguards mechanisms. States have to conclude an agreement for the application of safeguards in accordance with the NPT and the appropriate additional protocol. Parties must also adopt export control rules under which they will not provide source or any special fissionable material or related equipment to a NNWS that has not concluded an IAEA comprehensive safeguards agreement and additional protocol (Article 8).

Physical Protection of Nuclear Material and Equipment. Each party undertakes to apply measures of physical protection to nuclear material in domestic use, transport and storage, to nuclear material in international transport, and to nuclear facilities within its territory (Article 9).

Sub-Par. 6 Verification

Meetings. States parties accept to hold annual meetings as well as extraordinary meetings, at the request of any party, in order to review compliance with the treaty or other matters related to its implementation (Article 10).

Sub-Par. 7 Measures in the Event of Non-compliance/Settlement of Disputes

A party may bring an issue to the annual meeting or to an extraordinary meeting (Article 10). States have to use peaceful settlement of disputes mechanisms (Article 11).

Sub-Par. 8 Remarks

- The CANWFZ directly shares borders with two NWS: China and Russia.
- The CANWFZ Treaty does not establish an institution to ensure implementation and compliance/verification as in the case of Bangkok, Pelindaba, and Tlatelolco treaties, or 'control systems' as in the case of the Bangkok, Rarotonga and Tlatelolco treaties.
- Each party is allowed to make its own decision with regard to transit of nuclear weapons through its territory by air, land or water (Article 4). Only Turkmenistan has made a unilateral declaration to ban all transit of WMD.
- The treaty does not affect the rights and obligations of the parties under previous international agreements (Article 12). Therefore the 1992 Treaty on

Collective Security (also known as the Tashkent Treaty) is still applicable. This treaty allows Russia, under certain circumstances, to reintroduce nuclear weapons into the CANWFZ.

SECTION 4 LIST OF ABBREVIATIONS

ASEAN	Association of Southeast Asian Nations
ATS	Australian Treaty Series
CANWFZ	Central Asia Nuclear-Weapon-Free Zone
COCOM	Coordinating Committee for Multilateral Export Controls
COPUOS	Committee on Peaceful Uses of Outer Space
CTBT	Comprehensive Nuclear-Test-Ban Treaty
CTBTO	Comprehensive Nuclear-Test-Ban Treaty Organization
GPS	Global Positioning Satellite
IAEA	International Atomic Energy Agency
IGY	International Geophysical Year
ILM	International Legal Materials
IMS	International Monitoring System
LTBT	Limited Test Ban Treaty
MTCR	Missile Technology Control Regime
NBC	Nuclear, Biological and Chemical Weapons
NSG	Nuclear Suppliers Group
NWS	Nuclear-Weapons States
NWFZ	Nuclear-Weapons-Free Zone
NNWS	Non-Nuclear-Weapon States
NPT	Nuclear Non-Proliferation Treaty
OPANAL	Organismo para la Proscripción de las Armas Nucleares en la América Latina y el Caribe / Agency for the Prohibition of Nuclear Weapons in Latin America and the Caribbean
OPCW	Organization for the Prohibition of Chemical Weapons
OUA	Organization of African Unity
SALW	Small Arms and Light Weapons
UN	United Nations
UNGA	United Nations General Assembly
UNTS	United Nations Treaties Series
V2	Vergeltung 2
WMD	Weapons of Mass Destruction

SECTION 5 USEFUL INFORMATION

Sub-Section 1 Enforcement Authorities Contact Details

Name of Organization	*Association of Southeast Asian Nations (ASEAN)*
Postal Address	ASEAN Secretariat 70A, Jalan Sisingamangaraja Jakarta 12110 Indonesia
Telephone	+62 21 7262991
Fax	+62 21 739823
Website	www.aseansec.org

Name of Organization	*Australia Group*
Postal Address	No secretariat
Website	www.australiagroup.net

Name of Organization	*CTBTO Preparatory Commission*
Postal Address	Vienna International Centre PO Box 1200 A-1400 Vienna Austria
Telephone	+43 1 26030 6210
Fax	+43 1 26030 5897
Website	www.ctbto.org

Name of Organization	*IAEA* *International Atomic Energy Agency*
Postal Address	P.O. Box 100, Wagramer Strasse 5 A-1400 Vienna Austria
Telephone	+43 1 2600-0
Fax	+43 1 2600-7
Website	www.iaea.org

Name of Organization	*MTCR* *Missile Technology Control Regime*
Postal Address	No permanent secretariat
Website	www.mtcr.info

Name of Organization	*Nuclear Suppliers Group (NSG)*
Postal Address	No permanent secretariat
Website	www.nuclearsuppliersgroup.org

Name of Organization	*OPANAL* *Agency for the Prohibition of Nuclear Weapons in Latin America and the Caribbean*
Postal Address	Schiller 326 - 5° floor Col. Chapultepec Morales, Mexico City, 11570 Mexico, Mexico
Telephone	(52-55) 5255-2914
Fax	(52-55) 5255-3748
Website	www.opanal.org

Name of Organization	*OPCW* *Organization for the Prohibition of Chemical Weapons*
Postal Address	Johan de Wittlaan 32 2517 JR – The Hague The Netherlands
Telephone	+31 70 416 3300
Fax	+31 70 306 3535
Website	*www.opcw.org*

Name of Organization	*Pacific Island Forum Secretariat*
Postal Address	The Secretary General Forum Secretariat Private Mail Bag Suva, Fiji
Telephone	+679 3312 600
Fax	+679 3301 102
Website	www.forumsec.org.fj

Name of Organization	*Secretariat of the Antarctic City*
Postal Address	Maipú 757 Piso 4 C1006ACI - Buenos Aires Argentina
Telephone	+ 54 11 4320 4250
Fax	+ 54 11 4320 4253
E-mail	ats@ats.aq
Website	www.ats.aq/

Name of Organization	*United Nations*
Postal Address	UN Headquarters First Avenue at 46th Street New York, NY 10017 USA
Telephone	+ 1 212 963 4475
Fax	+1 212 963 0071
E-mail	inquiries@un.org
Website	www.un.org

Name of Organization	*UNIDIR* *United Nations Institute for Disarmament Research*
Postal Address	Palais des Nations 1211 Geneva 10 Switzerland
Telephone	+41 (0)22 917 31 86
Fax	+41 (0)22 917 01 76
E-mail	unidir@unog.ch
Website	www.unidir.org

Name of Organization	*UNOOSA* *Office for Outer Space Affairs*
Postal Address	United Nations Office at Vienna Vienna International Centre, P.O. Box 500, A-1400 Vienna AUSTRIA
Telephone	+43-1-260 60 4950
Fax	+43-1-260 60 5830
E-mail	oosa@unvienna.org
Website	www.unoosa.org

Name of Organization	*Wassenaar Arrangement Secretariat*
Telephone	+43 1 960 03
Fax	+43 1 960 031 or 032
E-mail	oosa@unvienna.org
Website	www.wassenaar.org/

Name of Organization	*Zangger Committee*
Postal Address	Secretary of the Committee Mr Tim Andrews Deputy Head of Mission UK Permanent Mission to the United Nations in Vienna Jauresgasse 12 A-1030 Vienna Austria
Telephone	+43 1 716 13 4232
Fax	+43 1 716 13 4900
E-mail	oosa@unvienna.org
Website	www.zanggercommittee.org

Sub-Section 2 Other

None.

CHAPTER 4
Brazil

Pedro Paulo Salles Cristofaro, Daniela Bessone, Daniel de Avila Vio & Thiago Dias Oliva

SECTION 1 TABLE OF CONTENTS

SECTION 2 EXECUTIVE SUMMARY

Brazil has committed itself to many treaties with a view to preventing the proliferation of mass destruction weapons, as well as the indiscriminate trade of arms. Generally speaking, Brazil avoids selling military and dual-use goods, as well as directly related services, to countries involved in external or internal conflicts - especially those which do not comply with the principle of non-intervention or which might endanger the military balance of a given region.

In order to ensure compliance with international embargoes and trade restrictions on the products mentioned above, Brazil has established complex mechanisms of export/import control. These mechanisms are built upon a great deal of fragmented and overlapping legislation, which establishes different definitions of products subjected to independent control regimes.

In brief, there are two main concepts covering military and dual-use products under Brazilian legislation: 'military use goods' (*material de emprego militar*) - i.e., particularly powerful or critical conventional weapons - and 'sensitive goods' (*bens sensíveis*) - nuclear, biological, chemical and missile products that might be employed for war purposes, even if originally meant for peaceful uses.

The procedures for the import/export of military use and sensitive goods are very similar, requiring - or, at least, enabling - the participation of several governmental bodies and secretariats, within different ministries. Both of them involve the participation of the Ministry of External Relations (MRE, in Portuguese) before the commencement of negotiations between supplier and purchaser. The import/export of military use goods, however, is subject to the final approval of the Ministry of Defence, while the import/export of sensitive goods requires the Ministry of Science, Technology and Innovation's assent.

The main piece of legislation governing the control regime applicable to the import/export of conventional weapon systems, containing some special provisions for controlled products that qualify as military use goods, is Decree No. 3,665 of 20 November 2000 (*R-105*). In addition, the General Guidelines of the National Policy for Exports of Military Use Goods (*Diretrizes Gerais da Política Nacional de Exportação de Material de Emprego Militar*; known as *DG/PNEMEM*) - a confidential document - still plays a major role on the import/export of military use goods.[248]

The control regime applicable to the export of sensitive goods is governed by Law No. 9,112, of 8 October 1995, and Decree No. 1,861, of 12 April 1996, as well as by several lower-rank resolutions. It is mostly conducted by a joint ministerial commission (*Comissão Interministerial de Controle de Exportação de Bens Sensíveis - CIBES*), chaired by the Ministry of Science, Technology and Innovation.

In order to assure compliance with the provisions and requirements set forth in such legislation, Brazilian Law establishes criminal and administrative sanctions imposed on violations thereof.

248. R-105, Article 177, Sole paragraph.

SECTION 3 INTRODUCTION – ELEMENTS OF CONTEXT

Sub-Section 1 Regime Overall Philosophy

Until the 1960s, Brazil did not have a significant local industry of military products and was heavily dependent on foreign supplies. However, the establishment of different research institutes coordinated by each of the branches of the armed forces (namely Navy, Army and Air Force) and their collaboration with the emerging industry, not to mention the particular geopolitical conditions of the period (Cold War and conflicts in the Middle East), allowed the country to very quickly affirm itself as a major producer and exporter of systems of medium level technology during the 1970s. The industry reached its peak during the 1980s, developing relatively sophisticated systems, such as combat vehicles and aircrafts.

Export of military products is generally perceived as a key instrument for the competitiveness and further development of the Brazilian arms industry, which otherwise would probably not be able to endure or thrive, given the limited value and number of purchases from the local government and the ensuing absence of adequate economics of scale. Brazilian external sales of weapons systems and military gear are often oriented, thus, by prevailingly economic objectives, rather than the direct intention of exercising a specific geopolitical influence over potential purchasers or their respective regions. This pragmatic approach, however, often requires a delicate balance with traditional fundamental principles of the Brazilian foreign policy, such as multilateralism, non-intervention and pacifism.[249]

This need of political assessment of more significant transactions – also discussed from a historical perspective in the following topic – associated with a tradition of very close governmental scrutiny on all phases of production, transportation and trade of weapons – covering even purely national/internal operations – entailed a multi-layered and prevailingly ‘product-oriented’ system of control. The system is multi-layered to the extent that applicable regulation is somewhat fragmented and that a single transaction may be simultaneously subject to the review of and prior approval by different authorities. Given the differences of scope in each assessment, the approval by one authority – even if higher ranking – will normally not exclude the need of authorization from the other ones. The Brazilian system can also be regarded as ‘product-oriented’ in that it is the nature of the exported/imported goods that will most often trigger the need of approval by specific authorities.

Sub-Section 2 Historical Outlook

Brazil has had a comprehensive regulation of the production, storage, transportation and trade – expressly encompassing all forms of international trade and customs clearance proceedings – of conventional weapons, explosives and other military

249. Article 4 of the Brazilian Federal Constitution of 1988 includes as elementary principles of the foreign policy of the country *inter alia* the prevalence of human rights, international self-determination, equality among sovereign States, promotion of peace, and the peaceful settlement of disputes.

systems - defined as 'controlled products' (*produtos controlados*) - since the mid-1930s.[250,251] This regulation and surveillance system, traditionally known as *R-105*, was, and still is, strongly centred in the Brazilian Army.

In the mid-1970s, as the country affirmed its role as a significant supplier of military goods, the military government felt the need for a national policy regarding the approval of more sensitive transactions, which could affect regional balances of power or otherwise damage Brazilian reputation in the international arena. Such transactions required a more sophisticated political assessment, with a larger input from non-military authorities, particularly diplomatic officers (diplomats, ambassadors and military attachés). The guidelines of such strategy were embodied in an internal (confidential) document entitled *DG/PNEMEM* or simply *PNEMEM*, approved in 1974.

In the late 1990s, several years after the end of the military rule in 1985, the Ministry of Defence was created as a civil and central authority overseeing the activities of the three branches of the Armed Forces (Navy, Army and Air Force). The new Ministry of Defence undertook since then the role of coordinating with other high-ranking federal authorities the issuance of export permits for particularly powerful or critical conventional weapons, now formally defined as 'military use goods' (*material de emprego militar*).[252]

With respect to weapons of mass destructions (WMD) and dual-use goods, two critical factors seem to have set the pace for the structuring of Brazilian regulation and international commitments in this field: (i) the often tense relations with Argentina and (ii) the country's ambition to develop local nuclear energy and space programmes.

Following a brief period of rivalry and regional arms race in the 1960s and 1970s, which included competing secret programmes for the development of nuclear weapons and launch vehicles, the Trilateral Agreement of 1979[253] paved the way for a new era of collaboration between Brazil and Argentina.[254]

In the 1990s, after having dealt with regional disputes and adopted a constitutional ban on nuclear weapons,[255] Brazil has actively sought to accede to the most

250. Decree No. 24,602/1934 (which was granted the status of ordinary law under the Brazilian Constitution of 1934) had its provisions detailed down and regulated by Decree No. 1,246/1936. The matter was subsequently addressed *inter alia* by Decrees Nos 55,649/1965, 64,710/1969, 2,998/1999 and 3,665/2000, the latter of which is still valid and effective.
251. Brazil has a tri-level federal system comprised of the Federal Government, Member States and Cities. Unless otherwise indicated, all acts, ordinances and regulations mentioned herein refer to the Federal Government. Article 21 of the Brazilian Federal Constitution confers upon the Federal Government exclusive authority to *inter alia*: safeguard national security, authorize and supervise the production and trade of military equipment, and explore nuclear services and facilities of any nature. In addition, there is a constitutional federal state monopoly on the research, mining, enrichment, reprocessing, industrialization and trade of nuclear minerals and their derivatives. In addition, Article 22 states that only the Federal Government shall enact legislation on military material and nuclear activities of any nature.
252. Decree No. 3,770/2001 and Joint Ministerial Ordinance MCT/MD No. 631/2001.
253. Executed by Argentina, Brazil and Paraguay on 19 Oct. 1979, regarding the use of resources of the Paraná River basin, which settled existing disputes concerning the binational Itaipu dam project, developed by Brazil and Paraguay.
254. As illustrated, for instance, by the execution, on 18 Jul 1991, of the Agreement between the Republic of Brazil and the Republic of Argentina for the Pacific Use of Nuclear Energy.
255. Brazilian Federal Constitution, Article 21, XXII, item 'a'.

important treaties regarding WMDs and sensitive goods. Many of these new undertakings did not impose more stringent obligations than those previously established in regional agreements and in Brazilian internal regulation. However, accession to such agreements was still essential in order to improve the international reputation of the country and formally secure access to sensitive technology, a critical aspect for the further development of its space and nuclear energy programmes. This seems to have been, for instance, the main driver for Brazilian accession to the Treaty on Non-Proliferation of Nuclear Weapons in 1998, as mentioned below.

Sub-Section 3 Participation to International Regimes

The following tables summarize Brazil's participation status to the most relevant export control related international treaties and programmes. It is also mentioned, when relevant, that Brazil is party to a treaty either by signature and ratification or by accession.

Par. 1 Treaties and Regimes Dealing with Specific Items and Technologies

Table 4.1 Nuclear Weapons Treaties

Treaty Name	*Overall Status*	*Specific Status*	*Enforceable in Brazil*
Limited Test Ban Treaty[256]	OS: 5 August 1963 EF: 10 October 1963	S: 9 August 1963 R: 15 December 1964	Yes
Nuclear Non-Proliferation Treaty[257]	OS: 1 July 1968 EF: 5 March 1970	A: 18 September 1998	Yes
Comprehensive Nuclear Test Ban Treaty[258]	OS: 24 September 1996 EF: not in force	S: 24 September 1996 R: 24 July 1998	No

OS: Opened for signature; EF: Entry into force; S/R: Signature/Ratification; A: Accession.

Table 4.2 Biological and Chemical Weapons Treaties

Treaty Name	*Overall Status*	*Specific Status*	*Enforceable in Brazil*
Geneva Protocol[259]	OS: 17 June 1925 EF: 8 February 1928	S: 17 June 1925 R: 28 August 1970	Yes

256. Treaty Banning Nuclear Weapon Tests in the Atmosphere, in Outer Space and Under Water, *U.N.T.S.*, vol. 480, p. 43.
257. Treaty on the Non-Proliferation of Nuclear Weapons, *U.N.T.S.*, vol. 729, p. 161.
258. U.N.G.A., resolution 50\245.
259. Protocol for the Prohibition of the Use in War of Asphyxiating, Poisonous or Other Gases, and of Bacteriological Methods of Warfare, 94, *League of Nations Treaty Series*, No. 2138 (1929).

Treaty Name	Overall Status	Specific Status	Enforceable in Brazil
Biological Convention[260]	OS: 10 April 1972 EF: 26 March 1975	S: 10 April 1972 R: 27 February 1973	Yes
Chemical Convention[261]	OS: 13 January 1993 EF: 29 April 1997	S: 13 January 1993 R: 13 March 1996	Yes

OS: Opened for signature; EF: Entry into force; S/R: Signature/Ratification; A: Accession.

Table 4.3 Other Treaties

Treaty Name	Overall Status	Specific Status	Enforceable in Brazil
The Arms Trade Treaty	OS: 3 June 2013 EF: not yet in force	S: 3 June 2013 R: -	No

OS: Opened for signature; EF: Entry into force; S/R: Signature/Ratification; A: Accession.

Table 4.4 Multilateral Export Control Regimes

Regime Name	Formation	Participation
Zangger Committee[262]	1971	No
Nuclear Suppliers Group	1974	Yes
Australia Group	1985	No
Missile Technology Control Regime	1987	Yes
Wassenaar Arrangement[263]	1994	No

Table 4.5 Others

Name	Adoption	Participation
UN Register on Conventional Arms	9 December 1991	Yes
Programme of Action on Small Arms and Light Weapons	20 July 2001	Yes
International Code of conduct[264]	25 November 2002	No

260. Convention on the Prohibition of the Development, Production and Stockpiling of Bacteriological (Biological) and Toxin Weapons and On Their Destruction, *U.N.T.S.*, vol. 1015, p. 163.
261. Convention on the Prohibition of the Development, Production, Stockpiling and Use of Chemical Weapons and on Their Destruction, Doc.CD/CW/WP.400/Rev.1.
262. Non-Proliferation Treaty Exporters Committee (also called the Zangger Committee).
263. Wassenaar Arrangement on export controls for conventional arms and dual-use goods and technologies.
264. Hague Code of Conduct against Ballistic Missile Proliferation, not yet published.

Par. 2 Treaties Dealing with Specific Areas

Table 4.6 International Zones

Treaty Name	*Overall Status*	*Specific Status*	*Enforceable in Brazil*
Antarctic Treaty[265]	OS: 1 December 1959 EF: 23 June 1961	A: 16 May 1975	Yes
Outer Space Treaty (OST)[266]	OS: 27 January 1967 EF: 10 October 1967	S: 30 January 1967 R: 5 March 1969	Yes
Sea Bed Arms Control Treaty[267]	OS: 11 February 1971 EF: 18 May 1972	S: 3 September 1971 R: 10 May 1988	Yes
Moon agreement[268]	OS: 18 December 1979 EF: 11 July 1984	-	No
Convention on the Law of the Sea[269]	OS: 10 December 1982 EF: 16 November 1994	S: 10 December 1982 R: 22 December 1988	Yes

OS: Opened for signature; EF: Entry into force; S/R: Signature/Ratification; A: Accession.

Table 4.7 Regional Nuclear Weapons-Free Zones

Treaty Name	*Overall Status*	*Specific Status*	*Enforceable in Brazil*
Treaty of Tlatelolco[270]	OS: 14 February 1967 EF: 22 April 1967	S: 9 May 1967 R: 29 January 1968	Yes

OS: Opened for signature; EF: Entry into force; S/R: Signature/Ratification; A: Accession.

265. 402, *U.N.T.S.*, 7.
266. Treaty on Principles Governing the Activities of States in the Exploration and Use of Outer Space, including the Moon and Other Celestial Bodies, *U.N.T.S*, vol. 610, p. 205.
267. Treaty on the Prohibition of the Emplacement of Nuclear Weapons and other Weapons of Mass Destruction on the Seabed and The Ocean Floor and in the subsoil thereof, *U.N.T.S.*, vol. 955, p. 115.
268. Agreement governing the Activities of States on the Moon and Other Celestial Bodies, *I.L.M.*, vol. 18, p. 1434.
269. Doc. A/CONF.62/122 and Corr.1-11.
270. Treaty for the Prohibition of Nuclear Weapons in Latin America and the Caribbean, *U.N.T.S.*, vol. 634, p. 326.

Table 4.8 Regional Arms Control Treaties and Bilateral Agreements

Treaty Name	*Overall Status*	*Specific Status*	*Enforceable in Brazil*
Inter-American Convention on Firearms[271]	OS: 14 October 1997 EF: 1 July 1998	S: 14 November 1997 R: 28 September 1999	Yes
Inter-American Convention on Transparency[272]	OS: 7 June 1999 EF: 21 November 2002	S: 7 June 1999 R: 14 December 2006	Yes
Pacific Use of Nuclear energy Agreement[273]	OS: 18 July 1991 EF: 12 December 1992	S: 18 July 1991 R: 11 December 1991	Yes

OS: Opened for signature; EF: Entry into force; S/R: Signature/Ratification; A: Accession.

SECTION 4 CONTROL REGIME

Sub-Section 1 Military Goods and Services

Par. 1 Overall Presentation

As briefly mentioned above, Brazilian control regime for import/export of conventional military goods is composed of two main overlapping levels of approval and surveillance: (i) the one applicable to 'controlled products' (*produtos controlados*) and (ii) the regarding materials that also qualify as 'military use goods' (*material de emprego militar*).

The Brazilian Army is the main authority with respect to the surveillance and approval of transactions concerning controlled products.[274] The list of 'controlled products' - a concept essentially covering firearms, ammunition, pyrotechnics items, gunpowder, explosives, as well as their components and accessories - is set forth in Annex I to R-105.[275] The definition of controlled products extends as well to aggressive chemical products and other materials that, given their destructive power or other properties, have their use restricted to certified individuals.[276]

271. Inter-American Convention Against the Illicit Manufacturing of and Trafficking in Firearms, Ammunition, Explosives, and Other Related Materials, *OAS*, A/53/78.
272. Inter-American Convention on Transparency in Conventional Weapons Acquisitions, *OAS*. Accessed on: http://www.oas.org/juridico/english/sigs/a-63.html.
273. Agreement between the Republic of Brazil and the Republic of Argentina for the Pacific Use of Nuclear Energy (*Acordo entre a República Federativa do Brasil e a República Argentina para o Uso Exclusivamente Pacífico da Energia Nuclear*).
274. R-105, Article 27, VIII and XII, as well as Article 177, main section; Decree No. 5,123 of 1 Jul 2004, Article 58.
275. As mentioned before, the current wording of R-105 was set forth by Decree No. 3,665/2000.
276. R-105, Article 3, LXIX.

Controlled products are subdivided into classes 1-5.[277] Imports of all classes require the approval of the Army's Supervision Board of Controlled Products (*Diretoria de Fiscalização de Produtos Controlados – DFPC*). At the same time, the export of products from classes 1, 3, 4 and 5 products depends on the consent of the Army's Supervision Service of Controlled Products in Military Districts (*Serviço de Fiscalização de Produtos Controlados das Regiões Militares – SFPC/RM*). The export (but not the import) of class 2 controlled products is the only form of international trading with such materials and equipment that does not require prior approval from SFPC/RM.[278] Article 10 of R-105 displays a table outlining the regulation of certain activities concerning 'controlled products':

Table 4.9 Regulation of Activities by DFPC and SFPC/RM

Class of the Products	*Activities under Control*						
	Manufacturing	*Use*	*Import*	*Export*	*Customs Clearance*	*Transport*	*Trade*
1	X	X	x	x	x	x	x
2	X	X	x	-	x	x	x
3	X	-	x	x	x	x	-
4	X	-	x	x	x	-	-
5	X	-	x	X	x	-	x

(x) – Activities under control.

(-) – Activities not subject to specific DFPC or SFPC/RM control.

'Controlled products' and 'military use goods' are distinct – although possibly overlapping – definitions. Each of such concepts, therefore, entails different and specific import/export requirements and restrictions. Transactions concerning materials that qualify not only as controlled products but also as military use goods are subject not only to DFPC's or SFPC/RM's consent but also to prior approval by other higher ranking federal authorities, in accordance with the PNEMEM principles and under coordination of the Ministry of Defence.[279]

Sub-Par. 1 Requirements Prior to Any Specific Import/Export

Prior registration with the Brazilian Army is a mandatory requirement for individuals or companies willing to manufacture, use in industrial processes, store, trade, export, import, handle, transport, maintain or recover 'controlled products'.[280]

277. The class of each controlled product is established in R-105, Annex I.
278. R-105, Articles 10 and 177, main section.
279. Decree No. 3.770/2001, Article 1, R-105, Article 177, sole paragraph, and Law No. 10,683 of 28 May 2003 (Article 27, VII, 'o', No. 1). For individual export transactions with an amount falling under USD 1,000,000.00, the capacity to grant approval can be assigned by the Ministry of Defence to other high-ranking federal authorities (Decree No. 3,770/2001, Article 1, sole paragraph).
280. R-105, Article 39.

Registration is formalized by means of the issuance of a 'title of registration' (*Título de Registro - TR*) or a 'certificate of registration' (*Certificado de Registro - CR*), both with a validity term of up to three years. A TR is always granted with reference to a specific production plant and entitles the relevant owner or operator to manufacture controlled products. A CR, on the contrary, allows individuals or legal entities to industrialize, store, trade, export, import, handle, transport, maintain, repair or restore such products.[281] In case a company already owns a valid TR and intends to export or import controlled products, it does not need to file a new registration request. In short, by holding a TR, an individual or legal entity is allowed to manufacture controlled products in a given production plant, as well as entitled to carry out ancillary activities, such as industrializing, storing, trading, exporting, importing, handling, transporting, maintaining, repairing or restoring the said items. By holding a CR, however, an individual or legal entity may develop some or all of the above-mentioned *ancillary* activities, to the extent specifically set forth in the relevant permit, with the exclusion of the manufacturing of controlled products.

Each issued TR or CR indicates the classes of controlled products its holder is entitle to operate with, as well as applicable symbols, technical (and commercial) names and applicable restrictions. In addition, both TR and CR must also clearly identify the relevant holder and its authorized activities.[282]

Individuals or companies seeking a CR must file a request with the relevant office of *DFPC* of the applicable military district (*Região Militar de vinculação* - or simply *RM*).[283] Within each RM, DFPC's local regional offices are known as Supervision Service of Controlled Products in Military Districts (*SFPC/RM*).

Such request must be presented in accordance with the template of Annex XVI to R-105 and is addressed to the Commander of the applicable RM. It must describe all activities that the individual or company intends to develop upon issuance of the requested CR. Moreover, all the following additional information and documents must be provided to the SFPC/RM:[284]

(a) Written good-standing statement (Annex V to R-105). If the registration request is filed by a State-owned company, a copy of the publication of the appointment of its representative shall suffice.

281. R-105, Articles 42 and 43.
282. R-105, Article 45.
283. In other words, the military district, or RM, where the activities will be developed. Brazilian territory is divided into twelve distinct military districts: RM1(States of Rio de Janeiro and Espírito Santo), RM2 (State of São Paulo), RM3 (State of Rio Grande do Sul), RM4 (State of Minas Gerais, with the exception of the 'Triângulo Mineiro' region), RM5 (States of Paraná and Santa Catarina), RM6 (States of Bahia and Sergipe), RM7 (States of Pernambuco, Rio Grande do Norte, Paraíba and Alagoas), RM8 (States of Pará and Amapá), RM9 (States of Mato Grosso do Sul and Mato Grosso), RM10 (States of Maranhão, Ceará and Piauí), RM11 (Distrito Federal, as well as the States of Goiás, Tocantins and the Triângulo Mineiro region) and RM12 (States of Amazonas, Acre, Rondônia and Roraima). Diretoria de Fiscalização de Produtos Controlados. '*SFPC em todo o Brasil*'. Accessed on: http://www.dfpc.eb.mil.br/index.php/features. R-105, Article 83.
284. R-105, Article 84.

(b) A copy of the operation licence of the relevant plant, storage area or office (a document, provided by either a State or municipal authority, allowing the company to develop its activities).
(c) A proof of registration under the Brazilian Taxpayers' Registry (*Cadastro Nacional de Pessoas Jurídicas – CNPJ*).
(d) Incorporation documents of the legal entity.
(e) Building drawings and photographs of storage areas, if applicable.
(f) Building drawings and photographs of storage areas where explosives are kept, in case the legal entity owns a quarry or an isolated storehouse.
(g) Written statement in the form and substance of Annex VI to R-105, which establishes the obligation to comply with all legal provisions regarding controlled products, as well as to allow Army inspections at any time.
(h) Filled questionnaire, the content of which varies according to the main activities to be developed by the individual or company: (i) Annex XVII (controlled products to be employed in production chain); (ii) Annex XVIII (controlled products to be employed in demolition, mining and road construction); (iii) Annex XIX (controlled products to be traded); (iv) Annex XX (weapons repair); (v) Annex XXI (shooting clubs); or (vi) a specific ad hoc questionnaire prepared by the relevant SFPC/RM.

Sub-Par. 2 Requirements at the Import and/or Export Stages

I Goods and services

Import (R-105, Article 9, III)

After the registration phase (i.e., TR or CR issuance), individuals and companies intending to import controlled products must apply with DFPC, before the materials are embarked in the port of origin,[285] for a specific import licence for each relevant transaction. In its assessment of the request, the Army (through DFPC) may consider the convenience of the transaction in light of the Brazilian national interest and security needs.[286]

It is important to underscore that the Army, whenever deemed appropriate, is entitled to establish import quotas for specific controlled products.[287] In addition, imports of controlled products already being manufactured in Brazil will be in principle forbidden or restricted, if the Army considers the relevant industry to be strategic for the country.[288] Even in such cases, however, imports may be exceptionally authorized if deemed appropriate by the Army.

285. Ordinance D-Log (Logistics Department of the Army) No. 9/2004, Article 7.
286. R-105, Article 183, main section.
287. R-105, Article 27, VIII.
288. R-105, Article 190.

R-105 also includes a principle of reciprocity, pursuant to which imports of a given controlled product will only be authorized if the country where the manufacturer is based allows the local purchase of similar items manufactured by Brazilian companies.[289]

The Navy and the Air Force do not need to obtain import licences for the acquisition of products for their own use.[290]

Licence requests[291] shall be directed to the head of DFPC, specifying the products to be imported and their names under the List of Controlled Products (Annex I to R-105), as well as their most relevant technical features.[292] Importers must file one request within each RM in the territory of which the relevant controlled products will be delivered. In case of approval, DFPC will emit an international certificate of import (*Certificado Internacional de Importação – CII*).[293] If requested by the country of origin, DFPC will issue a certificate of final user (*Certificado de Usuário Final*, Annex XXXI to R-105).

Before granting a CII, DFPC may, however, consult the Department of Foreign Trade Operations (*Departamento de Operações de Comércio Exterior – DECEX*)[294] of the Ministry of Development, Industry and Trade (*MDIC*). As further detailed in Section 6 below, the import permit will be denied whenever the country of origin is under a United Nations (UN) embargo, as reflected in rules enacted by the Secretariat of Foreign Trade (*Secretaria de Comércio Exterior – SECEX*).[295]

With respect to military use goods, the relevant customs clearance shall also be subject to specific regulation enacted by the Brazilian Federal Revenue (*Receita Federal do Brasil – RFB*),[296] pursuant to which the importing agency is required to register the transaction with customs authorities, by means of the electronic Foreign Trade Integrated Information System (*Sistema Integrado do Comércio Exterior – SISCOMEX*). The details of the SISCOMEX registration, as well as the relevant bill of lading, must be presented to customs authorities before the delivery of the imported goods at a customs clearance unit of RFB.[297]

R-105 does not contain specific provisions on international transactions aimed at the transfer of intellectual property or specialized consulting services regarding controlled products. Brazil has indeed been criticized in the past for the lack of more comprehensive regulation of intangible transfers of weapon technology.

289. R-105, Article 195.
290. R-105, Article 183, second paragraph.
291. Annex XXXII of R-105 – *Requerimento para Obtenção do CII.*
292. R-105, Article 191.
293. Annex XXXII of R-105, mentioned in Article 183 of the same regulation. The import permit granted by the Army remains valid for six months, counted from the date of grant (R-105, Article 184).
294. R-105, Articles 37 and 38.
295. Ordinance SECEX No. 23/2011, Article 66.
296. Ordinance (*Instrução Normativa SRF*) No. 74/1997.
297. Ordinance SRF No. 74/1997, Articles 5 and 6.

Export (R-105, Article 9, IV)

(a) Controlled Products

Permits for the export of controlled products shall be required to SFPC/RM.[298] At that opportunity, the exporter shall present a detailed list of goods to be exported, as well as the quantities thereof, total price, payment method and estimated time of delivery. The request shall be submitted with an import licence provided by an accredited body of the destination country or a certificate of final user,[299] if the importer is part of the local government. Whenever the country of destination lacks restrictions on imports of controlled goods, a statement of the Brazilian diplomatic mission in the country or the diplomatic mission of the importing country in Brazil shall suffice.[300]

Article 178 of R-105 establishes that Brazilian exporters of controlled products must comply with the local regulation in force in the country of destination. This means, in practical terms, that a breach of foreign law can also amount to a violation of R-105. As a result, foreign rules may have some effects within Brazilian territory.

As further detailed in Section 6 below, the export permit will be denied whenever the country of destination is under a UN embargo, as reflected in rules enacted by SECEX.[301]

After consultations, if the export is deemed convenient by the PNEMEM System,[302] SFPC/RM authorizes the operation, registering it at SISCOMEX.[303] For this purpose, exporters must list all products to be delivered in order to enable their identification, providing their brand, quantity, standard name, calibre and technical characteristics - as well as their commonly used names.[304] Upon registration, DECEX shall issue the export register.[305]

(b) Military use goods

If the goods to be exported qualify as well as military goods, the transactions shall be subject to additional requirements, related to the PNEMEM System.

First, after becoming aware of a business opportunity, the interested party shall submit to the *MRE* a request for permission to engage in preliminary negotiations. Requests of this kind shall specify the products to be negotiated and the value thereof. Such requests are to be analysed through the prism of Brazil's foreign affairs. In the absence of any objection to the negotiations raised by other members of the PNEMEM

298. R-105, Article 177. The export of 'category 2' controlled products do not require previous licence. The five different 'control categories' of all controlled products are stated in Annex I of R-105.
299. Annex XXXI of R-105.
300. R-105, Article 178, second paragraph.
301. Ordinance SECEX No. 23/2011, Article 66.
302. PNEMEM System consists of all governmental bodies that take part in the decision making procedures related to the export of military use goods.
303. R-105, Article 177.
304. R-105, Article 180.
305. R-105, Article 38.

System, MRE grants permission for the commencement thereof. The permission remains valid for a period of two years, unless the international scenario significantly changes in the meantime.

Second, in case negotiations lead to a concrete transaction, the interested party shall apply for an export permit to the Ministry of Defence. Should the importer be a company – rather than a foreign government – applications for export permits shall be substantiated with a governmental authorization issued by the country of destination, along with a declaration to the effect that the products will not be re-exported without prior governmental approval.[306] These requirements aim at mitigating the risk of transfers of military use goods to third parties by means of transactions not submitted to and approved by Brazilian authorities. At this point of the licensing procedure, intra-governmental consultations between PNEMEM System bodies – under the coordination of the Ministry of Defence – will take place.

Par. 2 Control Lists

As mentioned above, the term 'controlled products' is defined in Articles 3, LXIX and 8 of R-105 as materials that, given their destructive power or other properties, have their use restricted to certified individuals/companies.

Annex I to R-105 contains an exhaustive list of such products (and Annex II has a list of their common, commercial names), including essentially: aggressive chemical products, weapons, ammunition, military equipment, as well as ships, aircrafts, vehicles and other items which are typically used by Armed Forces. It should be noted that the Army has the authority to expand or amend such list whenever deemed necessary or appropriate.[307]

Same import/export restrictions are applicable to civilian versions of aircrafts, ships and other equipment designed for military purposes, whose marketing rights have not yet been transferred to private entities.

In addition, Joint Ministerial Ordinance MCT/MD No. 631/2001 contains a list of military use goods subject to PNEMEM.

Even though not directly related to the exports control regime, it is also important to mention the recently enacted legislation defining the concepts of 'defence product' (*produto de defesa*) and 'strategic defence product' (*produto de defesa estratégico*),[308] which entail special rules for *inter alia* taxation, public procurement and international joint ventures. An exhaustive list of strategic defence products is currently established by Ordinance MD No. 1,1016/2014.

The Brazilian government is reportedly studying the merger of the concept of 'military use goods' and 'defence products' in a new integrated regulation that will address both the export restriction and industry incentive policies aspects of the matter.

306. According to the Ministry of External Relations. *supra* p. 214-216.
307. R-105, Article 27, II.
308. Law No. 12,598/2013 and Decree No. 7,970/2013.

Par. 3 Licensing and Enforcement Authorities (Controlled Products)

Figure 4.1 Import/Export Flowchart: Controlled Products

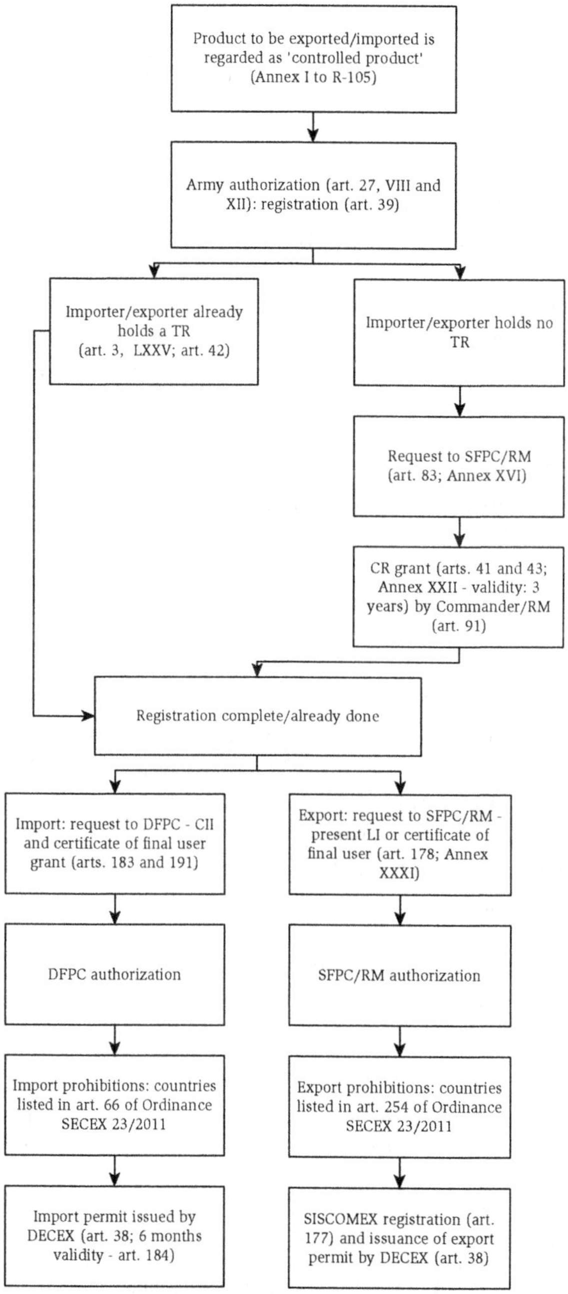

Par. 4 Sanctions and the Recourses of the Importer/Exporter

Sub-Par. 1 Administrative Sanctions

Under R-105, non-compliance with the provisions and requirements set forth therein shall give rise to one (or more) of the following sanctions:

(a) *warning*, in cases that involve minor violations to R-105 and provided that infringer has never violated R-105 before;
(b) *minimum simple fine (BRL 500.00*[309,310] *)*, in cases that involve up to two simultaneous violations to R-105;
(c) *medium simple fine (BRL 1,000.00*[311] *)*, in cases that involve up to three simultaneous violations to R-105;
(d) *maximum simple fine (BRL 2,000.00*[312] *)*, in cases that involve up to five simultaneous violations to R-105, as well as in cases that involve a major violation to R-105;
(e) *pre-interdiction fine (BRL 2,500.00*[313] *)*, in cases that involve more than five violations to R-105 within a two-year period, as well as in cases that involve a major violation to R-105 (even if said major violation is the first one committed by the infringer);
(f) *temporary suspension* of the infringer's activities pertaining to controlled products, in cases that involve (i) recidivism after infringer has been punished with the pre-interdiction fine sanction, or (ii) major violation to R-105 which may result in public calamity, or that causes infringer's operations to become detrimental to the public safety, or that puts under considerable risk the safety of the neighbouring population or buildings; and
(g) *revocation* of infringer's TR or CR, as the case may be, leading to the final cessation of the infringer's activities related to controlled products, in cases that involve (i) recidivism after infringer has been punished with the temporary suspension sanction, or (ii) major violation to R-105 that impairs infringer's integrity and good-standing.

Individuals and companies that participate or cooperate in violations to R-105 shall be also subject to the sanctions described above.

309. The amounts due to each type of fine are established in Law No. 10,834, of 29 Dec. 2003.
310. Approximately EUR 125.63. The amount in Euros is based on the Real-to-Euro exchange rate from 15 Apr. 2016 (About 3.98).
311. Approximately EUR 251.26. The amount in Euros is based on the Real-to-Euro exchange rate from 15 Apr. 2016 (About 3.98).
312. Approximately EUR 502.51. The amount in Euros is based on the Real-to-Euro exchange rate from 15 Apr. 2016 (About 3.98).
313. Approximately EUR 628.14. The amount in Euros is based on the Real-to-Euro echange rate from 15 Apr. 2016 (About 3.98).

Fines may be imposed severally or cumulatively with other sanctions (except for warning), in view of the gravity of the violation, and are independent of other penalties that may be provided by law.

Upon the revocation of the TR or CR, the relevant controlled products shall be seized (at the discretion of the Army, these products may be sold by their owners to other individuals or entities duly authorized to operate with controlled products). Also, the infringer shall be prevented from developing any activities involving controlled products and shall not be entitled to any indemnification.

A new TR or CR shall not be granted to companies having as a shareholder a former shareholder of a company that had a TR or CR previously revoked.

Sanctions can only be imposed under an administrative proceeding conducted with full observance of due process of law. An appeal is available to the same authority that imposed the sanction, except for the revocation of the TR or CR, in which case an appeal may be filed to the Commander of the Army.[314] Appeals must be filed within a ten-day term from the date on which infringer has been notified of the decision and (at least in theory) shall be decided within a thirty-day term from the delivery of the records of the case to the competent authority.

Decree No. 5,123, of 1 July 2004, contemplates the following pecuniary penalties imposed by the administrative agency in charge of inspection and control of activities pertaining to firearms and ammunition (without prejudice of the applicable criminal sanctions):

(a) BRL 100,000[315] on:
   (i) airlines, road transport companies, railway companies, shipping companies, river navigation companies, and lake navigation companies that allow the transport of firearms, ammunition and accessories, without proper authorization or in breach of safety standards; and
   (ii) companies engaged in the production or trade of arms that conduct advertising encouraging indiscriminate use of firearms, accessories and ammunition, except in specialized publications;
(b) *BRL* 200,000[316] on:
   (i) airlines, road transport companies, railway companies, shipping companies, river navigation companies, and lake navigation companies that deliberately carry out, promote or facilitate the transport of firearms, ammunition and accessories, without proper authorization or in breach of safety standards; and

314. The Commander is the highest authority within the Army and such position is reserved to the highest-raking officers of such branch of the Armed Forces. Since enactment of Complementary Law No. 97, of 9 Jun. 1999, each of the Armed Forces is headed by a Commander, who acts under coordination of the Minister of Defence (Article 3).
315. Approximately EUR 25,125.63. The amount in Euros is based on the Real-to-Euro exchange rate from 15 Apr. 2016 (About 3.98).
316. Approximately EUR 50,251.26. The amount in Euros is based on the Real-to-Euro exchange rate from 15 Apr. 2016 (About 3.98).

(ii) companies engaged in the production or trade of arms in case of recidivism in connection with advertising encouraging the indiscriminate use of firearms, accessories and ammunition; and

(c) BRL 300,000[317], in case of recidivism in connection with the conducts described above.

Sub-Par. 2 Criminal Sanctions

Under Article 253 of the Brazilian Penal Code, the 'production, supply, purchase, possession or transport, without licence from the competent authority, of explosive substance or device, toxic or asphyxiating gas, or materials used for the production thereof' qualify as a *crime* punishable with imprisonment from six months to two years plus a fine.

In addition, under Articles 17 and 18 of Law No. 10,826, of 22 December 2003, the following conducts are defined as *crimes*:

(a) 'To purchase, rent, receive, transport, carry, hide, store, disassemble, assemble, reassemble, tamper, sell, expose for sale, or otherwise use, in the interest of the perpetrator himself or others, in the exercise of a trade or industrial activity, firearms, firearm accessories or ammunition, without proper authorization or in breach of legal or regulatory determination', punishable with imprisonment from four to eight years plus a fine. For the purposes of this legal provision, the expression trade or industrial activity comprises irregular or clandestine rendering of services, manufacturing and trade of such products, even if conducted in the perpetrator's or third parties' residence.

(b) 'To import, export, favour the entry or exit from the national territory, in any way, firearms, firearm accessories or ammunition without authorization of the competent authority', punishable with imprisonment from four to eight years plus a fine.

Sub-Par. 3 Delegation of Authority

Brazilian Law does not allow for company directors to assign to another person within the company their liabilities as directors (civil and/or criminal) in respect to export control issues.

317. Approximately EUR 75,376.88. The amount in Euros is based on the Real-to-Euro exchange rate from 15 Apr. 2016 (About 3.98).

Sub-Section 2 Dual-Use Goods and Services

Par. 1 Overall Presentation

Brazil adopted on 8 October 1995, Law No. 9,112, which regulates the export of sensitive goods (*bens sensíveis*) and other directly related services. Sensitive goods, dual-use goods (*bens de uso duplo*) and directly related services are defined as those that can be used for war purposes, including the ones employed in nuclear, chemical and biological programmes somehow associated to war purposes.

The aforementioned legislation established a joint ministerial commission (*Comissão Interministerial de Controle de Exportação de Bens Sensíveis - CIBES*), whose main responsibility is to prepare a list containing all goods and services considered sensitive and, thus, subject to Law No. 9,112/1995. CIBES is composed by representatives of the following Ministries: (i) Ministry of Science, Technology and Innovation (that presides the commission); (ii) Ministry of Defence; (iii) Ministry of Development, Industry and Foreign Trade; (iv) Ministry of Finance; (v) Ministry of Justice; and (vi) Ministry of External Relations (Decree No. 4,214/2002). The sensitive goods are divided into four different groups, each of which has specific procedures of the granting of export authorization: nuclear field, biological field, missile field and chemical field. The formalities applicable to such four fields are outlined below.

Sub-Par. 1 Requirements Prior to Any Specific Import/Export

(a) Nuclear Field

Decree No. 1,861, enacted on 12 April 1996, regulates the export of nuclear sensitive goods and related services.

As a first step, exporters must submit a request to MRE in order to be able to negotiate products included in the list of the nuclear field. MRE shall then assess the request in light of Brazilian policies and foreign relation and decide whether or not the negotiation authorization should be granted. It is important to emphasize that a negotiation authorization issued by MRE does not represent an export permit: it only authorizes the beginning of discussions between the exporter and a foreign government or company.

(b) Biological Field

CIBES Resolution No. 21, of 19 July 2013, defines which products and materials qualify as sensitive goods (and related services) for the biological field.

Similar to the nuclear field, it is necessary to apply with MRE for an authorization to start negotiations with a foreign purchaser. In this case, however, MRE has the final authority to grant the authorization to start negotiations, in which case it will inform the General Department of Sensitive Goods (*Coordenação-Geral de Bens Sensíveis - CGBE*) about the possibility of a future export in this field.[318]

318. Item 2.1 of Annex II of CIBES Resolution No. 21/2013.

(c) Missile Field

CIBES Resolution No. 17, of 16 August 2012, establishes the general provisions for the export of goods and directly related services pertaining to the missile field. Such rules are almost identical to the ones set forth for products included in the biological field.

Sub-Par. 2 Requirements at the Import and/or Export Stages

I Goods and Services

(a) Nuclear Field

Once negotiations are concluded, an exporter must apply with CGBE for an export permit, presenting an end-user certificate.[319]

Furthermore, the State of destination of the export shall: (i) ensure the peaceful use of goods involved in the negotiation;[320] (ii) apply the safeguards required by *IAEA* (International Atomic Energy Agency);[321] (iii) ensure that it will not use the products for uranium enrichment beyond 20%.[322] In the process of taking its decision, CGBE consults with several entities, agencies and ministries (especially those already represented at CIBES). Upon the granting of the authorization, the export transaction shall be registered at SISCOMEX.

It should be noted that the export of nuclear materials – not necessarily qualifying as sensitive goods – can also be subject to the approval of the National Nuclear Energy Commission (*Comissão Nacional de Energia Nuclear – CNEN*).[323]

(b) Biological Field

Should CGBE notice any serious political, strategic or technological inconsistency when analysing the export permit request, CIBES must be consulted on the convenience of the granting thereof. In the event CIBES does not reach a consensus on the matter, the request shall be analysed by the President of the Republic. If CGBE understands there are no negative impacts, the export permit request may be granted.[324] It is worth noting that before granting an export permit request, CGBE may consult several governmental bodies, such as other secretariats and the Brazilian National Intelligence Agency (*ABIN*). Afterwards, once the application has been granted, the export transaction must be registered with SISCOMEX, in the same way as goods/services within the nuclear field.[325] Lastly, the export registration will be briefly analysed by MDIC, for the purposes of ratifying (or not) the export permit. The final approval of the transaction by MDIC shall be subsequently recorded with SISCOMEX.

319. Article 12, IV, (a), 4 of the Annex of the Decree No. 1,861.
320. Article 19, II of the Decree No. 1,861.
321. Article 12 of the Decree No. 1,861.
322. Article 13 of the Decree No. 1,861.
323. Law No. 4,118/1962, Article 2; Law No. 6,189/1974, Article 11.
324. Items 2.2.1.7, 2.2.1.8 and 2.2.1.9 of Annex II of CIBES Resolution No. 21/2013.
325. Item 2.2.1.10 of Annex II of CIBES Resolution No. 21/2013.

(c) Missile Field

The only difference in comparison with the biological field procedures worth noting is that CGBE may also consult the Brazilian Space Agency (*AEB*) before authorizing the export transaction.[326]

(d) Chemical Field

Ordinance No. 437, of 14 June 2012, of the Ministry of Science, Technology and Innovation (MCTI, in Portuguese) defines which products and materials qualify as sensitive goods (and related services) for the chemical field. Export operations of such products shall be analysed by the Supervision Board of Implementation, Follow Up and Control in the Chemical Field (*Coordenação de Implementação, Acompanhamento e Controle na Área Química*), pursuant to MCT Ordinance No. 753, of 3 October 2006. CGBE, after consulting several governmental bodies, grants the export permit.[327]

Par. 2 Control Lists

As explained above, sensitive and dual-use goods are those that might be employed for war purposes, even if originally developed for peaceful uses.

CIBES is the commission responsible for editing the control list of sensitive or dual-use goods. The List of Sensitive Goods is set forth in four provisions: Resolution CIBES No. 13/2010 (Biological Field);[328] Resolution CIBES No. 18/2012 (Missile Field);[329] Resolution CIBES No. 14/2011 (Nuclear Field)[330] and MCTI Ordinance No. 437/2012 (Chemical Field).[331]

The Biological Field list includes several types of bacteria, rickettsiae, fungi, viruses, phytoplasma, nematodes, toxins, genetic elements and equipment related to biology. The Missile Field list includes equipments, materials, software and technologies directly connected to the manufacture or use of missiles. Similarly, the Nuclear Field list contains equipment, systems, materials and technologies directly associated to the application in the nuclear field. Lastly, the Chemical Field list is composed by several chemical substances.

326. Item 2.7 of Annex of CIBES Resolution No. 17/2012.
327. Article 10 of MCT Ordinance No. 753 of 3 Oct. 2006; Article 5, VI of CIAD/CPAQ Resolution 1 of 14 Dec. 2006.
328. Accessed on: http://www.mct.gov.br/upd_blob/0216/216145.pdf, http://www.mct.gov.br/index.php/content/view/20047.html#ancora.
329. Accessed on: http://www.mct.gov.br/upd_blob/0226/226466.pdf.
330. Accessed on: http://www.mct.gov.br/index.php/content/view/331308/Lista_de_Controle_da_Area_Nuclear__.html.
331. Accessed on: http://www.mct.gov.br/index.php/content/view/339895.html#ancora.

Par. 3 Licensing and Enforcement Authorities

Figure 4.2 Export Flowchart: Sensitive Goods

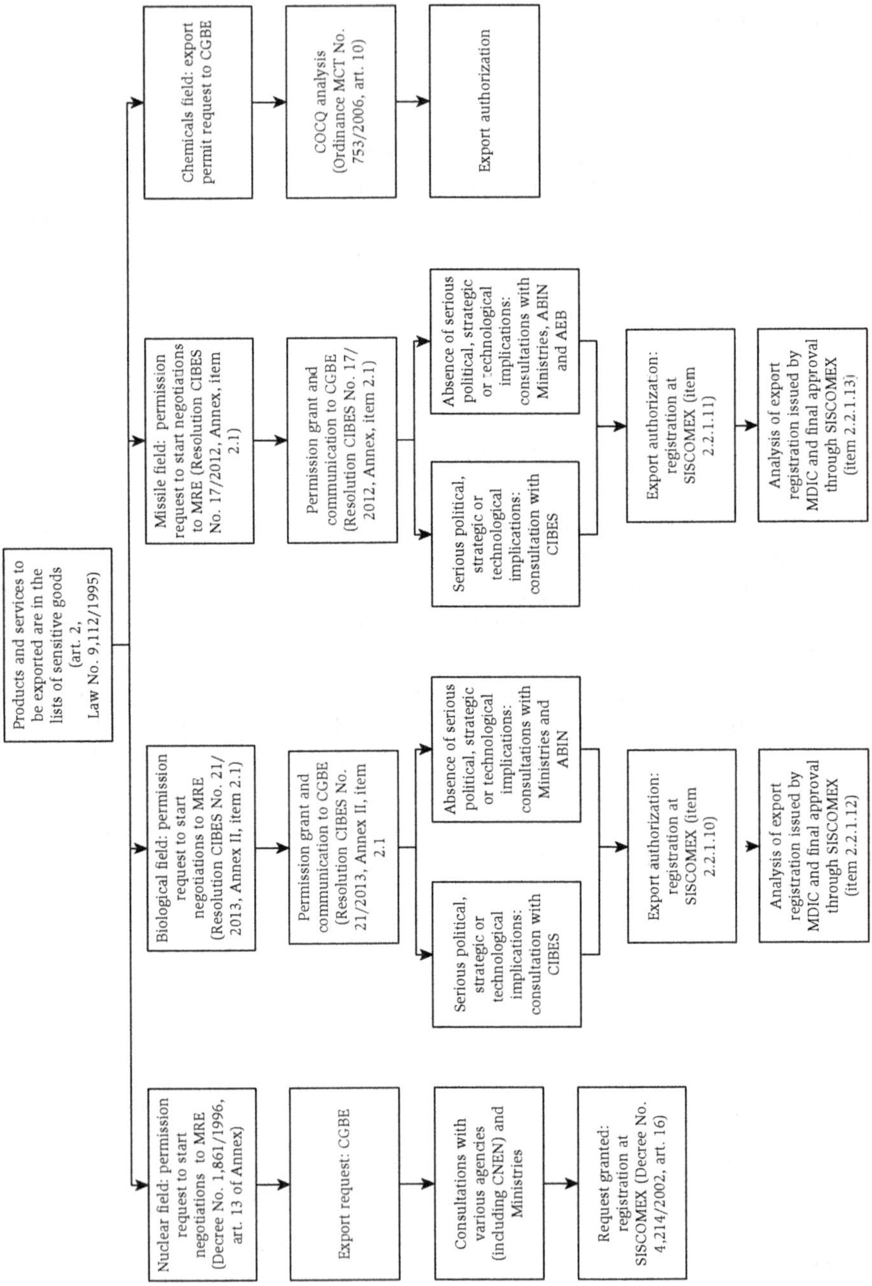

Par. 4 Sanctions and the Recourses of the Importer/Exporter

Sub-Par. 1 Administrative Sanctions

Under Law No. 9,112/1995, one (or more) of the following sanctions shall apply to the export of sensitive goods and services directly related thereto in violation of the provisions thereof and of the applicable regulation:

(a) warning, in cases that involve minor violations;
(b) fine in the amount of two times the transaction value;
(c) loss of the relevant sensitive goods;
(d) suspension of the right to export, for a period ranging from six months to five years; and
(e) revocation of the licence to engage in foreign trade, in the case of recidivism.

Sanctions referred to in (b), (c), (d) and (e) may be imposed severally or cumulatively, in view of the gravity of the violation and the prior conduct of the infringer, always under an administrative proceeding in which the due process of law shall be fully observed.

The very same approach is adopted by Law No. 11,254, of 27 December 2005, in connection with the Convention on the Prohibition of the Development, Production, Stockpiling and Use of Chemical Weapons and on Their Destruction (*CWC*).

In fact, omissions or inaccuracies in information to be provided to competent authorities, as well as non-cooperation with competent authorities during the exercise of their statutory functions shall give rise to the following administrative sanctions:

(a) warning in cases that involve minor violations;
(b) fine in an amount ranging from BRL 5,000[332] to BRL 50,000[333];
(c) loss of the goods related to the violation;
(d) suspension of the right to trade, for a period ranging from six months to five years; and
(e) revocation of the licence to trade, in the case of recidivism.

Sanctions referred to in (b), (c), (d) and (e) may be imposed severally or cumulatively, in view of the gravity of the violation and the prior conduct of the infringer, always under an administrative proceeding in which the due process of law shall be fully observed.

332. Approximately EUR 125.63. The amount in Euros is based on the Real-to-Euro exchange rate from 15 Apr. 2016 (About 3.98).
333. Approximately EUR 125.63. The amount in Euros is based on the Real-to-Euro exchange rate from 15 Apr. 2016 (About 3.98).

Sub-Par. 2 Criminal Sanctions

Under Article 253 of the Brazilian Penal Code, the 'production, supply, purchase, possession or transport, without licence from the competent authority, of explosive substance or device, toxic or asphyxiating gas, or materials used for the production thereof' qualify as a crime punishable with imprisonment from six months to two years plus a fine.

The export of sensitive goods and services directly related thereto in violation of the provisions of Law No. 9,112, of 10 October 1995, qualify as a crime, punished with imprisonment from one to four years. This provision reaches individuals who, directly or indirectly, by action or omission, cooperate in such violation.

Under Law No. 11,254, of 27 December 2005 (CWC), each of the following conducts qualifies as a crime punishable with imprisonment from one to ten years:

(a) 'To make use of chemical weapons or perform, in Brazil, activity involving the research, production, storage, acquisition, transfer, import or export of chemical weapons or chemical substances covered by the CWC for the purpose of producing such weapons'; and
(b) 'To cooperate, directly or indirectly, by action or omission, with the use of chemical weapons or the performance, either in Brazil or abroad, of the activities enrolled in the preceding item (please see (a) above).'

Sub-Par. 3 Delegation of Authority

Brazilian Law does not allow for company directors to assign to another person within the company their liabilities as directors (civil and/or criminal) in respect to export control issues.

SECTION 5 SPECIFICITIES/SPACE-RELATED PROVISIONS

Sub-Section 1 Specificities of the Control Regime

Decisions of the Army and the Ministry of Defence concerning export permits for controlled products and military use goods are generally confidential, i.e., cannot be disclosed to third parties unrelated to the holder of the licence.

Sub-Section 2 Space-Related Provisions in the Control Regime

Some space-related technologies and products are covered by the restrictions on sensitive goods pertaining to the Missile Field, discussed above.

SECTION 6 SANCTIONS AND EMBARGOES

Sub-Section 1 Participation of Brazil to Embargoes or Other Related Sanctions

Brazil has incorporated into its domestic law restrictions on sales/purchases of certain products approved by the Security Council of the UN. SECEX Ordinance No. 23, of 14 July 2011, consolidates these import and export restrictions.[334] The following table lists the countries subject to embargoes enforced by Brazil, as well as the international documents in which such embargoes have been established and the Decrees confirming the effectiveness of these import/export restrictions in Brazilian territory:

Table 4.10 Embargoes Brazil Is Participating in

Country	*Activities Forbidden*	*Embargoes Origin*	*Internalization*
Islamic Republic of Iran	Import/Export	S/RES/1835 (2008)	Decree No. 6,735 of 12 January 2009
Democratic People's Republic of Korea	Import/Export	S/RES/1718 (2006) S/RES/1874 (2009) S/RES/1928 (2010) S/RES/2087 (2013)	Decree No. 5,957 of 7 November 2006 Decree No. 6,935 of 12 August 2009 Decree No. 7,479 of 16 May 2011 Decree No. 8,007 of 15 May 2013
State of Eritrea	Import/Export	S/RES/1907 (2009)	Decree No. 7,290 of 1 September 2010
Iraq	Export	S/RES/1483 (2003)	Decree No. 4,775 of 9 July 2003
Liberia	Export	S/RES/1408 (2002) S/RES/1478 (2003) S/RES/1521 (2003) S/RES/1731 (2006) S/RES/1854 (2008) S/RES/1903 (2009) S/RES/1961 (2010)	Decree No. 4,299 of 11 July 2002 Decree No. 4,742 of 13 June 2003 Decree No. 4,995 of 19 February 2004 Decree No. 6,034 of 1 February 2007 Decree No. 6,936 of 13 August 2009 Decree No. 7,291 of 1 September 2010 Decree No. 7,444 of 25 February 2011

334. Articles 66 and 254.

Country	*Activities Forbidden*	*Embargoes Origin*	*Internalization*
Somalia	Export	S/RES/733 (1992) S/RES/1844 (2008)	Decree No. 1,517 of 7 June 1995 Decree No. 6,801 of 18 March 2009
Sierra Leone	Export	S/RES/1171 (1998)	Decree No. 2,696 of 29 July 1998
Republic of Ivory Coast	Export	S/RES/1572 (2004) S/RES/1727 (2006) S/RES/1842 (2008) S/RES/1893 (2009)	Decree No. 5,368 of 4 February 2005 Decree No. 6,033 of 19 February 2007 Decree No. 6,937 of 13 August 2009 Decree No. 7,289 of 1 September 2010
Democratic Republic of the Congo	Export	S/RES/1493 (2003) S/RES/1596 (2005) S/RES/1649 (2005) S/RES/1698 (2006) S/RES/1771 (2007) S/RES/1799 (2008) S/RES/1807 (2008) S/RES/1857 (2008) S/RES/1896 (2009) S/RES/1952 (2010)	Decree No. 4,822 of 28 August 2003 Decree No. 5,489 of 13 July 2005 Decree No. 5,696 of 7 February 2006 Decree No. 5,936 of 19 October 2006 Decree No. 6,358 of 18 January 2008 Decree No. 6,569 of 16 September 2008 Decree No. 6,570 of 16 September 2008 Decree No. 6,851 of 14 May 2009 Decree No. 7,149 of 8 April 2010 Decree No. 7,450 of 11 March 2011
Sudan	Export	S/RES/1556 (2004) S/RES/1591 (2005) S/RES/1945 (2010)	Decree No. 5,451 of 1 June 2005 Decree No. 5,470 of 16 June 2005 Decree No. 7,463 of 19 April 2011
Libya	Import/Export	S/RES/1970 (2011)	Decree No. 7,460 of 14 April 2011

Sub-Section 2 Regime of the Embargoes or Related Sanctions in Brazil

Under SECEX Ordinance No. 23 of 14 July 2011 (Section 66), import permits may not be issued regarding the following products and countries:

Table 4.11 Import Embargoes

Islamic Republic of Iran	*Weapons and Related Items*
Democratic People's Republic of Korea	Battle tanks, armoured combat vehicles, large calibre artillery systems, combat aircrafts, battle helicopters, warships, missiles or missile systems; and items, materials, equipment, goods and technology which might contribute to programmes of the Democratic People's Republic of Korea related to nuclear activities, missile ballistic or other mass destruction weapons.
State of Eritrea	Weapons and related items.
Libya	Weapons and related items.

A greater number of countries are submitted to export embargoes, as set forth by said SECEX Ordinance No. 23 of 14 July 2011 (Article 254). SECEX, in fact, forbids the issuance of export permits in connection with the cases indicated below:

Table 4.12 Export Embargoes

Islamic Republic of Iran	All items, materials, equipment, goods and technology that might contribute to uranium enrichment, reprocessing activities and heavy water projects, as well as to the development of nuclear weapons vectors; and tanks, armoured combat vehicles, large calibre artillery systems, combat aircraft, battle helicopters, warships, missiles or missile systems as well as related material, including spare parts.
Democratic People's Republic of Korea	Battle tanks, armoured combat vehicles, large calibre artillery systems, combat aircrafts, battle helicopters, warships, missiles or missile systems; luxury goods and items, materials, equipment, goods and technology which might contribute to programmes of the Democratic People's Republic of Korea related to nuclear activities, missile ballistic or other mass destruction weapons.
State of Eritrea	Weapons, military equipment, related material of all kind, including guns and ammunition, military and paramilitary vehicles, as well as equipment, and spare parts.
Iraq	Weapons and related material, except if required by the Authority, Unified Command of Occupying Powers.

Liberia	Weapons and war materials, including ammunition, military vehicles, paramilitary equipment and spare parts for such equipment.
Somalia	Weapons and military equipment.
Sierra Leone	Weapons or related material of all kind, including guns and ammunition, vehicles and military equipment, paramilitary equipment, and spare parts for the aforementioned material. Exception: exports to government entities.
Republic of Ivory Coast	Weapons or any related material, especially aircrafts and military equipment.
Democratic Republic of the Congo	Weapons and related material.
Sudan	Weapons and related material of all kind, including guns and ammunition, military vehicles and equipment, paramilitary equipment and spare parts.
Libya	Weapons or related material of all kind, including guns and ammunition, military vehicles and equipment, paramilitary equipment, and spare parts.

SECTION 7 LIST OF ACRONYMS

ABIN	Agência Brasileira de Inteligência
AEB	Agência Espacial Brasileira
IAEA	International Atomic Energy Agency
CGBE	Coordenação-Geral de Bens Sensíveis
CIBES	Comissão Interministerial de Controle de Exportação de Bens Sensíveis
CII	Certificado Internacional de Importação
COCQ	Coordenação de Implementação, Acompanhamento e Controle na Área Química
CNPJ	Cadastro Nacional de Pessoas Jurídicas
CR	Certificado de Registro
DECEX	Departamento de Operações de Comércio Exterior
DFPC	Diretoria de Fiscalização de Produtos Controlados
DG/PNEMEM	Diretrizes Gerais da Política Nacional de Exportação de Material de Emprego Militar
LI	Licença de Importação
MDIC	Ministério do Desenvolvimento, Indústria e Comércio Exterior
MRE	Ministério das Relações Exteriores
R-105	Regulamento para a Fiscalização de Produtos Controlados
RM	Região Militar de vinculação

SECEX	Secretaria de Comércio Exterior
SFPC/RM	Seção de Fiscalização de Produtos Controlados da Região Militar de vinculação
SISCOMEX	Sistema Integrado de Comércio Exterior
RFB	Receita Federal do Brasil
TR	Título de Registro

SECTION 8 REFERENCES

Sub-Section 1 Primary Documentation

Par. 1 Statutory Legislation

(a) Relating to the Export and Import Control Regime on Military Goods and 'Assimilated Goods':
- Federal Law No. 10,826 of 22 December 2003.
- Federal Law No. 10,683 of 28 May 2003.
- Federal Law No. 12,598 of 21 March 2012.
- Federal Decree No. 3,665 of 20 November 2000 (R-105).
- Federal Decree No. 3,770 of 12 March 2001.
- Federal Decree No. 5.123 of 1 July 2004.
- Federal Decree No. 7,970 of 28 March 2013.

(b) Relating to the Export and Import Control Regime on Sensitive and Dual-use Goods and Directly Related Services:
- Federal Law No. 4,118 of 27 August 1962.
- Federal Law No. 6,189 of 16 December 1974.
- Federal Law No. 9,112 of 10 October 1995.
- Federal Law No. 11,254 of 27 December 2005.
- Federal Law No. 12,598 of 21 March 2012.
- Federal Decree No. 1,861 of 12 April 1996.
- Federal Decree No. 4,214 of 30 April 2002.
- Federal Decree No. 6,759 of 5 February 2009.
- Federal Decree No. 7,970 of 28 March 2013.

Par. 2 Regulations

(a) Relating to the export and import control regime on military goods and 'assimilated goods':
- Joint Ministerial Ordinance MCT/MD No. 631/2001.
- SECEX Ordinance No. 23/2011.

- Federal Revenue Ordinance No. 74/1997.
- Ministry of Defence Ordinance No. 3,229/2013.

(b) Relating to the export and import control regime on sensitive and dual-use goods and directly related services:
- CIBES Resolution No. 17/2012.
- CIBES Resolution CIBES No. 21/2013.
- MCT Ordinance No. 753/2006.
- SECEX Ordinance No. 23/2011.

(c) The following documents, result from Decree No. 3,665 of 20 November 2000 (R-105), are available on a dedicated DropBox folder which can be accessed by following the link below: www.kluwerlawonline.com/eclrh-annexes:
- Annex IV - TR Request.
- Annex X - TR.
- Annex XXII - CR.
- Annex XXXI - Certificate of Final User.
- Annex XXXII - CII.

Sub-Section 2 Secondary Documentation

Par. 1 Internet Sites

- http://www4.planalto.gov.br/legislacao (official Internet site for Brazilian legislation)
- http://portal.in.gov.br/ (Internet site of the Brazilian Republic's official newspaper publishing the Brazilian legislation)
- http://www.eb.mil.br/ministerio-da-defesa (Internet site of the Ministry of Defence) http://www.mct.gov.br/index.php/content/view/43073.html (Internet site of the MCTI proving information and legislation on the control regime on sensitive and dual-use goods and directly related services)
- http://www.mdic.gov.br//sitio/interna/index.php?area=5 (Internet site of MDIC providing information on foreign trade)
- http://dai-mre.serpro.gov.br/ (Internet site of MRE providing information on the international treaties and agreements ratified by Brazil)
- http://www.sae.gov.br/site/ (Internet site of the Secretariat of Strategic Affairs)
- http://www.receita.fazenda.gov.br/Legislacao/LegisAssunto/Siscomex.htm (Internet site of the Federal Revenue with SISCOMEX legislation)
- http://www.portalsiscomex.gov.br/ (Internet site of SISCOMEX)
- http://www.brasilglobalnet.gov.br/frmPrincipal.aspx (Information on foreign trade provided by MRE)

Par. 2 Paper Publications

'A Indústria Brasileira de armas leves e de pequeno porte: Produção Legal e Comércio', Pablo Dreyfus, Benjamin Lessing and Júlio Cesar Purcena, in: Brasil: as armas e as vítimas, Rio de Janeiro, 7Letras, 2005, p. 64-125.

'Armas brasileiras na América Central um estudo sob a perspectiva da Política Nacional de Exportação de Material de Emprego Militar - PNEMEM (1974-1991)', Carlos Federico Domínguez Avila, in: Varia Historia, No. 41, v. 25, 2009, p. 293-314.

'Exposição do Ministro de Estado das Relações Exteriores, Embaixador Luiz Felipe Lampreia, perante a Comissão de Relações Exteriores da Câmara dos Deputados', in: Resenha de Política Exterior do Brasil, No. 77, 1995, p. 209-217.

'O Brasil, a política nacional de exportação de material de emprego militar - PNEMEM - e o comércio internacional de armas: um estudo de caso', Carlos Federico Domínguez Avila, in: Tempo, No. 30, v. 16, 2011, p. 221-241.

'Small Arms in Brazil: Production, Trade, and Holdings', Pablo Dreyfus, Benjamin Lessing, Marcelo de Sousa Nascimento and Júlio Cesar Purcena, Geneva, Small Arms Survey, 2010.

'The Brazilian Export Control System', Victor Zaborsky, in: The Non-proliferation Review, Monterey, James Martin Center for Non-proliferation Studies, 2003.

'Transparency Counts: Assessing State Reporting on Small Arms Transfers', Jasna Lazarevic, Geneva, Small Arms Survey, 2010.

SECTION 9 USEFUL INFORMATION

Sub-Section 1 Enforcement Authorities Contact Details

(a) Military Goods Exports

Name of Organization	*Diretoria de Fiscalização de Produtos Controlados (DFPC)*
Postal Address	Quartel General do Exército - Bloco H - 4° piso - Setor Militar Urbano, Brasília - DF, Brasil, CEP 70630-901
Telephone	+55 (61) 3415 6013
Website	http://www.dfpc.eb.mil.br/

(b) Sensitive and Dual-Use Goods and Directly Related Services

Name of Organization	*Coordenação-Geral de Bens Sensíveis (CGBE)*
Postal Address	Postal address: SPO - Área 05 - Quadra 03, Bloco F - 1° Andar, Brasília - DF, Brasil, CEP 70610-200
Telephone	+55 (61) 3411 5600
Facsimile	+55 (61) 2033 7453
Website	http://www.mct.gov.br/index.php/content/view/43073.html

(c) Other

Name of Organization	*Departamento de Operações de Comércio Exterior (DECEX)*
Postal Address	EQN 102/103, Lote 1, Asa Norte, Brasília - DF, Brasil, CEP 70722-400
Telephone	Export: +55 (61) 2109-7429 / 2109-7160 Import: +55 (61) 2109-7686 Head of department's office: +55 (61) 2027-7562 / 2027-7563
Facsimile	+55 (61) 2027-7188
Email address	decex.cgoc@desenvolvimento.gov.br / decex.gabin@mdic.gov.br
Website	http://www.mdic.gov.br//sitio/interna/index.php?area=5

Name of Organization	*Coordenação-Geral de Informação e Desenvolvimento do SISCOMEX (CGIS)*
Postal Address	EQN 102/103, Lote 1, Asa Norte, Brasília - DF, Brasil, CEP 70722-400
Telephone	+55 (61) 2027-8283
Facsimile	+55 (61) 2027-7188
Email address	siscomex@mdic.gov.br

Name of Organization	*Departamento de Promoção Comercial e Investimentos (DPR))*
Postal Address	Esplanada dos Ministérios, Bloco H, Anexo I, sala 534, Brasília - DF, Brasil, CEP 70170-900
Telephone	+55 (61) 2030-8794/8798
Facsimile	+55 (61) 2030-8790

Name of Organization	*Divisão de Operações de Promoção Comercial (DOC*
Postal Address	Esplanada dos Ministérios, Bloco H, Anexo I, sala 426, Brasília - DF, Brasil, CEP 70170-900
Telephone	+55 (61) 2030-8531
Facsimile	+55 (61) 2030-6007
Email address	doc@itamaraty.gov.br

Sub-Section 2 Other

None.

CHAPTER 5
China

Marion Feurtey

SECTION 1 TABLE OF CONTENTS

SECTION 2 EXECUTIVE SUMMARY

Over the last decades, China has developed an export control system for sensitive products and technologies. Regulations governing exports of nuclear and nuclear dual-use, biological dual-use, chemical, military, missile and related technologies are now in place. The State controls all exports of the above-mentioned items and technologies. Only entities designated by the State have the right to export such goods and technologies. Organizations not approved by the State are prohibited from exporting such materials. For each type of material to be exported, there is a different interagency system to examine applications of sensitive exports and implement and enforce the export control laws. The respective competent authorities also impose sanctions in addition to export licences. The licence procedures for dual-use materials are the same as for controlled materials and the sanctions are equally severe.

SECTION 3 INTRODUCTION: ELEMENTS OF CONTEXT

Sub-Section 1 Overall Philosophy

The Chinese military export control regime is restrictive in order to retain tight control of military goods entering or exiting the country. In fact, for national security reasons, the government imposes restrictions and prohibitions on a case-by-case basis. For all imports or exports of military goods, a specific licence is required and at the current time, only eleven entities are permitted to export or import such products.

The guiding logic of the Chinese export control regime focuses on the final destination and the central questions of the end-user, and how the items will be used. Supporting documentation must therefore be supplied to the relevant government agencies by the entity wishing to export and/or by the end-user, and in some cases by the government of the end-user country.

Sub-Section 2 Historical Outlook

Following the founding of the People's Republic of China (PRC) in 1949, the Chinese government began to transfer sensitive goods and services to neighbouring countries. During this period, China transferred, often free of charge, weapons and military goods to the States with which it had friendly relations. However, such transfer did not constitute commercial export since it resulted from political considerations. No formal export control regime was in existence at that time, but all decisions on such exports were made by the State.

China began to transition from a system of administrative controls to a system of legally based controls in the mid-1990s. Since the promulgation of the first Customs Law in 1987 and the Foreign Trade Law in 1994, the PRC has promulgated several regulations concerning the export of sensitive and authorized goods and technologies.

Sub-Section 3 Participation in International Regimes

The following tables display China's participation status as to export control related international treaties and programmes. It is also stated, when relevant, that China is a party to a treaty either by signature and ratification or by accession.

Par. 1 Treaties and Regimes Dealing with Specific Items and Technologies

Table 5.1 Nuclear Weapons Treaties

Treaty Name	*Overall Status*	*Specific Status*	*Enforceable in China*
Test Ban			
Limited Test Ban Treaty[335]	OS: 5 August 1963 EF: 10 October 1963	–	No
Comprehensive Nuclear Test Ban Treaty[336]	OS: 24 September 1996 EF: not in force	S: 24 September 1996	No
Non-proliferation			
Nuclear Non-Proliferation Treaty[337]	OS: 1 July 1968 EF: 5 March 1970	A: 9 March 1992	Yes
IAEA Comprehensive Safeguards Agreement(s)[338]	EF: 18 September 1989	N/A[339]	Yes
IAEA Model Additional Protocol[340]	S: 31 December 1998 EF: 28 March 2002	N/A[341]	Yes

Abbreviations: OS: Opened for signature; EF: Entry into force; S/R: Signature/Ratification; A: Accession.

335. Treaty Banning Nuclear Weapon Tests in the Atmosphere, in Outer Space and Under Water, *UNTS*, vol. 480, 43.
336. UNGA, resolution 50\245.
337. Treaty on the Non-Proliferation of Nuclear Weapons, *UNTS*, vol. 729, 161.
338. Agreement Between the Agency and States Required in Connection with the Treaty on the Non-Proliferation of Nuclear Weapons (NPT), INFCIRC/153 (Corrected).
339. This treaty is a bilateral one and, accordingly, the differences that apply to multilateral treaties (between the overall status and the specific status) do not apply.
340. Model Protocol Additional to the Agreement(s) between State(s) and the Agency for the Application of Safeguards, INFCIRC/540(Corrected).
341. This treaty is a bilateral one and, accordingly, the differences that apply to multilateral treaties (between the overall status and the specific status) do not apply.

Table 5.2 Biological and Chemical Weapons Treaties

Treaty Name	*Overall Status*	*Specific Status*	*Enforceable in China*
Geneva Protocol[342]	OS: 17 June 1925 EF: 8 February 1928	A: 24 August 1929	Yes
Biological Convention[343]	OS: 10 April 1972 EF: 26 March 1975	A: 15 November 1984	Yes
Chemical Convention[344]	OS: 13 January 1993 EF: 29 April 1997	S: 13 January 1993 R: 25 April 1997	Yes

Abbreviations: OS: Opened for signature; EF: Entry into force; S/R: Signature/Ratification; A: Accession.

Table 5.3 Conventional Arms

Treaty Name	*Overall Status*	*Specific Status*	*Enforceable in China*
Protocol on Firearms to the Convention against Transnational Organized Crime[345]	DA: 31 May 2001 EF: 3 July 2005	–	No
Convention on anti-personnel mines[346]	OS: 18 September 1997 EF: 1 March 1999	–	No

Abbreviations: OS: Opened for signature; DA: Date of adoption; EF: Entry into force; S/R: Signature/Ratification; A: Accession.

Table 5.4 Multilateral Export Control Regimes

Regime Name	*Formation*	*Participation*
Zangger Committee[347]	1971	Yes
Nuclear Suppliers Group	1974	Yes
Australia Group	1985	No

342. Protocol for the Prohibition of the Use in War of Asphyxiating, Poisonous or Other Gases, and of Bacteriological Methods of Warfare, 94, *League of Nations Treaty Series*, No. 2138 (1929).
343. Convention on the Prohibition of the Development, Production and Stockpiling of Bacteriological (Biological) and Toxin Weapons and On Their Destruction, *UNTS*, vol. 1015, 163.
344. Convention on the Prohibition of the Development, Production, Stockpiling and Use of Chemical Weapons and on Their Destruction, Doc.CD/CW/WP.400/Rev.1.
345. Protocol against the Illicit Manufacturing of and Trafficking in Firearms, Their Parts and Components and Ammunition, supplementing the United Nations Convention against Transnational Organized Crime, A/RES/55/225.
346. Convention on the Prohibition of the Use, Stockpiling, Production and Transfer of Anti-Personnel Mines and on their Destruction, *ATS, 1999, n°3.*
347. Non-Proliferation Treaty Exporters Committee (also called the Zangger Committee).

Regime Name	*Formation*	*Participation*
Missile Technology Control Regime	1987	No
Wassenaar Arrangement[348]	1994	No

Table 5.5 Others

Name	*Adoption*	*Participation*
UN Register on Conventional Arms[349]	9 December 1991	Yes[350]
Programme of Action on Small Arms and Light Weapons[351]	20 July 2001	Yes
International Code of Conduct[352]	25 November 2002	No

Par. 2 Treaties Dealing with Specific Areas

Table 5.6 International Zones

Treaty Name	*Overall Status*	*Specific Status*	*Enforceable in China*
Antarctic Treaty[353]	OS: 1 December 1959 EF: 23 June 1961	A: 8 June 1983	Yes
Outer Space Treaty[354]	OS: 27 January 1967 EF: 10 October 1967	A: 30 December 1983	Yes
Sea Bed Arms Control Treaty[355]	OS: 11 February 1971 EF: 23 June 1961	A: 28 February 1991	Yes
Moon Agreement[356]	OS: 18 December 1979 EF: 11 July 1984	S: December 1983	Yes
Convention on the Law of the Sea[357]	OS: 10 December 1982 EF: 16 November 1994	R: 7 June 1996	Yes

348. Wassenaar Arrangement on export controls for conventional arms and dual-use goods and technologies.
349. A/RES/46/36/L.
350. Information provided for the calendar years 1992-1996.
351. Programme of Action to Prevent, Combat and Eradicate the Illicit Trade in Small Arms and Light Weapons in All Aspects, A/CONF.1992/15.
352. The Hague Code of Conduct against Ballistic Missile Proliferation, not yet published.
353. 402, *UNTS*, 7.
354. Treaty on Principles Governing the Activities of States in the Exploration and Use of Outer Space, including the Moon and Other Celestial Bodies, *UNTS*, vol. 610, 205.
355. Treaty on the Prohibition of the Emplacement of Nuclear Weapons and other Weapons of Mass Destruction on the Seabed and The Ocean Floor and in the subsoil thereof, *UNTS*, vol. 955, 115.
356. Agreement governing the Activities of States on the Moon and Other Celestial Bodies, *ILM*, vol. 18, 1434.
357. Doc. A/CONF.62/122 and Corr.1-11.

Abbreviations: OS: Opened for signature; EF: Entry into force; S/R: Signature/Ratification; A: Accession.

Table 5.7 Regional Nuclear Weapons-Free Zones

Treaty Name	*Overall Status*	*Specific Status*	*Enforceable in China*
Treaty of Tlatelolco[358]	OS: 14 February 1967 EF: 22 April 1967	–	No[359]
Treaty of Rarotonga[360]	OS: 8 August 1985 EF: 11 December 1986	–	No[361]
Treaty of Bangkok[362]	OS: 15 December 1995 EF: 27 March 1997	–	No
Treaty of Pelindaba[363]	OS: 11 April 1996 EF: on the date of deposit of the twenty-eight instrument of ratification	–	No[364]

Abbreviations: OS: Opened for signature; EF: Entry into force; S/R: Signature/Ratification; A: Accession.

SECTION 4 CONTROL REGIME

Sub-Section 1 Military Goods and Services

Par. 1 Overall Presentation

Among the several key government departments involved in the deliberation of import/export military use goods and services, the Ministry of Commerce (MOFCOM) and the State Administration for Science, Technology and Industry for National Defence (SASTIND) are major players. MOFCOM is the primary Chinese government department tasked with export/import control administration for controlled goods and technologies. SASTIND is the primary government organ for licensing decisions for conventional military exports/imports, reporting directly to the Ministry of Industry and Information Technology (MIIT).

358. Treaty for the Prohibition of Nuclear Weapons in Latin America and the Caribbean, *UNTS*, vol. 634, 326.
359. China signed and ratified the Protocol II (S: 21 Aug. 1973, R: 12 Jun. 1974).
360. South Pacific Nuclear Free Zone Treaty, *ILM*, vol. 24, 1442.
361. China signed and ratified the Protocols II and III (S: 10 Feb. 1987, R: 21 Oct. 1988).
362. South East Asia Nuclear-Weapon-Free Zone Treaty, *ILM*, vol. 35, 635.
363. African Nuclear Weapon-Free Zone Treaty, *ILM*, vol. 35, 698.
364. China signed and ratified the Protocols I and II (S: 11 Apr. 1996, R: 10 Oct. 1997).

The importation and exportation of military goods and services are strictly regulated in China. At present, only eleven entities[365] in China are authorized to import or export military goods or services.

Sub-Par. 1 Requirements Prior to Any Specific Import/Export (i.e., Manufacturing Phase)

In China, several thousands of companies manufacture military items. As State-owned entities, they produce goods for the sole purpose uniquely for the Chinese government. Prior to any export or import of military goods, an importer/exporter must have been authorized by the State to trade and commercialize such goods.

Sub-Par. 2 Requirements at the Import and/or Export Stages

I Goods

A. General

The export of sensitive items and technologies are subject to examination and approval by the competent departments of the central government on a case-by-case basis. Should any of the following exports have a significant impact on State security, social and public interests or foreign policy, they may be elevated to the State Council or MFA's Department of Arms Control (DAC) for approval instead of the original interagency licence review process. No export is possible without a licence. The holder of an export licence must engage in export activities in strict compliance with the licence during its validity period. If any export items or contents are changed, the original licence must be returned and an application made for a new export licence. When the goods are physically leaving the country, an exporter must provide the export licence to the Customs, undergo Customs formalities as indicated in the Customs Law of the PRC, the relevant control regulations and control measures, and be subject to supervision and control by the Customs.

Export Registration System: All exporters of sensitive items or technologies must be registered with the competent departments of the Central Government. Without the registration, no entity or individual is permitted to engage in such exports. Only designated entities are authorized to handle nuclear exports and the export of controlled chemicals and military products. No other entity or individual is permitted to conduct trade activities in this field.

365. China Electronics Import and Export Company; China Aeronautical Technology Import and Export Company; China North Industries Company (NORINCO); China Vessels Industry Trading Company; China Precision Machines Import and Export Company; Poly Science and Technology Company; China Xinxing Import and Export Company; China Jing An Import and Export Company; China Electro-Sci-Tec International Trading Company; China Vessels Heavy Industry International Trading Company; and Aerospace Long March International Trading Company.

End-user and End-use Certification: An exporter of sensitive items and technologies is required to provide a certificate specifying the end-user and the end-use, which must be provided by the end-user that imports them. Different kinds of certificates must be produced, depending on the circumstances and the sensitivity of the exported items or technologies. In some cases, the certificates must be produced by the relevant government department of the importing country. The end-user must certify the identity of the end-user and end-use of the imported materials or technologies in the above-mentioned certificates, and guarantee that without permission from the Chinese government, it shall not use the relevant item provided by China for purposes other than the certified end-use, or transfer it to a third party other than the certified end-user.

B. Chemicals

The primary governing laws in this regard include the 1995 'Administration of Chemicals under Supervision and Control'[366] and the 1997 'Implementation Details on the Regulations on Monitored and Controlled Chemicals'. Only two entities have the right to import or export controlled chemicals, which are: the 'China National Chemicals Import & Export Corporation' (SINOCHEM), and the 'China Haohua Chemical Group'.

Co-coordinating closely with MOFCOM, the National CWC Implementation Office (NCWCIO) acts as the principal specialist body to authorize export licences for chemical items. The licence granting process is as described below. There are four categories of controlled chemical items:

- Schedule 1: chemicals with uses as chemical weapons
- Schedule 2: chemicals with uses as the precursors in the manufacture of chemical weapons
- Schedule 3: chemicals with uses as the primary materials in the manufacture of chemical weapons
- Schedule 4: discrete organic chemicals with the exception of explosives and pure hydrocarbon compounds.

For Schedule 1 items, the entities must submit an application to NCWCIO and provide a written guarantee from the recipient government. If NCWCIO approves, it will forward the application to the State Council for final approval. After the State Council approves the application, the entities may apply for a licence from MOFCOM. Only after having received the licence from MOFCOM may the entities apply to the Customs Administration for clearance.

For other categories, the process is the same, except that NCWCIO does not need to submit the application to the State Council.

366. State Council Decree No. 190.

C. Nuclear Materials and Equipment

In this field, the China Atomic Energy Agency (CAEA) acts as the principal specialist authority and China National Nuclear Corporation (CNNC) acts as the deputy. The primary applicable rules can be found in the Regulations on Nuclear Export Control.[367] Only competent entities designated by the State Council have the right to export nuclear items. The entities may apply directly to the CAEA in order to obtain an export licence.

An authorized nuclear exporter applies to the CAEA for a licence to export a controlled nuclear item. The CAEA is the lead agency regarding exports of nuclear materials, nuclear equipment and non-nuclear materials used for reactors. The export should also apply for a proxy licence to the CNNC. After receiving the Nuclear Export Application form and the documents required by Article 7 of the Regulations on the Control of Nuclear Export, the CAEA shall submit a review report and notify the applicant within fifteen working days after the receipt of the application. If approval is given after the review, the following procedures should be followed, according to the particular circumstances

- Licence application for export of nuclear materials shall be forwarded to the SASTIND for re-examination.
- Licence application for export of nuclear equipment or non-nuclear materials used for reactors, as well as their related technologies, shall be forwarded to MOFCOM for re-examination or MOFCOM will jointly re-examine the case with the SASTIND.

After such examination and re-examination process, which may take one or several forms depending on the circumstances, if the Nuclear Export Applications have been approved, MOFCOM will issue a Nuclear Export licence and send a notification to Customs. Only with the licence may the exporter apply to the Customs for clearance to export such items and equipment.

D. Military Items

The State Council and the Central Military Commission (CMC) promulgated the Regulations on the Control of Military Products Export.[368] Only eleven Military Products Trading Corporations designated by the authority may hold the status of a State Military Articles Trading Company, being granted the right to export military items.

The export of military products requires a military products export licence. The SASTIND acts as the competent authority to examine or approve the application. The

367. State Council Decree No. 230, issued in 1997 http://www.caea.gov.cn/n16/n1130/78790.html.

368. Promulgated on 22 Oct. 1997 by the PRC State Council and the PRC CMC under Order No. 234; revised according to the 'Decision of the State Council and the Central Military Commission on Amending the PRC Regulations on Control of Military Products Export' on 15 Oct. 2002 http://kjs.mofcom.gov.cn/article/Nocategory/200412/20041200324669.shtml.

DAC in the Ministry of Foreign Affairs (MFA) also participates in the licensing review process, as well as the implementation of China's international commitments and treaty obligations.

A Military Products Trading Company submits proposals for military products export in the form of an application for examination to SASTIND. If a proposal is approved, the exporter may then sign a contract with a foreign firm, after which the contract should be submitted to SASTIND for examination and approval. In addition, when the item to be exported could affect China's own military capability, the CMC is consulted to assess the impact on China's security interests. The contract shall be valid only once it has been approved.

For important military products export items, SASTIND will examine the application and then submit it to the State Council and the CMC for final approval. As there is no definition of the term 'important military export items' in the Regulation itself, it is in SASTIND's discretion whether such a contemplated export shall be deemed as an 'important' one. A Military Products Trading Company must provide the relevant military products export approval document to SASTIND for application for a military products export licence. Unlike with respect to most other items, licences for exporting military products are issued by SASTIND rather than MOFCOM. In case of disagreements, the State Council or the CMC have the final say. Only with the military products export licence can it apply to the Customs Administration to export the items.

E. Missiles and Missile-Related Items and Technologies

As in the case of the military items system, MOFCOM is the principal regulatory authority in this field. The relevant regulations are the 'Regulations of the PRC on Export Control of Missiles and Missile-related Items and Technologies'.[369] The export application forms can be obtained from the competent foreign economic and trade department of the State Council.

Exporters should first register themselves with MOFCOM and then submit the application. MOFCOM will make a decision of approval or denial, jointly with relevant departments of the CMC. If the application is approved, MOFCOM will issue a licence and notify the Customs Administration in writing. Once it has the licence, the exporter may apply to the Customs Administration to export the items.

II Services

The export of military services requires the same licensing and approval process as described above for military goods.

369. Promulgated on 22 Aug. 2002, http://www.npc.gov.cn/englishnpc/Law/2007-12/14/content_1384258.htm.

III Persons

Given the relatively controlled environment for Chinese Nationals to travel abroad and the discretionary authority the government has with regard to such approvals, one must assume that any travel abroad by persons with such sensitive knowledge will require approvals. In other words, the Chinese government can in its discretionary authority require a special approval for such persons with sensitive knowledge to travel abroad.

Par. 2 Control Lists

List Control Method: China has drawn up detailed control lists of sensitive materials, equipment and technologies.

In the nuclear, biological and chemical fields, the relevant lists cover virtually all of the materials and technologies included in the control lists of the Zangger Committee, the NSG, the Chemical Weapons Convention (CWC) and the AG (Nuclear Exports Control List 1996).[370]

In the missile field, the scope of the Chinese list is generally the same as the Technical Annex of the MTCR (the Missiles and Missile-related Items and Technologies Export Control List 2002).[371]

In the arms export field, the Chinese government also drew on the experience of the relevant multilateral mechanism and the relevant practice of other countries when it first formulated and issued the arms export control list in 2002 (Certain Chemicals and Related Equipment and Technologies Export Control List 2002).[372]

Par. 3 Licensing and Enforcement Authorities

MOFCOM, the General Administration of Customs (GAC) and the Ministry of Public Security (MPS) have the responsibility for enforcing export regulations the GAC works closely with MOFCOM and the CAEA. The GAC may detain items if they suspect a violation of the Customs Law of the PRC, and may detain individuals as criminal suspects for twenty-four hours, or hand them over to the judiciary authorities.

Figure 5.1 summarizes the licence application process and the authorities involved.

370. The Regulations of the PRC on Control of Nuclear Exports, http://english.mofcom.gov.cn/aarticle/policyrelease/domesticpolicy/200211/20021100049338.html.
371. Regulations of the PRC on Export Control of Missiles and Missile-related Items and Technologies, http://exportcontrol.mofcom.gov.cn/article/y/bi/200305/20030500093638.shtml.
372. http://english.mofcom.gov.cn/aarticle/policyrelease/domesticpolicy/200211/20021100049240.html.

Figure 5.1 Licence Application Process and Authorities Involved

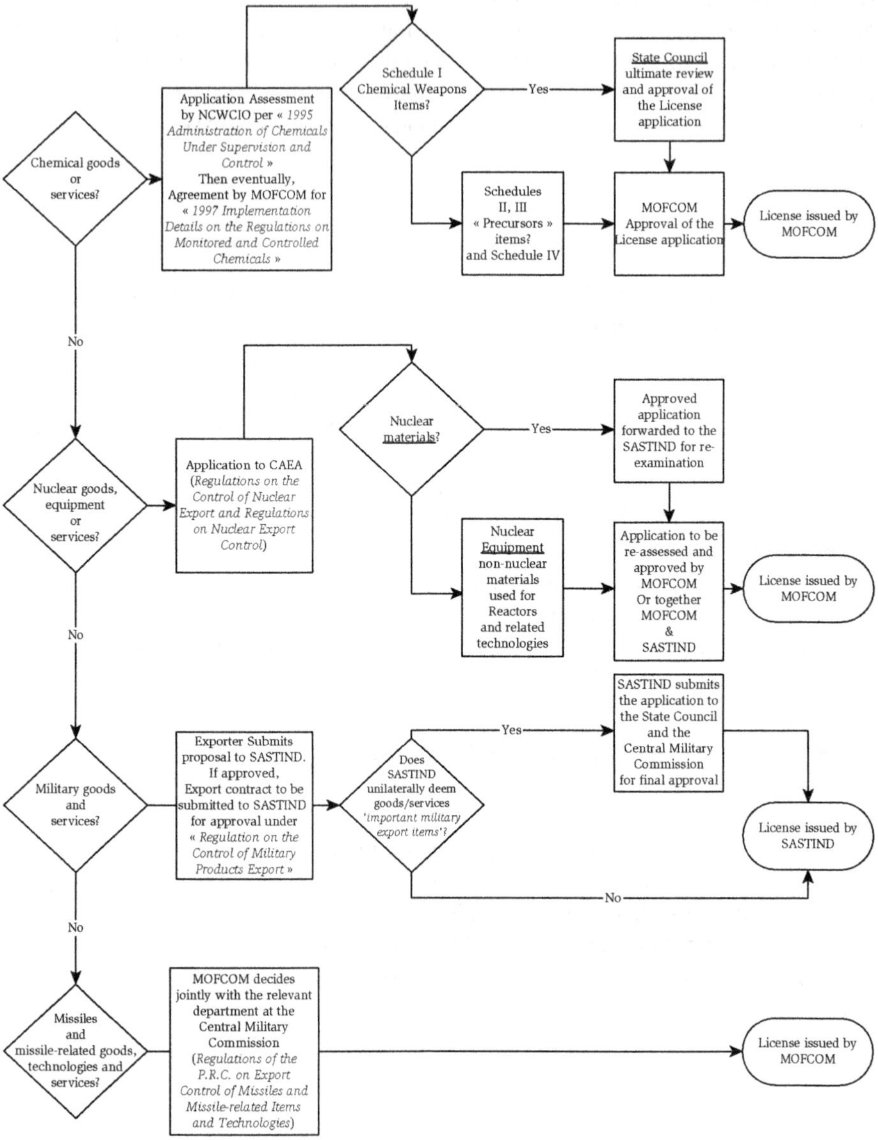

Par. 4 Sanctions and Recourses of the Importer/Exporter

Aside from the final examination by the Customs Administration, the specific authority for each export material has the authority to impose sanctions. MOFCOM issuing the export licence also has the right to investigate and impose sanctions ranging from monetary fines, suspension of export-import privileges to a full revocation of a business licence.

In all the export control legislation of the PRC, there are processes according to which exporters who export controlled items or technologies without approval, arbitrarily export items beyond the approved scope, or forge, alter, buy or sell export licences shall be investigated for criminal liability in accordance with the provisions of the PRC laws on smuggling, illegal business operation, disclosure of State secrets or other crimes. For cases that do not constitute crimes, the competent government department shall impose administrative sanctions, including warning, confiscation of illicit proceeds, fines ranging from a value equal to 30%-100% of the value of the goods, suspension or even revocation of foreign trade licences. An aggrieved importer/ exporter has a right to apply for administrative reconsideration or to sue the administrative authority in administrative proceedings.

Pursuant to the Criminal Code of China, smuggling of arms, ammunitions or nuclear materials shall be subject to a sentence of imprisonment for seven years, with a fine or forfeiture of property. For less serious offences, imprisonment could be for three years to seven years together with fines. Whoever forges or alters official documents, certificates or seals of State organs can be sentenced to not more than three years of imprisonment; when the circumstances are serious, the sentence is to be no less than three years but not more than ten years of imprisonment. Whoever shall purchase or sell import-export licences shall be sentenced to not more than five years of imprisonment and may be subject to a fine not less than 100% and not more than 500% of his illegal income. Where the circumstances are particularly serious, violators can be sentenced to not less than five years of imprisonment and a fine of not less than 100% and not more than 500% of his illegal income or the confiscation of his property. State personnel who seriously violate the Law of Protection of State Secrets[373] by intentionally or negligently revealing State secrets can be sentenced to not more than three years of imprisonment or criminal detention. Exceptionally serious violations are punishable by not less than three years and not more than seven years of imprisonment.

Chinese law does not specifically provide that a director of a company can pass their liability on to an employee who is responsible for such activities as obtaining the licences. However, according to the principles with regard to agency set forth in the General Principles of the Civil Law of the PRC, where employees have been delegated power to obtain licences, they shall perform acts in the company's name within the scope of the power of agency – i.e., obtaining licences. The company shall be liable for the employee's acts of agency unless the employee's act is beyond his power of attorney or after his power of agency has expired and the company does not ratify the act retroactively.

373. http://www.hrichina.org/en/implementation-regulations/2014-regulations-implementation-law-peoples-republic-china-guarding-state.

Where violations of Chinese law by Chinese citizens overseas constitute criminal acts that occur outside of the territory of China, Chinese citizens overseas may be subject to the Criminal Code of China pursuant to the general jurisdiction principles of such law.

Sub-Section 2 Dual-Use Goods and Services

Par. 1 Overall Presentation

The Chinese dual-use goods and services export control is composed of several main regulations and administrative measures. One, the Regulations on Nuclear Export Control, relates to the trade of nuclear dual-use items. Another, the Regulations of the PRC on Export Control of Dual-use Biological Agents and related Equipment and Technologies, relates to dual-use biological agents and related equipment and technologies. The third, the Administrative Measures on Import and Export Licences for Dual-use Items and Technologies, regulates the licensing for dual-use items and technologies.

Sub-Par. 1 Requirements Prior to Any Specific Import/Export (i.e., Manufacturing Phase)

The requirements prior to any specific export include the same registration, licensing and end-user certification as the ones for military use items and technologies abovementioned.

Sub-Par. 2 Requirements at the Import and/or Export Stages

I Goods

A. General

The Administrative Measures on Import and Export Licences for Dual-use Items and Technologies, which were promulgated jointly by MOFCOM and the GAC on 31 December 2005,[374] are expressly intended to cover both the import and export of the dual-use items and technologies. There are no similar laws or regulations specifically governing the import of military goods and services.

Pursuant to the Administrative Measures on Import and Export Licences for Dual-use Items and Technologies, Dual-use Items and Technologies Import or Export Licences are required for all importing and exporting of controlled dual-use items and technologies, as well as transiting through the territory of China or transferring or transporting controlled dual-use items and technologies in China.

374. Amended on 31 Dec. 2014, http://exportcontrol.mofcom.gov.cn/article/t/z/201412/20141200854684.shtml.

B. Biological Agents and Related Equipment and Technologies

In this field, the competent authority is the competent foreign economic and trade department of the State Council. The primary piece of legislation with respect to biological items is the Regulation of the PRC on Export Control of Dual-use Biological Agents and Related Equipment and Technologies, issued on 17 October 2002. As with the military control regime, only the same eleven entities may apply to export such items.

The State Council has a licensing system for the export of dual-use biological agents and related equipment and technologies. The exporters must register themselves with MOFCOM and provide a guarantee.[375] They should then complete the export application form produced by MOFCOM and submit it to MOFCOM for review. After having examined and approved the application, MOFCOM will issue an export licence. Only with the export licence may the exporter apply to the Customs Administration to export the items.

C. Nuclear Dual-Use Items and Related Technologies

In this field, the applicable law is the Regulations of the PRC on the Control of Nuclear Dual-use Items and Related Technologies Export.[376] The primary competent authority is MOFCOM.

After the exporting entities have registered and provided a guarantee[377] and completed the export application form, MOFCOM will approve or reject the application, jointly with the China Atomic Energy Authority (CAEA) within forty-five business days. If foreign policy concerns are involved, MOFCOM may seek an opinion from the MFA or from the other relevant State Council departments. If the exports contained in the application could have a significant impact on State security, MOFCOM shall submit it to the State Council for review and approval. If the application is approved, MOFCOM will issue an export licence, which the exporter may then present to the Customs Administration in order to export the items.

II Services

The export of services related to biological dual-use agents and nuclear items as well as scientific cooperation and aid must follow the same licensing and registration requirements as imposed on the dual-use biological agents.

---

375. Article 7 of the Regulations of the PRC on Export Control of Dual-Use Biological Agents and Related Equipment and Technologies, http://english.mofcom.gov.cn/aarticle/policyrelease/domesticpolicy/200211/20021100049225.html.
376. Adopted at the Fourth Executive Meeting of the State Council on 1 Jun. 1998, promulgated by Decree No. 245 of the State Council of the PRC, and revised in January 2007, http://english.mofcom.gov.cn/article/policyrelease/Businessregulations/201303/20130300047261.shtml.
377. Article 6 of the Regulations of the PRC on the Control of Nuclear Dual-Use Items and Related Technologies Export, http://english.mofcom.gov.cn/article/policyrelease/Businessregulations/201303/20130300047261.shtml.

III Persons

Pursuant to the Administrative Measures on Import and Export Licences for Dual-use Items and Technologies, the regime for issuance of Import and Export Licences shall apply for importing or exporting the controlled dual-use items and technologies in any way, and also applies to such items or technology passing through the territory of China or being transferred or transported within China. In view of the breadth of this licence regime, disclosure to a foreigner in China who will then leave China knowing such information would fall under the language of at least one of the regulations and may be treated as 'exporting in any way'. Accordingly, the conduct is highly likely to be subject to Chinese governmental control.

Par. 2 Control Lists

List Control Method: China has drawn up detailed control lists of sensitive materials, equipment and technologies.

In the nuclear, biological and chemical fields, the relevant lists cover virtually all of the materials and technologies included in the control lists of the Zangger Committee, the NSG, the CWC and the AG:

- Nuclear Dual-use Items and Related Technologies Control List (1998)[378]
- Dual-use Biological Agents and Related Equipment and Technologies Export Control List (2002).[379]

Par. 3 Licensing and Enforcement Authorities

MOFCOM, the GAC and MPS are the primary enforcement authorities for export control on dual-use goods and services. They may launch investigations into suspected violations. MOFCOM has the power to levy administrative sanctions, which range from monetary fines and suspension of export-import privileges to a full revocation of business licences.

In China, the applications and approvals remain non-public and neither third parties nor the public is able to access to such information. Due to the relatively bureaucratic characteristic and non-transparency of the decision-making process of the Chinese government, the internal deliberations remain non-public and the government does not publicly differentiate the military use of dual-use items.

Figure 5.2 summarizes the licence application process and the authorities involved.

378. The Regulations of the PRC on Control of Nuclear Exports, http://english.mofcom.gov.cn/aarticle/policyrelease/domesticpolicy/200211/20021100049338.html.
379. PRC Regulations on Export Control of Dual-Use Biological Agents and Related Equipment and Technologies, http://english.mofcom.gov.cn/aarticle/policyrelease/domesticpolicy/200211/20021100049225.html.

Figure 5.2 Licence Application Process and Authorities Involved

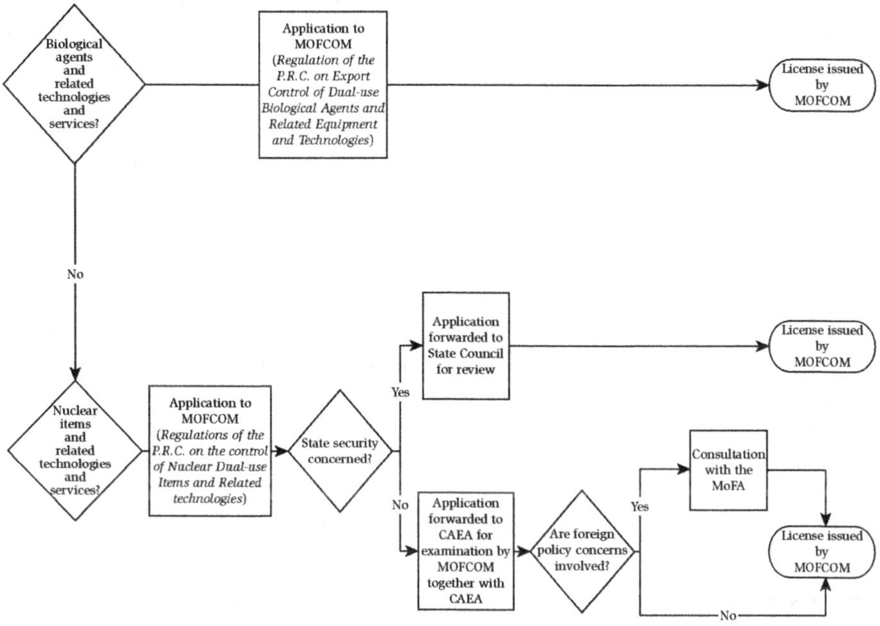

Par. 4 Sanctions and Recourses of the Importer/Exporter

Exporters or importers who export or import controlled dual-use items or technologies without approval, arbitrarily export items beyond the approved scope, or forge, alter, buy or sell export licences shall be investigated for criminal liability in accordance with the provisions of the laws on smuggling, illegal business operation, disclosure of State secrets or other crimes. For cases that do not constitute crimes, the competent government department may impose administrative sanctions, including warnings, confiscation of illicit proceeds, fines ranging from a value equal to 30% of the value of the goods to 100% of the value of the goods or suspension or revocation of foreign trade licences. An importer/exporter has the right to apply for administrative reconsideration or to sue the administrative authority in administrative proceedings.

Pursuant to the Criminal Code of China, smuggling arms, ammunitions or nuclear materials shall be subject to a sentence of imprisonment for seven years, with a fine or forfeiture of property. For less serious offences, imprisonment could be for from three years to seven years together with fines. Whoever forges or alters official documents, certificates or seals of State organs can be sentenced to not more than three years of imprisonment; when the circumstances are serious, the sentence is to be no less than three years but not more than ten years of imprisonment. Whoever shall purchase and sell import-export licences shall be sentenced to not more than five years of imprisonment and may be subject to a fine of not less than 100% and not more than 500% of their illegal income. Where the circumstances are particularly serious, violators can be sentenced to not less than five years of imprisonment and a fine of not less than 100% and not more than 500% of their illegal income or the confiscation of their property. State personnel who seriously violate the Law of Protection of State Secrets by intentionally or negligently reveal State secrets can be sentenced to not more than three years of imprisonment or criminal detention. Exceptionally serious violations are punishable by not less than three years and not more than seven years of imprisonment.

Chinese law does not specifically provide that a director of a company can pass their liability on to an employee who is responsible for such activities as obtaining the licences. However, according to the principles with regard to agency set forth in the General Principles of the Civil Law of the PRC, where employees have been delegated power to obtain licences, they shall perform acts in the company's name within the scope of the power of agency – i.e., obtaining licences. The company shall be liable for the employee's acts of agency unless the employee's act is beyond his power of attorney or after his power of agency has expired and the company does not ratify the act retroactively.

Where violations by Chinese citizens overseas constitute criminal acts that occur outside of the territory of China, Chinese citizens overseas may be subject to the Criminal Code of China pursuant to the general jurisdiction principles of such laws.

SECTION 5 SPECIFICITIES/SPACE-RELATED PROVISIONS

Sub-Section 1 Specificities of the Control Regime

The Chinese export control legal system has incorporated international standards and practices for non-proliferation export control, among others, including registration and licensing, control lists of equipment, materials and technologies as well as end-user and end-use certifications. The control regulations stipulate a catchall provision that allows the government to deny any export if the government deems it necessary, even for goods not specifically included on the control lists. China does not maintain a formal internal watch list of foreign countries and companies that are automatically barred from receiving sensitive exports, but it does monitor suspected Chinese companies to prevent illegal exports of controlled goods and services. (The list of such suspect companies is not public.)

In China, the licence applications and approvals remain non-public. Neither the third parties nor the public are able to access to such information.

Sub-Section 2 Space-Related Provisions in the Control Regime

SASTIND and the China National Space Administration (CNSA) have begun working on regulations to control the export of a variety of space items. The Chinese government is expected to control, for example, the export of high-resolution remote sensing satellites.

SECTION 6 LIST OF ABBREVIATIONS

AG	Australia Group
ATS	Australian Treaty Series
CAEA	China Atomic Energy Agency
CMC	Central Military Commission
CNSA	China National Space Administration
CNNC	China National Nuclear Corporation
CWC	Chemical Weapons Convention
DAC	Department of Arms Control and disarmament
GAC	General Administration of Customs
IAEA	International Atomic Energy Agency
ILM	International Legal Material
MCI	Ministry of the Chemical Industry
MFA	Ministry of Foreign Affairs
MIIT	Ministry of Industry and Information Technology
MOFCOM	Ministry of Commerce
MTCR	Missile Technology Control Regime
NCWCIO	National Chemical Weapons Convention Implementation Office
NSG	Nuclear Suppliers Group
PRC	People's Republic of China
SASTIND	State Administration for Science Technology and Industry for National Defence
SINOCHEM	China National Chemicals Import & Export Corporation
UNTS	United Nations Treaty Series

SECTION 7 REFERENCES

Sub-Section 1 Primary Documentation

All the export control laws are included in the links to the official website of MOFCOM (http://exportcontrol.mofcom.gov.cn), SASTIND (http://www.sastind.gov.cn/), and CAEA (www.caea.gov.cn).

Please be aware that some of the English translations of Chinese laws and regulations available on those sites (and more generally the sites that are referenced in the footnotes in the present chapter) are for reference only and are not official translation, and that they are also not always maintained up to date.

Par. 1 Statutory Legislation and Regulations

General	– Foreign Trade Law, 1994 (revised in 2004) – Customs Law, 1987 (revised in 2000) – Administrative Measures on Registration for Operation of Export of Sensitive Items and Technologies, 2002 – Provisional Administrative Measures on Export Licences for Sensitive Items and Technologies, 2003 – Category Subject to Export Licence for Sensitive Items and Technologies, 2003 – Administrative Measures on Import and Export Licences for Dual-use Items and Technologies, 2005, as amended 31 December 2014
Chemical and Dual-use	– Regulations on Administration of Controlled Chemicals, December 1995 – Implementation details of the above regulation March 1997 – A ministerial circular (executive decree) on strengthening chemical export controls, August 1997 – Decree n° 1 of the State Petroleum and Chemical Industry Administration (regarding chemical export controls) June 1998 (Note: These regulations have expanded the coverage of China's chemical export controls to include dual-use chemicals covered by the AG) – Measures on Export Control of Certain Chemicals and Related Equipment and Technologies, 19 October 2002 – Certain Chemicals and Related Equipment and Technologies Export Control List, 19 October 2002
Biological and Dual-use	– Regulations of the People's Republic of China on Export Control of Dual-use Biological Agents and Related Equipment and Technologies, 14 October 2002 – Dual-use Biological Agents and Related Equipment and Technologies Export Control List, 14 October 2002
Nuclear and Dual-use	– Circular on Strict Implementation of China's Nuclear Export Policy, May 1997 – Regulations on Nuclear Export Control, September 1997 (Note: The control list included in the 1997 regulations is identical to that used by the Nuclear Suppliers Group, to which China is not a member.) – Regulations on Export Control of Dual-use Nuclear Goods and Related Technologies, June 1998, as amended 26 June 2007 – Nuclear Export Control List as amended, 5 November 2006[380]

380. http://exportcontrol.mofcom.gov.cn/article/t/z/200612/20061203931782.shtml.

Military and Dual-use	- Regulations on Export Control of Military Items, October 1997 - Procedures for the Management of Restricted Technology Export, November 1998 (Note: The new regulations cover 183 dual-use technologies, including some on the Wassenaar Arrangement's 'core list' of dual-use technologies) - China's Ministry of Foreign Trade and Economics Cooperation, now MOFCOM, released a Catalogue of Technologies that are Restricted or Banned in China, 1998 - Decision of the State Council and the Central Military Commission Amending Regulations on Control of Military Products Export, 15 October 2002
Missile Systems and Components	- The Chinese government gave verbal assurance of its intention to adhere to the MTCR in November 1991, followed by written commitment in February 1992 - The U.S. and Chinese governments issued a joint statement on missile proliferation in October 1994. Beijing agreed to ban all MTCR-class missiles and agreed to use the 'inherent capability' principle in defining MTCR-class missile systems - The Chinese government issued a statement in November 2000 promising for the first time to promulgate missile export control regulations and to issue a control list - China announced the promulgation of the Regulations on Export Control of Missiles and Missile-related Items and Technologies and the related control list in August 2002
Encryption	- Regulations for the Administration of Commercial Encryption (State Council Decree 273), 7 October 1999

Par. 2 Annexes – Copies of Documents of Practical Use to the Importer/Exporter

A number of standard documents relevant for the import or export process in China (e.g., most current official application forms for import or export licences, templates of contractual undertaking, or regulation extracts) as well as other non-official documents are available on a dedicated DropBox folder which can be accessed by following the link below:

www.kluwerlawonline.com/eclrh-annexes

Sub-Section 2 Secondary Documentation

Par. 1 Internet Sites

- www.armscontrol.org (Arms control Association: the authoritative source on arm control)
- www.sipri.org/contents/expcon/china.html (Stockholm International Peace Research Institute)
- www.novexcn.com/customs_sez_inbound_outbou.html (NovexCn.com was originally established as a not-for-profit enterprise in order to fill a void that was experienced by lawyers, China scholars, academics, journalists and foreign governments)
- exportcontrol.mofcom.gov.cn

Par. 2 Paper Publications

Richard T. Cupitt, 'Non-proliferation Export Controls in the People's Republic of China', 2003.

SECTION 8 USEFUL INFORMATION

Sub-Section 1 Licensing and Enforcement Authorities Contact Details

Name of Organization	*SASTIND*
Postal Address	8, Fucheng Street Haidian District Beijing 100048 China
Telephone	+86 (10) 6605-8958
Website	www.sastind.gov.cn

Name of Organization	*CAEA*
Postal Address	8, Fucheng Street Haidian District Beijing 100048 China
Telephone	+86 (10) 6603-4714
Fax	+86 (10) 6603-4714
Email address	webmaster@caea.gov.cn
Website	www.caea.gov.cn/ecaea/index.asp

Name of Organization	*MOFCOM*
Postal Address	2, Dong Chang'an Avenue Beijing 100731 China
Telephone	+86 (10) 6718-4455/6708-1527
Fax	+86 (10) 6708-1513
Website	www.mofcom.gov.cn

Name of Organization	*Ministry of National Defence*
Postal Address	The Foreign Affairs Office 25 Huangsi Avenue Beijing 100011 China
Telephone	+86 (10) 6201-8356
Website	www.mod.gov.cn

Sub-Section 2 Other

None.

CHAPTER 6

The European Union

Arnaud Idiart & Marion Ringot

SECTION 1 TABLE OF CONTENTS

SECTION 2 EXECUTIVE SUMMARY

The need for greater harmonization of export control regulations in Europe regarding sensitive products (i.e., commodities, technologies, software and services) has long been acknowledged and asserted. Nonetheless, the binding set of export control provisions which the European Union (EU) has put in place since 1995 a strict

Regulation to cover the export of dual-use equipment only. It is only a Directive[381] – not a Regulation – which defines, since June 2009, a common list of products a common policy and related enforcement guide lines that controls Intra-Community Transfers (ICT)_ of 'Defence related Products'.

Member States had two years to implement this Directive that organize the ICT only; Member States keep the full control to export outside the EU.

The question of conventional arms and dual-use exports remains a sensitive issue. The EU plays no direct role in managing arms transfers inside or out of the Member States' national community. It has, however, pressed for discussion and cooperation in areas related to conventional arms transfers. The Code of Conduct has been adopted as a politically binding regulation by the Member States at the end of 2008.[382] The Letter of Intent (LoI) enforced in 1998 is also supported by the ICT Directive[383] as Article 1§4 which provides 'This Directive does not affect the possibility for Member States to pursue and further develop intergovernmental cooperation, whilst complying with the provisions of this Directive'. These two examples illustrate that Member States will coordinate their positions on and facilitate arms export controls. Although there is no common European regime for arms export, Council Regulation n° 428/2009[384] regulates exports of dual-use items. The Regulation establishes a hybrid system where both the EU and Member States are involved in its development and enforcement. The system is based on two core principles: the free transfer of dual-use goods and technologies within the EU, and the prohibition to export those items outside the EU without a national licence. This Regulation illustrates Member States will to both, control efficiently EU common dual-use goods exports and respect strictly their national obligations which derive from individual participation in international export control regimes.

SECTION 3 INTRODUCTION: ELEMENTS OF CONTEXT

Sub-Section 1 Overall Philosophy

Member States have always preferred to reserve the right to make decisions relating to domestic security issues at a national level. Article 346 Lisbon Treaty on the Functioning of the European Union[385] (TFEU) states that Member States may exempt the

381. Directive n° 2009/43/EC of the European Parliament and of the Council of 6 May 2009 simplifying terms and conditions of transfers of defence-related products within the Community, *Official Journal*, L 146, 10 Jun. 2009 (hereinafter the 'ICT Directive').
382. Common Position 2008/944 PESC of 8 Dec. 2008 of the European Council, OJEU L355/99, 99 of 13 Dec. 2008.
383. Directive n° 2009/43/EC.
384. Regulation (EC) n° 428/2009, *supra* n. 230.
385. Treaty on the Functioning of the European Union consolidated version; cf. OJEU n°2012/C 326/01, 26.10.2012, C 326/1 ((previously Article 296) Treaty Establishing the European Community, *Official Journal*, C 325 of 24 Dec. 2002 and before Article 223 of the Treaty of Rome) states:

production and trade of arms from the rules of the common market. The subsequent Treaty revisions (Maastricht, Amsterdam and Nice or Lisbon) did not modify this. European Member States wished to keep sovereignty over conventional arms transfer policy and practice. This explains why, as an organization, the EU plays a limited part in regulating arms transfers.

Export controls have an important economic impact, especially when it comes to technologies that have a dual-use (both civil and military). The competition rules in the common market do apply to dual-use goods[386] which, therefore, fall under the Trade Policy of the EU.

The question of conventional arms and dual-use exports remains, however, problematic, primarily because the issue of arms and dual-use exports involves two different European policies, which operate in radically different ways. Whereas arms exports fall under the security and defence policy of the EU, dual-use exports come within its Trade Policy. As a result, the institutional setting is rather complex since the commercial policy lies within the exclusive competence of the EU, while the security and defence policy remains an area of responsibility reserved for each Member States.

Sub-Section 2 Historical Outlook

Par. 1 Conventional Armaments

Generally speaking, questions which relate to security and defence armaments are of a national nature because they lie at the very heart of States' sovereignty. Several attempts to create the European Defence Policy were made in the 1950s and 1960s but

---

> 1. The provisions of this Treaty shall not preclude the application of the following rules: (a) No Member State shall be obliged to supply information the disclosure of which it considers contrary to the essential interests of its security; (b) Any Member State may take such measures as it considers necessary for the protection of the essential interests of its security which are connected with the production of or trade in arms, munitions and war material; such measures shall not adversely affect the conditions of competition in the common market regarding products which are not intended for specifically military purposes; 2. During the first years after the entry into force of this Treaty, the Council shall, acting unanimously, draw up a list of products to which the provisions of paragraph 1(b) shall apply; 3. The Council may, acting unanimously on a proposal from the Commission, make changes in this list.

386. Council Regulation (EC) n° 3381/94, *Official Journal*, L 367, 31 Dec. 1994, 0001–0007, in its Preamble reads:

> Whereas, in establishing the internal market, the free movement of goods, including dual-use goods, must be ensured in accordance with the relevant provisions of the Treaty; whereas intra-Community trade in certain dual-use goods is currently subject to controls by the Member States; whereas a condition for the elimination of such controls on intra-Community trade is the application by the Member States of the most effective controls possible, based on common standards, on the export of the aforesaid goods in the framework of a Community regime of exports controls for dual-use goods; whereas the elimination of such controls will improve the international competitiveness of European industry.

both the Pleven Plan[387] and the Fouchet plans[388] failed. A minority of Member States was opposed to transferring competence on such sensitive policies. It was not until the Treaty on European Union (TEU),[389] which entered into force in 1993, that Member States succeeded in creating a Common Foreign and Security Policy (CFSP).[390] Title V of the TEU placed these questions under a separate pillar, with a different decision-making body and an intergovernmental nature. Decisions are made by Member States through the Council, which is different to Trade Policy or the Single Market decisions process. The EU has started to develop Security and Defence Policy as a part of the CFSP, but the export/import of armaments are not yet covered by a European regulation. In other words, there is not one 'European common Licence' to replace twenty-seven nationals' authorizations for the export/import of conventional arm.[391]

The European Commission has, however, long been urging Member States to move towards greater transparency and harmonization of their export control regulations. In its Communication 'Towards a European Union Defence Equipment Policy',[392] dated 2003, the Commission re-emphasized the fact that lack of harmonization affects the competitiveness of Europe's industrial and technological base. Over time, the EU has exercised a larger influence over the conventional arms export systems of its Member States. In 1991, Member States adopted the Council Directive n° 91/477/EEC[393] on the control of the acquisition and possession of weapons, which aims to abolish intra-Community borders' controls on the possession of firearms and partially harmonize national laws on firearms. It lays down categories of firearms which acquisition and possession by private persons are either prohibited or subject to authorization or declaration.

Par. 2 Dual-Use Exports

Dual-use export controls are increasingly more complex and multifaceted than conventional armaments export controls because they fall under both common trade policy and foreign and security policy.

387. The Pleven plan proposed to create an integrated European Army under joint commandment. The negotiation around the plan led to the signature of the Treaty Establishing the European Defence Community. It never came into force because it was rejected by the French National Assembly in 1954.
388. The two Fouchet plans aimed at closer political cooperation, a union of States and a common foreign and defence policies.
389. TEU signed on 7 Feb. 1992 (known as the Maastricht Treaty), updated by 2012/C 326/01 available in its consolidated version at the following Internet Site: http://eur-lex.europa.eu/legal-content/EN/TXT/?uri=CELEX:12012M/TXT.
390. For more information regarding the CFSP please refer to the EU Internet Site at http://europa.eu/pol/cfsp/index_en.htm.
391. The ICT Directive does not include such a European licence (the licences will remain national).
392. Communication from the Commission to the Council, the European Parliament, the European Economic and Social Committee and the Committee of the Regions – European defence – Industrial and market issues – Towards an EU Defence Equipment Policy, n° COM/2003/0113 final, available at http://europa.eu/eur-lex/lex/LexUriServ/LexUriServ.do?uri=CELEX:52003DC0113:EN:HTML.
393. Council Directive n° 91/477/EEC of 18 Jun. 1991 on the control of the acquisition and possession of weapons, *Official Journal* L 256 of 13 Sep. 1991, Corrigendum: *Office Journal* L 299 of 30 Oct. 1991.

Article 296 of the TEC explicitly excludes from the trade competence of the EU certain military items; all other manufactured goods are subject to European law as a consequence a huge majority of product is subject to the common trade policy. Therefore, a specific regime has been implemented for the import/export of dual-use items and technologies in Europe. The first regime entered into force on 1 January 1995.[394] It established a common system to control the import/export of dual-use items to countries which lay outside the EU's common custom borders. The Regulation founds the principal that dual-use items, except those classified in the Regulation as the most sensitive,[395] could be transferred freely inside the EU.

The regime was composed, on the one hand, of a Council Decision n° 94/942/ CFSP and, on the other hand, of the Council Regulation (EC) n° 3381/94.[396] While the Regulation outlined the procedures and how the system worked, the lists of export destinations and controlled items were annexed to the Decision. As a result, the regime was based on two different decision mechanisms. The procedures set out in the Regulation were integrated into European law and placed under the responsibility of the Commission. The establishment, monitoring and updating of the lists was placed by the CFSP under the sole responsibility of the Member States, via the Council. All decisions relating to the lists were thus kept outside the Commission's competence because it was considered that decisions about the lists should be made by Member States given that they were of a strategic and political nature.[397]

In 2000, the regime was revised and a new Council Regulation was adopted.[398] The adoption of the Regulation followed two decisions of the European Court of Justice (ECJ),[399] which ruled that dual-use items were subject to the common Trade Policy. It determined that, while the individual security interests of Member States in this field should be taken into account, trade measures (including export controls) were in fact a matter of exclusive Community competence, under Article 133 (ex-113) TEU. The new Regulation thus abandoned the 'cross-pillar approach', and was adopted as a single document which placed both the control of dual-export procedures and the elaboration and revision of the lists under the sole responsibility of the Commission.

Such a decision opens a new approach of the Dual-Use Goods control Regime where National sovereignty applies only to the most sensitive items.

394. Council Regulation (EC) n° 3381/94, *supra* n. 386, and Council Decision n° 94/942/CFSP of 19 Dec. 1994 on the Joint Action adopted by the Council on the basis of Article J.3 of the TEU concerning the control of exports of dual-use goods (Council Decision 94/942/CFSP: *Office Journal* L 367 of 31 Dec. 1994; Bull. 12-1994, point 1.3.2).
395. See discussion *infra* Chapter 6, Section 4, Sub-Section 2.
396. Council Regulation (EC) n° 3381/94, *supra* n. 386.
397. *Ibid.* The Preamble of the Regulation reads:

> Whereas common lists of dual-use goods, destinations and guidelines are essential elements for an effective control system; whereas decisions concerning the content of these lists are of a strategic nature and consequently fall within the competence of the Member States; whereas those decisions are the subject of joint action pursuant to Article J.3 of the Treaty on European Union.

398. Regulation (EC) n° 1334/2000, (cf. *OJEU* L 159/1 of 30.6.2000).
399. See European Court of Justice (ECJ), Case C 83/94 *Leifer* Judgment of 17 Oct. 1995 and ECJ, Case C-70/94 *Werner*, Judgment of 17 Oct. 1995, Rec. I-3189.

Dual-Use items are today under the Commercial Regime even if related to Nuclear, stealth or space launchers and optic satellites.[400]

Sub-Section 3 Participation in International Regimes

Almost all EU Member States are parties to all international treaties concerning disarmament and non-proliferation. They are therefore committed to controlling imports/exports of goods in conformity with their international commitments.[401]

It is worth noting that all twenty-eight EU Member States are members of the Australia Group and the Nuclear Suppliers Group. Among the twenty-eight EU Member States, nine are not yet parties to the Missile Technology Control Regime (MTCR), but they have already joined the Wassenaar Arrangement. Within the framework of these arrangements, States have promised to each other that they will take steps to control the export and transfer of listed items and technologies. The EU Dual-Use Regulation is a reflection of Member States' participation in these regimes; it covers all the items and technologies listed under the said international regimes.

The European Community, as an organization, through the European Commission, participates in international export control regimes either as a member or as an observer.[402] The fact that, in most cases, the European Community is not a member of all these regimes, results in uncoordinated positions of the Member States. This is another illustration of the difficulty to ensure the balance between National Sovereignty and Community leadership.

However, unlike Council Regulation n° 428/2009,[403] none of these international export control regimes provide for the free circulation of the listed items between its members, neither do they provide for harmonized procedures.

SECTION 4 CONTROL REGIME

Sub-Section 1 Military Goods and Services

Par. 1 Overall Presentation

There exists no common regime in the EU for arms exports. Each Member State sets up its own policy and procedures for the export of arms.[404] However, since June 2009, the ICT Directive gives a real framework to the Member States to organize and implement their national export control common regime.

400. Amal Rakibi. *L'utilisation duale des technologies spatiales - Entre impératifs sécuritaires et émancipation commerciale.* Thèse: Université Paris XI, 2009, 606.
401. Please refer to the Chapter on international regimes.
402. See Chapter on international regimes. A member is considered by other members of the regime as an independent participant with full rights. A simple observer is allowed to participate with limited rights.
403. See *supra* n. 230.
404. Please refer to national legislations and foreign policies on arms exports, as well as to the national executive agencies responsible for carrying out specific tasks and implementing the domestic policy (some of which are covered in others Chapters of the present Handbook on Export Control).

Member States have long acknowledged that coherence is desirable. Such coherence is now to be reached through the implementation of ICT Directive including procedures to facilitate gradual harmonization, and to improve information sharing by circulation of national reports common works on arms export policies and practices.

The EU Code of Conduct for Arms Exports, adopted in 1998 under the CFSP, is a clear example of the determination of Member States to cooperate in the field of conventional armaments exports. It is intended to provide some guidelines for exports/ imports. This compensation has been improved by the adoption of the Common Position n° 944/2008 PESC which makes binding the recommendations of the Code of Conduct. In 2000, the six major arms producing European countries (France, Germany, Italy, Spain, Sweden and the United Kingdom (UK)) established a Framework Agreement[405] which is linked to a LoI, signed between the Defence ministries of such countries in 1998.[406] Farnborough Framework Agreement details the six partners' own rules on transfers and exports for both governmental and industrial cooperative programmes and other exchanges. Strictly speaking the LoI is not part of the CFSP Framework,[407] even if the ICT Directive provides that such cooperation is to be maintained.

Par. 2 Increased Discussion and Cooperation on Conventional Armaments in Europe

Sub-Par. 1 The Code of Conduct for Arms Exports[408]

The Common Position n° 944/2008[409] has reinforced the European Code of Conduct of Arms Exports which was adopted in June 1998 by the Member States as part of the

405. 'Farnborough Framework Agreement' concerning Measures to Facilitate the Restructuring and Operation of the European Defence Industry of 27 Jul. 2000 (available at the following Internet site: http://data.grip.org/documents/200904221112.pdf).
406. The Letter of Intent (LoI) of 6 Jul. 1998, signed by the Ministers of Defence of France, Germany, Italy, Spain, the United Kingdom and Sweden (which together represent 90% of the EU Defence-related material production) and the LoI related Framework Agreement of 27 Jul. 2000:

   > between the French Republic, the Federal Republic of Germany, the Italian Republic, the Kingdom of Spain, the Kingdom of Sweden and the United Kingdom of Great Britain and Northern Ireland, concerning Measures to Facilitate the Restructuring and Operation of the European Defence Industry.

407. Burkard Schmitt. *A Common European Export Policy for Defence and Dual-Use Items?* The Institute for security studies western EU, 2001. This paper was first published as *Working Paper* n° 9 by the Study Group on Enhancing Multilateral Export Controls for US National Security (The Henry L. Stimson Center/Center for Strategic and International Studies, April 2001), http://www.iss.europa.eu/fr/publications/detail-page/article/a-common-european-export-policy-for-defence-and-dual-use-items-1/.
408. Code of Conduct for Arms Exports, 8 Jun. 1998, *Official Journal*, 2003/C 320/01, also available at www.fas.org/asmp/campaigns/code/eucodetext.htm.
   The Council of European Union set up in 2009 guidelines for the utilization of the Code. Last update is available on http://register.consilium.europa.eu/pdf/en/09/st09/st09241.en09.pdf.
409. Common Position 2008/944 PESC of 8 Dec. 2008 of the European Council *Official Journal* L355/99, 99 of 13 Dec. 2008.

CFSP. This Code sets common standards for managing the control of imports/exports of conventional armaments. In particular, it lists eight criteria, which constitute the policy, sets out guidelines for the enforcement such as circumstances in which licences should not be granted. It also defines mechanisms for information exchange, consultation, and to follow-up procedures.

When examining an export application for conventional armaments, Member States take into consideration the following eight criteria:

(1) respect for the international commitments of EU Member States, in particular the sanctions decreed by the United Nations (UN) Security Council and those decreed by the EU, agreements on non-proliferation and other subjects, as well as other international obligations;
(2) respect for human rights in the country of final destination;
(3) awareness of the internal situation in the country of final destination, such as the existence of tensions or armed conflicts;
(4) preservation of regional peace, security and stability;
(5) national security of the Member States and of territories whose external relations are under the responsibility of a Member State, as well as that of friendly and allied countries;
(6) behaviour of the buyer country with regards to the international community, as regards in particular its attitude to terrorism, the nature of its alliances and respect for international law;
(7) existence of a risk that the equipment will be diverted within the recipient country or re-exported under undesirable conditions; and
(8) compatibility of the arms exports with the technical and economic capacity of the recipient country, taking into account the desirability that States should achieve their legitimate needs of security and defence with the least diversion of armaments of human and economic resources.

Along with these eight considerations, the Code establishes a denial information exchange and consultation rules with an undercut procedure. EU Member States circulate details of any licence refused for military equipment, and comments on the reasons why the licence has been denied. Before any Member State grants a licence that has been denied by another Member State (or States), within the last three years, for an 'essentially identical' transaction, it should first consult the Member State which issued the denial(s) to get a possible 'preliminary agreement'. If the (at least) two Member States cannot come to an agreement, the Member State which wants to export could nevertheless decide to approve the licence (undercut). In that case, the exporting Member State has to notify the Member State or States which issued the denial(s), giving a detailed justification of its decision. Ultimately, the final decision remains always at the national discretion of each Member State.

The Code is one of the pillars of the EU common policy for conventional arms export controls. The Code of Conduct provides the publication of an annual report by each Member State on its defence exports and Code enforcement. Such reports are discussed and approved in an annual meeting of the Council working group on conventional arm export (COARM).

The COARM plays a central role in the discussion of arms transfer issues within the EU; it is in charge of reviewing experiences in implementing the Code over the preceding year, and defining work programmes for the next twelve months. Since the discrepancies in national control lists have always been a major source of incoherence, the biggest success of the COARM to date has undoubtedly been the development of a common list of military equipment. The COARM list has been adopted by EU as the annex of the ICT Directive. The consequence is that the twenty-eight Member States have now a common Control List as reference for their licensing process.[410]

Sub-Par. 2 The Letter of Intent

Although the LoI was signed in 1998 and its Framework Agreement enacted in 2000, between the six major European arms producing countries in Europe (France, Germany, Italy, Spain, Sweden and the UK), it was not made by or under the authority of the EU. The so-called LoI is in fact a multilateral binding treaty that aims to facilitate the movement of defence goods and services among the six Partners and define common export procedures for mutual cooperation. It sets up a simplified transfers' regime for cooperative armament projects, introducing the Global Project Licence (GPL), which is granted for manufacturing transfers occurring in intergovernmental or industrial programmes and then streamline the export of such systems to third parties countries. In contrast to the dual-use regime, export provisions of the 'GPL' are applied differently to each and every operation and always operate on a case-by-case basis.

Sub-Par. 3 The Assessment of Community Initiatives Related to ICT of Defence Products and the ICT Directive[411]

On 4 December 2007, the European Commission proposed Directive on ICT. Industry underlined the importance of maintaining strict control of all exports of sensitive equipment and technologies and supported this initiative. As national procedures for ICT can advantageously be harmonized and streamlined, while keeping the full responsibility and authority for all export licensing decisions with Member State Governments.

410. Last update is part of the Directive 43/2009 amended by Directive 2014/108/UE, 12 Dec. 2014.
411. The Directive for Intra-Community Transfers (ICT) of military-related products aiming at streamlining and simplifying procedures for Member States is available at http://eur-lex.europa.eu/LexUriServ/LexUriServ.do?uri=OJ:L:2009:146:0001:0036:FR:PDF, amended by Directive 2014/108/UE, 12 Dec. 2014 (update of the controlled list) available at http://eur-lex.europa.eu/legal-content/EN/TXT/?qid=1421533620442&uri=CELEX:32014L0108.

The ICT Directive is an important contribution towards three important aims:

- Facilitating the efficient supply to Member States' Governments and/or Armed Forces of defence items (including goods, spares, services and information).
- Making more efficient the supply of sub-systems and components, usually from small and mid-size companies, to system-integrating companies.
- Enabling unencumbered EU-internal transfers of defence items as part of the integrated development and production processes in European defence companies.

Member States would be free, under national legislation, controls and procedures to use the process envisaged in the ICT Directive to licence imports by 'Certified Enterprises' of supplies from close allies (e.g., NATO).

Also all exporters could benefits from global or general licences to privileged countries.

Sub-Par. 4 Arms Brokering

With respect to arms brokering, the European Council has adopted a Common Position n° 2003/468/CFSP of 23 June 2003[412] which principles are the following:

- Brokering concerns activities of all persons (natural and entities).
- Negotiating or arranging transactions that may involve the transfer of items listed on the EU Common List of Defence-related products from one Third Country (i.e., Non-EU Member State) to any other Third Country or who buy, sell or arrange the transfer of such items that are in their ownership from a Third Country to any other Third Country.
- EU Member States are permitted to implement more stringent rules.

Sub-Section 2 Dual-Use Goods and Services

Par. 1 Overall Presentation

Sub-Par. 1 Scope and Definitions

In the EU Regulation (EC) n° 428/2009, dual-use items are defined as goods and technology developed for civilian uses, but which can be used for military applications and to produce weapons of mass destruction (WMD).[413] Dual-use items are not weapons and they are traded, sometimes very widely, for perfectly legitimate civilian purposes.[414] The EU Regulation (EC) n° 428/2009 also covers intangible transfers of

412. European Council Common Position n° 2003/468/CFSP 'regarding controls on armament brokering',adopted by the EU Member States on 23 Jun. 2003 (EU *Official Journal* L 156 of 25 Jun. 2003, 79).
413. See the Regulation (EC) n° 428/2009, *supra* n. 230, Article 2.
414. *Ibid.*

technology.[415] The control of intangible transfers has not been as efficient as for material, mainly because of the difficulty to clearly characterize all intangible transfers that can be done through traditional tangible means (the 'offline world' already covered by the previous regulation) and by new means of communication (fax, telephone or 'online' media such as emails).[416] The Report to the Commission noted that:

> in practice, the control procedures established at national level had to take account of the constant evolution of communications technology [...]. The basic rule contained in the Regulation is that the exports of items and technologies, including those by new means of communication, is subject to authorisation. However, the Regulation does not cover transfers that take place through the cross-border movements of natural persons (Article 3.3) or data in the public domain.[417]

The scope of the EU Regulation (EC) n° 428/2009 is laid down in its Article 3. It provides that the export of goods and technologies listed in Annex I requires an authorization of export. It further adds (Article 4.2) that goods not listed in this Annex can also sometimes be subject to authorization. It is of interest to note the evolution of the EU Regulation regarding DU Controls. The previous Regulation n° 1334/2000[418] did not address the brokering and transit issues; in the Regulation n° 428/2009, Articles 5 and 6 adds the licences requirements in these cases.

Whereas the general principles and the way of working of the Regulation n°428/2009 are still in force, this Regulation has been update from time to time, in order to fit the Regulations to the evolution of the state of the technology researches and of the Industry needs.

The Annex I listing the controlled items has been updated by a Regulation in 2012 (EC Regulations n° 388/2012, 19 April 2012).[419] These 2012 Regulations integrated in the European list of controlled items the evolution of the controlled lists of the different International Export Control Regimes of 2009 and 2010.

Then annual evolutions of the Annex I took place in 2014 and 2015 through the EC delegated Regulation n° 1382/2014, 22 October 2014 the Commission Delegated Regulation (EU) n° 2015/2420 of 12 October 2015 (cf. Official Journal of the European Union L 340/1 of 24 December 2015).[420] Once again, the purpose of this update of the Regulation was the integration of the evolution of the International Export Control Regimes.

---

415. *Ibid.*
416. Report to the European Parliament and the Council on the implementation of Council Regulation (EC) n° 1334/2000 setting up a Community regime for the control of exports of dual-use items and technology; October 2000-May 2004, 5, http://trade.ec.europa.eu/doclib/docs/2004/september/tradoc_118993.pdf.
417. The Regulation (EC) n° 428/2009, *supra* n. 230 does not apply to cross borders workers who would bring some 'restricted knowledge' to another country everyday (Article 7).
418. Council Regulation n° 1334/2000 of 22 Jun. 2000, *Official Journal*, L 159 of 30 Jun. 2000, 1.
419. EC Regulations n°388/2012, 19 Apr. 2012, http://eur-lex.europa.eu/LexUriServ/LexUriServ.do?uri=OJ:L:2012:129:0012:0280:EN:PDF.
420. EC delegated Regulation n°1382/2014, 22 Oct. 2014, http://eur-lex.europa.eu/legal-content/EN/TXT/?uri=OJ:JOL_2014_371_R_0001.

In addition, as the European Union with the Member States determined that some situations reflected a low degree of sensitivity, the number of Union General Export Authorisations (UGEA) has been increased through the EC Regulation n° 1232/2011, 16 November 2011. The Annex II has been modified in consequence to add five new General Authorisations. As consequence of those export facilities, the Regulation reinforced the obligations of reporting and transparency from the Member States.

In order to simplify the reading of the lecturers, the followings parts of this Chapter will refer only to the Regulation n° 428/2009, but this reference has to be understood as generic and meaning 'Regulation n° 428/2009 including all following updates', presented here above.[421]

Sub-Par. 2 Architecture of the Regulation

The architecture of the Regulation (EC) n° 428/2009 is quite complex. Two different elements have to be taken into account when determining export requirements for a dual-use item; the country of destination of the export and its level of sensitivity which are both equally important (particular consideration is made to the end-use and to the end-user). Specific procedures apply depending on the country of destination and the type of goods exported.

The first twenty-one provisions, following the Preamble lay out, among other things, the definition, scope, export authorizations (types of licences), control procedures, control measures, and cooperation between Member States. They are followed by four Annexes which complement and substantiate on the basic regime laid out in the first part of the document. Whereas Annex III contains Model Forms,[422] in its part (a) and (b), and in its part (c), common elements for publications of general export authorizations, Annexes I, II, and IV can be seen as concentric of sensitivity of the EU Dual-Use products list, with the most sensitive products at the centre (Annex IV), and the less sensitive at the border (Annex I).

Annex I is the cornerstone of the EC Regulation n° 428/2009 since it lists all dual-use items that need an authorization for export outside the EU. This list is a long and comprehensive classification of those dual-use items. The sensitivity of the goods is not taken into consideration in this Annex, goods and technologies are only listed according to their technical characteristics and field of application.[423] This list encompasses many items covered by the international treaties or agreements (e.g., MTCR, Wassenaar, NSG, etc.[424]) such as the core elements of nuclear weapon or equipment needed to build them; pieces of rockets, especially engines and guiding elements; radar stealth coating and other detection systems; bacteria which are particularly dangerous for human beings, animals and crops; space-grade electronic devices and remote sensing elements.

421. The current last Annex I update is of the EC Regulation 428/2009, can be found here: http://eur-lex.europa.eu/legal-content/EN/TXT/PDF/?uri=OJ:L:2015:340:FULL&from=FR.
422. *Ibid.*, at Annex III Part (a) and (b) (referred to in Article 10.1).
423. Categories under Annex I.
424. See Chapter on international regimes.

The most sensitive items of Annex I constitute the Annex IV. For those items, conditions for export are a lot stricter than for the rest of the goods and technologies listed in Annex I. For instance, all goods listed in Annex I can be transported freely within the EU which is not the case for those identified in Annex IV. Part I of Annex IV contains the most restricted devices (nuclear weapon cores and manufacturing equipments, and chemicals used in chemical weapons) whereas Part II contains goods such as missiles parts and stealth technology.

Annex II of the EC Regulation n° 428/2009 modified by EC Regulation n° 1232/2011 sets up the 'UGEA', described at Article 9 of this Regulation. The UGEAs could be described as a lighter regime for the export of the less sensitive dual-use items to certain destination.

Par. 2 Principles Underlying the Regime

The main principle underlying the Regulation n° 428/2009 is the free circulation of dual-use items (except for the most sensitive items listed in the Annex IV of the Regulation) within the twenty-eight Member States. According to this principle, dual-use goods move as freely between Member States as they do within each of them. Effective controls have been established among Member States which include common standards for export to non-European Member States. Exports to non-EU destinations are thus subject to an authorization, which is obtained in the form of a licence.

Sub-Par. 1 Licences for Dual-Use Exports

Articles 9 and 11 define the four different types of licences created under the Regulation (EC) n° 1334/2000.[425] Three of them (individual, national general and global authorizations) are granted by Member states for exports (outside of the EU) of all Dual-Use goods, or transfers within the EU of very sensitive dual-use items (listed in Annex IV) only. The fourth type is UGEA, issued by the European Union for exports and put in application by all Member States,

I UGEA Are Referred to in Article 9 and Detailed in Annex II of EC Regulation n° 428/2009, Modified by EC Regulation n° 1232/2011

This type of Authorisation is designed for export to specific destinations in designated situations which are considered as not so much sensitive.

Although the EU is the 'issuing authority',[426] the decision to grant a licence remains at the Member State level. In order to obtain an UGEA, an exporter must provide the administrative authorities of its Member State with a preliminary 'Internal Control Programme'.

425. *Ibid.*, at Articles 6 and 7.
426. Cf. EU Regulation EC 428/2009 - CHAPTER III : EXPORT AUTHORISATION AND AUTHORISATION OR BROKERING SERVICES – Article 9 1. : A Community General Export Authorisation

All the UGEAs are presented according to the same scheme in the regulation. The 1st part of the UGEA gives the list of items covered by the authorization. The 2nd part designates the eligible destinations and the 3rd precises 'the conditions and the requirements for use' which are different for each UGEA.

As of today, six different UGEAs are in place, each of them corresponds to a specific situation:

- UGEA n°001
  The UGEA n°001 (Annex IIa), inherited from the prior Regulation n° 1334/ 2000 has been reconducted by the EU Regulation n° 428/2009. It aims at facilitating the export of the majority of goods and technologies to seven 'privileged countries' (Australia, Canada, Japan, New Zealand, Norway, Switzerland (including Liechtenstein) and the United States of America). Part 2 of Annex IIa bars its application to the most sensitive goods, (i.e.: items listed in Annex IV and some few others).
  All the following UGEA have been introduced by the EC Regulation n°1232/ 2011, as the European Union determined the low sensitivity of certain exports, and decided to cover them with General Authorizations.
- UGEA n°002 (Annex IIb)
  This Authorisation covers some dual-use items (mainly from the categories 1 and 3) for certain destinations. The eligible products quantity is less wide than the UGEA 001 due to the fact that the listed destinations are allied countries but not at the same level than the seven countries of the UGEA 001.
- UGEA n°003 (Annex IIc)
  This Authorisation is linked to the export after repair or replacement of certain dual-use items (listed in the part 1) for certain destination (Part 2).
- UGEA n°004 (Annex IId)
  This Authorisation covers a large part of the Annex I items to be temporary exported for Exhibition or Fair to certain destination.
- UGEA n°005 (Annex IIe)
  This Authorisation is linked to some items of the Telecommunications category to be exported to certain destinations.
- UGEA n°006 (Annex IIf)
  This Authorisation is related to Chemicals (1C category mainly) to be exported to certain destinations.

---

for certain exports as set out in Annex II is established by this Regulation. 2. For all other exports for which an authorisation is required under this Regulation, such authorisation shall be granted by the competent authorities of the Member State where the exporter is established. Subject to the restrictions specified in paragraph 4, this authorisation may be an individual, global or general authorisation. All the authorisations shall be valid throughout the Community.

II Individual Export Licences (Referred to in Articles 9 and 14.1 and Annex IIIa of Regulation (EC) n° 428/2009)

Individual export licences are not defined by the EU Regulation n° 428/2009. National practices may differ from one Member State to another.[427] They are the most commonly issued type of licences; they could be delivered either for the export of items listed in Annex I or for transfer of very sensitive items listed in Annex IV and subject to the most strict controls. They are delivered to one exporter only for one specific transaction and one particular end-user. Individual licences are valid for, one year, one consignee and one country of destination only.

III General Export Licences (Referred to in Article 9 of EU Regulation n° 428/2009)

The general licence (also referred to as 'national general authorization') offers a simplified procedure for the export of controlled goods to certain destinations. The General Export licence already existed in some countries before the EU Regulation. Presently, it exists in Austria, Croatia, Cyprus, Estonia, Finland, France, Germany, Greece, Hungary, Ireland, Italy, Latvia, Lithuania, Luxembourg, Malta, Netherlands, Poland, Portugal, Romania, Slovakia, Slovenia, Spain, Sweden, United Kingdom[428] It is applicable: (i) to all exporters with respect to a type or category of dual-use goods except for the more dangerous; (ii) to the less sensitive listed destinations; and (iii) is valid to export from any of the twenty-eight EU Member States. The exporter using a general authorization must be registered with the licensing National authorities of the Member State where it resides, and keep records of its exports. When in force, these 'national general authorizations' have to be published in Member States' official journal according to conditions defined in Annex III c.

In addition Member States have to notify the European Commission of any issue or modification of a National General Export Authorization.

IV Global Export Licences (Referred to in Article 9 and Annex IIIa)

Global export licences are defined at Article 9.5[429] of the EC Regulation. Such licences are tailored and granted to one company that need to export regularly certain goods to certain destinations.

427. *Ibid.*, Article 19.
428. Cf. OJEU of 13.2.2015 – C 51/8; 'information note' on Council Regulation (EC) n° 428 /2009 (*supra* n. 230) Information on measures adopted by Member States in conformity with Articles 5, 6, 8, 9, 10, 17 and 22, (2015/C 51/08) §6. (Information provided by Member States in conformity with Article 9(4)(b) of the regulation (national general export authorizations).
429. See the Regulation (EC) n° 428/2009 *supra* n. 230 states that 'Member States shall maintain or introduce in their respective national legislation the possibility of granting a global authorisation' to a specific exporter with respect of a type or category of dual-use item which may be valid for exports to one or more specified countries.

Figure 6.1 explains how the licences are granted, depending on the types of goods and categories of countries the products are exported to.

Figure 6.1 EU Dual Use Goods and Technology Licensing System

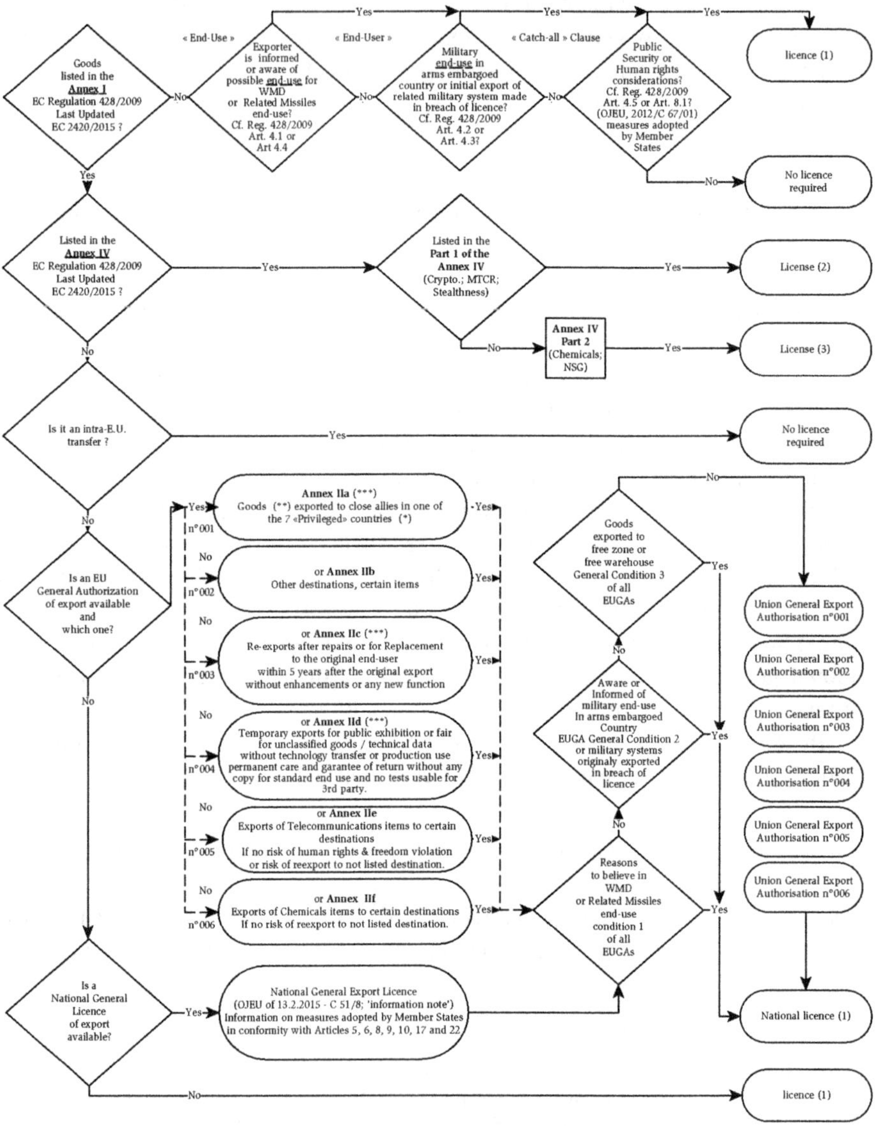

Please refer galley proof for source line format: provide one line space for

(1) Each EU Members states determines which type of EU licence (Individual or Global) is applicable.

(2) For goods and related technologies listed in Annex IV Part 1, Individual or Global EU licences are available.
(3) For goods and related technologies listed in Annex IV Part 2, only Individual licences are permitted.

(*) Seven countries listed in Annex IIa (EC) Regulation n° 428/2009 are the following: Australia, Canada, Japan, New-Zealand, Norway, Switzerland and US.
(**) Nearly all goods listed in Annex I except those listed in Annex IV and few others deemed very sensitive (cf. Annex g).
(***) cf. Annex IIg for possible other not authorized items.

Sub-Par. 2 Denial of a Licence

Member States are required to notify the European Commission when they refuse an export of goods either listed in the Annex I of the Regulation (EC) n° 428/2009[430] or covered by the 'catch-all' mechanism[431] of such a Regulation.[432] EU Member States also retain the individual right to refuse the transfer of certain dual-use items in order to safeguard public policy or public security. The implementation of these criteria is under the sole competence of each EU Member State. In fact, although the EU Regulation n° 428/2009 established that the dual-use export control system was part of the exclusive EU jurisdiction, it makes it clear that the key elements of the system will continue to be implemented at the Member State level, through Member State authorities which are required to provide its enforcement.[433] Hence, the criteria to grant a licence are not listed exhaustively in Article 12 of the Regulation (EC) n° 428/2009.

However, goods subject to control will not be exported as long as one the following concerns should exist:

(1) commitments under international agreements on non-proliferation;
(2) obligations under sanctions imposed by the UN Security Council;
(3) national foreign and security policy; and
(4) the intended end-use and risk of diversion.

States commit themselves to keep information and records about dual-use equipment exported in line with above listed criteria. If a Member State denies a transaction, the competent national authority has to notify its other EU Member States' counterparts, as well as the European Commission. Such exchange of information

430. *Ibid.*, Article 13.
431. *Ibid.*, Articles 4 and 8.
432. *Ibid.*, Articles 4 and 5.
433. *Ibid.* Preamble (recital *n*°5) states:

> The responsibility for deciding on individual, global or national general export authorisations, on authorisations for brokering services, on transits of non-Community dual-use items or on authorisations for the transfer within the Community of the dual-use items listed in Annex IV lies with national authorities. National provisions and decisions affecting exports of dual-use items must be taken in the framework of the common commercial policy, and in particular Council Regulation (EEC) No 2603/69 of 20 December 1969 establishing common rules for exports.

ensures that each licensing authority is kept aware of potential risks of proliferation and/or diversion.

I The 'No-Undercut' Principle

The no-undercut principle aims at preventing a company denied by its authorities to export the same item from another Member State. When an essentially identical transaction has been denied by one or more Member States in the three preceding years, the Member State assessing the new request for authorization has to consult with any Member State that previously denied such an authorization. In the event of disagreement, Member States can consult with the European Commission and justify their positions.[434]

II The Catch-All Clause

The Article 4 of the Regulation (EC) n° 428/2009 provides a mechanism commonly called 'catch-all clause'.

Such mechanism allows Member States to control any (non-sensitive) item and/or technology not listed in the Annexes I of the Regulation (EC) n° 428/2009, when they have reasons to believe that the use of these goods may be diverted for an illicit purpose. For instance, this will be the case when the exporter is informed by its authorities or just 'knows' that a good is intended to be used for a military purpose by a country subject to an arms embargo, or when it suspects a weapon of mass destruction end-use.[435] The provision obliges the exporter to exert extra caution when

434. *Ibid.*, Article 13.5.

435. *Ibid.*, paragraphs 4.1-4.5 list the cases in which the catch-all mechanism applies:

(1) An authorization shall be required for the export of dual-use items not listed in Annex I if the exporter has been informed by the competent authorities of the Member State in which he is established that the items in question are or may be intended, in their entirety or in part, for use in connection with the development, production, handling, operation, maintenance, storage, detection, identification or dissemination of chemical, biological or nuclear weapons or other nuclear explosive devices or the development, production, maintenance or storage of missiles capable of delivering such weapons.

(2) An authorization shall also be required for the export of dual-use items not listed in Annex I if the purchasing country or country of destination is subject to an arms embargo imposed by a decision or a common position adopted by the Council or a decision of the OSCE or an arms embargo imposed by a binding resolution of the Security Council of the United Nations and if the exporter has been informed by the authorities referred to in paragraph 1 that the items in question are or may be intended, in their entirety or in part, for a military end-use. For the purposes of this paragraph, 'military end-use' shall mean:
  (a) incorporation into military items listed in the military list of Member States;
  (b) use of production-, test- or analytical equipment and components therefore, for the development, production or maintenance of military items listed in the abovementioned list;
  (c) use of any unfinished products in a plant for the production of military items listed in the above-mentioned list.

(3) An authorization shall also be required for the export of dual-use items not listed in Annex I if the exporter has been informed by the authorities referred to in paragraph 1 that

exporting technologies. It is the export of goods as a whole that is to be considered by a Member State, either involving technology or not and even if sub-parts of the goods are not themselves controlled when standing alone.

If a Member State makes use of the provision in application of paragraphs 1-5 of Article 4 of the EU Regulation (EC) n° 428/2009, it shall inform the other Member States and the European Commission. The other Member States must give all due consideration to this information and inform, to all the extent possible, their customs offices and all other relevant national agencies.

In addition, Article 8 provides that a Member State may prohibit or impose an authorization to export items not listed in Annex I of the EU Regulation n° 428/2009, for national public security reasons or human rights considerations.

III Sanctions and Recourses of the Importer/Exporter

Sanctions for violations are dealt with by Article 24 of the Regulation (EC) n° 428/2009, and are imposed by Member States national authorities. Each Member State has to lay down in its national legislation the sanctions to be imposed in the event of violations of the EU dual-use export control Regulation. Although the nature of the penalties provided for does not differ much from a Member State to another, the amount of the fine or the duration of the imprisonment could differ dramatically from one Member State to another, which may create discrepancies.

Member States have agreed to respect the export licences commitments issued by any EU partner at the point where goods leave EU territory. In the event of uncertainty or a dispute over specific aspects of a transfer, to solve the case, the relevant national authority in the country from which the goods are to be exported contacts its counterpart which issued the licence. Alternatively, the European Commission can act as a 'clearing-house' to assist both Member States in resolving the case.

Sub-Par. 3 Space-Related Provisions in the Control Regime of Dual-Use Items

In Part I Annex IV of the Regulation (EC) n° 428/2009 (at the very end of part I), MTCR technology items are exempted from the application of Annex IV in four situations if a

the items in question are or may be intended, in their entirety or in part, for use as parts or components of military items listed in the national military list that have been exported from the territory of that Member State without authorization or in violation of an authorization prescribed by national legislation of that Member State.

(4) If an exporter is aware that dual-use items which he proposes to export, not listed in Annex I, are intended, in their entirety or in part, for any of the uses referred to in paragraphs 1, 2 and 3, he must notify the authorities referred to in paragraph 1, which will decide whether or not it is expedient to make the export concerned subject to authorization.

(5) A Member State may adopt or maintain national legislation imposing an authorization requirement on the export of dual-use items not listed in Annex I if the exporter has grounds for suspecting that those items are or may be intended, in their entirety or in part, for any of the uses referred to in paragraph 1.

contractual relationship linked to a space programme exist.[436] Hence, within the framework of a space contract or programme led either by the European Space Agency, a national space agency, or two or more Member State's governmental agencies, the EU Regulation offers a simplified procedure for the export of MTCR technology.

Sub-Par. 4 Reflexions of the European Union Related to the Needed Evolution of the Dual-Use Regulation

The use of the dual-use items is continuously evolving, due to the wide scope of application of those products and to the constant effort of every actors to push the technology researches. The military and dual-use sectors offer by essence a field of competition to the supremacy, and as consequence the regulations controlling the non-proliferation and the export of the related items has to evolve very quickly.

The European Union well understood this strategic dimension, in order to keep the regulation fitted with the industrial and research reality.

The EC Regulation n° 428/2009 in its Article 25 imposes the Commission to assess the implementation and the impact of the regulation through a report to the Parliament and the Council. This report has to be issued every three years, but the Commission has not waited three years to start to issue some communications. The Commission may propose amendments or evolutions to improve the European system of control.

The first demarche of an exam of the situation from the Commission came in 2011, through a Green Paper,[437] which has as purpose to launch a huge public consultation.

This debate led to a document (published by the Commission in 2013).[438] Compiling all the issues raised by about hundred actors who exposed potential regulatory evolutions according to their experiences. The common goal was to improve the regulations in order to lead to an efficient and integrated control, balancing security issues and non-distortion in competition.

436. See Regulation (EC) n° 428/2009 (*supra* n. 230) Annex IV: Exemptions: Annex IV does not control the following items of the MTCR technology that are transferred:

(1) on the basis of orders pursuant to a contractual relationship placed by the European Space Agency or that are transferred by European Space Agency to accomplish its official tasks;
(2) on the basis of orders pursuant to a contractual relationship placed by a Member State's national space organization or that are transferred by it to accomplish its official tasks;
(3) on the basis of orders pursuant to a contractual relationship placed in connection with a Community space launch development and production programme signed by two or more European governments;
(4) to a State-controlled space launching site in the territory of a Member State, unless that Member State controls such transfers within the terms of this Regulation.

437. Green Paper, COM(2011) 393, 30 Jun. 2011: http://trade.ec.europa.eu/doclib/docs/2011/june/tradoc_148020.pdf.
438. SWD(2013) 7, 17 Jan. 2013, http://trade.ec.europa.eu/doclib/docs/2013/february/tradoc_150459.pdf.

In parallel, the European Council reinforced in 2013 the importance of having an efficient control policy with adaptation capabilities.[439]

The heart of the efficiency of the control of dual-use items is the list of the concerned items. The controlled items are the ones representing a specific sensitivity. The technology evolution is very fast, and the preoccupation is to control the new and future dangerous products and to stop controlling obsolescent goods and technologies.

The International Export Control regimes update very regularly their list of control, with the contribution of their experts. The European Union, due to the complexity of regulations issuing process, had some difficulties to update immediately is own regulations to reflect evolutions; it happens that some items waited more than two years to be added in or suppressed from the European List. For the released items, this delay may have a big impact due to the fact that the exports are controlled until the official withdrawal of the list. This weakness has been identified and taken into account by the European Union.

In 2011, the Commission set up a proposition[440] giving it the possibility (on behalf of Parliament and Council) to update on its own the list of controlled dual-use items and to suppress some destinations or to decrease the scope of UGEAs, through 'Delegated Acts'. The Parliament adopted the proposition in the first lecture in October 2012. The proposition has finally been officially adopted through the EC Regulation n° 599/2014, 16 April 2014.[441] This new regulation have direct impact on the efficiency of the control due to the quasi immediate addition of new controlled items in the EU list of control. The Commission used this new possibility quite quickly, to implement the last update of the EU list. On 22 October 2014, the EC Delegated Regulation n° 1382/2014, adopted in furtherance of EC Regulation n° 599/2014, updated the Annex of the Dual-Use EU Regulation to reflect the last evolutions of the Wassenaar Arrangement.

The work of research of an efficient control is still continuing within the European Union, and more specifically through the Commission. Indeed, the Commission issued a Communication to the Parliament and to the Council in April 2014.[442] This new document restates the importance of several subjects which are at the heart of the preoccupation of the States, and presents some reflexions of the Commission:

(1) The continued effort to reduce the risk of proliferation by a 'smart security' approach, through an expert network giving an increased reactivity to the European Union to tackle the new tools and products used by the proliferant actors (cybersecurity, cloud computing, intangible technology transfer, etc.).

439. Council Conclusions on ensuring the continued pursuit of an effective EU policy on the new challenges presented by the proliferation of weapons of mass destruction (WMD) and their delivery systems, 21 Oct. 2013.
440. COM(2011) 704, 7 Nov. 2011, http://trade.ec.europa.eu/doclib/docs/2011/november/tradoc_148340.pdf.
441. EC Regulation n°599/2014, http://trade.ec.europa.eu/doclib/docs/2014/july/tradoc_152647.pdf.
442. COM(2014) 244, 24 Apr. 2014, http://trade.ec.europa.eu/doclib/docs/2014/april/tradoc_152446.pdf.

This will allow fitting the controls to the evolution of the technological, industrial and competitive development.

(2) The automatic update of the EU list of control to avoid any disparity with the various lists of the International Export Control Regimes.

(3) The evolution of terms from 'dual-use items' to 'strategic items', which is a larger notion than the potential use for military purpose or the non-proliferation research, and which includes a wider security concept.

(4) The potential new UGEA to put in place:
   - Low value export (already studied by a working group since 2013)
   - Cryptology
   - Technology transfer intra-enterprise
   - Intra-EU transfer of Annex IV items
   - Wide projects (consideration by the control authorities of a global situation rather than through numerous distinct requests).

(5) The consistent and efficient implementation of the European Regulations by all the Member States.

The evolutions of the European Regulations will certainly follow those reflexions in the coming years.

SECTION 5 LIST OF ABBREVIATIONS

CFSP	Common Foreign and Security Policy
COARM	Council working group on conventional arms
ECJ	European Court of Justice
EU	European Union
GPL	Global Project Licence
LoI	Letter of Intent
MTCR	Missile Technology Control Regime
OSCE	Organization for Security and Co-operation in Europe
TEU	Treaty on the European Union
UGEA	Union General Export Authorisation
WMD	Weapons of Mass Destruction

SECTION 6 REFERENCES

Sub-Section 1 Primary Documentation

Par. 1 Statutory Legislation

- Treaty establishing the European Community (consolidated text), *EU Official Journal*, C 325 of 24 December 2002.

- Treaty instituting the European Union signed on 7 February 1992 (known as the Maastricht Treaty), *EU Official Journal, C 191, 29 July 1992.*

Par. 2 Regulations

- Commission Directive 82/347/EEC of 23 April 1982 laying down certain provisions for implementing Council Directive 81/177/EEC on the harmonization of procedures for the export of Community goods, *EU Official Journal,* L 156, 7 June 1982, 0001–0005.
- Council Directive 81/177/EEC of 24 February 1981 on the harmonization of procedures for the export of Community goods, *EU Official Journal,* L 083, 30 March 1981, 0040–0047.
- Council Regulation (EC) n° 837/95 of 10 April 1995 amending Regulation (EC) n° 3381/94 setting up a Community regime for the control of exports of dual-use goods, *EU Official Journal,* L 090, 21 April 1995, 0001–0001.
- Council Regulation (EC) n° 3381/94 of 19 December 1994 setting up a Community regime for the control of exports of dual-use goods, *EU Official Journal,* L 367, 31 December 1994, 0001–0007.
- Council Directive n° 91/477/EEC of 18 June 1991 on the control of the acquisition and possession of weapons, *EU Official Journal,* L 256 of 13 September 1991; Corrigendum: *Official Journal* L 299, 30 October 1991, available at http://europa.eu.int/scadplus/leg/en/lvb/l14011.htm.
- Council Regulation (EC) n° 1334/2000 of 22 June 2000 setting up a Community regime for the control of exports of dual-use items and technology, *Official Journal,* L 159, 30 June 2000, 0001–0215 as amended and updated (last amendment and update to date by Council Regulation (EC) n° 394/2006 of 27 February 2006 (*Official Journal,* L 74/1, 13 March 2006)). Updated by Regulation n°428/2009 of 5 May 2009, Article 27, with effect from 27 August 2009.
- Council Regulation (EC) n° 1504/2004 of 19 July 2004 amending and updating Regulation (EC) n° 1334/2000 setting up a Community regime for the control of exports of dual-use items and technology, *Official Journal,* L 281, 31 August 2004, 0001–0225. Updated by Regulation n°428/2009 of 5 May 2009, Article 27, with effect from 27 August 2009.
- Council Regulation (EC) n° 1334/2000, amended by Regulation (EC) n° 149/2003: Information on measures adopted by Member States in conformity with Articles 5, 6, 13 and 21, *Official Journal,* C 273, 14 November 2003, 0002–0005. Updated by Regulation n°428/2009 of 5 May 2009, Article 27, with effect from 27 August 2009.
- Council Regulation (EC) n° 1183/2007 of 18 September 2007 amending and updating Regulation (EC) n° 1334/2000 setting up a Community regime for the control of exports of dual-use items and technology, *EU Official Journal* L 278, 22 October 2007, 1–240. Updated by Regulation n° 428/2009 of 5 May 2009, Article 27, with effect from 27 August 2009.

- Council Regulation (EC) n° 880/2002 of 27 May 2002 amending Regulation (EC) n° 1334/2000 setting up a Community regime for the control of exports of dual-use items and technology, *Official Journal* L 139, 29 May 2002, 0007–0008. Updated by Regulation n° 428/2009 of 5 May 2009, Article 27, with effect from 27 August 2009.
- Council Regulation (EC) n° 2432/2001 of 20 November 2001 amending and updating Regulation (EC) n° 1334/2000 setting up a Community regime for the control of exports of dual-use items and technology, *EU Official Journal*, L 338, 20 December 2001, 0001–0214. Updated by Regulation n° 428/2009 of 5 May 2009, Article 27, with effect from 27 August 2009.
- Council Regulation (EC) n° 458/2001 of 6 March 2001 amending Regulation (EC) n° 1334/2000 with regard to the list of controlled dual-use items and technology when exported, *EU Official Journal*, L 065, 7 March 2001, 0019–0019. Updated by Regulation n° 428/2009 of 5 May 2009, Article 27, with effect from 27 August 2009.
- Council Regulation (EC) n° 2889/2000 of 22 December 2000 amending Regulation (EC) n° 1334/2000 with regard to ICT and exports of dual-use items and technology, *EU Official Journal*, L 336, 30 December 2000, 0014–0014.
- Index of items listed in Annex I to Council Regulation n° 1334/2000 of 22 June 2000 setting up a Community regime for the control of exports of dual-use items and technology, *EU Official Journal*, C 241, 23 August 2000, 0001–0072. Updated with the Regulation n° 428/2009 of 5 May 2009, Article 27, with effect from 27 August 2009.
- Council Joint Action of 22 June 2000 concerning the control of technical assistance related to certain military end-uses, *EU Official Journal*, L 159, 30 June 2000, 0216–0217.
- Council Regulation (EC) n° 428/2009 of 5 May 2009 setting up a Community regime for the control of exports, transfers and brokerage of dual-use items, *EU Official Journal*, L 134, 1 of 29 May 2009.
- Regulation (EU) n° 1232/2011 of The European Parliament and of The Council of 16 November 2011 amending Council Regulation (EC) No 428/2009 setting up a Community regime for the control of exports, transfer, brokering and transit of dual-use items.
- Regulation (EU) n° 599/2014 – Delegated Acts: Regulation empowering the EU Commission to modify under certain conditions the EU control list (Annex I) and the list of destinations benefitting from EU-UGEAs (Annex II).
- Commission Delegated Regulation (EU) No 2420/2015 of 12 October 2015 amending Council Regulation (EC) n° 428/2009 setting up a Community regime for the control of exports, transfer, brokering and transit of dual-use item: a Commission Regulation updating the EU list of dual-use items has been published on 24 December 2015 (OJEU L340/1), and entered into force on 25 December 2015.

Par. 3 Other

- Code of Conduct for Arms Exports, 8 June 1998, (*Official Journal,* 2003/C 320/01 and also available at www.fas.org/asmp/campaigns/code/eucodetext .htm).
- Code of Conduct - Common Position 2008/944 PESC 8 December 2008 (OJEU L 335, 99 of 13 December 2008.
- The Council of the European Union defined common rules governing the control of exports of military technology and equipment (Council of European Union, 9241/2009, 29 April 2009, http://register.consilium.europa.eu/pdf/en /09/st09/st09241.en09.pdf).
- The LoI of 6 July 1998, signed by the Ministers of Defence of France, Germany, Italy, Spain, the UK and Sweden (can be found on the Internet site address: projects.sipri.se/expcon/loi/lointent.htm.
- FA of 27 July 2000 'between the French Republic, the Federal Republic of Germany, the Italian Republic, the Kingdom of Spain, the Kingdom of Sweden and the UK of Great Britain and Northern Ireland, concerning Measures to Facilitate the Restructuring and Operation of the European Defence Industry', (can be found on the Internet site address: http://projects.sipri.se/expcon/loi /indrest01.htm).
- Directive of the European Parliament and Council n° 43/2009 of 6 May 2009 'Simplifying terms and conditions of transfers of defence-related products within the Community' (OJEU L 146, 1 of 10 June 2009).

Sub-Section 2 Secondary Documentation

Par. 1 Internet Sites

- http://www.sipri.org/research/disarmament/dualuse (Stockholm International Peace Research Institute)
- http://europa.eu/index_en.htm (European Union)
- *http://ec.europa.eu/trade/import-and-export-rules/export-from-eu/dual-use-cont rols/* (European Union on dual-use export controls (under Trade))
- *http://eeas.europa.eu/non-proliferation-and-disarmament/arms-export-control/ index_en.htm* (European Union External Action)

Par. 2 Paper Publications

- Anthony Eckstein, S. & Zanders, J.P., 'Multilateral military-related export control measures', *S.I.P.R.I. Yearbook 1997.*
- Anthony, I., 'EU approaches to arms control, non-proliferation and disarmament', *S.I.P.R.I. Yearbook App.C, 2001*, available at the following Internet site: www.sipri.org/contents/expcon/08C.pdf.
- Kile, S. *Nuclear arms control.* S.I.P.R.I. Yearbook 1997: Armaments, Disarmament and International Security (Oxford: Oxford University Press, 1997).

- Report to the European Parliament and the Council on the application of Regulation (EC) n° 3381/94 setting up a Community system of export controls regarding dual-use goods, COM/98/0258 final, available at the following Internet site: http://europa.eu.int/eur-lex/lex/Result.do?direct=yes&lang=en&xsl=celex-som,celex-txt&PgSize=128&where=CC:02401030*.
- *The European Code of Conduct for Arms Exports* S.I.P.R.I. Yearbook 1999: Armament and Disarmament and International Security (Oxford: Oxford University Press, 1999).
- Schmitt B. *A Common European Export Policy for Defence and Dual-Use Items?* The Institute for security studies western European Union, 2001. This paper was first published as *Working Paper n° 9 by the Study Group on Enhancing Multilateral Export Controls for US National Security* (The Henry L. Stimson Center/Center for Strategic and International Studies, April 2001), available at www.iss-eu.org/occasion/occ25.html.
- Schmitt B. *From Cooperation to Integration: Defence and Aerospace Industries in Europe.* Chaillot Paper 40 (Paris, Institute for Security Studies of western European Union, July 2000).
- Rakibi A. *L'utilisation duale des technologies spatiales – Entre impératifs sécuritaires et émancipation commerciale.* Thèse, Université Paris XI, 2009, 606 p.

SECTION 7 USEFUL INFORMATION

Sub-Section 1 Enforcement Authorities Contact Details

EU Member States enforcement authorities contact details can be found at the following Internet site (please refer to the document entitled 'EU licensing authorities' contacts and websites'): http://trade.ec.europa.eu/doclib/docs/2011/july/tradoc_148094.pdf.

Please also refer to the chapters of this book dedicated to specific EU Members States regimes for further information.

Sub-Section 2 Other

None.

CHAPTER 7

France

Arnaud Idiart & Marion Ringot

SECTION 1 TABLE OF CONTENTS

SECTION 2 EXECUTIVE SUMMARY

In order to contribute to the strengthening of international security and stability, France has committed itself to many treaties which aim to prevent the proliferation of weapons of mass destruction (WMD), and is an active member of the various multilateral export control regimes. These international commitments and actions are given form in France's Military and Dual-Use Goods Export Control Regulations.

According to the French Code of Defence (CoD),[443] trade and brokering in war products,[444] whose list is defined by the French Code of Homeland Security (Code de la Sécurité Intérieure[445]), is strictly prohibited, unless a Minister of Defence's authorization granted. Only, the Import of 'war weapons/products' (i.e.: not all 'Military Goods') required an import licence granted by the Customs' Director acting upon an inter-ministerial consultation. Exports of all 'Military Goods' including their related components and technology, are prohibited, unless a licence is delivered by the Customs' Director. This licence follows an inter-ministerial consultation of the Inter-ministerial Commission for Evaluation of Exports of Military Goods (CIEEMG)[446] to get the final Prime Minister's agreement expressed by the General Secretary for National Defence and Security ('*Secrétaire Général de la Défense et de la Sécurité Nationale*' (SGDSN)). This systems applies for any export, including subcontracts for sourcing abroad studies and design of subsystems, answers to foreign requests for proposal (RFP), Such prohibition rules constitute a complete exception to the common freedom of trade and industry principle.

Indeed, a first export approval is mandatory for the negotiation and acceptance of any contract regarding the export of 'Military products/equipment' and afterwards a Licence is required for the shipment of the related deliverables. Up to June 2014, this export licensing process required one specific licence for each of these two steps ('pre' and 'post' acceptance of an order). Today, for business in military goods and exports the mandatory clearances are the following: (i) for 'war weapons/products' the Authorization of Manufacturing and/or Trading and/or Brokering on the French territory ('*Autorisation de Fabrication, de Commerce et d'Intermédiation*' (AFCI), granted by the Minister of Defence); (ii) for all military products (hardware, software

443. The CoD, legislative part, was adopted by Order n° 2004-1374 of 20 Dec. 2004 and ratified through the law by the French Parliament n° 1550 on 12 Dec. 2005. Its relevant provisions have thus replaced the fundamental Legislative Decree of 18 Apr. 1939 'creating a regime governing war material, arms and munitions', while maintaining the same basic rules.
444. In this chapter, (a) 'War products' or 'War Equipment' shall mean items specifically listed by the Article L.2331-I. 1° / category A2 of the CoD; the list of 'war materials, weapons and ammunitions and related elements' are more precisely defined by the Article 2 of the Decree n° 2014-1253 of 27 Oct. 2014, concerning the provisions of the books III, VI et VII of the Regulatory part of the Code of Home Security (JORF n° 0251 of 29 Oct. 2014, p. 7908).
445. Loi n° 2003-239 du 18 mars 2003 (JORF n° 66 of 19 mars 2003, p. 4761).
446. CIEEMG: Décret n° 2012-1176 of 23 Oct. 2012 'modifiant le décret n° 55-965 du 16 juillet 1955 portant réorganisation de la commission interministérielle pour l'étude des exportations de matériels de guerre' (JORF n° 0249 du 25 Oct. 2012, p. 16577).

and/or related technology and/or services), the export Licence ('la Licence'[447]). The Licence is a single document authorizing all commercial operations: from the negotiation through the acceptance of an export contract, to the shipment of the related products. The Licence is granted by the French Prime Minister in light of an inter-ministerial (CIEEMG) assessment of the whole operation. It is delivered by the Director General of Customs.[448] The existing strict legislative and regulatory framework has been adapted to comply with European rules and principles.[449]

The *export* control regime applies to 'Assimilated Goods'[450] (i.e., military goods not classified as 'war weapons/products') and 'war weapons/products'.[451]

For Dual-Use goods and technology, the French export control regime is also very stringent and formal. Dual-Use goods are controlled in France under an European

---

447. Hereinafter also referred to as 'Export Licence'. One unique licence replaces since 4 Jun. 2014, the two previous authorizations: the Prime minister '*Agrément Préalable*' (AP or Preliminary Agreement), and the '*Autorisation d'Exportation de Matériel de Guerre*' (Authorisation of Export of Military Good - AEMG).
448. The whole process involves the Prime Minister, the General Secretary for National Defence and Security ('*Secrétaire Général de la Défense et de la Sécurité Nationale*' - 'SGDSN'), the Ministry of Defence ('MoD' DGA/Division Internationale/sous-direction de la gestion des procédures de contrôle), the Ministry of Foreign Affairs and International Development (Sous-direction du contrôle des armements et de l'Organisation pour la sécurité et la coopération en Europe (OSCE); and the Ministry of Economy, Economic Regeneration and Digital Economy (a) the General Directorate of Treasury and Economy Policy DGTPE and (b) the General Directorate for Customs and Indirect Taxes ('*Direction Générale des Douanes et des Droits Indirects*' - 'DGDDI' - Sous-direction E. Commerce international).
449. These rules and principles result from the (EU) Code of Conduct (CoC) for Arms Exports of 8 Jun. 1998 (www.fas.org/asmp/campaigns/code/eucodetext.htm); *EU Official Journal*, 2003/C 320/01. In 2008, the CoC evolved into a legally binding Council Common Position, defining the common rules governing the control of exports of military technology and commodities (2008/944 CSEP). These documents establish eight common criteria applicable to national conventional arms export policies. Additional rules come from the implementation of the 'Letter of Intent' (LoI) of 6 Jul. 1998, signed by the Ministers of Defence of France, Germany, Italy, Spain, the United Kingdom and Sweden, which together represent 90% of the EU Defence-related production material. LoI principles have been enforced by the LoI Framework Agreement of 27 Jul. 2000:

    > between the French Republic, the Federal Republic of Germany, the Italian Republic, the Kingdom of Spain, the Kingdom of Sweden and the United Kingdom of Great Britain and Northern Ireland, concerning Measures to Facilitate the Restructuring and Operation of the European Defence Industry.

    Finally, in 2011, France transposed the EU Directive n° 2009/43 of 6 May 2009 simplifying terms and conditions of transfers of defence-related products within the Community.
450. In the present chapter, 'Assimilated Goods' means any elements related to 'Military Goods', that is to say components, elements, parts, sub-assemblies, subsystems and associated documentation software technology and services specifically designed for defence-related products (categories listed in the Decree 2014-1253. These 'assimilated' products are specified in the Order of 16 Mar. 2015; (*JORF n° 0065 du 18 mars 2015 page 5033) modifiant l'arrêté du 27 juin 2012 relatif à la liste des matériels de guerre et matériels assimilés soumis à une autorisation préalable d'exportation et des produits liés à la défense soumis à une autorisation préalable de transfert.*
451. *Note*: two main differences between 'Assimilated Goods' and 'Assimilated Goods': for the second category, (a) the AFC is not mandatory for trade on the French territory and (b), no import licence is required for their imports in France.

Union (EU) Regulations. Licences are required[452] for most 'sensitive' intra-Community transfers; i.e.: goods which are only listed in a specific control Annex of the EU Regulation.[453] Since 1995, this regime follows an European common law lastly recast by the Council Regulation (EC) n° 428/2009 of 5 May 2009.[454] DU licensing Sensitive cases follow an inter-ministerial process[455] but, (a) the export decision is always made by the Minister in charge of Industry (Ministry of Economy, Economic Regeneration and Digital economy),[456] and (b) the notification rests within the hands of the Customs General Directorate.

In respect of imports, only the products classified as 'war weapons/products'[457] (i.e.: not the 'assimilated' military products and/or Dual-Use goods) require an import licence.[458]

Imports of 'Assimilated Goods' as well as Dual-Use goods and technology do not require any specific import licence.

Criminal and administrative sanctions, applicable in case of failure, violation and/or non-compliance are foreseen by the CoD, the Criminal Code (Code penal) and the Customs Code.

In addition, France has specific intellectual property rules; accordingly transfers abroad of industrial property rights and/or intellectual elements (notably, know-how) must be declared with the French National Institute of Industrial Property.[459] There are also specific regulatory provisions addressing exports of Space-related goods. Civil and military remote-sensing satellites, military telecom satellites and launchers are dealt under the 'Military Goods' export procedure, whereas civil telecom satellites, related equipment and ground stations follow the Dual-Use Goods and Technology Export Control Regime.

452. The DU licence is mandatory only to ship goods (not for contract negotiation) consequently it could be granted after the contract has been signed.
453. Cf. Annex IV of the Council Regulation (EC) n° 428/2009, *supra* n. 230.
454. *Ibid.* Annexes (lists of DU goods and technologies) of this Regulation has been lastly updated by Commission Delegated Regulation (EU) n° 1382/2014 (cf. Official Journal of the European Union L 371/1 of 30.12.2014).
455. The standard process is less formal: the 'Service des Biens à Double Usage' (Service for Dual-Use Goods - SBDU) on behalf of the Ministry in charge of Industry, assesses the operation on its own. It possibly asks the support of one or two Agencies such as SGDSN, MoFA, MoD and Intelligence Services. The most sensitive cases are escalated by the SBDU to an inter-ministerial Commission (chaired by Foreign Affairs Ministry and including the following Departments: SGDSN, Economy (Industry, Commerce, Customs) Home Affairs, Health, Research, Defence, Agriculture, and Energy).
456. In French, 'Ministère de l'Économie, du Redressement productif et du Numérique'.
457. The control of *imports* of War Weapons/Products follows a process close to the one used for controlling the Military Goods *exports* and, in addition, it includes generally a consultation of the *'Ministère de l'intérieur'* (Home Affairs Department).
458. Importers have to (a) be authorized (the 'AFCI', granted by the Minister of Defence, is mandatory even on the French territory to manufacture and trade of 'War Products/ equipment'), and (b) to obtain an import licence from the General Director for Customs and Indirect Taxes (*'Directeur Général des Douanes et des Droits Indirects'* (DGDDI)).
459. INPI, 15 rue des minimes - 92677 Courbevoie Cedex - Phone: 0 820 213 213 - Mail: iledefrance@inpi.fr.

SECTION 3 INTRODUCTION: ELEMENTS OF CONTEXT

Sub-Section 1 Overall Philosophy

Par. 1 Export Control Regime for Military Goods

The French control regime for the export of military goods is based on the following strict legislative and regulatory general principal: *exports of Defence related products are 'prohibited unless and until authorized'*. The French Export control has a strong political dimension, closely linked to the National's foreign policy; in particular, France strictly observes the right of self-defence[460] of each and every UN Member State.

More and more, the French export control of military goods does not *primarily* focus on how sensitive the goods are, but rather gives importance to their destination (end-use and/or end-user). The level of scrutiny depends mainly on the sensitivity of the receiving persons (individuals, companies or governments). Moreover, a 'programme approach' is possible, so that, for instance, within the framework of the Ariane launcher, NH90 helicopter, A400M military transport aircraft, ... programmes, all exchanges of any products between Members States cooperating in the programme benefit from a general licence exemption according to the Arrêté of 2 June 2014 related to the licence exemption for exports out of the EU territory, 'war weapons/products, and ammunitions and other assimilated products'.[461]

Par. 2 Export Control Regime for Dual-Use Goods

The French export control regime for Dual-Use goods and technology follows the European regime, established by the Council Regulation (EC) n° 428/2009.[462] The ability of the French Government/Administration to establish their own rules regarding Dual-Use Exports still exists but is less and less used.

Par. 3 Military and Dual-Use Services

The export of military services and dual-use services is not specifically addressed in the present chapter, as for now there is no *specific* regulatory framework to cover this matter in France. However, this topic, closely linked to the issue of 'intangible transfers', is being studied by French authorities, in the coordination with international fora such as the Wassenaar Arrangement or the Missile Technology Control Regime (MTCR).

---

460. Upheld by Article 51 of the United Nations Charter (https://treaties.un.org/doc/publication/ctc/uncharter.pdf), signed at San Francisco on 26 Jun. 1945 that entered into force on 24 Oct. 1945.
461. Cf. 'Arrêté du 2 juin 2014 relatif aux dérogations à l'obligation d'obtention d'une licence d'exportation hors du territoire de l'Union européenne des matériels de guerre, armes et munitions et de matériels assimilés ou d'une licence de transferts intracommunautaires de produits liés à la défense' (JORF n° 0129 of 5 Jun. 2014, p. 9453).
462. Cf. Council Regulation (EC) n° 428/2009 *supra* n. 230.

Par. 4 Process to Be Followed by Exporters According to the French Control Regime

Before any export consideration regarding military or Dual-Use goods or technology, exporters must check whether Military Goods ('war weapons/products' and 'Assimilated'), or Dual-Use goods regulations, could apply.

Practically, exporters have first to check whether the goods they intend to export are, or not, listed by Regulations. For all classification issues, they can seek for guidelines and/or commodity jurisdiction from French officials: the Ministry of Defence (MoD) for 'Military Goods', and, for Dual-Use goods, Ministry of Economy, Economic Regeneration and Digital economy. Then, exporters are strongly encouraged to gather information as precise and comprehensive as possible on the end-user and final use of their goods.

Finally, exporters must check whether the goods to be exported contain, or not, any components, sub-parts, or 'embedded' software or 'commingled' technology which could be subject to specific constraints under foreign regulations (in particular, the American ones: International Traffic in Arms Regulations (ITAR) and/or Export Administration Regulations (EAR)[463]).

Sub-Section 2 Historical Outlook

Par. 1 Military Goods

Up to 2005, the cornerstone of the French control regime was the 'Legislative Decree' of 18 April 1939 'creating a regime governing war weapons/products, arms and munitions', which set up the current principle of 'prohibition': export of military items is forbidden, without a specific licence.[464] The Legislative Decree of 18 April 1939 was in a first step modified by the laws n° 2001-1062 of 15 November 2001[465] and n° 2003-239 of 18 March 2003, and was finally replaced by provisions of the 2004 CoD.[466] The Code is now referred to as the main text of the national regulatory framework on military goods control; CoD provisions are substantially similar to those of the above-mentioned 'Legislative Decree', and the basic principles remain the same. Since 2005, the Export control principles and rules are codified by the 'Code de la Defense'.

463. Cf. *infra* in this book the chapter on the United States of America export control regime.
464. Since 1939, Decrees and various Orders have been taken by the French government in application of the 'Legislative Decree', for example Decree n° 95-589 of 6 May 1995 for enforcement of the Legislative Decree and the Order of 17 Jun. 2009, which established the French export control list of war weapons/products and assimilated materials subject to the special export procedure.
465. OJ 266, 16 Nov. 2001, 18215.
466. The CoD, legislative part, was adopted by Ordinance n° 2004-1374 of 20 Dec. 2004 and last modified by the French Parliament on 28 Nov. 2005 (National Assembly/ adopted text n° TA 503) ratified by Law n° 2005-1550 of 12 Dec. 2005 (OJ 289, 13 Dec. 2005, p. 19160).

In October 2014, the new French classification of the war weapons/products and ammunitions was codified in the Code of Home Security (Article R311-2).[467]

By the end of the 1990s, France as well as the vast majority of the EU Member States has to compromise between its will and the necessity to build European common export control rules and its sovereignty regarding Military Goods transfers. Indeed the regulatory national autonomy automatically decreased as soon as each Member State commits itself to comply with EU common rules. For instance, since 1998, France adapted its control regime to comply with the recommendations of the EU Code of Conduct (CoC) for Arms Exports of 8 June 1998,[468] and the so-called Letter of Intent (LoI) of 6 July 1998,[469] and its related Framework Agreement of 27 July 2000.[470]

Par. 2 Dual-Use Goods

The French export control regime for Dual-Use goods and technology was originally based on a Decree of 1944. Since 1995, however, the regime is based on the European law, as updated by Regulation (EC) n° 428/2009.[471] Such Regulation is complemented in France by the Decree n° 2001-1192 of 13 December 2001 'relating to the control of exports, imports and transfers of Dual-Use goods and technology'.

Sub-Section 3 Participation in International Regimes

In order to contribute to the strengthening of international security and stability, France participates in the international fight against the proliferation of WMD and their means of delivery, and has committed itself to a number of international treaties. It is also an

467. This new codification was defined by the law n° 2012-304 of 6 Mar. 2012 related to the establishment of a simple and preventive control of modern arms (JORF n° 0057 du 7 mars 2012, p. 4200). Categories content were précised by the Decret 2014-1253 of 27 Oct. 2014. Regarding exports, today the list of the products subject to the special military export control procedure is given by the Arrêté of 27 Jun. 2015, lastly updated by the Arrêté of 16 Mar. 2015.
468. Code of Conduct (CoC) for Arms Exports of 8 Jun. 1998 (www.fas.org/asmp/campaigns/code/eucodetext.htm); (*EU Official Journal*, 2003/C 320/01). Since 2008, the CoC is a legally binding Council Common Position which defines the common rules governing the control of exports of military technology and equipment (2008/944 CSEP). These documents establish eight common criteria applicable to conventional arms national export policies.
469. *Ibid*. The 'Letter of Intent' (LoI) of 6 Jul. 1998, signed by the Ministers of Defence of France, Germany, Italy, Spain, the United Kingdom and Sweden, which together represent 90% of the EU Defence-related production material. Finally, in 2011, France transposed the EU Directive n° 2009/43 of 6 May 2009 simplifying terms and conditions of transfers of defence-related products within the Community.
470. *Ibid*. LoI principles have been enforced by the LoI Framework Agreement of 27 Jul. 2000:

> between the French Republic, the Federal Republic of Germany, the Italian Republic, the Kingdom of Spain, the Kingdom of Sweden and the United Kingdom of Great Britain and Northern Ireland, concerning Measures to Facilitate the Restructuring and Operation of the European Defence Industry.

This agreement entered into force on the 18 Apr. 2001 and was ratified by France through the Presidential Decree n° 2001-1075 of 16 Nov. 2001, (cf. OJ 291, 15 Dec. 2001, p. 19905).
471. Cf. EU chapter, *supra* n. 230.

active member of the various multilateral export control regimes and suppliers groups which establish common control rules, lists of sensitive materials whose exports are subject to strict control, and provide for partners exchanges of information.

These international commitments and actions are reflected in France's national military good and Dual-Use goods export control procedures.

The following tables display France's participation status to export control international treaties and programmes. For each one it is mentioned how France is part of it either by signature, ratification or by accession.

Par. 1 Treaties and Regimes Dealing with Specific Items and Technologies

Table 7.1 Nuclear Weapons Treaties

Treaty Name	*Overall Status*	*Specific Status*	*Enforceable in France*
	Test Ban		
Limited Test Ban Treaty[472]	OS: 5 August 1963 EF: 10 October 1963	–	No
Comprehensive Nuclear Test Ban Treaty[473]	OS: 24 September 1996 EF: not in force	S: 24 September 1996 R: 6 April 1998	No
	Non-proliferation		
Nuclear Non-Proliferation Treaty[474]	OS: 1 July 1968 EF: 5 March 1970	A: 2 August 1992	Yes
IAEA Comprehensive Safeguards Agreement(s)[475]	EF: 12 September 1981 S: 26 September 2000[476]	N/A[477]	Yes
IAEA Model Additional Protocol[478]	S: 22 September 1998 EF: 30 April 2004	N/A[479]	Yes

OS: Opened for signature; EF: Entry into force; S/R: Signature/Ratification; A: Accession.

472. Treaty Banning Nuclear Weapon Tests in the Atmosphere, in Outer Space and Under Water, *UNTS*, vol. 480, 43.
473. UNGA, resolution 50\245.
474. Treaty on the Non-Proliferation of Nuclear Weapons, *UNTS*, vol. 729, 161.
475. Agreement Between the Agency and States Required in Connection with the Treaty on the Non-Proliferation of Nuclear Weapons (NPT), INFCIRC/153 (Corrected).
476. The safeguards agreement referred to is pursuant to Additional Protocol I to the Treaty of Tlatelolco.
477. This treaty is a bilateral one and, accordingly, the differences that apply to multilateral treaties (between the overall status and the specific status) do not apply.
478. Model Protocol Additional to the Agreement(s) between State(s) and the Agency for the Application of Safeguards, INFCIRC/540(Corrected).
479. This treaty is a bilateral one and, accordingly, the differences that apply to multilateral treaties (between the overall status and the specific status) do not apply.

Table 7.2 Biological and Chemical Weapons Treaties

Treaty Name	*Overall Status*	*Specific Status*	*Enforceable in France*
Geneva Protocol[480]	OS: 17 June 1925 EF: 8 February 1928	S: 17 June 1925 R: 10 May 1926	Yes
Biological Convention[481]	OS: 10 April 1972 EF: 26 March 1975	A: 27 September 1984	Yes
Chemical Convention[482]	OS: 13 January 1993 EF: 29 April 1997	S: 13 January 1993 R: 2 March 1995	Yes

OS: Opened for signature; EF: Entry into force; S/R: Signature/Ratification; A: Accession.

Table 7.3 Conventional Arms

Treaty Name	*Overall Status*	*Specific Status*	*Enforceable in France*
Arms Trade Treaty (ATT),	DA: 2 April 2013 EF: 25 September 2013	S: 3 June 2013 R: 2 April 2014	Yes
Protocol on Firearms to the Convention against Transnational Organized Crime[483]	DA: 31 May 2001 EF: 3 July 2005	–	**No**
Convention on anti-personnel mines[484]	OS: 18 September 1997 EF: 1 March 1999	R: 23 July 1998	Yes

OS: Opened for signature; DA: Date of adoption; EF: Entry into force; S/R: Signature/Ratification; A: Accession.

480. Protocol for the Prohibition of the Use in War of Asphyxiating, Poisonous or Other Gases, and of Bacteriological Methods of Warfare, 94, *League of Nations Treaty Series*, n°. 2138 (1929).
481. Convention on the Prohibition of the Development, Production and Stockpiling of Bacteriological (Biological) and Toxin Weapons and On Their Destruction, *UNTS*, vol. 1015, 163.
482. Convention on the Prohibition of the Development, Production, Stockpiling and Use of Chemical Weapons and on Their Destruction, Doc.CD/CW/WP.400/Rev.1.
483. Protocol against the Illicit Manufacturing of and Trafficking in Firearms, Their Parts and Components and Ammunition, supplementing the United Nations Convention against Transnational Organized Crime, A/RES/55/225.
484. Convention on the Prohibition of the Use, Stockpiling, Production and Transfer of Anti-Personnel Mines and on their Destruction, *ATS*, 1999, n° 3.

Table 7.4 Multilateral Export Control Regimes

Regime Name	*Formation*	*Participation*
Zangger Committee[485]	1971	Yes
Nuclear Suppliers Group	1974	Yes
Australia Group	1985	Yes
Missile Technology Control Regime	1987	Yes
Wassenaar Arrangement[486]	1994	Yes

Table 7.5 Others

Name	*Adoption*	*Participation*
UN Register on Conventional Arms[487]	9 December 1991	Yes[488]
Programme of Action on Small Arms and Light Weapons[489]	20 July 2001	Yes
International Code of conduct[490]	25 November 2002	Yes

Par. 2 Treaties Dealing with Specific Areas

Table 7.6 International Zones

Treaty Name	*Overall Status*	*Specific Status*	*Enforceable in France*
Antarctic Treaty[491]	OS: 1 December 1959 EF: 23 June 1961	S: 1 December 1959 R: 16 September 1960	Yes
Outer Space Treaty[492]	OS: 27 January 1967 EF: 10 October 1967	S: 25 September 1967 R: 5 August 1970	Yes

485. Non-Proliferation Treaty Exporters Committee (also called the Zangger Committee).
486. Wassenaar Arrangement on export controls for conventional arms and dual-use goods and technologies.
487. A/RES/46/36/L.
488. Information provided for the calendar years 2001-2005.
489. Programme of Action to Prevent, Combat and Eradicate the Illicit Trade in Small Arms and Light Weapons in All Aspects, A/CONF.1992/15.
490. The Hague Code of Conduct against Ballistic Missile Proliferation, not yet published.
491. 402, *UNTS*, 7.
492. Treaty on Principles Governing the Activities of States in the Exploration and Use of Outer Space, including the Moon and Other Celestial Bodies, *UNTS*, vol. 610, 205.

Treaty Name	*Overall Status*	*Specific Status*	*Enforceable in France*
Sea Bed Arms Control Treaty[493]	OS: 11 February 1971 EF: 23 June 1961	–	No
Moon agreement[494]	OS: 18 December 1979 EF: 11 July 1984	S: 18 December 1979	No
Convention on the Law of the Sea[495]	OS: 10 December 1982 EF: 16 November 1994	R: 11 April 1996	Yes

OS: Opened for signature; EF: Entry into force; S/R: Signature/Ratification; A: Accession.

Table 7.7 Regional Nuclear Weapons-Free Zones

Treaty Name	*Overall Status*	*Specific Status*	*Enforceable in France*
Treaty of Tlatelolco[496]	OS: 14 February 1967 EF: 22 April 1967	–	No[497]
Treaty of Rarotonga[498]	OS: 6 August 1985 EF: 11 December 1986	–	No[499]
Treaty of Bangkok[500]	OS: 15 December 1995 EF: 27 March 1997	–	No
Treaty of Pelindaba[501]	OS: 11 April 1996 EF: not in force	–	No[502]

OS: Opened for signature; EF: Entry into force; S/R: Signature/Ratification; A: Accession.

493. Treaty on the Prohibition of the Emplacement of Nuclear Weapons and other Weapons of Mass Destruction on the Seabed and The Ocean Floor and in the subsoil thereof, *UNTS*, vol. 955, 115.
494. Agreement governing the Activities of States on the Moon and Other Celestial Bodies, *ILM*, vol. 18, 1434.
495. Doc. A/CONF.62/122 and Corr.1-11.
496. Treaty for the Prohibition of Nuclear Weapons in Latin America and the Caribbean, *UNTS*, vol. 634, 326.
497. France signed and ratified the Protocol I (S: 2 Mar. 1979, R: 24 Aug. 1992) and the Protocol II (S: 18 Jul. 1973, R: 22 Mar. 1974).
498. South Pacific Nuclear Free Zone Treaty, *ILM*, vol. 24, 1442.
499. France signed and ratified the Protocols I, II, III (S: 25 Mar. 1996, R: 20 Sep. 1996).
500. South East Asia Nuclear-Weapon-Free Zone Treaty, *ILM*, vol. 35, 635.
501. African Nuclear Weapon-Free Zone Treaty, *ILM*, vol. 35, 698.
502. France signed and ratified the Protocols I, II, III (S: 11 Apr. 1996, R: 31 Jul. 1997).

SECTION 4 CONTROL REGIME

Sub-Section 1 Military Goods and Services

Par. 1 Overall Presentation

The control regime applies to exports and imports of 'war weapons/products', but also to exports of all other military goods so-called 'Assimilated Goods'.[503]

The CoD states that all exports of 'war weapons/products' and 'Assimilated Goods' (Article L.2335-3), as well as all imports of 'war weapons/products' (Article L.2335-1), are prohibited unless a licence is obtained at ministerial level.

The control of 'war weapons/products' and 'Assimilated Goods' exports and 'war weapons/products' imports are carried out in France under a legal regime that constitutes a complete exception to the principle of free trade (including the freedom of manufacturing, exchanging, exporting and/or importing goods and services). Thus, the regime set up by the CoD (Legislative Part, Part 2, Book III, Titre III, Article L.2331-L.2371) applies to all 'war weapons/products' commercial steps, from their design, and manufacture up to their shipment abroad. The process relies on permanent inter-ministerial consultations through a multi-step licensing system: (a) the manufacturing authorization (for 'war weapons/products' arms and ammunitions – AFCI), (b) the export Licence granting simultaneously henceforth the Prime Minister's 'Preliminary agreement' to negotiate, tune final sale operations, initial and sign the export contract) and, ultimately, (c) the Customs' consent to ship the defence-related product.[504] The above-mentioned AFCI is also mandatory to import category A2 'war weapons/products' listed in the Article 311-2 of the 'Code of Homeland Security'. However, it should be noted that the import of 'Assimilated Goods' is not subject to any French specific import licensing constraint.

Sub-Par. 1 Requirements Prior to Any Import/Export (i.e., Manufacturing Stage)

The specific authorization (AFCI) granted by the Minister of Defence is mandatory for any natural or legal person who wish to manufacture, trade and/or exchange 'war weapons/products', even on or from the French territory (cf. Article L.2332-1 of the CoD).

---

503. Detailed export control rules applicable are specified by the Decree n° 2012-901 (codified by the Code de la Defence Article R2335-) related to imports and exports out of the EU of war weapons/products, ammunitions and assimilated material and to intra-community transfers of Defence related products (Décret n° 2012-901 du 20 juillet 2012 relatif aux importations et aux exportations hors du territoire de l'Union européenne de matériels de guerre, armes et munitions et de matériels assimilés et aux transferts intracommunautaires de produits liés à la défense (JORF n° 0169 du 22 juillet 2012, p. 12083).

504. Before 4 Jun. 2014, this last authorization known as Authorisation of Export of Military Good (AEMG) was an extra document delivered by the General Director of Customs after five to eight weeks.

By contrast, an AFCI is not necessary to manufacture or trade 'Assimilated Goods'; neither is it needed to import 'Assimilated Goods' in France nor to export it from the French territory.

Nonetheless, a specific authorization is required to carry out intermediary activities in either 'war weapons/products' or 'Assimilated Goods'.[505] The 'Intermediary activity' of Brokering is defined by the Annex of the Decree n° 2014-1253 of 27 October 2014 and the Article R311-1 for the Code of the Homeland Security, as an action, (a) made by a French person (physical or legal entity) or a foreign national person acting from the French territory, (b) which results in a benefit to this person (e.g.: payment of monies, increase of market share, increase of influence, etc.), and (c) occurs in the course of an exchange between a provider and a buyer, when they are both established outside of France.[506]

Therefore, any individual or legal entity, who intends (a) to get activity in manufacturing and trading 'War Equipment' or (b) to carry out an intermediary activity regarding any military good or any combination thereof, must apply for an (AFCI) at the Ministry of Defence/Directorate for General Armament/ Directorate of International development/ 'Sub-Directorate for management of Procedures of Control' - (MoD/DGA/DI/SD-GPC).[507] On average, it takes to the applicant about nine months to grant such a licence. The AFCI is granted by the MoD, after various inquiries made by all French security services (police, customs, intelligence,), and possibly, (for licences relating to cryptology) by the National Agency for Information Systems Security, (a Directorate of the SGDSN, a Prime Minister's Agency - SGDSN/ANSSI).

The licence validity cannot exceed five years but it is renewable. Ideally, for renewal, the request must be applied one year before the end of the current AFCI. Moreover, the AFCI is granted for one particular person (individual or legal), its update and/or renewal must be requested as soon as any change could happen; (e.g., for companies: new Corporate executive officer, chairman, and/or Director, new member

505. The French government adopted Decree n° 2002-23 of 3 Jan. 2002, concerning the control of 'intermediation' (OJ n° 5 of 6 Jan. 2002, 409), which amends Decree n° 95-589 of 6 May 1995 (*OJ* n° 108 of 7 May 1995, 7443) and defines and subjects to prior authorization by the State the exercise of intermediary and brokering activities held on the national territory, regardless of where third parties carry out their activities. Authorization commitment set up by the Article L.2332-1 of the CoD, concerns both intermediation in 'war weapons/products' and 'Assimilated Goods'. France also was closely associated in drawing up the European Council Common Position n° 2003/468/CFSP 'regarding controls on armament brokering', adopted by the EU Member States on 23 Jun. 2003 (EU *OJ* n° L 156/79 of 25 Jun. 2003). Detailed information on these requirements and related procedures is contained in the CoD (Legislative Part, Part 2, Book III, Title III, Chapter 2; Article L2332-1) and Articles 74 & 83 of the Decree n° 2013-700 of 30 Jul 2013 (JORF n° 0178 du 2 août 2013, p. 13194; lastly modified by the Decree 2014-1253 of 27 Oct. 2014 (JORF n° 0251 du 29 octobre 2014, p. 17908).

506. *1° Activité d'intermédiation: toute opération à caractère commercial ou à but lucratif dont l'objet est soit de rapprocher des personnes souhaitant conclure un contrat d'achat ou de vente de matériels de guerre, armes et munitions ou de matériels assimilés, soit de conclure un tel contrat pour le compte d'une des parties. Cette opération d'intermédiation faite au profit de toute personne quel que soit le lieu de son établissement prend la forme d'une opération de courtage ou celle d'une opération faisant l'objet d'un mandat particulier ou d'un contrat de commission.*

507. The DGA/DI/SD-GPC Directorate within the Ministry of Defence could hereinafter also refer to as 'DEF/DGA/SD-GPC' or 'MoD/DGA/SD-GPC'.

of the executive committee and/or the board, modification of the shareholding structure, geographical location of the legal HQ or any authorized facility).

Sub-Par. 2 Requirements at the Import/Export Stage

I Goods

A. AFCI

For the 'War Equipment' before issuing a 'Licence' and authorize imports or exports, French authorities check if the importer/exporter holds a valid AFCI.[508] Just before a 'War Equipment' exits or enters the French territory, Customs could check, the validity of the AFCI (*Note*: this is not the case for 'Assimilated Goods').

B. Prime Minister's Agreement

The obligation to apply for the export Licence is set forth in Article L.2335-2 of the CoD, for the export (outside of the EU) and in Article L.2335-10, for Intra-Community Transfers.

The exporter must file its Licence application either, electronically through 'SIGALE' (the dedicated inter-ministerial IT application) or, by mail sending the CERFA form n° 14942 duly completed to the 'Ministère de la défense, direction générale de l'armement, direction du développement international' (MoD/DGA/DI/SD-GPC, 60 boulevard Général Martial VALIN - CS 21623 75509 Paris Cedex 15.).[509]

The Article R2335-9 - I of the CoD lists the operations which are subject to an *export* Licence application and the Article R. 2335-21. – I. lists the operations subject to an EU Intra-Community *transfer* licence.[510]

One of the French export control system particularities is certainly to follow a two-step process. An exporter must apply for a Licence to cover two distinct phases of the export contract process: (i) Prior to signing the contract, the 'negotiation phase' which covers all commercial operations (i.e.: from the answer to a 'request for proposal' including technical data up to the initialization of the contract); and (ii) the final 'signature' of the contract, (i.e.: all last adjustments and eventually the signature[511]).

Then, for shipments, the export Licence is mandatory to physically export, military tangibles (including documents), and/or all related intangibles information and/or services.

508. Cf. CoD L.2335-1-III; (conditions and exceptions are set up by the cf. Decree n° 2013-700 of 30 Jul 2013 (Articles 75-77, lastly modified by the Decree 2014-1253 of 27 Oct. 2014).
509. According to the Arrêté du 14 avril 2014(JORF n° 0115 of 18 mai 2014, p. 8211) 'relatif aux modalités de demande de licences individuelles et globales d'exportation de matériels de guerre et matériels assimilés et aux modalités de demande de licences individuelles et globales de transfert de produits liés à la défense'.
510. CoD modification ordered by Decree n° 2012-901 of 20 Jul 2012 (Article 1).
511. Indeed, from June 2007 to speed up the process, the French Administration was used to deliver a unique Prime Minister's 'Agrément Préalable' (AP) valid to cover, up to three years, both contract negotiation and final signature phases. Since June 2014, the same Prime Minister's agreed 'Licence' covers all the exporting steps from contractual negotiations to final shipments.

Since 4 June 2014, (for any defence-related product, 'War Equipment' and/or 'Assimilated Goods') the French export Licence grants simultaneously the exporter, the French Prime Minister's 'preliminary agreement' authorising the company to negotiate and sign the contract and Customs to consent the exporting shipments of the military products. The contract signed by the exporter must be strictly compliant with the authorized scope of products, end-use and end-users. It must also fully and scrupulously abide the licence requirements restrictions and provisos.

In other words, the Prime Minister grants, once and simultaneously, through the 'one step' Licence delivered by the Customs: (i) the 'Preliminary Agreement' (valid up to three years, for both negotiating and signing the contract) and also (ii) the authorization to ship the products. This administrative simplification is to be considered as the major step made over the last ten years to improve and speed up the French licensing process.

Since 2002 and up to 4 June 2014, another main improvement had been made: the promotion and the generalization of bulk authorizations. As a direct consequence of the LoI/Framework Agreement,[512] at first in 2002 France implemented the 'Global Project Licence' (GPL).[513] This GPL was extended, in 2004, according to the Order of 29 July 2004[514] with the 'Global Preliminary Agreement' (APG) and related 'Global Authorisations of Export' (AGEMG)/Import (AGIMG)/Transit (AGTMG); allowing, under certain conditions, global exports or imports. Such 'global authorizations' (granted generally for three years), authorized exports of certain products to a limited list end-users, without any limitation in quantity and/or value. 'Global authorizations' were limited, at that time, by the French Administration to export 'non-sensitive' goods, to countries considered as 'friendly'. These Global licences have allowed French exporters to deliver not only to nationals of the six LoI/Framework Agreement partners but also to reliable companies in the United States of America, Australia, Canada, Switzerland, Japan, New Zealand and Norway. In 2009 the so-called EU 'ICT Directive' (n° 2009/43/EC of the European Parliament and of the Council of 6 May 2009, simplifying terms and conditions of transfers of defence-related products within the Community), recommended that Member States implement 'Global Licences' for intra EU 'transfers'. However the ICT global licences cannot be used to export to non-European major partners. This makes legally impossible for a company to refer to the sole ICT Directive for the needs of a programme including EU and third countries exports. Consequently, France decided to take the opportunity of the ICT transposition law,[515] to totally revisit, simplify, streamline and harmonize, both its export and transfer systems.

---

512. This position has been confirmed in the French transposition law (LOI n° 2011-702 du 22 juin 2011 relative au contrôle des importations et des exportations de matériels de guerre et de matériels assimilés, à la simplification des transferts des produits liés à la défense dans l'Union européenne et aux marchés de défense et de sécurité (JORF n° 0144 of 23 Jun. 2011, p. 10673) of the Directive 2009/43/EC of the European Parliament and of the Council of 6 May 2009 simplifying terms and conditions of transfers of defence-related products within the Community.
513. (Order of 28 Mar. 2002, OJ 76, 30 Mar. 2002, 5652).
514. OJ 178, 3 Aug. 2004, p. 13820.
515. Loi n° 2011-702 of 22 Jun. 2011, related to control of imports and exports of 'war weapons/ products' and 'Assimilated' and the simplification of Defence related products transfers within the EU and contracts for Defence and security; JORF n° 0144 of 23 Jun. 2011, p. 10673.

In a nutshell, implementation in France of 'GPL' was a requirement of the LoI/Framework Agreement,[516] to streamline the business between the six LoI European partners. France extended the LoI principles and possibilities even to non-EU countries partners in the United States of America, Australia, Canada, Switzerland, Japan, New Zealand and Norway.

However, despite these administrative simplifications the general licensing process did not change much. Currently, single licences for operations deemed simple (basic components for a legitimate end-use and a reliable end-user) need sometimes more than one month to be granted; 'sensitive' cases instruction could still stays over three months on average.[517]

A Licence (global or single) may impose additional restrictions or caveats. The exporter may be required to undertake additional commitments with regard to the intermediates consignees or end-user/use and/or the government of the country to which the goods are to be exported. It may be necessary, for instance, to include in the export contract a clause or a guarantee prohibiting the re-export of certain items,[518] or, to dictate the customer to provide all related Security documents in the event of exchanges of classified information.[519]

C. Import Licence ('AIMG')/Export Licence (former 'AEMG')

According to the Article L.2335-3 of the CoD, the export of 'War Equipment' or 'Assimilated Goods' requires a Licence. The exporter must lodge its export request with the MoD/DGA/DI/SD-GPC. Currently it takes on average five to eight weeks to obtain an export Licence.[520]

As regards imports, according to Articles L.2335-1 and R.2335-1 to 8, of the CoD, an Autorisation d'Importation de Matériel de Guerre (AIMG) is required for the import of 'War Equipment' (but not for the import of 'Assimilated Goods').

516. This position has been reiterated in the French transposition law (LOI n° 2011-702 du 22 juin 2011 relative au contrôle des importations et des exportations de matériels de guerre et de matériels assimilés, à la simplification des transferts des produits liés à la défense dans l'Union européenne et aux marchés de défense et de sécurité (JORF n° 0144 of 23 Jun. 2011, p. 10673) of the Directive 2009/43/EC of the European Parliament and of the Council of 6 May 2009 simplifying terms and conditions of transfers of defence-related products within the Community.
517. Time elapsed from the date the application is submitted to the date Customs deliver the shipping authorization.
518. Cf. Article R. 2335-16. of the CoD. In particular, 'non re-export and end-user certificate' takes the official form of the CERFA document n° 10 919*02 (it can be found at https://www.ixarm.com/-Bibliotheque- and is equivalent to a Government -to- Government commitment. Such a 'non re-export certificate' is also called 'complete', 'normal' or 'ordinary' non-re-export certificate. A non-re-export understatement is sometimes required from the recipient of the goods (it is generally the case with industrial customers who incorporate the related goods into their own products or systems). Such an 'Industry-to-Government commitment may be written simply as a letter on company headed paper; these non-re-export documents are known as 'commitment to non-re-export goods' *'as such'* or *'as it is'* (*'en l'état'*)'.
519. According to the principles of the Ministry of Defence *'Instruction particulière n°* 2560/DEF/C.23' of 21 May 1984, for industrial cooperation and contracts with foreign countries; this regulation in 2013 has been repealed however practically it keeps giving useful guidelines.
520. Time elapsed from the date of the export licence application filing to the signature of the exporting form by the General Director of Customs.

D. Export Certificate ('APD')[521]

This document is no more used since June 2012. All necessary shipment information have now to be reported, half yearly by the exporter, in the framework of the 'ex post' exporters' reporting obligations.

Sub-Par. 3 Services

The export or import of 'Military services' are not subject to specific national rules. This means that export of Services must follow the standard licensing procedure. Accordingly export authorizations for related services have to be requested at the same time and with the commodities application form.

Sub-Par. 4 Persons/Deemed Export

According to Article R. 2335-9.I. of the CoD a Licence is required to accept export contracts under which it will be possible to release information that could contribute to gives the possibility to copy or to impair the efficiency of war equipments and/or assimilated goods.

Release information to a foreign national is deemed an export and, for that reason, an export Licence is also mandatory to employ foreign national workers or for hosting visitors when they have a need to know about information related to defence-related products.

Par. 2 Control Lists

Checking if the goods they intend to export are listed or not, exporters can figure out by themselves the regulations they have to comply with. In case of doubt about the classification of a product, exporters can always ask the MoD's DGA/DI/SD-GPC. If the distinction between 'War Equipment' or 'Assimilated Goods' is not obvious, or when it is not possible to find easily the right category of 'arms, ammunition and/or military goods',[522] Administration (or the exporter directly) can submit the case to the Interministerial Commission for Classification ('*Commission Interministérielle de Classement*' (CIC)).[523]

521. Customs clearance certificate (Export Certificate). One specific APD was required for each shipment. APD refer to a correspondent AEMG and gave details for goods identity, quantities and values. APD was meant for final check by the Defence Protection and Security Directorate ('*Direction de la Protection et de la Sécurité de la Défense*' (DPSD)), after control by Customs.
522. Cf. Article L.2331-1 of the CoD which draws up the list of 'war weapons/products, and ammunitions and elements'; specified by the Décret n° 2014-1253 of 27 Oct. 2014 (JORF n° 0251 du 29 octobre 2014, p. 17908) as codified in the Article R311-2 of the Code of the Homeland Security.
523. Cf. Arrêté of 28 Aug. 2000, '*portant application du a) de l'article 5 du décret n° 95-589 du 6 mai 1995 modifié relatif à l'application du décret du 18 avril 1939 fixant le régime des matériels de guerre, armes et munitions*' (JORF n° 200 of 30 Aug. 2000, p. 13400); last modification by

The CoD, under Article L.2331-1, establishes in four categories[524] the list of items which are referred to in the Decree 2014-1253 of 27 October 2014 as codified in the Article R311-2 of the Code of the Homeland Security. 'War weapons/products' are listed in category A2: '*weapons classified as "war weapons/products", equipment intended to carry or to use, in the battlefield, firearms, equipment of protection against poison gases*'. Specific items related to 'war weapons/products' are called 'Assimilated Goods' they are export controlled and follow the same licensing process, rules and regulations as the 'war weapons/products'. Both 'war weapons/products' and 'Assimilated Goods' are listed in the Order of 9 June 2014.[525]

The Authority in charge of coordination of the Administration to determine the export control classification of goods is the MoD (DGA/DDI/SD/GPC). When making its decisions, the MoD applies the CoD provisions and can consult with technical experts of the MoD/DGA and operational specialists of Ministry of Defence Head Quarter (MoD/EMA).

Par. 3 Licensing and Enforcement Authorities

Sub-Par. 1 As Regards Requirements Preliminary to Any Specific Import/Export (i.e., Manufacturing Stage)

For 'war weapons/products', before the export takes place, the AFCI has to be granted by the MoD, after receiving the approval of the police regional authority ('*Préfet de Région/Département*') and conclusions of French security and intelligence services enquiries, plus as soon as cryptology is concerned, the agreement of the National Agency for Information Systems Security (SGDSN/ANSSI).[526]

Arrêté of 2 Sep. 2013 – Article 9 (JORF n° 0206 of 5 Sep. 2013, p. 14989). This Commission is chaired by the CGA and the time it takes generally to convene the commission is between one and three month(s); the decision is published in an administrative decision signed by the French Ministry of Defence.

524. Article L. 2331-1.-I. – The war weapons/products, the ammunitions and the elements listed by the present title are classified in the following categories:

   1° Category A: war weapons/products forbidden the acquisition and the detention of which is subject to provisions of the article L. 2336-1.
   This category includes:

   A1: weapons and elements of weapons forbidden for their acquisition and detention;
   A2: weapons classified as war weapons/products, equipment intended to carry or to use, *in the battlefield*, firearms, equipment of protection against poison gases;

   2° Category B: weapons subjected to authorization for the acquisition and the detention;
   3° Category C: weapons subjected to declaration for the acquisition and the detention;
   4° Category D: weapons subjected to recording and weapons and equipment among which the acquisition and the detention are free.

525. Cf. Arrêté 27 juin 2012 '*relatif à la liste des matériels de guerre et matériels assimilés soumis à une autorisation préalable d'exportation et des produits liés à la défense soumis à une autorisation préalable de transfert*'; last update by Arrêté of 16 Mach 2015 (JORF n° 0073 of 27 Mar. 2015, p. 5553). modifiant l'arrêté du 27 juin 2012, modifié.
526. Cf. CoD L.2335-1-III; (conditions and exceptions are set up by the Articles 75-77 of the Decree n° 2013-700 of 30 Jul 2013).

Sub-Par. 2 At the Import/Export Stage

Since 4 June 2014, to comply with the EU 'Intra-Community Transfers Directive' (ICT)[527] a unique 'Licence' substitutes for the two-step original French licensing process. A one-step assessment of the contemplated export/transfer operation is made, on behalf of the Prime Minister, by the General Secretary for the National Defence and Security (Secrétaire Général de la Défense et de la Sécurité Nationale (SGDSN)) who chairs the Inter-ministerial Commission to Evaluate Exports of Military Goods (*'Commission Interministérielle pour l'Etude des Exportations de Matériels de Guerre'* (CIEEMG)). Ministry of Foreign Affairs (MoFA), MoD and Ministry for Economy, Finance and Industry (MINEFI) representatives are the three full members of the CIEEMG;[528] they provide counsel to the French Prime Minister who ultimately takes the final decision to agree or deny the export/transfer. Accordingly, in the same meeting, the CIEEMG recommends, or not, (1) the Prime Minister to give politically, a positive signal to the customer's country and (2) to the General Director of Customs (head of DGDDI) to deliver the related administrative authorization of export/transfer. Practically the former Preliminary Agreement (*'Agrément Préalable'* (AP)) and the related former *Authorisation to Export Military Goods* (AEMG) are now combined into one unique document: the 'Licence'.

I Import Licence ('AIMG')

For imports only (AIMG does no more exist today for EU Transfers) AIMGs are granted by the General Director of Customs, acting on behalf of the Ministry of Economy, Economic Regeneration and Digital economy, after approval of the MoD, the Ministry of Home Affairs, the MoFA and ultimately the blessing of the SGDSN on behalf of the Prime Minister.

II Control at Customs: Export Licence, Reporting and Ex Post Controls

When Customs' clearance checks have been carried out to satisfaction by the local Customs Service, the individual Licence (specifying the quantities and values actually shipped) are completed and countersigned by the Customs Service, which then authorizes the export itself (shipping of the goods abroad). Exports made with a Global or a General Licence are also controlled. However Customs only check the nature of the product neither their quantity nor value.

527. Directive 2009/43/EC of the European Parliament and of the Council of 6 May 2009, *'Simplifying terms and conditions of transfers of defence-related products within the Community'*. (OJEU L 146 of 10.6.2009, p.1).

528. Indeed, many other agencies attend the CIEEMG meetings (customs, home office, security and intelligence services, police, space agency, ...) but only the three 'full' members vote to make a unanimous advise to the Prime Minister. (cf.: Decree n) 55-965 of 16 Jul. 1955 modified by the Decree n) 2012-929 of 31 Jul. 2012).

Sub-Par. 3 Export Control Regime Procedure Chart

Figure 7.1 summarizes according to the type of products what are the licensing commitments and export possibilities.

Figure 7.1 French Military Products Licensing System

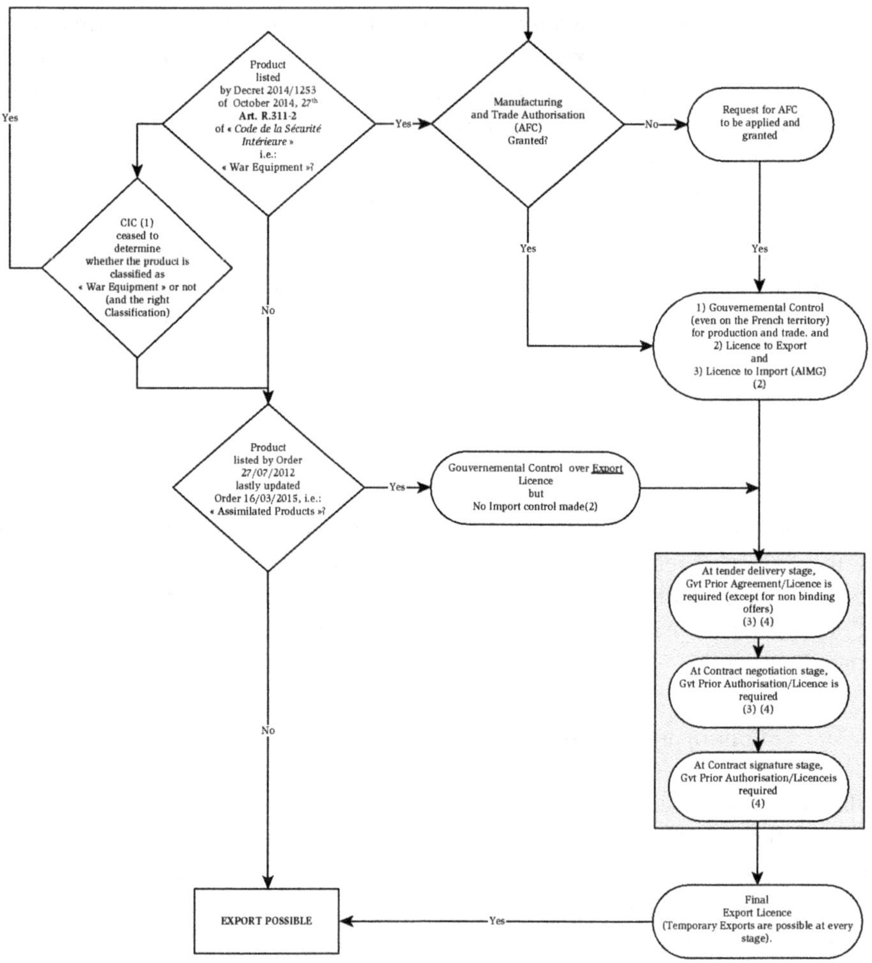

(1) In case of doubt about the classification of the good, exporters can ask the DGA (General Directorate for Armament) or the CGA (General Control of Armies) within the Ministry of Defence. If the classification is too difficult, the issue can be referred to the C1C (Inter-ministerial Commission for Classification) by the Administration or the company (exporter). The time generally needed to convene the CIC is between three and six months.
(2) Export without licence is prohibited (Articles L.2335-2 and L.2335-3 of the Code of Defence and Décret 901/2012 dated 20 July 2012); Import without licence is prohibited (Code of DefenceL2335-1).

(3) Processing time: standard cases are managed through the IT process 'SIGALE'; The current average elapsed time for a simple licensing operation is around thirty days, from the Licence application date to the Custom's Export Licence notification.
(4) Period of validity of the Licence, three years. The Licence covers sales, negotiations as well as temporary exports.

Par. 4 Sanctions for Non-compliance and Recourses of the Importer/Exporter

Sanctions for non-compliance with applicable regulations and procedures are laid down in the CoD, the customs regulations, the French Criminal Code and the Public Procurement Code.

Sub-Par. 1 Sanctions Contained in the CoD

Sanctions can be of a criminal and/or administrative nature. They are also set up in the Chapter VIII (criminal sanctions) of the Décret n° 2013-700 of 30 July 2013.[529]

I As Regards the AFCI

The relevant criminal sanctions are set out in Article L.2339-2 of the CoD, and the administrative sanctions in Article L.2332-11 of the CoD.

Article L.2339-2 of the CoD states that any individual or legal entity who manufactures or trades 'war weapons/products', or carries on an intermediary or brokering activity involving such goods, without being properly authorized to do so, is liable to imprisonment for up to seven years and a fine of EUR 100,000. The goods may also be confiscated.

Furthermore, if it is a legal entity which is in breach of the law, it may incur the penalties set out in Articles 131-38 and 131-39 of the French Criminal Code which provide for a fine of up to five times the amount provided for individuals (see Article L.2339-2 of the CoD).

Article L.2332-11 of the CoD provides for the withdrawal of the AFCI at any time, by the MoD (DGA/DI/SD/GPC), if the individual or legal entity infringes any of the provisions of Chapter 2 'Manufacture and Commerce' of the CoD or of the French labour Code.

Administrative decisions do not have to be supported with reasons. However, the authority in charge may be asked by the exporter/importer to reconsider its decision and, if necessary, the importer/exporter can appeal to the administrative courts within two months of the date the importer/exporter is notified of the decision.

In addition to the above, the AFCI will be withdrawn by the Administration (or will not be renewed) in the event the imprisonment sentence is in excess of three months.

529. Articles 175-178 of the Décret n° 2013-700 du 30 juillet 2013, '*portant application de la loi n° 2012-304 du 6 mars 2012 relative à l'établissement d'un contrôle des armes moderne, simplifié et préventif*', (JORF n° 0178 du 2 aout 2013, p. 13194).

II As Regards the Licences

Article L.2339-3 of the CoD states that accepting a purchase order for the export of military goods without having first obtained the required Licence (L. 2335-2), is punishable with up to five years imprisonment and a fine of up to EUR 75,000.

According to Article L.2339-10 of the CoD, importing or attempting to import goods of the categories A, B, C D, of the Decree n° 2014-1253 of 27 October 2014, without a licence (as demanded by Article L. 2335-1), is punishable with up to five years imprisonment and a fine of up to EUR 9,000.

Article L.2335-19 of the CoD specifies that disputes between exporters and the authorities regarding export/import of military goods are arbitrated by an 'arbitration committee' (*Comité de contestation en douanes*) under MoD jurisdiction.[530]

Sub-Par. 2 Sanctions Provided for in Customs Related Regulations

Additionally and according to Article 38 of the Customs Code, goods which import or export is subject to a licence are deemed prohibited when imported or exported without the required licence. Exporting or importing prohibited goods without a licence constitutes a first class customs offence, punishable with up to three years imprisonment, confiscation of the goods and a fine that can be up to twice the value of the goods (Article 414 of the Customs Code).[531]

Sub-Par. 3 Criminal Code

Article 411-6 of the French Criminal Code states:

> supplying or making accessible to a foreign power... information, processes, articles, documents, computerized data or files, the use, disclosure or collection of which could endanger the fundamental interests of the nation, is punished by fifteen years' criminal detention and a fine of € 225,000.[532]

530. Décret n° 2012-929 of 31 Jul. 2012 *'relatif à l'organisation et au fonctionnement du comité de règlement des contestations en douane'* (JORF n° 0178 du 2 août 2012, p. 12690).

531. Customs Code – Customs offences A. – first class. Article 414:

> *Are liable to a detention of three years, to a seizure of the object of fraud, the seizure of the means of transportation, the seizure of objects serving to mask the fraud, the seizure of the goods and the assets which are the direct or indirect product of the breach and a fine between one and two times the value of the object of the fraud, any smuggled fact as well as any fact of import or export without declaration when these breaches relate to goods of the category of those which are prohibited or strongly taxed in the sense of the present code. The prison sentence may be increased up to a maximal duration of five years and the fine can go three times to the value of the object of the fraud when the smuggled facts, of import or export concern Dual Use goods military and civilian whose circulation is subjected to limitation by the European regulations. The prison sentence may be increased up to a duration of ten years and the fine can go five times to the value of the object of the fraud either when the smuggled facts, of import or export concern dangerous goods for the health, the morality or laws and orders, the list of which is fixed by order of the Ministry in charge of customs, or when they are committed in organised group.*

532. Courtesy translation proposed by the authors.

Sub-Par. 4 Public Procurement Code

Exclusion by all French public procurement procedures could be decided by a judge as an additional sanction to a criminal offence. To our best knowledge, such possibility has never been applied in the context of export control laws and regulations.[533]

Sub-Section 2 Dual-Use Goods and Services

Par. 1 Overall Presentation

The French Dual-Use goods and technology export control is implemented in accordance with rules defined by the Council Regulation (EC) n° 428/2009 of 5 May 2009 'setting up a Community regime for the control of exports of dual-use items and technology';[534] this Regulation is directly applicable in each and every EU Member State. The Regulation (EC) n° 428/2009 defines, in its Article 2, the terms 'dual-use items and technology' (which include software and 'related' technology), and establishes in four annexes[535] the lists of controlled Dual-Use goods and technology.

According to the Regulation, each Member State is free to nationally choose the respective authorities in charge of the export licensing and to determine the scope, conditions and period of validity of their licences, as well, the procedures that exporters must follow to obtain and manage these licences. In France, implementation was achieved through the Decree n° 2001-1192 of 13 December 2001 'related to the control of exports, imports and transfers of Dual-Use goods and technology' and two Orders for its enforcement.[536]

533. Article L.131-39 of the Criminal Code.
534. Cf. *supra* n. 230.
535. *Annex I* (referred to in Article 3 of this Regulation) 'List Of Dual-Use Items'; *Annex IIa* (referred to in Article 9(1) of this Regulation); Union General Export Authorisation n° EU001: Exports to Australia, Canada, Japan, New Zealand, Norway, Switzerland, including Liechtenstein, and United States of America; *ANNEX IIb* (referred to in Article 9(1) of this Regulation); Union General Export Authorisation n° EU002; Exports of certain dual-use items to certain destinations; *Annex IIc* (referred to in Article 9(1) of this Regulation) Union General Export Authorisation n° EU003: Export after repair/replacement; *Annex IId* (referred to in Article 9(1) of this Regulation) Union General Export Authorisation n° EU004: Temporary export for exhibition or fair. *Annex IIe* (referred to in Article 9(1) of this Regulation); Union General Export Authorisation n° EU005: Telecommunications; *Annex IIf* (referred to in Article 9(1) of this Regulation); Union General Export Authorisation n° EU006: Chemicals. Annex IIg: List referred to in Article 9(4)(a) of this Regulation and Annexes IIa, IIc and IId to this Regulation. *Annex IIIa* (referred to in Article 14(1) of this Regulation): model for individual or global export authorization forms; *Annex IIIb* (referred to in Article 14(1) of this Regulation): model for brokering services authorization forms; *Annex IIIc* (referred to in Article 9(4)(b) of this Regulation): common elements for publication of national general export authorizations in national official journals; *Annex IV*: List referred to in Article 22(1) of this Regulation: *'An authorisation shall be required for intra-Community transfers of dual-use items listed in Annex IV...'.*; *Annex V*: Repealed Regulation with its successive amendments.
536. (i) Decree n° 2001-1192 of 13 Dec. 2001 (OJ n° 291 of 15 Dec. 2001, 19905) last modified by **Décret n°** 2010-292 of 18 Mar. 2010:

Sub-Par. 1 Requirements Prior to Any Specific Import/Export (e.g., Manufacturing Phase)

There is no specific authorization for imports of Dual-Use goods.

To assess export applications French authorities examine closely the sensitivity and the quantity of goods, the reliability of the end-users and the legitimacy of the declared end-uses. As a vast majority of Dual-Use goods are not exported to sensitive end-users for sensitive end-use, no specific preliminary requirements are necessary. Following the usual assessment process, licensing authorities only focus on the performances of the goods. The most sensitive cases (goods and related technology[537]) are handled under an inter-ministerial consultation, close to the one followed for export of military goods.

Practically, the benefit of a 'Union General Export Authorisation'[538] as well as a 'National General Licence'[539] or a national Global Licence[540] requires the exporter relies upon a sound 'Internal Control Programs'(ICP) – main requirements are the following: description of the company's export compliance policy, organization of the entity in charge of its enforcement, copies of the related main procedures and a self-commitment of the top management to comply fully with all the licence requirements.[541]

relatif aux procédures d'autorisation d'exportation, de transfert, de courtage et de transit de biens et technologies à double usage et portant transfert de compétences de la direction générale des douanes et droits indirects à la direction générale de la compétitivité, de l'industrie et des services.

(JORF n° 0067 du 20 mars 2010, p. 5633); (ii) Order related to the control over exports to third countries and over the transfer to Member States of the EU of dual-use goods and technology. (OJ 291, 15 Dec. 2001, 19911) last updated by Arrêté of 18 Mar. 2010 'relatif aux autorisations d'exportation, d'importation et de transfert de biens et technologies à double usage' (JORF n° 0067 du 20 mars 2010, p. 5636); and (iii) Order related to the issuance of an international import certificate and of a delivery verification certificate for import of dual-use goods and technology (OJ 291, 15 Dec. 2001, 19914); last update by Arrêté du 18 mars 2010 relatif aux autorisations d'exportation, d'importation et de transfert de biens et technologies à double usage (JORF n° 0067 du 20 mars 2010, p. 5636).

537. These most sensitive dual-use goods and technology are goods, technology and software required for producing weapons of mass destruction and their means of delivery, regardless of payload or range. They are precisely defined in Annex IV of the Council Regulation (EC) n° 428/2009 *supra* n. 230.
538. EU 001-EU 006 as set forth in annex II of the Council Regulation (EC) n° 428/2009 *supra* n. 230.
539. As set forth in Article 9.4 of the Council Regulation (EC) n° 428/2009, Article 3 of the Décret n° 2001-1192 of 13 Decembre 2001 and related Articles 7 and 10 of the Arrêté of 13 Decembre 2001.
540. As set forth in Article 9.5 of the Council Regulation (EC) n° 428/2009, *supra* n. 230, and in Article 3 and Article 6 of the Décret n° 2001-1192 of 13 Decembre 2001 ('relatif au contrôle à l'exportation, à l'importation et au transfert de biens et technologies à double usage') and related Arrêté of 13 Decembre 2001 (*'relatif au contrôle à l'exportation vers les pays tiers et au transfert vers les Etats membres de la Communauté européenne de biens et technologies à double usage').*
541. This ICP is also required to benefit from simplified export controls, taking into account the control of brokering and/or the management of intangibles.

Sub-Par. 2 Requirements at the Import/Export Stage

I Goods

A. Principles

Dual-Use goods and technology can be transferred freely within the EU, except for the most sensitive items, listed in Annex IV of the Regulation (EC) n° 428/2009, which do require a licence (Article 22 of the Regulation (EC) n° 428/2009). Moreover, it should be pointed out that, under the French Regime, exports of these sensitive items are subject to procedures very close to those which apply to the export of military goods (i.e.: inter-ministerial consultation).

As regards exports of Dual-Use goods and technology outside the EU (including transfers of software and technology by electronic means, fax, telephone, etc.), Article 3 of the Regulation (EC) n° 428/2009 provides that a licence must be obtained for all goods, technology and software listed in Annex I of the Regulation.

When necessary, France uses the 'catch-all clause', described in Article 4 of the Regulation (EC) n° 428/2009, which enables Member States to require a licence for the export of any item which is (or may be) intended for use in connection with WMD, or terrorism or when the destination is a country sanctioned by an arms embargo.

Under Article 8 of the Regulation (EC) n° 428/2009, France is also entitled (for reasons of public security, or for human rights considerations) to prohibit exports or to impose a national licence for shipments of dual-use items even if they are not listed in the Annex I. Accordingly, France currently requires an export licence for the following: (i) civilian helicopters and related parts,[542] (ii) tear gas and anti-riot agents,[543] (iii) mobile equipment for IT interception.[544] *Note*: Additionally, France issued two other National General Licences the first one related to fairs and expositions;[545] and the second to supply French military forces in operation wherever in the world with Dual-Use goods.[546]

542. Pease note that, since 8 Aug. 2014, a national general licence is available for these Civilian helicopters and spare parts; cf. Arrêté du 31 juillet 2014 relatif aux exportations d'hélicoptères et de leurs pièces détachées vers les pays tiers (OJ 182, 8 Aug. 2014, p. 13297).
543. Tear gas and anti-riot agents; cf. Arrêté du 31 juillet 2014 relatif aux exportations de gaz lacrymogènes et agents antiémeute vers les pays tiers (OJ n° 0182 du 8 Aug. 2014, p. 13295).
544. Mobile equipment for interceptions of telecommunications; cf. Avis aux exportateurs du 6 décembre 2012 (OJ 284 du 6 Dec. 2012, p. 19146). However, since 22 Oct. 2014, following a 2013 French proposal to the Wassenaar Arrangement, these products are controlled by the EU Regulation n° 428/2009), *supra* n. 230.
545. Reexports of goods temporarily imported for expositions and fairs; Arrêté du 31 juillet 2014 relatif à la licence générale 'Salons et Expositions' 'Exportations et transferts au sein de l'Union européenne de biens à double usage importés pour la tenue de salons et d'expositions sous le régime douanier de l'admission temporaire' (OJ 0182 du 8 août 2014, p. 13295).
546. Dual-Use goods for French military forces; Arrêté du 31 juillet 2014 relatif à la licence générale 'biens à double usage pour forces armées françaises' (OJ 0182 du 8 août 2014, p. 13294).

B. Different Type of Licences

The Union General Export Authorisation n° 001 was established by Regulation (EC) n° 1334/2000.[547] It allows, under specified conditions, Member States to export a huge majority of Dual-Use goods and technology[548] to designated non-EU countries:[549]

> Five Union General Export Authorizations have been added in 2011 to the Regulation 428/2009 by Regulation (EU) No 1232/2011:[550] EU 002: Exports of certain dual-use items to certain destinations;[551] EU 003: Export after repair/replacement[552]; EU 004: Temporary export for exhibition or fair;[553] EU 005: Telecommunications[554]; EU 006: Chemicals.[555]

In France, depending on the required scope of the licence and according to the Article 3 of the Decree n° 2001-1192 of 13 December 2001,[556] licences can be individual, global or general. The exporter[557] apply for the licence to a dedicated agency of the Ministry of Economy, Industry and Numerical business: 'Le Service des Biens à Double Usage' (SBDU)[558] belonging to the General directorate for competitiveness of Industry and Services (*Direction générale des Entreprises – DGE*).

An Order of 13 December 2001,[559] elaborated by the Minister in charge of Customs defines the conditions as well as the technical and practical requirements to manage these licences. 'Individual licence' are valid everywhere in the EU and last for one year. The Licence is granted for, (i) one or several listed Dual-Use goods, (ii) a specified value and (iii) a limited quantity, for (iv) a single transfer and (v) a single recipient; global and national general licences are more open.

The 'global licence' is valid for two years and enables to export, without any limitation of quantity or value, a limited list of dual-use good(s) to an agreed list of

547. Currently set out in the Annex IIa of the Regulation 428/2009, *supra* n. 230.
548. Only the most sensitive ones are excluded.
549. Switzerland, Norway, Canada, Japan, Australia, the United States of America and New Zealand.
550. Regulation (EU) n° 1232/2011 of the European Parliament and of the Council of 16 Nov. 2011, amending Council Regulation (EC) n° 428/2009 setting up a Community regime for the control of exports, transfer, brokering and transit of dual-use items. (OJEU L 326 of 8.12.2011, p. 26).
551. OJEU L 326 of 8.12.2011, p. 29.
552. OJEU L 326 of 8.12.2011, p. 31.
553. OJEU L 326 of 8.12.2011, p. 34.
554. OJEU L 326 of 8.12.2011, p. 37.
555. OJEU L 326 of 8.12.2011, p. 39.
556. Decree n° 2001-1192 of 13 Dec. 2001 (OJ n° 291 of 15 Dec. 2001, p. 19905) last modified by Décret n° 2010-292 of 18 Mar. 2010 (JORF n° 0067 du 20 mars 2010, p. 5633).
557. The same administrative document (CERFA n° 10994*04 form) is used whatever the type of applications could be: individual, global or general licence. These forms can be requested from the '*bureaux de l'Imprimerie Nationale*' and/or downloaded on the https://www.formulaires.modernisation.gouv.fr/gf/cerfa_10994.do and/or on the Customs' Internet site: www.douane.gouv.fr.
558. '*Service des Biens à Double Usage* (SBDU) http://www.dgcis.gouv.fr/biens-double-usage/accueil. (cf. details *infra* in Part 3: Licensing and Enforcement Authorities.
559. Order related to the control over exports to third countries and over the transfer to Member States of the EU of dual-use goods and technology. (OJ 291, 15 Dec. 2001, p.19911) last updated by Arrêté of 18 Mar. 2010 'relatif aux autorisations d'exportation, d'importation et de transfert de biens et technologies à double usage' (JORF n° 0067 du 20 mars 2010, p. 5636).

recipients. However, such licences are granted only after the exporter has provided the Administration with evidences of its compliance with export control regulations and commitment to fulfil all possible conditions and restrictions. Main requirements are the following: (i) have a sound organization and financial references, (2) appoint an entitled senior executive as 'export compliance officer' responsible to set up, enforce and promote an adequate export/import internal policy.

The 'national general licence' is valid for one year (but it is automatically renewable) and it enables, without any limitation of quantity or value, exports of listed categories of goods to listed destinations. The General licences take usually the form of Orders which, accordingly, are published on the Official Journal, they are open to all exporters. The exporter must commit to comply with the specific rules of the General licence. Currently in France seven national general licences are available. The three first were set up by three Orders of 18 July 2002[560] to cover 'industrial goods',[561] 'chemical products'[562] 'and graphite'.[563] The General licence n° 4, for biological products, was enforced by an Order of the 14 May 2007.[564]

An exporter who applies for an individual licence may be asked (i) to give supplementary information about the recipient and the end-user/end-use of the goods and (ii) to provide the Customs Administration with an 'end-user certificate' ('*Certificat d'Utilisateur Final*' (CUF)). Such a certificate must be signed by the recipient and the end-user and be fully consistent with the form set out under Annex II of the Order of 13 December 2001.[565]

560. Modified by Orders of 21 Jun. 2004 (13635 OJ 31 Jul. 2004,); lastly modified by Arrêté of 18 Mar. 2010 (JORF n° 0067 of 20 Mar. 2010, p. 5636).
561. Authorized countries are: South Africa, Argentina, Brazil, Bulgaria, Chilli, South Korea, Hong Kong, Island, Malaysia, Morocco, Mexico, Romania, Russia, Singapore, Taïwan, Thailand, Turkey, and Ukraine.
562. Authorized countries are South Africa, Argentina, Bulgaria, China, South Korea, Equator, Hong Kong, Indonesia, Island, Morocco, Mexico, Romania, Singapore, Taïwan, Tunisia, and Turkey.
563. Authorized countries are: South Africa, Argentina, Brazil, Bulgaria, South Korea, Hong Kong, Island, Malaysia, Mexico, Romania, Russia, Singapore, Taïwan, Turkey, and Ukraine.
564. OJ 114, 17 May 2007, 9555; lastly modified by Arrêté of 18 Mar. 2010 (OJ 67 of 20 Mar. 2010, p. 5636).

Authorized countries are: South Africa, Albania, Algeria, Antigua-et-Barbuda, Saudi Arabia, Argentina, Armenia, Australia, Azerbaijan, Bahamas, Bahrein, Bangladesh, Barbados, Belarus, Belize, Benin, Bhutan, Bolivia, Bosnia & Herzegovina, Botswana, Brazil, Brunei Darussalam, Bulgaria, Burkina Faso, Cambodia, Canada, Cabo-Verde, Chili, China, Cyprus, Colombia, Congo, Congo (Democratic Republic of), Korea (Republic of), Costa Rica, Croatia, Cuba, Dominica, El Salvador, Ecuador, United States of America, Ethiopia, Fiji, Gambia, Georgia, Ghana, Grenada, Guatemala, Guinea, Guinea-Bissau, Honduras, India, Indonesia, Iceland, Jamaica, Japan, Jordan, Kenya, Kirghizstan, Kuwait, Lao (Democratic Republic of), Lesotho, Lebanon, Libya, Liechtenstein, Macedonia (The Former Yugoslav Republic of), Malaysia, Maldives, Mali, Morocco, Mauritius, Mexico, Moldavia (Republic of), Mongolia, Nicaragua, Niger, Nigeria, Norway, New Zealand Oman, Uganda, Uzbekistan, Pakistan, Palau, Panama, Papua-New-Guinea, Paraguay, Peru, Philippines, Qatar, Dominican-Republic, Romania, Russia (Federation of), Rwanda, Santa-Lucia, San-Kitts-et-Nevis, San-Marin, San-Vincent-and the-Grenadines, Salomon (islands), São Tomé and Príncipe, Senegal, Serbia, Montenegro, Seychelles, Sierra Leone, Singapore, Sudan, Sri Lanka, Switzerland, Suriname, Swaziland, Tajikistan, Thailand, Timor-Leste (Democratic Republic of), Togo, Tonga, Tunisia, Turkmenistan, Turkey, Ukraine, Uruguay, Vanuatu, Venezuela, Viet-Nam, Yemen, Zimbabwe.
565. Published in OJ 291, 15 Dec. 2001, 19911; Form available at the following Internet address: //www.entreprises.gouv.fr/biens-double-usage/procedures-et-licences-et-circuit.

C. Specific Obligations Regarding Intra-Community Transfers of Dual-Use Goods Listed in Annex I of Regulation (EC) n° 428/2009

Exporters should comply with certain formalities before carrying out intra-community transfers of Dual-Use goods. They must clearly indicate on the relevant commercial documents (sales contracts, order confirmations, delivery slips, invoices, etc.) that the goods shall be subject to control if they are exported (outside of EU). Exporters must also keep the documents and registers related to these goods for at least three years, starting from the end of the calendar year during which the transfer occurred.

II Services

There is no specific French regulation to control the export of services. Regulation (EC) n° 428/2009 provides: 'This Regulation does not apply to the supply of services or the transmission of technology, if that supply or transmission involves cross-border movement of natural persons'.[566] Such a wording implies that, in all other cases, 'export' encompasses transmission of software or technology by electronic media, fax or telephone to a destination outside the Community.[567] The General Technology Note (GTN) of Regulation (EC) n° 428/2009 indicates: 'the export of "technology" which is "required" for the "development", "production" or "use" of goods controlled in categories 1 to 9, is controlled according to the provisions of Categories 1 to 9'.

Practically, the major difficulty here is to brief and manage properly all the natural persons of the company who could potentially provide services abroad. Indeed, there is always a risk for pieces of export controlled, information, technical data or know-how, to be orally disclosed, even if no physical software code or technical data sheets are communicated to unauthorized persons. Unfortunately this issue is a general one that Export compliance officers have to face daily, irrespective of the national regulations they must comply with.

III Persons/Deemed Export

Article 7 of Council (EC) Regulation n° 428/2009 provides: "*This Regulation does not apply to the supply of services or the transmission of technology if that supply or transmission involves cross-border movement of persons*". However, in France, deemed export are controlled (i) in the framework of the protection of the national scientific and technical potential, by the décret n° 2011-1425 of 2 November 2011[568] and the circulaire interministérielle de mise en oeuvre du dispositif de protection du potentiel scientifique et technique de la nation n° 3415/SGDSN/AIST/PST du 7 novembre 2012.

566. Cf. Article 7 of the Council Regulation (EC) n° 428/2009 *supra* n. 230.
567. Cf. recital (8) and Article 2 2. (iii) of the Council Regulation (EC) n° 428/2009; *supra* n. 230.
568. Décret n° 2011-1425 of 2 novembre 2011 '*for inforcement of the article 413-7 of Criminal Code and related to the protection of the scientific and technical national potentiel*'; (JORF n° 0256 du 4 Nov. 2011 p.18562) and the Arrêté of 3 Jul. 2012 '*related to the protection of the national scientific and technical potential*'; (JORF n° 0155 of 5 Jul. 2012, p. 11051).

Also, most sensitive cases and specially classified information, could be covered by the Criminal Code (Article 411).

Par. 2 Control Lists

The lists of controlled Dual-Use goods and technology are common to all EU Member States. They were established by Council Regulation (EC) n° 428/2009.[569] They are set out under a comprehensive document set forth in Annex I of the Regulation (EC) n° 428/2009; Each General Licence on Annex II lists articles of the Annex I which could benefit of Union General Export Authorisation n° 1 to 6 and Annex IV lists the most sensitive articles of the Annex I which require a licence, even for intra-Community transfers (as well as export to non-EU Member States).

These lists are regularly updated according to developments in international treaties and international non-proliferation regimes and export control arrangements to which EU Member States are parties or Participating States. In particular, the list object of the Annex I is based on a combination of existing international lists, which were drawn up to prevent proliferation of nuclear (Nuclear Suppliers Group (NSG)), chemical and biological (Australia Group (AG)) products, ballistic missiles (MTCR) and conventional arms and Dual-Use goods (Wassenaar Arrangement).

Last 16 April 2014, the Regulation EU n° 599/2014, modified the Article 15 of the Regulation 428/2009 and give the European commission the capacity to update the list of dual-use items set out in Annex I.[570]

Par. 3 Licensing and Enforcement Authorities

In France since March 2010, a new specialized Department the 'SBDU': Service des Biens à Double Usage (Service of Dual-Use goods) is the focal point for Dual-Use goods exporters.[571] The SBDU is a Service of the Ministry for Economy, Industry and Numerical business under the General Directorate for Competitiveness, Industry and Services (DGCIS).[572]

---

569. Cf. Council Regulation (EC) n° 428/2009; *supra* n. 230.
570. Cf. Regulation (EU) n° 599/2014 of the European Parliament and of the Council of 16 Apr. 2014, amending Council Regulation (EC) 428/2009 setting up a Community regime for the control of exports, transfer, brokering and transit of dual-use items. (OJEU L 173 of 12.6.2014, p. 79). Additionally, Article 9(1) is amended and, in cases of arms embargoes imperative grounds of urgency, the Commission is empowered to remove destinations from the scope of Union General Export Authorisations.
571. SBDU (a National competency Service) has been created under the authority of MINEFi, It is composed with around fifteen persons including experts from MoD, MoFA, Nuclear Agency (*Commissariat à l'Energie Atomique* (CEA)), and ministry of Ecology, sustainable development and Energy (Ministère de l'écologie, du développement durable et de l'énergie).
572. SBDU substitutes for 'SETICE' ('*Service des Titres du Commerce Extérieur*'; the old Customs Directorate's service under the Ministry of Budget. SBDU is responsible for the rational assessment of the technological risks of end-use diversion. It makes the interface between the business world and the Administration in the framework of the French, EU and International Laws, Regulations and Regimes. SBDU is also in charge of licensing Electronic technology (before 2010 such licences were under the '*Direction Générale de l'Industrie des Technologies de l'Information et des Postes*' ('DiGITIP')).

The 'SBDU' is responsible for coordinate investigations and to deliver 'Dual use goods' licences. The exporter is responsible to know about the right classification of the products to be exported. However the SBDU could provide guidelines and support exporters in case of difficulties.

Today, the licence application has to be sent to the SBDU by mail using the 'CERFA' form (three pages: 'Application' 'Exporter' & 'Licence').[573] A receipt is delivered and the applicant can check with the licensing officer if his/her request is well completed.[574]

The final export decision is in any case made by the Minister in charge of Industry. According to the complexity of the operation and after a first assessment by the SBDU's technical experts, the application file is either processed internally or transmitted to the 'Interministerial Commission' of the Dual-Use goods ('*Commission Interministérielle des Biens à Double Usage*' (CIBDU))[575] for a collective survey and a common advise to the Minister in charge of Industry.

The 'CIBDU' examines monthly all applications for sensitive operations (e.g., individual licences for goods listed in Annex IV, or relating to sensitive export destinations), and all initial requests for 'global' or 'general' licences.

Finally, the Minister's decision is communicated in a letter, to the exporter by the SBDU.

Licensing process time is closely linked to the complexity of the application; nevertheless, if the final decision has not been communicated to the applicant within a nine-month period, the application is deemed denied.

Figure 7.2 summarizes the licensing process and Figure 7.3 summarizes what are the licensing possibilities according to the products and end users.

573. CERFA form n° 109 94*04; https://www.formulaires.modernisation.gouv.fr/gf/cerfa_10994.do.
574. It is important to apply for the right type of licence. In particular, for the first application or for the first export of new products, companies shall apply for 'individual licences'.
575. Note: Within the MoD, intelligence and security services play an important role in examining the credibility of the end-use/end-user declared for the goods or technology, assessing the risk of diversion from the end-use, and determining the reliability of the recipients.

Figure 7.2 Dual Use Products Licence Assessment Rules in France

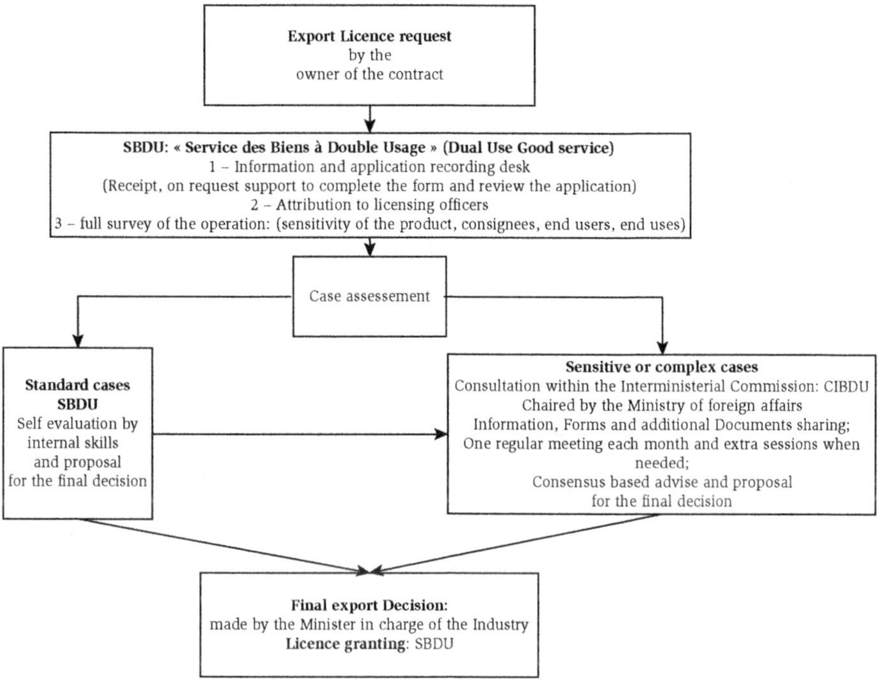

Figure 7.3 EU Dual Use Goods and Technology Licensing System

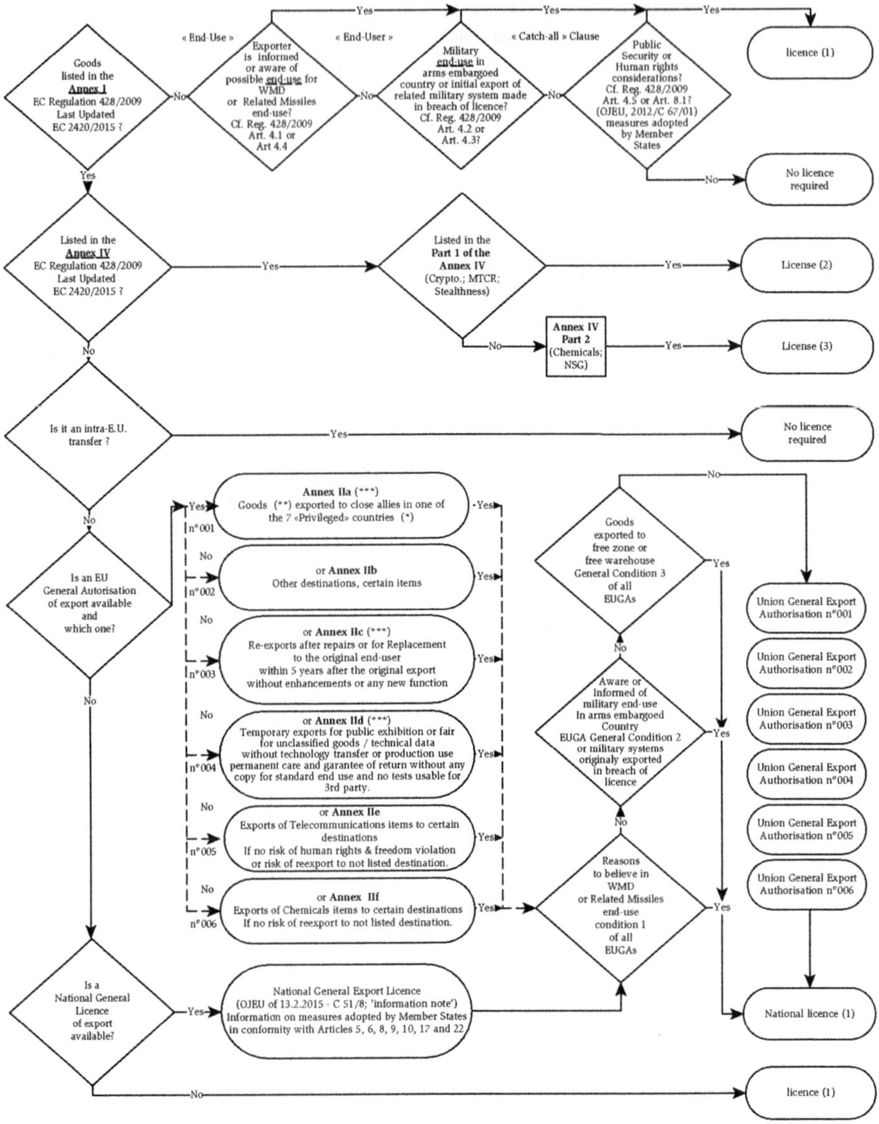

(1) Each EU Members states determines which type of EU licence (Individual or Global) is applicable.
(2) For goods and related technologies listed in Annex IV Part 1, Individual or Global EU licences are available.
(3) For goods and related technologies listed in Annex IV Part 2, only Individual licences are permitted.

(*) Seven countries listed in Annex IIa (EC) Regulation n° 428/2009 are the following: Australia, Canada, Japan, New-Zealand, Norway, Switzerland and US.

(**) Nearly all goods listed in Annex I except those listed in Annex IV and few others deemed very sensitive (cf. Annex g).
(***) cf. Annex IIg for possible other not authorized items.

Annex IIb Part 1 - Items:— 1A00I, — 1A003, — 1A004, — lC003b-c, — 1C004,— 1C005, — 1C006, — 1C008, — 1C009, — 2B008, — 3A001a3, — 3A001a6-12, — 3A002c-f, — 3C001, — 3C002, — 3C003, — 3C004, — 3C005, — 3C006.

Annex IIb Part 2 - Destinations: Argentina, Croatia, Iceland, South Africa, South Korea, Turkey.

Annex IIe Part 1 - Items: (a) the following items of Category 5, Part I: (i) items, including specially designed or developed components and accessories therefore specified in 5A001b2 and 5A001c and d; (ii) items specified in 5B001 and 5D001, where test, inspection and production equipment is concerned and software for items mentioned under (i);
(b) technology controlled by 5E00Ia, where required for the installation, operation, maintenance or repair of items specified under (a) and intended for the same end-user.

Annex IIe Part 2 - Destinations: Argentina, China (including Hong Kong and Macao), Croatia, India, Russia, South Africa, South Korea, Turkey, and Ukraine.

Annex IIf Part 1 - Items: 1C350: 1. Thiodiglycol (111-48-8); 2. Phosphorus oxychloride (10025-87-3); 3. Dimethyl methylphosphonate (756-79-6); 5. Methylphosphonyl dichloride (676-97-1); 6. Dimethyl phosphite (DMP) (868-85-9); 7. Phosphorus trichloride (7719-12-2); 8. Trimethyl phosphite (TMP) (121-45-9); 9. Thionyl chloride (7719-09-7); 10. 3-Hydroxy-1-methylpiperidine (3554-74-3); 11. N,N-Diisopropyl-(beta)-aminoethyl chloride (96-79-7); 12. N,N-Diisopropyl-(beta)-aminoethane thiol (5842-07-9); 13. Quinuclidin-3-ol (1619-34-7); 14. Potassium fluoride (7789-23-3); 15. 2-Chloroethanol (107-07-3); 16. Dimethylamine (124-40-3); 17. Diethyl ethylphosphonate (78-38-6); 18. Diethyl-N,N-dimethylphosphoramidate (2404-03-7); 19. Diethyl phosphite (762-04-9); 20. Dimethylamine hydrochloride (506-59-2); 21. Ethyl phosphinyl dichloride (1498-40-4); 22. Ethyl phosphonyl dichloride (1066-50-8); 24. Hydrogen fluoride (7664-39-3); 25. Methyl benzilate (76-89-1); 26. Methyl phosphinyl dichloride (676-83-5); 27. N,N-Diisopropyl-(beta)-amino ethanol (96-80-0); 28. Pinacolyl alcohol (464-07-3); 30. Triethyl phosphite (122-52-1); 31. Arsenic trichloride (7784-34-1); 32. Benzilic acid (76-93-7); 33. Diethyl methylphosphonite (15715-41-0); 34. Dimethyl ethylphosphonate (6163-75-3); 35. Ethyl phosphinyl difluoride (430-78-4); 36. Methyl phosphinyl difluoride (753-59-3); 37. 3-Quinuclidone (3731-38-2); 38. Phosphorus pentachloride (10026-13-8); 39. Pinacolone (75-97-8); 40. Potassium cyanide (151-50-8); 41. Potassium bifluoride (7789-29-9); 42. Ammonium hydrogen fluoride or ammonium bifluoride (1341-49-7); 43. Sodium fluoride (7681-49-4); 44. Sodium bifluoride (1333-83-1); 45. Sodium cyanide (143-33-9); 46. Triethanolamine (102-71-6); 47. Phosphorus pentasulphide (1314-80-3); 48. Di-isopropylamine (108-18-9); 49. Diethylaminoethanol (100-37-8); 50. Sodium sulphide (1313-82-2); 51. Sulphur monochloride (10025-67-9); 52. Sulphur dichloride (10545-99-0); 53. Triethanolamine hydrochloride (637-39-8); 54. N,N-Diisopropyl-(Beta)-aminoethyl chloride hydrochloride (4261-68-1); 55. Methylphosphonic acid (993-13-5); 56. Diethyl methylphosphonate (683-08-9); 57. N,Nimethylaminophosphoryl dichloride (677-43-0); 58. Triisopropyl phosphite (116-17-6); 59. Ethyldiethanolamine (139-87-7); 60. O,O-Diethylphosphorothioate (2465-65-8); 61. O,O-Diethyl phosphorodithioate (298-06-6); 62. Sodiumexafluorosilicate (16893-85-9); 63. Methylphosphonothioic dichloride (676-98-2).

1C450 a: 4. Phosgene: Carbonyl dichloride (75-44-5); 5. Cyanogen chloride (506-77-4); 6. Hydrogen cyanide (74-90-8); 7. Chloropicrin: Trichloronitromethane (76-06-2);

1C450 b: 1. Chemicals, other than those specified in the Military Goods Controls or in 1C350, containing a phosphorus atom to which is bonded one methyl, ethyl or propyl (normal or iso) group but not further carbon atoms;
2. N,N-Dialkyl [methyl, ethyl or propyl (normal or iso)] phosphoramidic dihalides, other than N,N-Dimethylaminophosphoryl dichloride which is specified in 1C350.57; 3. Dialkyl [methyl, ethyl or propyl (normal or iso)] N,N-dialkyl [methyl, ethyl or propyl (normal or iso)]-phosphoramidates, other than Diethyl-N,N-dimethylphosphoramidate which is specified in 1C350; 4. N,N-Dialkyl [methyl, ethyl or propyl (normal or iso)] aminoethyl-2-chlorides and corresponding protonated salts, other than N,N-Diisopropyl-(beta)-aminoethyl chloride or N,N-Diisopropyl-(beta)-aminoethyl chloride hydrochloride which are specified in 1C350; 5. N,N-Dialkyl [methyl, ethyl or propyl (normal or iso)] aminoethane-2-ols and corresponding protonated salts; other than N,N-Diisopropyl-(beta)-aminoethanol (96-80-0) and N,N-Diethylaminoethanol (100-37-8) which are specified in 1C350; 6.

N,N-Dialkyl [methyl, ethyl or propyl (normal or iso)] aminoethane-2-thiols and corresponding protonated salts, other than N,N-Diisopropyl-(beta)-aminoethane thiol which is specified in 1C350; 8. Methyldiethanolamine (105-59-9).

Annex IIf Part 2 – Destinations: Argentina, Croatia, Iceland, South Korea, Turkey, and Ukraine.

Annex IIg excluded – Items for UGEA 001, 003 & 004: — all items specified in Annex IV, And : — 0C001 'Natural uranium' or 'depleted uranium' or thorium in the form of metal, alloy, chemical compound or concentrate and any other material containing one or more of the foregoing, — 0C002'Special fissile materials' other than those specified in Annex IV, — OD001 'Software' specially designed or modified for the 'development', 'production' or '...' of goods specified in Category 0, in so far as it relates to 0C001 or to those items of 0C002 that are excluded from Annex IV, — 0E001 'Technology' in accordance with the Nuclear Technology Note for the 'development', 'production' or '...' of goods specified in Category 0, in so far as it relates to 0C001 or to those items of 0C002 that are excluded from Annex IV, — 1A102 Resaturated pyrolised carbon-carbon components designed for space launch vehicles specified in 9A004 or sounding rockets specified in 9A104, — 1C351 Human pathogens, zoonoses and 'toxins', — 1C352 Animal pathogens, - 1C353 Genetic elements and genetically modified organisms, — 1C354 Plant pathogens, — 1C450a.l. amiton: O,O-Diethyl S-[2-(diethylamino)ethyl] phosphorothiolate (78-53-5) and corresponding alkylated or protonated salts, — 1C450a.2. PFIB: 1,1,3,3,3-Pentaftuoro-2-(trifluoromethyl)-1-propene (382-21-8), — 7E104 'Technology' for the integration of flight control, guidance and propulsion data into a flight management system for optimization of rocket system trajectory, — 9A009.a. Hybrid rocket propulsion systems with total impulse capacity exceeding 1.1 MNs, — 9A117 Staging mechanisms, separation mechanisms and interstages usable in 'missiles'.

Par. 4 Sanctions for Non-compliance

Sanctions for non-compliance with applicable regulations and procedures are laid down in customs regulations.[576] There are also administrative sanctions in case of

576. *Customs offences A. – first class. Article 414*:

> *Are liable to a detention of three years, to a seizure of the object of fraud, the seizure of the means of transportation, the seizure of objects serving to mask the fraud, the seizure of the goods and the assets which are the direct or indirect product of the breach and a fine between one and two times the value of the object of the fraud, any smuggled fact as well as any fact of import or export without declaration when these breaches relate to goods of the category of those which are prohibited or strongly taxed in the sense of the present code. The prison sentence may be increased up to a maximal duration of five years and the fine can go three times to the value of the object of the fraud when the smuggled facts, of import or export concern Dual Use goods military and civilian whose circulation is subjected to limitation by the European regulations.*
>
> *The prison sentence may be increased up to a duration of ten years and the fine can go five times to the value of the object of the fraud either when the smuggled facts, of import or export concern dangerous goods for the health, the morality or laws and orders, the list of which is fixed by order of the Ministry in charge of customs, or when they are committed in organised group.*

The Criminal Code does not contain specific sanctions for irregular export of dual-use goods, (nevertheless, Art. 411 applies to illegal disclosure which could endanger the fundamental interests of the Nation) The sanctions provided for in customs regulations that are potentially applicable to breach of dual-use goods and Technology regulations are the same as the ones mentioned for military goods.

export irregularities or if the licence was obtained through misrepresentation. According to Article 1 of Decree n° 2001-1192 of 13 December 2001, the export licence may be suspended, modified, withdrawn or revoked by the Minister responsible for Customs. Finally, the sanctions already mentioned, which relate to National Security concerns, may also be imposed in situations involving Dual-Use goods of an intangible nature.

SECTION 5 SPECIFICITIES OF THE REGIME/SPACE-RELATED PROVISIONS

Sub-Section 1 Specificities of the Control Regime

Par. 1 Obligation to Notify Certain Exports to the National Institute of Industrial Property

According to Article R624-1 of the French Intellectual Property Code states:

> Any contract [...] having for its purpose the transfer by a natural or legal person, having his place of residence or business in France, to a natural or legal person, having his place of residence or business abroad, of industrial property rights and of all intellectual elements comprised in scientific or technical assistance of any nature, particularly know-how and engineering, shall be subject to declaration with the National Institute of Industrial Property.

Par. 2 Specific Sanctions for Non-compliance

Regarding military goods, an exporter may lose the AFCI in the event of a breach of the Labour Code.

In addition, AFCI may be withdrawn (or not be renewed) in the event of a condemnation to an imprisonment period of three months or more (suspended sentence or not).

Sub-Section 2 Space-Related Provisions in the Control Regime

Military space vehicles and equipment

Two categories of space-related goods are controlled in accordance with the Decree n° 2014-1253 of 27 October 2014 and the second part of the Arrêté of 27 June 2012[577] (which first part was last modified by the Arrêté of 16 March

577. Second part other assimilated products:

> 1.a) Satellite of detection or observation, their equipment of observation and photography as well as their ground stations, specifically, designed or modified for a military use or whose characteristics could confer them military capacities. When they are specially designed or modified for a military use, the spatial vehicles and other satellites, their ground stations and their equipment.

2015[578]) to update the French list of export controlled military goods and technologies.[579]

The first category 1.a is made of civil and military remote-sensing or observation satellites (and their observation or recording equipment, as well as their ground stations, designed or modified for a military use or whose characteristics could confer them military capacities). The 1.b consists of the military telecom satellites as well as their ground stations, conceived or modified for a military use and other satellites whose characteristics could confer them military capacities. The 1.c concerns the maintenance or environment of the two above paragraphs and the paragraph 1.d controls the manufacturing installations.

The second category 2.a concerns rockets, space launchers, and 2.b their equipment essential components, and specialized manufacturing testing tools and launching facilities.

To facilitate the Ariane VI programme and its numerous exchanges between the partners of the programme, a French General Licence (n° LGT110) has been granted last 28 July 2015.

Non-military space vehicles and equipment

Exports regarding civilian remote-sensing and telecom satellites (as well as their associated equipment, ground stations, facilities and services), are controlled in France under the Dual-Use goods and technology control principles described above.[580]

According to the law (Loi 2008/518 du 3 June 2008[581]) for spatial operations, the operator must grant a specific authorization before any launch or recuperation of a space object and the law *précises* the conditions of this authorization. Two Decrees define the export regime of spatial images: The Decree 2009-640 of 9 June 2009 (last

---

1.b) Engines and propulsion systems specially designed or modified for the materials of the paragraph 1.a above.
1.c) Other components, accessories and equipment of environment included specific equipment of maintenance of equipment listed in paragraphs 1a) as and 1b) above.
1.d) specialized equipment for manufacturing of products listed in paragraphs 1.a, 1.b and 1.c above.
2.a) rockets and spatial launchers with military ballistic capacities.
2.b) equipment, components, production, tests and launch installations, of the products listed in 2.a.

578. Cf. ML 11 Electronic products, 'spacecraft' and components not elsewhere listed in the common list of defence-related products annexed to the European Union ICT Directive, as follows: ... c) 'spacecraft' specially designed or modified for the military use and their components specially designed for the military use.
579. Décret n° 2014-1253 of 27 Oct. 2014 'relatif aux dispositions des livres III, VI et VII de la partie réglementaire du code de la sécurité intérieure' (modifying the Décret n° 2013-700 of 30 Jul. 2013 *'portant application de la loi n° 2012-304 of 6 March 2012 relative à l'établissement d'un contrôle des armes moderne, simplifié et préventif'* (JORF n° 0178 of 2 Aug 2013 p 13194)) and Arrêté of 27 Jun. 2012 *'relatif à la liste des matériels de guerre et matériels assimilés soumis à une autorisation préalable d'exportation et des produits liés à la défense soumis à une autorisation préalable de transfert'* (JORF n° 0151 of 30 juin 2012, p. 10702), last modified by Arrêté of 16 Mar. 2015 (cf. JORF n° 0073 of 27 Mar. 2015, p. 5553).
580. Cf. *supra* Section 4, Sub-Section 2.
581. LOI n° 2008-518 du 3 juin 2008 relative aux opérations spatiales (JORF n° 0129 du 4 Jun. 2008, p. 9169).

modified by the Decree 2013-653 of 19 July 2013)[582] sets the process and thresholds of each category of images and the Decree 2013-654 of 19 July 2013[583] establishes the role of the 'Commission Interministérielle des Données d'Origine Spatiale' (CIDOS) and related restrictions.

It must be underlined here that indeed, France has set up a 'trade freedom regime' to export satellite imagery. This regime is limited by the governmental capacity to freeze operations as soon as necessary. The 'CIDOS' can set up permanent restrictions regarding: images/data quality, end-uses/users. Additionally, on a case-by-case basis, CIDOS can also notify very sudden limitations depending on quick evolutions of the overall geopolitical climate or local changes.

SECTION 6 SANCTIONS AND EMBARGOES TO THIRD COUNTRIES

Today, France has to apply embargoes and restrictive measures to thirty countries[584] mostly based on United Nations Security Council (UNSC) resolutions or in the framework of EU decisions (I).

As it affects trade and exportations of military goods, any violation of those embargoes or restrictive measures may be sentenced on the basis of the CoD and the Code of Customs for transfers of Dual-Use goods or civil ones (II).

Sub-Section 1 Participation of France to Embargoes or Other Related Sanctions

An embargo has to be understood as restrictions applied to economic, trade or financial relations with a country in order to put it under diplomatic and political pressure. Embargoes or restrictive measures may be due to a unilateral decision from a specific country but most of the time, they are resulting from multilateral decisions.

In France, two types of restrictions are set up: restrictions decided by the UNSC under Chapter VII of the Charter, and restrictions decided by the EU.

The Treaty Establishing the European Community (Treaty of Rome of 1957), as amended by Lisbon Treaty of 2007, allows the EU Council to take restrictive measures against non-member countries on the basis of its economic and autonomous powers. It can be adopted in the framework of the Common and Foreign Security Policy (CFSP)

582. Décret n° 2009-640 du 9 juin 2009 portant application des dispositions prévues au titre VII de la loi n° 2008-518 du 3 juin 2008 relative aux opérations spatiales (JORF n° 0132 du 10 juin 2009, p. 9387); modified by Décret n° 2013-653 du 19 juillet 2013 modifiant le décret n° 2009-640 du 9 juin 2009 portant application des dispositions prévues au titre VII de la loi n° 2008-518 du 3 juin 2008 relative aux opérations spatiales (JORF n° 0168 of 21 Jul. 2013, p. 12190).

583. Décret n° 2013-654 du 19 juillet 2013 relatif à la surveillance de l'activité des exploitants primaires de données d'origine spatiale (JORF n° 0168 of 21 Jul. 2013, p. 12190).

584. *List of countries under French embargoes*: Afghanistan, Armenia, Azerbadjian, Belarus, Bosnia and Herzegovia, Central Africa Republic, China, Cote d'Ivoire, North Korea, Congo, Egypt, Eritrea, Guinea, Guinea Bisseau, Haiti, Iran, Iraq, Lebanon, Liberia, Libya, Moldova, Myanmar, Russia, Somalia, Sudan, Syrian Arabic Republic, Tunisia, Ukraine, Yemen, Zimbabwe.

under the Treaty on EU (Article 24[585]), or in the framework of the Trade and Economic Policy. EU decides restrictions regardless of the decisions taken by the UN Security Council. Whatever the framework, all sanctions must be adopted under a Common Position[586] (Article 29 TEU[587]).

But, Member States, as France, might also take unilateral measures if '*serious political reasons and grounds of urgency*' justify it, and if EU Council has not already taken such a measure (experience has shown that it is rarely used). Moreover, let us remember that arms sales are a Member State prerogative (Article 346[588]). France would take some embargoes or restrictive measures against countries regardless of EU decisions.

In addition, the Organization for Security and Cooperation in Europe (OSCE) imposes simultaneously other sanctions. For instance, France set up arms embargoes against Azerbaijan and Armenia in application of sanctions decided by OSCE.[589]

Concerning the nature of these sanctions, it is proportional to the gravity of the infraction committed. It can take the form of arms embargoes, general or specific trade restrictions (prohibition on exports and imports of Dual-Use goods or even purely civil goods), financial restrictions, assets freeze, entry and residence restrictions (ex: visa ban), etc.

In the same way as the UN, in the previous years, the EU and Member States had mostly applied arms embargoes or economic restrictions as restrictive measures. In case of terrorism, targeted financial sanctions can also be imposed. In this regard, the Article L. 562-1 of Monetary and Financial Code foresees asset freeze mechanisms in case of terrorist actions.

---

585. **Article 24 Treaty on EU** (ex Article 11 TEU):

> *1. The Union's competence in matters of common foreign and security policy shall cover all areas of foreign policy and all questions relating to the Union's security, including the progressive framing of a common defense policy that might lead to a common defense. The common foreign and security policy is subject to specific rules and procedures. It shall be defined and implemented by the European Council and the Council acting unanimously, except where the Treaties provide otherwise.*

586. **Common provision** is decided with unanimity in the Council but without any preliminary orientation of European Council. It binds Member States of EU. Contrary to the 'common action', the implementation of this common position is a Member States initiative.
587. **Article 29** of **Treaty on EU** (ex Article 15 TEU): '*The Council shall adopt decisions, which shall define the approach of the Union to a particular matter of a geographical or thematic nature. Member States shall ensure that their national policies conform to the Union positions.*'
588. *Article 346 of Treaty on the Functioning of the European Union (ex Article 223 Treaty Establishing European Community):*

> *1. The provisions of the Treaties shall not preclude the application of the following rules: (a) no Member State shall be obliged to supply information the disclosure of which it considers contrary to the essential interests of its security; (b)* ***any Member State may take such measures as it considers necessary for the protection of the essential interests of its security which are connected with the production of or trade in arms, munitions and war material****; such measures shall not adversely affect the conditions of competition in the internal market regarding products which are not* ***intended for specifically military purposes****. 2. The Council may, acting unanimously on a proposal from the Commission, make changes to the list, which it drew up on 15 April 1958, of the products to which the provisions of paragraph 1(b) apply.*

589. The only embargo decided by OSCE concerned armed forces engaged in Nagorno-Karabakh area.

The implementation of those sanctions depends on the scope of its field of competence. UNSC Resolution may be transposed directly by EU but it may also depend on Member States competences. It involves transposing the resolution by an EU regulation or a national act. Note that EU Regulations enter into force on the day of their publication in the national legal order. Most of EU regulations contain annexes that foresee the authorities in charge of sanctions in France, for example, the General Directorate of the Treasury[590] for questions linked to financial aspects or the French Customs and Indirect Taxation authority called 'DGDDI'[591] for customs matters.

According the nature of restrictions, Member States have to define sanctions in case of non-compliance, provide derogations by the same decision, write a report to the Commission to explain the national implementation, etc.

Sub-Section 2 Regime of the Embargo or Related Sanctions in France

Violations of embargoes may come from States which do not apply international decisions, but also from non-governmental organizations or groups, and natural or legal entities such as individuals or companies. Re-exportation circuits exist and may contribute to the failure of embargoes. Therefore, a repressive regime is required.

Awaiting a new legislation proposal, the current French legal framework imposes different types of sanctions. First of all, concerning the armament industry, the 'Code de la Défense'[592] has to be applied. Then, the 'Code des Douanes' also imposes sanctions for violation of embargoes notably concerning dual-use products. All precisions about those sanctions can be found under *Section 4, Parts 4 of Sub-Section 1 and 2, and Section 5, Part 2 of Sub-Section 1* of this chapter.

SECTION 7 LIST OF ABBREVIATIONS

AEMG	Autorisation d'Exportation de Matériel de Guerre
AFCI	Autorisation de Fabrication, de Commerce etd'Intermédiation
AG	Australia Group
AIMG	Autorisation d'Importation de Matériel de Guerre
AP	Agrément Préalable
APD	Attestation de Passage en Douane
ATS	Australian Treaty Series
BTWC	Biological and Toxic Weapons Convention
CGA	Contrôle Général des Armées
CIBDU	Commission Interministérielle des Biens à Double Usage

590. All request can be sent to: sanctions-gel-avoirs@dgtresor.gouv.fr and information can be found on: https://www.tresor.economie.gouv.fr/.
591. All information can be found on http://www.douane.gouv.fr/accueil.
592. Notably the Sections 1 and 2 of the Chapter IX of the Title III concerning war materials, arms and munitions set up the procedure and the different sanctions in case of non-compliance.

CIC	Commission Interministérielle de Classement
CIDOS	Commission Interministérielle des Données d'Origine Spatiale
CIEEMG	Commission Interministérielle pour l'Etude des Exportations de Matériels de Guerre
CoD	Code of Defence
CTBT	Comprehensive Test Ban Treaty
CUF	Certificat d'Utilisateur Final
CWC	Chemical Weapons Convention
DGA/DI/SD-GPC	Direction Générale de l'Armement/ Direction Internationale/ Sous-Direction de la Gestion des Procédures de Contrôle
DGA/DI/SDGQ/AE	Délégation générale pour l'Armement/Direction Internationale /Sous-Direction Politique d'Exportation/ Bureau des Analyses Economiques et des Statistiques
DGDDI	Direction Générale des Douanes et des Droits Indirects
DCE	Direction générale des entreprises (ex DGCIS)
DiGITIP	Direction Générale de l'Industrie des Technologies de l'Information et des Postes
EC	European Community/European Communities
EU	European Union
IAEA	International Atomic Energy Agency
ICP	Internal Control Program
ILM	International Legal Material
LoI	Letter of Intent
MoFADI	Ministry of Foreign Affairs and International Development
MINEFE[593]	Ministry for Economy, Finance and Employment
MINEFI	Ministry for Economy, Finance and Industry
MoD	Ministry of Defence ('Déf.' in French)
	Missile Technology Control Regime
NPT	Nuclear Non-Proliferation Treaty
NSG	Nuclear Suppliers Group
OJEU	Official Journal of the European Union
OJRF	Official Journal of the French Republic
OST	Outer Space Treaty
SBDU	Service des Biens à Double Usage
SGDSN	Secrétariat Général de la Défense et de la sécurité Nationale
UNTS	United Nations Treaty Series
WMD	Weapons of Mass Destruction

593. Before 19 Jun. 2007 MINEFi encompassed both the Finance Ministry and the Budget Ministry.

SECTION 8 REFERENCES

Sub-Section 1 Primary Documentation

Par. 1 Statutory Legislation

Sub-Par. 1 Relating to the Export and Import Control Regime on Military Goods and 'Assimilated Goods'

- *Code of Defence*: The CoD legislative part, was adopted by Ordinance n° 2004-1374 of 20 December 2004 (OJ, 21 December 2004). The CoD has been last modified by the French Parliament on 28 November 2005 (National Assembly, adopted text n° TA 503). Ordinance n° 2004-1374 has been ratified (including last modifications) by the Law n° 2005-1550 of 12 December 2005 (OJ 289, 13 December 2005, 19160). relevant provisions of the CoD for export purposes are set forth in *Partie 2, Livre III, Titre III.*
  Note: Legislative Decree/ 'Decret-loi' of 18 April 1939 creating a regime governing war weapons/products, arms and ammunition (OJ Lois et Décrets, 13 June 1939, 7463) has been integrated into the CoD.
- *Code of Internal Security* created by the Law n° 2003/239 of the 18 March 2003.
- *Law n° 2012- 304 of 6 March 2012* concerning control and classification of military goods.

Sub-Par. 2 Relating to the Export Control Regime on Dual-Use Goods and Technology

- *Council Regulation (EC) n° 428/2009 of 5 May 2009 setting up a Community regime for the control of exports, of dual-use items* and technology (OJEU *L.134, p. 1 of 29 May 2009)*, as subsequently amended.
- *Iran: Regulation* EU n° 267/2012 of 23 March 2012 concerning restrictive measures against Iran and repealing Regulation (EU) No 961/2010.
- *Syria: Regulations* EU n° 36/2012 of 18 January 2012 concerning restrictive measures in view of the situation in Syria and repealing Regulation (EU) No 442/2011.
- *Russia: Regulation* EU n° 833/2014 concerning restrictive measures in view of Russia's actions destabilizing the situation in Ukraine of 31 July 2014 amended by Regulation EU n° 960/2014 of 8 September 2014.

Par. 2 Regulations

Sub-Par. 1 Relating to Classification, Management, Export and Import Control Regime of Defence Related Goods, War Weapons/Products and Assimilated Products and Technology

Decree n° 1253/2014 of 27 October 2014 which was incorporated in the Code of internal security in its article R. 311-2 classing the different arms, ammunition and war materials (regulatory section).

- *Decree n° 2013-700 of 30 July 2013 for enforcement of the law n° 2012-304 of 6 March 2012 relative to the establishment of a modern, simplified and preventive control of weapons* (JORF n° 0178 of 2 August 2013 p. 13194), amended and repealed by the Decree n° 1253/2014 of 27 October 2014 which was incorporated in the Code of internal security in its article R. 311-2 classing the different arms, ammunition and war materials (regulatory section),

  Note: the 'perennial' Decree, 'Décret pérenne,' n° 901-2012 of 20 July 2012 related to the procedure applicable to the import, export and transfer outside of the EU territory of war equipment, arms and ammunition, assimilated products and Defense related goods (JORF n° 0169 of 22 July 2012 p. 12083), was incorporated in the Code of Defense since July 2014 (Regulatory Section – Title III of Book III of Part II, Chapter V: Imports and Exports – EU Transfers),
- *Decree n° 2012/1176 of 23 October 2012* for the reorganization of inter-ministerial commission to review exports of war materials (CIEEMG) (JORF n° 0249 du 25 October 2012 p. 16577 text n° 1), amending the Decree n° 55-965 of 16 July 1955,
- *Decree n°2012-929 of 31 July 2012* concerning organization and working of Committee for custom disputes (JORF n° 0178 of 2 August 2012 p. 12690 text n° 48),
- *Order of 2 September 2013* ***amending historical and collection arms and ammunition legal regime*** (JORF n° 0206 of 5 September 2013 p. 14985, Text n° 17),
- *Inter-ministerial Order of 2 June 2014* concerning derogations to the obligation of export licensing for arms, ammunition and war materials from EU territory or licenses for intra-community transfers of defense-related products, (JORF n° 0129 du 5 June 2014 p. 9453, Text n° 51),

  Note: Notice to exporters of war materials and assimilated products of 1 November 2014 (JORF n° 0254 du 1 November 2014 p. 18464, Text n° 140) listing countries which have been excluded of derogations,
- *Order from DGDDI*[594] *(Directorate General for Customs) and DGA*[595] *(the French defense procurement agency) of 14 April 2014* concerning licenses request, (JORF n° 0115 du 18 May 2014 p. 8211, Text n° 8),
- *Order of 1 October 2014* designing the members of the Committee for a posteriori controls, (JORF n° 0245 of 22 October 2014, Text n° 68),
- *Order of 2 September 2013*, for coordination of orders classing certain arms and ammunition, (JORF n° 0206 du 5 September 2013, p. 14988, Text n°18),
- *Order of 2 September 2013*, relative to the establishment of a modern, simplified and preventive control of weapons in application of Law n°2012-304 of 6 March 2012, p. 14989, Text n°19), for manufacturing and marketing Authorizations procedures
- *Order of 2 September 2013* relative to the rank of ammunition in application of Article 2, 10°) Category B and 7°) Category C of Decree n° 2013-700 of 30 July 2013 establishing war materials, arms and ammunition regime, (JORF n° 0206 du 5 September 2013, p. 15019, Text n° 20),
- *Inter-ministerial Order of 16 July 2012* as amended by Order of 2 June 2014 concerning imports reporting conditions and incoming transfers,

594. In French: Direction Générale des Douanes et Droits Indirects.
595. In French: Direction Générale de l'Armement.

- *Order from DGDDI of 20 June 2012* repealing 2ter dispositions concerning EU transfers of military products. The same order set up for an international import certificate (CII) and a delivery verification certificate (CVL) conditions, and forms concerning the Global Authorization for exports of military goods (called AGEMG[596]) and the Global Authorization for transit of military goods (called AGTMG[597]),
- *Order of 27 June 2012* concerning the list of war equipment and assimilated products subject to export prior authorization and defense-related products subject to transfer prior authorization (JORF n° 0151 of 30 June 2012 p. 10702), last updated by Order of 16 March 2015 (JORF n° 0073 of 27 March 2015, p. 5553 Text n° 56),
- *Order of 30 November 2011* concerning declaration for restrictions of re-export, *cf. Article 10 of Directive n° 2009/43/EC simplifying terms and conditions of transfers of defense-related products within the Community,*[598]
- *Order of 30 November 2011* organizing the on-the-spot-checks by Ministry of Defense ***in application of article L. 2339-1 of the Code of defense,***
- *Order of 30 November 2011,* concerning the certification procedure for companies wishing to purchase military products, (JO 8 December 2011),
- *Order 30 November 2011* relating to declaration modalities set up under article L.2335-7 of Code of Defense, (JO of 8 December 2011)
- *Inter-ministerial Orders of 6 January 2012* relating to the general license for EU transfers of military products for demonstrations and evaluations nearby EU companies, as amended by the Order of 6 June 2014 relating to general licenses for exports from EU territory of military products and assimilated ones and EU transfers of defense related products:

  LGT 101: Armed forces procurement
  LGT 102: Certified companies
  LGT 103: Fairs and exhibitions
  LGT 104: Demonstrations and evaluations for armed forces
  LGT 105: Demonstrations and evaluations for EU private companies
  LGT 106: Police and customs procurement

- *Inter-ministerial Order of 3 June 2013* relating to the general license for the transfer of military products and spatial materials transferred temporally in France from another EU Member State, as amended by Order of 6 June 2014:

  LGT: 107 Returns,

- *Inter-ministerial of 6 June 2013* relating to the general licenses for transfer of defense-related products and ground station for exploitation of satellites, for French armed forces located in another EU Member State, amended by the Order of 6 June 2014:

---

596. In French: '*Autorisation Globale d'Exportation de Matériel de Guerre*' (AGEMG).
597. In French: '*Autorisation Globale de Transit de Matériel de Guerre*' (AGTMG).
598. Article 10 (Export Limitations):

> *Member States shall ensure that recipients of defense-related products, when applying for an export license, declare to their competent authorities, in cases where such products received under a transfer license from another Member State have export limitations attached to them, that they have complied with the terms of those limitations, including, as the case may be, by having obtained the required consent from the originating Member State.*

LGT 108: French Army in EU
LGE 201: French Army outside the EU,

- *Inter-ministerial Order of 14 November 2014* relating to the general license for defense-related products' technologies for armed forces or contracting authorities in the defense area and for companies of a Member State:

  LGT 109: Transfers of technologies
  LGT 110: Ariane VI

Sub-Par. 2 Relating to the Export Control Regime of Dual-Use Goods and Technology

- *Decree n° 2001-1192 of 13 December 2001* relating to the control of exports, imports and transfers of dual-use goods and technology (OJ n°291, 15 December 2001, p. 19905); amended by Decree n° 2010-292 of 18 March 2010 relating to procedures of, export, transfer, of brokering and transit authorization of Dual Use goods and Technologies and transferring the control competency from the General Customs Directorate and indirect taxes to DGE competency (ex- Directorate General for Competitiveness, Industry and Services (DGCIS), since 2014), (OJ n° 0067 of 20 March 2010 p. 5633),
- *Orders of 13 December 2001*, allowing the enforcement of Decree n° 2001-1192 of 13 December 2001:
  1. Order related to the control over exports to third countries and over the transfer to Member States of the EC of dual-use goods and technology (OJ 291, 15 December 2001, p. 19911)
  2. Order related to the issuance of a CII and of a CVL for import of dual-use goods and technology (OJ 291, 15 December 2001, 19914); updated by ***Order of 18 March 2010 related to export, import and transfer authorizations of Dual Use goods and Technology*** (OJ n°0067 of 20 March 2010 p. 5636).
- Orders concerning exemptions:

  Order of 31 July 2014 for exports of helicopters and its spare parts to Non-Member State (OJ, 8 August 2004, p. 13297),
  Order of 31 July 2014 for tear gases exports to Non-member State,
  Note: those orders set up that there is no licensing obligation for that kind of products, excepted for the listed countries, for which an individual authorization is necessary,

- *Orders concerning the national general licenses*:

  Order of 31 July 2014 providing the national general licenses for 'dual-use goods for armed forces', (JORF n°0182 of 8 August 2014 p. 13294, Text n° 18),
  Order of 31 July 2014 providing the national general licenses for exhibitions and fairs, (OJ, 8 August 2004, p. 13294 and 13295),
  Order of 14 May 2007 providing the national general licenses for biological products exports, (OJ, 17 May 2007 p. 9555),
  Order of 18 July 2002 providing the national general licenses for industrial goods exports, (JORF n°176 du 30 July 2002 p. 12972, text n° 11),

Par. 3 Other

Sub-Par. 1 Military Goods

- The EU CoC for Arms Exports of 5 June 1998 (EU – The Council – 8675/2/98 – DG E – PESC IV) (Official Journal, 2003/C 320/01) and also available at: http://projects.sipri.se/expcon/eucode.htm.
- CoC – Common Position 2008/944 PESC 8 December 2008 (OJEU L 335 99, 13 December 2008.
- The Council of the European Union defined common rules governing the control of exports of military technology and equipment (Council of the European Union, 9241/2009, 29 April 2009, http://register.consilium.europa .eu/pdf/en/09/st09/st09241.en09.pdf).
- LoI of 6 July 1998 'between Six Defence Ministers on Measures to facilitate the Restructuring of the European Defence Industry' (can be found on the Internet site address: projects.sipri.se/expcon/loi/lointent.htm).
- Framework Agreement Concerning Measures to Facilitate the Restructuring and Operation of the European Defence Industry of 27 July 2000, (can be found on the Internet site address: projects.sipri.se/expcon/loi/indrest 01.htm).
- Council Common Position 2003/468/CFSP on the control of arms brokering of 23 June 2003, (OJ L 156/79, 25 June 2003).

Sub-Par. 2 Dual-Use Goods and Technology

Directive of the European Parliament and Council n° 43/2009 of 6 May 2009 'Simplifying terms and conditions of transfers of defence-related products within the Community' (OJEU L 146, 1 of 10 June 2009).

Bulletin officiel des douanes (Official Bulletin of the Customs) on the regulation related to Dual-Use goods and technology (n° 6590 of 26 January 2004, Text n° 03-077), which can be found on the following Internet site address: www.douane.gouv.fr

Par. 4 Annexes – Copies of Documents of Practical Use to the Importer/Exporter

A number of standard documents relevant for the import or export process in France (e.g., most current official application forms for import or export licences, templates of contractual undertaking, or regulation extracts) as well as other non-official documents are available on a dedicated DropBox folder which can be accessed by following the link below: www.kluwerlawonline.com/eclrh-annexes.

Sub-Section 2 Secondary Documentation

Par. 1 Internet Sites

Sub-Par. 1 Legislation and Regulations

- www.legifrance.gouv.fr (official Internet site for French legislation and regulations)
- www.journal-officiel.gouv.fr (Internet site of the French Republic's official newspaper publishing)

Sub-Par. 2 Miscellaneous

- www.ladocfrancaise.gouv.fr (Internet site providing quantity of French documentation on various topics such as Law, Economics, Politics, Institutions)
- www.sipri.org (Internet site of the Stockholm International Peace Research Institute, which conducts research on questions of conflict and cooperation for international peace and security)
- www.diplomatie.gouv.fr (Internet site of Foreign Affairs Ministry, stating regulations for military goods)
- www.entrerprises.gouv.fr (Internet site of Directorate General for Enterprises, stating regulations for dual-use items)
- www.defense.gouv.fr (Internet site of Ministry of Defence)

Par. 2 Paper Publications

- '*Report to Parliament on armament exports from France*' Ministry of Defence, June 2015(can be found on the Internet Site: http://www.ladocumentationfrancaise.fr/rapports-publics/154000378/index.shtml), 'Les exportations d'armement' http://www.ixarm.com/-Les-exportations-d-armement- 'Guide sur les exportations de biens et technologies à double usage', Direction générale des douanes et des droits indirects – Sous-direction du commerce international – Bureau E2 Prohibitions (can be found on the following Internet site: http://www.douane.gouv.fr/Portals/0/fichiers/2015-fevrier-guide-bdu.pdf).
- General Information for private companies about arm, ammunition and war material can be found on Directorate General for International Relations and Strategy (Direction générale des relations internationales et de la stratégie, DGRIS) website: www.defense.gouv.fr.
- '*Export control of dual-use goods and technologies*' / '*Le contrôle de l'exportation des biens et technologies à double usage*', by SBDU[599] (Service for Dual-Use goods), Directorate General for Enterprises (DGE) of Ministry of Economy and Industry, (Internet site: www.entreprises.gouv.fr).

599. In french: *Service des Biens à double usage.*

SECTION 9 USEFUL INFORMATION

Sub-Section 1 Licensing and Enforcement Authorities Contact Details

Par. 1 Military Goods Exports

Name of Organization	*Ministère de la Défense (MoD) Délégation Générale pour l'Armement/ Direction Développement International (DGA/DDI Sous-direction de la Gestion des Procédures de contrôle (SD/GPC))*
Postal Address	DGA/DI/SPEM/SDGPC/Bureau des licences - 60 boulevard du général Martial Valin – CS 21623 – 75509 Paris CEDEX 15
Telephone	+33 (0)9 88 68 51 05 / +33 (0)9 88 68 51 03 / +33 (0)9 88 68 50 79 / +33 9 88 68 50 80
Facsimile	+33 (0) 9 88 68 94 33
Website	http://www.defense.gouv.fr/english

Par. 2 Dual-Use Goods and Technology

Name of Organization	*Ministère de l'Economie, de l'industrie et du numérique Direction générale des Entreprises (DGE) Service des Biens à Double Usage (SBDU)*
Postal Address	67 rue Barbès – BP 80001 94200 IVRY-SUR-SEINE Cedex
Telephone	+33 (0) 1 79 84 34 10
Courriel	doublusage@finances.gouv.fr
Website	http://www.entreprises.gouv.fr/biens-double-usage/accueil

Name of Organization	*Ministère des Finances et des Comptes publics Direction Générale des Douanes et des Droits Indirects (DGDDI) Sous-direction du commerce international Bureau E2 (Prohibition et protection du consommateur)*
Postal Address	11 rue des deux communes 93558 Montreuil Cedex
Telephone	+33 (0)1 44 74 46 73 / (0) 1 44 74 43 98
Mail	dg-e2@douane.finances.gouv.fr
Website	www.douane.gouv.fr

Name of Organization	*Infos Douane Service (questions douanières générales)*
Telephone	0.811.20.44.44 (numéro Azur, coût d'un appel local depuis un poste fixe
Mail	ids@douane.finances.gouv.fr
Website	*www.douane.gouv.fr*

Par. 3 Miscellaneous

Name of Organization	*Secrétariat Général de la Défense et de la Sécurité Nationale (SGDSN) Direction des affaires Internationales Stratégiques et Technologiques*
Postal Address	51, boulevard de La Tour-Maubourg 7500 PARIS 07 SP France
Telephone	+33 (0)1 71 75 80 51
Fax	+33 (0)1 71 75 80 60
Website	http://www.sgdsn.gouv.fr/site_rubrique87.html

Name of Organization	*Secrétariat Général de la Défense et de la Sécurité Nationale (SGDSN) Agence Nationale de la sécurité des systèmes d'information (for cryptology, IT and cyber security)*
Postal Address	51, boulevard de La Tour-Maubourg 75700 PARIS 07 SP France
Telephone	+33 (0)1 71 75 82 75
Fax	+33 (0)1 71 75 82 60/84 00
Website	www.ssi.gouv.fr

Name of Organization	*Ministère des Affaires Etrangères (MoFA) Direction des affaires stratégiques de sécurité et du désarmement*
Postal Address	37, Quai d'Orsay 75700 PARIS 07 SP France
Telephone	+33 (0)1 43 17 43 08
Fax	+33 (0)1 43 17 49 52/+33 (0) 1 43 17 43 14
Website	www.diplomatie.gouv.fr

Sub-Section 2 Other

None.

CHAPTER 8
Germany

Henrik Brethauer[*]

SECTION 1 TABLE OF CONTENTS

* Henrik Brethauer, LL.M. (Canterbury) is member of the Group Export Compliance Office of Airbus Group in Germany.

SECTION 2 EXECUTIVE SUMMARY

Germany is a strong supporter of 'free foreign trade', being one of the biggest exporting countries in the world. Therefore, generally trade will only be restricted under the aspects of the protection of the security, foreign interests and international commitments.

As a member of the European Union (EU), the North Atlantic Treaty Organization (NATO) and the United Nations (UN), Germany considers the criteria for international security in an extensive way. It is one of the core objectives of Germany's foreign policy to strengthen international security and stability through active participation in international organizations.

Germany is a member of all international agreements which aim to regulate the trade of conventional arms as well as fight against international terrorism and the proliferation of weapons of mass destructions[600] (WMD).

UN resolutions, NATO Policy, EU Legislation/Council decisions and the international export control regimes/treaties are the backbone of the German export control policy, which mainly relates to: (i) deliveries of military goods,[601] war weapons[602] and dual-use goods[603] as well as the provision of associated technical assistance and other services in foreign countries.

The main relevant legislation for exporting companies of the defence sector consists of:

- European Parliament and Council Directive n° 2009/43/EC ('*ICT-Directive*').
- European Parliament and Council Regulation (EU) n° 258/2012 ('*Feuerwaffenverordnung der EU*').
- The German Foreign Trade and Payment Act ('*Außenwirtschaftsgesetz*' - 'AWG'), including the corresponding Foreign Trade and Payments Ordinance ('*Außenwirtschaftsverordnung*' - 'AWV').
- The War Weapons Control Act ('*Kriegswaffenkontrollgesetz*' - 'KWKG').

The relevant legislation for exporting companies in the civil/dual-use sector is:

- The Council Regulation (EC) n° 428/2009 ('*EC Dual-use Regulation*') which replaced Regulation (EC) n° 1334/2000.

600. The term 'weapons of mass destructions' covers nuclear, biological and chemical weapons.
601. The term 'military goods' covers armaments and firearms pursuant to Annex I, Part I, Section A of the Foreign Trade and Payments Ordinance ('*Anlage AL zur Außenwirtschaftsverordnung, Teil I, Abschnitt A*'). The term 'good' in conjunction with the terms 'military' or 'dual use' includes commodities, technology and data processing programmes.
602. Pursuant to §1(1) War Weapons Act, the term 'war weapons' means armaments comprised by the Annex to the War Weapons Act ('*Anlage zu §1 Absatz 1 des Kriegswaffenkontrollgesetzes*').
603. See: Article 2, paragraph 1 of the Council Regulation (EC) n° 428/2009 *supra* n. 230.

- Some national amendments to this regulation.

A major reform of the German export control law was carried out in 1991 which introduced the following new rules and procedures:

- The end-use control for unlisted goods by 'catch all clauses', which later became part of the Council Regulation (EC) n° 428/2009.
- The concept of the nomination of an 'Officer responsible for Exports' ('*Ausfuhrverantwortlicher*' - 'AV')[604] within exporting companies, who must be a member of the 'Top Management'.

A further reform of the German export control laws was carried out in 2013. Both rules and the structure of AWG and AWV were simplified and streamlined in order to facilitate the use of such legal texts. The legal wording was modernized and regulations of little or no relevance were deleted. Also specific national regulations which gave disadvantages to German exporting companies in comparison to exporting companies from other EU Member States were removed. The reform, moreover, comprised modifications of the provisions on administrative and criminal sanctions.

The 2013 reform of AWG and AWV did not impact the general structure or the principles of the German export control regime. The most relevant rules for exporting companies remained unchanged. In particular the reform did not lower the control standards for the export of war weapons or military goods.

A major role in the application of the German export control laws regarding defence products have the 'Political Principles of the German Government for export of War Weapons and other Military Equipment (Guidelines)',[605] which were first released in 1982 and updated in January 2000. Pursuant to such guidelines:

- Export licences are generally granted for deliveries of war weapons and military goods if:
  (i) the final destination is a NATO or NATO-equivalent state;[606]
  (ii) if the export is undertaken in the frame of government-to-government cooperation; or
  (iii) if it is carried out in scope of a governmentally approved industrial cooperation between companies located in the above-mentioned states.
- Decision-making on export licences for shipments to all other countries is subject to the principle of restraint. Licences to these destinations are only granted after detailed assessment, if it is ensured that the export is compliant with all national and international interests and commitments.

604. The legal basis for the concept of the AV is included in §8(2) AWG and in the Principles of the Federal Government to check the reliability of exporters' of 25 Jul. 2001.
605. The 'EU Code of Conduct on Arms Exports' of 5 Jun. 1998 became an integral part of those guidelines by the 2000 revision.
606. Such as: Switzerland, Australia, New Zealand and Japan.

In the area of exports of dual-use goods, the Common Position n° 944/2008[607] plays a comparable role as the Political Principles. It covers criteria which must be considered in the context of decision-making on licence requests and, thus, serves as a guideline for the approval of export cases.

SECTION 3 INTRODUCTION – ELEMENTS OF CONTEXT

Sub-Section 1 Regime Overall Philosophy

The overall philosophy of the German export control system is defined by three principles.

Par. 1 Principle 1: 'Free Trade'[608]

In Germany the trade in goods, services, capital assets, payment transactions and any other types of trade with foreign economic territories as well as the trade in foreign valuables and gold between German residents (foreign trade and payments) is generally not restricted.

However, trade may be subject to requirements which are included in the AWG or which are laid down in statutory orders.

Par. 2 Principle 2: 'Protection of Security and External Interests'[609]

Legal transactions and activities related to foreign trade and payments may be subject to limiting conditions in order to:

- Meet international Commitments.
- Guarantee the vital security interests of Germany.
- Avoid a disturbance of the peaceful coexistence between nations.
- Prevent a major disruption of the foreign relations of Germany.
- Maintain the public security and order in accordance to Article 36, Article 52 (1) and Article 65 (1) of the Treaty on the Functioning of the European Union (TFEU).
- Prevent shortages in essential needs for the German population in accordance to Article 36 of the TFEU or for protection of the population's health and safety.

607. Council Common Position 2008/944/CFSP of 8 Dec. 2008 defining common rules governing control of exports of military technology and equipment, OJ L 335/99.
608. §1 AWG.
609. §4(1) (2) AWG.

Par. 3 Principle 3: 'Export Control Is the Responsibility of the Top Management'[610]

The Top Management of exporting companies has to guarantee compliance with the applicable European and German export control laws. Each exporting company has to nominate a member of the Board of Directors of the Executive Management as an 'Officer responsible for Exports', who has to ensure the establishment and maintenance of a reliable and compliant export control organization in the company. The nomination of such officer is a prerequisite for the receipt of export related licences.

Sub-Section 2 Historical Outlook

Par. 1 The National Elements

After the Second World War until 1955, any West-German activities regarding the foundation of military forces or the establishment of a defence industry have been forbidden by the former occupying powers USA, France and Great Britain.

With the Korean War and the gradual intensification of the Cold War between the communist Soviet Bloc and the Western Countries, the political scenario changed drastically. The Federal Republic recovered its full sovereignty. It became a member of the NATO and built up new military forces ('Bundeswehr'). In this context West-Germany was able to re-establish its national defence industry. The political objective for the defence industry was to provide an industrial and technological contribution for the armament of the West-German and the allied NATO military forces.

The re-establishment of the West-German defence industry was achieved largely through participation in government-to-government defence cooperation. This bilateral and multilateral approach served as a political measure to avoid the impression among the neighbour countries that a purely 'national' oriented defence industry would be established in Germany only short after the end of the Second World War.

As a consequence of the strategic reorientation of the Western and the West-German foreign and security policy, the Parliament ('Bundestag') of the Federal Republic approved and implemented in 1961 the relevant legislation related to exports of military goods and the production and handling of war weapons.

The following laws were imposed:

- The war weapons list (*'Kriegswaffenliste'* - 'KWL'), 20 April 1961 (which became later a part of the KWKG).
- The KWKG, 1 June 1961.
- The AWG, 28 April 1961 (in 1986 the AWG was amended by the AWV, which regulates in detail the different licence procedures regarding approval and denial).

610. See 'Principles of the Federal Government to check the reliability of exporters' of 25 Jul. 2001.

In the context of the KWKG, in 1978 the Federal Republic introduced, as one of the first countries in the world, provisions on brokering.[611] According to such rules, brokering activities undertaken on domestic territory require a licence if the activities refer to the delivery of war weapons from a location outside the domestic territory to another third country. The political intention was to restrict the trade of war weapons primarily to companies that were under contract with the government and, therefore, being controlled by it (i.e.: under the security regulations).

In 1982 the government of the Federal Republic established the 'Political Principles for the export of War Weapons and other Military Equipment (Guidelines)'. These guidelines which were confirmed in 2000 became important for the application of the German export control laws. They are considered in the scope of all licence issuing processes related to war weapons or military goods. The purpose of the guidelines is to facilitate trade which is in the interest of the NATO and NATO-equivalent states and to implement a restrictive policy for trade with countries outside the NATO alliance. In particular the guidelines include that exports are not approved if there is 'sufficient reason' to suspect that the exported goods will be used for internal repression or for any other human rights violations. Also other criteria laid down in the guidelines are of importance for the decision-making process, such as: the internal situation in the country of final destination resulting from tensions or armed conflicts, the preservation of peace, security and stability in a region, the purchasing country's stance towards the international community, especially its position on terrorism and its compliance with international non-proliferation obligations, or the risk of the equipment being diverted when arriving in the purchasing country.

Par. 2 The European Elements[612]

After the German reunification in 1989 and the EU summits of Maastricht and Helsinki, the EU Member States accepted to take over a bigger responsibility with respect to the international foreign and security policy. In this context it was decided to foster coherence and harmonization among the export control regimes of the EU Member States.

In 1998 the EU Code of Conduct for Arms Exports was adopted by the European Council in the framework of the Common Foreign and Security Policy. Such Code sets out common principles to be respected by EU Members States in the context of the decision-making on export/import of defence goods and war weapons. Additionally, in 2000 the six biggest arms producing EU Member States (France, Germany, Italy, Spain, Sweden and the United Kingdom) signed the Letter of Intent (LoI) 'Framework Agreement Concerning Measures to Facilitate the Restructuring and Operation of the European Defense Industry[613] (FA)'. Part 3 of the FA provides for special licence procedures to facilitate stronger governmental and industrial European defence cooperation.

611. See: §4a KWKG.
612. Please refer to the Chapter on the European Union.
613. Signed at the Farnborough Air Show on 27 Jul. 2000.

The principles of the EU Code of Conduct which were reinforced by the Common Position n° 944/2008[614] and the proposed procedures of the FA are fully implemented in the German export control procedures and export control policy.

Further coherence among the export control regimes of the EU Member States was established by the European Parliament and Council Directive n° 2009/43/EC since 2009. The Directive includes procedures to facilitate exports of defence goods within the EU and covers measures for harmonization.

Sub-Section 3 Participation to International Regimes

The following tables display Germany's participation status to export control related international treaties and programmes. It is also stated, when relevant, that Germany is party to a treaty either by signature and ratification or by accession.

Par. 1 Treaties and Regimes Dealing with Specific Items and Technologies

Table 8.1 Nuclear Weapons Treaties

Treaty Name	*Overall Status*	*Specific Status*	*Enforceable in Germany*
Limited Test Ban Treaty[615]	OS: 5 August 1963 EF: 10 October 1963	S: 19 August 1963	Yes
Nuclear Non-Proliferation Treaty[616]	OS: 1 July 1968 EF: 5 March 1970	S: 24 September 1996	No
Comprehensive Nuclear Test Ban Treaty[617]	OS: 24 September 1996 EF: not in force	R: 20 August 1998	

OS: Opened for signature; EF: Entry into force; S/R: Signature/Ratification; A: Accession.

Table 8.2 Biological and Chemical Weapons Treaties

Treaty Name	*Overall Status*	*Specific Status*	*Enforceable in Germany*
Geneva Protocol[618]	OS: 17 June 1925 EF: 8 February 1928	S: 17 June 1925 R: 30 May 1931	Yes

614. The Common Position constituted a significantly updated and upgraded instrument which replaced the EU Code of Conduct on Arms Exports of 5 Jun. 1998.
615. Treaty Banning Nuclear Weapon Tests in the Atmosphere, in Outer Space and Under Water, *U.N.T.S.*, vol. 480, p. 43.
616. Treaty on the Non-Proliferation of Nuclear Weapons, *U.N.T.S.*, vol. 729, p. 161.
617. U.N.G.A., resolution 50\245.

Treaty Name	*Overall Status*	*Specific Status*	*Enforceable in Germany*
Biological Convention[619]	OS: 10 April 1972 EF: 26 March 1975	S: 10 April 1972 R: 7 April 1983	Yes
Chemical Convention[620]	OS: 13 January 1993 EF: 29 April 1997	S: 13 January 1993 R: 12 August 1994	Yes

OS: Opened for signature; EF: Entry into force; S/R: Signature/Ratification; A: Accession.

Table 8.3 Multilateral Export Control Regimes

Regime Name	*Formation*	*Participation*
Zangger Committee[621]	1971	Yes
Nuclear Suppliers Group	1974	Yes
Australia Group	1985	Yes
Missile Technology Control Regime	1987	Yes
Wassenaar Arrangement[622]	1994	Yes

Table 8.4 Other

Name	*Adoption*	*Participation*
International Code of conduct[623]	25 November 2002	Yes

Par. 2 Treaties Dealing with Specific Areas

Table 8.5 International Zones

Treaty Name	*Overall Status*	*Specific Status*	*Enforceable in Germany*
Antarctic Treaty[624]	OS: 1 December 1959 EF: 23 June 1961	A: 5 February 1979	Yes

618. Protocol for the Prohibition of the Use in War of Asphyxiating, Poisonous or Other Gases, and of Bacteriological Methods of Warfare, 94, *League of Nations Treaty Series*, No. 2138 (1929).
619. Convention on the Prohibition of the Development, Production and Stockpiling of Bacteriological (Biological) and Toxin Weapons and On Their Destruction, *U.N.T.S.*, vol. 1015, p. 163.
620. Convention on the Prohibition of the Development, Production, Stockpiling and Use of Chemical Weapons and on Their Destruction, Doc.CD/CW/WP.400/Rev.1.
621. Non-Proliferation Treaty Exporters Committee (also called the Zangger Committee).
622. Wassenaar Arrangement on export controls for conventional arms and dual-use goods and technologies.
623. Hague Code of Conduct against Ballistic Missile Proliferation, not yet published.
624. 402, *U.N.T.S.*, 7.

Treaty Name	Overall Status	Specific Status	Enforceable in Germany
Outer Space Treaty (OST)[625]	OS: 27 January 1967 EF: 10 October 1967	R: 10 February 1971	Yes
Sea Bed Arms Control Treaty[626]	OS: 11 February 1971 EF: 23 June 1961	S: 8 June 1971 R: 18 November 1975	Yes
Moon agreement[627]	OS: 18 December 1979 EF: 11 July 1984	-	No
Convention on the Law of the Sea[628]	OS: 10 December 1982 EF: 16 November 1994	R: 10 October 1994	Yes

OS: Opened for signature; EF: Entry into force; S/R: Signature/Ratification; A: Accession.

Table 8.6 Regional Nuclear Weapons-Free Zones

Treaty Name	Overall Status	Specific Status	Enforceable in Germany
Treaty of Tlatelolco[629]	OS: 14 February 1967 EF: 22 April 1967	-	No
Treaty of Rarotonga[630]	OS: 6 August 1985 EF: 11 December 1986	-	No
Treaty of Bangkok[631]	OS: 15 December 1995 EF: 27 March 1997	-	No
Treaty of Pelindaba[632]	OS: 11 April 1996 EF: not in force	-	No

OS: Opened for signature; EF: Entry into force; S/R: Signature/Ratification; A: Accession.

625. Treaty on Principles Governing the Activities of States in the Exploration and Use of Outer Space, including the Moon and Other Celestial Bodies, *U.N.T.S.*, vol. 610, p. 205.
626. Treaty on the Prohibition of the Emplacement of Nuclear Weapons and other Weapons of Mass Destruction on the Seabed and The Ocean Floor and in the subsoil thereof, *U.N.T.S.*, vol. 955, p. 115.
627. Agreement governing the Activities of States on the Moon and Other Celestial Bodies, *I.L.M.*, vol. 18, p. 1434.
628. Doc. A/CONF.62/122 and Corr.1-11.
629. Treaty for the Prohibition of Nuclear Weapons in Latin America and the Caribbean, *U.N.T.S.*, vol. 634, p. 326.
630. South Pacific Nuclear Free Zone Treaty, *I.L.M.*, vol. 24, p. 1442.
631. South East Asia Nuclear-Weapon-Free Zone Treaty, *I.L.M.*, vol. 35. p. 635.
632. African Nuclear Weapon-Free Zone Treaty, *I.L.M.*, vol. 35, p. 698.

SECTION 4 CONTROL REGIME

Sub-Section 1 Military Goods and Services

Par. 1 Overall Presentation

Pursuant to §2(21) AWG deliveries from the German territory to countries outside the EU customs territory are determined as 'exports', while deliveries from the German territory to the EU customs territory are called 'transfers'. Such distinction of the terms requires a further legal differentiation between transfers where the goods remain in the EU and those followed by an export to countries outside the EU. The transfer of military goods is subject to licence just like their export. The differentiation between exports and transfers, however, gains importance with respect to the delivery of dual-use goods.[633]

Sub-Par. 1 Requirements Prior to Any Specific Import/Export (i.e., Construction Phase)

The development, production and maintenance of military goods must generally not be legitimated on the basis of licences. In this phase, however, licence requirements must be considered when the goods, parts of them or technology and software related to the goods are exchanged between different countries. Such exchanges which are legally determined as exports or transfers occur regularly in transnational producing companies. The provision of software and technology in the companies' intranets or in the internet is also subject to licensing if the access to software and technology is possible from third countries.

All industrial activities in relation to war weapons, such as development, production, maintenance or transport, require governmental licence. Companies that want to engage in those activities must hold specific war weapons licences. For instance, pursuant to §3 KWKG any domestic transport of war weapons between companies or between two sites of one company can only be undertaken when specific licences for the transport are in place (in case the transport occurs between two companies both companies involved in the transport need a specific licence).

Sub-Par. 2 Requirements at the Import and/or Export Stages

The German export policy is primarily 'end-user/end-use' oriented based on: (i) governmental guidelines, (ii) international sanctions/embargoes, (iii) Common Position 2008/944/CFSP, (iv) Article 6 and Article 7 of the Arms Trade Treaty. As consequence, licence for exports and transfers of military products are in general granted:

633. See *infra* Section 4, Sub-section 2.

- In the scope of government-to-government cooperation for defence programmes.
- When the 'end-user/end-use' destination is situated in an EU Member State, a NATO or NATO-equivalent state.
- Within the framework of a governmentally approved industrial cooperation between companies located in the above-mentioned states, especially between companies of the FA Member States.

Regarding exports to all other destinations generally a more restrictive licence policy is administered. The decision about such exports is conducted after detailed assessment on a case-by-case basis.

I Goods

All exports and transfers of military goods need an licence pursuant to the AWG and the AWV. No licences are needed for (i) submission of proposals or (ii) negotiation and signature of sales contracts for military goods as long as no controlled technical data is provided as part of these activities. German companies regularly include a clause in their sales contracts stipulating that the delivery obligation expires if not all respective export or transfer licences are granted.

In addition, as no export or transfer licence is necessary in the context of the submittal of a proposal, companies can apply for a so called 'export advice' ('*Voranfrage*') to check if the contemplated export or transfer will be permitted in the case that a contract is signed. The request for an export advice will be processed as if it was a licence application.

Pursuant to §§2 to 4a KWKG any activities regarding war weapons such as production, maintenance, transport, import, export as well as brokering and trafficking must be legitimated on the basis of licences.

II Services

Also certain services related to military goods and war weapons can be subject to export control restrictions.

§§49-52 AWV include information and licence requirements for the provision of technical assistance in another country. The term 'technical assistance' comprises any technical service, as repair, maintenance, development, but also transfer of practical skills and knowledge, i.e.: by consultation and training. Technical assistance can also be granted in oral or electronic form, by telephone or fax.

The BAFA decides whether an licence for the provision of the technical assistance is required. An licence shall be sought when the service provider was informed by BAFA or already knows that the technical assistance is granted in connection with the development, production, handling, operation, maintenance, storage, detection, identification or dissemination of WMD or with a military end-use in a purchasing country or country of destination that is subject to an arms embargo. These licence requirements apply to all domestic residents and all German nationals. The transfer of information that is available 'in the public domain' or is a part of basic scientific research is exempt from the licence requirement.

Moreover, §§46 and 47 AWV and §4a KWKG stipulate that licensing requirements apply to certain brokering services with regard to military goods and war weapons. Pursuant to such provisions, generally a brokering licence must be obtained when a person or company undertakes any supporting activities towards the delivery of military goods or war weapons from a location outside Germany to a destination in another third country. There are various ways of arranging or concluding a contract, such as:

- The brokering of a contract on the acquisition or disposal of military goods or war weapons.
- The proof of an opportunity to conclude such a contract.
- The conclusion of a contract on the disposal of military goods or war weapons.

III Persons

The concept of 'deemed export' is not contained in the German export control regime. However, the release of certain information classified as national confidential can be considered as illegal disclosure of secrets which is subject to the German Criminal Code.

Par. 2 Control Lists

Military goods and war weapons are mainly included in the following lists:

- List with military goods (*'Anlage AL zur Außenwirtschaftsverordnung, Teil I, Abschnitt A'*).
- List with war weapons (*'Anlage zu §1 Absatz 1 des Kriegswaffenkontrollgesetzes'*).

The Military goods list covers defence products as well as parts and components thereof in 22 sections (numbers 0001 to 0022). Such list correlates with the list of the Wassenaar Arrangement. The war weapons list covers primarily lethal weapon systems, their subsystems and components.

Moreover, the list of Regulation (EU) No. 258/2012 must be considered. Such list includes firearms, parts and components thereof as well as ammunition in this respect.

Par. 3 Licensing and Enforcement Authorities

Sub-Par. 1 Application for and Granting of Licences Regarding Export and Brokering of Military Goods

I Licensing Process

The BAFA manages all export and transfer licences related to military goods. This also includes licences for brokering, technical assistance as well as export advices. BAFA prepares based on the application documents: (i) a review under technical and legal aspects and (ii) a recommendation/justification for an approval or denial.

For exports or transfers with a final 'end-user/end-use' destination in the EU, in NATO or NATO-equivalent States, the BAFA had the mandate to take decisions about the issuance of licences independently. These competences for autonomous decision-making were withdrawn during the current legislative period.

Consequently, as applicable for all other destinations, recommendations for further consultation have to be submitted to the:

- Federal Ministry for Economic Affairs and Energy ('*Bundesministerium für Wirtschaft und Energie*' - 'BMWi').
- Federal Foreign Office ('*Auswärtiges Amt*' - 'AA').

In the following consultation process the ministries unanimously approve or deny the recommendation given by BAFA with regard to a certain export or transfer. They also involve other Ministries, such as: the Federal Ministry of Defence ('*Bundesministerium der Verteidigung*' - 'BMVg') and public agencies, if additional advice is necessary. BAFA has to respect the decision taken on ministerial level and execute it in the licence application process by issuance of a formal licence or a licence denial.

If the ministries do not agree on a common position or the export is considered as sensitive, the case must be submitted to the 'National Security Council' under the presidency of the German Chancellery. The council meets four to five times a year. In secret discussions the council members decide about export cases as last political instance. Only approved export cases are disclosed to the German Parliament.

In the event a licence application is denied, companies have the right to appeal against the decision to BAFA. If BAFA does not address the appeal within a reasonable period of time or persists in the denial of the licence the exporting company can seek judgment from the responsible Administrative court ('*Verwaltungsgericht*').

II Existing Types of Licence

The following export and transfer licence types exist:

- Individual Export/Transfer Licences (The basic type of export licence is the individual licence. It permits the shipment of one or several goods to one consignee, based on one order. The so-called maximum amount licence, being a special type of individual licence, license the shipment to one consignee up to an amount which is determined in the licence.).

- Global Project Licences (GPL) (Privileged licence type for reliable exporting companies and related to government-to-government cooperation or for governmentally approved industrial cooperation.).
- Open General Licences (The exporter does not need to apply for utilization of this licence type. It is sufficient if the exporter registers as the user. The licences are provided with additional terms and conditions by BAFA and published in the Federal Gazette. Each licence is only valid for the specific items and countries.).
- Trafficking and Brokering Licences (The licences legitimate trafficking and brokering activities in individual cases).

III Application Procedure

Applications for export or transfer licences can be filed electronically through the BAFA export portal ELAN K2 (Electronic Application Registration and Communication) or in paper form. The ELAN K2 is accessible on the BAFA homepage. Application forms are available from most of the Chambers of Industry and Commerce. Instructions on how to complete the forms are provided on the BAFA homepage.

Pursuant to 21 (1) (2) AWV an 'end-use-certificate' must be enclosed with the application for export or transfer licences. With respect to such certificates it must be distinguished between private and official end-use certificates as well as governmental end-use certificates (*'International Import Certificates'* – 'IC'). Both private and official end-use certificate contain statements by the consignee or end-user, referring to the final destination and use of the goods to be delivered. The official end-use certificate is only required if the goods are provided to a governmental end-user. It must include a confirmation on the intended end-use by a government licence, but can also include a statement of an involved private entity. In contrast to official end-use certificate, ICs comprise only an official declaration by the recipient country that it took note of the intended import of items and that a possible subsequent re-export will be monitored in accordance with its export control regulations.[634]

Besides end-use certificates, companies have to submit information with their applications which allow a technical assessment of the goods to be transferred or exported.

634. Australia, Austria, Belgium, Canada, China ('Importer Statement on End-User and End-Use'), Czech Republic, Denmark, Finland, France, Greece, Hungary, Ireland, Italy, Japan, Luxembourg, the Netherlands, New Zealand, Norway, Poland, Portugal, Singapore, Slovak Republic, Spain, Special Administrative Region of Hong Kong, Sweden, Switzerland, Turkey, United Kingdom and United States of America.

Sub-Par. 2 Application for and Granting of Licences Regarding Activities with War Weapons (KWKG)

In general applications for the issuance of war weapons licences must be submitted to the BMWi. This includes licences for the manufacturing, the transport/transit, import, export or brokering of such weapons. If a certain war weapon, however, is subject to a government-to-government cooperation programme, licence applications must be filed with the BMVg. The AA must only be contacted in case exporting companies seek to receive an export advice prior to their shipment activities.

Figure 8.1

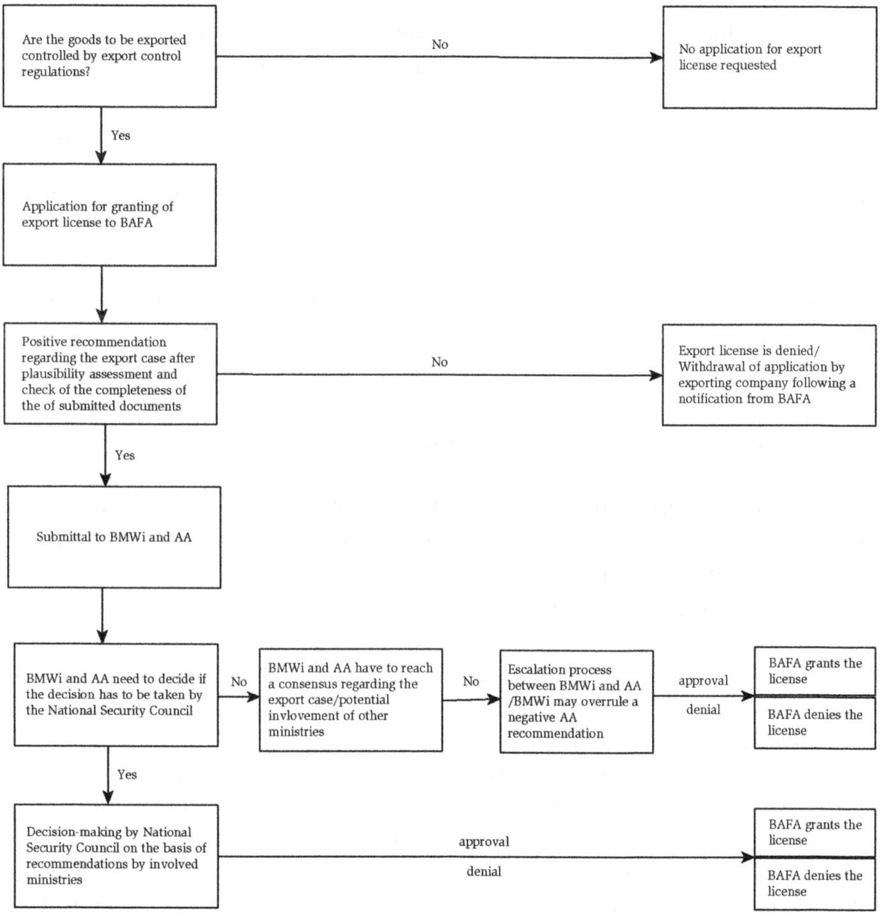

Par. 4 Compliance Review/Enforcement Authorities

German companies which hold licences for exports or transfers of military goods shall generally be audited every two years by the German Customs Authorities (*'Hauptzollämtern'*). Prepared audit reports are submitted to the BAFA for comments. In the event of severe failures to comply with laws or with the conditions or provisos of a granted licence, the report is provided to the Prosecution Office (*'Staatsanwaltschaft'*) for further evaluation and the initiation of additional measures (i.e.: opening of criminal investigations).

Also BAFA can withdraw licences (in particular when a licence was granted on the basis of misleading statements given by the exporting company) and reject the issuance of any new licences to companies which are guilty of legal infringements. Such companies are considered by the BAFA as 'unreliable exporters'. BAFA may demand from those 'unreliable' companies the nomination of a new 'Officer responsible for Exports' and the taking of actions for improving their export control organizations substantially.

Moreover, companies that obtained GPL are audited by the BAFA about every two year in order to check the quality of the companies' export control organizations. Such audits are executed on the basis of the licence conditions under which GPL are issued. GPL can be withdrawn by BAFA, if deficiencies are revealed during the audit.

Companies that hold war weapons licences are reviewed by a special group of the BAFA on average every two years. In case of revealed non-compliance with war weapons provisions, companies have to bear comparable legal procedures and consequences as described above in the context of military goods.

Par. 5 Sanctions and the Recourses of the Importer/Exporter

§§80-82 AWV impose administrative and criminal sanctions for infringements of provisions in the context of the export of military goods. Fines can reach up to EUR 500,000 per breach of the law. Imprisonment can be up to five years.

Pursuant to §§22a and 22b KWKG, breaches of laws in relation to war weapons can also result in fines or in imprisonment.

As an additional sanction, companies condemned under the AWG or KWKG will be listed on a Central Federal Register (*'Bundeszentralregister'*). Such companies may be banned from public procurement contracts.

Since the AWG and AWV reform in 2013, pursuant to §22(4) AWG companies which have violated export control provisions can submit voluntary disclosures regarding their misconduct to the customs Authorities. The possibility to submit a voluntary disclosure is restricted to various cases that are laid down in §19(2)-(5) AWG. Companies can only file a voluntary disclosure if the violation was uncovered independently. The customs Authorities shall not impose administrative fines against the company, if the violation happened due to negligent behaviour and if the company took measures to prevent the occurrence of similar violations in the future.

Sub-Section 2 Dual-Use Goods and Services

Par. 1 Overall Presentation

Dual-use goods are subject to the internal EU market and therefore subject to the EU jurisdiction. Nearly all of the dual-use goods can be exchanged freely within the EU. Exports of dual-use goods are governed in accordance with Council Regulation (EC) n° 428/2009. Such regulation comprises a harmonized list of items (Annex I to Council Regulation (EC) n° 428/2009), licensing requirements and procedures for the export and transfer of dual-use goods in all EU Member States. It also contains provisions on brokering activities related to dual-use goods and prohibitions of their transit. The main objective is to prevent the proliferation of WMD and their means of delivery as well as illegitimate military end-to-end.

In Germany the BAFA manages the issuing of licences related to exports of dual-use goods.

Sub-Par. 1 Requirements Prior to Any Specific Import/Export (i.e., Construction Phase)

In general, no specific requirements occur in connection with the import of dual-use goods. During development or manufacturing phase, however, licence requirements may occur if dual-use goods are exchanged between different sites of a company, when one of the sites is located outside the EU customs territory or the exchanged goods are considered as most sensitive.[635]

Sub-Par. 2 Requirements at the Import and/or Export Stages

I Goods

Exports of dual-use goods are restricted on the basis of the provisions included in the Council Regulation (EC) n° 428/2009. The term export is defined in Article 2 (2) of the Council Regulation (EC) n° 428/2009 referring to the dual-use items listed in its Annex I. In simple terms, export means the shipment of goods from the domestic territory or EU customs territory to a third country. A licence must be obtained for any export, irrespectively of whether the good was delivered to an EU Member State before. Under certain circumstances, however, transfers to another EU Member State do not require an licence even though, when it is known that the dual-use goods will be exported to a third country at a later stage. In this context a licence is not needed when the following conditions are met:

635. See *supra* n. 37.

- The good is integrated into a larger product prior to the export.
- The value of the goods comprises not more than then 30% of the value of the larger product and the delivered goods are not essential for its functioning.[636]
- The good is not easily retrievable from it.
- The good does not fall under Annex 4 of the EU dual-use regulation.

Furthermore, the Council Regulation (EC) n° 428/2009 stipulates licence requirements for transfers of special sensitive goods[637] from one EU Member State to another. Such most sensitive dual-use goods are listed in Annex IV of Council Regulation (EC) n° 428/2009.

In addition, it is up to the Member States to supplement the list of Annex I to Council Regulation (EC) n° 428/2009 by national goods. The German government identified certain additional dual-use goods (so-called 900 numbering range) and included them into a national applicable list (*'Anlage AL zur Außenwirtschaftsverordnung, Teil I, Abschnitt B'*). The export of such goods is subject to licence requirements.

II Services

Under Article 5 of the Council Regulation (EC) n° 428/2009 controls of trafficking and brokering activities related to dual-use goods apply in conjunction with the model of Article 4 (1) of the Council Regulation (EC) n° 428/2009. According to such model, licence and information are only required if the domestic resident has been informed by BAFA or knows that the goods are utilized in connection with the development, production, handling, operation, maintenance, storage, detection, identification or dissemination of WMD or with a military end-use in a purchasing country or country of destination that is subject to an arms embargo. Thus this model applies as in the context with 'technical assistance'.

III Persons

Pursuant to Article 3 of the Council Regulation (EC) n° 428/2009, the supply of services and the transmission of technology are not subject to this regulation if the supply or transmission involves cross-border movement of natural persons.

Par. 2 Control Lists

When checking which listed dual-use goods are subject to export or transfer licence, it is necessary to consider Annex I and Annex IV to the Council Regulation (EC) n° 428/2009 and the national applicable list with most sensitive dual-use goods.

636. Calculated on price basis, without spares and services.
637. These most sensitive dual-use goods and technologies include goods, technologies and software required for producing weapons of mass destruction and their means of delivery, regardless of payload or range.

Most importantly is Annex I to the Council Regulation (EC) n° 428/2009 in this regard. It covers about 650 items and contains goods of the following areas:

- Nuclear materials, plant and equipment.
- Materials, chemicals, micro-organisms and toxins.
- Materials processing.
- General electronics.
- Computers.
- Telecommunications, information security.
- Sensors and lasers.
- Aviation electronics and navigation.
- Oceanographic and naval technology.
- Propulsion systems, spacecraft and related equipment.

Companies may require an official technical assessment from BAFA ('*Auszug zur Güterliste*') if they have doubts whether a certain good is covered by the lists with dual-use goods or even the list with military goods.

Par. 3 Licensing and Enforcement Authorities

The BAFA is responsible for the issuance of all types of licences with respect to export related activities. Generally the decision about the granting of licences is made by BMWi and AA. The BAFA has the competence to decide about less sensitive exports autonomously.

As already mentioned above in connection with military goods, the following licence types exist with respect to exports and transfers of dual-use goods:

- Individual Export/Transfer Licences.
- GPL.
- Open General Licences.
- Trafficking and Brokering Licences.

Applications for licences must be filed to the BAFA in paper form or through the ELAN K2. Also it is necessary to provide with the application technical information about the good to be exported or transferred as well as an appropriate end-use certificate.

Figure 8.2

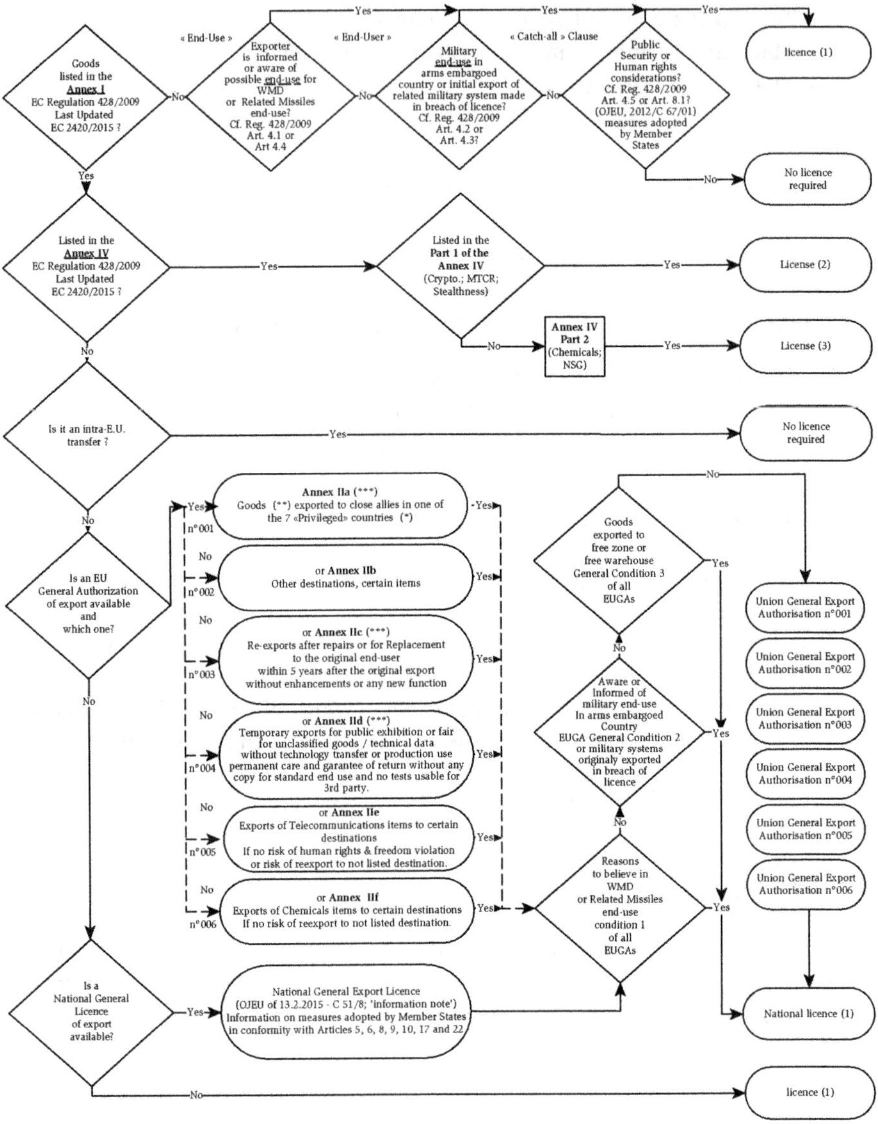

(1) Each EU Members states determines which type of EU licence (Individual or Global) is applicable.
(2) For goods and related technologies listed in Annex IV part 1, Individual or Global EU licences are available.
(3) For goods and related technologies listed in Annex IV part 2, only Individual licences are permitted.

(*) Seven countries listed in Annex IIa (EC) Regulation n° 428/2009 are the following: Australia, Canada, Japan, New-Zealand, Norway, Switzerland and US.

(**) Nearly all goods listed in Annex I excepted those listed in Annex IV and few others deemed very sensitive (cf. Annex g).
(***) cf. Annex 1Ig for possible other not authorized items.

Par. 4 Sanctions and the Recourses of the Importer/Exporter

As explained in the context of military goods, §§80-82 AWV include administrative and criminal sanctions for infringements of export control laws and regulations. Such provisions are also applicable in the context with dual-use goods.

SECTION 5 SPECIFICITIES/SPACE-RELATED PROVISIONS

Sub-Section 1 Specificities of the Control Regime

Companies which have doubts about the legitimacy of an intended export or transfer may request the issuance of a 'blank notice' ('*Null-Bescheid*') by BAFA in a formal administrative procedure. A blank notice is a legally binding administrative act indicating that an intended export or transfer is neither prohibited nor subject to licensing. It applies to a specific delivery at a definite period of time when the application was filed and is not transferrable to other or future transactions. Applications for the granting of a blank notice can be submitted via ELAN K2 or in paper form.

Sub-Section 2 Space-Related Provisions in the Control Regime

There is no specific space-related provision in German export control regime.

SECTION 6 SANCTIONS AND EMBARGOES

Sub-Section 1 Participation of Germany to Embargoes or Other Related Sanctions

Table 8.7

Countries/Non-State Entities/Individuals	*Restrictive Measures*
Al-Qaeda and associated individuals and entities	EU restrictive measures against certain persons
Armenia	OSCE arms embargo
Azerbaijan	OSCE arms embargo
Belarus	1. EU arms embargo 2. EU restrictive measures against certain persons

Countries/Non-State Entities/Individuals	*Restrictive Measures*
Central African Republic	1. EU arms embargo 2. EU restrictive measures against certain persons
People's Republic of China	Arms embargo following a declaration of the European Council of Ministers
Côte d' Ivoire	1. EU arms embargo 2. EU restrictive measures against certain persons
Democratic Republic of Congo	1. EU arms embargo 2. EU restrictive measures against certain persons.
Haiti	EU restrictive measures which prohibit the satisfying of claims by the Haitian Authorities with regard to contracts and transactions under UN sanctions.
Egypt	EU restrictive measures against certain persons
Eritrea	1. EU arms embargo 2. EU restrictive measures against certain persons
Former Socialist Federal Republic of Yugoslavia	EU restrictive measures against certain persons
Individuals suspected of involvement in the assassination of Rafiq Hariri	EU restrictive measures against certain persons
Individuals suspected of involvement in terror groups	EU restrictive measures against certain persons
Iran	1. EU arms embargo and sanctions including the prohibition to supply various dual-use goods and civil items as well as to provide certain services. 2. EU restrictive measures against certain persons
Iraq	EU arms embargo (non-government forces)
Lebanon	EU arms embargo (non-government forces)
Liberia	1. EU arms embargo 2. EU restrictive measures against certain persons
Libya	1. EU arms embargo 2. EU restrictive measures against certain persons
Moldavia	EU restrictive measures including travel bans
Myanmar	EU arms embargo and sanctions including the prohibition to supply goods that can be used for internal repression

Countries/Non-State Entities/Individuals	*Restrictive Measures*
North Korea	1. EU arms embargo and sanctions including the prohibition to supply various dual-use goods and civil items as well as to provide certain services. 2. EU restrictive measures against certain persons
Russia	1. EU arms embargo and sanctions including the prohibition to supply some dual-use goods and civil items as well as to provide certain services. 2. EU restrictive measures against certain persons
Somalia	1. EU arms embargo 2. EU restrictive measures against certain persons
South Sudan	EU arms embargo
Sudan	1. EU arms embargo 2. EU restrictive measures against certain persons
Syria	1. EU arms embargo and sanctions including the prohibition to supply various dual-use goods and civil items as well as to provide certain services. 2. EU restrictive measures against certain persons
Tunisia	EU restrictive measures against certain persons
Ukraine	EU restrictive measures against certain persons
Zimbabwe	1. EU arms embargo 2. EU restrictive measures against certain persons

Sub-Section 2 Regime of the Embargoes or Related Sanctions in Germany

The embargoes against other countries applied by Germany differ widely with respect to involved restrictions and prohibitions. Such embargoes impose, for instance, restrictive measures on the supply, import and transit of goods, the provision of services, investments and payment transactions. Often the embargoes include prohibitions to directly or indirectly supply natural or legal persons with economic resources and financial assets. In few cases they cover also rules on travel bans for certain persons.

Also Germany enforces restrictive measures, adopted by the EU,[638] to combat terrorism. Pursuant to these sets of regulations, it is prohibited to directly or indirectly provide certain natural or legal persons, or organizations, listed in the Annexes to the regulations, with economic resources and financial assets. In addition, the property of these persons and organizations is frozen. In this context the term economic resources includes any type of financial assets, regardless of tangible or intangible, movable or immovable forms that may be used for the purchase of money, goods or services. Therefore the direct or indirect delivery of goods to persons, entities or organizations mentioned in those lists is prohibited regardless of the country of destination.

The embargoes and sanctions applied by Germany are available on the BAFA homepage. Sections 74-77 AWV contain the legal transformation of embargo provisions into national law.

SECTION 7 LIST OF ACRONYMS

AA	*Auswärtiges Amt*/Federal Foreign Office
AG	Australia Group
AL	Export control lists/*Ausfuhrliste*
AV	*Ausfuhrverantwortlicher*/Officer responsible for Exports
AWG	*Außenwirtschaftsgesetz*/Foreign Trade and Payments Act
AWV	*Außenwirtschaftsverordnung*/Foreign Trade and Payments Ordinance
ATS	Australian Treaty Series
ATT	Arms Trade Treaty
BAFA	*Bundesamt für Wirtschaft und Ausfuhrkontrolle*/Federal Office of Economics and Export Control
BMWi	*Ministerium für Wirtschaft und Energie*/Federal Ministry of Economics and Energy
BMVg	*Bundesministerium der Verteidigung*/Federal Ministry of Defence
CWC	Chemical Weapons Convention
EU	European Union
FA	Framework Agreement for Restructuring of the European Defence Industry
GPL	Global Project Licences
IAEA	International Atomic Energy Agency
ILM	International Legal Material
LoI	Letter of Intent
KWL	*Kriegswaffenliste*/War Weapons List
KWKG	*Kriegswaffenkontrollgesetz*/War Weapons Control Act

638. Council Regulations (EC) n° 881/2002, (EC) n° 2580/2001 and (EC) n° 753/2011.

MTCR	Missile Technology Control Regime
NATO	North Atlantic Treaty Organization
NPT	Nuclear Non-Proliferation Treaty
NSG	Nuclear Suppliers Group
OJEU	Official Journal of the European Union
OSCE	Organization for Security and Co-operation in Europe
OST	Outer Space Treaty
SIPRI	Stockholm International Peace Research Institute
UN	United Nations
UNTS	United Nations Treaty Series
WMD	Weapons of Mass Destruction

SECTION 8 REFERENCES

Sub-Section 1 Primary Documentation

Par. 1 Statutory Legislation

- *Außenwirtschaftsrecht, Kriegswaffenkontrollrecht: (AWG, AWV, KWKG)*. A book comprising all legal texts of AWG, AWV and KWKG is published and regularly updated by the *C.H. Beck Verlag*, München, Germany. Also such legal texts are available on internet at: http://www.gesetze-im-internet.de or http://www.ausfuhrkontrolle.info/ausfuhrkontrolle/de (BAFA homepage).
- *Sammlung Güterlisten*. The book includes all applicable export control lists. It is published and regularly updated by *Bundesanzeiger Verlag*, Köln, Germany. Such lists are available on internet at: http://www.ausfuhrkontrolle.info/ausfuhrkontrolle/de (BAFA homepage).
- Council Regulation (EC) n° 428/2009 of 5 May 2009 setting up a Community regime for the control of exports, transfer, brokering and transit of dual-use items, OJ L 134/1.

Par. 2 Regulations

- Principles of the Federal Government to check the reliability of exporters of 25 July 2001: *http://www.verwaltungsvorschriften-im-internet.de/bsvwvbund_25072001_VB4500917.htm.*
- Council Common Position 2008/944/CFSP of 8 December 2008 defining common rules governing control of exports of military technology and equipment, OJ L 335/99.
- Political Principles of the German Government for export of War Weapons and other Military Equipment: http://www.bmwi.de/BMWi/Redaktion/PDF/A/aussenwirtschaftsrecht-grundsaetze,property = pdf,bereich = bmwi2012,sprache = de,rwb = true.pdf.

Par. 3 Annexes – Copies of Documents of Practical Use to the Importer/Exporter

A number of standard documents relevant for the import or export process in Germany (e.g., most current official application forms for import or export licences, templates of contractual undertaking, or regulation extracts) as well as other non-official documents are available on a dedicated DropBox folder which can be accessed by following the link below: www.kluwerlawonline.com/eclrh-annexes.

Par. 4 Other

- Council Common Position 2003/468/CFSP on the control of arms brokering of 23 June 2003, OJ L 156/79.
- EU Code of Conduct for Arms Exports of 5 June 1998 (EU- The Council – 8675/2/98-DG E -PESC IV): http://www.consilium.europa.eu/uedocs/cmsUpload/08675r2en8.pdf.
- LoI of 6 July 1998 'between Six Defence Ministers on Measures to the facilitate the Restructuring of the European Defence Industry': http://data.grip.org/documents/200904230933.pdf.
- LoI 'Framework Agreement Concerning Measures to Facilitate the Restructuring and Operation of the European Defence Industry of 27 July 2000': http://data.grip.org/documents/200904221112.pdf.
- 2013 Reform of the German Foreign Trade and Payments Act and the Foreign Trade and Payment Ordinance:

  http://www.ausfuhrkontrolle.info/ausfuhrkontrolle/de/arbeitshilfen/merkblaetter/merkblatt_awgnovelle_aenderungsuebersicht.pdf
  http://www.bmwi.de/BMWi/Redaktion/PDF/Gesetz/faq-awg-novelle,property=pdf,bereich=bmwi2012,sprache=de,rwb=true.pdf.

Sub-Section 2 Secondary Documentation

Par. 1 Internet Sites

- http://www.ausfuhrkontrolle.info/ausfuhrkontrolle/de/ (BAFA homepage)
- http://www.bmwi.de/ (BMWI homepage)
- www.sipri.org (Stockholm International Peace Research Institute homepage)

Par. 2 Paper Publications

- Wolffgang, Prof. Dr Hans-Michael/Simonsen, *AWR – Kommentar, Kommentar für das gesamte Außenwirtschaftsrecht*, vol. 1-3. The book includes detailed commentary on the German export control laws and on the administrative processes. It is published by Bundesanzeiger Verlag, Köln, Germany.

- *HADDEX – Handbuch der deutschen Exportkontrolle.* A detailed handbook about German and European export control laws, regulations and administrative processes. The handbook is edited by the BAFA and published by *Bundesanzeiger Verlag,* Köln, Germany.
- Steindorf, Joachim/Potrykus, Gerhard, *Waffenrecht: Waffengesetz, Beschussgesetz, Kriegswaffenkontrollgesetz einschliesslich untergesetzlichem Regelwerk und Nebenbestimmungen,* 8th edition, 2007. The book covers a commentary on the KWKG and is published by *C.H. Beck Verlag,* München, Germany.

SECTION 9 USEFUL INFORMATION

Sub-Section 1 Enforcement Authorities Contact Details

Name of Organization	*Bundesministerium für Wirtschaft und Energie (BMWi) – Office in Berlin*
Postal Address	Scharnhorststraße 34-37, 10115 Berlin, Germany
Telephone	+49 30/18 615-0
Fax	+49 30/18 615-7010
Website	www.bmwi.de

Name of Organization	*Bundesministerium für Wirtschaft und Energie (BMWi) – Office in Bonn*
Postal Address	Villemombler Straße 76, 53107 Bonn, Germany
Telephone	+49 228/99 615-0
Fax	+49 228/99 615-4436
Website	www.bmwi.de

Name of Organization	*Bundesamt für Wirtschaft und Ausfuhrkontrolle (BAFA)*
Postal Address	Frankfurter Straße 29-35, 65760 Eschborn, Germany
Telephone	+ 49 6196/908-0
Fax	+ 49 6196/908-800
Website	www.ausfuhrkontrolle.info

Name of Organization	*Auswärtiges Amt (AA) – Office in Berlin*
Postal Address	Werderscher Markt 1, 10117 Berlin, Germany
Telephone	+ 49 30/5000-02475

Name of Organization	*Auswärtiges Amt (AA) – Office in Berlin*
Fax	+ 49 30/1817-3402
Website	www.auswaertiges-amt.de

Name of Organization	*Bundesministerium der Verteidigung (BMVg) – Office in Berlin*
Postal Address	Stauffenbergstraße 18, 10785 Berlin
Telephone	+49 (0) 30/18 - 24 - 00
Fax	+49 (0) 30/18 - 24 - 53 57
Email address	poststelle@bmvg.bund.de
Website	www.bmvg.de

Name of Organization	*Bundesministerium der Verteidigung (BMVg) – Office in Bonn*
Postal Address	Hardthöhe, Fontainengraben 150, 53123 Bonn, Germany
Telephone	+49 228/12-00
Fax	+49 228/12- 5357
Email address	poststelle@bmvg.bund.de
Website	www.bmvg.de

Sub-Section 2 Other

None.

CHAPTER 9

India

Anand Prasad & Samsuddha Majumder

SECTION 1 TABLE OF CONTENTS

SECTION 2 EXECUTIVE SUMMARY

Although India is not a signatory to any of the international export control regimes, it has had an export control system in place since independence from British rule in 1947. This is because India views itself as a responsible international player and its foreign policy has historically been one of non-alignment with either the United States of America (USA) led or the then Union of Soviet Socialist Republic (USSR) led group of countries. Although India has yet to consolidate its export control policies into one legislation, control over exports has historically been exercised through a patchwork of laws, government regulations, notifications, circulars, etc., with separate laws governing nuclear, chemical and biological export controls. Since the enactment of the Foreign Trade (Development and Regulation) Act, 1992 (FTDRA), import and export controls are chiefly regulated by the Indian Tariff Classification (Harmonized System) (ITC (HS)), published by the Ministry of Commerce and Industry, which specifies the goods that can be imported to or exported from India and which applies to civilian, military and dual-use items. The ITC (HS) classification also specifies whether there are any conditions/restrictions associated with the goods sought to be imported/exported.

With respect to dual-use items, a significant step towards developing a unified control list of all dual-use items was taken in 2003, when the Special Chemicals, Organisms, Materials, Equipment and Technologies (SCOMET) list was created as part of the ITC (HS) classification.[639] The export of items listed in SCOMET is either prohibited, or permitted only under licence, and the grant of licence depends on various factors, primary among them are the end-use *cum* end-user certification. A further important step in export controls was made in 2005 with the enactment of the Weapons of Mass Destruction and their Delivery Systems (Prohibition of Unlawful Activities) Act, 2005 (WMDA), which criminalizes the possession of weapons of mass destruction (WMD) by unauthorized individuals and entities. It applies to the 'export, transfer, re-transfer, transit, and trans-shipment of material, equipment, or technology' related to WMD.

In the area of defence and atomic energy, the central government has maintained control over exploration, research, imports, and exports of fissile minerals and technology. It has also maintained direct or indirect control of research, development, and production of almost all defence-related items. The government has retained direct oversight over missile research and development by restricting these activities to national laboratories and restricting production to Defence Public Sector Undertakings (DPSUs). The government also maintains indirect control over the research and development and production of conventional arms by reserving these activities to government-owned and managed ordnance factories.[640] However, the defence sector has been opened up to 100% private participation from 2001.[641]

639. Schedule 2, Appendix 3 of the ITC (HS) classification.
640. Ordnance factories means factories dealing with manufacture and storage of military stores.
641. See *infra* Chapter 9, Section 4.

SECTION 3 INTRODUCTION – ELEMENTS OF CONTEXT

Sub-Section 1 Overall Philosophy

Unlike most developed western countries or countries such as Australia or Japan which are members of, or are otherwise associated with, various export control regimes, India is not a party to any of the following four multilateral export control regimes for trade and transfer of sensitive technologies: (i) the Nuclear Suppliers Group (NSG), (ii) the Australia Group (AG), (iii) the Missile Technology Control Regime (MTCR) and (iv) the Wassenaar Arrangement (WA). However, on 6 September 2008, the NSG granted a waiver to India from certain existing rules, allowing India to indulge in, *inter alia*, nuclear trade for peaceful purposes.

Further, although India is a signatory to the Chemical Weapons Convention (CWC) and the Biological and Toxin Weapons Convention, it is not bound by any treaty obligation regarding nuclear and missile trades. Notwithstanding the fact that it is not a party to the treaties/conventions relating to non-proliferation, India has always sought to project itself as a responsible global player in achieving non-proliferation, and as encouraged by the regimes mentioned above, India does exercise restraint in its military and dual-use export policies.

Unlike the USA, United Kingdom or France which have specific export/import laws relating to arms, military goods and technologies that could possibly be used for military purposes, export and import controls in India are regulated by a combination of municipal legislation,[642] rules, regulations, appendices and government circulars and notifications. There is no unified and comprehensive export control law, and separate laws govern nuclear, chemical and biological export controls. The lack of such specific laws on the export/import of arms and military products could be said to result from the nascent stage of the Indian defence industry and the fact that until recently the production of defence items was in the exclusive domain of government undertakings, which produced items essentially for consumption by the Government of India (GoI). However, with the growth of the domestic industry and with the development of science and technology, including in the sphere of non-conventional military technology, India has taken steps to regulate the export and/or import of such dual-use materials and technologies. A significant step towards developing a unified control list for export of all dual-use items was taken in 2003 with the creation of a single unified control list, namely, the SCOMET list, which is a part of the ITC (HS).[643] The export of items listed on SCOMET is either prohibited or permitted only under licence. The grant of a licence for SCOMET items depends on various factors, including, importantly end-use *cum* end-user certification.

642. See *infra*, Section 4.

643. The ITC (HS) classification specifies the goods that can be imported to or exported from India and apply to both civilian and military items. The ITC (HS) classification also specifies whether there are any conditions/ restrictions associated with the goods sought to be imported/ exported.

A number of factors are expected to dictate India's future policies on export control. Since the economic reform of 1991, the private sector has increased its involvement of dual-use goods. Further, increasing pressure to generate additional revenues on GoI entities in the defence sector may prompt India to adopt export control policies that are designed to assist in generating revenues for its defence industry. Such policies may gradually weaken GoI's control over exports of such products. Additionally, the recent growth of Indian industry has significantly benefited the Indian private sector, giving it access to information technology and a database, thereby enabling the private sector's research and development of advanced pharmaceutical, biotechnology, bioinformatics, software, information technology, chemical and biological sectors.

While there are special laws that govern the export/import of goods from and to India, restrictions vary according to the parties involved in the particular export/import activity. The GoI is exempted from any requirement to obtain an Importer-Exporter Code (IEC) number certificate.[644] Further, the Foreign Trade (Exemption from Application of Rules in Certain Cases) Order, 1993 provides that the Foreign Trade (Regulation) Rules, 1993[645] do not apply to import by agencies/undertakings controlled by the GoI for defence purposes.[646] The export of any goods by or under the authority of the GoI is also exempt from the application of the Foreign Trade Regulation Rules.[647]

While an import to or export from India would require compliance with Indian laws, an export from a country outside India to India of specified capital goods, raw materials, components may also require compliance with the laws of the exporting country. Specifically, if exports from the country of origin were not in compliance with its export laws, then it would also be an offence in India to import such goods. For example, any export from the USA would be subject to the export control regulations of the USA. In such a case, the supplier who is based in the USA would be required to obtain an export licence based on the import certificate furnished by the Indian importer to the supplier. In the case of military goods, the Ministry of Defence, GoI (MoD) is the import certificate issuing entity.[648] Thus, any non-compliance by the USA exporter with the laws of the USA would make the import of such items into India an offence, in addition to it being an offence in the USA as well.

Sub-Section 2 Historical Outlook

Exports, in general, have always been subject to extensive controls in India and its export control policies have been largely unilateral, owing to the fact that India believes

644. Discussed in more detail below.
645. Made under the Foreign Trade (Development and Regulation) Act, 1992, which *inter alia* prescribe the manner in which import and export licences are granted.
646. Paragraph 3(1)(a), Foreign Trade (Exemption from Application of Rules in Certain Cases) Order, 1993.
647. Paragraph 3(1)(a), Foreign Trade (Exemption from Application of Rules in Certain Cases) Order, 1993.
648. Paragraph 2.11, Handbook of Procedures, Foreign Trade Policy, 2009-2014.

that its domestic capabilities in the defence sector should not undermine regional instabilities or international security. Evidence of this is India's strong commitment to the non-aligned movement, i.e., the refusal to align with either the USA or the former USSR led group of countries.

Until 1992, the Imports and Exports (Control) Act, 1947 (IECA) regulated India's import/export laws. Over the years various amendments were made to the IECA to reflect the changing policies of the GoI. The early 1990s saw the GoI making a policy shift in many important sectors, including the economic sector. Changes in laws regulating foreign investment in India and private participation in various sectors were part of this policy shift. Such policy shift warranted a significant overhaul of the IECA. Accordingly, the IECA was superseded by the FTDRA. The FTDRA now regulates India's export/import control laws. Every five years, the GoI frames the export-import policy of India (EXIM Policy)[649] under the FTDRA. Additionally, the ITC (HS) classification referenced above is also provided for under the FTDRA.

The lack of specific legislation on dual-use goods prompted the GoI in early 1993 to establish the 'Small Group on Strategic Export Controls' with the goal of beginning the process of institutionalizing a system of controls over strategic exports from India. The group finalized a list, namely the 'Special Materials, Equipment and Technology' (SMET),[650] of items whose export will be subject to licensing.

As the CWC required India to list dual-use chemicals set out in the schedules to the CWC, the GoI issued another notification (through the Directorate General of Foreign Trade (DGFT) in March, 1993) identifying a list of dual-purpose chemicals, the export of which was either prohibited or permitted only under licence (the DGFT is the sole authority mandated with the powers relating to issuance of all export/import licences in India).

While conventional military trade, in the real sense, only developed after India's independence in 1947, India has been engaged in the commercial exploitation of atomic minerals since the 1930s, and has the oldest atomic energy programme among developing countries. The Atomic Energy Act, 1948 (AEA 48) was created to regulate the exploration, research, import and export of atomic minerals and technology. The AEA 48 also allowed the GoI to exercise strict control over all issues relating to atomic minerals. However, subsequent changes in the field of atomic energy as well as the implementation of future programmes relating to atomic energy precipitated the Atomic Energy Act, 1962 (AEA 62). The AEA 62 has also been amended from time to time to keep pace with changing requirements. One of the more significant amendments to the AEA 62 was made in 1995;[651] such amendment resulted in the creation of a detailed list of 'prescribed substances' which are or may be used for the production or use of atomic energy or research into matters connected therewith. The amendment was significant because it resulted in the GoI exercising complete control over all matters relating to atomic energy. Further, the Department of Atomic Energy (DAE)

649. Now known as Foreign Trade Policy.
650. Notified in the EXIM Policy announced on 31 Mar. 1995, effective 1 Apr. 1995 (Public Notice 68 EXP (PN)/ 92-97).
651. Notification AEA / 27/ 1/ 95-ER, dated March 1995.

which is the main agency in matters of atomic substances issued a notification, effective 1 April 1995, under the AEA 62, identifying equipment and substances that are subject to export licensing by the DAE with the most recent notification issued on 20 January, 2006. To further regulate the exports of these items, the DAE issued a notification on 1 February 2006 formulating a set of 'Guidelines for Nuclear Transfers (export) to any country'. The guidelines specify transfer of prescribed substances, equipment and related technology only upon formal governmental assurances from recipients explicitly excluding any uses which would result in any nuclear explosive device. The DAE, further, formulated guidelines for 'implementation of arrangements for cooperation concerning peaceful uses of atomic energy with other countries' on 4 June 2010,[652] under which the Government has allowed supply of certain listed items which include, *inter alia*, nuclear material, information and technology from countries willing to trade, without a formal bilateral agreement of cooperation with such countries. However, such transfer is subject to certain conditions which include peaceful assurances, application of International Atomic Energy Agency (IAEA) safeguards, etc. These guidelines also specify that an authorization would be required from the GoI for any commercial relations for such transfer.

The GoI has traditionally maintained control over the development and manufacture of defence-related items. However, with the change in India's foreign policies and economic growth, export control laws have also undergone changes. The current EXIM Policy (framed under the FTDRA) permits free exports of certain listed low technology military stores.[653] All other military stores that are not specified in the list require a 'no-objection certificate' from the Department of Defence Production and Supplies (DDP&S), MoD. This permission depends on inter-agency consultations and also end-user certification and may also impose a restriction on transfer to third parties within or outside the recipient country.

On 18 July 2005 India and the USA issued a joint statement on nuclear cooperation, and the GoI reached an agreement on a number of undertakings related to export controls. In these commitments, the GoI agreed to, among other things, take steps that will bring it into the international non-proliferation mainstream, including placing its civilian nuclear facilities and programmes under IAEA safeguards and adhering to the guidelines of the NSG and the MTCR. Both the countries have agreed to support efforts to limit the spread of enrichment and reprocessing technologies and also support the conclusion of a Fissile Material Cut-off Treaty. This eventually culminated in India and the USA signing the US–India Civil Nuclear Agreement in 2008, under which both the parties are to facilitate nuclear trade between themselves for peaceful use, while also highlighting that authorizations (including import and export licence) should not be used to restrict trade. India also joined the USA, Russia, the European Union, Japan, the Republic of Korea, and China as an **International Thermonuclear Experimental Reactor (ITER)** member.

652. Available at http://dae.nic.in/sites/default/files/Resolution_English.pdf.
653. This list is specified in Appendix 3 to Schedule 2 of the ITC (HS) Classifications of Export and Import Items, 2009-20014.

Sub-Section 3 Participation to International Regimes

India is not a party to any of the four multilateral export control regimes for trade and transfer of sensitive technologies; however, India has participated in a limited number of international export control related treaties and agreements.

The following tables identify India's participation status in export control related international treaties and programmes. The tables also indicate whether India is a party to a treaty either by signature and ratification or by accession.

Par. 1 Treaties and Regimes Dealing with Specific Items and Technologies

Table 9.1 Nuclear Weapons Treaties

Treaty Name	*Overall Status*	*Specific Status*	*Enforceable in India*
Limited Test Ban Treaty[654]	OS: 5 August 1963 EF: 10 October 1963	S: 8 August 1963 R: 10 October 1963	Yes
Nuclear Non-Proliferation Treaty[655]	OS: 1 July 1968 EF: 5 March 1970	-	No
Comprehensive Nuclear Test Ban Treaty[656]	OS: 24 September 1996 EF: not in force	-	No

OS: Opened for signature; EF: Entry into force; S/R: Signature/Ratification; A: Accession.

Table 9.2 Biological and Chemical Weapons Treaties

Treaty Name	*Overall Status*	*Specific Status*	*Enforceable in India*
Geneva Protocol[657]	OS: 17 June 1925 EF: 8 February 1928	S: 17 June 1925 R: 9 April 1930	Yes
Biological Convention[658]	OS: 10 April 1972 EF: 26 March 1975	S: 15 January 1973 R: 15 July 1974	Yes
Chemical Convention[659]	OS: 13 January 1993 EF: 29 April 1997	S: 14 January 1993 R: 3 September 1996	Yes

OS: Opened for signature; EF: Entry into force; S/R: Signature/Ratification; A: Accession.

654. Treaty Banning Nuclear Weapon Tests in the Atmosphere, in Outer Space and Under Water, *UNTS*, vol. 480, p. 43.
655. Treaty on the Non-Proliferation of Nuclear Weapons, *UNTS*, vol. 729, p. 161.
656. UNGA, resolution 50\245.
657. Protocol for the Prohibition of the Use in War of Asphyxiating, Poisonous or Other Gases, and of Bacteriological Methods of Warfare, 94, *League of Nations Treaty Series*, No. 2138 (1929).
658. Convention on the Prohibition of the Development, Production and Stockpiling of Bacteriological (Biological) and Toxin Weapons and On Their Destruction, *UNTS*, vol. 1015, p. 163.
659. Convention on the Prohibition of the Development, Production, Stockpiling and Use of Chemical Weapons and on Their Destruction, Doc.CD/CW/WP.400/Rev.1.

Table 9.3 Multilateral Export Control Regimes

Regime Name	*Formation*	*Participation*
Zangger Committee[660]	1971	No
Nuclear Suppliers Group	1974	No
Australia Group	1985	No
Missile Technology Control Regime	1987	No
Wassenaar Arrangement[661]	1994	No

Table 9.4 Other

Name	*Adoption*	*Participation*
International Code of conduct[662]	25 November 2002	No

Par. 2 Treaties Dealing with Specific Areas

Table 9.5 International Zones

Treaty Name	*Overall Status*	*Specific Status*	*Enforceable in India*
Antarctic Treaty[663]	OS: 1 December 1959 EF: 23 June 1961	A: 19 August 1983	Yes
Outer Space Treaty (OST)[664]	OS: 27 January 1967 EF: 10 October 1967	S: 3 March 1967 R: 18 January 1982	Yes
Sea Bed Arms Control Treaty[665]	OS: 11 February 1971 EF: 23 June 1961	A: 20 July 1973	Yes
Moon agreement[666]	OS: 18 December 1979 EF: 11 July 1984	S: 18 January 1982	No

660. Non Proliferation Treaty Exporters Committee (also called the Zangger Committee).
661. Wassenaar Arrangement on export controls for conventional arms and dual-use goods and technologies.
662. Hague Code of Conduct against Ballistic Missile Proliferation, not yet published.
663. 402, *UNTS*, 7.
664. Treaty on Principles Governing the Activities of States in the Exploration and Use of Outer Space, including the Moon and Other Celestial Bodies, *UNTS*, vol. 610, p. 205.
665. Treaty on the Prohibition of the Emplacement of Nuclear Weapons and other Weapons of Mass Destruction on the Seabed and The Ocean Floor and in the subsoil thereof, *UNTS*, vol. 955, p. 115.
666. Agreement governing the Activities of States on the Moon and Other Celestial Bodies, *ILM*, vol. 18, p. 1434.

Treaty Name	*Overall Status*	*Specific Status*	*Enforceable in India*
Convention on the Law of the Sea[667]	OS: 10 December 1982 EF: 16 November 1994	R: 29 June 1995	Yes

OS: Opened for signature; EF: Entry into force; S/R: Signature/Ratification; A: Accession.

Table 9.6 Regional Nuclear Weapons-Free Zones

Treaty Name	*Overall Status*	*Specific Status*	*Enforceable in India*
Treaty of Tlatelolco[668]	OS: 14 February 1967 EF: 22 April 1967	-	No
Treaty of Rarotonga[669]	OS: 6 August 1985 EF: 11 December 1986	-	No
Treaty of Bangkok[670]	OS: 15 December 1995 EF: 27 March 1997	-	No
Treaty of Pelindaba[671]	OS: 11 April 1996 EF: 15 July 2009	-	No

OS: Opened for signature; EF: Entry into force; S/R: Signature/Ratification; A: Accession.

SECTION 4 CONTROL REGIME

India does not have a single, unified import/export control law in relation to military and dual-use goods. Controls are imposed by a combination of municipal legislation, rules, regulations, appendices and government circulars and notifications. The import/ export of military and dual-use goods is governed by the following major laws:

(a) The FTDRA: This act forms the basis of the GoI's power to prohibit, restrict and regulate imports and exports. It provides for the formulation of the EXIM Policy. The EXIM Policy lays down the procedures for classifying items for import/ export purposes from India. The EXIM policy is modified from time to time and entities interested in exporting to or importing products from India would need to be apprised of the most recent EXIM Policy requirements.[672] By an amendment in 2010, provisions of the WMDA were

667. Doc. A/CONF.62/122 and Corr.1-11.
668. Treaty for the Prohibition of Nuclear Weapons in Latin America and the Caribbean, *UNTS*, vol. 634, p. 326.
669. South Pacific Nuclear Free Zone Treaty, *ILM*, vol. 24, p. 1442.
670. South East Asia Nuclear-Weapon-Free Zone Treaty, *ILM*, vol. 35. p. 635.
671. African Nuclear Weapon-Free Zone Treaty, *ILM*, vol. 35, p. 698.
672. Section 5 of the Foreign Trade (Development and Regulation) Act, 1992 provides that the Central Government may, from time to time, formulate and announce by notification in the

incorporated into the FTDRA, which expanded the scope of control on strategic trade in India by expanding the definition of exports and imports within the FTDRA to include 'services' and 'technologies,' which were previously identified only in the WMDA.

(b) The AEA 62: This Act regulates the use and trade of atomic minerals and technologies and specifies the list of commodities which are under the exclusive control of the GoI for production, manufacture, purchase, acquisition and disposal. Contravention of the provisions of the AEA 62 is punishable with fine and/or imprisonment of up to five years.

(c) The WMDA: This Act criminalizes the possession of WMD by unauthorized individuals and entities. Additionally, the Act updates the present system of export controls in India with a view to making it more contemporary, by introducing transit and trans-shipment controls, re-transfer provisions, technology transfer controls, brokering controls and end-use based controls. It prohibits the export of any goods or technology from India if the exporter knows that it is intended to be used in any WMD programme. It regulates its flow by introducing 'transfer controls' over such technologies. It regulates the flow of sensitive and dual-use technologies and know-how from India, or by Indians abroad. It also seeks to regulate the flow of such goods and technology to foreigners while in India. The provisions of this Act apply to citizens of India outside India, Indian companies with branches or subsidiaries abroad, persons in the service of the GoI, within and beyond India, and foreigners while in India. The Act imposes a general prohibition on brokering, by Indians or foreign nationals in India, in any such transaction that is prohibited or regulated under the Act. Regulation of transfers of sensitive and dual-use technologies has assumed importance in view of the increasing capability of India to produce such technologies, though the originators of such technologies continue to be overwhelmingly parastatal in India. The requirement to regulate also arises out of the need to ensure comprehensive control over unique or closely held, indigenously developed technology or know-how. It also meets the requirement to ensure that such technologies do not fall into the wrong hands.

(d) The Arms Act, 1959: This relates to arms and ammunition. The Act imposes a prohibition on possession of and dealing in arms and ammunition without a licence. Contravention of the provisions of the Act leads to both civil and criminal penalties.

(e) The CWC Act, 2000: The Act seeks to give effect to the Convention on the Prohibition of the Development, Production, Stockpiling and Use of Chemical Weapons and on their Destruction. It applies to citizens of India outside India and associates, branches or subsidiaries, outside India of companies or bodies corporate, registered or incorporated in India. Penalty for contravention of the provisions of the Act are civil and criminal.

Official Gazette, the export and import policy and may also, in the like manner, amend that policy. The current Foreign Trade Policy is valid from 2015 to 2020.

(f) The Explosives Act, 1884 and the Explosives Rules, 2008 require licensing of export, import, and manufacturing activities involving explosives.
(g) In addition to the above, the Customs Act, 1962 also deals with control of trade in defence and dual-use goods. Under the Customs Act, such goods can be confiscated if attempted to be imported/ exported contrary to any prohibition or the provisions of the Customs Act or any other act or regulation.[673] Civil and criminal liabilities may be imposed for contravening provisions of the Customs Act.[674] The Environment Protection Act, 1986, while primarily intended to be a legislation protecting India's environmental resources also provides for procedures assuring the security of and oversight over pathogens, micro organisms, genetically modified organisms, and toxins at any stage of production, import, export, use, or research.

Sub-Section 1 Military Goods and Services

An important aspect of the export control of military goods is the fact that the GoI has maintained control over the development and manufacture of almost all defence-related items. The GoI has also exercised control over the research and development and production of conventional arms by restricting these activities to government-owned and managed ordnance factories.[675] Missile research and development is also restricted to laboratories under the direct control of the GoI and the production of missiles can only be carried out by DPSUs (the ordnance factories are also DPSUs).

Prior to the year 2001, production of defence items was restricted only to the DPSUs and the role of the private sector was limited to the supply of raw materials, components, and sub-assemblies as input material for production in the ordnance factories and DPSUs. This situation changed in 2001, when the defence industry sector was opened to private participation.[676]

Par. 1 Overall Presentation

Sub-Par. 1 Requirements Prior to Any Specific Import/Export (i.e., Manufacturing Phase)

Indian private sector participants can now invest up to 100% in the defence industry while Foreign Direct Investment (FDI) is allowed up to a limit of 26%. In certain cases, the limit can exceed 26%, wherever it is likely to result in access to modern and 'state-of-art' technology in the country. This would depend on the approval from the Cabinet Committee on Security on a case to case basis. In both these cases, a licence

673. Section 111(d) and 113(d) of the Customs Act, 1962.
674. Section 112, 114, 114A, 114AA and 117 of the Customs Act, 1962.
675. For recent developments, please see below.
676. No. 5(6)/ 2000-FC I, dated 21 May 2001, Ministry of Commerce and Industry.

has to be obtained before any investment can be made. The licence is given by the Department of Industrial Policy and Promotion, Ministry of Commerce and Industry, GoI (DIPP) in consultation with MoD.[677] In cases involving FDI, the matter will also be considered by the Foreign Investment Promotion Board (FIPB), under the Department of Economic Affairs, Ministry of Finance, GoI.[678] Further, the FDI Policy, 2014, also permits import of equipment for pre-production activity including development of a prototype. It must be noted that while the defence industry sector has been opened up for private participation, FDI in the atomic energy sector is still not permitted.[679]

The First Schedule to the Industries (Development and Regulation) Act, 1951 (IDRA) specifies certain industries that cannot be established without obtaining an industrial licence. Among such industries is the arms and ammunition industry. To obtain this licence, the undertaking is required to submit an application to the Secretariat of Industrial Assistance, DIPP.[680]

In addition, the guidelines for the production of arms and ammunition, issued by the DIPP[681] *inter alia*, provide that:

(a) The applicant should be an Indian company/partnership firm, the management of the applicant company/partnership is required to be in Indian hands and a majority of the board of directors as well as the chief executive of the company/partnership firm are required to be resident Indians.
(b) The GoI has the right to verify the antecedents of the foreign collaborators and domestic promoters, including their financial standing and credentials in the world market.
(c) Preference would be given to original equipment manufacturers or design establishments, and companies having a good track record of past supplies to the armed forces, space and atomic energy sectors and having an established research and development base.
(d) Though there is no requirement of minimum capitalization in the case of FDI, assessment could be carried out by the applicant company depending upon the intended product and the intended technology. The licensing authority has the right to satisfy itself of the adequacy of the net worth of the foreign investor taking into account the product category and the intended technology.

677. No. 5(37)/ 2001-FC I, dated 4 Jan. 2002. This Notification was passed in order to lay down the guidelines for the licensing of production of arms and ammunitions.
678. The policy states that the GoI decision on applications to FIPB for FDI in defence industry sector will be normally communicated within a time frame of ten weeks from the date of acknowledgement by the Secretariat for Industrial Assistance in the Department of Industrial Policy & Promotion. However, in practice, the FIPB may take more time in coming out with the decision.
679. Annexure A to Schedule I, FEMA Notification No. FEMA 20/ 2000-RB, dated 3 May 2000.
680. The form is available at the SIA, at all outlets dealing in Government Publications, Indian Embassies, and can also be downloaded from the web site of the SIA (http://dipp.nic.in/English/Investor/Forms/Forms.aspx).
681. No. 5(37)/ 2001-FC I dated 4 Jan. 2002.

(e) There is a three year lock-in period for transfer of equity from one foreign investor to another foreign investor and such transfer would be subject to prior approval of the FIPB and the GoI.
(f) The capacity norms for production would depend on the recommendations of the MoD. This would involve comparison with similar existing capacities and allied products.
(g) The testing standards and procedures for items produced under licence from foreign collaborators or from indigenous research and development will have to be provided by the licensee to the GoI. Self-certification is considered on a case to case basis, which may involve either individual items, or group of items manufactured by the licensee.
(h) Purchase and price preference may be given to government-owned entities in accordance with GoI guidelines.

Sub-Par. 2 Requirements at the Import and/or Export Stages

I Goods

Export and import licences are necessary prior to any specific import/export except for the items which are designated as freely imported/exported.[682] Licences are issued by the DGFT in consultation with the relevant agencies of the GoI (if atomic materials are involved, the licensing authority is the DAE). In such case, the DAE reviews the end-user information supplied by the exporting entity. Further, depending on the product other departments such as the Department of Science and Technology, the Department of Electronics, and the DIPP (Technical) may also be consulted.

Chapter 93 of Schedule 1 of the ITC (HS) classification deals with the import of arms and ammunitions and restricts the import of goods such as military weapons, firearms, bombs, grenades, etc. The export of military stores is permitted subject to the issue of a No Objection Certificate (NOC) from the DDP&S.[683] However, the export of certain non lethal, low tech military stores, as specified by the GoI from time to time, is permitted without the requirement of an NOC.

Along with the application for a licence, the applicant should attach the IEC certificate – essentially a code/number. The DGFT issues the IEC certificate and import or export cannot be made without furnishing the IEC certificate.[684] The GoI, as discussed above is exempted from obtaining the IEC certificate.[685] Once the application is made to the DGFT, it has the power to either grant the licence or to reject the

682. 'Any goods / service, the export or import of which is "Restricted" may be exported or imported only in accordance with an Authorization / Permission/ License or in accordance to the procedure prescribed in a notification / public notice issued in this regard.' Chapter 2, paragraph 2.7, Foreign Trade Policy 2009-2014. Paragraph 2.8 of the Foreign Trade Policy, 2015-2020.
683. Schedule 2, Appendix 1, ITC (HS) Classification, 2015-2020.
684. Section 7, Foreign Trade (Development and Regulation) Act, 1992.
685. Chapter 2, paragraph 2.7, Foreign Trade Policy 2004-2009. Paragraph 2.7, Hand Book of Procedures, 2015-20.

application. In addition to this, the DGFT also has the power to cancel a licence or to refuse its renewal.[686] The DGFT is required to give the holder of the licence an opportunity to present its case prior to taking a decision on suspension or cancellation.[687]

It may be noted that unlike the private exporter or importer, the GoI and state government entities enjoy special privileges in the matter of export/import as Foreign Trade (Regulations) Rules framed under the provisions of the FTDRA do not apply to these bodies.[688] While the FTDRA exempts government-owned and/or related entities from the rigours of the export/import licensing requirements, the Defence Procurement Manual, 2009 and the Defence Procurement Procedure, 2013, Defence Procurement Procedure, 2016 set out the procedure to be followed by the government entities for procuring items. These documents are available from the website of the MoD.

In addition to the specific guidelines that are issued by the MoD, any procurement by the government entities as a general rule has to comply with the guidelines/policies set out by the Department of Expenditure.[689] Foreign suppliers who want to sell their stores and equipments can either do so directly or through an authorized representative.[690] A foreign firm wishing to appoint an authorized representative has to formally inform the MoD and has to furnish certain information, professional background and details of the nature of business undertaken by the authorized representative.[691]

II Services

Military services require the same licensing process as designated above for military goods.

III Persons/ Deemed Exports

According to EXIM Policy 'deemed exports' refer to those transactions wherein the goods supplied do not leave the country and payment for such supplies is received either in Indian Rupees or foreign currency. Supply of goods to Export Oriented Units,

686. Paragraph 2.9, Foreign Trade Policy 2009-2014. Paragraph 2.14, Foreign Trade Policy, 2015-20.
687. Section 9(4), Foreign Trade (Regulation and Development) Act, 1992.
688. Paragraph 3(2), Foreign Trade (Exemption from application of Rules in certain cases) Order, 1993.
689. No. F-23(1)-E.II(A)/ 89, dated 31 Jan. 1989, issued by the Department of Expenditure, Ministry of Finance.
690. An individual, a partnership, an association of persons, a limited company private or public can be appointed as authorized representative\agent\sales consultant\adviser of a foreign supplier\suppliers, who is either paid a retainer or is reimbursed his expenses or paid commissions or a combination of either, on completion of a specified obligation, by the original equipment manufacturer.
691. These details include the following information: whether functioning as an individual, a partnership, a private limited company, etc.; since when established; registered address, names and addresses of Directors; Chief Executive and executives of the company, specifically indicating those who are retired civilian or Defence Service Officers; principal place of business; whether the company has any partner/ agency/ office abroad; if so, full details thereof etc. Notification: No. 3(2)/ PO(Def)2001 dated 2 Nov. 2001, MoD.

Software Technology Parks, Electronic Hardware Technology parks, Biotechnology parks, projects financed by multilateral or bilateral agencies, amongst others, are regarded as deemed exports.

Par. 2 Control Lists

The ITC (HS) classification lists the various items that may be exported/imported with the restrictions, if any on the trade of such items. The classification contains two Schedules: Schedule 1 and Schedule 2. Chapter 93 of Schedule 1 deals with restrictions relating to the import of arms and armaments. Only certain items such as muzzle loading firearms are permitted for import without a licence, but there are conditions that the purchaser or user of that item must obtain a licence from the relevant authority under the provisions of the Arms Act, 1959. With regard to exports, all the items classified in Appendix 3 of Schedule 2 (the SCOMET list) require the exporters to obtain a licence. The licensing process is the same for military or dual-use goods. Appendix 1 of Schedule 2 lays down the provisions relating to the export of military stores. All military items, not specifically identified in the ITC (HS) classification require an NOC from the MoD in addition to the licensing process.

Par. 3 Licensing and Enforcement Authorities

Since there are a multitude of laws/departments that deal with the import and export of military stores and dual-use items, the licensing and enforcement authorities also tend to be multiple, each of the government agencies having the power to take necessary action within the scope of their authority. Overall, it would be fair to state that the MoD has the supervising role. The departments that would come into the picture, other than the MoD, in case of an enforcement related issue would, *inter alia*, be the DGFT, Customs, DAE, Ministry of Commerce and Industry, the Department of Revenue Intelligence, Reserve Bank of India and the local police.

At the outset, officials use the lack of export and import licences as evidence of illegality. Other documents that are used for this purpose are the Bill of Entry, the Shipping Bill, or any other document prescribed under the Customs Act 1962, which must have the IEC certificate number, issued by the designated offices of the DGFT. The IEC certificate number is used by the customs authorities, also to confirm that the approvals and licences are valid as on the date of export/import of the goods. Further, in cases where the materials are nuclear-related, the officials of customs and excise department (as well as the local police) are authorized to seize and send them to the DAE, and to arrest the persons concerned. In such cases, final investigation and a decision about their sensitivity is made by DAE, but the arresting agency is responsible for bringing the charges before the courts.

Par. 4 Sanctions and the Recourses of the Importer/Exporter

Sub-Par. 1 Sanctions

Implementation and enforcement of export laws fall primarily within the jurisdiction of the Central Board of Excise and Customs (CBEC) and its subordinate body, the Directorate General of Revenue Intelligence (DGRI), an organ of the Ministry of Finance. In addition, designated officials have the authority to enter suspect premises and inspect and seize materials prescribed by the FTDRA. Both CBEC and DGRI derive their statutory and prosecutorial authority from the Conservation of Foreign Exchange and Prohibition of Smuggling Activities Act, 1974. The Act empowers CBEC to formulate policy regarding the 'levy and collection of Customs and Central Excise duties, prevention of smuggling, and administration of matters relating to Customs, Central Excise and Narcotics (i.e., those under CBEC purview).'

The sanctions for violations typically would be: (1) cancellation of the export/ import related permission; (2) imposition of an internal travel ban on the key persons of the importing/ exporting entity; (3) impounding of such person(s) passport and (4) possibly custody of such person(s) during the pre trial stage. Depending on the seriousness of the offence, upon conviction the punishment could be a simple fine or fine with imprisonment. The duration of imprisonment also depends on the nature of offence. Sealing of the business premises of the entity concerned is also a possibility in addition to the above stated actions by the government authorities. For example, the Customs Act provides for confiscation of goods improperly exported/ or imported including a penalty; the FTDRA specifies that an export or attempt to export in violation of any of the conditions of licence shall invite civil and/or criminal prosecution, the AEA 62 prescribes a punishment of one to five years and/or fine.

In cases where the DGFT refuses to grant or renew a licence, or when it suspends or cancels the licence, the importer/exporter has the option of filing an appeal against the said order. Different level of appeals would be available including approaching the courts.[692]

There is no statutory provision which specifically provides for 'black listing' from public procurement contracts. However, there have been instances where MoD has been known to have issued internal circulars banning any kind of dealings with certain entities.

Sub-Par. 2 Recourses

Usually, most statutes provide for an appeal process, however the WMDA provides that in case of any offence under this Act, no court shall entertain any petition without the previous approval of the GoI. Under the Act the penalties include imprisonment for a term exceeding five years extendable to imprisonment for life, and fine against any person, who transfers, acquires, possesses, or transports fissile or radioactive material,

692. Section 15, Foreign Trade (Regulation and Development) Act, 1992.

to cause death or to intimidate people or to coerce a government in India or in any foreign country. Additionally, punishment for an unauthorized export may attract imposition of a fine not less than INR 0.3 million up to INR 2 million.

Sub-Section 2 Dual-Use Goods and Services

The first attempt at consolidating dual-use items into one list for export control purposes resulted in a list dubbed Special Materials, Equipment, and Technology, or SMET, which was incorporated into the EXIM Policy in 1995-1996. This extensive listing in the ITC (HS) classification of export and import items was amended in 1998 and 2000. Minor amendments and additions culminated in the latest version of the EXIM Policy or the ITC (HS) classification, 2015-20. Sensitive items, and the conditions under which they can be exported, have now been consolidated on the SCOMET list.

In relation to intangible technology transfers, the EXIM Policy provides that all intangible transfers must be reported quarterly (post facto) to the concerned Export Promotion Council.[693] The GoI has decided not to require licences in respect of intangible technology transfers. The WMDA provides a comprehensive definition of 'technology,' incorporating intangible technology transfers by Indian citizens abroad and by foreign nationals studying or working in India.[694] It also establishes specific civil and criminal penalties for violations[695] and expands liability for WMD export control violations to all individuals involved in a particular business enterprise.[696]

Par. 1 Overall Presentation

Sub-Par. 1 Requirements Prior to Any Specific Import/Export (i.e., Manufacturing Phase)

As mentioned earlier, the IDRA lists the industries in respect of which industrial undertakings can be established only after obtaining a compulsory industrial licence. The requirement of industrial licensing in the case of dual-use goods would therefore depend on whether an industrial undertaking proposed to be set up for the manufacture of such dual-use goods falls within the schedule to the IDRA. Similarly, whether or

693. According to paragraph 2.54 of Handbook of Procedures, vol. 1, 2009-20014, Chapter 2:

> All the exports made in non physical form by using communication links including high speed data communication links, internet, telephone line or any other channel which do not involve the Customs authorities have to be compulsorily reported on quarterly basis to concerned Export Promotion Council (Para 3.12 of FTP) as given in Appendix 19C.

694. Section 4L of the WMDA.
695. Sections 14-19 of the WMDA.
696. Section 20 of the WMDA.

not private participation and FDI will be allowed in the production of the dual-use good will also depend on the sector in which the said good is sought to be used.[697]

Sub-Par. 2 Requirements at the Import and/or Export Stages

I Goods

Since the SCOMET identifies the list of restricted items, it is essential to procure a licence by making an application to the DGFT. Once it is received by the DGFT, the application is circulated to the concerned agencies in the GoI who are involved with the goods sought to be exported, such agencies could include the Ministry of External Affairs (MEA), MoD, CBEC, and concerned Ministries/Departments (e.g., DAE/Space/ Defence Research and Development Organization (DRDO)/Department of Chemicals and Petro-chemicals/Department of Biotechnology), as required, for technical advice.[698]

If the concerned agency grants the NOC, then the DGFT forwards the application to the Inter-Ministerial Working Group (IMWG), which decides, by consensus, on whether or not to approve a particular export. The IMWG is composed of a core group which includes representatives from the MEA, DGFT, DRDO, DAE, Department of Space, Department of Customs, etc. The decision of the IMWG is communicated in the form of an 'Export Licence' with the conditions subject to which the licence is granted. In the event that the IMWG is unable to agree on a licensing decision, the matter is referred to a 'higher-level committee' for final resolution.

It must be noted that goods covered under Category 0 of the SCOMET list, (i.e., nuclear materials, facilities and related equipments) are governed by the provisions of the AEA 62[699] and applications regarding this category of goods are processed differently from all the other SCOMET categories. Applications for Category 0 items are submitted by the exporter directly to the DAE, which issues the NOC and the export licence based on its review of the exporter's track record and of the end-user information supplied by the exporter. The approval to export might also depend on formal assurances from the recipient state regarding non-use in any nuclear explosive device and additional end-use conditions may be stipulated in the authorizations.

Furthermore, exports of items not on SCOMET list may also be regulated under provisions of the WMDA.

II Services

Dual-use services require the same licensing process as designated above for dual-use goods.

697. The FDI caps and the list of industries in which FDI is not permitted are laid down in the Annexures to the FEMA. Notification No. FEMA 20/ 2000-RB, dated 3 May 2000.
698. http://dgft.gov.in/exim/2000/download/Appe&ANF/ANF2E.pdf.
699. Paragraph 2.50, Handbook of Procedures, Volume I. Paragraph 2.74 (V) of the Hand Book of Procedures, 2015-20.

III Person/Deemed Exports

Same as for Chapter 9, Section 4, Sub-Section 1, Par. 2.

Sub-Par. 3 Control Lists

The SCOMET list is available as a part of the Export Policy in Appendix 3 of Schedule 2 of the ITC (HS) classification of Export and Import Items for 2009-2014. The current SCOMET list contains all dual-use items and technologies. The categories contained in the list are set out in Annex A.

Sub-Par. 4 Licensing and Enforcement Authorities

Same as for Chapter 9, Section 4, Sub-Section 1, Par. 3.

Sub-Par. 5 Sanctions and Recourses of the Importer/Exporter

Same as for Chapter 9, Section 4, Sub-Section 1, Par. 4.

SECTION 5 SPECIFICITIES/ SPACE RELATED PROVISIONS

Sub-Section 1 Specificities of the Control Regime

India no longer has any blacklist, as such, of countries to which exports are prohibited. The Foreign Trade Policy one time prohibited export of 'arms and related materials' to Iraq and Libya. However, in 2004, the prohibition with respect to Libya was lifted. Hence, currently with the exception of Iraq,[700] Democratic People's Republic of Korea, Iran,[701] Somalia[702] and subject to compliance with all licensing requirements, military and dual-use goods may be exported to any country. Unofficially, however, the GoI continues to exercise vigilance and influence with respect to the grant of licences for export to certain 'suspect nations' and exports to certain countries that are within United Nations purview are also closely scrutinized.[703]

700. Chapter 2, paragraph 2.1.1, Foreign Trade Policy 2009-14; the ban on import and export was in relation to arms and related material. Paragraph 2.16 of the Foreign Trade Policy, 2015-20.
701. Chapter 2, paragraphs 2.1.2 and 2.1.3, Foreign Trade Policy 2009-14. Paragraph 2.17 and 2.18 of the Foreign Trade Policy, 2015-20.
702. Chapter 2, paragraph 2.1.4, Foreign Trade Policy 2009-14; the ban on import and export was in relation to charcoal. Paragraph 2.19 of the Foreign Trade Policy, 2015-20.
703. This of course is a matter of policy, and hence no exclusive list can be drawn up in this regard but can be said to include Libya, North Korea, Saudi Arabia and some other countries in the Middle East.

Sub-Section 2 Space-Related Provisions in the Control Regime

There is no specific legislation in India governing the export and import of space-related equipment. Import and export of space-related equipment is primarily regulated by the EXIM Policy and the Foreign Trade Policy of the GoI. According to the EXIM Policy, 2009-2014, certain items such as spacecraft (including satellites), helicopters, airplanes and suborbital and spacecraft launch vehicles, etc., which are restricted under the ITC (HS) classification can be imported or exported only in accordance with a special procedure such as licence, permission, certificate or public notice issued in this behalf, as the case may be.

Further, Category 5 of SCOMET lists items relating to aerospace systems and equipment, including production and test equipment and related technology, which includes rocket systems, unmanned aerial vehicles, manned aircraft, aero-engines, related equipment and components, micro-light aircraft and powered 'hang-gliders', etc. The export of such items would require an export licence and the same has to be obtained in the same manner as for other items listed in SCOMET.

SECTION 6 SANCTIONS AND EMBARGOS

Sub-Section 1 Participation of India to Embargos or Other Related Sanctions

India has incorporated into its domestic law restrictions on imports/exports of certain products approved by the Security Council of the United Nations. Notifications issued under the FTDRA read with the Foreign Trade Policy 2015-2020, consolidate these import and export restrictions. The following table lists the countries subject to embargos enforced by India, as well as the international documents in which such embargos have been established and the notifications confirming the effectiveness of these import/export restrictions in the Indian territory:

Table 9.7 Embargos India Is Participating to ...

Country	*Activities Forbidden*	*Embargos Origin*	*Internalization*
Islamic Republic of Iran	Import/Export of all items that could contribute to Iran's war or nuclear-related activities	INFCIRC/254/Rev.9/ Part 1 INFCIRC/254/Rev.7/ Part 2 S/Res/63 (2006)	DGFT Notification No. 89 (RE-2013) / 2009-2014 dated 6-08-2014 DGFT Notification No. 79 (RE-2013) / 2009-2014 dated 30-04-2014

Country	*Activities Forbidden*	*Embargos Origin*	*Internalization*
			DGFT Notification No. 17 (RE-2013)/2009-2014 dated 10-06-2013 DGFT Notification No. 105(RE-2010)/ 2009-2014 dated 05-03-2012
Iraq	Import/Export of Arms and related material	S/RES/1483 (2003)	DGFT Notification No. 67 (RE-2013) / 2009-2014 dated 12-02-2014 DGFT Notification No. 68 (RE-2013) / 2009-2014 dated 12-02-2014
ISIL and ANF etc. associated with Al Qaida	Import/Export of oil and related material and items of cultural, scientific and religious importance	S/RES/2199 (2015)	DGFT Notification No. 14/ 2015-2020 dated 30-06-2015
Democratic People's Republic of Korea	Import/Export of any material mentioned in the resolutions relating to nuclear armament of DPRK	S/2006/814, S/2006/815 (including S/2009/205), S/2009/364 and S/2006/853 INFCIRC/254/Rev.9/ Part1a INFCIRC/254/Rev.7/ Part 2a (IAEA documents)	DGFT Notification No. 17/2009-2014 dated 27-10-2009
Somalia	Import of charcoal	Foreign Trade Policy, 2015-2020 UNSC 2036 / 2012	NA

SECTION 7 LIST OF ACRONYMS

AEA 48	Atomic Energy Act, 1948
AEA 62	Atomic Energy Act, 1962
AG	Australia Group
CBEC	Central Board of Excise and Customs

CWC	Chemical Weapons Convention
DAE	Department of Atomic Energy
DDP&S	Department of Defence Production and Supplies
DGFT	Directorate General of Foreign Trade
DGRI	Directorate General of Revenue Intelligence
DIPP	Department of Industrial Policy and Promotion
DPSUs	Defence Public Sector Undertakings
DRDO	Defence Research and Development Organization
EXIM	Export-Import
FDI	Foreign Direct Investment
FIPB	Foreign Investment Promotion Board
FTDRA	Foreign Trade (Development and Regulation) Act, 1992
GoI	Government of India
IAEA	International Atomic Energy Agency
IDRA	Industries (Development and Regulation) Act, 1951
IEC	Importer-Exporter Code
IECA	Imports and Exports (Control) Act, 1947
IMWG	Inter-Ministerial Working Group
ITC (HS)	Indian Tariff Classification (Harmonized System)
ITER	International Thermonuclear Experimental Reactor
MEA	Ministry of External Affairs
MoD	Ministry of Defence
MTCR	Missile Technology Control Regime
NSG	Nuclear Suppliers Group
OST	Outer Space Treaty
NOC	No Objection Certificate
SCOMET	Special Chemicals, Organisms, Materials, Equipment and Technologies
SMET	Special Materials, Equipment and Technology
UNTS	United Nations Treaty Series
USA	United States of America
USSR	Union of Soviet Socialist Republics
WA	Wassenaar Arrangement
WMD	Weapons of Mass Destruction
WMDA	The Weapons of Mass Destruction and their Delivery Systems (Prohibition of Unlawful Activities) Act, 2005

SECTION 8 REFERENCES

Sub-Section 1 Primary Documentation

Par. 1 Statutory Legislation

- Foreign Trade (Development and Regulation) Act, 1992.
- The Customs Act, 1962.
- The Atomic Energy Act, 1962.
- The Weapons of Mass Destruction and their Delivery Systems (Prohibition of Unlawful Activities) Act, 2005.
- The Arms Act, 1959.
- The Chemical Weapons Convention Act, 2000.
- The Environment Protection Act, 1986.
- The Industries (Development and Regulation) Act, 1951.

Par. 2 Regulations/ Orders/ Notifications

- ITC (HS) classification.
- Foreign Trade Policy Handbook of Procedures (Vols 1 and 2).
- Foreign Trade Policy, 2009-2014.
- Foreign Trade Policy, 2015-20.
- Foreign Trade (Exemption from application of Rules in certain cases) Order, 1993.
- Public Notice 68 EXP (PN)/ 92-97.
- Notification AEA / 27/ 1/ 95-ER, dated March 1995.
- No. 5(6)/ 2000-FC I, dated 21 May 2001.
- No. 5(37)/ 2001-FC I, dated 4 January 2002.
- Notification No. FEMA 20/ 2000-RB, dated 3 May 2000.
- No. F-23(1)-E.II (A)/ 89, dated 31 January, 1989.
- No. 3(2)/ PO (Def) 2001 dated 2 November, 2001.

Par. 3 Annexes – Copies of Documents of Practical Use to the Importer/Exporter

A number of standard documents relevant for the import or export process in India (e.g., most current official application forms for import or export licences, templates of contractual undertaking, or regulation extracts) as well as other non-official documents are available on a dedicated DropBox folder which can be accessed by following the link below: www.kluwerlawonline.com/eclrh-annexes.

Sub-Section 2 Secondary Documentation

Par. 1 Internet Sites

- www.dipp.nic.in - website of the DIPP
- www.cbec.gov.in - website of the CBEC
- www.mod.nic.in - website of the MoD
- www.commerce.nic.in - website of the Ministry of Commerce and Industry, Department of Commerce
- www.eximkey.com - informational website relating to customs, excise and other trade related issues
- www.dgftcom.nic.in - website of the Ministry of Commerce and Industry, DGFT

Par. 2 Paper Publications

Seema Gahlaut & Anupam Srivastava, *Non-Proliferation Export Controls in India: Update 2005*. Centre for International Trade and security, University of Georgia, Athens, 2005.

SECTION 9 USEFUL INFORMATION

Sub-Section 1 Licensing and Enforcement Authorities Contact Details

Name of Organization	*Directorate General of Foreign Trade*
Postal Address	Udyog Bhawan, H-Wing, Gate No. 2, Maulana Azad Road, New Delhi -110011, India
Telephone	+91 11 23061562
Fax	+91 11 2306 2225
Email address	**dgft@nic.in**
Website	www.dgftcom.nic.in

Name of Organization	*Directorate General of Revenue Intelligence*
Postal Address	7th floor, D Block, IP Bhawan, IP Estate, New Delhi - 110002, India
Telephone	+91 11 23378629/23379871
Fax	+91 11 23370954
Email address	**drihqrs@nic.in**
Website	www.dri.nic.in

Name of Organization	*Central Board of Excise and Customs*
Postal Address	North Block, New Delhi -110001, India
Telephone	+91 11 23092849 (Chairman)
Fax	+91 11 23092890
Website	www.cbec.gov.in

Sub-Section 2 Other

None.

CHAPTER 10

Israel

*Doron Hindin**

SECTION 1 TABLE OF CONTENTS

* The author would like to express his thanks to Mr Daniel Reisner, a partner at Herzog Fox and Neeman, Israel's leading law firm, and to Mr Innokenty Pyetranker, for their invaluable contributions to this chapter. The information herein does not constitute legal advice and should not be relied upon as such. To contact the author, please email dhindin@gmail.com.

SECTION 2 EXECUTIVE SUMMARY

Geographically small, with a population of approximately 8 million and relatively few natural resources, Israel's economy is heavily dependent upon exports of goods, technologies and services. At the same time, since its inception in 1948, Israel has faced existential national security threats from neighbouring states and terrorist organizations. This tension between economic dependency on exports and the pressing need to maintain a qualitative-military-edge over surrounding adversaries has profoundly shaped Israel's relatively nascent trade control systems. For example, the ongoing struggle with national security threats has led to a highly-developed private sector defence industry, the sustainability and success of which is reliant upon exports. And while this sector receive substantial support and incentives from the Israeli government, policy makers have simultaneously endeavoured to curtail the proliferation of Israeli defence and dual-use goods and technologies to support national security and foreign policy interests. An additional reflection of this tension between economic needs and security interests is Israel's unique non-member status with respect to many of the major multilateral export control arrangements. Although Israel's domestic law incorporates many of the international control lists and while the government participates in multilateral discussions concerning those lists, Israel is formally not a member in the lists' associated organizations – primarily due to a fear that membership could undermine Israel's unique national security and foreign policy needs.

This dialectic between Israel's economic dependency on exports and its national security interests, together with certain recent developments discussed below, has resulted in an export control system comprised of four distinct export frameworks.

First, Israel's defence export control regime is administered by Israel's Defense Export Control Agency (DECA) within the Israeli Ministry of Defense (MOD) and constitutes Israel's most robust export control system. Subject to certain exceptions, licences are required for exports of defence goods and technologies, for transfer of related 'know-how', and for the provision of related services outside of Israel or to foreign nationals within Israel. In addition, licences must usually be obtained prior to conducting marketing and promotional activities for the above conduct even if no exports actually take place.

Second, Israel's civilian export control regime, administered by the Israeli Ministry of the Economy (MOE), controls the export of dual-use goods, technologies, and services not intended for security or defence end-users or end-uses. This regime also controls goods, technologies, and services related to chemical, biological, and nuclear technology and launch systems.

A third regime – the encryption control regime – is again administered by the MOD, and governs all activities relating to encryption-capable hardware and software, including their import, export, sale, development, and other activities. As such, encryption control in Israel is not a trade control regime, but is rather a system regulating a broader range of activities.

Finally, through a system of sanctions and restrictive trade measures, Israel prohibits its nationals from trading or otherwise engaging with a list of enemy countries and a variety of designated unlawful entities.

With respect to imports into Israel, the general rules governing customs and taxes and, where relevant, standards-compliance, apply equally to both civilian military and dual-use goods. Nevertheless, regulations identify a variety of sensitive items (including munitions) for which import licensing or import permits are required.

SECTION 3 INTRODUCTION – ELEMENTS OF CONTEXT

Sub-Section 1 Regime Overall Philosophy

Freedom of occupation is a constitutional right in Israel, enshrined in the country's Basic Law: Freedom of Occupation. In this vein, there exists a right to freely export and import goods and technologies and, more generally, to participate in international trade and commerce. Thus, all exporting activity by private individuals is permitted, unless specific legislation states otherwise.[704] Similarly, the majority of goods may be imported freely without prior governmental authorization, and import permits or licences are never required for intangible imports.[705] Notwithstanding, these rights are limited in a variety of ways to sustain the basic balance between the individual's freedom of occupation, the country's economic reliance on foreign markets for exports, the country's involvement in international and intergovernmental organizations, and Israel's existential need to maintain qualitative technological leverage over hostile countries and non-state actors.

Beyond these very high-level themes, however, it is difficult to identify a single overall philosophy common to Israel's various trade control frameworks. Indeed, upon analyzing the country's specific trade control regimes, a somewhat fragmented system appears. This fragmentation is most apparent with regard to the striking regulatory differences that exist with respect to the export and trade of military, dual-use, and encryption goods and technologies. Each of these regulatory regimes provides specialized requirements that are monitored and enforced by different bodies, and careful attention must be paid in order to remain compliant across these dissimilar systems. Notwithstanding, one unexpected common denominator between these otherwise disparate frameworks is that while Israel has refrained from obtaining membership in all of the primary multinational export control organizations, it in fact strictly abides by those organizations' control lists. For example, Israel is not a member of the Wassenaar

704. See Section 2 of the Free Export Order, 5767-2006, which provides the rule that ' … all goods are permitted for export'.

705. See Section 2 of the Free Import Order, 5774-2014, which freely permits import of almost all goods listed in Israel's Custom Tariff – subject to prior authorizations with respect to specific imports.

Arrangement or the Missile Technology Control Regime (MTCR). Nevertheless, Israel's legislature has bound its regulators to strict observance of these organizations' control lists. Thus, under Israeli law, changes to the Wassenaar and MTCR control lists are automatically and almost instantly incorporated in Israel and immediately bind local exporters and regulators.[706] Whereas in other jurisdictions changes to international control lists may be implemented gradually or following publication of local regulatory guidance, the Knesset (Israel's Parliament) has not afforded similar prerogatives to the Israeli exporters and regulators, upon whom changes to these control lists are instantaneously imposed.

Par. 1 Export Control Regime for Military Goods

Israel's defence export control regime is by far the most robust and restrictive of all of Israel's trade control regimes and DECA is recognized as Israel's predominant export control regulator. As such, other Israeli authorities, both as a matter of practice and law, turn to DECA prior to making licensing decisions.[707]

However, despite the central export control role of DECA, the agency and the regime that it administers have existed for less than a decade and the agency is constantly evolving and improving its policies and procedures. For example, the MOD has invested considerable funds into creating an online licensing platform similar to the United States' DTrade or SNAP-R, but to date applications must be submitted via postal mail or hand delivery.[708] Substantively, certain features of Israel's defence export control system can particularly confound exporters in their compliance efforts, potentially leading to inadvertent export compliance violations. By way of illustration, a unique DECA feature is that specific permits must be obtained prior to conducting most forms of 'defence marketing' or promotional activities.[709] Defence marketing is defined broadly to include any activity aimed at promoting a transaction involving the export of defence equipment, the transfer of defence know-how, or the provision of defence services.[710] The guiding rationale behind this requirement was to curtail proliferation as early as the marketing stage.[711] However, this approach has spawned a highly

706. See Section 2(a) of the Defense Export Control Order (Controlled Dual-Use Equipment), 5768-2008 and Section 2(a) of the Defense Export Control Order (Missile Equipment), 5768-2008; these regulations, which implement the Wassenaar Arrangement's dual-use list and the MTCR Annex respectively, provide that the control lists are binding in Israel ' ... as updated from time to time ...'.
707. See, e.g., Sections 4-7 of the Import and Export Order (Control of Dual-Purpose Goods, Services and Technology Exports), 5766-2006.
708. A 2013 report by Israel's State Comptroller and Ombudsman office pointed to various additional areas that required improvement within DECA. For example, the report criticized DECA enforcement authorities for relying on whistleblowers and informers, rather than DECA's investigative initiatives, for information regarding alleged export control violators. In practice, the whistleblowers and informers are often exporters seeking to obtain a commercial advantage over competitors. See 'State Comptroller and Ombudsman Annual Report 2013-963B', 17 Jul. 2013.
709. Article 14 of the Defense Export Control Law, 5766-2007.
710. *Ibid.*
711. See, e.g., Legislative Notes to Government Bill Number 274, 19 Dec. 2006, at pp. 191-192.

restrictive defence export control system, one in which activities as trivial as the posting of a picture of a defence product on a website or the referencing of a controlled item at a conference without a licence can constitute criminal legal violations. An additional anomaly that Israeli defence-exporters must confront relates to a variety of catch-all clauses in regulations and control lists that empower the government to assert control over items that are almost entirely civilian in nature, but that in some way serve the defence or homeland security sector.[712] As a result, certain items that might not be subject to any significant export controls in other jurisdictions may be subject to extensive DECA control once they reach Israeli soil or otherwise develop an Israeli nexus.

Par. 2 Export Control Regime for Dual-Use Goods

A key feature of Israel's dual-use export control regime is that goods and technologies appearing on the Wassenaar Arrangement's dual-use list are regulated by two different organizations. Dual-use technologies and goods intended for civilian end-use and end-users are regulated by Israel's Ministry of Economy (MOE), whereas dual-use technologies and goods intended for defence end-use *or* end-users are regulated by the far stricter DECA system.[713] Thus, if a company self-determines that it is subject to licensing for a particular dual-use export, it may yet be unclear as how to proceed, as the distinction between civilian end-use (subject to MOE licensing) and defence end-use (subject to DECA licensing) may be quite ambiguous. For instance, if a dual-use item is bought by a civilian to be used for a civilian purpose, then MOE licensing would be required. If, however, a defence-related end-user purchases the very same product, then the company is required to undergo the far more onerous DECA licensing process, even if this defence end-user intends to make purely civilian use of the product. Exporters naturally prefer to be subject to the regime of the MOE rather than DECA. In practice, however, it is DECA and the MOD - and not the exporters - that ultimately decide which regime will apply.

Sub-Section 2 Historical Outlook

Israel's trade control system dates back to before the state's inception in 1948.[714] Following World War I, the area known today as Israel was governed by the British Mandate for Palestine. At the outbreak of World War II, the UK enacted strict controls over trade and commerce, partially in the form of the Import, Export and Customs Powers (Defence) Act of 1939. To avoid legal lacunas, the nascent State of Israel broadly adopted the laws in effect prior to independence, including the strict trade laws

712. See, e.g., *Sections 21-22 of the Annex to the Defense Export Control Order (Combat Equipment), 5768-2008; Article 2 of the Defense Export Control Law, 5766-2007, providing a very broad definition of the term of 'defense knowhow'.*
713. See Article 2 of the Defense Export Control Law, 5766-2007, providing the definition and scope of 'Controlled Dual-Use Equipment'.
714. Israel declared independence on 14 May 1948.

that reflected the WWII reality from which Israel emerged.[715] Thereafter, Israel began enacting its own legislation, slowly replacing and updating earlier British and Ottoman laws. Throughout its first decades, Israel was reluctant to ease control over imports and exports, due mostly to the then-stagnant economy that was struggling to cope with continuing influxes of Jewish refugees, an unrelenting Arab boycott, devastations from the Israeli War of Independence, and other economically attenuating factors. In 1979, the UK's restrictive 1939 law – incorporated into Israeli law in 1948 as the Import, Export and Customs Powers (Defence) Ordinance of 1939 – was replaced by the Import and Export Ordinance [New Version] 5739-1979 (Import Export Ordinance). A similar process took place with respect to customs regulations, a topic first governed by diffuse British orders but eventually consolidated into Israel's current Custom Ordinance [New Version] of 1957. The Import Export Ordinance and the Customs Ordinance, and the array of subsidiary control orders that have been enacted under these laws, currently form the basis of Israel's contemporary civilian import and export control system.

Israel's defence export control system essentially shared the history described above until less than a decade ago when a new, independent legal regime was formed.[716] Historically, the export of defence equipment and the provision of defence services were strictly controlled through the 1939 Ordinance (later replaced by the Import Export Ordinance) and a 1957 law entitled the Control over Commodities and Services Law, 5717-1957 (Control Law).[717] At the outset of the twenty-first century, however, the Knesset came to the conclusion that these outdated laws could no longer serve as the source of control over Israel's highly-developed, export-oriented defence and dual-use industries. As a result, the Defense Export Control Law, 5766-2007 (DECL) was enacted, ushering in reforms to the export control system to which the local defence market is still adjusting. According to its legislative notes, three primary factors spurred the Knesset towards enacting the DECL.[718] First, the law was explained in light of Israel's commitments towards non-proliferation, international peace and stability, and a desire to cooperate with international export control regimes. Second, the Control Law upon which Israeli export control orders had previously been based was originally enacted to be temporary in nature – contingent upon a state of

715. Israel's first piece of legislation, promulgated by the provisional legislative council of the nascent country, was the Law and Administration Ordinance, 5708-1948. Article 11 of the law provides that:

> [t]he law which existed in the Land of Israel [on 14 May 1948] shall remain in force, insofar as there is nothing therein that is contrary to this Ordinance or to the other laws which may be enacted by or on behalf of the Provisional Council of State, and subject to such modifications as may result from the establishment of the State and its authorities.

716. Note that imports of defense goods into Israel are still regulated primarily by the Import and Export Ordinance, together with other customs, tax, standards-compliance, and other legislation.
717. The Control Law, enacted in 1957, aimed to consolidate the various British control orders that had been issued in the context of WWII and subsequently adopted by the State of Israel See, e.g., Legislative Notes to Bill Number 58, 12 Nov. 1950.
718. See Legislative Notes of Government Bill Number 274, 19 Dec. 2006.

emergency - and the DECL was preferred as a more stable piece of legislation.[719] Finally, in the early 1990s, Israel underwent a constitutional reformation in which, *inter alia*, the freedom of occupation was given constitutional legal status. The Knesset therefore felt it necessary to entrench control over export activity - control that by its nature impinges upon one's freedom of occupation - in primary legislation as opposed to the secondary orders and regulations that had previously been the basis of control.

Two additional factors, not mentioned in the legislative notes, further served as powerful catalysts for the DECL's promulgation. First, prior to the DECL's establishment of DECA, export permits were issued by the SIBAT, the division within the MOD responsible for assisting local industry with defence exports.[720] This was perceived to constitute an inherent conflict of interest, as the entity established to support exporters and foster Israel's private sector defence market was the same entity responsible for administering the regulations aimed at restricting export activity. Lastly, a final impetus for the creation of the DECL was likely strained US-Israel relations in the early twenty-first century.[721] In the mid-1990s, despite strong opposition from Washington, Israel began negotiating a multi-billion dollar sale of Israeli-developed Phalcon Airborne Early Warning Systems to the Chinese government. Persistent US pressure eventually convinced Israeli leaders to renege on the deal, profoundly impairing Sino-Israeli military cooperation. Although the sale did not ultimately transpire, the near release of sensitive aerospace technology to China elicited US scepticism over military aid to Israel. Against this backdrop, the DECL legislation enacted in the aftermath of the Phalcon crisis was, at least in part, aimed at reassuring the US of Israel's commitment to export oversight and at restoring US-Israel defence cooperation. A DECL provision that may be evocative of the Phalcon crisis is the requirement that DECA obtain extremely high-level approval prior to authorizing any defence exports based on a bilateral agreement that exceed NIS 200 million.[722] Authority in such cases rests with an inter-ministerial committee comprising the Israeli Prime Minister, the Minister of Defence, the Foreign Minister, the Minister of Justice, and the Minister of the Treasury.[723]

In short: like Israel itself, domestic controls over trade emerged from the WWII era. Since that time, and through a process spanning several decades, Israel has developed a modern, albeit somewhat perplexing, legal lattice of import and export control laws and regulations, many of which are elaborated upon throughout this chapter.

---

719. See Article 2 of the Control Law, conditioning the Control Law on a declared state of emergency. Since 1948, such a state of emergency has been continually declared, initially pursuant to Article 9(A) of the Law and Administration Ordinance, 5708-1948 and currently under Article 38 of Israel's Basic Law: The Government.
720. See generally, 'Sibat Homepage', http://en.sibat.mod.gov.il/Pages/home.aspx.
721. See Amnon Barzilai, 'The Phalcons Didn't Fly', *Ha'aretz*, 28 Dec. 2001; Jonathan Adelman, 'The Sino-Israeli-American Triangle', Jerusalem Center for Public Affair, Jerusalem Letter / Viewpoints No. 473, 1 Mar. 2002.
722. See Article 47(c) of the DECL; Defense Export Control Regulations (Scope of Defense Exports Pursuant to an Agreement between Israel and Another State to be Brought for Approval by the National Security Ministerial Committee), 5768-2008.
723. See Article 14(c) of the DECL.

Sub-Section 3 Participation to International Regimes

In Israel, internal domestic legislation is generally required to implement international agreements. Accordingly, Israel is generally categorized as a 'dualist' country in terms of international law.[724] The following tables display Israel's participation status to export control related international treaties and programmes. It is also stated, when relevant, whether Israel is party to a treaty either by signature and ratification or by accession. The tables show that Israel tends to refrain from binding itself to trade-related treaties. At the same time, however, the control lists and other regulatory features of many of these treaties are in fact operative in Israel via domestic legislation, jurisprudence, and practice.

Par. 1 Treaties and Regimes Dealing with Specific Items and Technologies

Table 10.1 Nuclear Weapons Treaties

Treaty Name	*Overall Status*	*Specific Status*	*Enforceable in Israel*
Limited Test Ban Treaty[725]	OS: 5 August 1963 EF: 10 October 1963	S: 8 August 1963 R: 15 January 1964	Yes
Nuclear Non-Proliferation Treaty[726]	OS: 1 July 1968 EF: 5 March 1970	-	No[727]
Comprehensive Nuclear Test Ban Treaty[728]	OS: 24 September 1996 EF: not in force	S: 25 September 1996	No[729]

OS: Opened for signature; EF: Entry into force; S/R: Signature/Ratification; A: Accession

724. Under black-letter law in Israel, the President is authorized to ratify treaties accepted by the Knesset. See Article 11(5) of Israel's Basic Law: The President of the State. However, as a common law country, the doctrine of *stare decisis* has established legal precedent accepting decisions of government bodies to bind the country to international agreements relevant to particular government body's area of activity. See, e.g., Criminal Appeal 131/67 *Hishmat Kmiar v. State of Israel*; HCJ 5167/00 *Prof. Hillel Weiss v. Prime Minister*; Ruth Lapidoth, 'Israel', in *National Treaty Law and Practice*, 2nd ed., ed. M. Leigh, M. Blakeslee & L.B. Ederington (Leiden: Martinus Nijhoff Publishers, 2003), 379-413.
725. Treaty Banning Nuclear Weapon Tests in the Atmosphere, in Outer Space and Under Water, *U.N.T.S.*, vol. 480, p. 43.
726. Treaty on the Non-Proliferation of Nuclear Weapons, *U.N.T.S.*, vol. 729, p. 161.
727. Israel has not signed the Nuclear Non-Proliferation Treaty (NPT), but the Export Order (Control of Chemical, Biological and Nuclear Exports), 5764-2004 expressly forbids any export of goods, services, and technologies intended for purposes of development or production of nuclear weapons.
728. U.N.G.A., resolution 50\245.
729. Although Israel has not ratified the Comprehensive Test Ban Treaty (CTBT), it does implement elements of the CTBT. For example, Israel's Atomic Energy Commission maintains facilities that comprise part of the International Monitoring System of the CTBT Organization (CTBTO). In addition, Israel participates in the CTBTO via the 'Israeli Mission to the International Atomic Energy Agency and the CTBTO', within the Embassy of Israel in Vienna, Austria.

Table 10.2 Biological and Chemical Weapons Treaties

Treaty Name	*Overall Status*	*Specific Status*	*Enforceable in Israel*
Geneva Protocol[730]	OS: 17 June 1925 EF: 8 February 1928	A: 20 February 1969[731]	No
Biological Convention[732]	OS: 10 April 1972 EF: 26 March 1975	-	No[733]
Chemical Convention[734]	OS: 13 January 1993 EF: 29 April 1997	S: 13 January 1993 R: Not Ratified	No[735]

OS: Opened for signature; EF: Entry into force; S/R: Signature/Ratification; A: Accession

Table 10.3 Multilateral Export Control Regimes

Regime Name	*Formation*	*Participation*
Zangger Committee[736]	1971	No
Nuclear Suppliers Group	1974	No[737]
Australia Group	1985	No[738]

730. Protocol for the Prohibition of the Use in War of Asphyxiating, Poisonous or Other Gases, and of Bacteriological Methods of Warfare, 94, *League of Nations Treaty Series*, No. 2138 (1929).
731. A reservation was made by Israel upon accession according to which Israel committed to applying the treaty only with respect to other signatories that ratified the treaty and that reciprocate its implementation vis-à-vis Israel.
732. Convention on the Prohibition of the Development, Production and Stockpiling of Bacteriological (Biological) and Toxin Weapons and On Their Destruction, *U.N.T.S.*, vol. 1015, p. 163.
733. Despite having not signed the Biological Convention, Israel's Export Order (Control of Chemical, Biological and Nuclear Exports), 5764-2004 expressly forbids any export of goods, services and technologies intended for purposes of development or production of biological weapons.
734. Convention on the Prohibition of the Development, Production, Stockpiling and Use of Chemical Weapons and on Their Destruction, Doc.CD/CW/WP.400/Rev.1 (CWC).
735. Despite having not signed the Chemical Weapons Convention, Israel's Export Order (Control of Chemical, Biological and Nuclear Exports), 5764-2004 expressly forbids any export of goods, services and technologies intended for purposes of development or production of chemical weapons. Furthermore, under MOE Director General Directive 2.3, the MOE will endorse CWC end-use certificates only after being convinced that no diversion risks exist. Such certificates are required under Parts VII and VIII of the CWC, prior to controlled transfers by exporters from CWC Member States to recipients in states not party to the convention.
736. Non-Proliferation Treaty Exporters Committee (also called the Zangger Committee).
737. While not formally a member, Israel adheres to the Nuclear Supplier control lists, generally incorporated in Israel through the Export Order (Control of Chemical, Biological and Nuclear Exports), 5764-2004 and its schedules.
738. While not formally a member, Israel adheres to the Australia Group (AG) Common Control Lists, incorporated in Israel through the Export Order (Control of Chemical, Biological and Nuclear Exports), 5764-2004, the Free Export Order, 5767-2006, and the Free Import Order, 5774-2014. Furthermore, under MOE Director General Directive 2.3, a process has been established whereby the MOE can endorse particular local importers as eligible to receive exports covered by the AG. Such endorsement may at times be necessary to alleviate concerns of an AG Member State authority and demonstrate that export to the particular Israeli importer in fact conforms to the AG Guidelines.

Regime Name	Formation	Participation
Missile Technology Control Regime	1987	No[739]
Wassenaar Arrangement[740]	1994	No[741]

Table 10.4 Other

Name	Adoption	Participation
International Code of conduct[742]	25 November 2002	No

Par. 2 Treaties Dealing with Specific Areas

Table 10.5 International Zones

Treaty Name	Overall Status	Specific Status	Enforceable in Israel
Antarctic Treaty[743]	OS: 1 December 1959 EF: 23 June 1961	-	No
Outer Space Treaty (OST)[744]	OS: 27 January 1967 EF: 10 October 1967	S: 27 January 1967 R:2 February 1977	Yes
Sea Bed Arms Control Treaty[745]	OS: 11 February 1971 EF: 23 June 1961	-	No
Moon agreement[746]	OS: 18 December 1979 EF: 11 July 1984	-	No

739. While not formally a member, Israel adheres to the MTCR's Missile Technology Annex, incorporated in Israel through Defense Export Control Order (Missile Equipment), 5768-2008.
740. Wassenaar Arrangement on export controls for conventional arms and dual-use goods and technologies.
741. While not formally a member, Israel maintains ongoing dialogue with the Wassenaar Secretariat and adheres to the Wassenaar Arrangement's dual-use and munitions lists under the laws and regulations discussed throughout this chapter.
742. Hague Code of Conduct against Ballistic Missile Proliferation, not yet published.
743. 402, *U.N.T.S.*, 7.
744. Treaty on Principles Governing the Activities of States in the Exploration and Use of Outer Space, including the Moon and Other Celestial Bodies, *U.N.T.S*, vol. 610, p. 205.
745. Treaty on the Prohibition of the Emplacement of Nuclear Weapons and other Weapons of Mass Destruction on the Seabed and The Ocean Floor and in the subsoil thereof, *U.N.T.S.*, vol. 955, p. 115.
746. Agreement governing the Activities of States on the Moon and Other Celestial Bodies, *I.L.M.*, vol. 18, p. 1434.

Treaty Name	*Overall Status*	*Specific Status*	*Enforceable in Israel*
Convention on the Law of the Sea[747]	OS: 10 December 1982 EF: 16 November 1994	-	No[748]

OS: Opened for signature; EF: Entry into force; S/R: Signature/Ratification; A: Accession

Table 10.6 Regional Nuclear Weapons-Free Zones

Treaty Name	*Overall Status*	*Specific Status*	*Enforceable in [Country]*
Treaty of Tlatelolco[749]	OS: 14 February 1967 EF: 22 April 1967	-	No
Treaty of Rarotonga[750]	OS: 6 August 1985 EF: 11 December 1986	-	No
Treaty of Bangkok[751]	OS: 15 December 1995 EF: 27 March 1997	-	No
Treaty of Pelindaba[752]	OS: 11 April 1996 EF: not in force	-	No

OS: Opened for signature; EF: Entry into force; S/R: Signature/Ratification; A: Accession

SECTION 4 CONTROL REGIME

Sub-Section 1 Military Goods and Services

Par. 1 Overall Presentation

No single Israeli law is exclusively dedicated to controlling the import of military goods and services into the country. By contrast, Israel's defence export control regime is administered by DECA pursuant to the provisions of the DECL and various subsidiary regulations.

Article 1 of the DECL provides that Israel's defence export control regime was created to '...regulate state control of the export of defense equipment, the transfer of defense know-how and the provision of defense services, for reasons of national

747. Doc. A/CONF.62/122 and Corr.1-11 (UNCLOS).
748. Despite not having signed the UNCLOS, Israel implements elements of the treaty in its domestic legislation. See, e.g., the Law on Sub-Marine Territory, 5713-1956; the Coastal Waters Law, 5713-1956; Marine Zones Bill, 5774-2013, recently introduced and aimed primarily at adopting certain UNLCOS EEZ provisions.
749. Treaty for the Prohibition of Nuclear Weapons in Latin America and the Caribbean, *U.N.T.S.*, vol. 634, p. 326.
750. South Pacific Nuclear Free Zone Treaty, *I.L.M.*, vol. 24, p. 1442.
751. South East Asia Nuclear-Weapon-Free Zone Treaty, *I.L.M*, vol. 35. p. 635.
752. African Nuclear Weapon-Free Zone Treaty, *I.L.M.*, vol. 35, p. 698.

security considerations, foreign relations considerations, international obligations and other vital interests of the State'.[753] Thus, these three activities - export of defence equipment, transfer of defence know-how, and provision of defence services - all require DECA licensing. Each one of these regulated actions, together with 'defence-brokering', will be discussed in detail below, although the DECL regulates a variety of other activities as well.

Sub-Par. 1

I Export of Defence Equipment

Under Article 15(a)(1) of the DECL, defence equipment and technologies or products containing such items as components may not be exported from Israel to foreign territory without a licence. Regarding export of defence equipment, in contrast to the transfer of defence know-how and the provision of defence services, export licences are generally not required for 'deemed exports', i.e., exports to foreigners within Israel. Nevertheless, licences are required prior to providing defence equipment to diplomatic or consular representatives of foreign states within Israel and before exporting defence equipment to areas under Palestinian control. As described below, defence equipment consists of goods and technologies found on the various control lists in effect pursuant to the DECL, collectively known as Defence Equipment.[754]

II Transfer of Defence Know-How

A licence is generally required prior to the release of any defence-related know-how of Israel origin in a foreign territory or within Israel to any non-Israeli citizen or resident or to a foreign corporation.[755] The mode of release is immaterial, and can be through an electronic medium, verbally (as in a presentation or exhibit) or in any other manner. The term 'Defense Know-how' is defined broadly under the DECL and includes all:

> information that is required for the development or production of Defense Equipment or its use, including information referring to design, assembly, inspection, upgrade and modification, training, maintenance, operation and repair of Defense Equipment or its handling in any other way.[756]

As a result, the term 'Defense Know-how' encompasses technology, technical data, and technical assistance related to controlled Defence Equipment, and requires licensing if transferred from Israel or within Israel to a foreign entity.

753. Quoted sections from the DECL throughout this chapter are taken from the DECL's unofficial English translation, available on the website of DECA.
754. See, *infra*, Section Par. 2 of Sub-section 1 of this Section 4, providing the scope of the term 'Defense Equipment' through reference to control lists.
755. Article 15(a)(2) of the DECL.
756. Article 2 of the DECL.

The term 'Defense Know-how' additionally extends to:

> [k]nowhow relating to defense forces, including know-how concerning their organization, build-up and operation, combat doctrine or training and drill methods, defense policy or their methods of action, as well as knowhow relating to defense policy, anti-terror combat, and security methods.[757]

Consequently, know-how not of a technical nature - that is, know-how not associated with any particular entry on the various export control lists - may nevertheless be deemed 'controlled' if it relates to the broader defence-related and security-related fields mentioned above. In practice, this inclusive language gives DECA broad discretion to determine whether the transfer of any particular know-how falls within its regulatory purview.

III Provision of Defence Services

Under Article 15(a)(3) of the DECL, every Israeli resident and 'Israeli Corporation' must obtain a licence before providing 'Defense Services' outside the territory of Israel or within Israel to a non-Israeli citizen or resident or to a foreign corporation. A Defence Service is defined as a:

> service relating to Defense Equipment, including its design, development production, assembly, review, upgrade, modification, repair, maintenance, operation and packaging, as well as instruction related to said equipment, and service regarding Defense Knowhow, including instruction, training and consulting regarding said Knowhow.[758]

Unlike for the export of Defence Equipment and transfer of Defence Know-how, DECA requires licences for the provision of Defence Services if any entity engaging in the activity is an Israeli resident or corporation, even if the relevant goods or technologies are entirely foreign and are not being exported from Israel. Moreover, companies anywhere in the world - even those not formally registered in Israel - require DECA licensing prior to providing Defence Services if such companies constitute 'Israeli Corporations'. As defined in Article 2 of the DECL, an Israeli Corporation includes, '(1) A corporation incorporated in Israel; or (2) A corporation that has its center of business in Israel, and which the Control over it is, directly or indirectly, by an Israeli citizen or resident'.[759] Consequently, if the ultimate beneficial owners of a foreign company are Israeli citizens or residents and if that company's centre of business is, in practice, Israel, that company would be subject to DECA requirements for the provision of Defence Services.

757. *Ibid.*
758. Article 15(a)(3) of the DECL.
759. Article 2 of the DECL.

IV Defence Marketing Licences

Israeli export control law is unique in that, in general, prior to being eligible to receive export licences for the above activities, marketing permits must have first been issued by DECA.[760] Specifically, Israeli citizens and residents, as well as Israeli Corporations, must obtain marketing permits prior to conducting marketing activities aimed at promoting transactions involving the export of Defence Equipment, the transfer of Defence Know-how, or the provision of Defence Services. There is no requirement that such marketing be conducted from Israel; instead, the key requirement is that the marketing relate to one of the three above-mentioned regulated activities, and that the marketing entity be an Israeli citizen or resident or an Israeli Corporation.

V Brokering Defence Contracts and Other Controlled Activities

Under Article 21 of the DECL, every Israeli resident and Israeli Corporation must obtain a licence before undertaking international brokering activities related to foreign Defence Equipment. Put differently, Israeli brokers - such as agents, intermediaries, finders, etc. - require licences even with respect to transactions that do not involve any Israeli products or companies. However, while Article 21 could have significant ramifications to the extent any sales, negotiating, or other commercial activities relating to Defence Equipment are conducted by Israeli residents, the Israeli government has officially decided not to implement the international brokering regulations for the time being.[761]

Sub-Par. 2 Requirements Prior to Any Specific Import/Export (i.e., Construction Phase)

I Generic Requirements for Conducting Business in Israel

First and foremost, companies doing business in Israel are typically required to register with the Israeli Registrar of Companies as well as with the Israeli Tax Authority's Department of Customs and Value Added Tax (VAT) within the Israeli Ministry of Finance.[762]

760. Articles 14 and 16 of the DECL.
761. Under Article 49(2) of the DECL, Article 21 is to take effect thirty days after the promulgation of relevant regulation by the Minister of Defense. Such regulation is subject to prior consultation with the Israeli Ministry of Foreign Affairs and the parliamentary Foreign Affairs and Defense Committee.
762. See, e.g., Article 346 of the Israeli Companies Law, 5759-1999, requiring that even foreign companies register with the Israeli Corporations Authority as a condition to conducting business in Israel; See generally Value Added Tax Law 5763-1975.

II Requirements Specific to Regulated Industries

Beyond generic commercial and tax requirements, certain sector specific laws and regulations exist. Thus, under the Israeli Firearms Law, 5709-1949, licences must be obtained from the Israeli Ministry of Public Security (IMPS) for 'conducting business activities related to firearms', as these terms are defined broadly in the law. Under the Explosives Regulations (Commerce, Transport, Manufacturing, Storage and Use), 5754-1994, and the Explosives Law, 5714-1954, it is prohibited to conduct certain activities with explosive devices without first obtaining the requisite permits from the Regional Workplace Inspector within the MOE's Administration of Occupational Safety and Health. Pursuant to the Licensing of Businesses Law, 5728-1968, the Israeli Minister of the Interior enacted the Licensing of Businesses Regulations (Dangerous Factories), 5753-1993, which requires companies to obtain specific permits and maintain heightened compliance standards prior to conducting activity with dangerous goods.[763] Similarly, under Category 9 of the Annex to the Licensing of Businesses Order (Businesses Requiring Licensing), 5773-2013, commercial activity related to defence articles requires specific licensing from the Ministry of the Interior, which is permitted to issue such licences only following consultation with the IMPS.

III Requirements Related to Commission Rates for Defence Brokering

Up until 2014, Israel's Control Law maintained strict requirements related to broker and agent commissions for the sale of foreign military equipment to the MOD or to various other Israeli security agencies. However, in 2014, Amendment Number 22 to the Control Law took effect and entirely voided these requirements.[764] The amendment reflected the Knesset understanding that controlling commission rates were anachronistic, overly paternalistic and possibly inconsistent with the constitutionally-protected freedom of occupation. Thus, following this significant amendment to the law, the Control Law no longer prohibits or otherwise applies restrictions or conditions to agency commissions for sales of defense equipment to Israeli authorities.[765]

763. Examples of these types of goods include items with designated UN ID numbers under the UN model regulations on the Transport of Dangerous Goods and items listed in the annex to specific Israeli regulations.
764. See Legislative Proposal Control over Commodities and Services Law, (Amendment No. 22) (Voiding of Chapter Two 3), 5772-2012, in Israel's Legislative Gazette, No. 694 (18 July 2012), implemented by Control over Commodities and Services Law, (Amendment No. 22) (Voiding of Chapter Two 3), 5774-2014, in Israel's Legislative Record (Sefer Ha'Hukim), No. 2458, 15 Jul. 2014.
765. See Bill for Control over Commodities and Services Law (Amendment No. 22) (Voiding of Chapter 3.2), 5772-2012.

Sub-Par. 3 Requirements at the Import and/or Export Stages

I Import

Items - be they military or civilian in nature - are released by Israeli customs authorities once the necessary import formalities, including payment of customs duties and indirect taxes, have been dealt with; for items subject to specific standards, release occurs once there is confirmation that all relevant standards are in compliance. Beyond these basic customs and tax formalities, imports to Israel are generally freely permitted and not subject to prior government authorizations. Notwithstanding this general rule, exceptions do exist according to which import permits (Import Permits) or import licences (Import Licences) must be obtained or other requirements and preconditions must be met with respect to imports. Thus, the first schedule to Israel's Free Import Order, 5774-2014, enumerates goods – including munitions, arms, and a variety of additional defence and dual-use goods – that require specialized Import Licences prior even to making arrangements for shipment to Israel. Import Permits, required for items listed in the second schedule to the Free Import Order, 5774-2014, as well as for a variety of other items, must be obtained as a condition to release from Israeli customs. The relevant government agency responsible for issuing these authorizations varies based upon the nature of the item designated for import. Accordingly, importers of certain aerospace vehicles and machinery are required to obtain licensing from the Israeli Ministry of Transport and Road Safety and imports of firearms require Import Licences from the MOE, although such a licence will be issued only if the applicant is able to first evidence requisite licensing from the IMPS.[766] In addition to these product-specific import permit requirements, imports from countries that do not maintain diplomatic relations with Israel typically also require an Import Licence, although a set of exemptions have been published in this regard.[767] There are many other governmental agencies that issue product-specific authorizations, and by inputting an item's Harmonized System (HS) number on the website of the Israeli Tax Authority, one can generally identify which, if any, additional authorizations are necessary under the Free Import Order, 5774-2014.[768] Finally, it is worth noting that pursuant to an MOE directive, the MOE may exempt an importer from import permit

766. Note that a variety of other specific licences or permits may be required from different governmental agencies under laws not discussed here, such as the Customs Ordinance [New Version] and its subsidiary legislation.

767. See Section 6(3)(a) of the Free Import Order, 5774-2014, derogating imports from countries with which Israel does not maintain diplomatic ties and that prohibit imports from Israel; imports from such countries typically require MOE licensing. Notwithstanding, Section 2 of 'MOE Directive No. 2.4 – Import of Goods from Countries to which the Free Import Order does not Apply', designates several states from which imports into Israel are freely permitted despite these states meeting the criteria for derogation under Article 6(3) of the Free Import Order, 5774-2014.

768. See the Customs Tariff page of the website of the Israeli Tax Authority, http://taxes.gov.il/customs/CommercialImport/Pages/CustomsTariffIF.aspx, although licensing requirements described adjacent to the Customs Tariff entries on the Israeli Tax Authority website pertain to the Free Import Order, 5774-2014 and do not outline import licensing requirements that may be required by other laws and regulations.

requirements for the import of '[m]ilitary equipment intended for the Ministry of Defense, the Israeli Police, or an alternate governmental body'.[769]

The import-related laws and regulations described in the paragraph above apply strictly to tangible imports and do not apply to intangible imports, which are not subject to import requirements.

II Exports under DECA Licensing Process

Under DECA, licensing is a multi-staged process with four core phases.

First, all defence-exporters must register with a specialized registry maintained by DECA. Registration is a prerequisite for filing requests for licences and only those individuals registered with DECA on behalf of a specific exporting company may benefit from the company's licences and engage in marketing and exporting activity on its behalf.

Second, following registration, any controlled product, know-how, or service that a company wishes to market or export abroad must receive a sensitivity classification from DECA. The classification determination relates to the confidentiality and sensitivity level of the item and has considerable ramifications for future licensing, as DECA will apply stricter procedural and substantive conditions to more highly classified and sensitive products. Following the sensitivity classification process, a specific product number is assigned and used by DECA for identifying the product, know-how, or service for all future regulatory purposes. Changes to the product after it has been assigned a registration number may necessitate a de novo assessment of the changed product by DECA.

Third, the arguably most significant phase involves obtaining a licence to market the proposed export, referred to as a Marketing Licence. Any marketing action aimed at promoting a defence export transaction requires a specific Marketing Licence detailing the specific goods, services, or know-how being marketed, listing the potential end-users, and designating the countries in which the marketing activity is supposed to take place. Under the DECL, unless a regulatory exemption has been made, no defence export is permitted and no export licence will be issued without the exporter first having obtained the appropriate Marketing Licence.[770] In practice, DECA has issued a variety of Marketing Licence exemptions and exceptions that facilitate compliance and expedite export licensing processes.[771]

Finally, actual defence export activities require an Export Licence specific to the items and customer in question. Export Licences include, *inter alia*, a monetary value

769. See 'MOE Directive 2.6 – Exemptions Granted under Section 2(c) (2) of the Free Import Order'.
770. Article 16 of the DECL.
771. See, e.g., Defense Export Control Regulations (Marketing Licence Exemption), 5770-2010; Defense Export Control Regulations (Marketing Licence Exemption), 5768-2008.

limit and once that value has been exceeded, a new permit is required. Marketing Licences are typically valid for up to three years, while Exporting Licences generally expire after two years.[772]

Par. 2 Control Lists

Under the DECL, Defence Equipment falls into three categories: (1) Missile Equipment; (2) Combat Equipment; and (3) Controlled Dual-Use Equipment. Each term is defined in the DECL with reference to one or more control lists.

Sub-Par. 1 Israel's Munitions List

Israel's Munitions List (IML) is found in the annex to the Defense Export Control Order (Combat Equipment), 5768-2008. All goods and technologies referenced in the IML constitute regulated Defence Equipment. The IML generally incorporates the entries designated under the Munitions List developed by the Wassenaar Arrangement, but further includes certain catch-all entries and a set of designations added by DECA that are not found in the Wassenaar Arrangement's Munitions List.

For instance, Section 21 of the IML reflects one of the primary Israeli additions to the Wassenaar Munitions List and is drafted quite broadly to include '[e]quipment, means and accessories especially planned or adapted for use by entities involved in internal security or for anti-terror units, in their operations ... '. The term 'equipment, means and accessories' is explained through an open list of examples that include riot control equipment, non-lethal weapons, dogs, protective gear, equipment for disposal or activation of explosives, and other similar means and equipment. By contrast, no legislative guidance is given with respect to the terms 'internal security' and 'anti-terror units', which have been often applied to civilian police and even prison services. Accordingly, the extremely inclusive language of this IML entry can lead to a variety of goods, technologies, and services that are essentially civilian in nature being classified by DECA as Defence Equipment due to remote or negligible defence applications. In practice, Section 21 has led to exporters of innocuous civilian goods being exposed to DECA enforcement actions despite the exporters having been entirely unaware that their products constituted Defence Equipment.[773]

Additional examples of IML entries that do not appear in the Wassenaar Munitions List include civilian space vehicles and auxiliary equipment; various manned and unmanned air, land and sea vehicles; certain military and non-military

772. Timeframes are established pursuant to the Defense Export Control Regulations (Licensing), 5768-2008.
773. Notably, the MOD and other Israeli government and parliamentary offices are having ongoing discussions regarding replacing the Hebrew IML with the official Wassenaar Munitions List. Entries that today are unique to the IML and that do not appear on the Wassenaar Munitions List would be incorporated in Hebrew into a separate order. This decision, which is as of mid-2014 not yet finalized, apparently stems from the interpretational difficulties arising out of translating the Wassenaar Munitions List into Hebrew.

electronic recording equipment; products or technological means associated with information security, communications interception, and data protection; and several additional entries that are similarly controlled as Defence Equipment under Israel's defence export control regime.[774]

Sub-Par. 2 Dual-Use Equipment for Defence End-Users or End-Uses

The DECL asserts control over 'Controlled Dual-Use Equipment' – a term that encompasses the majority of listings in the Wassenaar Arrangement's List of Dual-Use Goods and Technologies – provided they are intended for a defence end-use or end-user. Specifically, under the Defense Export Control Order (Controlled Dual-Use Equipment), 5768-2008, all goods and technologies found in categories one through nine of the Wassenaar dual-use list – to the exclusion of Category 5 Part 2, entitled 'Information Security' – are controlled for export by DECA when the end-user or end-use is defence-related. If the end-user and the end-use are civilian, jurisdiction rests with the MOE. Encryption items found in Category 5 Part 2, regardless of the nature of the end-use or end-user, are controlled by the MOD's Encryption Control Department, a separate division within DECA.

Sub-Par. 3 Missile Equipment

Regarding missile equipment, the Defense Export Control Order (Missile Equipment), 5768-2008, enacted pursuant to Article 2 of the DECL, extends DECA control to listings in the Equipment, Software and Technology Annex of the MTCR.

Par. 3 Licensing and Enforcement Authorities

Import Licences or Import Permits, when necessary, are issued by the authorized government body through a process that is generally expeditious and relatively straightforward. By contrast, DECA licensing system is more complex.

DECA was established in 2006 within the MOD, shortly before the promulgation of the DECL.[775] It is a developed agency within the MOD and maintains departments employing policy makers, technical experts and skilled investigators. When resources or expertise are insufficient, DECA utilizes other MOD capabilities, such as those of the MOD's Administration for the Development of Weapons and Technological Infrastructure (Maf'at). Hierarchically, the director of DECA is bound by the decisions of the General Director of the MOD, who in turn answers to the Minister of Defence. As a matter of law, DECA licensing decisions are subject to consultation with the Israeli

774. See Sections 9, 10, 11 and 22 of the IML.
775. DECA was founded on 2 Jul. 2006.

Ministry of Foreign Affairs (IMFA) and to general oversight by an interagency commission consisting of representatives from the MOD, the IMFA, the MOE, and from designated defence and homeland security agencies.[776] DECA has a strong influence on all of Israel's other export control regulators which as a matter of practice and, at times, as a matter of law, turn to DECA prior to making export control related decisions.[777]

Licensing processes at DECA are often quite lengthy. Registration of new companies, personnel, and products may take weeks or months, especially if the product is deemed highly classified or otherwise sensitive. Timeframes are largely dependent on the availability of government resources to conduct required security assessments, background checks, and product reviews. Under the Defence Export Control Regulations (Licensing), 5768-2008, Marketing Licences for registered Defence Equipment, services, and know-how that are designated as 'unclassified' must be issued by DECA within forty days of submission of an application, shortened from sixty days pursuant to Defence Export Control Regulations (Licensing), 5775-2015.[778] Marketing Licences for exports subject to higher classification levels or that are intended for countries designated as problematic by DECA must be issued within 120 days of submission of an application.[779] Export Licences are issued within shorter timeframes, between thirty and forty-five days depending on the specific export licence.[780] Despite these statutory timeframes, it often takes DECA longer periods to issue licences, requiring exporters to begin the licensing processes well in advance of any regulated marketing or export activity.

The two figures below offer a bird's-eye view of the process through which DECA handles requests for Marketing and Export Permits.[781]

Finally, as part of licensing, beneficiaries of DECA licences are typically required to comply with various reporting and recordkeeping obligations.[782] In addition, companies are subject to audits by DECA and must provide it with information upon request.[783] Marketing Licences are typically valid for up to three years, while Exporting Licences generally expire after two years.[784] A relatively recently development, emblematic of DECA's central export position, is that certain exporters must demonstrate that they have adequate anti-corruption and bribery procedures in place as a

776. Article 24 of the DECL.
777. See, e.g., Section 6 of the Import and Export Order (Control of Dual-Purpose Goods, Services and Technology Exports), 5766-2006, which imposes upon the MOE to consult with DECA prior to issuing various licensing-related decisions and rulings.
778. Section 14(a)(1) of the Export Control Regulations (Licensing), 5768-2008.
779. *Ibid.* at sub-section (2).
780. *Ibid.* at sub-sections (3)-(5).
781. These charts are loosely based on Hebrew-language diagrams available on the website of DECA, and in particular in a presentation given in February 2011. These and other presentation can be found at the following address: http://www.exportctrl.mod.gov.il/ExportCtrl/Hadrachot/Mazagot/.
782. See Article 28 of the DECL.
783. See Article 29 of the DECL.
784. Timeframes are established pursuant to the Defense Export Control Regulations (Licensing), 5768-2008.

precondition to DECA licensing. Anti-corruption and bribery declarations and commitments have further been incorporated into several of DECA's export control licence application forms. These requirements reflect part of Israel's commitments under the OECD's treaty forbidding foreign corrupt practices.[785]

Figure 10.1 DECA Process for Handling Applications for Defence Marketing Licences

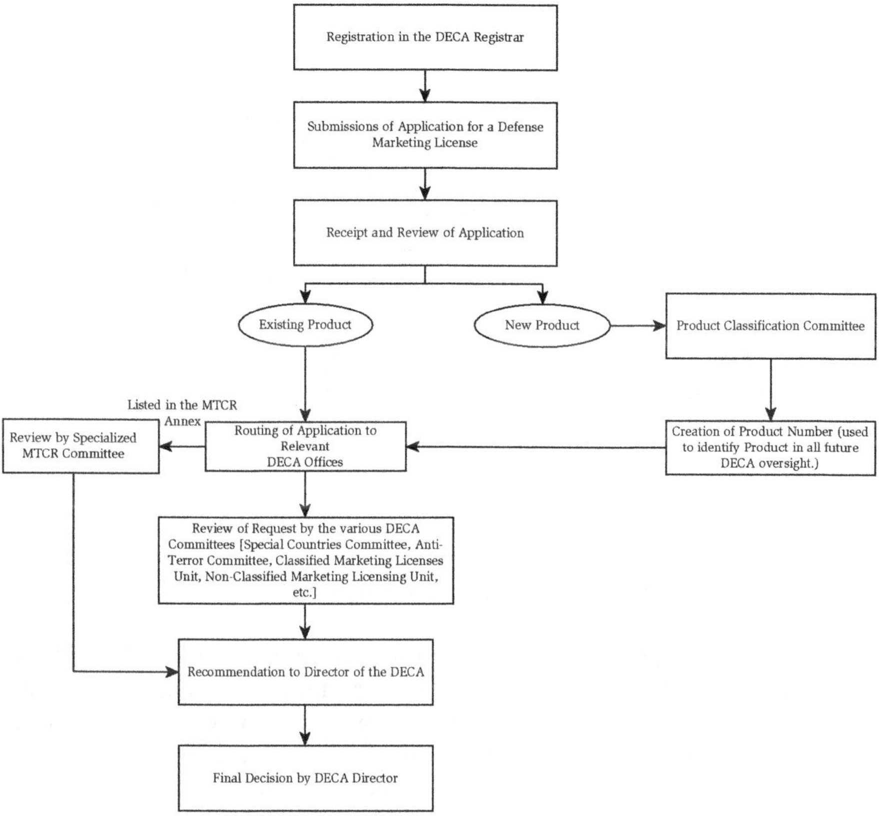

785. Israel, an OECD member, ratified the Convention on Combating Bribery of Foreign Public Officials in International Business Transactions in 2009. Under Israeli law, bribery of foreign public officials is primarily prohibited by Article 291A of the Penal Code, 5737-1977.

Figure 10.2 DECA Process for Handling Applications for Defence Export Licences

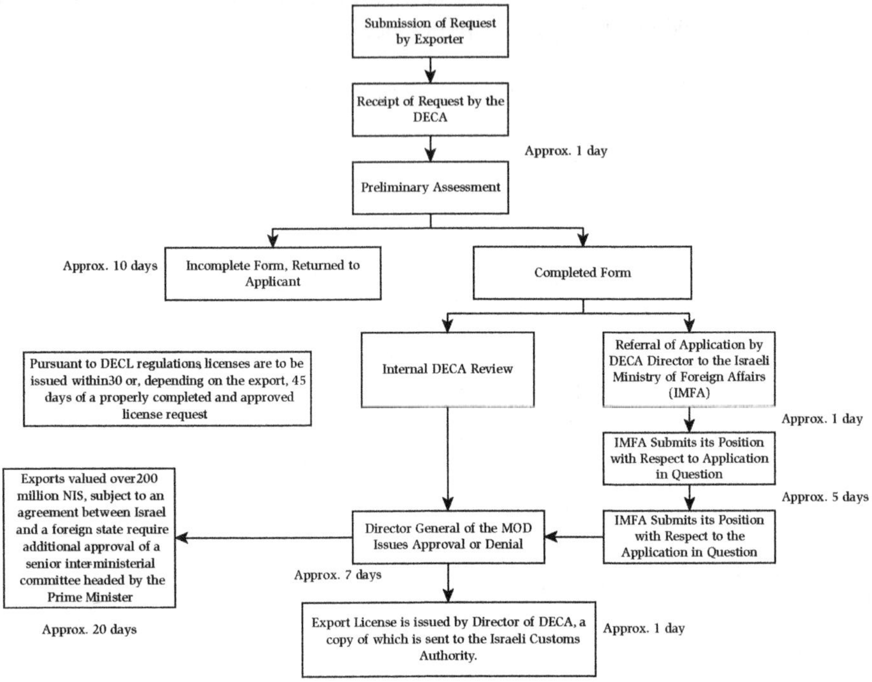

Par. 4 Sanctions and the Recourses of the Importer/Exporter

In addition to confiscation and seizure of goods, penalties for violating Israeli import laws include up to two years of imprisonment per violation and fines of up to three times the value of the imported goods.[786] Enforcement of import violations is led by the Tax Authority, and, at times, by the Ministry of Justice. With respect to exports, DECA has a developed enforcement branch consisting of engineers, investigators, and additional auxiliary personnel. In cases of violations, the DECL imposes (1) criminal liability for those legal and natural persons deemed in violation of the DECL; (2) 'strict liability' criminal responsibility for company officers; (3) administrative fines; and (4) financial sanctions.

Violators of the DECL are generally subject to up to three years imprisonment or a fine of up to NIS 6.8 million.[787] However, if the crimes were committed under 'Severe Circumstances', imprisonment is extended to five years and the fine increased to NIS 11.3 million.[788] Severe circumstances include: cases in which unlicensed marketing

786. See Article 7 of the Import Export Ordinance of 1979.
787. See Article 32 of the DECL.
788. See Article 33 of the DECL.

activity was undertaken for the purpose of promoting an export to an 'Enemy State';[789] cases in which unlicensed marketing activity was undertaken to promote an export to an entity subject to UN Security Council sanctions adopted by Israel; cases involving a 'classified' product; and cases involving the violation of a licence-specific provision of a particular Marketing or Export Licence.

Notably, the DECL creates strict liability obligations that are applicable to company officers, requiring them to supervise and do all reasonably possible to prevent defence marketing and export violations. In the event of criminal export conduct, the burden of proof rests upon each officer to prove that he or she fulfilled this obligation. Otherwise, the officer may be personally fined up to NIS 226,000 per violation.[790] In practice, written export control manuals, enforced export policies, and remedial procedures are essential tools used for alleviating this burden of proof.

Moreover, beyond the criminal liability mentioned above, DECA is empowered to impose a fine of up to NIS 1.017 million for violations of the marketing and exporting provisions of the DECL.[791] For violations of the law's reporting and recordkeeping obligations, a financial sanction of between NIS 22,590 and NIS 226,000 can be imposed, depending on the specific violation.[792] Continued violations are subject to a daily increase of one-fiftieth of the amounts listed above.[793]

Finally, in addition to statutory sanctions, compliance failures can lead to denial of export permits and other business disruptions.

Sub-Section 2 Dual-Use Goods and Services

Par. 1 Overall Presentation

Under Article 2 of the Import Export Ordinance, the Minister of Economy is authorized to regulate import and export of goods and technology into and out of Israel. Under this primary legislation, two central export control orders were enacted. Besides these two export orders, there are no orders or other laws or regulation that are dedicated and specific to dual-use goods or technologies; accordingly, there are no requirements prior to any specific dual-use import/export (i.e., at the construction phase) or requirements with respect to imports of specific dual-use items.

789. The DECL defines 'Enemy State' through reference to the Trading with the Enemy Ordinance, 1939.
790. See Article 34 of the DECL.
791. See Article 35 of the DECL.
792. See Article 36 of the DECL.
793. See Article 37 of the DECL.

Sub-Par. 1 Requirements at the Import and/or Export Stages

I Goods

A. Imports

No law is exclusively dedicated to controlling the import of dual-use goods and technologies into Israel. In practice, however, dual-use goods generally do not benefit from the Free Import Order, 5774-2014, and importers would therefore be required to obtain proper Import Licences or Import Permits from the MOE or from other relevant government bodies.[794]

At the same time, a process does exist for imports controlled under the Chemical Weapons Convention (CWC) and the Australia Group (AG), both of which mandate that certain precautionary measures be undertaken when transferring controlled toxins, precursors, pathogens, and other associated goods and technologies to non-participating states, such as Israel.[795] As of 1998, by virtue of MOE Director General's Directive 2.3, the MOE has had a process in place to produce government endorsed end-use certificates to local importers of goods and technologies controlled by the CWC and AG.[796] The signed certificate is aimed primarily at alleviating diversion concerns of regulatory authorities of CWC and AG Member States. By submitting an application to receive such a certificate from the MOE, an Israeli importer commits to subjecting itself to ongoing MOE reporting requirements and authorizes the MOE to conduct sampling of its chemicals, onsite factory audits, and other oversight activities.

B. Wassenaar Dual-Use Exports

Exports of certain dual-use goods and technologies are regulated pursuant to the Import and Export Order (Control of Dual-Purpose Goods, Services and Technology Exports), 5766-2006, commonly referred to as the 'Wassenaar Order'. Its first schedule incorporates the nine categories of controlled items set out in the Wassenaar Arrangement's List of Dual-Use Goods and Technologies. Any product designated on this list, or any product incorporating such a designation as a subcomponent, and the provision of services related to such products will be controlled for export by the MOE, provided that the intended end-use and end-user is civilian. An export listed on the Wassenaar Arrangement's dual-use list intended for a defence-related end-use or end-user will be controlled for export by DECA. A further caveat to MOE control is that entries listed in Category 5 Part 2 of the Wassenaar dual-use list, entitled 'Information Security', are controlled by the MOD's Encryption Control Department and excluded from MOE jurisdiction.

794. See *supra* Section 4, Sub-Section 1, Sub-par. 1 (discussing general import requirements for both military and dual-use goods and services).
795. See 'Guidelines for Transfers of Sensitive Chemical or Biological Items'; Parts VII and VIII to the Verification Annex to the CWC, detailing the requirements of the end-user certificates.
796. See 'MOE Directive No. 2.3 – Control over Imports of Goods in the Framework of the CWC'.

C. Chemical, Biological and Nuclear Exports

An array of goods and technologies related to chemical, biological and nuclear exports are controlled pursuant to the Free Export Order, 5767-2006, and the Import and Export Order (Control of Chemical, Biological and Nuclear Exports), 5764-2004 (CBN Order). Under these regulations, it is categorically forbidden for entities to export from Israel any goods, technology, or services knowing that they are intended for use in the development or the production of chemical, biological, or nuclear weapons. Exports not intended for these purposes may be permitted subject to requisite MOE approvals and licensing.

II Services

The Wassenaar Order as well as the CBN Order pertaining to chemical, biological and nuclear exports require licences for the 'exportation of goods specified in the lists, or technology or services related to such goods'.[797] Thus, the three forms of controlled civilian dual-use exports relate to (1) 'goods', (2) 'technologies related to such goods' and (3) 'services related to such goods'. 'Goods', as used in the relevant regulations, refers to a variety of goods referenced in the relevant control lists discussed below. The term 'technology related to such goods' is defined as:

> specific information required for the development, production, or use of any item included [in the control lists], except for information which is Part of the Public Domain or is Basic Scientific Research; this information may take the form of technical data or technical assistance.[798]

In contrast to the definitions of 'goods' and 'technology', the concept of 'services related to such goods' is undefined by the relevant laws and regulations. Accordingly, there is little legal clarity as to what type of activity would constitute 'services' requiring MOE licensing.[799] In practice, there may be conflicting positions on this matter and any determination by Israel's regulators are case-specific. Regarding deemed exports, the relevant MOE legislation and regulation is similarly vague. In contrast to the DECL, the Import Export Ordinance and its subsidiary legislation do not address the release of controlled goods, technology, or know-how within Israel to foreign nationals.

Finally, it is worth noting that the MOE regime, as opposed to its MOD counterpart, does not require a permit for marketing activities.

797. See Section 3(a) of the Import and Export Order (Control of Dual-Purpose Goods, Services and Technology Exports), 5766-2006; Section 4(a) of the Import and Export Order (Control of Chemical, Biological and Nuclear Exports), 5764-2004.
798. See Section 1 of the Import and Export Order (Control of Dual-Purpose Goods, Services and Technology Exports), 5766-2006; Section 1 of the Import and Export Order (Control of Chemical, Biological and Nuclear Exports), 5764-2004.
799. Article 2 of the Import Export Order [New Version], 5739-1979 defines '*Services*' as 'Providing a service to another, including in relation to Goods and Know-How', but it is difficult to glean any clear understanding from this definition.

Par. 2 Control Lists

The Wassenaar Arrangement's dual-use list, excluding Category 5 Part 2, is controlled by the MOE in cases in which the intended end-use and end-user are civilian in nature.

Additionally, Schedules 1 and 2 of the CBN Order list items over which Israel applies export controls. Specifically, these schedules reference items subject to control by the Nuclear Suppliers Group, the AG, the NPT, the Biological Weapons Convention (BWC), and the CWC. The 'Complete List of Source Items and Dual Use Items' is maintained by the MOE and published on its website. Furthermore, Article 2(a)(3) of the Free Export Order, 5767-2006, establishes that the nearly sixty types of chemicals designated in the Order's third Schedule require licensing for export. The export of any product containing these chemicals in any form requires licensing from the MOE's Chemistry and Environment Administration. While the Free Export Order, 5767-2006 is in Hebrew, all but two of the chemicals designated in the third Schedule are listed in English; the two chemicals listed in Hebrew translate to, 'Phosphorous' and 'Hydrogen Chloride.'

Finally, the Free Export Order, 5767-2006, ostensibly assert MOE control over exports listed in the MTCR Equipment, Software and Technology Annex, provided that '... the item is not for use by armed forces or defense forces or for military or defense use'. However, in practice, as of the promulgation of the DECL in 2007, this clause, while still on the books, has been superseded by DECA licensing which today covers all MTCR exports, including those to civilian end-users and for civilian end-uses.

Par. 3 Licensing and Enforcement Authorities

Export application forms for Wassenaar dual-use goods, technologies, and services as well as for controlled chemical, biological, and nuclear exports must be submitted both electronically and by physical mail to the MOE's Chemistry and Environment Administration.

The process and timeframes for licensing dual-use exports under the Wassenaar Order are presented in the flow chart below, although timeframes may be slightly extended in extenuating circumstances.[800] There is also an expedited track through which the MOE will issue licences within five days of application requests for exports of Wassenaar dual-use goods and technologies to civilian end-users in the following countries: Austria, Finland, France, Germany, Greece, Australia, Belgium, Bulgaria, Canada, Croatia, the Czech Republic, Denmark, Austria, Portugal, Romania, Latvia, Lithuania, Luxemburg, Mexico, Holland, New Zealand, Norway, Poland, Hungary, Ireland, Italy, Japan, Slovakia, Slovenia, Spain, Sweden, Switzerland, Britain and the US.

The process described in the figure is very similar to the licensing process for exports subject to the CBN Order.

800. See Sections 4(d) and 6(C) of the Wassenaar Order.

Figure 10.3 Flow Chart of MOE Licensing of Dual-Use Exports

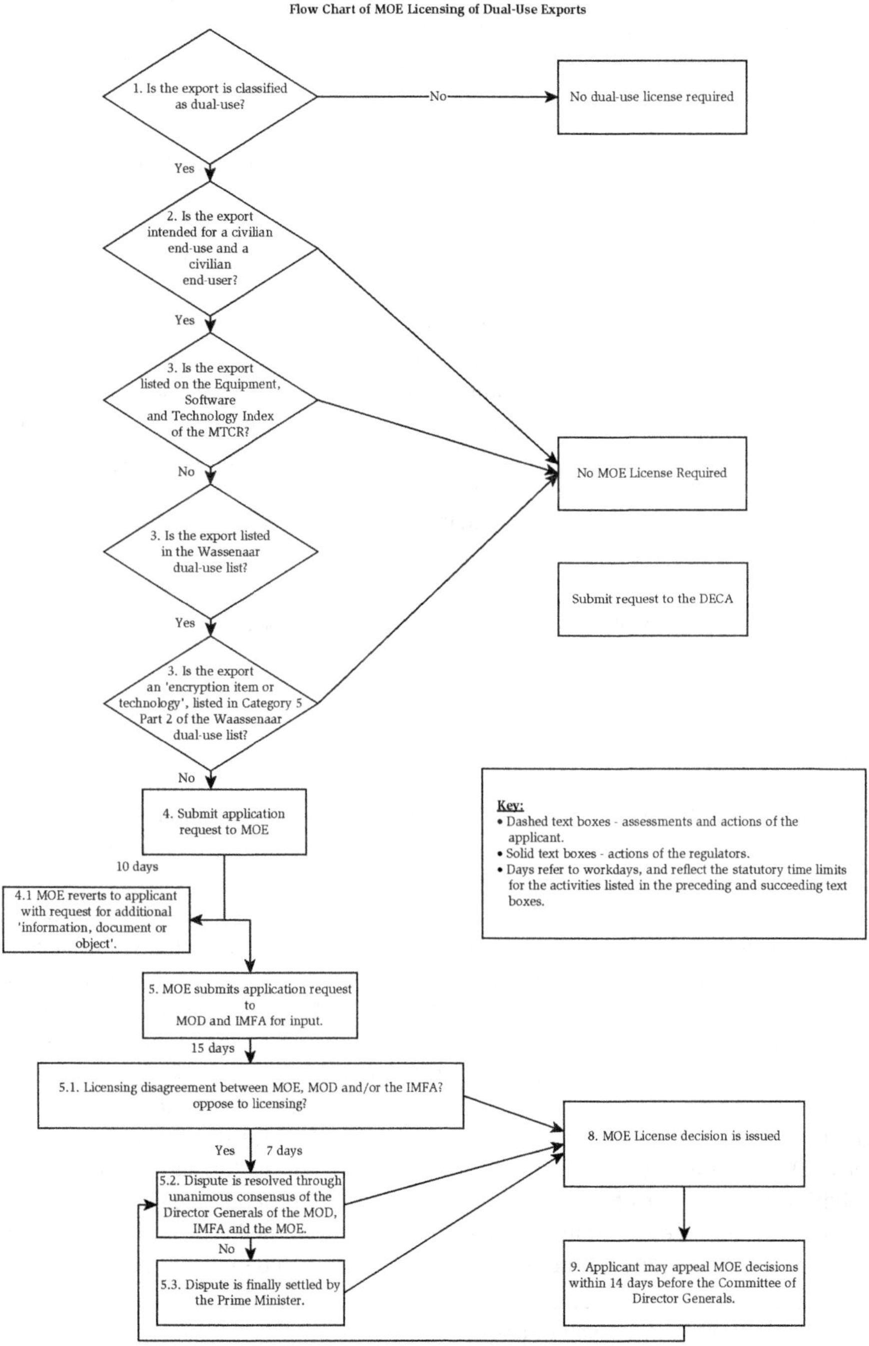

Par. 4 Sanctions and the Recourses of the Importer/Exporter

The Import Export Ordinance, under which MOE licensing is regulated, provides for administrative seizures as well as criminal liability. Specifically, if goods were shipped in contravention of an MOE order (such as the Free Export Order, 5767-2006, the CBN Order, or the Wassenaar Order), the goods themselves are subject to confiscation. Under certain conditions, the means of transport of the goods is also subject to administrative seizure. Criminally, the exporter as well as its agent or forwarder are subject to two years imprisonment or a fine of the greater value of either three times the cost of the unlawfully shipped goods or of their means of transportation.[801]

Additionally, under Article 11 of the Import Export Ordinance, exporters or forwarders must be prepared to submit proof to customs officials that (1) their exports are not destined for and did not in fact arrive in the hands of an enemy national or enemy state and (2) that they took all necessary steps to ensure that the goods will or have arrived only at permitted locations. Failure to produce a sufficient response to a request for such proof of compliance can result in seizure of the goods prior to shipment and, following shipment, a monetary fine. Customs officials are also entitled to require proof that exports are in compliance with applicable export control laws. If sufficient proof is not offered, the Israeli Customs Authority is entitled to seize the goods pursuant to directives of the MOE.

SECTION 5 SPECIFICITIES/SPACE-RELATED PROVISIONS

Sub-Section 1 Specificities of the Control Regime

Par. 1 Encryption Control in Israel

Under the Control Law, the Minister of Defence was given the authority to issue the Control of Commodities and Services Order (Engagement in Encryption Items), 5734-1974 (Encryption Order). The Encryption Order was issued in conjunction with the Declaration Governing the Control of Commodities and Services (Engagement in Encryption Items), 5734-1974 in which 'engagement in encryption items' was declared a service subject to governmental control. Thus, virtually all forms of engagement with cryptographic-related products are controlled in Israel. As such, encryption control in Israel is not exclusively an export control regime but rather a broad regulatory framework. Generally, the following encryption-related activities are regulated: (1) use, (2) import, (3) export, (4) sale, (5) development, (6) production, (7) modification, (8) integration, (9) purchase, (10) holding, (11) transfer (between places or persons), (12) conduct of negotiations, and (13) distribution. Engaging in any of these activities without first obtaining the requisite encryption control licence or without benefiting from a licence exemption or exception is prohibited. The licensing authority in this regard is the Encryption Control Department, an independent body within the

801. Article 7 of the Import Export Ordinance.

MOD's DECA. The Encryption Control Department possesses licensing authority over, *inter alia*, information security listings in Category 5 Part 2 of the Wassenaar Arrangement's dual-use list, supplanting MOE and DECA jurisdiction for encryption purposes. Licence applications are reviewed by the Encryption Control Division and ultimately issued by the Director General of the MOD.

Depending on the sensitivity of an application request, as determined by the Encryption Control Division, one of three licences may be issued. A General Licence authorizes most forms of engagement with a particular encryption product but excludes modification and integration that essentially create a new product. Such a licence is typically valid for an unlimited period of time and the associated product-name is generally published on the publicly available 'Free Means List' - a list of products that have essentially been decontrolled by the MOD. A Restricted Licence is the standard licence issued and is valid for one year. While the MOD may impose licence-specific restrictions on any particular 'Restricted Licence', standard restrictions for a licence of this type generally include a categorical prohibition on exports to Iran, Lebanon, Sudan, Syria, North Korea and Cuba; a limited restriction on exports to Iraq, Libya and to areas under Palestinian control without a Special Licence (as defined below); and (c) a restriction on transferring know-how and technology to third parties without first obtaining a Special Licence. 'Know-how' refers to source-code and other information and technology needed for the de novo development or manipulation of the encryption item. Finally, the third licence type, a Special Licence, is a licence issued in particularly sensitive scenarios. As a rule, a Special Licence is valid for one year and contains unique - and often quite strict - requirements and conditions.

Under the Control Law, violations of Israel's Encryption Order can lead to penalties of up to three years imprisonment or a fine of up to NIS 75,300.[802] If such an offence was committed under aggravating circumstances, the offender may be subject to a penalty of up to five years imprisonment or a fine of up to NIS 226,000.[803] Moreover, senior officials of any corporation that has violated the Control Law are personally liable unless they can prove that (1) the violations took place unbeknownst to them and (2) they took all reasonable means to assure compliance with the Control Law.[804] A lower standard exists with respect to employees personally involved in violations of the Control Law, who avoid liability upon proving that they were acting in accordance with their employer's directives and that they believed in good faith that their actions were not in violation of the Control Law.[805]

While the Encryption Order asserts very broad control, there are in fact various licence exemptions and exceptions that can obviate the need for licensing in select situations.

802. Article 39(b) of the Control Law.
803. *Ibid.*
804. *Ibid.* at Articles 39A.
805. *Ibid.* at Articles 39B and 39C.

Par. 2 Corporate Matters

Beyond the trade control matters discussed above, a range of laws and practices impose further context-specific restrictions on local defence companies.

For example, private defence companies, and particularly those providing services to Israeli government agencies, are often subject to confidential compliance requirements imposed by the MOD's Director of Security for the Defense Establishment (MaLma'B). Such requirements may, for example, entail having an MOD representative conduct ongoing onsite security checks or requiring employees of a defence company to undergo periodic background checks and screenings.

Additionally, Israel's Law on Defense Corporations (Protection of Defense Interests), 5766-2006, empowers a committee of senior government members to prevent share or asset transfer activity (i.e., mergers and acquisitions or M&A activity) of companies identified as bearing implications on the defence interests of the State of Israel. DECA itself can similarly impose a variety of conditions that could prevent or otherwise limit mergers and acquisitions of DECA regulated companies.[806] An additional body that has some authority over private defence companies is – somewhat unexpectedly – the Israeli Patent Office which, at the request of the MOD, is empowered to deny registering a patent with defence or homeland security applications.[807]

Licensing and enforcement decisions of the Israeli authorities (such as DECA, the MOE, MaLma'b and the Patent Authority) are often classified and disclosed only on a need-to-know basis to entities possessing adequate security clearances.

Par. 3 Anti-Boycott Legislation

Israel maintains anti-boycott legislation in the form of the Law to Prevent Damage to the State of Israel Through Boycotts, 5711-2011. Enacted in 2011 in response to anti-Israel boycott activity, the law establishes that calls to take part in broadly-defined 'anti-Israel boycotts' constitute a civil tort. The law further clarifies that entities calling for participation in anti-Israel boycotts are not entitled to a defence that they were acting on justified grounds if sued for 'tortuous interference'. Finally, the law authorizes the Minister of Finance, in consultation with the Minister of Justice, to deny tax credits, subsidies, and other incentives as well as bar participation in public tenders to any entity calling for or committing to participate in an anti-Israel boycott. In bill form, the law sought to criminalize boycott behaviour,[808] similar to the regime in the US under the Export Administration Regulations.[809] However, during the legislative process, the bill lost its criminal dimension and retained only the civil and administrative sanctions described.

806. Article 28(d) requires DECA registered companies to submit a notification following any change of control. Beyond this requirement, however, change of control over regulated company assets could require additional DECA licensing.
807. See Chapter Six of the Patent Law, 5727-1967.
808. See Knesset Bill P/18/2505 Prohibition on Boycott Bill, 5770-2010.
809. See 15 CFR Part 760, Restrictive Trade Practices or Boycotts.

Sub-Section 2 Space-Related Provisions in the Control Regime

In contrast to some other jurisdictions, Israeli export control law regulates most space-related exports under the MOD regime, even in cases in which the end-use and end-user are entirely civilian. Specifically, Section 22 of the IML provides that 'spacecraft', including 'communications satellites', as well as auxiliary equipment and products are deemed Defence Equipment. '[L]aunch systems' and 'systems intended for spacecraft positioning', 'telemetry ground stations', and even 'spacecraft imageries' are similarly considered Defence Equipment subject to strict DECA marketing and export licensing.

SECTION 6 SANCTIONS AND EMBARGOES

Sub-Section 1 Participation of Israel to Embargoes or Other Related Sanctions

Israeli law proscribes engagement with a variety of designated enemy states and unlawful entities. These states and entities are identified through domestic law and do not, for the most part, directly mirror listings of international or intergovernmental organizations. Nevertheless, under certain domestic Israeli laws, fast-track procedures are available for blacklisting entities already subject to UN Security Council sanctions.[810]

Sub-Section 2 Regime of the Embargoes or Related Sanctions in Israel

Par. 1 Enemy states and Designated Unlawful Entitles

The primary sanctions law in Israel is the Trading with the Enemy Ordinance, 1939 (Ordinance), prohibiting actual and attempted 'trading' with an 'enemy' and defines both terms broadly. Violations of the Ordinance constitute a criminal offence punishable by up to ten years imprisonment and a fine of up to NIS 1,130,000 if committed by a natural person or NIS 2,260,000 if committed by a corporation. In addition, the Ordinance empowers the Israeli government to seize any assets used in violation of the Ordinance. As of early-2016, designated enemy states include Iran, Syria, and Lebanon. Iraq is also formally considered an 'enemy state' under the Ordinance, but Israel-Iraq trade has been officially permitted by virtue of an exception granted by the Minister of Finance. In addition, pursuant to Article 4(2) of the Ordinance, the Minister of Finance issued a list designating many, mostly Iran-related, individuals and private and public entities as 'enemies' on 28 July 2011. Recently, the Ordinance has been amended to require reporting to the Israeli Police when an individual or company receives a request

810. See, e.g., Article 2(a)(1a) of the Prohibition of Financing Terrorism Law, 5765-2007; Article 3(a)(2) of the Law on the Struggle against the Iranian Nuclear Program, 5772-2012.

for trade in circumstances in which reasonable suspicion arises that the requests originate from enemy states or enemy nationals.[811]

In addition, Israel's Defence (Emergency) Regulations, 1945 and the Prevention of Terrorism Ordinance, 5708-1948, authorize the Minister of Defence to designate entities as 'unlawful associations', 'terrorists' and 'terrorist organizations'. Pursuant to the above legislation, several lists are maintained by the MOD, collectively designating hundreds of individuals and organizations with which nearly all types of engagement, such as providing material support, are prohibited.

Furthermore, under the Prohibition of Financing Terrorism Law, 5765-2007, the Security Cabinet of Israel has authority to declare individuals and organizations as designated terrorist entities on the basis of their being so designated by other countries or organizations (such as the UN Security Council). Accordingly, a declaration made in 2008 designated thirty-five terrorist organizations and a 2009 declaration designated a further fifty organizations. These two lists refer to organizations active mainly in Pakistan, Afghanistan, and North African countries and which direct their activities against Western elements, and not necessarily against Israel.

Under the Law on the Struggle against the Iranian Nuclear Program, 5772-2012, certain Israeli government committees are empowered to designate and prohibited engagement with entities deemed to be supporting Iran's nuclear program.[812]

Additional restrictive trade regulations require import permits for goods originating in certain countries that do not maintain diplomatic ties with Israel.[813] Finally, a range of anti-money laundering laws and regulations limit or otherwise regulate the conduct of business in or related to designated high-risk jurisdictions.[814]

SECTION 7 LIST OF ACRONYMS

AG	Australia Group
BWC	Biological Weapons Convention
CBN Order	Import and Export Order (Control of Chemical, Biological and Nuclear Exports), 5764-2004
Control Law	Control over Commodities and Services Law, 5717-1957

811. See Article 5A of the Ordinance.
812. See also Regulations on the Prohibition of Investment in Corporations that Maintain Commercial Relationships with Iran (List of Corporations and Procedures of the Implementing Committee), 5772-2012; Regulations on the Struggle against the Iranian Nuclear Program (Issuing Notifications and Procedures), 5774-2014.
813. See Section 6(3)(a) of the Free Import Order, 5774-2014, establishing that despite the general free import framework, specialized authorization is nevertheless required prior to imports from countries with which Israel does not maintain diplomatic ties and that prohibit imports from Israel.
814. See Prohibition on Money Laundering Law, 5760-2000, and the various regulations and orders enacted thereunder. The Israel Money Laundering and Terror Financing Prohibition Authority, Israel's 'Financial Intelligence Unit', designates jurisdictions as high-risk based upon the most current declarations by the Financial Action Task Force.

CWC	Chemical Weapons Convention
DECA	Defense Export Control Agency
DECL	Defense Export Control Law, 5766-2007
Encryption Order	Order Regarding the Control of Commodities and Services (Engagement in Encryption Items), 5734-1974
HS	Harmonized System
IMFA	Israeli Ministry of Foreign Affairs
IML	Defense Export Control Order (Combat Equipment), 5768-2008
Import Export Ordinance	Import and Export Ordinance [New Version] 5739-1979
IMPS	Israeli Ministry of Public Security
Maf'at	MOD's Administration for the Development of Weapons and Technological Infrastructure
MaLma'B	MOD's Director of Security for the Defense Establishment
MOD	Ministry of Defense
MOE	Ministry of Economy
MTCR	Missile Technology Control Regime
NPT	Nuclear Non-Proliferation Treaty
Ordinance	Trading with the Enemy Ordinance, 1939
OST	Outer Space Treaty
SIBAT	The International Defense Cooperation Agency of the Israeli Ministry of Defense

SECTION 8 REFERENCES

Sub-Section 1 Primary Documentation

Par. 1 Statutory Legislation

- Basic Law: Freedom of Occupation.
- Basic Law: The Government.
- Basic Law: The President of the State.
- Coastal Waters Law, 5713-1956.
- Companies Law, 5759-1999.
- Control over Commodities and Services Law, 5717-1957.
- Control over Commodities and Services Law, (Amendment No. 22) (Voiding of Chapter Two 3), 5774-2014.
- Custom Ordinance [New Version] of 1957.
- Defense Export Control Law, 5766-2007.
- Explosives Law, 5714-1954.
- Import and Export Ordinance [New Version], 5739-1979.

- Import, Export and Customs Powers (Defence) Ordinance of 1939.
- Israeli Firearms Law, 5709-1949.
- Law and Administration Ordinance, 5708-1948.
- Law of the Licensing of Businesses, 5728-1968.
- Law on Defense Corporations (Protection of Defense Interests), 5766-2006.
- Law on Sub-Marine Territory, 5713-1956.
- Law on the Struggle against the Iranian Nuclear Program, 5772-2012.
- Law to Prevent Damage to the State of Israel Through Boycotts, 5711-2011.
- Licensing of Businesses Order (Businesses Requiring Licensing), 5773-2013.
- Patent Law, 5727-1967.
- Penal Code, 5737-1977.
- Prevention of Terrorism Ordinance, 5708-1948.
- Prohibition of Financing Terrorism Law, 5765-2007.
- Prohibition of Money Launder Law, 5760-2000.
- Trading with the Enemy Ordinance, 1939.
- Value Added Tax Law, 5763-1975.

Par. 2 Regulations

- Control of Commodities and Services Order (Engagement in Encryption Items), 5734-1974.
- Defense (Emergency) Regulations, 1945.
- Defense Export Control Order (Combat Equipment), 5768-2008.
- Defense Export Control Order (Controlled Dual-Use Equipment), 5768-2008.
- Defense Export Control Order (Missile Equipment), 5768-2008.
- Defense Export Control Regulations (Licensing), 5768-2008.
- Defence Export Control Regulations (Licensing), 5775-2015
- Defense Export Control Regulations (Marketing Licence Exemption), 5770-2010.
- Defense Export Control Regulations (Marketing Licence Exemption), 5768-2008.
- Defense Export Control Regulations (Scope of Defense Exports Pursuant to an Agreement between Israel and Another State to be Brought for Approval by the National Security Ministerial Committee), 5768-2008.
- Explosives Regulations (Commerce, Transport, Manufacturing, Storage and Use), 5754-1994.
- Free Export Order, 5767-2006.
- Free Import Order, 5774-2014.
- Import and Export Order (Control of Chemical, Biological and Nuclear Exports), 5764-2004.
- Import and Export Order (Control of Dual-Purpose Goods, Services and Technology Exports), 5766-2006.
- Licensing of Businesses Regulations (Dangerous Factories), 5753-1993.

- MOE Directive 2.6 – Exemptions Granted under Section 2(c)(2) of the Free Import Order.
- MOE Directive No. 2.3 – Control over Imports of Goods in the Framework of the CWC.
- MOE Directive No. 2.4 – Import of Goods from Countries to which the Free Import Order does not Apply.
- Order Regarding the Control of Commodities and Services (Engagement in Encryption Items), 5734-1974.
- Prohibition of Money Laundering Order (Identification Requirements, Reporting and Recordkeeping by Investment Managers, for the Prevention of Money Laundering and Terrorist Financing), 5771-2010.
- Regulations on the Prohibition of Investment in Corporations that Maintain Commercial Relationships with Iran (List of Corporations and Procedures of the Implementing Committee), 5772-2012.
- Regulations on the Struggle against the Iranian Nuclear Program (Issuing Notifications and Procedures), 5774-2014.

Par. 3 Annexes – Copies of Documents of Practical Use to the Importer/Exporter

A number of standard documents relevant for the import or export process in Israel (e.g., most current official application forms for import or export licences, templates of contractual undertaking, or regulation extracts) as well as other non-official documents are available on a dedicated DropBox folder which can be accessed by following the link below: www.kluwerlawonline.com/eclrh-annexes.

Sub-Section 2 Secondary Documentation

Par. 1 Internet Sites

- http://www.exportctrl.mod.gov.il/ExportCtrl/Hadrachot/Mazagot/, website of DECA, offering export control educational materials
- http://taxes.gov.il/customs/CommercialImport/Pages/CustomsTariffIF.aspx, website of the Israeli Tax Authority where one can identify which, if any, import permits are required for particular goods
- http://www.moital.gov.il/NR/exeres/1507E1CF-E607-4409-9BD6-C141F7273F07.htm, website of the MOE providing information regarding dual-use licensing
- http://www.moital.gov.il/NR/exeres/08CBCB87-2408-475C-9DD2-EEFFC6C4DB73.htm, website of the MOE providing information regarding control over chemical, biological and nuclear goods, technologies and services

SECTION 9 USEFUL INFORMATION

Sub-Section 1 Enforcement Authorities Contact Details

Name of Organization	*Defense Export Control Agency*
Postal Address	Israeli Ministry of Defense, Defense Export Control Agency HaKirya, P.O. Box 7093, Tel-Aviv Israel, Postal Code 647324.
Telephone	+972-3-777-6707 (Sunday through Thursday between 08:30 and 16:00)
Fax	+972-3-697-6030
Email address	Api_Deca@mod.gov.il
Website	http://www.exportctrl.mod.gov.il/ExportCtrl

Name of Organization	*Ministry of Economy, Dual-Use Export Licensing Department*
Postal Address	Commissioner of Licensing for the Chemistry and Environment, MOE, Bank of Israel St. 5, Jerusalem Israel, Postal Code 91036.
Telephone	+972-2-6662419 or +972-2-6662417
Website	http://www.moital.gov.il/NR/exeres/1507E1CF-E607-4409-9BD6-C141F7273F07.htm (Hebrew)

Sub-Section 2 Other

Name of Organization	*SIBAT*
Postal Address	HaKirya, Tel Aviv 64734, Israel
Telephone	972-3-6084548
Fax	972-3-6084529
Email addresses available at	http://en.sibat.mod.gov.il/Sibat/Pages/Contact-Us.aspx
Website	http://en.sibat.mod.gov.il/OurServices/Pages/OpeningDoors.aspx

Name of Organization	*Israel Money Laundering and Terror Financing Prohibition Authority*
Postal Address	125 Menachem Begin Rd, P.O.B. 7330, Tel Aviv, Israel
Telephone	972-3-7632480
Fax	972-3-7632430
	mail@impa.justice.gov.il
Website	http://index.justice.gov.il/En/Units/IMPA/Pages/Default.aspx

CHAPTER 11

Italy

Stefano Tosi & Anna Chiara Mazza

SECTION 1 TABLE OF CONTENTS

SECTION 2 EXECUTIVE SUMMARY

International cooperation has become a standard for the major weapons programmes, which are – more than in the past – complex and expensive. Italy has several ongoing International partnerships in the defence sector and despite the economic crisis, the defence industry is certainly one of the most dynamic in the country. This scenario, characterized by more frequent contacts among national defence industries and consequent transfers of military goods (i.e. hardware, software) and know-how had the effect to accelerate the renovation of the Italian regulatory framework.

In June 2012, the Italian Government adopted the Legislative Decree n. 102, which transposes the Directive 2009/43/CE, amending the Italian Law n. 185 of the 1990,[815] in the respect of the principles of the same Law and of both the Common Positions 2003/468/PESC[816] and 2008/944/PESC.[817] Then, in 2013, the Ministerial Decree n. 19 (the so-called Implementing Regulation) has been adopted to implement the innovations with a range of information whose purpose was to explain and implement certain aspects of the regulations on military goods.

The most significant innovation of the reform was the appointment of the Ministry of Foreign Affair – Authorization Unit of the Armament Materials (MAE-UAMA) as National Authority competent for issuing of the Licences to Market (Authorization to contractual negotiations) and of the Export/Import Licences and responsible to coordinate the activities of all the Ministries (Ministry of Defence, Ministry of the Economy and Finance, Ministry of the Interior, Ministry of Economic Development) involved in the different authorization processes regulated by Italian Law n. 185.

The authorization process, laid down on the Law n. 185 requires specific licences for each different stage of the manufacturing and import/export chain as well as for the provision of related services and with the reform of the 2012, ad hoc rules for intra-community transfers entered into force. The aim of this amendment, made in order to transpose new European Union (EU) legislation, was to simplify commercial procedures among European Member States.

Export and import of military goods (defence articles, armament materials) and related services, so as their production, are submitted to the registration of the relevant Italian company on a national register[818] kept by the Italian Ministry of Defence (MoD).

The Italian regulatory framework also recognizes the control of dual-use goods of the utmost importance. The regime applicable to the export of dual-use goods follows the European law, and notably the Council Regulation (EC) n° 428/2099 of 5 May 2009, as amended in 2011 (Reg. n. EU 1232/2011) and in 2012 (Reg. n. EU 388/2012). The Italian Ministry of Economic Development is the competent governmental body appointed to supervise the control activities, with the target to operate in order to fight

815. Law n. 185, 9 Jul. 1990, 'New rules controlling the export, import and transit of armaments materials'.
816. Common Position on the control of arms brokering.
817. Common Position defining common rules governing the control of export of military technology and equipment.
818. RNI – National Register of (Defence) Company.

against terrorism and contrast the proliferation of weapons of mass destruction (WMD). According to the Annual Report 2013 (activities of 2012) to the Italian Parliament (*ex* Par. 5, Law n. 185), a total number of 1.294 requests were submitted to the Ministry of Economic Development for a value of *EUR* 1,288,961,609 and 202 opinions were released. Moreover, still in 2012, the Ministry frequently applied the 'catch-all' clause so to put under authorization the export of goods not listed in the dual-use list but considered, in any case, to be 'sensitive'.

SECTION 3 INTRODUCTION: ELEMENTS OF CONTEXT

Sub-Section 1 Overall Philosophy

The Italian control regime for the export of military goods and dual-use items is a regime of prohibition: with the exception of some well-identified cases, exports are prohibited unless the competent administrative bodies give authorization. As a consequence, the control regime – which has a strong political feature – is based on a strict legislative and regulatory framework and the non-compliance with the rules is liable to punishment by criminal and administrative sanctions.

Article 1, Par. 6, Law n. 185, states that export, transit, intra-community transfer and brokering[819] of military goods have to be considered prohibited when direct to:

(a) Countries in conflict and/or in contrast with the principles of the Article 51 of the Charter of the United Nations (UN), except when activities must be performed to respect international treaties or in the event of resolutions of the Italian Council of Ministers, to be adopted only after positive opinion of Italian Parliament.
(b) Countries whose policies is in contrast with the principles of the Article 11 of the Italian Constitution.
(c) Countries against whom have been declared the partial or total war supplies embargo by UN or OCSE (Organizzazione per la cooperazione e lo sviluppo economico – Organisation for Economic Co-operation and Development (OECD)).
(d) Countries responsible for serious violations of the human rights.
(e) Countries that receiving aid from Italy under the Italian Law n. 49,[820] devote resources to its military budget in excess of the defence needs of the country; according to the same Law n. 49, assistance is suspended, with the exception of natural events and/or disasters.

819. Brokerage Activities are defined by Law n. 185 as activities of (i) negotiation or organization of transactions that may involve the transfer of military goods from one State to another; (ii) buying, selling or transferring military goods in the company's possession from one State to another on behalf of third parties.
820. Law n. 49, 26 Feb. 1987, 'Italian Cooperation with developing countries'.

Moreover, the Italian regulatory framework prohibits the manufacture, the import, the export, the transit, the intra-Community transfer and the brokering of anti-personnel landmines, cluster munitions, biological weapons, chemical and nuclear weapons, as well as the development and export of related technology.

Generally speaking, the Italian control systems is based on the Italian Constitution, the EU PESC (Politique Etrangère et de Sécurité Commune) and the main International Treaties and Regimes on arms.

Sub-Section 2 Historical Outlook

The Italian Constitution of 1947 states in its Article n. 11 that 'The Italian State repudiates war [...]'. This sentence shows how sensitive is the issue of war and that of arms in Italy, due to historical reasons. Nowadays, Italy has a well-structured export control system with well-defined authorization processes and a clear assignment of political and administrative responsibilities; but it wasn't always so! For a long time, in fact, the export of military goods had been governed by general foreign trade rules, due to the reason that defence articles were considered as 'normal' commodities. In this context the trade of armaments and the relevant export rules were covered by Secret of State, according to Article 1, Royal Decree n. 1161 of 1941.

In 1975, two Ministerial Decrees have been issued on Export Table and Export Goods Rules (M.D. 10/01/1975, revoked in 1989) and on War Material Export Rules (M.D. 20/03/1975, never published in the Italian Official Journal). Still in 1975, the Italian Law n. 110 gave a definition of 'war weapons' and ' common firearms' for the first time.

In 1990, Law n. 185 has been the first law to introduce a modern defence articles and services export control system with principles of rigour and transparency, eliminating existing uncertainties that had existed in the law up to that point, except as indicated by the Article 28,[821] Royal Decree n. 773 of the 1931 (so-called Testo Unico Leggi di Pubblica Sicurezza (TULPS), Text of the Laws of Public Security), still effective.

The Law n. 185 has been modified over the years in order to incorporate international agreements to which Italy is party (in particular, the Framework Agreement (FA) of Farnborough,[822] introduced into Italian law in 2003[823]) and, as above described, in order to adopt the changes imposed by the EU. Despite changes, Law n. 185 is (still) considered a 'good law' by operators and NGOs.

821. Pursuant to Article 28 of TULPS, the manufacture, assembly, collection, possession and sale of war weapons and similar arms, whether Italian or foreign, parts thereof, ammunition, military uniforms or other items intended to arm or equip Italian or foreign armed forces are prohibited without a licence from the Ministry of the Interior. The licence is valid for two years.
822. FA between the French Republic, the Federal Republic of Germany, the Italian Republic, the Kingdom of Spain, the Kingdom of Sweden, and the United Kingdom of Great Britain and Northern Ireland concerning Measures to Facilitate the Restructuring and Operation of the European Defence Industry.
823. Law 148, 17 Jun. 2003, GU n° 146, 26 Jun. 2003.

Sub-Section 3 Participation in International Regimes

The following tables display Italy's participation status in export control related international treaties and programmes. The tables also show, where relevant, whether Italy is party to a treaty by signature and ratification, or by accession.

Par. 1 Treaties and Regimes Dealing with Specific Items and Technologies

Table 11.1 Nuclear Weapons Treaties

Treaty Name	*Overall Status*	*Specific Status*	*Enforceable in Italy*
		Test Ban	
Limited Test Ban Treaty[824]	OS: 5 August 1963 EF: 10 October 1963	S: 5 August 1963 R: 10 December 1964	Yes
Comprehensive Nuclear Test Ban Treaty[825]	OS: 24 September 1996 EF: not in force	S: 24 September 1996 R: 1 February 1999	No
		Non-proliferation	
Nuclear Non-Proliferation Treaty[826]	OS: 1 July 1968 EF: 5 March 1970	S: 28 January 1969 R: 2 May 1975	Yes
IAEA Comprehensive Safeguards Agreement[827]	EF: 21 February 1977	N/A[828]	Yes
IAEA Model Additional Protocol[829]	S: 22 September 1998 EF: 30 April 2004	N/A[830]	Yes

Abbreviations: OS: Opened for signature; EF: Entry into force; S/R: Signature/Ratification; A: Accession.

824. Treaty Banning Nuclear Weapon Tests in the Atmosphere, in Outer Space and Under Water, *UNTS*, vol. 480, 43.
825. UNGA, resolution 50\245.
826. Treaty on the Non-Proliferation of Nuclear Weapons, *UNTS*, vol. 729, 161.
827. Agreement Between the Agency and States Required in Connection with the Treaty on the Non-Proliferation of Nuclear Weapons (NPT), INFCIRC/153 (Corrected).
828. This treaty is a bilateral one and, accordingly, the differences that apply to multilateral treaties (between the overall status and the specific status) do not apply.
829. Model Protocol Additional to the Agreement(s) Between State(s) and the Agency for the Application of Safeguards, INFCIRC/540(Corrected).
830. This treaty is a bilateral one and, accordingly, the differences that apply to multilateral treaties (between the overall status and the specific status) do not apply.

Table 11.2 Biological and Chemical Weapons Treaties

Treaty Name	*Overall Status*	*Specific Status*	*Enforceable in Italy*
Geneva Protocol[831]	OS: 17 June 1925 EF: 8 February 1928	S: 17 June 1925 R: 3 April 1928	Yes
Biological Convention[832]	OS: 10 April 1972 EF: 26 March 1975	S: 10 April 1972 R: 30 May 1975	Yes
Chemical Convention[833]	OS: 13 January 1993 EF: 29 April 1997	S: 13 January 1993 R: 8 December 1975	Yes

Abbreviations: OS: Opened for signature; EF: Entry into force; S/R: Signature/Ratification; A: Accession.

Table 11.3 Conventional Arms

Treaty Name	*Overall Status*	*Specific Status*	*Enforceable in Italy*
Protocol on Firearms to the Convention against Transnational Organized Crime[834]	DA: 31 May 2001 EF: 3 July 2005	-	No
Convention on anti-personnel mines[835]	OS: 18 September 1997 EF: 1 March 1999	R: 23 April 1999	Yes

Abbreviations: OS: Opened for signature; DA: Date of adoption; EF: Entry into force; S/R: Signature/Ratification; A: Accession.

Table 11.4 Multilateral Export Control Regimes

Regime Name	*Formation*	*Participation*
Zangger Committee[836]	1971	Yes
Nuclear Suppliers Group	1974	Yes
Australia Group	1985	Yes

831. Protocol for the Prohibition of the Use in War of Asphyxiating, Poisonous or Other Gases, and of Bacteriological Methods of Warfare, 94, *League of Nations Treaty Series*, No. 2138 (1929).
832. Convention on the Prohibition of the Development, Production and Stockpiling of Bacteriological (Biological) and Toxin Weapons and On Their Destruction, *UNTS*, vol. 1015, 163.
833. Convention on the Prohibition of the Development, Production, Stockpiling and Use of Chemical Weapons and on Their Destruction, Doc.CD/CW/WP.400/Rev.1.
834. Protocol against the Illicit Manufacturing of and Trafficking in Firearms, Their Parts and Components and Ammunition, supplementing the United Nations Convention against Transnational Organized Crime, A/RES/55/225.
835. Convention on the Prohibition of the Use, Stockpiling, Production and Transfer of Anti-Personnel Mines and on their Destruction, *ATS, 1999, n°3*.
836. Non-Proliferation Treaty Exporters Committee (also called the Zangger Committee).

Regime Name	Formation	Participation
Missile Technology Control Regime	1987	Yes
Wassenaar Arrangement[837]	1994	Yes

Table 11.5 Other

Name	Adoption	Participation
UN Register on Conventional Arms[838]	9 December 1991	Yes[839]
Programme of Action on Small Arms and Light Weapons[840]	20 July 2001	Yes
International Code of conduct[841]	25 November 2002	Yes

Par. 2 Treaties Dealing with Specific Regions

Table 11.6 International Zones

Treaty Name	Overall Status	Specific Status	Enforceable in Italy
Antarctic Treaty[842]	OS: 1 December 1959 EF: 23 June 1961	A:18 March 1981	Yes
Outer Space Treaty[843]	OS: 27 January 1967 EF: 10 October 1967	S: 27 January 1967 R: 4 May 1972	Yes
Sea Bed Arms Control Treaty[844]	OS: 11 February 1971 EF: 23 June 1961	S: 11 February 1971 R: 3 September 1974	Yes
Moon agreement[845]	OS: 18 December 1979 EF: 11 July 1984	-	No

837. Wassenaar Arrangement on export controls for conventional arms and dual-use goods and technologies.
838. A/RES/46/36/L.
839. Information provided for the calendar years 1992-2005.
840. Programme of Action to Prevent, Combat and Eradicate the Illicit Trade in Small Arms and Light Weapons in All Aspects, A/CONF.1992/15.
841. The Hague Code of Conduct against Ballistic Missile Proliferation, not yet published.
842. 402, *UNTS*, 7.
843. Treaty on Principles Governing the Activities of States in the Exploration and Use of Outer Space, including the Moon and Other Celestial Bodies, *UNTS*, vol. 610, 205.
844. Treaty on the Prohibition of the Emplacement of Nuclear Weapons and other Weapons of Mass Destruction on the Seabed and The Ocean Floor and in the subsoil thereof, *UNTS*, vol. 955, 115.
845. Agreement governing the Activities of States on the Moon and Other Celestial Bodies, *ILM*, vol. 18, 1434.

Treaty Name	*Overall Status*	*Specific Status*	*Enforceable in Italy*
Convention on the Law of the Sea[846]	OS: 10 December 1982 EF: 16 November 1994	R: 13 January 1995	Yes

OS: Opened for signature; EF: Entry into force; S/R: Signature/Ratification; A: Accession.

Table 11.7 Regional Nuclear Weapons-Free Zones

Treaty Name	*Overall Status*	*Specific Status*	*Enforceable in Italy*
Treaty of Tlatelolco[847]	OS: 14 February 1967 EF: 22 April 1967	–	No
Treaty of Rarotonga[848]	OS: 6 August 1985 EF: 11 December 1986	–	No
Treaty of Bangkok[849]	OS: 15 December 1995 EF: 27 March 1997	–	No
Treaty of Pelindaba[850]	OS: 11 April 1996 EF: not in force	–	No

OS: Opened for signature; EF: Entry into force; S/R: Signature/Ratification; A: Accession.

SECTION 4 CONTROL REGIME

Sub-Section 1 Military Goods and Services

Par. 1 Overall Presentation

Article 2, Law n. 185 defines 'armaments' as all materials which, due to their technical characteristics, are considered to have been manufactured mainly for military use or for use by Armed Forces or by the police; so-defined materials are detailed and listed by a Decree of the Ministry of Defence (enacted in agreement with MAE, the Ministry of the Interior, MEF and the Ministry of Production Activities), which also provide to update the categories and lists contained therein, in order to be in step with the industrial production, technology and international agreements.[851]

In addition, the authorization processes indicated in Law n. 185 must also be applied to the defence-related products, as referred to in Directive 2009/43/EU. Always

846. Doc. A/CONF.62/122 and Corr.1-11.
847. Treaty for the Prohibition of Nuclear Weapons in Latin America and the Caribbean, *UNTS*, vol. 634, 326.
848. South Pacific Nuclear Free Zone Treaty, *ILM*, vol. 24, 1442.
849. South East Asia Nuclear-Weapon-Free Zone Treaty, *ILM*, vol. 35, 635.
850. African Nuclear Weapon-Free Zone Treaty, *ILM*, vol. 35, 698.
851. The current list has been published with Ministerial Decree 7 May 2014.

under Article 2, par. 4, Law n. 185, spare parts and specific components of armaments materials and defence-related products, to be used in the production phase, are considered military goods only for the purposes of exports and transfers to other EU Member States, in addition to drawings, diagrams and all the other kinds of documents and information necessary for their manufacture, utilization and maintenance.

Sub-Par. 1 Requirements Prior to Any Specific Import/Export (i.e., Manufacturing Phase)

I Common Requirements to Companies Dealing with Arms

Once companies have obtained authorization to produce, import, export or transport arms by the relevant Prefecture, in compliance with Article 28 TULPS, they must, in addition, register themselves in the 'National Register of (Defence) Companies' (hereafter referred to as the 'National Register'), which is maintained by the Italian MoD.[852] Copies of the National Register are transmitted to the Ministry of Foreign Affairs, the Interior, Finance, Industry and Trade, and Foreign Trade (i.e., all the ministries directly or indirectly interested in the import or export of armaments).

Pursuant to Article 123 of Presidential Decree n. 90, a Commission chaired by a Council of State judge is responsible for keeping the National Register. The Commission resolves on registrations or re-registrations, prepares opinions for submission to the MoD for undertakings to be struck-off or suspended from the Register (if the undertaking's circumstances have changed and it no longer meets the requirements for registration). Company registration is valid for three years and its renew provide for the submission of a renewal form six months prior its expiry date. The documents specified here-below must be submitted to MoD for registration or for the renewal of registration:

- Application on unstamped paper containing all the information and declarations requested in the facsimile on the Ministry website.
- General information about the undertaking and its trading and banking position, in duplicate.
- Self-certifications regarding the natural persons that are materially applying for registration.
- Certificate released by the Chamber of Commerce (C.C.I.A.A.).
- Proof of payment of annual fees.
- Copy of the Company's Bylaws.
- Certification of the Italian Security Authority.
- List of Military Goods with the indication of the items that the company exports.
- Information regarding licences pursuant to Article 28 TULPS (failing this, the company may be registered subject to a condition precedent with respect to sites not yet licensed).

852. Office of the Secretary-General, National Armaments Director.

The MoD is in charge of specifying, by decree, the procedure for gaining admission to the National Register.[853] In order to be admitted, the applicant must fulfil certain criteria.[854]

For a one-man firm or partnership, the owner or legal representative must either be an Italian National or be resident in Italy. If the owner or legal representative is not Italian, it must be a national of a country with which Italy has signed a Treaty of judicial cooperation.

For limited companies, if they are incorporated in Italy and perform their activities relating to armaments in Italy, the company's legal representatives must be resident in Italy, and be Italian nationals or nationals of countries with which Italy has signed a Treaty of judicial cooperation.

A Consortium of Companies, if it consists of one or more Companies registered on the National Companies Register, may also be registered on the National Register, provided that the legal representative of the consortium fulfils the same eligibility requirements as have been described for limited companies.

Admission to the National Register is also subject to the payment of an annual fee which amount is determined by a decree of the MoD and usually published in the Italian Official Journal by 31 October of the year which precedes the year to which the fee refers.

Sub-Par. 2 Requirements at the Import and/or Export Stage

I Goods

In addition to the above-mentioned requirement to be enlisted in the National Register, Companies wishing to obtain a licence to export/import military goods and related services or to grant an intellectual or industrial property rights licence (and related services) to a foreign manufacturer for the production of armaments in such manufacturer's Country, have to follow a procedure which is divided into several phases.

A. Authorization to Contractual Negotiation Phase (Licence to Market)

• *General Rules Applicable to the Contractual Negotiation Phase*

If a company wishes to export or import arms to non-EU Countries, it requires authorization not only for the export or import stage, but also to be able to negotiate the contract for the sale of the arms. The company must notify both the Ministry of Foreign

853. http://www.google.it/url?sa=t&rct=j&q=&esrc=s&frm=1&source=web&cd=1&ved=0CC4QFjAA&url=http%3A%2F%2Fwww.difesa.it%2FSegretario-SGD-DNA%2FSGD-DNA%2FVice_SG_DNA%2FReparto_Politica_degli_Armamenti%2FRNI%2FDocuments%2FIstruzioni%2520RNI%2520Aggiornate%2520CS%2520070212.doc&ei=WOmCU7HOB4TH7Aa76oCoDg&usg=AFQjCNGU8ZZPKuDNHNcV_rokQSQWWutSIA&bvm=bv.67720277,d.ZWU.
854. Law 185, Articles 3 and 4.

Affairs and the MoD that it wishes to enter into negotiations for the export, import and transit of armaments.[855] The Ministry of Foreign Affair - UAMA is the competent Authority to release the authorization.

The notification must specify supporting information, which includes but is not limited to information about the entities with which negotiations are being held, the end-user, the approximate value of the products and services under negotiation, the items quantities to be exported/imported[856] and all the countries to which the armaments are destined. If information supplied change during the negotiation phase, the competent Ministry may require that the whole process be relaunched as if the foreseen transaction was a new one.

The Ministry of Foreign Affairs is in charge of authorizing the negotiation of contracts for the export or import or arms to non-EU Countries. The Ministry is entitled, within sixty days, to prohibit further negotiations, or to impose conditions or limitations on the activities involved.[857] The opinion of the Ministry of Defence must be obtained during the authorization process.

If the Ministry refuses authorization or imposes conditions on the activities, it must motive the denial and it must communicate it to the Company concerned.[858]

The licence to initiate negotiations is valid for three years and may be renewed. It does not confer any subsequent right to import, export or transport the armaments[859] since a Company in force of the licence to market and of the following contract/order signed have to specially apply for the moving of the military goods and related services according to the authorized provision.

The Decree of the President of the Council of Ministries dated 14 January 2005, specifies that during the time frames referred to in this section the relevant company must not disclose to the other party to the negotiation any classified information, nor any information loosely described as being of 'national interest'.

References to 'specific inter-governmental agreements' in Law n. 185 refer to agreements Italy enters into with another state to open the way for the exchange of arms between the two countries. The Italian export rules states that the Ministry of Foreign Affairs is in charge of the qualification of such agreements as 'specific inter-governmental agreements'. In particular, the Ministry considers such agreements as 'specific inter-governmental agreements' if they state that an exchange is contemplated between Italy and the nominated state or between Italy and a private company authorized by its government to take part in such an exchange. Furthermore, such an agreement must state that the two countries shall not re-export the exchanged armaments without the prior consent of the country which originally exported the goods.[860]

855. Law 185, Article 9.1.
856. The value and the quantities must be considered limits 'up to' for the following licence request.
857. Law 185, Article 9.2.
858. *Ibid.*, Article 7.
859. *Ibid.*, Article 10.1.
860. *Ibid.*, Article 5.3.

• *Exception to the General Rules Applicable to the Contract Negotiation Phase*

The import or export of the products listed below (hereafter referred to as the 'Operations having the benefit of simplified processes') is simply subject to clearance by the MoD (so-called Nulla-Osta):[861]

(1) spare parts, components and services for maintaining and repairing materials forming the subject matter of previously authorized contracts;
(2) materials already lawfully exported and which need to be re-imported or temporarily re-exported, for repair or maintenance, to other countries;
(3) materials that have been imported, and exported where relevant, and which have to be returned to the manufacturers because of defects, unsuitability, or for similar reasons;
(4) equipment intended to be exported or imported temporarily simply for the purposes of installing, commissioning, or testing materials already authorized for import or export, but for which the related documents made no specific provisions;
(5) armaments intended only for exhibitions or technical demonstrations; their manuals and technical descriptions, and any other material required for their presentation, as well as samples to be used for bids and tenders, and evaluation trials.

In 2003, following incorporation of the FA into the Italian regime,[862] Article 9.7-*bis* was inserted into Law n. 185. According to the article, the above-mentioned rules relating to the contract negotiation phase do not apply to operations carried out within the framework of common intergovernmental programmes, or to the development or production of armaments in cooperation with companies from EU or NATO Member States, with which Italy has established specific agreements relating to the import or export of arms.[863]

• *The Contractual Negotiation Phase in case of the Intra-Community Transfers*

As described in the previous pages, the reform of Law n. 185 – introduced by Legislative Decree n. 105 – laid down ad hoc rules for intra-community transfers (Articles 10-*bis* to 10-*octies*, Law 185). In particular, three types of licences are provided for and their characteristics will be examined further on.

When the previous regulatory framework was in force, the authorization to negotiate was an obligatory step of the authorization process. With the reform, with a view to simplifying procedures, the legislator decided not to require this step for intra-community transfers. That said, none of the formalities described in Article 9 of Law n. 185 are necessary in this kind of operation.

861. Law 185, Article 9.5.
862. Law 148, 17 Jun. 2003, GU n° 146, 26 Jun. 2003.
863. Law 185, Article 9.5-*bis*.

In case of classified items to be transferred to a EU Member State, the operator must submit a preliminary request to the National Authority (that forward the instance to the Security National Authority - ANS), in order to obtain the authorization to the transfer of such information and materials before the signature of the relative agreement and the submission of the export/import licence request.

B. Applying for a Licence: Preparing the Application File

• *General Rules Applicable to a Licence Application*

An application for authorization to export or import armaments must be submitted by the relevant company to the Ministry of Foreign Affairs. The application must be signed by the legal representative of the company, or a person designated by him for the purpose.[864] Before submitting the request, the Company must pay the relative fee as indicated in the Inter Ministerial Decree (Minister of Foreign Affair and Minister of Economy and Finance) n. 16492 of the 18 June 2013. A copy of the payment receipt must be attached to the application.

The documents required in order to complete the application file for both import and export must include information on the type and quantity of the armaments in question, the different part-numbers, the value of the proposed transaction, the final country of destination for the material, and the name of the intended recipient.[865]

In addition, the companies applying for a licence to export have to include other information in their application file and, notably a copy of the authorization or clearance to conduct negotiations, and a copy of the commercial and financial terms (translated into Italian) in the contract, or the sub-contract, for the supply, purchase or transport of arms.[866]

If the country of destination has entered reciprocal agreements with Italy in relation to the control of arms exports, the exporting company must provide an 'international import certificate'(IIC) issued by the governmental authorities of that country.[867] If there is no reciprocal government-to-government agreement and/or no import certificate is available, the exporting company must include an 'end-user certificate' (EUC), which has been issued by the governmental authorities of the country of destination, certifying that the use of the material will be restricted to the stated end-use and shall not be re-exported without the prior authorization of the Italian authorities.[868] The end-user certificate must be authenticated by the Italian diplomatic or consular authorities accredited in the issuing country.[869]

• *Exceptions to the General Rules Applicable to Licence Applications*

Law n. 185 does not require such information for the export and import to or from North Atlantic Treaty Organization (NATO) countries, or for operations which benefit

864. *Ibid.*, Article 11.2.
865. The list of the information to be provided is set out in Law 185, Article 11.
866. Law 185, Article 11.3.
867. *Ibid.*, Article 11.3.c.1.
868. *Ibid.*, Article 11.3.c.2.
869. *Ibid.*, Article 11.4.

from the simplified process.[870] However the 'competent administrative bodies are entitled to require further documented information', the competent authority being the Ministry of Foreign Affairs. On the basis of such provision, the Ministry of Foreign Affairs can require such information to the companies wishing to proceed with an exportation or importation NATO countries.

If the relevant company requests a Global Project Licence[871] for the export or import of armaments within the framework of a common intergovernmental or industrial research programme, or for the development or production of armaments in cooperation with companies from EU or NATO Member States, with which Italy has established specific agreements relating to the import or export of arms, according to Law n. 185, the application should include the following:[872]

- a description of the common programme, and in particular of the kind of arms which will be produced;
- information about the relevant company of the country of destination or of origin of the item to be exported or imported. If said company is not known at the date of application, its identity shall be communicated to the Ministry of Foreign Affairs within ninety days of the day on which it became known;
- details of the addressee (i.e., the governmental authority, or the public or private entity) participating in the common programme.

According to Article 2, par. 4, Law. 185/90, no licence is required for the import of spare parts and specific components for the production and of drawings, diagrams and all the other kinds of documents and information necessary for manufacture, utilization and maintenance of armament materials and defence-related products.

Moreover, no licences are required for the import of defence articles from a Member State. The importer has to notify to Minister of Foreign Affair – UAMA a 'entry note' with the indication of the items involved and of the relative economics information.

• *Three 'new types' of licences – Intra European Community Transfer*

According to Article 10-*ter* of Law 185/90, the General licence for intra-community transfers is published by the Member State (in Italy, by a Decree issued by MAE-UAMA). This form of licence is not issued after the submission of a specific request but it is published on the EU Member State's initiative. In order to be able to use a general licence, an Italian Defence company must be registered with the RNI, must have obtained a certification of reliability and must comply with the terms and conditions set out from time to time in the clearance order. If the company meets these requirements, the operator is entitled to use the authorization, by notifying Minister of Foreign Affair

870. *Ibid.*, Article 5.
871. Introduction in the Italian regime of the FA by Law 148, 17 Jun. 2003, GU n° 146, 26 Jun. 2003.
872. Law 185, Article 11.5-*bis*.

- UAMA and Minister of Defence, with a written communication, that it intends to transfer defence articles under the relevant General Licence (within the period of thirty days before first using).

The Global licence, which is regulated by Article 10-*quater* of Law n. 185, unlike the general licence, is granted by MAE-UAMA at the request of the individual supplier. The authorization can be used for the transfer of specific military goods, without any restriction on quantity or value, in favour of authorized recipients.

Article 10-*quinquies* of Law n. 185/90 regulates individual licences for intra-community transfers. These are issued by MAE-UAMA, at the request of individual suppliers, for the transfer of a specified quantity of military goods of a specific value to a specified recipient.

In view of the tendency for global and general licences to allow an indefinite number of operations, after the reform introduced by Legislative Decree n. 105/2012, single licences are now destined to play a marginal role.

• *Company Certification*

Article 10-*sexies*, Law n. 185 describes the certification system adopted by the Italian export control system due to the implementation of the European Directive n. 49. The certification is valid for at most three years (renewable) and attests the reliability of the operator - among other - to comply with the restrictions imposed by another Member State in using a general transfer licence.

Undertakings may apply for this certification if it satisfies two preliminary conditions:

- at the time of the application, they must have a digital link to Minister of Foreign Affair - UAMA - according to the directives laid down by the same Minister;
- they must have a senior executive that is personally responsible for the office which handles intra-community transfers, imports and exports of military goods.

The competent Authority is the Ministry of Foreign Affair - UAMA.

When all the requirements and conditions are met, the undertaking can request to the Ministry of Foreign Affair to be assessed with a plant visit and a preliminary investigation, by presenting a questionnaire regarding the activities conducted in connection with the military goods.

The assessment criteria are the following:

- proven experience in activities related to Defence, particularly with respect to the extent to which the undertaking complies with restrictions on export, any court orders in connection with the matter, licences to manufacture or sell military goods and the employment of experienced senior executive staff;
- industrial activity relevant to the military goods sector within the EU and particularly the capacity to integrate systems or sub-systems;

- the appointment of a senior executive as the person solely and personally responsible for transfers and exports;
- written commitment by the undertaking, signed by the senior executive, to the effect that it takes all the necessary steps to comply with all the special conditions on the end-use and export of each of the components or products received;
- written commitment by the undertaking, signed by the senior executive, to use due care in providing the office that issues the certification with detailed information regarding the end-users or the end-use of all the products exported, transferred or received when using a licence to have them transferred from another Member State;
- a description, countersigned by the senior executive, of the internal compliance programme or transfer and export management system adopted by the undertaking. The description must state the organizational, human and technical resources allocated to the management of transfers and exports, the chain of responsibility in the structure of the undertaking, the internal audit procedures, the measures taken to enhance the awareness of its personnel and give them training and the regulations regarding physical and technical security, the keeping of registers and the traceability of transfers and exports.

The Minister of Foreign Affair-UAMA, in consultation with MoD, within thirty days after receiving the application, releases the certification. The certification document reports the competent authority that issues the certificate, the name and address of the recipient, the recipient's statement of compliance with assessment criteria, the date of issue and terms of the certificate.

In case of not complete request, the Minister can ask for additional documents to be submitted and in this case the time limit is suspended. The application can also be refused in case the operator is non-compliance with the law requirements.

The certification can be also revoked by UAMA, always in consultation with Minister of Defence, if the operator no longer satisfies the assessment criteria. In this event the European Commission and the other Member States are promptly informed. Moreover, in order to verify that the undertaking complies with the conditions laid down in the certification, inspectors designated by the competent Authority (MAE-UAMA) are entitled to enter all the relevant premises and examine and take copies of registers and all the documents concerning activities performed on the basis of a General Licence.

UAMA publishes and updates the list of Italian certified undertakings, giving notice thereof to the European Commission, the European Parliament and the other Member States.

• *Authorization of brokerage*

The Legislative Decree n. 105 has introduced new rules for the discipline of the so-called active intermediation. The Law n. 185 provides also a definition of the active intermediation that consists in circumstances in which a company contributes materials or goods of its own manufacture to the movement of the goods concerned, or confines itself to putting demand and supply into contact with each other.

So as to limit the proliferation of intermediaries and to provide an increasing degree of transparency in the movements of military items, only registered Defence Company (with the RNI) can carry out 'active' intermediation activities.

An authorization to contractual negotiation is always required (also for EU countries) before performing brokerage activities and the relevant application must be submitted to Minister of Foreign Affairs - UAMA (competent Authority to release the authorization) and (copied for information) to Minister of Defence. Each request must be complete of the following information:

- state of destination;
- state of dispatch;
- identification of the recipient and sender;
- details of registration with the RNI;
- type of military goods and related customs position;
- security classification of goods;
- financial settlement methods;
- certificate of import or end-user certificate;
- details and type of contractual commitment;
- amounts of brokerage fees;
- contract value;
- quantity of goods and related measurement unit;
- licence of export from the State of dispatch or equivalent documentation;
- reference to the authorization to contractual negotiations.

• *Authorizations for workshops, study visits and tours*

Article 21, Law n. 185 states that an operator may ask the President of the Council of Ministers to authorize seminars, study visits and tours abroad by Italian citizens and in Italy by foreign citizens with respect to materials protected by a security classification.

A distinction is made between visits that are envisaged in intergovernmental agreements and those that are not.

National Security Authority (ANS) is competent to release the authorizations according to the procedures and time limits complying with the provisions laid down in the intergovernmental understandings.

In case of events that are not under an intergovernmental understandings, organizers must submit an application to National Security Authority (ANS) at least thirty days before the visit, specifying the information required by the Authority

The ANS usually release the 'green light' within fifteen days after the receipt of the application, complete in all the attachments: the clearance document states the relative provisos and indicates the period of validity. If legal requirements are not met, the National Security Agency informs the applicant that authorization can't be released, clarifying the reasons of the decision.

C. Notification Relating to Carriers and Shippers[873]

Except for exports made on behalf of the Italian Government, the exporting company must:

- For operations for which the exporter is required to ship and deliver to their destination any armaments: the exporters must obtain from the shippers and carriers all relevant information concerning the mode of transport, the routing and any variations that may have occurred during shipment. The relevant documents must be kept in the records of the exporter for a period of ten years.
- For all operations for which the delivery is 'ex works' or 'ex warehouse':[874] the legal representative – or a person designated by him – of the exporter company must simultaneously notify the Ministers of Foreign Affairs, MoD, the Interior and Finance of the date and the procedures for the delivery, together with any other relevant information on the shipper or the carrier responsible for the operation. Such notification is to be made, at the latest, three days from the date the said company has been notified that the addressee or the carrier, commissioned by the exporter company, has collected the shipment.

D. Use of Licences and Permits[875]

Except for operations performed on behalf of the Government, a company authorized to export or transport armaments through Italy must:

- 'Promptly' notify the Ministry of Foreign Affairs – UAMA of the conclusion, including the partial conclusion, of the authorized operations.
- Send to the Ministry of Foreign Affairs – UAMA the verification forms, or the customs docket, evidencing the entry of the shipment into the recipient's country, or the documentation which certifies the importer received the shipment; or equivalent documentation issued by the local government authorities. The shipment must be made at the latest 180 days after the conclusion of the relevant authorized operation. The company is entitled to apply to the Minister of Foreign Affairs, at least thirty days before the expiry of the 180 days period, for an extension of ninety days. However, the exporter must give reasons for its request, providing what Law 185 calls 'good and documented grounds'. Such grounds will be considered by the Minister of Foreign Affairs, in consultation with the Consultative Committee. The

873. Law 185, Article 19.
874. 'Ex Works' is an Incoterm (i.e., an international commercial term defined by the International Chamber of Commerce). A good is delivered 'Ex Work' when the seller (exporter) makes the good available to the buyer (importer) at the seller's premises. As a consequence, the buyer is responsible for all transportation costs and accepts the risks of loss of the good immediately after the good is purchased and placed outside the factory door.
875. Law 185, Article 20.

exporter will not receive any extension of its authorization to export, until the relevant documentation has been received by the Minister of Foreign Affairs.
- If the Italian exporter cannot obtain the documents from the relevant foreign authorities, it must explain why it is unable to do so. The Consultative Committee will consider its reasons and decide whether they constitute sufficient justification.

According to the Interministerial Decree (Minister of Foreign Affair and Minister of Economy) dated 26 April 2013, a company which doesn't submit the documentation of arrival at destination within 180 days and is not able to justify this lack of documentation, can be punished by fine of up to EUR 1,500. In case of multiple violations, the UAMA's Director can decide to suspend the validity of the relative export licence until all necessary documentation is presented to the National Authority.

II Services

The provision of services for training and maintenance, to be effected in Italy or abroad, if not already authorized together with the export of the armaments, requires only clearance from the MoD, after consultation with the Minister of Foreign Affairs and the Minister of the Interior, provided that it is the continuation of an existing lawfully authorized agreement.

Law n. 185 does not specify the procedure to be followed if the services are not in the continuation of 'an existing lawfully authorized agreement'.

However, specific clearance is required before any negotiations are begun for the transfer of technology. 'Technology' includes, among other things, technical assistance and consultancy.

Par. 2 Sanctions

In the event of breach of export control rules of military goods, the regulatory framework in force until 2012 envisaged penal sanctions – Articles 23-25 of Law n. 185. These fines are still applicable in the case of intra-Community transfers, but with the Legislative Decree n. 105 new administrative sanctions come into force – Article 25-*bis* of Law n. 185 – when circumstances do not constitute a criminal offence.

Here below two schemes to quickly summarize the sanctions now in place. Consider that some sanctions are still expressed in Lire (ITL), the Italian currency before the Euro. The exchange rate between Euro and ITL is: 1 Euro = 1.936,27 ITL.

Table 11.8

Cases		*Criminal Sanctions*	
False documents	Obtaining the forms of clearance referred to in Articles 10-*bis* or 13, Law n. 185, or renewing them, on the basis of untrue information supplied with wilful misconduct	From two to six years' imprisonment or a fine of from 1/10 to 3/10 of the contract value	
	Untrue information that is conclusive for the purposes of registration with the RNI or obtaining a permit (Article 9, paragraph 5, Law n. 185)	Fine of from ITL 50-300 million	
Non-compliance with administrative provisions	Transactions carried out in breach of delivery conditions specified in the application for authorization as referred to in Article 13, Law n. 185, or in authorizations referred to in Article 10-*bis,* Law n. 185	Imprisonment up to five years or Fine of from 2/10 to 5/10 of the contract value	
No authorization	Transactions carried out without authorization (Articles 10-*bis* or 13, Law n. 185)	From 3 to 12 years' imprisonment or a fine of from ITL 50 to 500 million	The materials for export or intra-community transfer for which there is no authorization are confiscated
	Negotiations put in place without relative authorization (Article 9, Law n. 185)	Imprisonment up to four years or Fine of from ITL 50 to 500 million	

Cases	*Administrative Penalties*		
Failure to notify the recipients of the terms and conditions of the licence	Payment of an amount between EUR 5,000 and EUR 20,000	If the offence is repeated, the penalty of the two-year suspension from the RNI is also imposed on the supplier	Penalties are imposed by MAE-UAMA, in agreement with MD. D issues a decree suspending the supplier from the RNI
Register of Transfers incorrectly kept or not kept	Payment of an amount between EUR 5,000 and EUR 20,000		
Failure to send the documents regarding the conclusion of the operations within 180 days, unless there are justified reasons	Payment of an amount between EUR 150 and EUR 1,500		

• ***Banking transactions rules under Law n. 185***

The reform in 2012 also affected the Articles 27 of the Law n. 185, relating to authorizations of banking transactions connected to military goods activities. The ratio of the new rules was to modify the controls over bank operations from an *ex ante* to an *ex post* system.

Before 2012, all bank transactions were first to be notified to the Ministry of Economy and Finance, which had to authorize the operations within thirty days after notification with the Legislative Decree n. 105, operators must only submit a declaration to the banks regarding each transaction and the bank is in charge to forward the document to the Minister of Economy and Finance. The described *iter* has to be completed within thirty days after the bank transaction has been executed.

The declaration presented by operators to the bank must contain the following information:

- details of registration with the register;
- goods and services covered by the transaction and corresponding amount;
- financial settlement methods;
- State of origin and destination of goods and services;
- Identity of the purchaser or supplier, debtor or creditor;
- details of the corresponding licence or permit;
- nature and amount of related banking transactions, including accessory operations.

In the event that no declaration is presented to the bank, the operator can be punished with a pecuniary sanction, the amount of which vary between *EUR* 5,000 and *EUR* 25,000.

Moreover, the reform introduced in the Law n. 185 the Article *27-bis* that provides a new mechanism of control to counteract the financing of terrorism and the activities of States that threaten peace and international security in accordance with the resolutions of the UN or the deliberations of the EU.

The Minister of Economy and Finance is required to verify and analysed in detail all the notifications received by banks regarding the financing activities under Law n. 185; the activities are conducted in collaboration with the Italian Finance Police. Violations are punished with pecuniary administrative penalty of from *EUR* 10,000 to *EUR* 100,000.

• ***Revolving Door (The movement of high-level employees from public sector jobs to private sector jobs and vice versa)***

Public sector employees and military officers employed in functions associated with the application of Law n. 185 in the two years prior to the termination of the employment relationship, for the following three years from termination, cannot be part of the boards, assume positions of president, vice president, chief director, managing director and director general of a Defence Company as well as take consulting assignments, except those character from operations specifically related to technical design or testing.

Companies that violate the provisions shall be cancelled for two years from the National Register.

• ***Additional activities under Law n. 185***

In 2012, additional activities related to military goods were put under Law n. 185. The consequence was that all these activities became subject to the general export rules, as described in the previous pages:

- *Transfer of production*: Transfer licences for the production of military goods in a foreign country.
- *Delocalization of production*: Transfer by an Italian enterprise of production processes or manufacturing phases, related to military goods.
- *Intangible transfer:* Transmission of software or technology with electronic means as fax, telephone, email and other including, electronic transmission.

The Minister of Foreign Affair – UAMA has recently issued the Directive n. 2393 that provides some dedicated rules for intangible transfer. No authorizations to contractual negotiations are required but all Defence Companies are obliged to submit to the Minister of Foreign Affair – UAMA (for approval) their internal procedures dedicated to the management of the 'intangible transfers'. Moreover, each Company has to create an electronic register where to annotate all transfers; the electronic register must be accessible from UAMA. If a Company doesn't meet the requirements above described, no export licences for intangible transfers can be released by the National Authority.

Figure 11.1 Preliminary Formalities

Chart 1 – Preliminary formalities

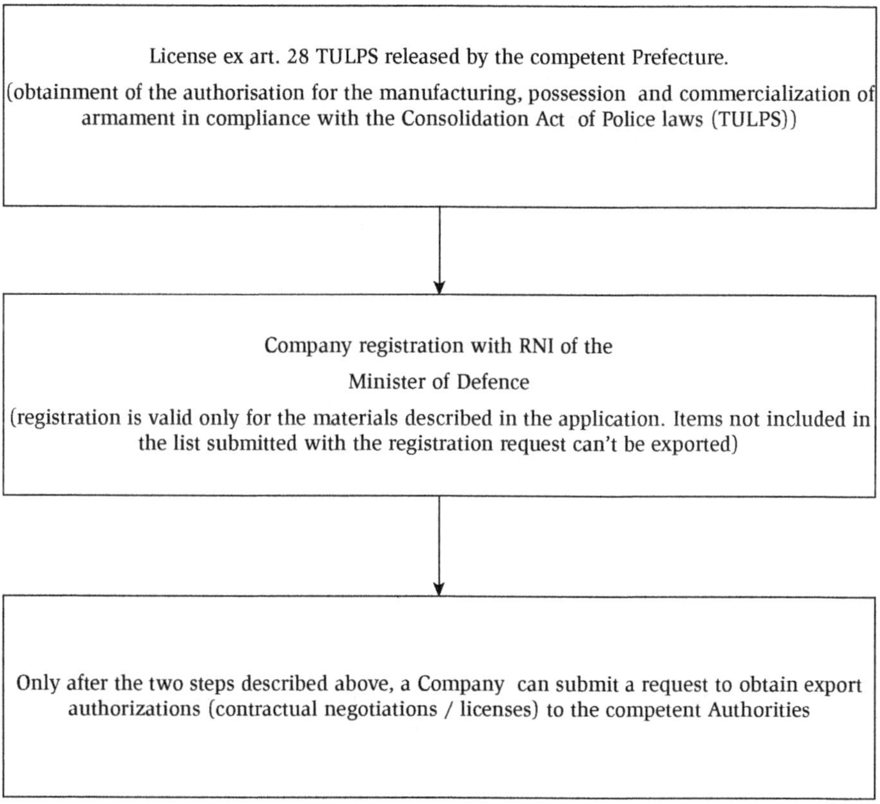
License ex art. 28 TULPS released by the competent Prefecture.
(obtainment of the authorisation for the manufacturing, possession and commercialization of armament in compliance with the Consolidation Act of Police laws (TULPS))
Company registration with RNI of the Minister of Defence
(registration is valid only for the materials described in the application. Items not included in the list submitted with the registration request can't be exported)
Only after the two steps described above, a Company can submit a request to obtain export authorizations (contractual negotiations / licenses) to the competent Authorities

Figure 11.2a Authorization to Contractual Negotiations – Att. 1

Chart 2 – Authorization to contractual negotiations – Att. 1

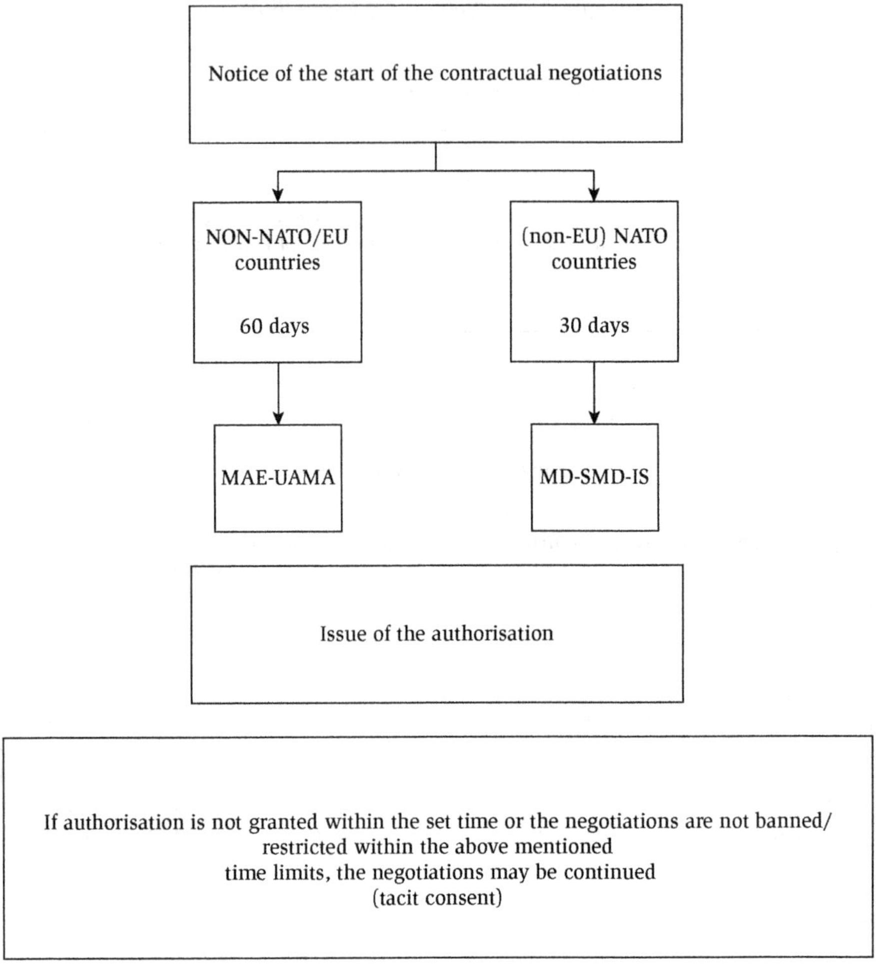
Notice of the start of the contractual negotiations
NON-NATO/EU countries
60 days
(non-EU) NATO countries
30 days
MAE-UAMA
MD-SMD-IS
Issue of the authorisation
If authorisation is not granted within the set time or the negotiations are not banned/ restricted within the above mentioned time limits, the negotiations may be continued (tacit consent)

Figure 11.2b Bis – Nulla – Osta – Att. 2

Chart 2 bis – Nulla – Osta – Att. 2

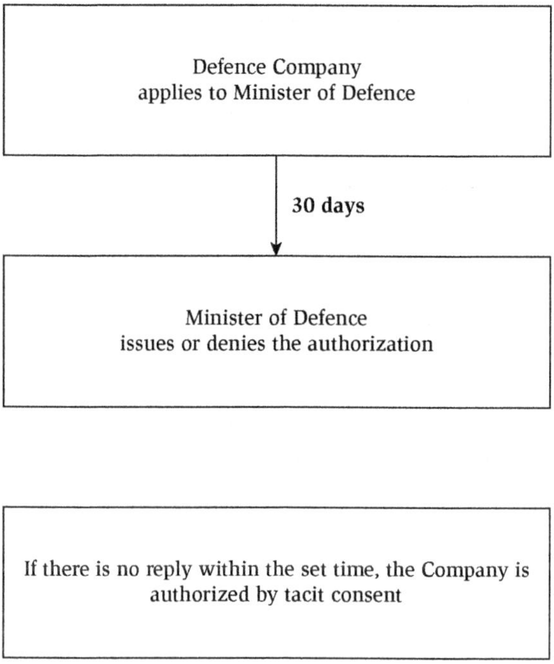

Figure 11.3 Intra-Community Transfers: General Licence

Chart 3 – Intra-community transfers: general licence

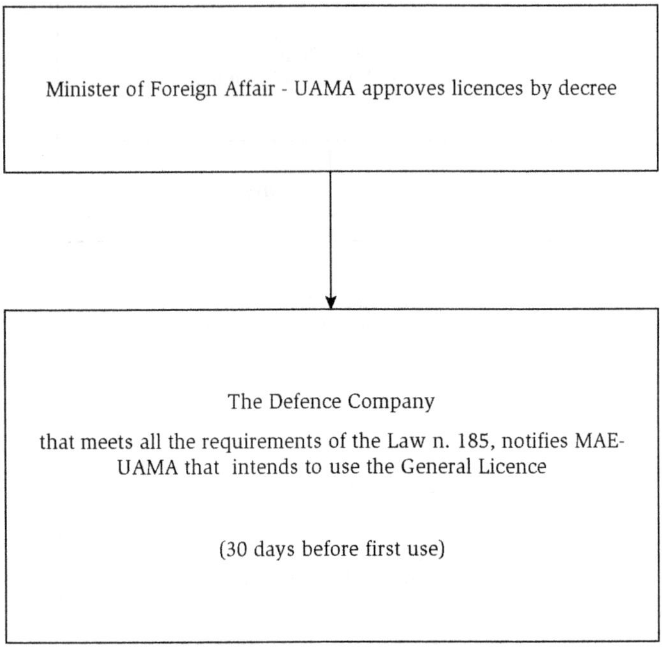

Figure 11.4 Intra-Community Transfers: Global Licence and Individual Licence

Chart 4 – Intra-community transfers: global licence and individual licence

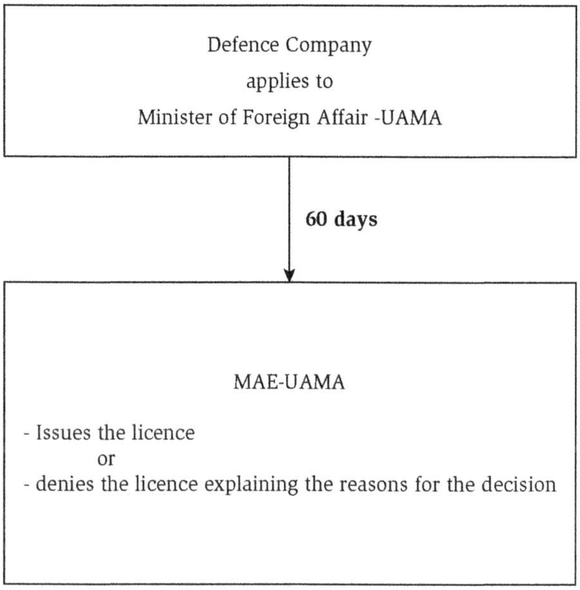

Figure 11.5 Non-EU Transactions – Individual Licence – Att. 3 e 4

Chart 5 – Non-EU transactions – Individual licence – Att. 3 e 4

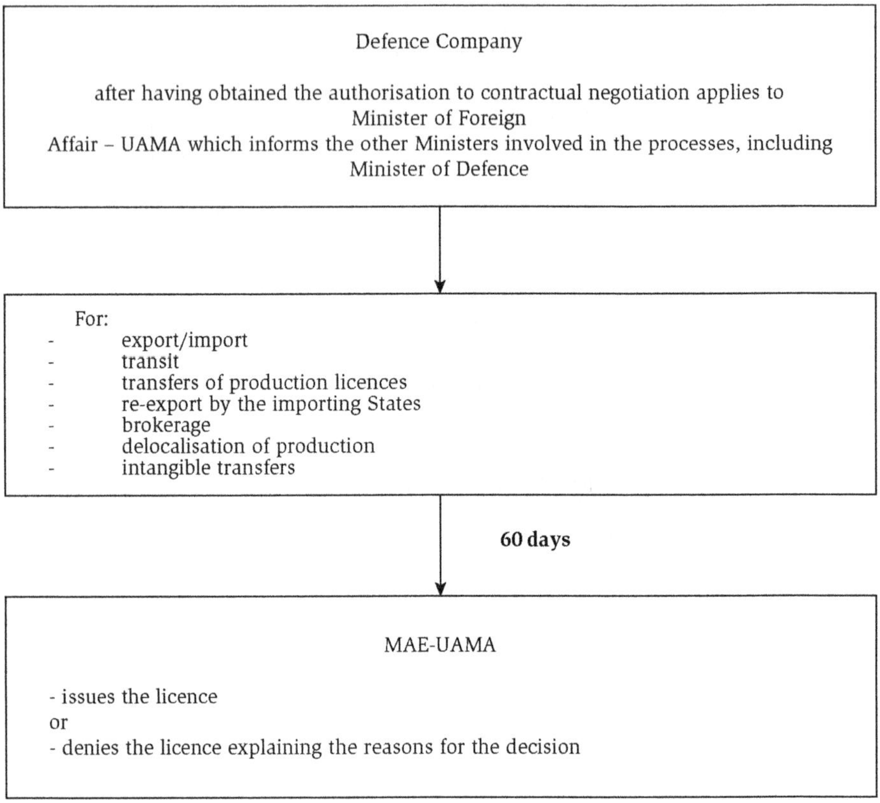

Sub-Section 2 Dual-Use Goods and Services

Par. 1 Overall Presentation

Dual-use items shall mean items, including software and technology, which can be used for both civil and military purposes, and shall include all goods which can be used for both non-explosive uses and assisting in any way in the manufacture of nuclear weapons or other nuclear explosive devices.

As in all EU Member States, the control regime of Italy for the export of dual-use goods and services is based principally on Council Regulation (EC) n° 428 of the 2009 setting up a Community regime for such control (hereafter 'the Regulation'). has been amended twice since it was issued, by Regulation (EU) n° 1232/2011 and Regulation (EU) n° 388/2012, which, however, did not make any substantial changes to the rules, as amendments were made to:

(i) the introduction of the community general authorization referred to in Annex II-*bis* to *octies* (Regulation (EU) n° 1232/2011);
(ii) the list of dual-use goods under Annex I attached to Regulation (EC) no. 428/2009 (Regulation (EU) n° 388/2012).

Several Italian legislative and Ministerial decrees complete the European Regulation. These decrees specify which national authority is in charge of which area of control, the different kinds of authorization each authority delivers and the sanctions incurred in the event of any violation of the regime.

On the website of the Italian Minister of Economic Development is possible to read:[876]

> *The export of goods and dual use technologies is governed by a variety of rules, criteria and procedures that meet the needs of national and international security, as follows:*
>
> *Regulation (EC) 428 /09 and amended by Regulation (EU) 388/12, which establishes a Community regime for the control of exports of dual-use goods and technology listed in the Annex I. In Italy, the provisions of Regulation 428 /09 have been transposed by the DL n. 96 of 09/04/2003 still in force. The list in the Annex I list represents the sum of the choices made by the following control regimes:*
>
> *Wassenaar ARRANGEMENT (high-tech sector)*
> *Group MTCR (Missile products sector)*
> *Group NSG (Nuclear)*
> *Australia Group (chemical biological).*

The control only applies to the exports of dual-use items which are implemented in accordance with the Regulation. However, this does not exclude the application of the legislation on military goods to the import of some dual-use goods which are listed in the relevant national control list of military goods. Imports of dual-use goods and technology are not controlled.

Sub-Par. 1 Requirements Prior to Any Specific Export (i.e., Manufacturing Phase)

Italian legislation does not set out specific requirements prior to the export of dual-use items. Then, and as a difference from the regime applicable to military goods, no requirement is set out for the production of dual-use items.

Sub-Par. 2 Requirements at the Export Stage

The Legislative Decree n. 96 of 9 April 2003 names the Ministry of Production Activities – Department for Internationalization – as the Authority in charge of implementing the

876. http://www.sviluppoeconomico.gov.it/index.php?option = com_content&view = article&viewType = 0&idarea1 = 564&idarea2 = 700&idarea3 = 0&andor = AND&sectionid = 2,12&andorcat = AND&idmenu = 1406&partebassaType = 0&MvediT = 1&showMenu = 1&showCat = 1&id = 2022475&idarea4 = 0&idareaCalendari.

transport control of dual-use goods and services. An Advisory Committee within the Ministry helps the Minister for Production Activities establish the procedure for authorizing applications.

Licences for the export of dual-use goods issued in Italy are regulated by Legislative Decree n. 96 of the 2003 and by Regulation (EC) n° 428 of the 2009 and are:

- *Individual Specific Licence:* Issued to an exporter for one specified end-user and for a determinate quantity and value of goods. This licence is valid for a set time which may be extended on application at least thirty days before it expire. The licence can be denied, suspended or revoked. In any case, the authorization is released only on the basis of a specific contract that provides operations for which licence is required.
- *National General Authorization*: This authorization is issued for all products in Annex I, Reg. n. 428, for exports direct to Argentina, South Korea, Turkey and Antarctica (Italian Base), for an indefinite period of time except for what is indicated in Annex II-*bis* to *octies* attached to Reg. n. 1232/2011 that amended the Reg. n. 428/2009. It may be used by all exporters permanently established or resident in the Member State that issues the authorization and in compliance with the conditions laid down in Regulation (EC) n° 428 of the 2009 and in national law.
- *European Union General Authorization*: The authorizations are valid in all Member States and may be used if are met all the conditions and the requirements listed in Annexes II-*bis* to II-septies attached to Regulation (EC) n° 1232 of the 2011, except for what is indicated in the Annex 2 octies of the same Regulation. The exporter who wants to use the authorization must notify this intention to the Minister within thirty days before the export activities are put in place.
- *Individual Global Authorization*: Issued to a single exporter for types or categories of dual-use goods (Annex I- Reg. n. 428/09), for one or more specified countries of destination, but without stating any quantity, value or end-user. The validity period cannot be more than three years but the authorization may be renewed if the request is submitted at the latest within thirty days before the expiry date. The licence can be denied, suspended or revoked.

According to the Law, the Minister has up to 180 days after the submission of the application to issue the licence; generally, the licence is issued within thirty/sixty days.

I Individual Specific Licence

The Individual Specific Licence is granted to an individual exporter for the export of items, falling within the first four categories of dual-use items as listed in Annexes I and IV of the Regulation, and for a specified end-user. The licence is issued or rejected after the Advisory Committee has stated its opinion. It is granted for a limited period but can be extended if an application is made within thirty days of the licence expiry date.[877]

Applications for authorization should be filed with the Ministry of Production Activities, using the form contained in Annex III-(a) of the Regulation.

The application file must contain a declaration of the end-user, which should include the following information:[878]

- the exact name or company name of the end-user, the exact indication of the registered office and the type of activity of the end-user carries out;
- a description of the imported items, including their quantity and value, and details of the relevant contract, or a copy of it;
- an indication of the specific civil use the items will be put to and their precise destination;
- a commitment not to use such items for military applications or nuclear explosives;
- a commitment not to re-export, transfer or deviate the imported items during their transit.

This declaration must be dated, sealed and signed by a legal representative of the end-user.[879]

The Ministry of Production Activities is also allowed to ask the exporter for an international import certificate and/or a certificate of end-use, issued by the relevant administrative authority in the end-user's own country.[880]

Applications should be made on the proper Community form.[881] The exporter is responsible for the quality of the data and information submitted in the application, and in any attachment. If it is incomplete or erroneously completed, the applicant has the right to correct the application.[882]

An application must include a declaration, signed by the exporter's legal representative, that it will use, on each export operation, only the dual-use items for which the licence was granted, and that it will only export those items to the destination indicated on the licence.[883]

Within thirty days of the end of each calendar semester the exporter shall transmit to the Ministry, by post, email or fax, a summary of the export transactions it has made using an Individual Global Licence.[884]

877. *Ibid.*, Article 4.2.
878. *Ibid.*, Article 4.4.
879. *Ibid.*, Article 4.5.
880. *Ibid.*, Article 4.6.
881. Please further see the Chapter on the European Union export control legislation.
882. Legislative Decree n° 96, 9 Apr. 2003, GU n° 102, 5 May 2003, Article 5.3.
883. *Ibid.*, Article 5.5.
884. *Ibid.*, Article 5.6.

II National General Export Licence

The National General Export Licence can be used for export activities direct to specified countries (Turkey; South Korea; Argentina and the Italian Base in Antarctica)[885] and for all the items goods listed in the Annex I - Reg. 428 of the 2009 - except for what is indicated in the Annex II octies of the Reg. n. 1232/2011 and of the goods and countries listed in the Annexes II bis, ter, quarter, quinques, sexies and septies of the same Reg. n. 1232/2011.

An application for such authorization should be submitted to the Ministry of Production Activities, having been signed by a legal representative of the exporter. It must state the name or company name of the exporter, the address of its registered office, and the names of its legal representatives.[886]

The names of all exporters intending to export items under such a licence are entered in the 'Register of Entities Exporting under the Terms of the National General Licence'.[887]

Within thirty days of the end of each calendar semester, the exporter must send the Ministry by post, email or fax, a brief list of all export transactions made under such a licence. Such list shall indicate the entries of invoice and contract, quantity and value of the items, categories and sub-categories of reference, corresponding customs tariff section, country of destination, identities of the consignee and of the end-user, date of sending, type of export (final, temporary, transit).[888]

III EU General Licence

The EU General Licences automatically cancel the Community General Licences. The authorizations are valid in all Member States and may be used if are met all the conditions and requirements listed in Annexes II-*bis*, ter, quarter, quinques, sexies and septies attached to Regulation (EC) n° 1232 of the 2011 that modified the Regulation (EC) n° 428 of the 2009. The names of all exporters intending to export items under such a licence are entered in the relative Register. Moreover, within thirty days of the end of each calendar semester, the exporter must send the Ministry by post, email or fax, a brief list of all export transactions made under such a licence.

IV Individual Global Licence

The Individual Global Licence is granted to individual exporters for the export of items, falling within the dual-use items as listed in Annexes I of the Regulation, to one or more specified countries of destination.[889] This authorization cannot be issued in favour of

885. *Ibid.*, Article 2.
886. Legislative Decree n° 96, 9 Apr. 2003, GU n° 102, 5 May 2003, Article 6.2.
887. *Ibid.*, Article 6.3.
888. *Ibid.*, Article 6.5.
889. *Ibid.*, Article 5.1.

occasional operators.[890] It is granted for a maximum of three years after hearing the opinion of the Advisory Committee. It can be extended under the same conditions as those which apply to the Individual Specific Licence.[891]

Par. 2 The 'Catch-All' Clause

Article 4 of Regulation (EC) n° 428 regulates the so-called catch-all clause and according to it, the products that are not included in the dual-use goods list may also be considered dual-use items in the case that the exporter has been informed by the competent authorities of the Member State that they may be used, even indirectly, in programmes involving the production of chemical, biological or nuclear weapons or for the development, production, maintenance or storage of missiles, or for the delivery of such weapons.

The catch-all clause can also operate 'if the purchasing country or country of destination is subject to an arms embargo (...) and if the exporter has been informed by the authorities that the items in question are or may be intended, in their entirety or in part, for a military end-use.'

In case of application of the clause, the Authority shall inform the company and the Customs Agency that a certain operation requires to be authorized. The company, if still interested in the transaction, shall start the authorization process as if the asset was in the dual-use list. At the end of the process, if the Authority issues the authorization, the company is allowed to export.

The catch clause has a validity period of three years and during this period all the similar operations must be authorized by the Minister before exporting procedures are performed.

Par. 3 Brokering Services

Regulation (EC) n° 428/2009 also requires that brokering services must be authorized and according to Article 2 of Regulation (EC) n° 428 of the 2009, brokering services shall mean any business transactions that allow the purchase, sale, supply and export of dual-use goods.

This type of services shall also include the negotiation or arrangement of transactions for the purchase, sale or supply of dual-use items from a non-EU State to any other non-EU State.

Broker shall mean any natural or legal person or partnership resident or established in a Member State of the Community that carries out brokering services from the Community into the territory of a non-EU State.

890. *Ibid.*, Article 5.4.
891. *Ibid.*, Article 5.2.

The broker is required to keep trade registers and to maintain documents relating to brokering services so as to prove, if required: (i) the description of the dual-use goods involved in brokering services; (ii) the period in which the products have been involved in said services; (iii) their destination, as well as; (iv) the countries involved in said brokering services.

If a broker has been informed by the competent authorities that dual-use products are the objects of the transfer, or that the goods are intended for countries under an embargo, the broker must inform the Minister of the Economic Development providing all the necessary information, including: (i) the exact details of the location of the dual-use products in the non-EU State of origin; (ii) a clear description of the products and the quantity concerned; (iii) any third parties involved in the transaction; (iv) the non-EU State of destination; (v) the end-user in this country; and (vi) the exact place in which the end-user is established.

After this the Minister of the Economic Development considers whether to issue the authorization: if it decides to do so, clearance is granted for a set number of specified products moving among two or more other third countries, and is valid all over Community territory.

Par. 4 Customs Procedures

Dual-use Export rules oblige the exporter to provide the relative licences to the competent local customs office when completing the formalities for the export of dual-use items.

The export of the items, however, may still be suspended or prohibited if relevant information has not been taken into consideration during the authorization procedure and/or the factual and legal circumstances on the basis of which the authorization was issued have changed.

If one of the two cases referred to in (i) or (ii) arise, Customs office contact the Ministry which must consider the information received and must decide whether to confirm, cancel, suspend or revoke the licence. The Authority has ten working days to reply. The deadline can be extend up to thirty days in some exceptional cases. In case of no reply within the specified time, the dual-use goods may be exported.

Furthermore, Article 17 of Regulation (EC) n° 428 of the 2009 allows the single Member States to provide that customs formalities may be completed only at specific customs offices. In this case, they shall inform the European Commission of the list of duly empowered customs offices and the Commission shall publish the information in the C series of the Official Journal of the EU.

Figure 11.6 EU Dual Use Goods and Technology Licensing System

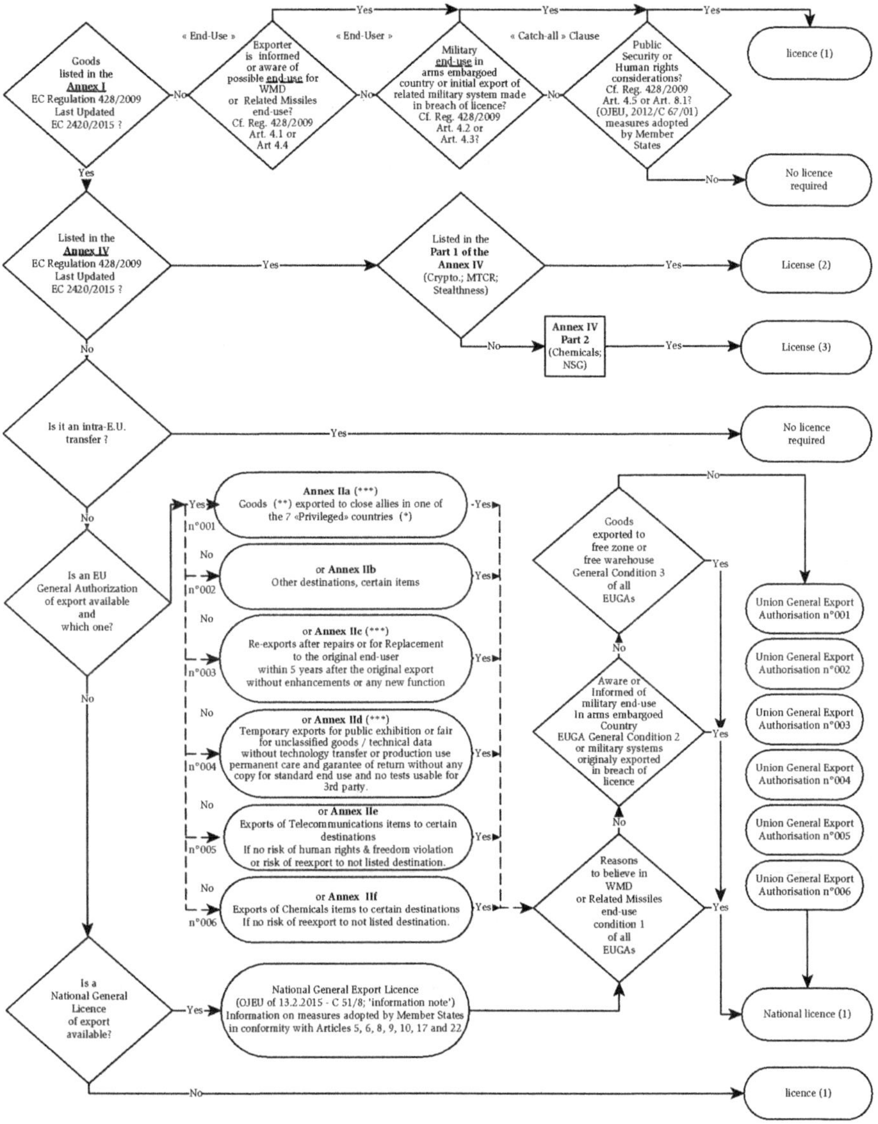

(1) Each EU Members states determines which type of EU licence (Individual or Global) is applicable.
(2) For goods and related technologies listed in Annex IV part 1, Individual or Global EU licences are available.
(3) For goods and related technologies listed in Annex IV part 2, only Individual licences are permitted.

(*) Seven countries listed in Annex IIa (EC) Regulation n° 428/2009 are the following: Australia, Canada, Japan, New-Zealand, Norway, Switzerland and US.

(**) Nearly all goods listed in Annex I excepted those listed in Annex IV and few others deemed very sensitive (cf. Annex g).
(***) cf. Annex 1Ig for possible other not authorized items.

Figure 11.7   Individual Specific Licence

Diagram 1 – Individual specific licences

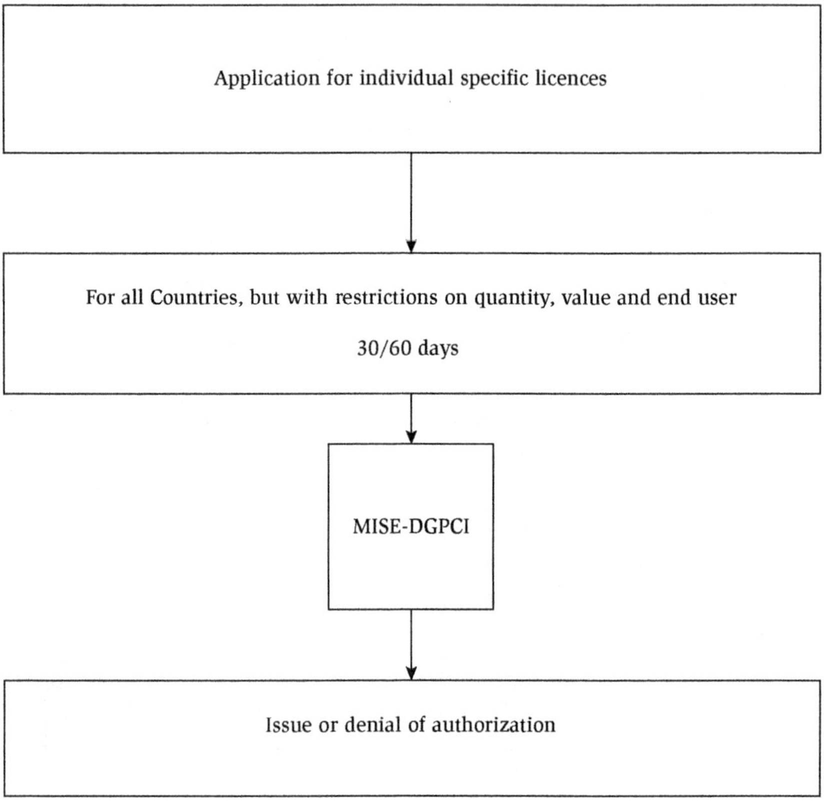

Figure 11.8 Individual Global Authorizations

Diagram 2 – Individual global authorisations

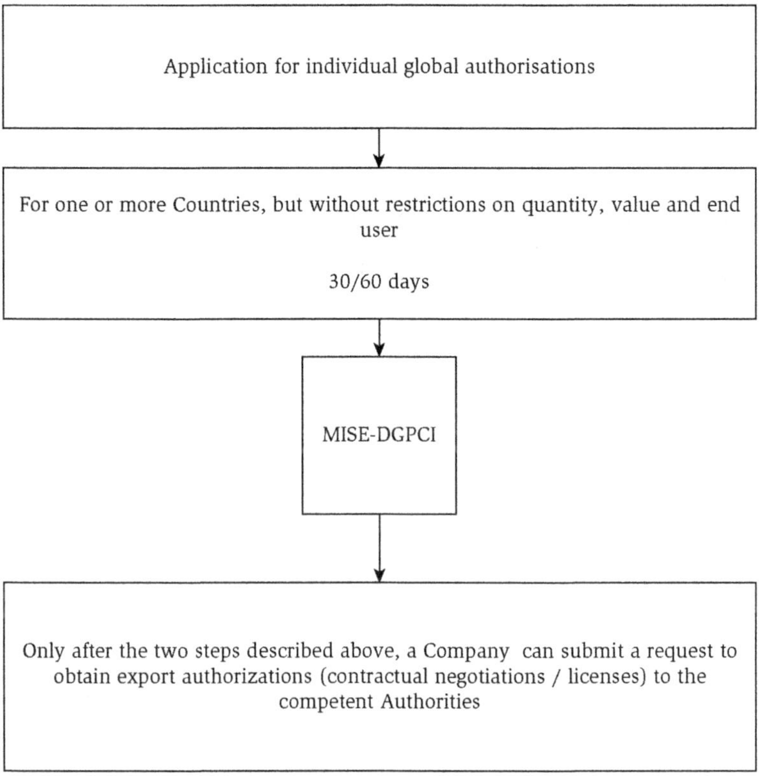
Application for individual global authorisations
For one or more Countries, but without restrictions on quantity, value and end user
30/60 days
MISE-DGPCI
Only after the two steps described above, a Company can submit a request to obtain export authorizations (contractual negotiations / licenses) to the competent Authorities

Figure 11.9 National General Authorizations

Diagram 3 – National general authorisations

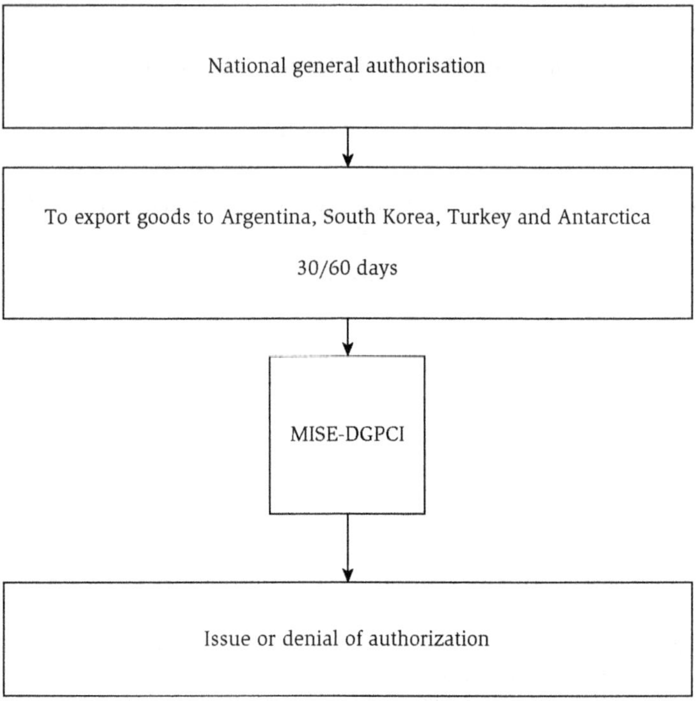

Figure 11.10 Community General Authorizations

Diagram 4 – Community general authorisations

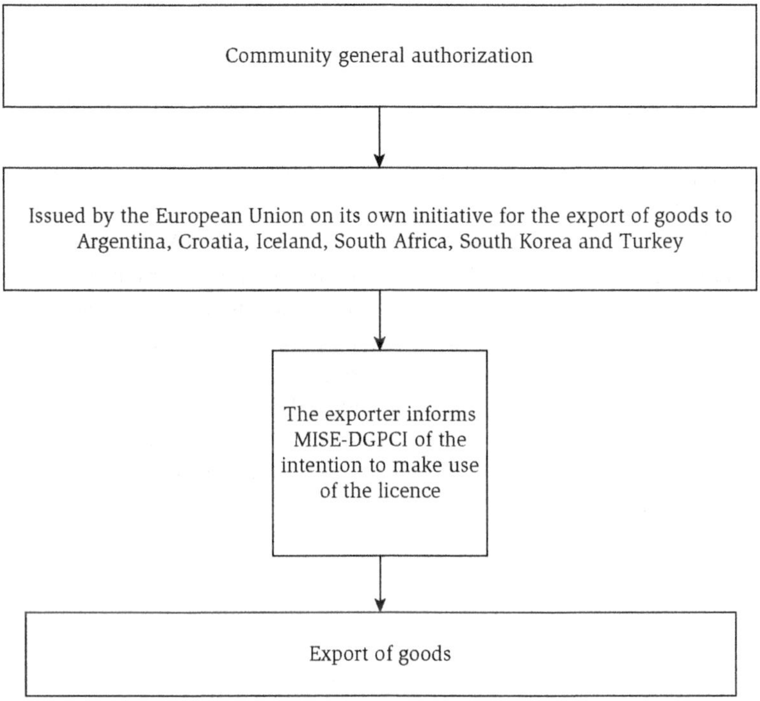
Community general authorization
Issued by the European Union on its own initiative for the export of goods to Argentina, Croatia, Iceland, South Africa, South Korea and Turkey
The exporter informs MISE-DGPCI of the intention to make use of the licence
Export of goods

Par. 5 Sanctions and Recourses of the Importer/Exporter

The export of dual-use items without the necessary licences, or under a licence which was obtained by supplying false information or documents, is punishable with imprisonment for a term of two to six years, or a fine ranging from EUR 25,000 to EUR 250,000.[892]

The Italian regime also imposes sanctions on the failure to provide the Ministry of Production Activities with the required information by an imprisonment of maximum two years.

892. Legislative Decree n° 96, 9 Apr. 2003, GU n° 102, 5 May 2003, Article 16.1.

SECTION 5 SPECIFICITIES/SPACE-RELATED PROVISIONS

Sub-Section 1 Details of the Control Regime

Par. 1 Restricted Information

Italian law does not allow the export of classified information nor that information widely described as being of 'national interest'. Such prohibition is still effective during the time period existing between the request of an authorization to start negotiations for the export of import of arms and the granting of such authorization by the competent body.

In addition, the Article 15 of the Legislative decree of 9 April 2003 applicable to the export of dual-use items specifies that a preliminary authorization shall be required for the transmission, by Internet or by other electronic media, fax or telephone, of any project, design, formula, software and technology which is related to the development, production or use of dual-use items contained in Annexes I and IV of the Regulation. The second paragraph of such Article 15 specifies that such preliminary authorization is not needed for the commercial advertisement of dual-use items, except if such advertisement includes the dissemination of the product's technical characteristics.

Par. 2 Obligations on Companies

Sub-Par. 1 Transport of Arms within the Italian Territory

Information must be given to the competent Prefecture of any intention to transport arms across Italy as part of commercial transactions between non-residents. The Prefect is entitled to issue a specific licence,[893] similar to the one granted to manufacture arms, but is also entitled to prevent the arms from entering Italian territory, for reasons of public order or public security.

Sub-Section 2 Space-Related Provisions in the Control Regime

The Italian regime does not set out specific processes or rules for goods or services related to space activities other than those mentioned in the Council Regulation (EC) n° 428/2009.

893. Text of the Laws of Public Security (*Testo Unico delle Leggi di Pubblica Sicurrezza*), GU n° 146, 26 Jun. 1936, Article 28.

SECTION 6 SANCTIONS AND EMBARGOES

Sub-Section 1 Participation of Italy to Embargoes or Other Related Sanctions

EU Member States have committed themselves to a Common Foreign Security Policy (CFSP) for the EU with the target, among others, to strengthen the role of the EU in the prevention of conflicts and in the management of the crisis. The application of the principles and objectives of the CFSP is pursued also with the application of a wide range of sanctions, even as consequences of the implementation of the resolutions of the UN Security Council.

The sanctions to apply in order to cause changes in activities such as violations of international law, human rights and - in general - of democratic principles, can include embargoes on the sale of arms, trade sanctions, financial restrictions, travel restrictions and other restrictive measures as the boycott of sport or cultural events. The application of the different sanctions must be driven by the valuation of the measures considered most appropriate to get the target. The effectiveness of sanctions is also guaranteed by a consistent implementation, enforcing and monitoring of the measures with an important role played by the competent Authorities of Member States that are generally responsible for the determination of penalties for violations of the sanctions in force.

Sub-Section 2 Regime of the Embargoes or Related Sanctions in Italy

In the light of the described scenario, Italy follows the regulation in place by the EU (and UN) and the trade sanctions and export restrictions to be applied are consequently drawn from European rules. Updated lists of the restrictive measures in force with the indication of all the targeted individuals, groups and bodies are available on the following websites:

http://www.esteri.it/mae/en/politica_europea/misure_deroghe
http://www.sviluppoeconomico.gov.it/index.php/it/commercio-internazionale/import-export/embarghi

SECTION 7 LIST OF ABBREVIATIONS

ANS	(Italian) National Security Agency
ATS	Australian Treaty Series
AG	Australia Group
ATS	Australian Treaty Series
COCOM	Coordinating Committee for multilateral strategic export control
CWC	Chemical Weapons Convention

DPCM	Decree of the President of the Council of Ministries - Decreto del Presidente del Consiglio dei Ministri
EC	European Community
EU	European Union
FA	Framework Agreement
GU	Italian Official Journal - GazzettaUfficiale
IAEA	International Atomic Energy Agency
ILM	International Legal Material
MTCR	Missile Technology Control Regime
MoD	Ministry (or Minister) of Defence
NATO	North Atlantic Treaty Organization
NSG	Nuclear Suppliers Group
OST	Outer Space Treaty
RNI	National Register of (Defence) Company
UAMA	Armaments Authorization Unit - Unità per le Autorizzazioni di Materiale di Armamento
UCPMA	Armaments Production Coordination Office - Ufficio per il Coordinamento della Produzione dei Materiali d'Armamento
UNTS	United Nations Treaty Series
WMD	Weapons of Mass Destruction

SECTION 8 REFERENCES

Sub-Section 1 Primary Documentation

Par. 1 Statutory Legislation

- Text of the Laws of Public Security (*Testo Unico delle Leggi di Pubblica Sicurrezza - TULPS)*, G.U. n° 146, 26 June 1936.
- Law 185, 9 July 1990, G.U. n° 163, 14 July 1990.
- Law 148, 17 June 2003, G.U. n° 146, 26 June 2003.
- Legislative Decree n° 96, 9 April 2003, G.U. n° 102, 5 May 2003.
- Legislative Decree n. 105, 22 June 2012, G.U. n°169, 21 July 2012.

Par. 2 Regulations, Decrees, Directives and Procedures

- Decree of Minister of Productive Activities, 11 July 2003.
- Decree 13 June 2003, G.U. n° 171, 25 July 2003.
- Decree 4 August 2003, G.U. n° 202, 1 September 2003.
- DPCM n° 93, 1 January 2005, n° 93, G.U. n° 127, June 2005.
- Circular UAMA n° 15894, 7 June 2013.
- Circular UAMA n° 16718, 17 June 2013.

- Inter Ministerial Decree n° 19 dated, 7 January 2013, G.U. n°53, 4 March 2013.
- Inter Ministerial Decree n° 16942, 18 June 2013.
- Directive UAMA n° 16755, 18 June 2013.
- Procedure UAMA n° 27007, 22 October 2013.
- Directive UAMA n° 30427, 25 November 2013.
- Directives UAMA n° 32040 e 32041, 9 December 2013.
- Directive UAMA n° 2393, 30 January 2014.

Par. 3 Annexes – Copies of Documents of Practical Use to the Importer/Exporter

A number of standard documents relevant for the import or export process in Italy (e.g., most current official application forms for import or export licences, templates of contractual undertaking, or regulation extracts) as well as other non-official documents are available on a dedicated DropBox folder which can be accessed by following the link below: www.kluwerlawonline.com/eclrh-annexes.

Sub-Section 2 Secondary Documentation

Par. 1 Internet Sites

- www.attivitaproduttive.gov.it
- www.difesa.it
- www.esteri.it
- www.governo.it
- www.mef.gov.it
- www.sicurezza-industriale.com
- www. sviluppoeconomico.gov.it

Par. 2 Paper Publications

'*Controlling the transfer of Military Equipment and technologies in Italy*', Centro Militare di Studi Strategici, edited by Alberto Traballesi, December 2004.

SECTION 9 USEFUL INFORMATION

Sub-Section 1 Licensing and Enforcement Authorities Contact Details

Name of Organization	*Ministry of Defence – Ministero della Difesa*
Postal Address	Palazzo Barachini Via XX Settembre 8, 00187 Roma, Italy
Website	www.difesa.it

Name of Organization	*General Secretary of Defense – Segretariato Generale della Difesa e DNA III Reparto Armaments Policy, International Cooperation and control on Arms, National Industry Register Service*
Postal Address	Via XX Settembre, 123/A - 00187 Roma, Italy
Website	urni@sqd.difesa.it

Name of Organization	*Ministry of Foreign Affairs – Ministero degli Affari Esteri*
Postal Address	Piazzale della Farnesina, 1, 00194 Roma, Italy
Website	www.esteri.it

Name of Organization	*Ministry of Economy and Finance – Ministero dell'Economia e delle Finanze*
Postal Address	Via XX Settembre, 97, 00187 ROMA
Website	www.mef.gov.it

Name of Organization	*Ministry of Productive Activities – Ministero Attività Produttive*
Postal Address	Via Veneto, 33, 00187 Roma
Website	www.attivitaproduttive.gov.it/

Name of Organization	*Presidency of the Council of Ministries – Presidenza del Consiglio dei Ministri*
Postal Address	Palazzo Chigi Piazza Colonna 370 00186 Roma – Italy
Website	www.governo.it

Sub-Section 2 Other

None.

CHAPTER 12

Japan

Shinji Itoh & Takehiro Fujita

SECTION 1 TABLE OF CONTENTS

SECTION 2 EXECUTIVE SUMMARY

The nature of Japan's export control laws and regulations has arisen from the specific situation in Japan following the Second World War and the resulting limitations on military capacity. The Government of Japan has been dealing carefully with 'arms' exports in accordance with the '3 principles on Arms Exports' policy guidelines in order to avoid any possibility of aggravating international conflicts.

In fact, arms exports are regulated in a strict manner, and therefore except for the Mutual Defence Assistance Agreement (the MDA Agreement) and the Exchange of Notes concerning the Transfer of Military Technologies concluded in 1983 under the MDA Agreement (the 1983 Exchange of Notes) between Japan and the United States (US), the export of arms by Japan to other destinations is very limited.

However, signs of change from a strict interpretation of pacifism to a more relaxed one are perceptible in Japan. In the first place, this concerns the exchange of technology with the US. In 2006, following the missile launch test fired by North Korea over Japanese seas, the Japanese government decided to accelerate the development of its advanced next generation missile interceptors with the US. For this occasion, the Japanese authorities declared that the Three Principles would not apply to US-Japan missile defence cooperation.

Along with those pressures, Japanese authorities themselves tend to be feeling the necessity to open arms exchanges with Europe more acutely than ever. The reason being that until now, historical ties and the legal framework has created a situation where Japanese defence purchasing has relied exclusively on the US. Those purchased technologies have often included technical solutions to which Japan has no access. The monopoly of US manufacturers also leads to much higher prices than those that could be expected as result of international competition.

The Japanese press announced in May 2009 that the government has decided to relax the ban on arms exports and allow Japanese companies to join international weapons development programmes. This would 'enable shipments to countries with which Japan co-develops arms', the economic newspaper Nikkei said, adding that 'The move is aimed at reducing procurement costs and stimulating the domestic defence industry by promoting joint development and production of key arms, such as next generation fighter jets, with the US and Europe.' The move notably allowed Japan to join the US controlled F-35 joint strike fighter project.[894]

In this way, the Japanese government has taken exemption measures with respect to the '3 principles on Arms Exports,' depending on the necessity in each individual case. In fact, there have been twenty-one cases of such exemptions since the three principles were established. Under these circumstances, there have been discussions in the government about the necessity for clear guidelines for approving transfers of defence equipment to overseas. Finally, on 1 April 2014, in accordance with the National Security Strategy adopted on 17 December 2013, the Japanese government decided to review the government's existing policy guidelines on overseas transfers of

894. Japan to relax arms export ban, Nikkei reports, 25 May 2009, www.japantoday.com/category/politics/view/japan-to-relax-arms-export-ban-nikkei-reports.

defence equipment, and accordingly announced the 'Three Principles on Transfer of Defense Equipment and Technology', namely: (i) Clarification of cases where transfers are prohibited, (ii) Limitation to cases where transfers may be permitted as well as strict examination and information disclosure, and (iii) Ensuring appropriate controls regarding extra-purpose uses or transfers to third parties.

At the same time as the announcement of the Three Principles on Transfer of Defense Equipment and Technology, the guidelines for said Three Principles were also implemented. These guidelines shall be referred to when adopting the Foreign Exchange and Foreign Trade Law, which governs export control systems.

By the adoption of the Three Principles on Transfer of Defense Equipment and Technology as well as the implementation of the subject guidelines, the Japanese government has clearly indicated the cases where overseas transfers of defence equipment and technology may be permitted. Considering that historically there have been no official standards or guidelines to permit such transfers, these new measures will presumably affect the regulation system of export control in Japan in the future (but it should be noted that the changes have not yet been implemented into laws, such as the Foreign Exchange and Foreign Trade Law).

For the time being, the regulation system stipulated in the Foreign Exchange and Foreign Trade Law does not create specific procedures for the authorization of arms exports other than the above new guidelines implemented on 1 April 2014. The procedures are the same for arms and dual-use items exports.

SECTION 3 INTRODUCTION: ELEMENTS OF CONTEXT

Sub-Section 1 Overall Philosophy

The devastating experience of Hiroshima and Nagasaki and the unconditional surrender in 1945 shook the cultural foundations of Japan. In fact, with regards to the arms export control policy, Japan has stuck to a cautious stance as a pacific nation in order to prevent aggravation of an international conflict by exporting arms. Article 9 of the Japanese Constitution states that 'aspiring sincerely to an international peace based on justice and order, the Japanese people forever renounced to war as a sovereign right of the nation and to the threat or use of force as means of settling international disputes'. Article 9 of the Constitution further states that 'in order to accomplish the aim of the preceding paragraph, land, sea, and air forces, as well as other war potential, will never be maintained. The right of belligerency of the state will not be recognized'.

Through such articles, Japan does not only renounce the right of belligerency to settle international disputes, but it also strictly limits Japanese military forces to 'self-defence' roles. The clearest links between the anti-military cultural norms of Japan and its trade policies exist in the area of arms exports. In practice, Japan's guidelines about export control have prohibited all arms exports until recently. Apart from arms and technologies exports to the US and relatively minor loopholes in arms export control, there has been almost no arms export from Japan since the Second World War. Prior to the adoption of the Three Principles on Transfer of Defense

Equipment and Technology, some exceptions existed; for example: facing the challenge of insecurity along of vital sea lanes, Japan decided in 2006 to provide three patrol vessels to Indonesia navy.

These vessels have been used to prevent piracy, maritime terrorism and proliferation of weapons in the Strait of Malacca. As it is expressly mentioned by the Ministry of Foreign Affairs (MOFA) in its website, such vessels fall under the category of 'military vessels' stipulated by the Export Control Trade Ordinance because they have been bullet-proofed to protect their crew members. They are defined as 'arms' in the Three Principles regarding Arms Exports. At the time of the agreement, the Japanese government issued a statement announcing that Japan would regard the provision of these vessels as an exception to the Three Principles.[895]

Sub-Section 2 Historical Outlook

In the 1950s, there was a considerable debate about the role of defence industries in the economic future of Japan. By the mid-1960s, consistent pressure from anti-militarist opposition parties and the fear that Japanese support to the American military might involve Japan in the Vietnam conflict were an incentive for the Liberal Democratic Party leaders to take a stronger stance against arms exports. Ultimately, in April 1967 Prime Minister Eisaku Sato explained the 'Three Principles on Arms Exports' (TPAE)[896] which determined the Japanese policy of arms exports. Furthermore, Prime Minister Takeo Miki augmented the Three Principles in February 1976 with policy guidelines that Japan would avoid arms exports to other areas and Japan would apply the same treatment to items related to the production of arms. The consolidated government view of arms control of the Miki administration[897] consists of the following three principles:

- the export of arms to the area subject to TPAE shall be prohibited;
- the export of arms to other areas, which are not subject to TPAE, shall be restrained in line with the spirit of the Constitution and the Foreign Exchange and Foreign Trade Act;[898]
- equipment related to arms production shall be treated in the same category as arms.

However, with the assurance of the US military protection, successive post-war Japanese governments made economic growth their primary security objective. In

895. MOFA, Grand Aid to Indonesia for the Project for Construction of Patrol Vessels for the Prevention of Piracy, Maritime Terrorism and Proliferation of Weapon, 16 Jun. 2009, www.mofa.go.jp/announce/announce/2006/6/0616-3.html.
896. The TPAE states the government will not permit exports to three categories of countries: the communist bloc countries, the countries to which the export of arms is prohibited according to the United Nations resolutions, the countries which are actually involved or likely to become involved in international conflict.
897. Takeo Miki was chosen as the Party's seventh President on 4 Dec. 1974 and formed a new 'Clean Cabinet' (*Kuriin naikaku*).
898. Law No. 228 of 1949, as amended.

particular, Japanese officials sought to use exports as an engine of economic prosperity. With such a strategy, Japan became a leading economic power, especially in the production and export of high-technology products.

Distinguishing between military and commercial items, however, has become much more difficult in recent decades. As the contributions of dual-use goods, technologies and services became increasingly important in modern weapons and logistical systems, the 'arms' export distinction in Japanese policy grew less meaningful. In 1983, Japan also formally exempted technology transfers to the US based on a strict interpretation of its 'TPAE'.

However, as mentioned above, the Japanese government adopted the Three Principles on Transfer of Defense Equipment and Technology on 1 April 2014 followed by implementation of new guidelines clarifying the cases in which overseas transfers of defence equipment and technology may be permitted under and subject to a strict examination and information disclosure. In this regard, it can be said that the situation has changed quite recently. Actually, the Japanese government, under this Three Principles, approved the export of parts of missiles to the USA as well as cooperative research on missile technology with the United Kingdom (UK) in July 2014.

Sub-Section 3 Participation in International Regimes

The following tables display Japan's participation status to export control related international treaties and programmes. It is also stated, when relevant, that Japan is party to a treaty either by signature and ratification or by accession.

Par. 1 Treaties and Regimes Dealing with Specific Items and Technologies

Table 12.1 Nuclear Weapons Treaties

Treaty Name	*Overall Status*	*Specific Status*	*Enforceable in Japan*
Test Ban			
Limited Test Ban Treaty[899]	OS: 5 August 1963 EF: 10 October 1963	S: 14 August 1963 R: 15 June 1964	Yes
Comprehensive Nuclear Test Ban Treaty[900]	OS: 24 September 1996 EF: not in force	S: 24 September 1996 R: 8 July 1997	No

899. Treaty Banning Nuclear Weapon Tests in the Atmosphere, in Outer Space and Under Water, *UNTS*, vol. 480, 43.
900. UNGA, resolution 50\245.

Treaty Name	*Overall Status*	*Specific Status*	*Enforceable in Japan*
Test Ban			
Nuclear Non-Proliferation Treaty[901]	OS: 1 July 1968 EF: 5 March 1970	S: 3 February 1970 R: 8 June 1976	Yes
IAEA Comprehensive Safeguards Agreement[902]	EF: 2 December 1977	N/A[903]	Yes
IAEA Model Additional Protocol[904]	OS: 4 December 1998 EF: 16 December 1999	N/A[905]	Yes

Abbreviations: OS: Opened for signature; EF: Entry into force; S/R: Signature/Ratification; A: Accession.

Table 12.2 Biological and Chemical Weapons Treaties

Treaty Name	*Overall Status*	*Specific Status*	*Enforceable in Japan*
Geneva Protocol[906]	OS: 17 June 1925 EF: 8 February 1928	S: 17 June 1925 R: 21 May 1970	Yes
Biological Convention[907]	OS: 10 April 1972 EF: 26 March 1975	S: 10 April 1972 R: 8 June 1982	Yes
Chemical Convention[908]	OS: 13 January 1993 EF: 29 April 1997	S: 13 January 1993 R: 15 September 1995	Yes

Abbreviations: OS: Opened for signature; EF: Entry into force; S/R: Signature/Ratification; A: Accession.

901. Treaty on the Non-Proliferation of Nuclear Weapons, *UNTS*, vol. 729, 161.
902. Agreement Between the Agency and States Required in Connection with the Treaty on the Non-Proliferation of Nuclear Weapons (NPT), INFCIRC/153 (Corrected).
903. This treaty is a bilateral one and, accordingly, the differences that apply to multilateral treaties (between the overall status and the specific status) do not apply.
904. Model Protocol Additional to the Agreement(s) Between State(s) and the Agency for the Application of Safeguards, INFCIRC/540 (Corrected).
905. This treaty is a bilateral one and, accordingly, the differences that apply to multilateral treaties (between the overall status and the specific status) do not apply.
906. Protocol for the Prohibition of the Use in War of Asphyxiating, Poisonous or Other Gases, and of Bacteriological Methods of Warfare, 94, *League of Nations Treaty Series*, No. 2138 (1929).
907. Convention on the Prohibition of the Development, Production and Stockpiling of Bacteriological (Biological) and Toxin Weapons and On Their Destruction, *UNTS*, vol. 1015, 163.
908. Convention on the Prohibition of the Development, Production, Stockpiling and Use of Chemical Weapons and on Their Destruction, Doc.CD/CW/WP.400/Rev.1.

Table 12.3 Multilateral Export Control Regimes

Regime Name	*Formation*	*Participation*
Zangger Committee[909]	1971	Yes
Nuclear Suppliers Group	1974	Yes
Australia Group	1985	Yes
Missile Technology Control Regime	1987	Yes
Wassenaar Arrangement[910]	1994	Yes

Table 12.4 Others

Name	*Adoption*	*Participation*
UN Register on Conventional Arms[911]	9 December 1991	Yes[912]
Programme of Action on Small Arms and Light Weapons[913]	20 July 2001	Yes
International Code of conduct[914]	25 November 2002	No

Japan is currently leading the projects of the Arms Trade Treaty (ATT), that have been adopted on 2 December 2009 as well as on 3 April 2013 by the United Nations General Assembly (UNGA). Japan signed the ATT on 3 June 2013 and submitted an instrument of ratification to the UN on 10 May 2014.[915] The ATT will go into effect with ratification in at least fifty countries, among which Japan is the 32nd signatory.

909. Non-Proliferation Treaty Exporters Committee (also called the Zangger Committee).
910. Wassenaar Arrangement on export controls for conventional arms and dual-use goods and technologies.
911. A/RES/46/36/L.
912. Information provided for the calendar years 1992 up to 2005.
913. Programme of Action to Prevent, Combat and Eradicate the Illicit Trade in Small Arms and Light Weapons in All Aspects, A/CONF.1992/15.
914. The Hague Code of Conduct against Ballistic Missile Proliferation, not yet published.
915. MOFA, Adoption of the Conventional Arms Resolutions by the United Nations General Assembly, 3 Dec. 2009 Submission of an instrument of ratification to the United Nations, 3 May 2014, http://www.mofa.go.jp/mofaj/press/release/press4_000869.html, www.mofa.go.jp/announce/announce/2009/12/1197775_1148.html.

Par. 2 Treaties Dealing with Specific Areas

Table 12.5 International Zones

Treaty Name	*Overall Status*	*Specific Status*	*Enforceable in Japan*
Antarctic Treaty[916]	OS: 1 December 1959 EF: 23 June 1961	S: 1 December 1959 R: 4 August 1960	Yes
Outer Space Treaty[917]	OS: 27 January 1967 EF: 10 October 1967	S: 27 January 1967 R: 10 October 1967	Yes
Sea Bed Arms Control Treaty[918]	OS: 11 February 1971 EF: 23 June 1961	S: 11 February 1971 R: 21 June 1971	Yes
Moon agreement[919]	OS: 18 December 1979 EF: 11 July 1984	-	No
Convention on the Law of the Sea[920]	OS: 10 December 1982 EF: 16 November 1994	R: 20 June 1996	Yes

Abbreviations: OS: Opened for signature; EF: Entry into force; S/R: Signature/Ratification; A: Accession.

Table 12.6 Regional Nuclear Weapons-Free Zones

Treaty Name	*Overall Status*	*Specific Status*	*Enforceable in Japan*
Treaty of Tlatelolco[921]	OS: 14 February 1967 EF: 22 April 1967	-	No
Treaty of Rarotonga[922]	OS: 6 August 1985 EF: 11 December 1986	-	No
Treaty of Bangkok[923]	OS: 15 December 1995 EF: 27 March 1997	-	No

916. 402, *UNTS*, 7.
917. Treaty on Principles Governing the Activities of States in the Exploration and Use of Outer Space, including the Moon and Other Celestial Bodies, *UNTS*, vol. 610, 205.
918. Treaty on the Prohibition of the Emplacement of Nuclear Weapons and other Weapons of Mass Destruction on the Seabed and The Ocean Floor and in the subsoil thereof, *UNTS*, vol. 955, 115.
919. Agreement governing the Activities of States on the Moon and Other Celestial Bodies, *ILM*, vol. 18, 1434.
920. Doc. A/CONF.62/122 and Corr.1-11.
921. Treaty for the Prohibition of Nuclear Weapons in Latin America and the Caribbean, *UNTS*, vol. 634, 326.
922. South Pacific Nuclear Free Zone Treaty, *ILM*, vol. 24, 1442.
923. South East Asia Nuclear-Weapon-Free Zone Treaty, *ILM*, vol. 35, 635.

Treaty Name	*Overall Status*	*Specific Status*	*Enforceable in Japan*
Treaty of Pelindaba[924]	OS: 11 April 1996 EF: not in force	–	No

Abbreviations: OS: Opened for signature; EF: Entry into force; S/R: Signature/Ratification; A: Accession.

Table 12.7 Other Alliance Coordination Mechanism

Other Regional Treaties	*Overall Status*
US-Japan defence technology agreement	S/R August 1983
The Japan-US Agreement on Cooperation in Science and Technology	S/R: 29 November 1988
Agreement between the Government of Japan and the Government of the US concerning Reciprocal Provision of Logistic Support	S/R: 15 April 1996
Supplies and Services between the Self-Defence Forces of Japan and the Armed Forces of the US	S/R: 28 April 1998
Japan-EU Joint Declaration on Disarmament and Non-proliferation	EF: 22 April 2004

Abbreviations: OS: Opened for signature; EF: Entry into force; S/R: Signature/Ratification.

SECTION 4 CONTROL REGIME

Sub-Section 1 Military Goods and Services

Par. 1 Overall Presentation

The legal framework for Japanese non-proliferation export controls can be found in the Foreign Exchange and Foreign Trade Control Act. For the export as well as import of arms or arms production-related equipment, the permission of the Ministry of Economy, Trade and Industry (METI) is required.

Supporting the Foreign Exchange and Foreign Trade Control Act are three Cabinet Orders, the Export Trade Control Order (*Yushutsu-Kanri-rei*),[925] the Foreign Exchange Control Order (*Gaikoku Kawase Kanri-rei* or *Gaitame-rei*),[926] and the Import

924. African Nuclear Weapon-Free Zone Treaty, *ILM*, vol. 35, 698.
925. Order No. 378 of 1 Dec. 1949.
926. Order No. 260 of 11 Oct. 1980.

Trade Control Order (*Yunyu Kanri-rei*).[927] Further, articles for which there is a prohibition on importing are also listed by the Customs Tariff Act.[928]

Sub-Par. 1 Requirements Prior to Any Specific Import/Export (i.e., Manufacturing Phase)

According to Article 3 of the Law for Manufacturing Arms,[929] any person wishing to manufacture arms or arms-production-related equipment has to obtain the permission of METI. However, Article 4 of said Law provides that no licence is required for a person, institution or company wishing to trial-produce the arms. Article 3 of said Law stipulates the following process to obtain the licence:

(1) Complete and submit the application form for an Arms Manufacturing Licence to METI, Manufacturing Industries Bureau.
(2) Documents to be attached to the Application for an Arms Manufacturing Licence are the following:
  (a) Report on the business project.
  (b) Industrial establishment plan.
  (c) Manufacturing blue print for the arms.
  (d) Report on the Applicant Company's current business plan.
  (e) Applicant Company's article of association.
  (f) Financial report of the Applicant Company.

Sub-Par. 2 Requirements at the Import and/or Export Stages

I Goods

Article 48 of the Foreign Exchange and Foreign Trade Control Act[930] stipulates that a licence from METI is required to export military goods. The Export Trade Control Order Attachment List I, listing all controlled items and technology says that Arms and Weapons are controlled goods under its item I. However there is no detailed list available.

Under Article 52 of the Foreign Exchange and Foreign Trade Control Act[931] and Article 9 of the Import Trade Control Order, some items (weapons, firearms) are exempted from import liberalization obligations implemented under the General Agreement on Tariffs and Trade (GATT) because they may be a threat to public safety. Thus, any importer who intends to import these items must be allocated an import quota by METI.

927. Order No. 414 of 29 Dec. 1949.
928. Law No. 54 of 1910.
929. Law No. 145 of 1953, as amended.
930. See *supra* n. 898.
931. See *supra* n. 898.

The procedure to obtain an export licence is as follows:

(1) Complete and submit the application form to the Security export Licensing Division of the Trade and Economic Cooperation Bureau of METI or the nine regional Bureaus of Economy, Trade and Industry.[932]
(2) Documents to be attached to the Application for an Export Licence.

Items (1)-(4) below are required for all applications. Other documentation may be required in some cases in order to verify the end-use and other information included in the application form, and so forth.

(1) 'Supplementary Details regarding the Export Licence Application' Items such as the following are included in the above document:
    (a) information on the good itself including number of model or type;
    (b) section/item in the Export Control Order Table No. 1 applicable to the good;
    (c) name of manufacturer;
    (d) quantity and value;
    (e) name, address and activities of the importer (business activities, number of employee, capital, fund, portfolio, annual sales, annual output, etc.);
    (f) name and address of the plant where the goods are to be installed or used; and
    (g) outline of the end-use (purpose and use of the goods).
(2) A copy of the contract.
(3) Technical evaluation form.
(4) Catalogues or other supplementary information on the specification of the good.

One must know that the procedure can be long and troublesome. Basically, METI may ask for any kind of complementary documents. Examples of other documents which may be requested by METI are:

(i) End-user statement.
    Contents of the end-user statement:
    - Names and addresses of the importer and end-user.
    - Location where the goods are to be installed/used, and the purpose of use Pledge by the importer and/or end-user that the goods will be used for civil use only and will not be used for the development or production of weapons of mass destruction (WMD) (nuclear weapons, biological weapons and chemical weapons) and missiles which are capable of delivering WMD.
    - Restriction on re-exports.
    - Signature by the representative, his title and date.

932. Kanto: Kanto Bureau of Economy, Trade and Industry.

(ii) Materials relating to the business which are public information such as company pamphlets or annual reports, or formal documents such as certificates of registration and tax payment.
(iii) Document containing location, outline of the business, structure, capital relationship, major customers.
(iv) Documents including the purpose and use of the goods/technologies, the location for installation.

II Services

Not only items but also technologies are controlled and require an export licence. Technology can be any specific piece of information required for the development, production or use of any items under the Export Control Principles. Technologies may take the form of technical data (blue prints, software, etc.) or technical assistance (instructions to develop skills, training, etc.).

Paragraph 1 of Article 25 of the Foreign Exchange and Foreign Trade Control Act[933] stipulates that a licence from METI is required for military related technology and/or goods transaction:

- Transactions for which the objective is the design, manufacture, or provision of technology (hereinafter called 'designated technologies') in designated regions, for use in relation thereto of types of products as designated by Cabinet Order[934] which are deemed to prevent the maintenance of international peace and order.
- Transactions involving the movement of goods between foreign countries related to trading of goods, which as set by Cabinet Order,[935] are deemed to prevent the maintenance of international peace and order.

With regard to the paragraph below III. Persons/Deemed export, when a Japanese resident, with a non-resident, makes a technology transaction, it is necessary to obtain permission from METI. In that case, all regions are subject to the first paragraph of Article 25 of the Foreign Exchange and Foreign Trade Control Act.[936]

III Persons/Deemed export

Under paragraph 2 of the Article 25 of the Foreign Exchange and Foreign Trade Control Act,[937] any resident who intends to make specified technology and/or enter a goods[938] transaction with a non-resident including Japanese persons must obtain a licence from

933. See *supra* n. 898.
934. Appended Table 1 to the Export Trade Control Order, see *infra*: www.mofa.go.jp/policy/un/disarmament/policy/annex1.html.
935. *Ibid.*
936. See *supra* n. 898.
937. *Ibid.*
938. Any goods and technology listed in the Appended Table 1 to the Export Trade Control Order.

METI. With regards to Japanese export control laws and regulations, the nationality of a person who intends to make a transaction is not important.

However, a non-resident Japanese national, who is working for the diplomatic services of Japan abroad, is considered as 'non-resident' in the sense of Article 25 of the Foreign Exchange and Foreign Trade Control Act.[939]

Persons having Japanese nationality are considered 'non-residents' when they:

(1) go to a foreign country with an aim to work at the overseas bureau and stop at there;
(2) go to foreign country and plans to stay more than two years;
(3) have already resided in a foreign country for over two years;
(4) fall under items (1) from (3), but return home temporarily for less than six months.

A resident, not having Japanese nationality:

(1) who works within the bureau in Japan or;
(2) who has stayed in Japan over six months does not require a permission to make a specified technology/goods transaction.

In the case of a company, a resident means legal person:

(1) duly organized and existing under the laws of Japan;
(2) not being duly registered under the laws of Japan, but having overseas offices in Japan;
(3) a Japanese diplomatic establishment abroad.

A non-Japanese national can become a Japanese resident by staying in Japan for more than six months. Fear has been growing at METI that foreigners could take this opportunity to acquire sensitive technology without any control and reuse it in the interest of his or her country of origin. Therefore, METI is considering quickly addressing this matter, as it appears to be a loophole in the legislation.

Par. 2 Control Lists

Today, Japan controls a sixteen-item category list for security purposes, which are listed in Appended Table 1 to the Export Trade Control Order (*Yushutsu-Kanri-rei*)[940] as undermining the maintenance of international peace and safety (Article 48 of the

939. See *supra* n. 898.
940. The categories are: 1 – Weapons; 2 – Nuclear Weapons (N.S.G. Part 1 and Part 2 items); 3 and 3-2 – Biological and Chemical Weapons (CWC and AG items); 4 – Missiles (MTCR items); 5 – Advanced materials; 6 – Materials processing; 7 – Electronics; 8 – Computers; 9 – Telecommunications; 10 – Sensors and lasers; 11 – Navigation and avionics; 12 – Marine; 13 – Propulsion; 14 – Munitions; 15 – Sensitive Items; 16 – Complementary export controls.

Foreign Exchange and Foreign Trade Control Act). Examples (taken from Appended Table 1 of the Export Trade Control Order) are: weapons (1); items related to nuclear power (2); items related to chemical or biological weapons (3 and 3-2); items related to missiles; (4) conventional weapons (5-15); and items covered under supplementary export regulations (16).

The list of controlled technologies appears in the Appended Table 1 to the Foreign Exchange Control Order (*Gaitame-rei*)[941] and various Ministerial Ordinances (*Sho-rei*). The categories parallel those for goods. So any technology necessary for production or use of the goods listed in Appended Table 1 to the Export Trade Control Order can be controlled by METI.

The overall list corresponds to the current NSG/Zangger Committee, the Australia Group (AG), the Missile Technology Control Regime (MTCR), and, initially, the list of the Coordinating Committee for multilateral strategic export control (COCOM). To reflect the control lists and procedures of the Wassenaar Arrangement, the government amended the Foreign Exchange Control Order (*Gaitame-rei*) and relevant Ministerial Ordinances (*Sho-rei*) effective as of 13 September 1996. Among other things, this created an additional category (i.e., category fifteen, the 'very sensitive' list).

The lists are updated regularly to take into account, in particular, changes in Japan's international obligations. It added new agents in line with the Chemical Weapons Convention (CWC), for example, while it also modified the criteria for chemical agents in line with AG guidelines.

Par. 3 Licensing and Enforcement Authorities

The Customs Department (under the authority of the Ministry of Finance (MOF)) is in charge of checking at the border whether the goods to be exported are subject to controls and whether an export licence has been obtained. The law enforcement authorities (i.e., the police and the public prosecutors' office) also have the authority to enforce all laws in Japan including the Foreign Exchange and Foreign Trade Law.

The Export Division of METI (*Anzen Hosho Boeki Kanri-ka* or *Ampo-ka*) coordinates Japanese commercial exports and arms control policies. The *Ampo-ka* administers security-based export licences, negotiates and cooperates with foreign counterparts, and analyses security information for METI.

METI also has a CWC Office responsible for domestic compliance in CWC-related activities, including preparing industries for undergoing inspections by the CWC Secretariat. Security export control officials maintain frequent contact with other divisions within METI (including the Nuclear Energy Industry Division, the Material for Chemical Weapons and Drug Control Office, the Biochemical Industry Division and the Aircraft, Defence Products and Space Industry Division), especially since they may have served in or with someone in those offices under the frequent system of rotation used in the Japanese public service.

941. The list is available at following internet site address: www.meti.go.jp/policy/anpo/apply01.html (only in Japanese).

The MOFA is one of the participants in the Japanese export control system. Article 69-4 of the Foreign Exchange and Foreign Trade Control Act (*Gaitame-hou*),[942] specifies that METI may ask MOFA to comment on export licence applications. In practice, MOFA has a formal right to express an opinion on exports, and METI usually respects the position of MOFA. METI will grant a licence without consultation, but *Ampo-ka* will not issue a licence without consultation if they have any concerns about international repercussions, the need to refer to concerned countries and so forth.

Within MOFA, the Non-proliferation Bureau takes the leading role in licensing issues and cooperation with METI officials regarding international export control arrangements. Several other units in MOFA play a part in the process, such as the Nuclear Energy Division, which handles NSG Part I items (the Non-Proliferation Bureau handles Part II items), and the CWC Division, which works on legal issues of the CWC. Both units, however, work closely with the Non-proliferation Bureau.

The Customs Department (under the authority of the MOF) are in charge of checking whether the goods to be exported are subject to controls and whether an export licence has been obtained. The law enforcement authorities (i.e., the police and the public prosecutors' offices) also have the authority to enforce all laws in Japan including the Foreign Exchange and Foreign Trade Act.[943]

As far as licensing procedures are concerned, the application is submitted to the Security Export Licensing Division of the Trade and Economic Cooperation Bureau of METI or to one of the nine Regional Bureaus of economy, Trade and Industry. Within the Security Export Licensing Division, licensing officials are divided into several groups. Each group examines export licence applications of a specific category, such as advanced materials, material processing, electronics and computers, telecommunications, and so on.

Upon the adoption of the Three Principles on Transfer of Defense Equipment Technology, it was announced that in some cases when particularly careful consideration is required for the application of the conditions for approving the transfers such as overseas transfers of defence equipment and technology, the deliberations will take place at the National Security Council (NSC), which was launched as a venue for such deliberations in December 2013. Therefore, in the event that the application submitted to METI is recognized as a case which requires deliberation at the NSC according to the guidelines of said Three Principles, such application will be examined at the NSC and METI will give due consideration to the deliberation.

Figure 12.1 summarizes the licence application process and the authorities involved.

942. See *supra* n. 898.
943. *Ibid.*

Figure 12.1. Catch-All Control System

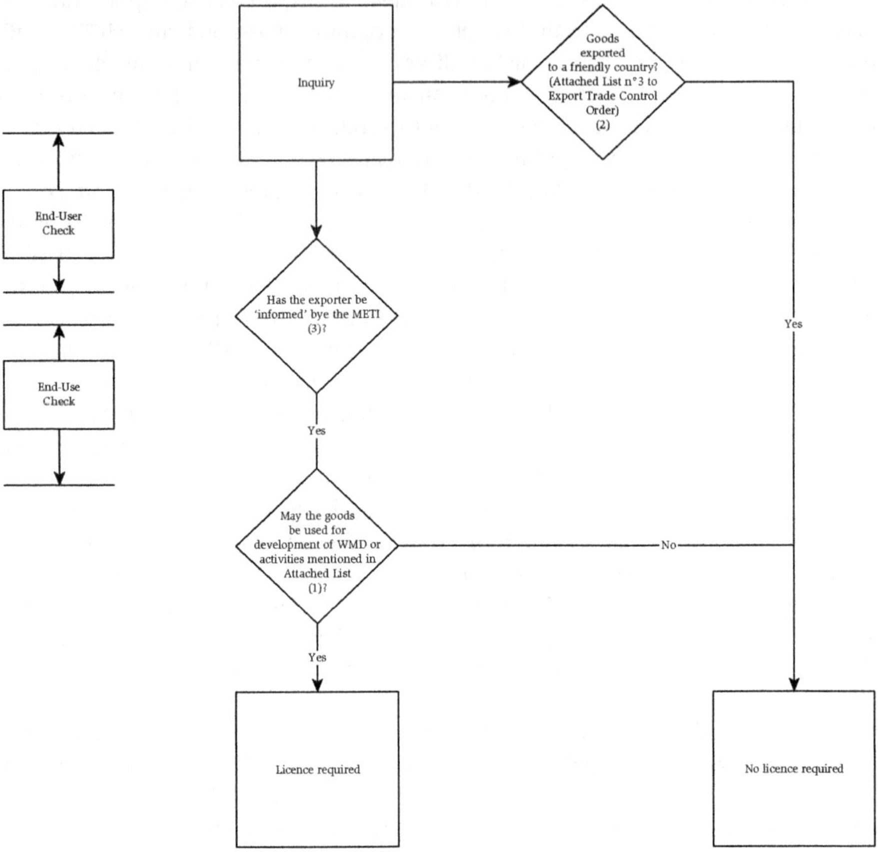

Figure 12.2. Export Control System

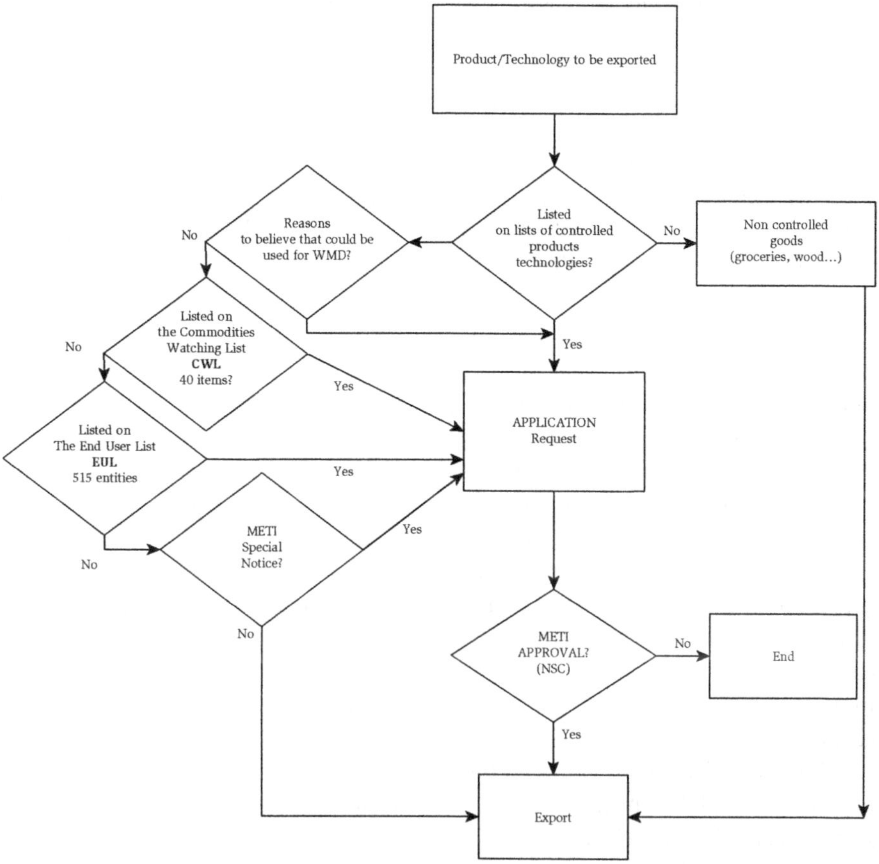

Par. 4 Sanctions and Recourses of the Importer/Exporter

In Japan, the following prison terms, fines, or both may be imposed in accordance with the Foreign Exchange and Foreign Trade Act[944] on those who have exported controlled items without obtaining a licence.

Sub-Par. 1 Criminal Penalties

The past years have witnessed an outburst of scandals involving Japanese companies violating the arms export prohibition, toward countries involved in WMD proliferation.

944. *Ibid.*

For instance, the International Atomic Energy Agency (IAEA) inspectors have discovered Tokyo Vacuum and Nakano Corporation products in North Korean nuclear facilities.[945] The criminal penalties related to those violations have consequently been enhanced.

According to Article 69-6 of the Foreign Exchange and Foreign Trade Act, violators may face imprisonment of up to seven years and fines of up to JPY 7,000,000 (approximately EUR 50,274) or up to five times the value of the exported goods, if it is exceeding JPY 7,000,000. The last update of the Foreign Exchange and Foreign Trade Law was enforced on April 2010 and includes heavier sanctions: the potential imprisonment has been expanded up to ten years and the fine has been raised up to JPY 10,000,000 (approximately EUR 71,850).

Sub-Par. 2 Administrative Sanction

Under Article 25-2 of the Foreign Exchange and Foreign Trade Act,[946] METI can curtail the export privileges of a violator for up to three years for the export of technology without a licence or the export of weapons.

Under Article 53 of the Foreign Exchange and Foreign Trade Act,[947] METI can prohibit exports of goods by a violator for up to three years. Penalties for filing false reports (or no reports), obstructing spot inspections or making false statements include up to six months imprisonment and fines of no more than JPY 500,000 (approximately EUR 3,590) under Article 72. On 14 August 2009, Horkos Corp., a high precision manufacturer in Japan, was sanctioned with a total export prohibition of five months (from 21 August 2009 to 20 January 2010), for having exported high specification machine tool to South Korea and China without an export licence from METI.[948]

METI also has the authority to impose other administrative sanctions. The said sanction may prohibit any good exports or any technology transfers, including those of goods or technology which are already licensed or which do not need to be licensed, for a period not exceeding three years.

945. Masako Toki and Stephanie Lieggi, Japan's struggle to limit illegal dual-use exports, http://thebulletin.org/japans-struggle-limit-illegal-dual-use-exports, 5 Sep. 2008.
946. *Ibid.*
947. *Ibid.*
948. 'Horkos illegally exported approximately 650 units of numerically controlled machine tools (machining centers, etc.) that can be used for developing nuclear weapons to South Korea and other regions from 2000 to 2008, without obtaining necessary permission from the Minister of Economy, Trade and Industry, by falsifying measurement data and thereby intentionally under representing the machines' performance.'

Sub-Section 2 Dual-Use Goods and Services

Par. 1 Overall Presentation

Sub-Par. 1 Requirements Prior to Any Specific Import/Export (i.e., Manufacturing Phase)

There are no specific requirements under Japanese export control laws and regulations for a person which would want to manufacture in Japan some dual-use equipment or to provide some dual-use related services.

Sub-Par. 2 Requirements at the Import and/or Export Stages

After a lengthy back and forth process between businesses and government, a 'catch-all' regulation was introduced on 1 April 2002. As a general rule, export of all goods and technologies, including concrete salt, cement, medical supplies, plastic products, rubber goods, fibre products, glassware, pottery porcelain items and metal products, tools, musical instruments and clocks, toys, pearls and jewels, to the entire world is subject to the catch-all regulation.

Exporters are required to apply for export licences in cases where items or technologies are not on control lists but could contribute to WMD proliferation programmes.

There are two main tools that allow the exporter to determine if he needs to apply for a licence or not. The first tool is a list called 'The End User list' released by METI and which contains names of foreign entities or persons that are believed to be involved with WMD. The list contains 515 entities. It is not an embargo list. However, a person wanting to export to one of the listed entities has to apply for a licence, unless it is apparent that the exported items will not be used for WMD purpose.[949] The second tool is the Commodity Watch List (CWL). It contains examples of forty items with a high risk of diversion for development. If an item is on the list, it does not mean that it is banned but it would be considered as sensitive.

If METI informs an exporter of the necessity to obtain a licence, the exporter must obtain the licence prior to exportation. Further, if an exporter has information that exported goods or technologies may be used for development, manufacture, use storage and so forth of nuclear, biological or chemical weapons, or missiles, or by an user which did such development, etc., in the past, the exporter must obtain the licence prior to exportation. Provided, however, that, if the destination of goods or technologies is any of the specified twenty-seven countries, including the US, Canada, UK, Australia or Korea, the licence is not necessary for exportation.

Japan also has a set of 'After-the-fact inspections' which aims at checking the legitimacy of export shipments, based on Article 7 of the Export Control Order in Japan.

949. The list is available in following METI website in pdf and MS-Excel format. http://www.meti.go.jp/policy/anpo/law05.html#gaikokuuserlist.

METI can request exporters to submit the reports on export shipments (Article 55-8 of the Foreign Exchange and Foreign Trade Control Act[950]) and/or to conduct on-the-spot inspections of the exporter's office and other locations related to the export.

Par. 2 Control Lists

As mentioned in the above, METI established a seventeen category list of items for security purposes.[951] Appended Table 1 of the Export Trade Control Order provides for such seventeen categories and corresponds to the current NSG/Zangger Committee, AG and MTCR control lists. The last category has been the list of Catch-all controlled products, where each and every exportable item, excluding foodstuff and lumber was included. In addition to these items, the technology related to the design, production and use of these goods is subject to regulations in a similar manner.

Such control lists constitute two types of categories depending on the regulatory framework. One is 'List Control' which is in connection with the categories from 1 to 15 on Appended Table 1 of the Export Trade Control Order and Foreign Exchange Order. The other is 'Catch-all Control' which is in connection with the last category listed on said Appended Table 1.

First, List Control is a regulation depending on the type of product. In other words, in the event that the items are listed in any categories from 1 to 15 of Appended Table 1 of the Export Trade Control Order, or the technologies are listed in a category from 1 to 15 of Appended Table 1 of the Foreign Exchange Order, the exporter is required to obtain a licence from METI. Second, even in the cases where the items and/or technologies are not controlled by the List Control, the Catch-all regulations will apply ('Catch-all Control'). Since 2008, METI completed the former through the implementation of a 'conventional weapon catch-all control', aiming at limiting the misappropriation of dual-use goods by terrorists or countries developing WMD. This regulation is the transposition of the Wassenaar arrangement on the export of dual-use goods into Japanese Law.

Catch-all Control is distinguishing between those countries with restrictions and the so-called white countries. The restricted countries list is composed of Afghanistan, Democratic Republic of the Congo, Eritrea, Ivory Coast, Iraq, Lebanon, Liberia, Libya, North Korea, Somalia and Sudan.

The 'white countries' list which is composed of friendly countries abiding by international laws: Argentina, Australia, Austria, Belgium, Bulgaria, Canada, Czech Republic, Denmark, Finland, France, Germany, Greece, Hungary, Ireland, Italy,

950. *Ibid.*
951. Within the list, the categories related to dual-use goods are: Item 2 Nuclear related goods; Item 3 and 3-2 Biological and chemical agents and related items (Items related to WMD); Item 4 Missiles and related items; Item 5 Advanced materials; Item 6 Materials processing; Item 7 Electronics; Item 8 Computers; Item 9 Telecommunications [Items related to conventional]; Item 10 Sensors and lasers arms; Item 11 Navigation and avionics; Item 12 Marine; Item 13 Propulsion; Item 14 Munitions; Item 15 Sensitive items; Item 16 Catch-all export controls items [Other Items (specified by H.S. Codes)].

Republic of Korea, Luxemburg, Netherlands, New Zealand, Norway, Poland, Portugal, Spain, Sweden, Switzerland, UK, and the USA.

Exporting an item listed on the product list category 16 in Export Trade Control Order Appended Table 1 and in Foreign Exchange Order Attachment List to a 'white country' does not require a licence. Yet, the exporter will have the responsibility to apply for a licence if he trades with the countries on the UN arms embargo countries related list. In case the exporter comes to know under the normal course of business that any goods or technology in category 16 will be exported to UN arms embargo countries for the development, manufacturing and use for conventional arms, the export licence is required and the exporter needs to submit licence application to METI for their review.

When the end-user is not located in one of the 'white countries' group, but however not in one of the countries under any UN arms embargo, the exporter will need a licence if and only if he is 'informed' by METI that there is a risk of 'proliferation'. In that case, the 'catch all' process applies and a licence is required for such countries.

Any exported good entering the country is the subject of catch-all regulation, excluding the foodstuff and the lumber. In addition, the technology related to the design, production and use of these goods becomes the subject of regulation.

Par. 3 Licensing and Enforcement Authorities

All the Japanese lists are made by METI for all products, including not only the military weapons but also the Dual-Use Goods and the so-called non-listed sensitive products object of the 'CWL'.

Consequently, for all controlled products METI is involved into the licensing process and deliberation of NSC is required for some cases. Also, METI coordinates with MOFA and Customs (MOF) for the enforcement.

Par. 4 Sanctions and Recourses of the Importer/Exporter

Articles 25-2, 53, 69-6, and 72 of the Foreign Exchange and Foreign Trade Law of the Foreign Exchange and Foreign Trade Act,[952] concerning the sanctions for those who have exported controlled items without obtaining a licence, apply equally for the issues related to dual-use goods or services.

Special case: Subsidiaries

On 20 November 2009, Japanese government has created a new type of bulk export licence called the 'Special Subsidiary Bulk Licence'. It is dedicated to Japanese intra-company export (from the mother company to its overseas subsidiaries). With a bulk export licence, a company is allowed to make multiple exports of certain controlled items regulated by international regimes such as Nuclear Suppliers Group,

952. *Ibid.*

AG, MTCR and Wassenaar Arrangement, to certain destinations without obtaining individual licence by METI. However, the licence is only valid for the 'use' of technology and not for preliminary stages like 'design and manufacturing'.

SECTION 5 SPECIFICITIES/SPACE-RELATED PROVISIONS

Sub-Section 1 Specificities of the Control Regime

Japan has effective tools within private companies in order to have effective export controls (Internal Compliance Programmes (ICP)). Therefore, the licensing authorities give guidelines to the private entities in order to interpret and implement export control policies. Since 2007, Japanese companies have had to create or strengthen their ICP to be granted bulk licences.

The Centre for Information on Security (later strategic) Trade Control (CISTEC) is the body enabling the information to flow between METI and the industry. CISTEC makes contributions in wide range of activities including compilation and submission of industry's opinions, organization of seminars, publication of guidebooks and answering of inquiries regarding technical specifications of controlled items and internal export controls.

Sub-Section 2 Space-Related Provisions in the Control Regime

There is no specific space-related provision in Japanese export control laws or regulations.

SECTION 6 SANCTIONS AND EMBARGOES

Sub-Section 1 Participation of Japan to Embargoes or Other Related Sanctions

(1) North Korea

The Government of Japan has imposed sanctions specific to North Korea. In particular, various sanctions were imposed response to its launching of missiles in July 2006, January and February 2016, and to its performance of nuclear bomb tests in October 2006, May 2009, February 2013 and January 2016.

The majority of sanctions that the Japanese Government imposes are, in general, measures which are taken after the passing of a particular resolution by the UN Security Council. The background related to this is that, until 2004, economic sanctions could not be implemented under the Foreign Exchange and Foreign Trade Act without the passing of a resolution by the UN Security Council, or international pressure for action. However, in response to the various incidents concerning North Korea, several laws were enacted or amended in 2004 so that the Japanese Government could implement sanctions independently without, for example, a UN Resolution. For this reason, the Japanese Government has imposed unique sanctions specifically against North Korea, as indicated below.

(a) Sanction Measures implemented independently by Japan

- Prohibition against any North Korean ship from entering a Japanese port, except for cases where the ship in question enters a Japanese port for the purpose of delivering goods necessary for humanitarian reasons, to individuals in North Korea.
- Prohibition in principle against any officers of North Korean authorities from entering into Japan.
- Prohibition against the exportation of any goods to North Korea.
- Prohibition against the importation of any goods whose place of origin or shipping area is North Korea.
- Prohibition against any trade involving a transfer of goods between North Korea and a third country, and against any transaction (intermediary trade transaction) related to a loan or a donation.
- Prohibition against payments for the importation of goods whose place of origin or shipping area is North Korea, performed without the prior consent of Japanese authorities.

(b) Sanction Measures upon the resolution of UN Security Council (except for asset-freezing measures)

(i) UN Resolutions 1718

- Prohibition against any exports of luxury goods to North Korea without permission from METI in accordance with the Foreign Exchange and Foreign Trade Act. The same applies to intermediary trade transactions related to luxury goods exported from a third country to North Korea, which require permission from METI.
- Prohibition against any exports of goods related to WMD to North Korea without permission from METI in accordance with the Foreign Exchange and Foreign Trade Act.

(ii) UN Resolutions 1874

Concerning the transfer of assets related to WMD: pursuant to the Foreign Exchange and Foreign Trade Act, the Cabinet took the following measures to prevent any activities that could contribute to activities or plans related to North Korea's nuclear, Ballistic missile and other WMD:

- Restrictions on payments.
- Restrictions on importation and exportation such as means of payment.

- Restrictions on capital transactions.
- Restrictions on service transactions.

(iii) UN Resolutions 2094

Concerning transactions with North Korean financial institutions:

- Prohibition against correspondent banking relationships with any North Korean financial institutions.
- Prohibition against the transfer of equity to any North Korean financial institutions.
- Prohibition against the establishment in Japan of a branch office of any North Korean financial institutions.
- Strict implementation of the obligation to report any suspicious transactions and to scrutinize customer identifications.

(c) Asset-freezing measures against those designated as 'involved in North Korea's missiles or any other WMD programs,' pursuant to the Foreign Exchange Act

(i) Based on UN resolutions:
   - Measures taken based on UN Resolution 1695: Currently, fifteen entities and one individual are so designated. Among all the targets, fourteen organizations located in North Korea are also registered on the End-User List (reviewed on 4 February 2014) published by METI.
   - Measures taken based on the UN Resolutions 1718, 1874, 2087 and 2094: Currently, nineteen entities and twelve individuals are so designated. Among the targets, nineteen organizations are also registered on the End-User List (reviewed on 4 February 2014) published by METI.

(ii) Based on Japan's cooperation with the US and the European Union for international peace: Currently, ten entities and six individuals are so designated. Among the targets, ten organizations are also registered on the End-User List (reviewed on 4 February 2014) published by METI.

(2) Iran

The Government of Japan had been implementing various sanctions based on the UN Security Council Resolutions as indicated below. However, many of these sanctions were lifted on 22 January 2016.

(a) Measures taken by the Cabinet, other than asset-freezing, based on UN Resolutions 1737, 1747, 1929, and pursuant to the Foreign Exchange Act:
   - Prevention against any transfer of funds made for the purpose of contributing to 'the development of means for carrying nuclear weapons and proliferation-sensitive nuclear activities in Iran'.

- Prohibition against the provision from Iran of items related to 'the development of means for carrying nuclear weapons and proliferation-sensitive nuclear activities in Iran'.
- Prohibition against the provision from Iran of weapons and other related goods.
- General prohibition against capital transactions and domestic direct investments pertaining to investments by a related party of Iran in any Japanese stock.
- Permission system for payments made to and received from Iran, for insurance underwritten by Japanese companies, and for intermediary transactions by Japanese companies concerning securities issued by a related party of Iran, in connection with certain activities such as 'activities related to the supply of Iran's large conventional weapons'.
- Prohibition against any individual designated as 'a person involved in the development of means for carrying nuclear weapons and in Iran's proliferation-sensitive Nuclear activities' from entering into or transiting (i.e., getting connecting flights) in Japan. Currently, sixty-five individuals are so designated.
- Strict implementation of Iran's transfer controls, including regulations related to chemical, biological and nuclear matters.
- Request for report regarding the acceptance of any payment made from Japan to Iran or from Iran to Japan.
- Request for voluntary ban when concluding a correspondent contract with a financial institution banking facility of Iran.
- Prohibition against the establishment of a corporation or a branch office in Iran of a Japanese financial institution banking facility, and prohibition against the establishment of a corporation or a branch office in Japan of a financial institution banking facility of Iran.
- Request for a strict implementation of the obligation to report any suspicious transactions and to scrutinize customer identifications.
- Suspension of any new provision or acceptance of mid-term (more than two years) export credits to Iran (for short-term, they are dealt with following the adequate fulfilment of acceptance requirements and a strict inspection).
- Suspension of any new investment in oil and gas areas.
- Alert concerning Iran-related transactions in the industrial world, especially in the oil and gas areas.

(b) Asset-freezing measures that the Cabinet took against entities and individuals, based on UN Resolutions 1737, 1747, 1803 and 1929, and pursuant to the Foreign Exchange Act:
   - Asset-freezing measures against 'those involved in Iran's proliferation-sensitive nuclear activities and in the development of means for carrying nuclear weapons': Currently, seventy-eight entities (including two banks) and forty-three individuals are so designated.

- Asset-freezing measures against 'entities, other than banks, and individuals who could contribute to Iran's proliferation-sensitive nuclear activities and development of means for carrying nuclear weapons.' Currently 194 entities (other than banks) and twenty-five individuals are so designated.
- Implementation of measures of suspension of correspondent banking relationships through asset-freezing, against any bank designated as 'a bank that could contribute to Iran's nuclear activities and development of means for carrying nuclear weapons' and against two banks that have been designated as 'involved in Iran's nuclear activities and development of means for carrying nuclear weapons.' Currently seventeen banks have been designated as 'banks that could contribute to Iran's nuclear activities and development of means for carrying nuclear weapons,' and, with the two banks designated as 'involved in Iran's nuclear activities and development of means for carrying nuclear weapons,' there are a total of nineteen banks subject to these measures.

(3) Other Countries – Asset-Freezing Measures

The Government of Japan has been implementing asset-freezing measures by imposing the following two restrictions under the Foreign Exchange and Foreign Trade Control Act as listed in the table 12.8 (as of 20 August 2014).

(a) Payment Restrictions

All payments to any of the entities or individuals specified by the MOFA's notification referred to above must obtain the prior approval of the Government of Japan.

(b) Restrictions on Capital Transactions

All capital transactions with any of the entities or individuals specified by the MOFA's notification referred to above (including deposit contracts, trust contracts, and money loan contracts) must obtain the prior approval of the Government of Japan.

Table 12.8 Sanctions on Individual/Entity

Restricted Individual/Entity	*Implemented Since*	*Number of Related UN Security Council Resolutions*
Milosevic Slobodan, a former President of the Federal Republic of Yugoslavia and individuals designated as being associated with him	February 2001	N/A (Corporation with USA, EU, etc. for international peace)
Taliban-associated entities and others designated by the UN Security Council	September 2001	1267, 1333, 1390

Restricted Individual/Entity	*Implemented Since*	*Number of Related UN Security Council Resolutions*
Terrorists and others designated by the UN Security Council	December 2001	1373
Agencies and Senior Officials of the Former Iraqi Government and Related Individuals designated by the UN Security Council	May 2003	1483
Senior officials of the former Liberian regime or associates thereof designated by the UN Security Council	August 2004	1532
Violators of arms embargo on the Democratic Republic of the Congo, as designated by the UN Security Council	November 2005	1596
Persons/parties who threaten peace on the Ivory Coast	March 2006	1975, 1572
Violators of Peace in Darfur on Republic of the Sudan	June 2006	1591
Violators of Embargoes in arms transportation to Somalia	June 2010	1844
Leading revolutionaries for Muammar Al Qadthafi in Libya and associated entities or individuals for such movement	March 2011	1970, 1973, 2009
Bashar al-Assad, the president of Syria, and associated entities or individuals	September 2011	N/A (Corporation with USA, EU, etc. for international peace)
Individuals for whom there is suspicion of direct involvement in the Crimea Annexation or instability in the East Ukraine	August 2014	N/A (Corporation with USA, EU, etc. for international peace)
Entities and individuals involved in the Violation of Peace in Central African Republic	August 2014	2127, 2134

Sub-Section 2 Regime of the Embargoes or Related Sanctions in Japan

(1) Sanctions based on UN resolutions or international needs

The Japanese government has been implementing various sanctions under the Foreign Exchange and Foreign Trade Law, based on UN resolutions or international pressure for cooperation. The Foreign Exchange and Foreign Trade Law stipulates that when the following requirements are met, the Japanese Government can take appropriate measures, and said UN resolutions or international requirements are considered to fulfil them:

- such measures are necessary for sincerely fulfilling obligations under the treaties and other international agreements which Japan has signed; or
- such measures are particularly necessary for Japan to be able to make a contribution to international efforts for achieving international peace.

(2) Sanctions implemented independently by Japan

The amendment of the Foreign Exchange and Foreign Trade Law in 2004 allows the Japanese government to impose economic sanctions upon Cabinet decisions when it is particularly necessary to maintain peace and security in Japan. However, in such case, the Japanese government shall submit the implementation of the countermeasures to the Diet within twenty days from the day when it took the countermeasures in order to seek approval of the Diet, and upon the passing of a resolution of disapproval, the government shall promptly terminate the measures.

Additionally, in June 2004, the Act on Special Measures concerning Prohibition of Entry of Specified Ships into Ports was enacted. It allows the Japanese government to prohibit a ship of a particular country from entering a Japanese port upon Cabinet decisions when it is particularly necessary to maintain peace and security in Japan.

SECTION 7 LIST OF ABBREVIATIONS

AG	Australia Group
CISTEC	Centre for Information on Security Trade Control
COCOM	Coordinating Committee for multilateral strategic export control
CWC	Chemical Weapons Convention
GATT	General Agreement on Tariffs and Trade
HS Code	Harmonized System Code
IAEA	International Atomic Energy Agency
ICP	Internal Compliance Programmes
ILM	International Legal Material
JAXA	Japan Aerospace Exploration Agency
MDA	Mutual Defence Assistance
METI	Ministry of Economy, Trade and Industry
MITI	Ministry of International Trade and Industry
MOF	Ministry of Finance
MOFA	Ministry of Foreign Affairs
MTCR	Missile Technology Control Regime

NPT	Nuclear Non-Proliferation Treaty
NSG	Nuclear Suppliers Group
TPAE	Three Principles on Arms Export
UNTS	United Nations Treaty Series
US	United States
WMD	Weapons of Mass Destruction

SECTION 8 REFERENCES

Sub-Section 1 Primary Documentation

Par. 1 Statutory Legislation

(1) Foreign Exchange and Foreign Trade Control Act (*Gaitema-hou,* Law n° 228 of 1 December 1949).

(2) Export Trade Control Order (*Yushutsu-rei,* Order n°. 378 of 1 December 1949).

(3) Several Ministerial Ordinances also apply to the licensing of sensitive exports in Japan.

- Export Trade Control Regulation (Ministry of International Trade and Industry (MITI) Ordinance n° 64 of 1 December 1949).
- Ministerial Ordinance Concerning Foreign Exchange Control (MOF Ordinance n° 44 of 15 November 1980).
- Ministerial Ordinance Defining Goods and Technology on the basis of the Provisions of Supplement No. 1 of Export Trade Control Order and Supplement of Foreign Exchange Order (MITI Ordinance n° 49 of 14 October 1991).
- Ministerial Ordinance Defining Goods Pursuant to Provisions of Supplement No. 2 and Supplement No. 7 of the Export Trade Control Order (MITI Ordinance n° 38 of 19 June 1992).
- Ministerial Ordinance Concerning Invisible Trade Transaction Relating to Foreign Trade (MITI Ordinance n° 8 of 4 March 1998).
- Ministerial Ordinance Defining the Cases Where Exported Commodities are Suspected to Be Used for the Development, Production or Use of Nuclear Weapons or the Like (METI Ordinance n° 249 of 28 December 2001).

(4) Import Trade Control Order (Order n° 414 of 29 December 1949).

Par. 2 Annexes – Copies of Documents of Practical Use to the Importer/Exporter

A number of standard documents relevant for the import or export process in Japan (e.g., most current official application forms for import or export licences, templates of contractual undertaking, or regulation extracts) as well as other non-official documents are available on a dedicated DropBox folder which can be accessed by following the link below: www.kluwerlawonline.com/eclrh-annexes.

Sub-Section 2 Secondary Documentation

Par. 1 Internet Sites

- www.k-faz.co.jp/e-faz/import/imp-5a.html (Items prohibited for importation)
- *www.jmcti.org/jmchomepage/english/index.htm (Japan Machinery Canter for Trade and Investment)*
- *www.mofa.go.jp/policy/un/disarmament/index.html (MOFA/Arms Control, Disarmament and Non-Proliferation)*
- *www8.cao.go.jp/kisei-kaikaku/oto/otodb/english/houseido/hou/lh_08010.html (Foreign Exchange and Foreign Trade Law)*
- www8.cao.go.jp/kisei-kaikaku/oto/otodb/english/houseido/image/08010-1.pdf (Flowchart of Import Trade Control)
- www.meti.go.jp/policy/anpo/englishpage.html (Outline of Export Control)
- www.meti.go.jp/policy/anpo/law_document/tutatu/t11kaisei/boueisoubiitensangensoku_honbun_english.pdf (Three Principles on Transfer of Defense Equipment and Technology)
- *www.meti.go.jp/policy/anpo/law_document/tutatu/t11kaisei/boueisoubiitensangensoku_unyoushishin_english.pdf (Implementation Guidelines for the Three Principles on Transfer of Defense Equipment and Technology)*

Par. 2 Paper Publications

L'espace, Enjeux Politiques (Paris, Hermès 34, 2002).
Mabito Yoshida, *Information Security Policies in Japan*, www.itu.int/osg/spu/cybersecurity/presentations/session7_yoshida.pdf.

SECTION 9 USEFUL INFORMATION

Sub-Section 1 Licensing and Enforcement Authorities Contact Details

Name of Organization	*Ministry of Economy, Trade and Industry (METI)*
Postal Address	1-3-1 Kasumigaseki, Chiyoda-ku, Tokyo 100-8901, Japan
Telephone	(General METI Inquiries): +81-(0)3-3501-1511
Website	www.meti.go.jp

Name of Organization	*Trade and Economic Cooperation Bureau*
Postal Address	1-3-1 Kasumigaseki, Chiyoda-ku, Tokyo 100-8901, Japan
Telephone	(General METI Inquiries): +81-(0)3-3501-1511
Website	www.meti.go.jp/english/aboutmeti/data/aOrganizatione/2007/03_trade_and_economic_cooperation.html

Name of Organization	*Trade Control Policy Division, Security Export Control Policy Division, Regional Bureaux of Economy, Trade and Industry, Division in Charge of Security Export Controls*
Postal Address	1-3-1 Kasumigaseki, Chiyoda-ku, Tokyo 100-8901, Japan
Telephone	+81-(0)3-3501-2800 / +81-(0)3-3501-2801 / +81-(0)3-3501-2841 / +81-(0)3-3501-0538 / +81-(0)3-3501-3679,
Email address	qqfcbf@meti.go.jp
Website	www.meti.go.jp/policy/anpo/index.html

Name of Organization	*Ministry of Foreign Affairs (MOFA)*
Postal Address	Kasumigaseki 2-2-1, Chiyoda-ku, Tokyo 100-8919, Japan
Telephone	+81-(0)3-3580-3311
Email address	webmaster@mofa.go.jp
Website	www.mofa.go.jp/policy/un/disarmament/index.html

Name of Organization	*Japan Ministry of Defence*
Postal Address	5-1, Honmura-cho, Ichigaya, Shinjuku-ku, Tokyo 162-8801, Japan
Telephone	+81-(0)3-5366-3111
Fax	+81-(0)3-5261-8018
Email address	infomod@mod.go.jp
Website	www.mod.go.jp/e/index.html

Name of Organization	*Japan Aerospace Exploration Agency (JAXA)*
Postal Address	7-44-1 Jindaiji Higashi-machi, Chofu-shi, Tokyo 182-8522, Japan
Telephone	+81-(0)422-40-3000
Website	http://global.jaxa.jp/

Name of Organization	*Japan Customs (Customs and Tariff Bureau)*
Postal Address	3-1-1 Kasumigaseki, Chiyoda-ku, Tokyo 100-8940, Japan
Telephone	(General MOF Inquiries): +81-(0)3-3581-4111
Website	http://www.customs.go.jp/english/index.htm

Sub-Section 2 Other

Name of Organization	*Center for Information on Security Trade Control (CISTEC)*
Postal Address	4F Shin-Toranomon Jitsugyou-Kaikann, 1-1-21 Toranomon Minato-ku Tokyo 105-0001, Japan
Website	http://www.cistec.or.jp/english/export/index.html

Name of Organization	*General Affairs Department*
Postal Address	
Telephone	+81-(0)3-3593-1148
Fax	+81-(0)3-3593-1137
Website	

Name of Organization	*Center for International Cooperation on Security Export Control*
Postal Address	
Telephone	+81-(0)3-3593-1149
Fax	+81-(0)3-3593-1642
Name of Organization	*Research Department*
Postal Address	
Telephone	+81-(0)3-3593-1146
Fax	+81-(0)3-3593-1138
Name of Organization	*Export Control Consulting Section, Exporter Services Department*
Postal Address	
Telephone	+81-(0)3-3593-1145
Fax	+81-(0)3-3593-1136
Website	

Name of Organization	*Japan Machinery Center for Trade and Investment*
Postal Address	4F Kikai-Shinkou-Kaikan, 3-5-8 Shiba-Koen, Minato-ku, Tokyo 105-0011, Japan
Telephone	+81-(0)3-3593-1145
Fax	+81-(0)3-3436-6455
Email address	info@jmcti.or.jp / kanemaru@jmcti.or.jp / hashimoto@jmcti.or.jp / arai@jmcti.or.jp
Website	www.jmcti.org/jmchomepage/english/index.htm

Name of Organization	*Kanto Bureau of Economy, Trade and Industry*
Postal Address	Saitama-Shintoshin Joint Government Building No. 1, 1-1 Shintoshin, Chuo-ku, Saitama-shi, Saitama 330-9715, Japan
Telephone	+81-(0)48-600-0262
Fax	+81-(0)48-601-1306
Website	http://www.kanto.meti.go.jp/data/english/index.html

Name of Organization	*Kansai Bureau of Economy, Trade and Industry*
Postal Address	2F, 3F and 5F Joint Government Building No. 1, 1-5-44 Ohtemae, Chuo-ku, Osaka 540-8535, Japan
Telephone	+81-(0)6-6966-6031 / +81-(0)6-6966-6032
Fax	+81-(0)6-6966-6087
Website	http://www.kansai.meti.go.jp/english/index.html

CHAPTER 13
Russian Federation

Iliya Zotkin, Ivan Davydov & Clémence Bastien

SECTION 1 TABLE OF CONTENTS

SECTION 2 EXECUTIVE SUMMARY

After the collapse of the Soviet Union in the early nineties, the Russian Federation progressively reshaped a comprehensive legal framework for export control. To govern the export of military products, the lower chamber of the Russian Parliament adopted on 3 July 1998 a Federal Law on 'Military-Technical Cooperation with Foreign States', which sets out the regulatory principles. Only state-owned or state-controlled companies which are authorized by virtue of the Federal Law on 'Military-Technical Cooperation with Foreign States' or by the President of the Russian Federation to participate in military-technical cooperation (MTC) are entitled to ship military products abroad. Moreover, the export control procedure requires not only authorization for the right to conduct foreign trade activities involving goods of a military nature but also the licensing of the actual import and export of such products. As for dual-use items, a 1999 Federal Law 'On Export Control' sets up a system in which a subject of licence is not a company but an export operation. Export control law goes beyond trade in physical goods and addresses foreign economic activity involving intellectual property, and establishes a 'catch-all' rule.

SECTION 3 INTRODUCTION: ELEMENTS OF CONTEXT

Sub-Section 1 Overall Philosophy

The Russian Federation is an important actor on the export control scene because it holds vast amounts of nuclear materials, weapons of mass destruction (WMD), dual-use technology and related know-how, and extensive stockpiles of weaponry. Export control policy contributes to international stability by establishing cooperation in areas such as reducing threats to global security and the use of WMD. Moreover, Russian export control regulation in particular acts as a barometer to gauge the state of Russia's relationship with the United States (US).

Russia was also motivated by economic reasons to set up a comprehensive export control regime, since the export control legislation permits a trade regulation rooted in criteria other than tariff policies. The objective is to enable Russian exporters actively to sell goods on foreign markets, while preventing dissemination of the knowledge behind those domestic technologies, which are the source of the country competitiveness. Controls on technologies are seen as particularly sensitive and of a great importance for Russia's competitiveness.

Sub-Section 2 Historical Outlook

Par. 1 Export Control Regimes within the Borders of the Former Soviet Union

Within the borders of the former Soviet Union, the transfer of military and dual-use goods is a very serious issue because illegal re-exports are known to take place (mainly in Central Asia). For this reason, the US provided export control support to the Russian Federation, Belarus, Kazakhstan and Ukraine (Nunn-Lugar Cooperative Threat

Reduction Program). The international community has called for the harmonization of export control procedures in the countries of the former Soviet Union. On 19 April 1999, an agreement between the Russian Federation and Belarus, calling for the development of a single procedure for export controls in both countries, entered into force. Further developments in the field of unification of the export control regime on the territory of the former Union of Soviet Socialist Republics (USSR) included the launch in 2010 of the Eurasian Economic Community Customs Union with participation of Russia, Belarus and Kazakhstan (the Customs Union). Within the framework of the Customs Union, Russia, Belarus and Kazakhstan have made certain efforts to create a unified export control system which resulted in the draft Agreement on the Procedure for Transfer of Military Goods between Customs Union Member States as well as across the Customs Border of the Customs Union. Currently this draft agreement is still under review by the Customs Union, but given the developments that have already taken place one can reasonably expect it to be adopted and come into effect in the foreseeable future.

Until then Russia as well as Belarus and Kazakhstan will rely on and utilize their internal export control systems based on the national legislations.

Par. 2 Legislative Changes in the Russian Federation

Before 1998, the Russian Federation did not have a comprehensive export control law. The Soviet Union did not feel that it was necessary to control the provision of military or dual-use goods. The legal basis for export control procedures rested on several presidential decrees, government regulation and a law on state regulation of foreign economic activity (1995). At the time, Russian exporters of controlled items were required to obtain two licences, one from the Federal Service for Currency and Export Control (VEK, under the authority of the Ministry of Defence (MoD)), and another from the Ministry of Trade. Since 1 December 2000 (the date on which the President of the Russian Federation adopted Decree n° 1953 'On Matters of Military-Technical Cooperation of the Russian Federation with Foreign Sates', which established the Russian Federation Committee for MTC with Foreign States), the only body competent to deliver a licence, i.e., the Russian Federation Committee for MTC with Foreign States (subsequently replaced by the Federal Service for MTC) has operated under the authority of the president of the Russian Federation and is a subordinate to the MoD.

With regard to dual-use goods and services, the Russian government issued a 'catch all' export control regulation on 22 January 1998 in the form of Governmental Decree n° 57 'On strengthening of control over export of dual-use goods and services associated with weapons of mass destruction and means of their delivery'. Under the decree, Russian firms are forbidden from selling dual-use goods if they know they will be used for WMD, even if the items are not specifically mentioned on 'control lists'. On 15 August 2005, the above regulation was substituted by a government Decree n° 517, which, however, retained the said 'catch all' rule. A comprehensive Federal Law 'On export control' took effect on 29 July 1999. The law provides, in its Article 6, that export control lists are drawn up by the federal executive bodies of the Russian Federation in consultation with the Parliament and industry representatives, and should be approved by the President. In this respect, the law provides a new foundation for export control policy, empowering other actors than those from simply the executive branch. Since August 2004, it has been the Federal Technical Export Control Service (FTECS), a successor to the Ministry of Economic Development and Trade (MEDT), operating under the authority of the President of the Russian Federation and being subordinate to the MoD, which is responsible for issuing licences.

Sub-Section 3 Participation in International Regimes

The following table displays the Russian Federation's participation status in existing export control related international treaties. Information is also given, where relevant, of the fact that the Russian Federation may have only acceded to a treaty (i.e., when it is not a founding member of the treaty or has not ratified it).

Where the treaty in question pre-dates 1991, it means that the Russian Federation inherited the status of the USSR.

Par. 1 Treaties and Regimes Dealing with Specific Items and Technologies

Table 13.1 Nuclear Weapons Treaties

Treaty Name	*Overall Status*	*Specific Status*	*Enforceable in the Russian Federation*
		Test Ban	
Limited Test Ban Treaty[953]	OS: 5 August 1963 EF: 10 October 1963	S: 5 August 1963 R: 10 October 1963	Yes
Comprehensive Nuclear Test Ban Treaty[954]	OS: 24 September 1996 EF: not in force	S: 24 September 1996 R: 30 June 2000	No
		Non-proliferation	
Nuclear Non-Proliferation Treaty[955]	OS: 1 July 1968 EF: 5 March 1970	S: 7 January 1970 R: 5 March 1970	Yes
IAEA Comprehensive Safeguards Agreement[956]	EF: 10 June 1985	N/A[957]	Yes

953. Treaty Banning Nuclear Weapon Tests in the Atmosphere, in Outer Space and Under Water, *UNTS*, vol. 480, 43.
954. UNGA, resolution 50\245.
955. Treaty on the Non-Proliferation of Nuclear Weapons, *UNTS*, vol. 729, 161.
956. Agreement Between the Agency and States Required in Connection with the Treaty on the Non-Proliferation of Nuclear Weapons (NPT), INFCIRC/153 (Corrected).
957. This treaty is a bilateral one and, accordingly, the differences that apply to multilateral treaties (between the overall status and the specific status) do not apply.

Treaty Name	*Overall Status*	*Specific Status*	*Enforceable in the Russian Federation*
IAEA Model Additional Protocol[958]	OS: 22 March 2000 EF: not in force	N/A[959]	No

Abbreviations: OS: Opened for signature; EF: Entry into force; S/R: Signature/Ratification; A: Accession.

Table 13.2 Biological and Chemical Weapons Treaties

Treaty Name	*Overall Status*	*Specific Status*	*Enforceable in the Russian Federation*
Geneva Protocol[960]	OS: 17 June 1925 EF: 8 February 1928	A: 5 April 1928	Yes
Biological Convention[961]	OS: 10 April 1972 EF: 26 March 1975	S: 10 April 1972 R: 26 March 1975	Yes
Chemical Convention[962]	OS: 13 January 1993 EF: 29 April 1997	S: 13 January 1993 R: 5 November 1997	Yes

Abbreviations: OS: Opened for signature; EF: Entry into force; S/R: Signature/Ratification; A: Accession.

Table 13.3 Conventional Arms

Treaty Name	*Overall Status*	*Specific Status*	*Enforceable the Russian Federation*
Protocol on Firearms to the Convention against Transnational Organized Crime[963]	DA: 31 May 2001 EF: 3 July 2005	-	No

958. Model Protocol Additional to the Agreement(s) Between State(s) and the Agency for the Application of Safeguards, INFCIRC/540 (Corrected).
959. This treaty is a bilateral one and, accordingly, the differences that apply to multilateral treaties (between the overall status and the specific status) do not apply.
960. Protocol for the Prohibition of the Use in War of Asphyxiating, Poisonous or Other Gases, and of Bacteriological Methods of Warfare, 94, *League of Nations Treaty Series*, n° 2138 (1929).
961. Convention on the Prohibition of the Development, Production and Stockpiling of Bacteriological (Biological) and Toxin Weapons and On Their Destruction, *UNTS*, vol. 1015, 163.
962. Convention on the Prohibition of the Development, Production, Stockpiling and Use of Chemical Weapons and on Their Destruction, Doc.CD/CW/WP.400/Rev.1.
963. Protocol against the Illicit Manufacturing of and Trafficking in Firearms, Their Parts and Components and Ammunition, supplementing the United Nations Convention against Transnational Organized Crime, A/RES/55/225.

Treaty Name	*Overall Status*	*Specific Status*	*Enforceable the Russian Federation*
Convention on anti-personnel mines[964]	OS: 18 September 1997 EF: 1 March 1999	–	No
Arms Trade Treaty	OS: 3 June 2013 EF: not in force	–	No

Abbreviations: OS: Opened for signature; DA: Date of adoption; EF: Entry into force; S/R: Signature/ Ratification; A: Accession.

Table 13.4 Multilateral Export Control Regimes

Regime Name	*Formation*	*Participation*
Zangger Committee[965]	1971	Yes
Nuclear Suppliers Group	1974	Yes
Australia Group	1985	No[966]
Missile Technology Control Regime	1987	Yes
Wassenaar Arrangement[967]	1994	Yes

Table 13.5 Others

Name	*Adoption*	*Participation*
UN Register on Conventional Arms[968]	9 December 1991	Yes[969]
Programme of Action on Small Arms and Light Weapons[970]	20 July 2001	Yes
International Code of Conduct[971]	25 November 2002	Yes

964. Convention on the Prohibition of the Use, Stockpiling, Production and Transfer of Anti-Personnel Mines and on their Destruction, *ATS, 1999, n°3.*
965. Non-Proliferation Treaty Exporters Committee (also called the Zangger Committee).
966. Russia does not participate in the A.G. but complies with the rules.
967. Wassenaar Arrangement on export controls for conventional arms and dual-use goods and technologies.
968. A/RES/46/36/L.
969. Information provided for the calendar years 1992 up to 2005.
970. Programme of Action to Prevent, Combat and Eradicate the Illicit Trade in Small Arms and Light Weapons in All Aspects, A/CONF.1992/15.
971. The Hague Code of Conduct against Ballistic Missile Proliferation, not yet published.

Par. 2 Treaties Dealing with Specific Areas

Table 13.6 International Zones

Treaty Name	*Overall Status*	*Specific Status*	*Enforceable in the Russian Federation*
Antarctic Treaty[972]	OS: 1 December 1959 EF: 23 June 1961	S: 12 January 1959[973] R: 21 June 1960	Yes
Outer Space Treaty[974]	OS: 27 January 1967 EF: 10 October 1967	S: 27 January 1967 R: 10 October 1967	Yes
Sea Bed Arms Control Treaty[975]	OS: 11 February 1971 EF: 23 June 1961	S: 11 February 1971 R: 18 May 1972	Yes
Moon agreement[976]	OS: 18 December 1979 EF: 11 July 1984	-	No
Convention on the Law of the Sea[977]	OS: 10 December 1982 EF: 16 November 1994	S: 10 December 1982 R: 22 January 1997	Yes

Abbreviations: OS: Opened for signature; EF: Entry into force; S/R: Signature/Ratification; A: Accession.

Table 13.7 Regional Nuclear Weapons-Free Zones

Treaty Name	*Overall Status*	*Specific Status*	*Enforceable in the Russian Federation*
Treaty of Tlatelolco[978]	OS: 14 February 1967 EF: 22 April 1967	-	No[979]
Treaty of Rarotonga[980]	OS: 6 August 1985 EF: 11 December 1986	-	No[981]
Treaty of Bangkok[982]	OS: 15 December 1995 EF: 27 March 1997	-	No

972. 402, *UNTS*, 7.
973. The Russian Federation succeeded the USSR.
974. Treaty on Principles Governing the Activities of States in the Exploration and Use of Outer Space, including the Moon and Other Celestial Bodies, *UNTS*, vol. 610, 205.
975. Treaty on the Prohibition of the Emplacement of Nuclear Weapons and other Weapons of Mass Destruction on the Seabed and The Ocean Floor and in the subsoil thereof, *UNTS*, vol. 955, 115.
976. Agreement governing the Activities of States on the Moon and Other Celestial Bodies, *ILM*, vol. 18, 1434.
977. Doc. A/CONF.62/122 and Corr.1-11.
978. Treaty for the Prohibition of Nuclear Weapons in Latin America and the Caribbean, *UNTS*, vol. 634, 326.
979. The Russian Federation signed and ratified the Protocol II (S: 18 May 1978, R: 8 Jan. 1979).
980. South Pacific Nuclear Free Zone Treaty, *ILM*, vol. 24, 1442.
981. The Russian Federation signed and ratified the Protocols II and III (S: 15 Dec. 1986, R: 21 Apr. 1988).

Treaty Name	*Overall Status*	*Specific Status*	*Enforceable in the Russian Federation*
Treaty of Pelindaba[983]	OS: 11 April 1996 EF: not in force	–	No[984]

Abbreviations: OS: Opened for signature; EF: Entry into force; S/R: Signature/Ratification; A: Accession.

On December 1992, the Parliament of the Republic of Tatarstan declared the region a nuclear-weapon-free zone, thereby committing itself to not producing or storing fissionable material or components of WMD.

SECTION 4 CONTROL REGIME

Sub-Section 1 Military Goods and Services

Par. 1 Overall Presentation

As far as military commodities are concerned, the State Duma, the lower chamber of the Russian Parliament, adopted on 3 July 1998[985] a Federal Law n° 114-FZ 'On Military-Technical Cooperation with Foreign States' setting the regulatory principles.[986] Under such federal law, only the following legal entities are entitled to participate in foreign trade activities in relation to military commodities:[987]

- 'national negotiators', i.e., specialized federal state unitary enterprises or, as the case may be, open joint-stock companies wholly owned by the federal Government or by a state corporation (today Rosoboronexport, which is owned by Russian Technologies State Corporation (RosTech) (see below)), which have permanent Presidential authorization to conduct foreign trade activities in the military sphere.
- RosTech.
- Russian developers and manufacturers of military products which have received an authorization (the duration of which does not, as a general rule, exceed five years) from the President of the Russian Federation.[988]

982. South East Asia Nuclear-Weapon-Free Zone Treaty, *ILM*, vol. 35, 635.
983. African Nuclear Weapon-Free Zone Treaty, *ILM*, vol. 35, 698.
984. The Russian Federation signed the Protocols I and II (S: 5 Nov. 1996).
985. Approved by the Federation Council, the upper chamber of the Russian Parliament, on 9 Jul. 1998.
986. Implemented by the Presidential Decree n° 1062 on 10 Sep. 2005.
987. The list of authorized legal entities is available at the official web page of the Federal Service on Military-Technical Cooperation with Foreign States (FSMTC) at http://www.fsvts.gov.ru/materials/2457DFEC607E6BC6C32575FA0024FB41.html/.
988. Russian developers and manufacturers of weapons and military products are entitled to conduct foreign trade activities with respect to military goods, provided that the federal

Each of the above legal entities must obtain a licence every time it wishes to export or import a specific item or service.[989] This licence is granted with reference to two lists: the 'state list' (which refers to the country of destination) and the 'equipment list' (which refers to the item itself).[990] The Federal Service on Military-Technical Cooperation with Foreign States (FSMTC) has a prominent role in the implementation of the MTC and is the body which ultimately issues the licence.[991] Russian arms export has been steadily growing during the last years and according to the Russian President, Mr Vladimir Putin, has reached USD 15.7 billion in 2013. Mr Putin has also reported increase of total portfolio of export orders which exceeded USD 49 billion.[992]

Anybody who breaches Russian law governing the export or import of military items exposes themselves to civil, administrative, and criminal law sanctions.

Sub-Par. 1 Requirements Prior to Any Specific Import/Export (i.e., Manufacturing Phase)

According to the Federal Law 'On Weapons', dated 13 December 1996, n°. 150-FZ, and the Federal Law 'On Licensing of Certain Types of Activities', dated 4 May 2011, n° 99-FZ development and manufacturing of weapons are subject to licensing. The aforementioned licensing is effected by the Ministry of Industry and Trade of the Russian Federation.

Sub-Par. 2 Requirements at the Import and/or Export Stage

I Goods

Imports are generally subject to the same regime as exports. Currently, there are no specific provisions as far as imports of military goods are concerned.

The export control of weapons and military equipment, as well as information, work, services, and results of intellectual activity and relevant exclusive rights, which are for military use, is conducted in accordance with laws of the Russian Federation in the sphere of MTC.[993]

In the military field, the import/export procedure is at once an authorization and a licence-based one. The Government has the power to issue any related regulation it deems necessary. A two-step procedure is in force. Once a national negotiator or a

Government owns at least 51% of the relevant developer's/manufacturer's shares and provided further that the remaining participation in such companies is held by Russian persons (legal entities and/or individuals).

989. Article 1 of the Federal Law 'On Military-Technical Cooperation with Foreign States'.
990. Article 6 of the Federal Law 'On Military-Technical Cooperation with Foreign States'.
991. Presidential Decree n° 1062, 10 Sep. 2005.
992. 'Vzglyad' business newspaper, 25 Apr. 2014, available at http://www.vz.ru/news/2014/4/25/683960.html/.
993. Federal law of the Russian Federation, adopted by the State Duma on 3 Jul. 1998 and approved by the Federation Council on 9 Jul. 1998 'On Military-Technical Cooperation of the Russian Federation With Foreign States'.

developer and/or manufacturer of military products[994] has obtained authorization from the President to conduct foreign trade activities involving military items, it must obtain a licence from the FSMTC,[995] to be able to export or import the items.

The FSMTC, operating under the authority of the President and being subordinate to the MoD, is the authority in charge of delivering licences, and checking whether the items to be exported are on the control lists. Licences for export and import on military goods shall be issued by the FSMTC on the basis of the decisions made by the President of the Russian Federation, or the federal Government, or the FSMTC. A single copy of the licence is issued and it cannot be transferred to a third party. It is compulsory for the importer/exporter to be in a position to produce the original copy of the licence in order to pass the customs check carried out by the Federal Customs Service.

II Services

Like goods, services related to military activities are subject to export control. Article 1 of the Federal Law 'On Military-Technical Cooperation with Foreign States' lists what such services are. Among them are:

- training in the development, production, operation, maintenance, modernization, and servicing of arms and military equipment;
- training and instruction of military and military-technical personnel of foreign states; and
- performance and/or participation in the performance of research, testing, development, and engineering in the creation, modernization and/or destruction of military products and means of protecting against WMD and conventional arms.

III Persons/Deemed Export

The release of certain technologies or products to a foreign national in the Russian Federation is 'deemed' to be an export to the home country of the foreign national, and triggers the export control procedures.

994. Noteworthy, since Russian Technologies State Corporation (RosTech) by virtue of the Federal Law 'On Military-Technical Cooperation with Foreign States' is expressly vested with the right to participate in MTC, it does not require a specific authorization to exercise such right.
995. The Federal Service for Military-Technical Cooperation (under the MoD). On 9 Mar. 2004 (Presidential Decree n° 314), it replaced the Russian Federation Committee for Military-Technical Cooperation with Foreign States (KVTS) established by the Presidential Decree n° 1953 on 1 Dec. 2000.

Par. 2 Control Lists

Equipment list:[996] the list of military products authorized for transfer to foreign entities is drawn up on the basis of recommendations by the Government. However, the President must approve the list.

State list:[997] the list of states to which the transfer of military products is authorized must also be approved by the President. He/she can restrict the number of partners for MTC by proscribing those destinations he/she deems unsafe.

The President can thus restrict or expand both the type of weapons transferable to selected countries, and the list of countries to which the listed military products can be transferred.

Par. 3 Licensing and Enforcement Authorities

MTC with other countries is regulated and implemented as described below.

The President of the Russian Federation is in charge of setting content and procedure guidelines in this field. He approves, enlarges or restricts the equipment and state lists, and establishes federal bodies to deal with MTC.

The Government of the Russian Federation implements the presidential guidelines, has the authority to conclude international agreements, and regulates domestic and foreign prices for military products.

Federal executive bodies implement presidential decisions and governmental regulations.

Russian MoD as well as any other state customer placing orders for military products also plays a significant role in the process. They receive a document package from the FSMTC and approve/disapprove the licence issuance. Their opinion is final. If their decision is negative, the applicant cannot be granted a licence. Before they make their decision, however, the licence applicant is entitled to submit further explanatory documents to support the application. During the review, the reviewing authorities will take into account the end-users, the technology involved and the item to be exported.

The FSMTC is ultimately in charge of issuing licences for military goods.

The procedure to import and export defence goods is summarized in Figure 13.1.

996. List of military products authorized for transfer to foreign entities, provided by the Governmental Decree n° 831 on 1 Dec. 2007 (List n° 1).
997. List of states to which the transfer of military products is authorized, provided by the Presidential Decree n° 831 on 1 Dec. 2007 (List n° 2).

Figure 13.1

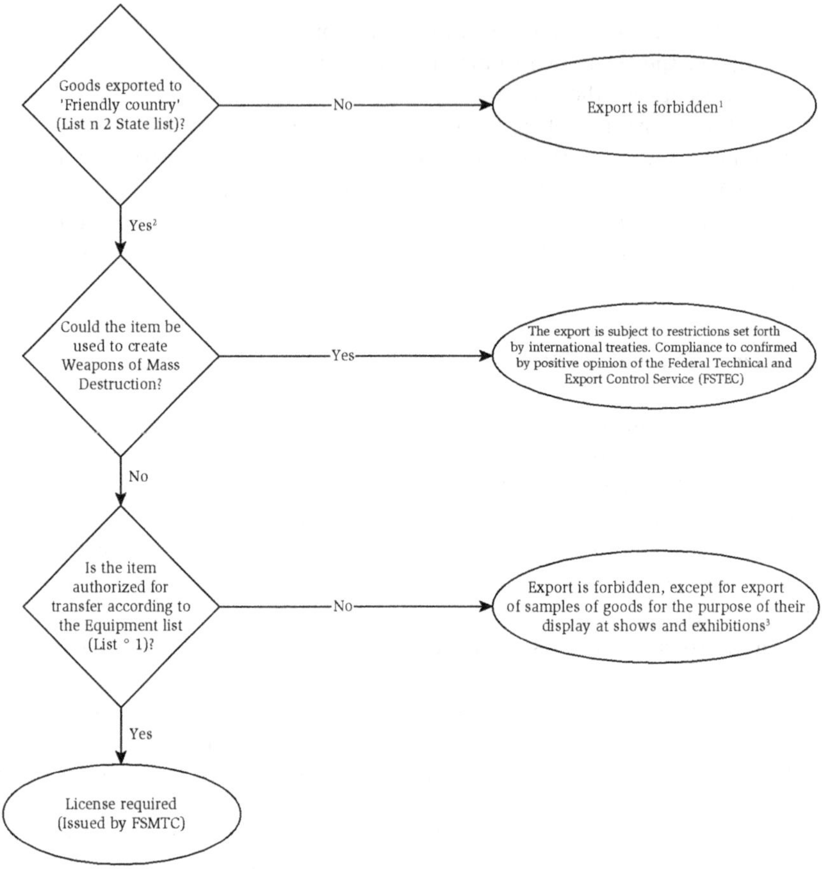

1. By way of exception the President of the Russian Federation can permit export of goods to countries not on List n° 2.
2. By way of exception the President of the Russian Federation can limit export of certain goods to selected 'Friendly countries'.
3. By way of exception the President of the Russian Federation can permit export of certain goods that are included into the Equipment list.

Par. 4 Sanctions, and Recourses Available to the Importer/Exporter

Anybody who breaches Russian law governing the export or import of military items exposes themselves to civil, administrative, and criminal law sanctions.

Sub-Par. 1 Export Control and the Criminal Code

Even before the existence of a consistent federal law, in July 1998, President Yeltsin had asked the Government to amend the Criminal Code 'regarding responsibility for the illegal distribution of technology, scientific and technical information, and services related to the manufacture of WMD and delivery missiles'. On 7 May 2002, President Putin signed a federal law[998] which amended Articles 188 and 189 of the Criminal Code and introduced new sanctions for trafficking and illegal exports of controlled items. Amendments to Article 188 expanded the list of items, the illicit trafficking of which is subject to criminal prosecution, to include radiation sources, fissile materials, and WMD. Article 189 was amended to expand the list of activities considered a crime under the Criminal Code and now includes any export or transaction by any person that may contribute to the development of WMD. Subsequently, Article 188 of the Criminal Code was declared void and substituted with Article 226.1. Article 226.1 has not changed the list controlled items, the illicit trafficking of which is subject to criminal prosecution as compared to the one previously stated in Article 188. Instead it has changed the scope of punishable illicit trafficking which now includes not only illicit trafficking of controlled items through the customs border of the Russian Federation but also illicit trafficking of controlled items through customs borders of the Customs Union (i.e., customs borders of Belarus and Kazakhstan).

Article 226.1 of the Criminal Code states that any party found guilty can be imprisoned for the term from three to seven years and additionally fined up to RUB 1 million (approximately EUR 21,000), or the amount of their entire income for the past five years. The sanctions take the form of a fine and/or a prison sentence (of up to twelve years). Persons found guilty for illegal exports of items contributing to development of WMD under Article 189 of the Criminal Code can be prohibited to occupy certain positions, imprisoned for the term of up to seven years or a fined up to RUB 1 million (approximately EUR 21,000), or the amount of their entire income for the past five years.

Sub-Par. 2 Export Control and Administrative Penalties

The Administrative Code of the Russian Federation entered into force in July 2002. Its Article 14.20 outlines penalties for violations of export control procedures. It states that transfers of goods, information or services, which can be used to develop WMD, without a licence (where licensing is required), in violation of the terms of a licence, or with an illegally obtained licence, are subject to penalties equal to the value of the goods, the information, and/or the services concerned with the illegal transaction, as well as optional confiscation of such goods and assets. A violation of the established accounting procedures for foreign transactions will result in penalties of up to RUB 2,000 (approximately EUR 42) for officials and up to RUB 20,000 for corporations (approximately EUR 420).

998. Adopted by the State Duma on 5 Apr. 2002, approved by the Federation Council on 23 Apr. 2002, and signed by Russian President Putin on 7 May 2002.

Sub-Section 2 Dual-Use Goods and Services

Par. 1 Overall Presentation

Federal Law n° 183-FZ 'On Export Control' (18 July 1999)[999] sets out Russia's dual-use export control policy, the competencies state bodies are vested with, and the rights, obligations and responsibilities of those wishing to carry out dual-use export activities. The law extended the scope of the control regime so that now not only is trade in physical goods subject to control but also foreign economic activity which involves an exchange of intellectual property. The law also established a 'catch-all' rule. If a product must be submitted to export control, a state assessment takes place to determine whether to issue a licence or not.[1000] The state assessment is conducted by the FTECS[1001] of the MoD, which is also the authority that will ultimately issue the licence.

Sub-Par. 1 Requirements Prior to Any Specific Import/Export (i.e., Manufacturing Phase)

Dual-use goods and services are referred to in the Federal Law 'On Export Control' as follows:

> crude resources, materials, equipment, scientific and technical information, work, services, and the results of intellectual activity (rights to them) that could, by virtue of their distinctive features and properties contribute substantially to the development of WMD, their delivery systems, and other types of weapons and military equipment, as well as products which are especially dangerous in terms of preparation and (or) execution of acts of terrorism.[1002]

The Federal Law 'On Export Control' establishes certain specific pre-export requirements relating to general licences for the export of dual-use commodities, i.e., licences which for a fixed period of time export of specified items to particular foreign end-users,[1003] without the need for additional governmental approvals.

999. With changes and updates: law n° 196-F3, 30 Dec. 2001, law n° 58-F3, 29 Jun. 2004, law n° 90-F3, 18 Jul. 2005, law n° 283-FZ, 29 Jun. 2007, law n° 318-FZ, 1 Dec. 2007, law n° 89-FZ, 7 May 2009, law n° 169-FZ, 1 Jul. 2011, law n° 242-FZ, 18 Jul. 2011 and law n° 409-FZ, 6 Dec. 2011.
1000. Article 21 of the Federal Law 'On export control', see *supra* n. 993.
1001. Decree of the President of the Russian Federation n° 1085, 16 Aug. 2004.
1002. Article 1 of the Federal Law 'On Export Control'.
1003. Noteworthy, general licences can only be issued if the dual-use goods that are subject to export and the relevant country of destination are included into the respective lists of goods and countries of destination with respect to which general licences may be issued and which are approved by the Government of the Russian Federation. Please see Article 19 of the Federal Law 'On Export Control'.

In particular, Article 19 of the law states that general licences will only be issued to legal entities with accredited Internal Compliance Programmes (ICP). These programmes are supposed to speed up the licence-delivering process.

No general licence will be delivered to an exporter which has not implemented an accredited ICP. An exporter without an accredited ICP is required to obtain a special single-use licence, which covers only one given product and destination.

Sub-Par. 2 Requirements at the Import and/or Export Stage

I Goods

In order to determine whether dual-use goods or technology are subject to export control (and therefore whether an import/export licence is needed), it is necessary to obtain an independent classification of the item.[1004] This classification stage is compulsory.[1005] The item may be classified through the exporter's ICP[1006] or by contracting with an organization authorized to grant official classifications. For the purpose of the classification assessment, the exporter must provide a series of documents, which include information on the destination state and, if available, information on an end-user.

Transactions involving controlled products are subject to state expertise carried out by expert groups at the FTECS,[1007] as per the general rule, within thirty days. Expertise of transactions is carried out on grounds of the documents submitted for the purposes of obtaining of a relevant export control licence.[1008]

As per the general rule, an export licence issued by the FTECS is required for the purposes of export of controlled goods. Certain controlled goods may be temporarily exported from the Russian Federation without actual transfer to a foreign party on grounds of an authorization of the Export Control Commission (ECC).[1009]

1004. The assessment procedure is ruled by Governmental Decree n° 477, 21 Jun. 2001, modified by Governmental Decree n° 731, 3 Oct. 2002, Decree n° 54, 4 Feb. 2005, Decree n° 384, 22 May 2008, Decree n° 654, 3 Sep. 2008, Decree n° 484, 15 Jun. 2009, Decree n° 1002, 8 Dec. 2010, Decree n° 1201, 30 Dec. 2010, Decree n° 712, 23 Aug. 2011, Decree n° 1105, 22 Dec. 2011 and Decree n° 730, 5 Sep. 2011, http://fstec.ru/component/content/article/99-eksportnyj-kontrol/zakonodatelstvo/postanovleniya/332-postanovlenie-pravitelstva-rossijskoj-federatsii-ot-21-iyunya-2001-g-n-477.

1005. Article 24 of the Federal Law 'On export control', see *supra* n. 993.

1006. FTECS delivers accreditation to enterprises which established internal compliance programmes.

1007. 'Rules for conducting state expertise of foreign trade transactions with goods, information, works, services and results of intellectual activity (right to them) subject to export control' approved by Governmental Decree n° 294, 16 Apr. 2001.

1008. Item 4 of 'Rules for conducting state expertise of foreign trade transactions with goods, information, works, services and results of intellectual activity (right to them) subject to export control'.

1009. Item 13 of 'Regulations on exercise of control over foreign economic activities with involving dual-use goods and technologies which may be used for production of weapons and military equipment' approved by the Governmental Decree n° 447, 7 Jun. 2001.

The documents that an exporter must submit to obtain an export licence include the elements below:[1010]

- An official application form, duly completed.
- A copy of the export/import contract. The contract must specify the end-user, the purpose of the export/import, and the country in which the end-use will take place.
- A copy of the agreement between the importer and the exporter, if the person asking for a licence is an intermediary.
- Written obligations by an end-user in relation to use of controlled products and, in certain cases, a document by governmental authority of a relevant state, supporting such end-user's obligations.
- Various other supporting documents about the person asking for a licence.

Article 20 of the Federal Law 'On export control' is a 'catch-all' clause. Russian exporters are required to renounce contacts with foreign parties:

> if they have valid reasons to believe that the goods, information, work, service and the results of intellectual activity will be used by a foreign party for the development of WMD and their delivery systems or for the purpose of preparation and (or) implementation of acts of terrorism.

Russian authorities understand this provision to mean that exporters should ensure that their foreign partners will use the technology acquired for civil purposes only.

After reviewing the documents, the FTECS decides whether or not to issue the licence. The initial licence period cannot exceed twelve months but the national negotiator can apply for extensions. As discussed above in Sub-Par. 1. of Par. 1. of this Sub-Section 2, the export licences delivered are of two types: general licences and single-use licences.

For import activities, import of controlled goods and technologies in cases where it is necessary to ensure the security of the state and the performance of international obligations of the Russian Federation, is subject to licensing. Relevant list of goods and technologies, imports of which is subject to licensing is approved by the Government of the Russian Federation on grounds of the lists of controlled goods and technologies.[1011]

According to the Russian Tax Code,[1012] which among other things, establishes the amounts of fees and duties collected by the state authorities for performance of their functions, the licensing fee amounts to RUB 6,000 (approximately EUR 126).

1010. Items 8-10 of 'Regulations on licensing of foreign economic operations involving goods, information, works, services and results of intellectual activity (right to them) subject to export control', approved by Governmental Decree n° 691, 15 Sep. 2008.
1011. Article 19 of the Federal Law 'On Export Control'.
1012. Item 92 Article 333.33 of the Tax Code of the Russian Federation.

Controlled goods are always subject to customs clearance and inspection, which customs officials initiate after the entity authorized to participate in operations with controlled goods has shown them original copy of a licence or an authorization.

According to the Federal Law 'On Export Control', the decision whether to issue the licences has to intervene before forty-five days[1013] from the date of receipt of licence application material (these forty-five days include the thirty days mentioned above and dedicated to the independent classification). However, the period of time can be shorter or can take up to three months, depending on whether the exporter is new to the process, the end-user is known and the file is complete. Industrials report that over the past few years, there has been no significant improvement in shortening the time of the licensing process.

II Services, Tangible and Intangible Data

Like goods, services, tangible and intangible data are subject to export control.

Russian authorities pay particular attention to technology transfers. 'Technology' is defined as any information necessary to the production, elaboration or use of any military product. A technology transfer can take the form of a 'data transfer', but it can also take the form of any 'technical help'. The following are considered to be 'data': technical drawings, diagrams, printed copies, models, formulae, charts, technical specifications and instructions (either on paper or in any other means). The following is considered to be 'technical help': staff training, education, exchange of production knowledge and consulting services.

The control of intangible technology is complicated because the means of conveying it are difficult to identify and control (software medium, specific context of the transfer...). The Russian Federation has attempted as far as possible to subject to control as wide a range as possible of intangible technology transfers: for example, exchange of data through any form of visual contact (at scientific conferences, meetings, talks, scientific exchanges, lectures, consultations, demonstrations, the education of foreign students, etc.), and any form of electronic/electric transmission (fax, telephone, emails) requires a licence (the same licence as for military goods transfers).

However, elements dealing with fundamental scientific research are not explicitly included in the scope of export control. This creates the difficulty of having to distinguish between fundamental science and applicable science, and the boundary between the two is sometimes blurred and constantly moving.

III Persons/Deemed Export

The release of certain technologies or products to a foreign national in the Russian Federation is 'deemed' to be an export to the home country of the foreign national, and triggers the export control procedures. The Federal Law 'On Export Control' deals not

1013. Forty-five days is a general term that may be changed by the underlying legislation.

only with the supply of goods and technology to foreign countries but also with their transfer to foreigners on the territory of the Russian Federation.

In addition to the concept of 'deemed export', the Russian Federation law does not require a licence from the FTECS for the temporary export of goods to a Russian person (body or entity) outside of the territory of the Russian Federation, but only an authorization from the ECC.[1014]

Par. 2 Control Lists

The President, at the Government's request, approves the lists of controlled goods and technologies by issuing an edict. Currently, 'special' (as opposed to 'general') licences are required if the item falls within one of the six lists below.

- List of the dual-use goods and technologies which can be used for the manufacturing of armaments and military hardware and which are subject to export control.[1015]
- List of equipment, materials and technologies used in developing missile weapons and which are subject to export control.[1016]
- List of microorganisms, toxins, equipment and technologies subject to export control.[1017]

  List of chemicals, equipment and technologies with potential use in the development of chemical weapons and which are subject to export control.[1018]
- List of the dual-use equipment, materials and technologies which can be used for nuclear purposes and which are subject to export control.[1019]

1014. Presidential Decree n° 468, 25 Apr. 2005, http://fstec.ru/component/content/article/98-eksportnyj-kontrol/zakonodatelstvo/ukazy/317-ukaz-prezidenta-rossijskoj-federatsii-ot-25-aprelya-2005-g-n-468 (in Russian). For the composition of the ECC, see http://fstec.ru/component/content/article/98-eksportnyj-kontrol/zakonodatelstvo/ukazy/320-ukaz-prezidenta-rossijskoj-federatsii-ot-17-sentyabrya-2008-g-n-1380.
1015. Presidential Decree n° 1661, 17 Dec. 2011, http://fstec.ru/component/content/article/98-eksportnyj-kontrol/zakonodatelstvo/ukazy/319-ukaz-prezidenta-rossijskoj-federatsii-ot-17-dekabrya-2011-g-n-1661 (in Russian). Noteworthy, Section 5 of the relevant List expressly lists dual-use goods import of which is subject to control (in the form of licensing) necessary to ensure security of state.
1016. Presidential Decree n° 1005, 8 Aug. 2001, //fstec.ru/component/content/article/98-eksportnyj-kontrol/zakonodatelstvo/ukazy/322-ukaz-prezidenta-rossijskoj-federatsii-ot-8-avgusta-2001-g-n-1005 (in Russian).
1017. Presidential Decree n° 1083, 20 Aug. 2007, http://fstec.ru/component/content/article/98-eksportnyj-kontrol/zakonodatelstvo/ukazy/318-ukaz-prezidenta-rossijskoj-federatsii-ot-20-avgusta-2007-g-n-1083 (in Russian).
1018. Presidential Decree n° 1082, 28 Aug. 2001, http://fstec.ru/component/content/article/98-eksportnyj-kontrol/zakonodatelstvo/ukazy/314-ukaz-prezidenta-rossijskoj-federatsii-ot-28-avgusta-2001-g-n-1082 (in Russian).
1019. Presidential Decree n° 36, 14 Jan. 2003, http://fstec.ru/component/content/article/98-eksportnyj-kontrol/zakonodatelstvo/ukazy/325-ukaz-prezidenta-rossijskoj-federatsii-ot-14-yanvarya-2003-g-n-36 (in Russian).

- List of nuclear materials, equipment, special non-nuclear materials and corresponding technologies subject to export control.[1020]

Par. 3 Licensing and Enforcement Authorities

The different missions of governmental entities in the sphere of export control are defined in Article 8 through Article 11 of the Federal Law 'On Export Control'.

The President defines basic policy guidelines, ensures coordination between the various governmental agencies involved in the process of export control and approves the lists of controlled goods.

The Government implements export control policy (including compliance with international regimes) and determines procedures for conducting foreign trade in controlled items.

The FTECS[1021] under the authority of the MoD plays a prominent role: it issues licences for the export of dual-use and critical nuclear materials. The FTECS has seven regional branches across the territory of the Russian Federation.[1022]

The ECC coordinates policy, implements legislation and settles disputes between different administrative bodies.

A series of ministries and federal agencies intervene in the licence-delivering process: they receive the document package from the FTECS and approve/disapprove the licence issuance. Their opinion is mandatory. In the event of a negative decision, the applicant will not be granted a licence. The applicant has, at this stage of the process, the opportunity to support its case by submitting explanatory documents. When deciding whether the licence should be granted, the bodies involved in the inter-agency review take into account several criteria. They consider the end-user, the technology and the item to be exported.

Par. 4 Sanctions and Recourses Available to the Importer/Exporter

Chapter VI of the Federal Law 'On Export Control'[1023] describes the following types and forms of violations in the sphere of export control, the commitment of which entails imposition of sanctions:[1024]

- performance, without a licence or permit, of foreign economic operations involving goods, information, work, services, and the results of intellectual activity which are subject to export control;

1020. Presidential Decree n° 202, 14 Feb. 1996, http://fstec.ru/component/content/article/98-eksportnyj-kontrol/zakonodatelstvo/ukazy/324-ukaz-prezidenta-rossijskoj-federatsii-ot-14-fevralya-1996-g-n-202 (in Russian).
1021. Presidential Decree n° 1085, 16 Aug. 2004.
1022. For the locations, addresses and phone number, see http://fstec.ru/obshchaya-informatsiya/struktura#.
1023. See *supra* n. 993.
1024. Article 30 of the Federal Law 'On export control'. See *supra* n. 993.

- submission of forged documents, or documents containing false information, to obtain a licence or permit for foreign economic operations with goods, information, work, services, and the results of intellectual activity subject to export control;
- violation of the requirements and terms of licences or permits for foreign economic operations with goods, information, work, services, and the results of intellectual activity subject to export control;
- non-compliance or improper compliance with the instructions of the special authorized federal agency of the executive branch in the sphere of export control;
- creation of obstacles to keep the officials of federal agencies from the executive branch, exercising powers in the sphere of export control, from performing their duties;
- unwarranted refusal to furnish information, which has been requested by federal agencies of the legislative and executive branches for the purposes of export control, or the deliberate distortion or concealment of this information;
- violation of the established procedure for keeping records of foreign economic transactions with goods, information, work, services, and the results of intellectual activity, for the purposes of export control.

Officials of organizations and citizens who are guilty of violating the law of the Russian Federation with respect to export control of controlled goods and services will be subject to criminal, administrative, and civil legal penalties.[1025] An organization violating the law can be deprived of the right to exercise some foreign economic/trade activities, for a maximum duration of three years.[1026] The possibility of recourse exists in the event the above-mentioned sanctions are applied.[1027]

The procedure to import and export dual-use goods is summarized in Figure 13.2.

1025. Article 31 of the Federal Law 'On export control'.
1026. Article 32 of the Federal Law 'On export control'.
1027. Article 33 of the Federal Law 'On export control'.

Figure 13.2

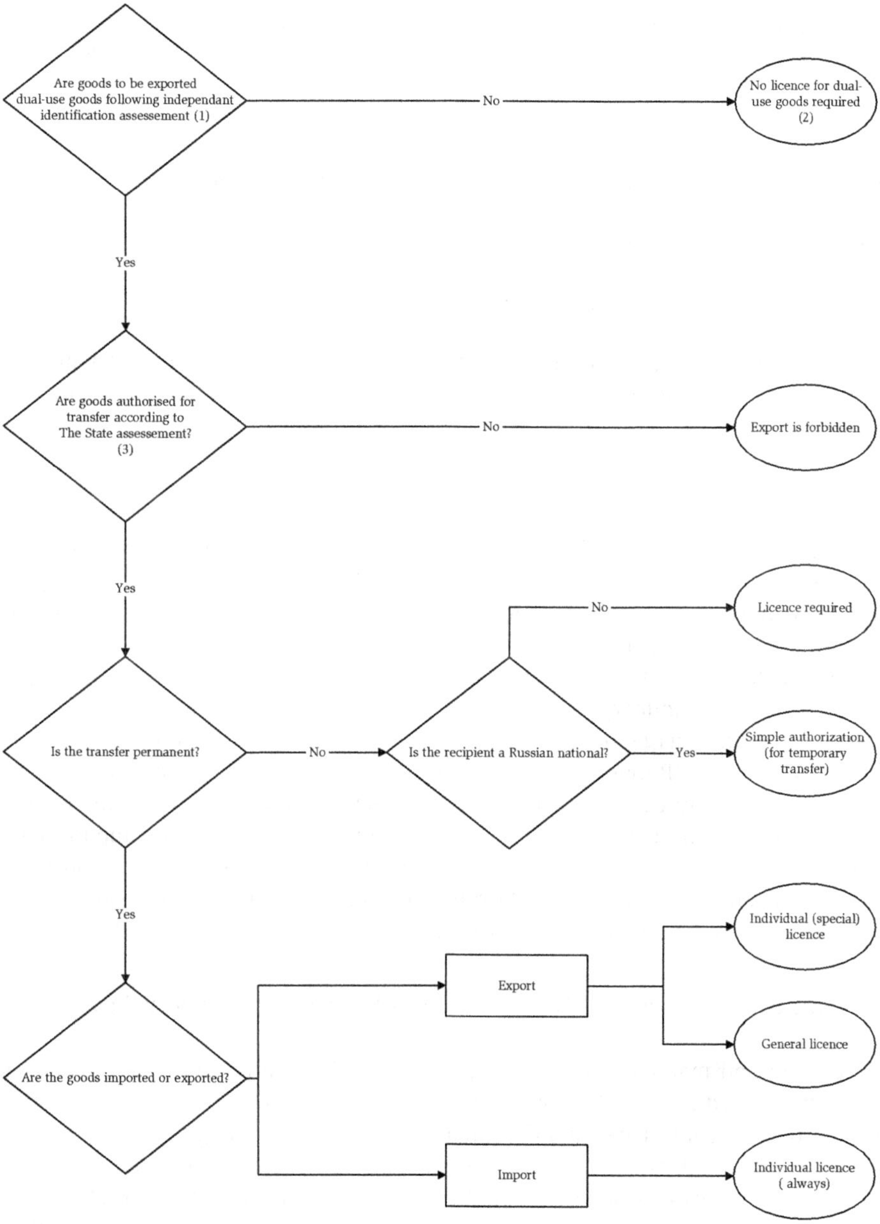
Are goods to be exported dual-use goods following independant identification assessement (1)
No
No licence for dual-use goods required (2)
Yes
Are goods authorised for transfer according to The State assessement? (3)
No
Export is forbidden
Yes
No
Licence required
Is the transfer permanent?
No
Is the recipient a Russian national?
Yes
Simple authorization (for temporary transfer)
Yes
Individual (special) licence
Export
General licence
Are the goods imported or exported?
Import
Individual licence (always)

1) Decree n°477 on 21 June 2001 (modified by Decree n°731 on 3 October 2002 and n°54 on 4 February 2005).
2) Export is not subject to control (other rules may apply):
   (i) military use regime;
   (ii) quotas and licence for some specific economical operations;
   (iii) spedfic control regime (metals, precious stones, narcotics containing products, etc);
   (iv) export free of control (customs only).

See military goods flow chart supra.

SECTION 5 SPECIFICITIES/SPACE-RELATED PROVISIONS

Sub-Section 1 Specificities of the Control Regime

Par. 1 Military Goods and Services

Only certain specific persons (state-owned or state-controlled companies which are specially authorized to conduct such activities) have the right to ship military products abroad.

Sub-Par. 1 Government Intermediary

Presidential Decree n° 162, dated 10 September 2005, sets out the actors in charge of controlling the export and import of military goods. Rosoboronexport State Corporation, which was founded by a presidential order, replaced a collection of state intermediaries ('Rosvoorouzhenie', 'Promexport', 'Rossiskie Tekhnologii'), and became the sole arms trade intermediary state agency ('national negotiator') with respect to the full scope of military goods/services that may be exported and/or imported. It results from the merger in 2000 of two Federal State Unitary Enterprises ('Rosvoorouzhenie' and 'Promexport'). It operates in more than seventy countries, and is controlled by the MoD. Rosoboronexport accounts for more than 80% of the Russian Federation's military exports.[1028] It is officially involved in the export/import operations for military goods/services only. It is also entitled to deal with dual-use products, but it has no enforcement powers. The remaining Russian military exports is conducted by developers and manufacturers of weapons and military products and RosTech.

Sub-Par. 2 Developers and Manufacturers of Weapons and Military Products

Developers and manufacturers of weapons and military products have the right to conduct foreign trade activities, on condition that the federal Government owns at least 51% of the company shares and that the rest of the shares belong to Russian persons (entities and/or individuals). Russian individuals are not allowed to conduct MTC.

At the end of the Nineties, about fifteen firms were given the right to get involved in foreign trade, and to sell their products abroad directly. Such companies include Antei (missiles, Moscow), Arsenyev Company (military helicopters, Arsenyev, Primorsky krai), Gidromash (plane mechanics, Nizhni Novgorod), Murom (armoured vehicle

1028. Official web page of Rosoboronexport http://www.roe.ru/roe/rus_status.html/.

and tanks, Murom, Vladimirskaia oblast, Rubin (submarines, St Petersburg) and Metrovagonmash (air defence, Moscow). The list of persons that possess the right to engage in MTC was subsequently refined and currently includes eighteen developers and manufacturers of weapons and military products including (among others):[1029] Russian Aircraft Corporation MiG (Military aircraft, Moscow), OJSC NPO Pribor (small caliber ammunitions, Moscow), Gas-Turbine Engineering Research and Production Center 'Salut' (aircraft engines, Moscow), Scientific Research and Production Center 'Kvant' (radio-electronic warfare products, Veliky Nogorod), JSC Concern 'Almaz-Antey' (anti-aircraft defence systems, Moscow) and Admiralty Shipyard (naval war-ships, Saint Petersburg).

Sub-Par. 3 Russian Technologies State Corporation

RosTech was founded in 2007 to, among other things, promote the development, production and export of high-tech industrial products for the defence sector and was thus granted the same year the status of a person eligible to participate in MTC.[1030] The activities of RosTech in the sphere of MTC follow its principal function stated above and are limited to advertising activities, marketing activities as well as organizing, holding and participating in exhibitions of military goods.

Par. 2 Re-exports and Temporary Exports

The Russian government established procedures for the temporary export and the re-export of controlled items.

According to the Federal Law 'On Export Control',[1031] temporary exports of controlled goods that do not involve a transfer to a foreign party (particularly if the goods are intended for display in exhibits or for personal use), do not require a licence, but only require an authorization. The only conditions are that the goods remain under the direct control of the Russian party taking them out of the Russian Federation, and that they are returned in due time.

As regards re-exports, re-exports are covered under the same rules as exports.

Par. 3 Intellectual Property and Patent Rights

Sub-Par. 1 FAPRID and the Licensing Process

In September 1998, government resolution[1032] established that intellectual property rights related to military, nuclear, and dual-use technologies that are developed with

1029. The list of persons authorized to engage in MTC is available at the official web page of Federal Service on Military-Technical Cooperation at: http://www.fsvts.gov.ru/materials/2457DFEC607E6BC6C32575FA0024FB41.html (in Russian).

1030. Federal law n° 271-FZm dated 26 Nov. 2007 'On introduction of amendments into Articles 9 and 12 of the Federal Law 'Military-Technical Cooperation with Foreign States''.

1031. Article 19 of the Federal Law 'On export control'.

1032. Resolution n° 1132 on 29 Sep. 1998.

the help of State funding belong to the State. The Federal Service for Intellectual Property is in charge of dealing with the government's interest in this field, through its intermediary agency the Federal Agency for the Legal Protection of the Results of Intellectual Activity in the Sphere of Military, Special, and Dual-Use Technology (FAPRID).

The FAPRID has a consultative role in the licence attribution process: it approves the export and submits its approval to the licence-delivering authority. Further, it has a monopoly over the right to register intellectual property rights and gather 'royalties' from the exporters on behalf of the state.

Sub-Par. 2 Patent Regulation

In 1999, FAPRID investigated cases[1033] in which Russian citizens had illegally patented Russian technology with potential applications in the military field. Official representatives said those who had filed the patents in the US could be charged with violating Article 189 of the Russian Criminal Code (which prohibits the illegal export of technologies used in the production of WMD).

Par. 4 Means of Submitting Licence Applications

There are currently no electronic licensing procedures. Most of the time, the exporters must physically carry licence applications and other documents to Moscow in order to obtain the required signature.

Par. 5 Effectiveness of the Implementation of the Russian Export Control Rules

The Russian Federation has made great progress in improving its system of laws and regulations with respect to the licensing and controlling of its sensitive exports. Nonetheless, it faces major problems in implementing its system of controls.[1034] Implementation could be improved if the actors involved were aided in understanding the system. Thinking along these lines, the Russian government established and authorized[1035] twenty-one regional Classification Centres, in order to assist exporters

1033. Yuriy Gaydukov, general director of the FAPRID, told a press conference on 3 Jun. 1999, Vremya-MN newspaper reported.

1034. 'Nuclear Non-Proliferation Concerns and Export Controls in Russia, Testimony before the Governmental Affairs Subcommittee on International Security, Proliferation, and Federal Services', by David Albright, President, Institute for Science and International Security (ISIS), 6 Jun. 2002.

1035. In accordance with Governmental Decree n° 477, 21 Jun. 2001. The current list of classification centres is available at the official web of FTECS at http://fstec.ru/eksportnyj-kontrol/nezavisimaya-identifikatsionnaya-ekspertiza/.

and customs officials in determining whether items are subject to licensing. Until now, only the Russian Academy of Science (Moscow, Novosibirsk, Vladivostok), the Centre for Industry Development Projects (Saint Petersburg), Ural Federal University named after the first President of Russia B. N. Yeltsin (Yekaterinburg), Samara State Technical University (Samara), FGUP 'Gostekhstroy' (Moscow), Central Research and Development Institute for Chemistry and Mechanical Science (Moscow), South Ural State University (Chelyabinsk) and Southern Federal University (Rostov-on-Don) have an expertise covering the full range of controlled goods. All other Classification Centres have limited scope of review associated with their field of specialization.

Sub-Section 2 Space-Related Provisions in the Control Regime

Par. 1 Roles of the Licensing and Enforcement Authorities

As far as export control is concerned, the Federal Space Agency cooperates closely with the FSMTC, the licence-delivering authority for military products.

The MoD certifies space technologies intended for use in a military context. The aim of this certification is to check that space technologies match the requirements of federal laws.

Par. 2 Details of the Regime Relating to Space Activities

In the Russian Federation, space activities are subject to a special licence, which is issued only once an investigation has been carried out. This investigation is specific to the context of space technologies and is different to the investigation carried out for the export control of other products. It aims, among other things, at establishing whether the item is subject to control or not.

No separate department has been specifically created in the Russian Space Agency (Roskosmos) to deal with export control issues. The department that deals with international cooperation also covers export control matters.

SECTION 6 SANCTIONS AND EMBARGOES

Sub-Section 1 Participation of the Russian Federation in Embargoes and Other Related Sanctions

The following table displays the Russian Federation's participation in embargoes and other related sanctions imposed in relation to military goods and services and dual-use goods and services as at.

Table 13.8

Country Affected	*Sanctions Introduced*	*Term of Effect*
The Islamic Republic of Iran[1036]	prohibition of export, transit and transfer of certain nuclear materials, related goods and technologies, certain military goods which may make activities of Iran in the nuclear sphere possible and promote development of missile weapons and prohibition of technical, financial or other assistance associate with supply, export, transfer manufacturing or use of aforementioned above; prohibition of investment by Iran, its citizens and companies and controlled entities in any business activity located in Russia and relating to extraction of uranium, production or use of nuclear materials and technologies, delivery systems and special controlled non-nuclear materials and technologies; prohibition of entry and transit of listed individuals; limitations in relation to Iranian banks and other listed entities; restriction of certain activities in Iran where there are grounds to believe that such activities will favour sensible Iranian nuclear related activity or development of nuclear weapon delivery systems.	until special resolution
Liberia[1037]	prohibition of sale, supply or transportation by Russian air and sea vessels of weapons and related goods and prohibition of any assistance (including, amongst other, financial) relating to military activities to any non-governmental parties or individuals operating in Liberia; prohibition of entry and transit of certain individuals.	until special resolution

1036. In accordance with Presidential Decree n° 1593, 28 Nov. 2007 'On measures for implementation of resolutions of the UN Security Council n° 1737 of 23 Dec. 2006 and n° 1747 of 24 Mar. 2007'; Presidential Decree n° 682, 5 May.2008 'On measures for implementation of resolution of the UN Security Council n° 1803, 3 Mar. 2008'; Presidential Decree n° 1154, 22 Sep, 2010 'On measures for implementation of resolution of the UN Security Council n°1929, 9 Jun, 2010'.

1037. In accordance with Presidential Decree n° 1051, 23 Aug. 2010 'On measures for implementation of resolution of the UN Security Council n° 1903, 17 Dec. 2009'; Presidential Decree n° 297, 2 Mar. 2004 'On measures for implementation of resolution of the UN Security Council n° 1521, 22 Dec. 2003'; Presidential Decree n° 911, 21 Aug. 2006 'On measures for implementation of resolutions the UN Security Council n° 1683 of 13 Jun. 2006 and n° 1689 of 20 Jul. 2003'.

Country Affected	*Sanctions Introduced*	*Term of Effect*
Eritrea[1038]	prohibition of export, sale, supply or transportation to Eritrea by Russian air and sea vessels and specified individuals and entities of weapons, related goods and military equipment and prohibition of any assistance (including, amongst other, financial) relating to military activities; prohibition of purchase of any goods or receipt of assistance specified above from Eritrea; prohibition of entry and transit of certain individuals; prohibition of financial operations with assets of specified individuals and entities.	until special resolution
Somalia[1039]	prohibition of export to Somalia of any military goods; prohibition of financing of purchases and deliveries of military goods to Somalia or specified individuals or rendering any assistance (including, amongst other, financial) of military technical nature or services relating to training of military and military-technical personnel; prohibition of entry and transit of certain individuals; prohibition of financial operations with assets of specified individuals and entities.	until special resolution
Democratic People's Republic of Korea[1040]	prohibition of purchase in DPRK and transportation by Russian air and sea vessels of any weapons and related goods and of any assistance (including, amongst other, financial) in connection with manufacturing, sales, delivery or operation of weapons or related goods; prohibition of export and transit to DPRK, transportation by Russian air and sea vessels of any weapons or related goods and of rendering of any assistance (including, amongst other, financial) in connection with manufacturing, sales, delivery or operation of weapons or related goods, except for firearms, light weapons and related goods;	until special resolution

1038. In accordance with Presidential Decree n° 933, 22 Jul. 2010 'On measures for implementation of resolution of the UN Security Council n° 1907, 23 Dec. 2009'.

1039. In accordance with Presidential Decree n° 516, 24 Apr. 2010 'On measures for implementation of resolution of the UN Security Council n° 1844, 20 Nov. 2008'.

1040. In accordance with Presidential Decree n° 381, 27 Mar. 2010 'On measures for implementation of resolution of the UN Security Council n° 1874, 12 Jun. 2009'; Presidential Decree n° 665, 27 May 2007 'On measures for implementation of resolution of the UN Security Council n° 1718, 14 Oct. 2006'.

Country Affected	*Sanctions Introduced*	*Term of Effect*
	prohibition of export and transit to DPRK, transportation by Russian air and sea vessels of listed goods, materials, equipment and technologies determined by the UN Security Council and its Committee, which may facilitate DPRK's nuclear, ballistic missiles or other WMD related programmes, except for certain goods used for medical purposes; prohibition of rendering financial services, transfers of any financial or other assets or resources to, through or from Russia or to Russian individuals or entities, which may facilitate DPRK's nuclear, ballistic missiles or other WMD related programmes; prohibition to undertake obligations relation to disbursement of subsidies, financial assistance or preferential loans to DPRK, except for purposes relating to humanitarian activities, denuclearization or the needs of civilians; prohibition of any financial assistance to trade with DPRK, if such may facilitate DPRK's nuclear, ballistic rockets or other WMD related programmes; prohibition of entry and transit of listed individuals.	
Democratic Republic of Congo[1041]	prohibition of export and transit, transportation by Russian air and sea vessels of any weapons to Congolese militia and military groups, expect for the Government of Congo, and of rendering any military assistance to and training of such parties; prohibition of entry and transit of listed individuals; freezing of cash and other assets of certain listed individuals.	until special resolution

1041. In accordance with Presidential Decree n° 1490, 17 Oct. 2008 'On measures for implementation of resolution of the UN Security Council n° 1807, 31 Mar. 2009'.

Sub-Section 2 Regime of the Embargoes and Related Sanctions in the Russian Federation

The regime of the embargoes and related sanctions is governed by Federal Law n° 164-FZ dated 9 Dec. 2003 'On principles of state regulation of foreign economic activity' (as subsequently amended) and Federal Law n° 281-FZ dated 30 Dec. 2006 'On special economic measures'.

Pursuant to Federal Law n° 164-FZ dated 8 December 2003 'On principles of state regulation of foreign economic activity', the President of the Russian Federation is entitled to restrict foreign trade in goods, services and intellectual property if required to ensure participation of the Russian Federation in international sanctions imposed in accordance with the UN Charter. The Government of the Russian Federation is entitled to adopt restrictive measures in order to support the equilibrium of the payment balance of the Russian Federation. Additionally, reciprocal restrictive measures may be adopted by the Government of the Russian Federation, including but not limited to the case where a foreign state is in breach of its obligations under international treaties, undertakes measures, which contradict the economic interests of the Russian Federation or its constituent entities or political interests, or fails to provide adequate and effective protection of interests of Russian parties.

Pursuant to Federal Law n° 281-FZ dated 30 December 2006 'On special economic measures', relevant measures are aimed at the protection of the interests and the security of the Russian Federation, mitigation or minimization of threats to rights and freedoms of its citizens. Special economic measures may be introduced by the President of the Russian Federation. The scope of such measures includes prohibition of actions in relation to a foreign state, foreign entities, citizen or persons without citizenship residing in at the territory of a foreign state, positive obligation or other restrictions. Special economic measures may be aimed, amongst other, at suspension of programmes in the area of economic, technical or military assistance or cooperation, prohibition or limitation of financial operations, prohibition or limitation of foreign economic operations, termination or suspension of international trade agreement or other agreements in the area of foreign economic activity.

SECTION 7 LIST OF ABBREVIATIONS

ATS	Australian Treaty Series
AG	Australia Group
BTWC	Biological and Toxic Weapons Convention
COCOM	Coordinating Committee for multilateral strategic export control
CTBT	Comprehensive Test Ban Treaty
CWC	Chemical Weapons Convention
ECC	Export Control Commission
FAPRID	Federal Agency for the Legal Protection of the Results of Intellectual Activity in the Sphere of Military, Special, and Dual-Use Technology

FSMTC	Federal Service on Military-Technical Cooperation with Foreign States
FTECS	Federal Technical Export Control Service
IAEA	International Atomic Energy Agency
ICP	Internal Compliance Programme
ILM	International Legal Material
MEDT	Ministry of Economic Development and Trade
MoD	Ministry of Defence
MTC	Military-Technical Cooperation
MTCR	Missile Technology Control Regime
NIS	Newly Independent States
NPT	Nuclear Non-Proliferation Treaty
NSG	Nuclear Suppliers Group
OST	Outer Space Treaty
US	United States
USSR	Union of Soviet Socialist Republics
UNTS	United Nations Treaty Series
VEK	Federal Service for Currency and Export Control
WMD	Weapons of Mass Destruction

SECTION 8 REFERENCES

Sub-Section 1 Primary Documentation[1042]

Par. 1 Statutory Legislation

- Federal Law n° 114-FZ 'On Military-Technical Cooperation with Foreign States', adopted by the Russian Parliament (State Duma and Federation Council) on 9 July 1998.
- Federal Law n° 183-FZ 'On Export Control', adopted by the Russian Parliament on 18 July 1999, with changes and updates: law n° 196-FZ, 30 December 2001, law n° 58-FZ, 29 June 2004, law n° 90-FZ, 18 June 2005, law n° 283-FZ, 29 November 2007, law n° 318-FZ, 1 December 2007, law n° 89-FZ, 7 May 2009, law n°169-FZ, 1 July 2011, law n° 242-FZ, 18 July 2011 and law n° 409-FZ, 6 December 2011.
- Federal Law n° 164-FZ 'On principles of state regulation of foreign economic activity', adopted by the Russian Parliament (State Duma and Federation Council) on 26 November 2003, and signed by the President of the Russian Federation on 8 December 2003, with changes and updates: law n° 122-FZ, 22

1042. For an exhaustive and up dated list of all the norms (directly or indirectly related to export control) in force, see (in Russian) http://fstec.ru/eksportnyj-kontrol/zakonodatelstvo. The full text of all the norms can be found (in Russian) through this page.

August 2004, law n° 117-FZ, 22 July 2005, law n° 19-FZ, 2 February 2006, law n° 285-FZ, 3 November 2010, law n° 336-FZ 8 December 2010, law n° 200-FZ, 11 July 2011, law n° 409-FZ, 6 December 2011, law n° 137-FZ, 28 July 2012, and law n° 318-FZ, 30 November 2013.

- Federal Law n° 281-FZ 'On special economic measures' adopted by the Russian Parliament (State Duma and Federation Council) on 27 December 2006, and signed by the President of the Russian Federation on 30 December 2006.
- Federal law adopted by the State Duma on 5 April 2002, approved by the Federation Council on 23 April 2002, and signed by the President of the Russian Federation on 7 May 2002, amending the Criminal Code on export control related matters.

Par. 2 Regulations

- Presidential Decree n° 314, 9 March 2004, creating the Committee for MTC Service (under the authority of the MoD). It replaces Presidential Decree n° 1953, 1 December 2000.
- Presidential Decree n° 1062, 10 September 2005, implementing the Federal Law 'On Military-Technical Cooperation with Foreign States'.
- Presidential Decree n° 1085, 16 August, 2004, creating the FTECS.
- Presidential Decree n° 556, 14 May 1998, 'On the Legal Protection of the Results of Scientific, Experimental, and Technological Work with Military, Special, and Dual-Use Applications', creating FAPRID.
- Governmental Resolution n° 1132, 29 September 1998, implementing the directives issued by Presidential Decree n° 556, 14 May 1998.
- Governmental Decree n° 477, 21 June 2001, creating eight regional classification centres.

Par. 3 Annexes – Copies of Documents of Practical Use to the Importer/Exporter

A number of standard documents relevant for the import or export process in Russia (e.g., most current official application forms for import or export licenses, templates of contractual undertaking, or regulation extracts) as well as other non-official documents are available on a dedicated DropBox folder which can be accessed by following the link below: www.kluwerlawonline.com/eclrh-annexes.

Sub-Section 2 Secondary Documentation

Par. 1 Internet Sites

(a) Official Authorities

- www.fstec.ru: Federal Technical and Export Control Service
- www.fsvts.gov.ru: FSMTC with Foreign States
- www.mil.ru: the MoD
- www.fsb.ru: Federal Security Service
- www.gov.ru: the best governmental site to get in touch with any official authority
- www.www.roe.ru: Rosoboronexport
- www.roscosmos.ru: National Space Agency
- www.government.ru: Official site of the Russian Government
- www.mid.ru: Ministry of Foreign affairs

(b) Other Internet Sites

- http://fstec.ru/eksportnyj-kontrol/zakonodatelstvo: for any reference to any legal text
- www.expcon.ru: TsPEK (Center on export control issues)
- http://mdb.cast.ru/mdb/3-2001/ec/lfrae/: for military goods regime
- www.sipri.org: Stockholm International Peace Research Institute (SIPRI)
- www.uga.edu/cits/database/xcdb.htm: Center for International Trade and Security (CITS), School of public and international affairs, University of Georgia
- www.uga.edu/cits/programs/national_evaluations: CITS

Par. 2 Paper Publications

- Michael Beck, Maria Katsva & Igor Khripunov. *Nonproliferation Export Controls in Russia*, in *To Supply or To Deny*. Kluwer Law International, 2003.
- Michael Beck. *Russia and Efforts to Establish Export Controls*, 1998, online on: www.uga.edu/cits/documents/html/nat_eval_russia.htm.
- David Albright., *Nuclear Non-Proliferation Concerns and Export Control in Russia, Testimony before the Governmental Affairs Subcommittee on International Security, Proliferation and Federal Services*, Institute for Science and International Security, 6 June 2002, online on: http://exportcontrols.info/testimony.html.
- Elena Kiritchenko, Director of the Research Center on North-American studies (IMEMO), *Speech at the Moscow Physico-Technical Institute*, 21 April 2005. Online in Russian on: www.armscontrol.ru/course/lectures05a/evk050421.htm.
- *The Nonproliferation Review*, Spring/Summer 1995; online on: http://cns.miis.edu/npr/pdfs/lawall23.pdf.

– NIS Export Control Observer, August 2004: http://cns.miis.edu/observer/pdfs/ob_0408e.pdf.

SECTION 9 USEFUL INFORMATION

Sub-Section 1 Licensing and Enforcement Authorities Contact Details

Федеральная служба по военно-техническому сотрудничеству, ФСВТС: Адрес: 115324Москва, Овчинниковская наб.,д.18/1 Телефон: +7 (495) 950-98-08	**Federal Service on Military-Technical Cooperation, FSMTC: Address: 115324 Moscow, Ovchinnikovskaia nab., 18/1 Tel.: +7 (495) 950-98-08**
Федеральная служба безопасности, ФСБ Адрес: 107031Москва, ул. Кузнецкий мост, д. 22 Телефон: +7 (495) 224-70-69	**Federal Security Service, FSB Address: 107031 Moscow, Kouznetskii most St., 22 Tel.: +7 (495) 224-70-69**
Территориальные управления ФСТЭК России	**FTECS regional branches**
Центральный Адрес: 117342г. Москва, Севастопольский пр-т.,д. 56/40 Телефон/ факс: +7 (495) 334-16-21 Факс: +7 (095)	**For the Central Region Address: 117342 Moscow, Sevastopolsiy prospekt, 56/40 Tel./Fax: +7 (495) 334-16-21 Fax: +7 (095) 334-16-21**
Северо-западный Адрес: 190000,г. Санкт-Петербург, Исаакиевская пл.,д.11 Телефон/ факс: +7 (812) 312-55-29	**For the North-West Region Address: 190000, Saint Petersburg, Isaakievskaia Plochad, 11 Tel./Fax: +7 (812) 312-55-29**
Южный и северо-кавказский Адрес: 344079, г. Ростов-на-Дону, ул. Ярослава Галана, д.1е/25 Телефон: +7 (863) 200-46-10 Факс: +7 (863) 200-75-38	**For the South and North Caucasus Region Address: 344079, Rostov-on-Don, Yaroslava Galana St., 1 e/25 Tel.: +7 (863) 200-46-10 Fax: +7 (863) 200-75-38**
Приволжский Адрес: 603104,г. Нижний Новгород, пр-т. Гагарина, д.60, к. 11 Телефон/ факс: +7 (831) 439-68-79	**For the Volga Region Address: 603104, Nizhni-Novgorod, Prospekt Gagarina, 60, bld. 11 Tel./Fax: +7 (831) 439-68-79**
Уральский Адрес: 620078,г. Екатеринбург, ул. Гагарина, д.28б Телефон: +7 (343) 372-18-53 Факс: +7 (343) 362-43-03	**For the Urals Region Address: 620078, Ekaterinburg, Gagarina St., 28b Tel.: +7 (343) 372-18-53 Fax: +7 (343) 362-43-03**
Сибирский Адрес: 630091,г. Новосибирск, Красный проспект, д. 41 Телефон/ факс: +7 (383) 203-54-07	**For the Siberian Region Address: 630091, Novosibirsk, Krasniy Prospect, 41 Tel./Fax: +7 (383) 203-54-07**

Дальневосточный **Адрес: 680030 г. Хабаровск, ул. Ленина, д. 37** **Телефон/факс: +7 (4212) 91-10-23**	**For the Far East Region** **Address: 680030, Khabarovsk, Lenina Oulitsa, д. 37** **Tel./Fax: +7 (4212) 91-10-23**

Sub-Section 2 Other

None.

CHAPTER 14
Spain

David de Terán

SECTION 1 TABLE OF CONTENTS

SECTION 2 EXECUTIVE SUMMARY

The Spanish export control regime was established by the Law 53/2007 of 28 December and Royal Decree (RD) n° 679/2014 of 1 of August 2014 ('RD n° 679/2014' hereon). It comprises all items related to the import and export of defence and dual-use goods, it has four appendices that must be observed for each import/export activity and it is in force in the whole Spanish territory.

Law 53/2007 has the aim to contribute for a better regulation of the foreign trade of defence and dual-use good and technology.

Law 53/2007 is applicable and mandatory for any person or company who export or transfer, in the Spanish territory, items, goods, documentation or technology of defence or dual-use.

The purpose of the Law 53/2007 is to set forth the guidelines of the export or transfer of defence and dual-use goods in a normative with a level of a law. The Law 53/2007 was approved by the Spanish Parliament. Before the Law 53/2007, the Spanish Export Control Regulation was only regulation approved by Spanish Government (Royal Decree: e.g., RD n° 1782/2004).

The RD n° 2061/2008 was a development of the Law 53/2007.

RD n° 2061/2008 provided the obligation of having a licence in order to do the import/export activity. Prior to the application licence request, the importer/exporter must to be registered in the special registry of (import/export) operators.

RD n° 2061/2008 established five different types of licences and the Previous Agreement (PA). The licensing procedure is similar in both cases; it means defence and use dual goods, and it is carried out by the same authority. The authority in charge of issuing the licence is the General Secretary of Foreign Trade but before responding to a licence application, it must obtain the prior consent of the Inter-Ministerial Regulatory Board on Foreign Trade in Defence and Dual Use Goods. The General Secretary of Foreign Trade has the power to resolve all disputes related to import/export licences.

RD n° 2061/2008 aimed at setting forth the requirements and procedures to export and to import defence material and dual-use goods and technology.

The RD n° 844/2011 amended the RD n° 2061/2008 in order to implement the Directive of 2009/43/EC, of 6 May 2009.

Finally, the RD n° 679/2014 consolidates the RD n° 2061/2008 and RD n° 844/2011 in one document.

SECTION 3 INTRODUCTION: ELEMENTS OF CONTEXT

Sub-Section 1 Overall Philosophy

The purpose of the Spanish export control Regulation is to lay down the conditions, requirements and procedure by which to control external trade in defence material, other material and dual-use items and technologies including intangible transfers.

The Spanish export control regime takes into account Spain's national defence and state policy interests, Spain's international commitments, European Union (EU) legislation (especially the criteria's adopted in the European Councils of Luxembourg in June 1991 and Lisbon June 1992) as well as North Atlantic Treaty Organization (NATO) arms embargoes and United Nations (UN).

The export control Regulation applies in the whole of Spanish territory (i.e., legislation that is issued by the Spanish Government, not by a local government or autonomous region).

The Spanish export control regime prohibits imports or exports of controlled goods unless an authorization is obtain, except in cases established in RD n° 679/2014 or other laws.

The political objective of the Spanish legislator reflected in the Law 53/2007 and RD n° 679/2014 coincides with the criteria of the EU for the import/export of defence and dual-use goods.

The Law 53/2007 and the RD n° 679/2014 try to implement and develop the European policy on defence and dual-use goods in Spain. The legislation permits a degree of flexibility in its application. Flexibility lies in the different forms of licences that the authorities can grant, the possibility to extend the expiration date in some licences, the exemptions of the registration, and so forth.

Also, the Royal Decree 844/2011 of 17 June ('RD n° 844/2011' hereon) was a development of the Law 53/2007 and the implementation of the Directive of 2009/43/EC, of 6 May 2009. The RD n° 844/2011 tried to facilitate and integrate the European Defence Industry

In addition to Law 53/2007 and the RD n° 844/2011, other texts apply (e.g., the Order of the Ministry of Commerce and Tourism of 14 July 1995,[1043] the Order of the Ministry of Economy of 24 November 1998,[1044] as well as Law n° 30/1992 of 26 November 1992,[1045] which sets forth the Legal Regime of the Public Administrations and the Common Administrative Procedure).

Sub-Section 2 Historical Outlook

The Spanish export control regime was established by the RD n° 491/1998 of 27 March 1998[1046] and the RD n° 1315/2001 of 30 November 2001.[1047] Such decrees are no longer in force as they have been repealed by RD n° 1782/2004.

Other important pieces of legislation, which contribute to the Spanish export control regime, was the Organic Laws n° 3/1992[1048] of 30 April 1992, now repealed by Law 53/2007 and n° 12/1995[1049] of 12 December 1995. The Organic Law 12/1995 lays out what will happen if items are imported or exporter without a licence or without the importer/exporter having adequately complied with the licence conditions.

1043. 'Boletin Oficial del Estado' (BOE) n° 179 of 29/07/95 (BOE is Spain's official journal).
1044. BOE n° 289 of 03/12/98.
1045. BOE n° 285 of 27/11/92.
1046. BOE n° 84 of 8/4/98.
1047. BOE n° 303 of 19/12/01.
1048. BOE n° 105 of 1/5/92.
1049. BOE n° 297 of 13/12/95.

As a result of the modifications made by the EU in relation to the import and export control of dual-use goods, Spain reviewed and updated its domestic regulation regarding the controlled movement of import/export of defence goods in order to conform to international commitments.

RD n° 1782/2004[1050] was the next Spanish Export Control Regulation. The RD n° 1782/2004 was the conditions of export control of defence and dual-use goods and technology.

RD n° 1782/2004 came into force on 30 July 2004 and it replaced the preceding regulations which was contradictory (e.g., it left untouched the Ministerial Orders of 14 July 1995[1051] and 24 November 1998[1052]).

The Law 53/2007 and the RD n° 844/2011 are the latest Spanish Regulation establishing the actual conditions of export control of defence goods, both in import and export stage, and it follows the EU standards of control on use dual material, other goods and technology.

The Law 53/2007 came into force on 29 January 2008 and it replaced preceding regulations which was contradictory (e.g., the Organic Law n° 3/1992 of 30 April 1992).[1053]

The RD n° 2061/2008 came into force on 7 February 2009 and it replaced the RD n° 1782/2004.[1054]

The RD n° 844/2001 came into force on 2 July 2011.

The RD n° 679/2014 came into force on 26 August 2014.

Sub-Section 3 Participation in International Regimes

The following tables display the degree of Spain's participation status in international to export control treaties. Information is also given, when relevant, of the fact that Spain may have only accede to a treaty (i.e., when it is not founding member of the treaty or has not ratified it).

Par. 1 Treaties and Regimes Dealing with Specific Items and Technologies

Table 14.1 Nuclear Weapons Treaties

Treaty Name	*Overall Status*	*Specific Status*	*Enforceable in Spain*
Test Ban			
Limited Test Ban Treaty[1055]	OS: 5 August 1963 EF: 10 October 1963	S: 13 August 1963 R: 17 December 1964	Yes

1050. BOE n° 210 of 31/8/2004.
1051. See *supra* n. 1043.
1052. See *supra* n. 1044.
1053. BOE n° 312 of 29/12/07.
1054. BOE n° 6 of 7/01/09.
1055. Treaty Banning Nuclear Weapon Tests in the Atmosphere, in Outer Space and Under Water, *UNTS*, vol. 480, 43.

Treaty Name	Overall Status	Specific Status	Enforceable in Spain
Comprehensive Nuclear Test Ban Treaty[1056]	OS: 24 September 1996 EF: not in force	S: 24 September 1996 R: 31 July 1998	No
Test Ban			
Nuclear Non-Proliferation Treaty[1057]	OS: 1 July 1968 EF: 5 March 1970	A: 5 November 1987	Yes
IAEA Comprehensive Safeguards Agreement[1058]	A: 5 April 1989	N/A[1059]	Yes
IAEA Model Additional Protocol[1060]	OS: 22 September 1998 EF: 30 April 2004	N/A[1061]	Yes

Abbreviations: OS: Opened for signature; EF: Entry into force; S/R: Signature/Ratification; A: Accession.

Table 14.2 Biological and Chemical Weapons Treaties

Treaty Name	Overall Status	Specific Status	Enforceable in Spain
Geneva Protocol[1062]	OS: 17 June 1925 EF: 8 February 1928	S: 17 June 1925 R: 22 August 1929	Yes
Biological Convention[1063]	OS: 10 April 1972 EF: 26 March 1975	S: 10 April 1972 R: 20 June 1979	Yes
Chemical Convention[1064]	OS: 13 January 1993 EF: 29 April 1997	S: 13 January 1993 R: 3 August 1994	Yes

Abbreviations: OS: Opened for signature; EF: Entry into force; S/R: Signature/Ratification; A: Accession.

1056. UNGA, resolution 50\245.
1057. Treaty on the Non-Proliferation of Nuclear Weapons, *UNTS*, vol. 729, 161.
1058. Agreement Between the Agency and States Required in Connection with the Treaty on the Non-Proliferation of Nuclear Weapons (NPT), INFCIRC/153 (Corrected).
1059. This treaty is a bilateral one and, accordingly, the differences that apply to multilateral treaties (between the overall status and the specific status) do not apply.
1060. Model Protocol Additional to the Agreement(s) Between State(s) and the Agency for the Application of Safeguards, INFCIRC/540 (Corrected).
1061. This treaty is a bilateral one and, accordingly, the differences that apply to multilateral treaties (between the overall status and the specific status) do not apply.
1062. Protocol for the Prohibition of the Use in War of Asphyxiating, Poisonous or Other Gases, and of Bacteriological Methods of Warfare, 94, *League of Nations Treaty Series*, No. 2138 (1929).
1063. Convention on the Prohibition of the Development, Production and Stockpiling of Bacteriological (Biological) and Toxin Weapons and On Their Destruction, *UNTS*, vol. 1015, 163.
1064. Convention on the Prohibition of the Development, Production, Stockpiling and Use of Chemical Weapons and on Their Destruction, Doc.CD/CW/WP.400/Rev.1.

Table 14.3 *Conventional Arms*

Treaty Name	*Overall Status*	*Specific Status*	*Enforceable in Spain*
Protocol on Firearms to the Convention against Transnational Organized Crime[1065]	DA: 31 May 2001 EF: 3 July 2005	–	No
Convention on anti-personnel mines[1066]	OS: 18 September 1997 EF: 1 March 1999	R: 19 January 1999	Yes
The Arms Trade Treaty	DA: 2 April 2013		Yes

Abbreviations: OS: Opened for signature; DA: Date of adoption; EF: Entry into force; S/R: Signature/ Ratification; A: Accession.

Table 14.4 *Multilateral Export Control Regimes*

Regime Name	*Formation*	*Participation*
Zangger Committee[1067]	1971	Yes
Nuclear Suppliers Group	1974	Yes
Australia Group	1985	Yes
Missile Technology Control Regime	1987	Yes
Wassenaar Arrangement[1068]	1994	Yes

Table 14.5 *Others*

Name	*Adoption*	*Participation*
UN Register on Conventional Arms[1069]	9 December 1991	Yes[1070]
Programme of Action on Small Arms and Light Weapons[1071]	20 July 2001	Yes
International Code of conduct[1072]	25 November 2002	Yes

1065. Protocol against the Illicit Manufacturing of and Trafficking in Firearms, Their Parts and Components and Ammunition, supplementing the United Nations Convention against Transnational Organized Crime, A/RES/55/225.
1066. Convention on the Prohibition of the Use, Stockpiling, Production and Transfer of Anti-Personnel Mines and on their Destruction, *ATS, 1999, n°3.*
1067. Non-Proliferation Treaty Exporters Committee (also called the Zangger Committee).
1068. Wassenaar Arrangement on export controls for conventional arms and dual-use goods and technologies.
1069. A/RES/46/36/L.
1070. Information provided for the calendar years 1994-2005.
1071. Programme of Action to Prevent, Combat and Eradicate the Illicit Trade in Small Arms and Light Weapons in All Aspects, A/CONF.1992/15.
1072. The Hague Code of Conduct against Ballistic Missile Proliferation, not yet published.

Par. 2 Treaties Dealing with Specific Areas

Table 14.6 International Zones

Treaty Name	*Overall Status*	*Specific Status*	*Enforceable in Spain*
Antarctic Treaty[1073]	OS: 1 December 1959 EF: 23 June 1961	A: 31 March of 1982	Yes
Outer Space Treaty[1074]	OS: 27 January 1967 EF: 10 October 1967	A: 27 November 1968	Yes
Sea Bed Arms Control Treaty[1075]	OS: 11 February 1971 EF: 23 June 1961	A: 15 July 1987	Yes
Moon agreement[1076]	OS: 18 December 1979 EF: 11 July 1984	–	No
Convention on the Law of the Sea[1077]	OS: 10 December 1982 EF: 16 November 1994	R: 15 January of 1997	Yes

Abbreviations: OS: Opened for signature; EF: Entry into force; S/R: Signature/Ratification; A: Accession.

Table 14.7 Regional Nuclear Weapons-Free Zones

Treaty Name	*Overall Status*	*Specific Status*	*Enforceable in Spain*
Treaty of Tlatelolco[1078]	OS: 14 February 1967 EF: 22 April 1967	–	No
Treaty of Rarotonga[1079]	OS: 6 August 1985 EF: 11 December 1986	–	No
Treaty of Bangkok[1080]	OS: 15 December 1995 EF: 27 March 1997	–	No
Treaty of Pelindaba[1081]	OS: 11 April 1996 EF: not in force	–	No

Abbreviations: OS: Opened for signature; EF: Entry into force; S/R: Signature/Ratification; A: Accession.

1073. 402, *UNTS*, 7.
1074. Treaty on Principles Governing the Activities of States in the Exploration and Use of Outer Space, including the Moon and Other Celestial Bodies, *UNTS*, vol. 610, 205.
1075. Treaty on the Prohibition of the Emplacement of Nuclear Weapons and other Weapons of Mass Destruction on the Seabed and The Ocean Floor and in the subsoil thereof, *UNTS*, vol. 955, 115.
1076. Agreement governing the Activities of States on the Moon and Other Celestial Bodies, *ILM*, vol. 18, 1434.
1077. Doc. A/CONF.62/122 and Corr.1-11.
1078. Treaty for the Prohibition of Nuclear Weapons in Latin America and the Caribbean, *UNTS*, vol. 634, 326.
1079. South Pacific Nuclear Free Zone Treaty, *ILM*, vol. 24, 1442.
1080. South East Asia Nuclear-Weapon-Free Zone Treaty, *ILM*, vol. 35. 635.
1081. African Nuclear Weapon-Free Zone Treaty, *ILM*, vol. 35, 698.

SECTION 4 CONTROL REGIME

Sub-Section 1 Military Goods and Services

Par. 1 Overall Presentation

Sub-Par. 1 Requirements Prior to Any Specific Import/Export (i.e., Manufacturing Phase)

Before obtaining the licence to import or to export defence and dual-use goods, the importer/exporter (operator) must register all its personal information on the registry of foreign trade operators at the General Secretary of Foreign Trade by filling out a form founded in Appendix IV.15 of the RD n° 844/2011 as a prerequisite for the issuance of any administrative import, export or brokering authorization with respect to materials, products and technologies referred to in such Regulation.

The following exemptions exist with respect to the obligation to be registered on the registry of foreign operators:

- Administrative bodies belonging to the Armed Forces, State Law enforcement officials under the auspices of the National Government, law enforcement bodies belonging to the autonomous communities and local police forces.
- Export by natural persons of controlled arms when not done as part of a recurring economic or commercial activity.

In the Spanish Registry of import/export Operators of defence and dual-use goods, it is not necessary to be a Spanish citizen. Both, Spanish nationals and foreign nationals can be registered. Nevertheless, a foreign national must first obtain Spanish residence[1082] in accordance with Spanish law. Spanish law provides that at the time of import and export defence or dual-use goods, the nationality of the end-user and the destination country must be taken into account, but not the nationality of the importer/exporter itself.

In the case of companies where the main shareholder is a foreign person, an authorization pursuant to the RD n° 664/1999, of 23 April[1083] of foreign investments will be necessary: an authorization is not necessary up to 5%, and for more than 5%, the authorization of the Spanish Government will be necessary.

In case of transfer or export of weapons, the person who wants to transfer the weapons will need the prior authorization like gunsmith's by the General Director of Police and the Guardia Civil.

Once a person is registered in the Spanish Registry of import/export Operators, it may carry out any import/export activity and not need to register itself again. One registration on the registry is enough to cover any subsequent import/export activities.

1082. Residence means the legal right to live in Spain granted by the competent authority.
1083. BOE n° 106 of 4/05/99.

Each time an operator wishes to undertake a new import or export activity should include in the licence application its registration number.

According to the Article 2 of RD n° 844/2011, it is imperative to have a licence issued by the competent authority in order to be able to import and to export such items.

Sub-Par. 2 Requirements at the Import/Export Stage

To be able to undertake export activities, a licence applicant must first have obtained one of the following control documents:

- The International Import Certificate or equivalent document (except in the case of weapons of war dealt with below) issued by the competent authorities of the importing country: applicable to exports destined for any of the EU Member States or to the countries listed in Annex IIa of Council Regulation (EC) n° 428/2009, 5 May 2009 as amended.[1084]
- End-user undertaking issued by the competent authorities of the importing country (except in the case of weapons of war dealt with below) or by the end-user: applicable to exports intended for countries not mentioned in the foregoing paragraph. The said undertaking shall at least include a commitment on the part of the recipient to import the defence goods or goods subject to control in the exporting country and to not re-export it without the prior written authorization of the competent Spanish authorities and to use the said goods for the end-use declared.[1085]
- End-use certificate issued by the competent authorities of the importer country: applicable to exports of the defence material included on the list of weapons of war. The said certificate shall at least reflect the commitment to import the goods or technology to the expedition country and to not re-export it without the prior written authorization of the competent Spanish authorities and to use the said goods or technology for the end-use declared.
- In case so requiring, the department in charge of export control licensing process within the Department of Defence ('JIMDDU') may call for support documentation proving that the defence goods which export is contemplated, have indeed been imported in the territory of the country of destination. Such documentation consists of the entrance verification certificate or the equivalent customs release document.

It will be necessary to include the technical documentation to analyse and identify the goods object to export or import.

1084. See *supra* n. 230.

1085. Article 30 of the RD n° 679/2014: Prior to the import, the recipient must sign an End-User undertaking in which it undertakes to not re-export without the prior written authorization of Spanish authorities and to use the goods for the end-use declared.

I Goods

In addition, and prior, to receiving a licence (which will be dealt with further down in this section), the RD n° 679/2014 sets forth the 'Previous Agreement' (PA) to import and to export defence and dual-use goods. The conditions for applying for a PA are established in Article 27 for defence and dual-use. The applications requirements for both types of goods are the same.

The PA on the export of defence and other material implies Government consent in principle with the transactions deriving from such PA.

The PA is used when there is a project of import or export of defence or dual-use goods to a country with which a contract is already signed or is being negotiated, but requires a long period of implementation. The PA will have a term of validity not exceeding three years. If the contract in force or in negotiation needs a long period, it will be possible to authorize in exceptional circumstances a longer term of validity.

The activities which derive from a PA still require a licence before the import or export can go ahead. The PA will not by itself permit shipment of the goods across the customs boundary because an export licence is still required. PA application is made by filling out the following forms: 'PA of Transfer of Defence and Dual-use Goods' or 'PA of Global License of Project of Transfer of Defensive Goods', which are contained in Appendices VI.5 and VI.6 of the RD n° 679/2014.

The export control regime in Spain is determined by the provisions of the RD n° 679/2014. It is comprises twenty-two appendices which must be filled out by the operator (importer/exporter) with the required information, in order to apply for a licence to import or to export defence and dual-use goods. As set out in Article 1 of the RD n° 679/2014 the aim is to establish the requirements and the procedures for the import/export control of defence and dual-use goods. According to the Article 2 of RD n° 679/2014, it is imperative to have a licence issued by the competent authority in order to be able to import and to export such items.

The Spanish law contemplates three types of licences: (i) Definitive authorizations; (ii) Temporary authorizations; and (iii) Authorizations deriving from a temporary import when the country of destination does not coincide with the country of origin or when the defence or other material intended for export does not coincide with that declared on the temporary import introduction.

Authorizations are either:

(a) individual export-expedition licence of defence and other material;
(b) global export-expedition licence of defence and other material;
(c) Global Project Licence (GPL) for defence material; or
(d) general authorization;
(e) brokering authorization;
(f) general licence for Defence material;
(g) global licence for components of Defence material.

The types of licences are the same for defence and dual-use goods or services at the import and the export stages with the exception of the GPL, which is only available for defence goods.

Types of licence

(a) Individual Licence

For import or export of defence and dual-use goods, the individual licence allows one or several deliveries of the licensed goods up to a specified limit, to one specified country, through one specified custom (boundary) and within a period of one year. In the case that the import or the export, depending of the case, has a temporary activity, the importer/exporter does the import/export within a period of six months. Upon substantiated request by the exporter, extensions of the validity period of the licence may be authorized.

In the case of weapons included in Annexes II and III of the RD n° 679/2014, it will be necessary import licence of the country of destiny. However, if the exporter is just cause a natural person, it is a temporary export and the temporary export is not as part of a recurring economic or commercial activity, it will be necessary only a statement signed by the exporter, including the country of destiny and type of weapon.

If the material intended for export contains materials which are contained on the list of defence or other material (Annexes I and II of the RD n° 679/2014) originally coming from foreign countries, the applicant must identify the said materials on a separate document (which takes the form of an annex to the application) specifying the proportion of the goods intended for export.

(b) Global Licence

Such licence allows the import/export of an unlimited number of specified goods of a value up to a specified amount, through one or several customs, to one or several addressees in one or several specified countries up to the amount allowed in the licence and within a period of three years. It is possible to extend this limitation period once.

A global licence will be granted when the relationship between the exporter and the recipient of the goods falls into of the following categories:

- a parent company and one of its subsidiaries or between subsidiaries of the same company;
- a manufacturer and his exclusive distributor;
- a contractual framework entailing a regular commercial relationship between the exporter and the final user of the exported material.

The global licence is possible for weapons listed in Annexes II and III of the RD n° 679/2014, but in this case it will necessary to include in the application form, the import licence of the country of destination.

In case of exports, the licence-holder must submit to the Secretary-General of Foreign Trade a half-yearly summary of the exports undertaken for each country of destination.

If, among the items to be exported, there are materials included on the defence material list or in Annexes I or II of RD n° 679/2014 which originally come from foreign countries, the petitioner must list the said materials on a separate document (as an annex to the application) specifying the proportion of the total amount of goods intended for export.

(c) Global Project Licence

Such a licence allows the import/export activity of goods under practically the same conditions as the global licence. In other words, it allows an unlimited number of the type of delivery established in the licence, of goods up to a specified value, through one or several customs, to one or several addressees in one or several specified countries but for a period of five years. Such period can also be extended once. GPL is only available for defence goods. They are governed by Article 24 of the RD n° 679/2014 and issued for the following cases:

- Those arising from an international defence cooperation programme endorsed by the Spanish Government pursuant to the framework Agreement of 27 July 2000, or any other international defence cooperation programme endorsed by the Spanish Government or by one or several companies established in Spain.
- Those deriving from a non-governmental defence material development or production programme in which one or several trans-national defence companies (TDC)[1086] established in Spain participates to so-called Letter of Intent (LoI) of 6 July 1998,[1087] and its related Framework Agreement of 27 July 2000.[1088] Concerning measures to facilitate the restructuring and operation of the European defence industry, providing that the company or companies have been granted authorization from the Ministry of Defence demonstrating that the programme in question meets the requirements laid down in the Framework Agreement.
- At the initial development phase of industrial cooperation, the export of equipment and components to other companies participating in the said phase.

1086. Referred to in Article 2 of the *Acuerdo Marco relative a las medidas encaminadas a facilitar la restructuración y funcionamiento de la industria europea de defensa.*

1087. The Letter of Intent (LoI) of 6 Jul. 1998, signed by the Ministers of Defence of France, Germany, Italy, Spain, the United Kingdom and Sweden, which together represent 90% of the EU Defence-related material production (can be found on the Internet Site: http://projects.sipri.se/expcon/loi/lointent.htm).

1088. LoI related Framework Agreement of 27 Jul. 2000:

> between the French Republic, the Federal Republic of Germany, the Italian Republic, the Kingdom of Spain, the Kingdom of Sweden and the United Kingdom of Great Britain and Northern Ireland, concerning Measures to Facilitate the Restructuring and Operation of the European Defence Industry.

(This can be found on the Internet Site: http://projects.sipri.se/expcon/loi/indrest01.htm.)

- Items returned to their place of origin and temporary exports for the purpose of repair, testing and homologation of the materials initially described in the GPL.

The applicant must provide a breakdown of the components, their value per item and in total, for each company and country of destination.

If the item, product or technology intended for export contains materials which figure on the defence material list and originates from other countries, the applicant must list the said materials on a separate sheet specifying their proportion of the total volume of goods destined for export.

(d) General Authorization

Such an authorization is issued for import or export activities pursuant to Council Regulation (EC) n° 428/2009, of 5 May 2009, Article 91.

In such case, the operator must explicitly commit to:

- Undertake export/import operations with end-users which are exclusively those indicated on to the Spanish authorities.
- Carry out individualized management of the documentation required for the exports, including, at least, a description of the goods including the corresponding sub-article as per the Annex I of the Council Regulation (EC) n° 1183/2007, of 18 September 2007, the amounts individually exported and the date, name and address of the exporter as well as the name and address of the recipient, the user and the end-use where applicable.
- Make available, to the Secretariat-General for Foreign Trade (GSFT) and the Department of Customs and Excise Duties of the National Tax Administration Agency, the documentation described in the foregoing paragraph and any other relevant information concerning the exports undertaken in order to allow for necessary verifications.
- Put the following legend on invoices and transport documents accompanying the goods and procure a related commitment of compliance from the recipient: 'The export of these items is undertaken by means of a general authorization and may only be addressed to the specified recipient. The items may not be re-exported without the authorization of the national authorities of the country in question'.
- Inform the authorities and suspend the export until an express authorization is obtained if it is discovered that the products or technologies are being used or could be used, either totally or partially, for the development, production, handling and operation, maintenance, stockpiling, detection, identification or dissemination of chemical, biological or nuclear weapons.
- If the items to be exported incorporate materials included in Annex I of Council Regulation (EC) n° 1183/2007, of 18 September 2007 and originate from foreign countries, the licence applicant must list the said items on a separate document specifying how much their value represents in the overall total amount of goods intended for export.

(e) Brokering Authorization

This authorization is approved for the activities set forth in the Article 2.1.c of RD nº 679/2014. The application will include the following information:

- equipment, materials or technologies;
- persons involved in the transaction;
- countries of origin and destination, and countries of transit;
- transport and finance plan.

Before the authorization, the Secretariat-General for Foreign Trade will exchange information with other countries of the EU, pursuant to Article 5 of Council Common Position 2003/468/CFSP of 23 June 2003 on the control of arms brokering.

(f) General Licence for Defence material

Only for the materials described in the list of articles of the Annex IV of the RD 679/2014.

Types of General Licences

- When the destinations are the Army Forces of the countries of the EU or a contractor when the only use is for the Army Forces of the EU.
- When a destination is a certified company for the competent authorities of the countries of the EU.
- Temporary export for exhibition, test and demonstration.
- For maintenance and repair.
- When the export is part of the activities of the Spanish Ministry of Defence or Spanish companies in activities or operation of the NATO or NAMSA.

Obligations of the General Licences

- Only for the materials, destinations and addressees approved in the General licence.
- To fulfil the terms and conditions, limitations and provisos issued in the General licence.
- Specific management of the documentation under a General licence, including description of the material, quantity and value, date of the export, name and address of the exporter, name and address of the destination.
- Every six months, to report to the competent Spanish authorities the documentation described above and any other relevant information requested by the Spanish authorities.
- To include in all the customs invoices a statement indicating the material is being exported under a General licence and only for the countries of the EU.

Certified companies

As part of the General Licence, the General Secretary of Foreign Trade could certify companies for the reception of defence material under a General Licence. In this case, the requirements of the companies to be certified are:

- To prove the experience of the company in Defence activities, especially in the export of defence goods or technology and to get the authorization to produce and sale defence goods and technology.
- To prove that the company has a industrial capacity for defence activities.
- To appoint a Director, responsible of the export of the Defence goods and technology.
- This Director has to sign a statement declaring that the company shall implement all the policies and resources in order to fulfil all the terms and conditions and obligations of the General Licence, reporting to the relevant authorities.
- To provide the policies and procedures of the company, including material and human resources, security policies, etc for the fulfilment of the obligations of the General licence.

The certification is only valid for five year. At least every three years, the General Secretary of Foreign Trade has the obligation to audit the certified companies and in case that these companies does not fulfil the requirement, it is possible to suspend or revoke the certification.

(g) Global licence for components of Defence material

Only for the parts, components, replacement and services described in the list of articles of the Annex V of the RD n° 679/2014.

The Global licence is only valid for three years, with the possibility of renewal.

The destinations are the Army Force of the countries signatories of the Framework agreement of 27 July 2000 or companies in these countries when these companies an agreement with these countries and the end-user of the materials are for the Army Forces of these countries.

II Services

The export of defence material, including technical assistance, which is not explicitly contained on the list of defence material, is subject to authorization in the following cases:

(1) If the exporter is established in Spain and has been informed by the competent authorities of Spain that the items to be exported are or may be intended, in whole or in part, for use in connection with the development, production, handling, operation, maintenance, storage, detection, identification or dissemination of chemical, biological or nuclear weapons or other nuclear

explosive devices or the development, production, maintenance or storage of missiles capable of delivering such weapons.

(2) If the purchasing country or country of destination is subject to an arms embargo decided by a common position or joint action adopted by the European Council or a decision of the Organization for Security and Co-operation in Europe (OSCE) or an arms embargo imposed by a binding resolution of the Security Council of the UN and if the exporter has been informed by Spanish authorities that the items to be exported are or may be intended, in whole or in part, for a military end-use. For the purposes of this paragraph, 'military end-use' shall mean: Incorporation into military items listed in the military list contained in RD n° 679/2014; use of production, test or analytical equipment and components, for the development, production or maintenance of military items listed in the above-mentioned list; use of any unfinished products in a plant for the production of military items listed in the above-mentioned list.

(3) If the exporter has been informed by the Spanish authorities that the items to be exported are or may be intended, in whole or in part, for use as parts or components of military items listed in the national military list that have been exported from the Spanish territory without authorization or in violation of an authorization prescribed by Spanish legislation.

(4) When the exporter either knows or has reason to suspect that these items are intended or could be intended, totally or partially, for any of the uses referred to in paragraph 1 above.

Defence services mean the furnishing of assistance (including training) to foreign persons, whether in Spain or abroad in the design, development, engineering, manufacture, production, assembly, testing, repair, maintenance, modification, operation, demilitarization, destruction, processing or use of defence articles.

III Persons/Deemed Export

Spanish law generally controls the destination, use of the items subject to export control (Hardware, Technology and Services) and also the nationalities of the recipients.

The main mechanism of the law is the application of the control through a case-by-case export authorization (*erga omnes*) provided for in Article 2 of RD n° 679/2014.

Spanish law provides that at the time of import and export defence or dual-use goods, the following must be taken into account:

(1) Article 2.1.a.4.i) of RD n° 679/2014 – The use of the item: If the exporter has been informed by the competent authorities of the Member State in which he is established that the items to be exported are or may be intended, in whole or in part, for use in connection with the development, production, handling,

operation, maintenance, storage, detection, identification or dissemination of chemical, biological or nuclear weapons or other nuclear explosive devices or the development, production, maintenance or storage of missiles capable of delivering such weapons.

(2) Article 2.1.a.4.ii) of RD n° 679/2014 – The destination country: If the purchasing country or country of destination is subject to an arms embargo decided by a common position or joint action adopted by the European Council or a decision of the OSCE or an arms embargo imposed by a binding resolution of the Security Council of the UN and if the exporter has been informed by Spanish authorities that the items to be exported are or may be intended, in whole or in part, for a military end-use. For the purposes of such paragraph, 'military end-use' means: incorporation into military items listed in the military list; Use of production, test or analytical equipment and components therefore, for the development, production or maintenance of military items listed in the above-mentioned list; Use of any unfinished products in a plant for the production of military items listed in the above-mentioned list.

(3) Article 2.1.a.4.iii) of RD n° 679/2014 – Use of the item exported without authorization: If the exporter has been informed by the Spanish authorities that the items in question are or may be intended, in whole or in part, for use as parts or components of military items listed in the national military list that have been exported from the Spanish territory without authorization or in violation of an authorization prescribed by Spanish legislation.

(4) Article 2.1.a.4.iv) of RD n° 679/2014. When the exporter either knows or has reason to suspect that these items are intended or could be intended, totally or partially, for any of the uses referred to in Article 2.1.d.1 of RD n° 679/2014.

Par. 2 Control Lists

Export of defence materials which require a licence are listed in Appendix I of the RD n° 679/2014. The list corresponds to the classification established in Article 22 of the Wassenaar Agreement.

Import of defence goods which require a licence are listed in Appendix III.2 of the RD n° 679/2014.[1089]

1089. Fire arms (12.7 mm calibre and less) and canon arms (20 mm calibre and less); arms (12.7 mm calibre and more); arms canon (20 mm calibre and superior); components and munitions; bombs, rockets and missiles; target direction systems; military terrestrial vehicles; toxicological agents and radioactive materials; energy materials (gas and military explosives); war tanks; military airplanes; electronic equipments; arms systems; re-enforced equipments and constructions; simulations and test equipments; measures equipments; smelt equipments; different materials and equipments; production equipments; arms systems of directed energy; cryogenics and superconductors equipments; software and technology.

Par. 3 Licensing and Enforcement Authorities

The General Secretary of Foreign Trade is the government authority in charge of issuing import and export licences for defence and dual-use goods.[1090] It is also empowered to deny licences or to cancel licences already in force.

If the General Secretary of Foreign Trade wishes to authorize the import/export, it must first have obtained the green light from the JIMDDU, which forms part of the Ministry of Economy and Competitiveness. The JIMDDU has a duty to review every import/export activity of defence and dual-use goods. In doing so, it must take into account any international commitments of Spain, the Code of Conduct[1091] criteria, the nature of the goods, the country of destination, the final use of the goods and any previous licence refusals of the importer/exporter to or from Spain (in line with the 'no undercut' principle as provided for by EU law[1092]).

The General Secretary of Foreign Trade is required to process a licence application within six months. If it remains silent beyond that period, the application demanded has been denied. All applications must be filled out on the forms established by the RD n° 679/2014 and its appendices, in order to ensure that the destination and final use of the products match those specified in the licence.

In the event that several Member States participate in the control of the same brokering transaction, consultations must immediately be made with competent authorities of the Member State or States involved furnishing them with all pertinent information. Possible objections lodged by the Member State or States shall be binding on the authority granting the authorization for the brokering activity in question (Article 9 of the RD n° 679/2014). If no objections have been lodged within ten working days, it shall be assumed that the Member State or States consulted do not have any objection to the contemplated brokering transaction (Article 9 of the RD n° 679/2014).

The General Secretary of Foreign Trade supervises and controls the use of the licence. The licensee must keep all the documents related to the import/export activity of defence and dual-use during four years, starting as from the expiration date of the licence validity.

The procedure to import and export defence and dual-use goods is summarized.

1090. Except for the materials that have been entered into Zone Franc Deposits and when the competence to issue the authorization belongs to the Department of Customs and Taxes. A Zone Franc means a delimited area of the Spanish territory which has been delimited in order to promote and to develop the industrialization of exportable goods and services in order to benefit the exchanges rates, taxes, customs and export trades.

1091. EU Code of Conduct for Arms Exports, 8 Jun. 1998, available at http://projects.sipri.se/expcon/eucode.htm.

1092. For further details on this matter, please refer to the chapter on European Union.

Figure 14.1

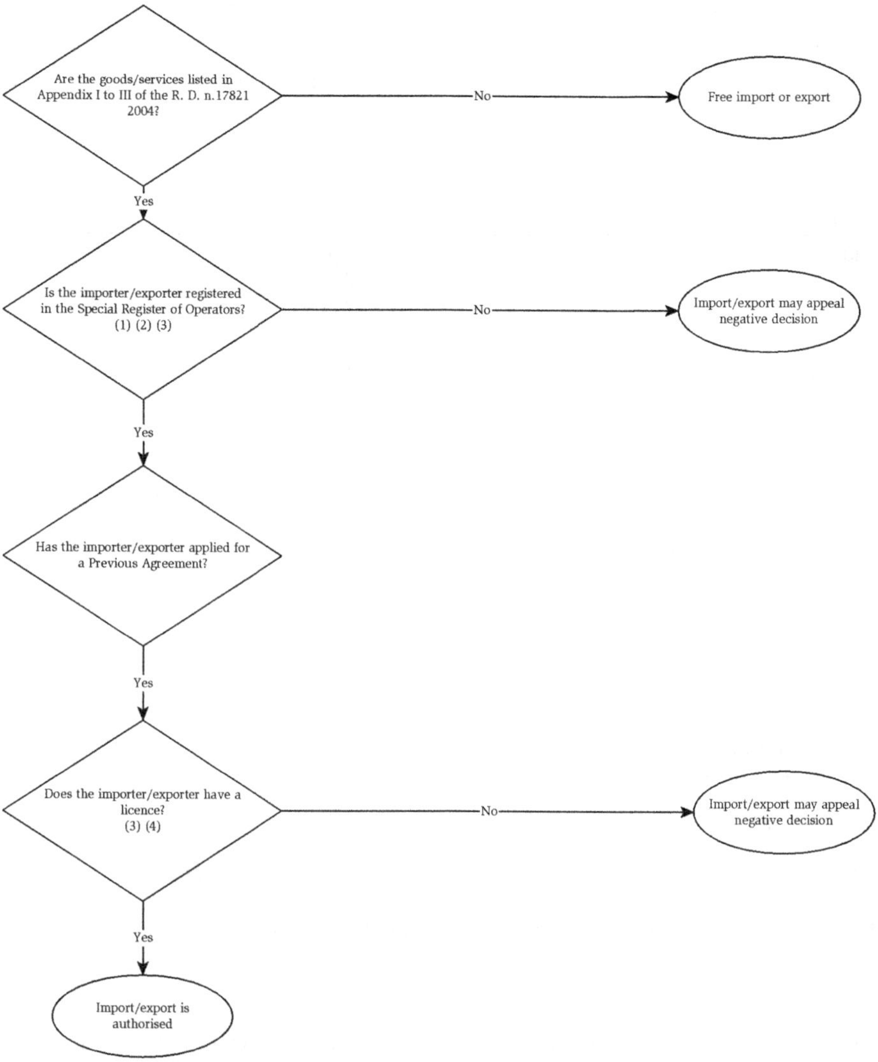

(1) Exemptions in respect to the obligation to be registered: (i) Administrative bodies belonging to the Armed Forces, State Law enforcement officials under the auspices of the National Government,law enforcement bodies belonging to the autonomous communities and local police forces; (ii) Transactions regarding dual-use items and technologies covered by a General authorization; and (iii) export by natural persons of controlled arms when not done as part of a recurring economic orcommercial activity.
(2) The importer/exporter must fill in for contained in appendix IV.8 of the RD n°1782/2004.
(3) GSFT must take a decision on registration application within sixty days following the prior consent issued by JIMDDU.
(4) The Prior Agreement is available within the framework of a contract, either signed or under negotiation, which requires a long period of execution.

(5) The determination of the relevant licence application for (as contained in the appendices of the RD n°1782/2004) depends on the nature of the activity. Type of export/import licence of Defence goods: (i) Individual License (ii) Global License (iii) Global Project License; or General License.

(See further chart below for more details)

Table 14.8 indicates which annex of the RD n° 679/2014 is to be used for which type of import or export.

Table 14.8

Type of Licence	*Export*	*Import*
Individual Licence	Ap. VI.1 Ap. VI.2 Ap. VI.3 *	Ap. VI.1 Ap. VI.2 Ap. VI.3
Global Licence	Ap. VI.9 Ap. VI.10 *	Ap. VI.9 Ap. VI.10
Global Project Licence	Ap. VI.6 Ap. VI.7 *	Ap. VI.6 Ap. VI.7
General Authorization	N/A	N/A
Brokering Authorization	Ap. IV.1 Ap. IV.2	N/A
Previous Agreement	Ap. VI.8	Ap. VI.8
General Licences for Defence Material	Ap. VI.9	N/A
Global licence for components of Defence material	Ap. VI.13	N/A
Additional Documents**	Aps. VI. 15 to 22	Aps. VI.15 to 22

Abbreviation: Ap.: Appendix.
* It means that Ap. IV.9 and IV.11 must fill out if JIMDDU request them.
** In some cases, JIMDDU may be request additional documents, which are established in those Ap.

Par. 4 Sanctions and Recourses of the Importer/Exporter

Sub-Par. 1 Criminal and Civil Sanctions

Organic Law n° 6/2011 related to the crime of trafficking provides that it is an offence to import/export defence and dual-use activities without the required licence. It is also an offence, if the licence has been obtained by false or incomplete declarations. Such acts are punished with imprisonment (one to five years in prison) and fines of between two to six times the amount of the good exported.[1093] It is necessary, however, that the goods, merchandise, objects, constituting the offence/crime, are of a value higher than EUR 50,000.

In addition, penalties entailing deprivation of rights can be imposed (on the basis of the seriousness of the crime), for example, special incapacitation for use or public charge, profession, industrialist, commerce or office, or any other law.

1093. Article 3 of the Organic Law 6/2001 (BOE n° 156 of 1 Jul. 2011).

In addition to the criminal sanctions, the exporter or importer can incur a civil responsibility equivalent to damages in the amount that can be applied as a result of the application of the customs code/regulations.

Finally, additional penalties (belong to a particular category[1094]) can be imposed consisting in the confiscation from the merchandise, materials and means of transport.

Sub-Par. 2 Administrative Sanctions

Import/export of defence and dual-use activities without the required licence or when the licence has been obtained by false or incomplete declarations, and the value of the goods, merchandise or effects contraband object is not higher than EUR 50,000 (above EUR 18,000, sanctions are no longer administrative but become criminal and are treated under criminal law) can be categorized as follows:

(a) Very serious, when the value of the goods, merchandise or object trafficking is higher to EUR 12,000.00.
(b) Serious: when the value is equal or higher to EUR 1,000.00 and equal or inferior to EUR 12,000.00.
(c) Slight: when the value is less than EUR 1,000.00.

The sanction will consist of a fine in relation to the value of the goods, merchandise exported in fraud, within the following limits:

(a) Very serious: 250%-350%.
(b) Serious: 150%-250%.
(c) Slight: 100%-150%.

The graduation of the sanctions will depend on the reiteration, the resistance, refusal or obstruction to the investigation, the fraudulent means use or the commission of the infraction by means of interposed person, the nature of the goods, merchandise or effects object of the fraudulent export.

It is important to indicate that, in order to apply for an export or import licence, the operator (importer/exporter) must obtain a registration on to the special Register of Foreign Trade Operators in defence and dual-use items. This Registry is made up of the data furnished by the operator, as well as any other data relative to the activities related to the operations controlled as per RD n° 679/2014. Therefore, any prior convictions will be taken into account for registration on the Registry (or for the withdrawal from such Registry). The General Secretariat-General for Foreign Trade and the JIMDDU has the possibility of successfully obtaining information from other Administrations on a given importer/exporter.

Finally, in addition to the company itself, company management can be imposed criminal or administrative sanctions in the event they supported the commission of the

1094. Article 9 of the Organic Law 6/2001 (BOE n° 156 of 1 Jul. 2011).

crime or the infraction or if, within the scope of their responsibilities, they did not make the efforts or acts necessary to avoid the commission of the crime or the infraction.

The General Secretary of Foreign Trade, besides having to obtain the prior consent of the JIMDDU, must take into account when deciding whether to grant or deny a licence: (i) the existence of reasonable grounds for believing that defence and dual-use might be employed in actions that may disturb the peace, or disrupt regional or global stability and security, or that the export of such goods may disturb Spanish international commitments; and (ii) Spain's overall national interest and foreign policy.

Article 8 of the RD n° *679/2014, of 1st Aug. 2014* provides that the importer/exporter may appeal from decisions of the General Secretary of Foreign Trade or the Customs and Taxes Department (in situations where the latter has granted the licence).

The operator can apply to the Ministry of Economy and Competitiveness if it feels that the decision was not valid.[1095]

Sub-Par. 3 Rectification of the Export or Import Licences

When changes arise in the circumstances of the transaction during the effective term of the defence material export or import licence, to the extent it has already been issued, the Secretary-General for foreign Trade, duly informed by the JIMDDU, may authorize the rectification of the particular requirements or conditions of the licence providing that they do not relate to the following points: specification of the goods; export or import country of destination; or export or import consignee and end-user, if relevant.

In the case of global licences and GPLs for the export of defence material, only the following rectifications may be made: the country-by-country breakdown of the quantities of products or technologies provided that this does not affect the licence's maximum quantity and value, and the customs departure point.

No rectification may be made in the PA and General Licence.

Sub-Section 2 Dual-Use Goods and Services

Par. 1 Overall Presentation

Sub-Par. 1 Requirements Prior to Any Specific Import/Export (i.e., Manufacturing Phase)

The requirements are the same established to the export or import of defence goods, except for the fact that, in the case of dual-use related goods, it is not necessary to register in the Special Register of foreign trade Operators in defence and dual-use items.

1095. Article 8 of the RD n° *679/2014, of 1st Aug 2014*, following the process developed in the Article 114 of the Spanish law n° 30/1992 of 26 Nov. 1992 (BOE 27/11/92).

Sub-Par. 2 Requirements at the Import/Export Stage

I Goods

(a) The requirements for importing and exporting dual-use goods are described in Section 4 Sub-section 2 Par. 3 of this chapter. Import/export activities can be permanent, temporary or result from one temporary import activity. The types of licences available (individual, global, and general licence) are the same as for defence goods. The specific conditions are established in Article 25 of the RD n° 679/2014.

(b) The difference with the defence classifications types of licences are in the case of general licences, where the person interested in doing the import/export activity must fill the conditions set forth in Regulation (EC) n° 428/2009 as amended[1096] for both import and export. In the case of dual-use goods, the GPL is not applicable.

II Services[1097]

The Spanish regulation does not contain any specific provisions relating to the export/import of services.

III Persons/Deemed Export

See above: Section 4, Sub-section 1.

Par. 2 Control Lists

Export of dual-use goods that require a licence are listed in Appendices I, II and IV of the EU Regulations (EC) n° 428/2009 as amended.[1098]

Imports of dual-use goods which require a licence are set out in list (1), (2) and (3) of the Chemical Arms Convention and are divided into ten categories.[1099] Imports of substances to use in the production of chemical arms are listed in Appendix III.3 of the RD n° 844/2011.

For transactions involving dual-use items and technologies, the said authorization holders shall also be subject to the control measures laid down in Council Regulation (EC) N° 1334/2000 of 22 June 2000 setting up a Community regime for the control of exports of dual-use items and technology and Council Regulation (EC) N° 1504/2004 of 19 July 2004 amending and updating the former.

1096. See *supra* n. 230.
1097. See Chapter 6, Section 4, Sub-Section 2, Par. 1.
1098. *Ibid.*
1099. Nuclear materials, installations and equipments; toxins materials and chemical substance; materials treatment; electronics; computers; telecommunications and information security; sensors and lasers, navigation and airplane, navy, propulsion systems, spatial vehicles and related equipments.

Par. 3 Licensing and Enforcement Authorities

See *supra* Chapter 14 Section 4. Sub-Section 1. Par. 3.

Figure 14.2 summarizes the licence application process and the licensing/enforcement authorities involved.

Figure 14.2 EU Dual Use Goods and Technology Licensing System

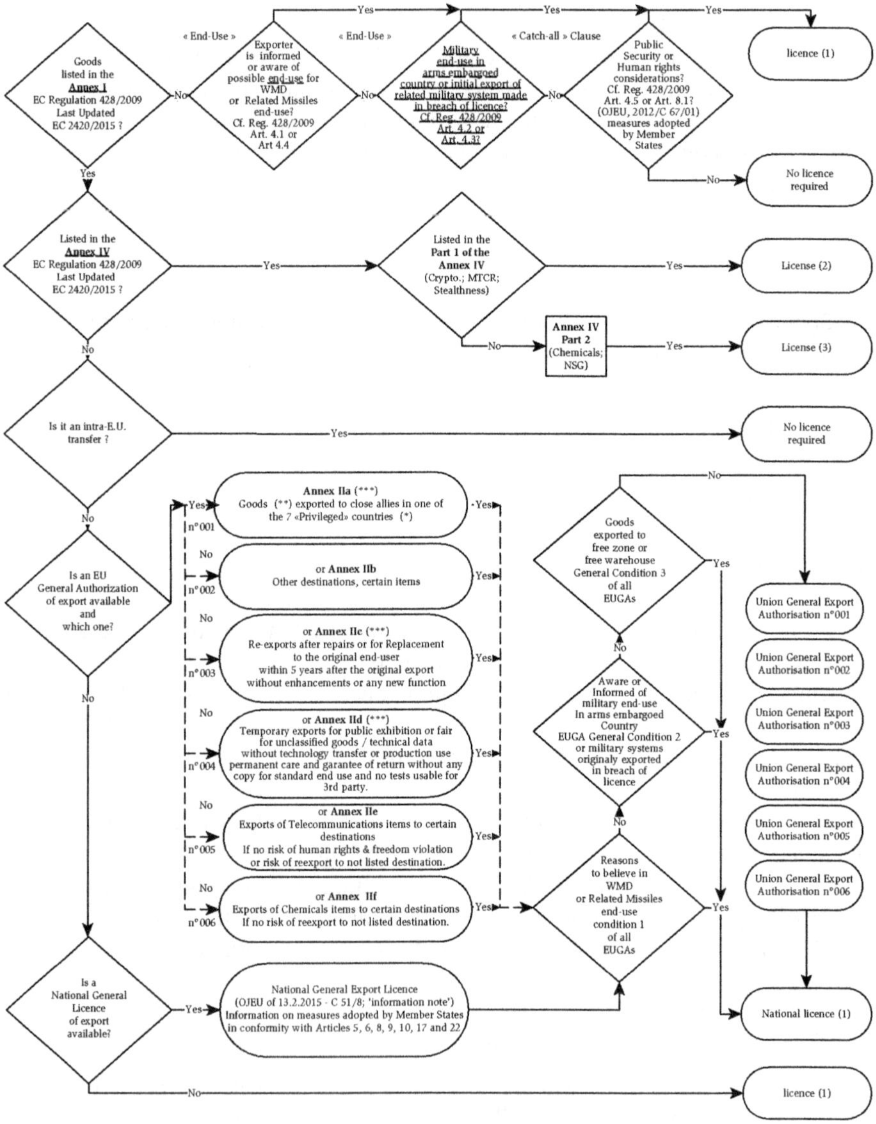

(1) Each EU Members states determines which type of EU licence (Individual or Global) is applicable.
(2) For goods and related technologies listed in Annex IV Part 1, Individual or Global EU licences are available.
(3) For goods and related technologies listed in Annex IV Part 2, only Individual licences are permitted.

(*) Seven countries listed in Annex IIa (EC) Regulation n° 428/2009 are the following: Australia, Canada, Japan, New-Zealand, Norway, Switzerland and US.
(**) Nearly all goods listed in Annex I excepted those listed in Annex IV and few others deemed very sensitive (cf. Annex g).
(***) cf. Annex 1Ig for possible other not authorized items.

Table 14.9 indicates which annex of the RD n° 679/2014 is to be used for which type of import or export.

Table 14.9

Type of Licence	*Export*	*Import*
Individual Licence	Ap. VI.1 Ap. VI.2 Ap. VI.3	Ap. VI.1 Ap. VI.2 Ap. VI.3
Global Licence	Ap. VI.9 Ap. VI.10	Ap. VI.9 Ap. VI.10
Global Project Licence	N/A	N/A
General Authorization	Ap. VI.11	There is no Ap. Established
Brokering Authorization	N/A	N/A
Previous Agreement	N/A	N/A
Additional Documents*	Aps. VI. 15 to 22	Aps. VI. 15 to 22

Abbreviation: Ap.: Appendix.

* In some cases, JIMDDU may be request additional documents, which are established in those Ap.

Par. 4 Sanctions and Recourses of the Importer/Exporter

See this Chapter 14 on Section 4 Sub-Section 1 Par. 4 supra.

SECTION 5 SPECIFICITIES/SPACE-RELATED PROVISIONS

Sub-Section 1 Specificities of the Control Regime

The Spanish regime is structured in a simple way; one text governs both imports/exports of military and dual-use products and the same authorities are in charge of implementing the procedure which is common to both import and exports and to both military and dual-use products.

Sub-Section 2 Space-Related Provisions in the Control Regime

There are no specific provisions under Spanish law for space-related export/import of equipment.

SECTION 6 LIST OF ABBREVIATIONS

ATS	Australian Treaty Series
BOE	*Boletin Oficial del Estado*
EC	European Community/European Communities
EU	European Union
GSFT	General Secretary of Foreign Trade
IAEA	International Atomic Energy Agency
ICE	*Información Comercial Española*
ILM	International Legal Material
JIMDDU	*Junta Inter-Ministerial de Defensa y Uso Doble*
NATO	North Atlantic Treaty Organization
LoI	Letter of Intent
OSCE	Organization for Security and Co-operation in Europe
PA	Previous Agreement
RD	Royal Decree
TDC	Trans-national Defence Companies
UNTS	United Nations Treaty Series

SECTION 7 REFERENCES

Sub-Section 1 Primary Documentation

Par. 1 Statutory Legislation

Organic Law n° 12/1995 of 12 December 1995 establishes the repression to trafficking crimes. It has been published in BOE n° 297 of 13 December 1995.

Par. 2 Regulations

- Law 53/2007, of 28 December 2007, about the control of foreign trade of Defence and Dual-Use goods. It has been published in BOE n° 312 of 29 December 2007.
- RD n° 844/2011 of 12 December 2001 regulates foreign trade on defence goods, material of use dual and other goods and technology of use dual. It has been published in BOE n° 6 of 7 January 2009.
- RD n° 844/2011 of 17 June 2011 to amend the RD n° 844/2011 and to implement the Directive of 2009/43/EC, of 6 May 2009.

- RD n° 679/2014 of 1 of August, for the amendment and compilation of the RD 2061/2008 and RD 844/2011 in order to have one RD.

Par. 3 Other

Regulation EC n° 428/2009 of the Council 5 May 2009 establishes the European Community regime for the control of exports of dual-use goods and technologies of use dual.[1100]

Par. 4 Annexes – Copies of Documents of Practical Use to the Importer/Exporter

A number of standard documents relevant for the import or export process in Spain (e.g., most current official application forms for import or export licences, templates of contractual undertaking, or regulation extracts) as well as other non-official documents are available on a dedicated DropBox folder which can be accessed by following the link below: www.kluwerlawonline.com/eclrh-annexes.

Sub-Section 2 Secondary Documentation

Par. 1 Internet Sites

- http://noticias.juridicas.com: Internet site which offers the most up to date state of Spanish laws and regulations as well as other information such as jurisprudence and doctrine.
- www.datadiar.com: Internet site of Spanish company which offers law services in different fields. In this site we can find law regulation and official bulletins among others.
- http://www.mineco.gob.es/: Internet site of the Minister of Economy and Competitiveness where can be found the information of the State Secretary of Tourism and Trade.
- www.igsap.map.es: Internet site containing the administrative information centre of the Minister of Public Affairs of Spain.
- www.maec.es: Internet site containing information of the Minister of Foreign Affairs of Spain.
- www.mde.es: Internet site containing information of Minister of Defence of Spain.
- http://www.comercio.mineco.gob.es/es-ES/Paginas/default.aspx: Internet site with information of the Spanish General Secretary of Foreign Trade.
- http://europa.eu.int: Internet site of the EU where can be found different sorts of information such as the acts related to the external trade and import market of goods and technology of dual-use.

1100. See *supra* n. 230.

- www.aeat.es: Internet site of the tax agency of Spain which contains the tax information and links to Span Ministry of Economy, among other things.
- www.boe.es: Internet site of the State Official Bulletin of Spain, within the Ministry of the Presidency in charge of the printing, distribution and sale of the official diary, BOE, and so forth.

Par. 2 Paper Publications

Annual report by Spanish Government published in the 'Boletin Economico' of ICE (Commercial Information of Spain) issued by the Ministry of Economic and Treasury Ministry normally in November every year.

SECTION 8 USEFUL INFORMATION

Sub-Section 1 Licensing and Enforcement Authorities Contact Details

Name of Organization	*General Secretary of Foreign Trade (Secretaría General de Comercio Exterior)*
Postal Address	Paseo de la Castellana, 162. 28046 – Madrid, Spain
Telephone	+ 34 915835284
Fax	+ 34 915835619
Email address	buzon.oficial@sgdefensa.secgcomex.sscc.mineco.es
Website	http://www.comercio.gob.es/es-ES/Paginas/default.aspx

Name of Organization	*Inter-Ministerial Regulatory Board of Foreign Trade of Defence and Use Dual Goods Junta Interministerial Reguladora del Comercio Exterior de Material de Defensa y de Doble Uso)*
Postal Address	Paseo de la Castellana, 160. 28071- Madrid, Spain
Telephone	+ 34 902 446006
Fax	+ 34 91 4578066
Website	http://www.comercio.gob.es/es-ES/Paginas/default.aspx

I *Other*

Name of Organization	*Department of Customs and Taxes (Departamento de Aduanas e Impuestos Especiales)*
Postal Address	C/ Guzmán el Bueno, 139. 28003 – Madrid, Spain
Telephone	+ 34 91 5826805

Name of Organization	*Department of Customs and Taxes (Departamento de Aduanas e Impuestos Especiales)*
Fax	+ 34 91 3937553
Email address	dri12000@correo.aeat.es
Website	www.aeat.es

Sub-Section 2 Other

None.

CHAPTER 15
Sweden

Mattias Hedwall[*]

SECTION 1 TABLE OF CONTENTS

[*] This chapter is co-written with Olof Konig previously an associate at Baker & McKenzie in Stockholm.

SECTION 2 EXECUTIVE SUMMARY

Sweden applies a strict legislative and regulatory framework to control export of products and services deemed sensitive.[1101] Sweden, as many other countries applies the general rule 'prohibited unless and until authorized'. The export regime in Sweden is closely linked to the political agenda and Sweden actively participates in the development of the European export control system. The Swedish export control regime for Dual-Use Technology closely follows the European regime and the Swedish Government has refrained from imposing any additional rules regarding Dual-Use export. Sweden has, e.g., not included any additional products to the list of Dual-Use Goods included in the European regime.[1102] Sweden applies an export control of certain types of technical assistance in relation to Military Goods which is similar to the concept applied within the Dual-Use control. Sweden applies the same view as the other Member States in relation Dual-Use Services. Thus, at the present time, there is no specific regulatory framework which deals with Dual-Use Services in Sweden.

The export control process for Military Goods is based on the Swedish Military Equipment Act. The Government's export principles guide the assessment on a case-by-case basis and include several conditions that should be met in order for an Export Licence to be granted. The Swedish Military Equipment Act applies to Defence Materials including both Military Goods used in combat and other Military Goods listed in the appendix to the act. The Swedish list of controlled Military Goods mainly consists of the European Union (EU) Military List[1103] with only a few exceptions.

To be able to produce or develop Defence Materials it is necessary to apply for a Production Permit. A licence is required for the production of any material or components listed as Defence Material. The Production Permit also grants the right to sell the same Defence Materials to third parties. A company that only intends to sell and market Defence Materials needs to apply for a Supply Permit. If a company wants to export Defence Materials or services out of Sweden, it is necessary to apply for an Export Licence. There are three types of Export Licences available in Sweden; General, Individual and Global Export Licence.

All companies that have been granted a Production Permit or a Supply Permit are obliged to report all marketing efforts outside of Sweden. Furthermore, it is necessary to inform the Swedish Agency for Non-Proliferation and Export Control, *Inspektionen för Strategiska Produkter* (ISP), before entering into any binding contracts or submitting

1101. In this chapter, (a) 'good(s)' or 'product(s)' shall refer collectively to hardware, software and technology; Defence Material will refer as generic expression to all equipment specially designed or modified for military purpose; (b) 'Military Goods' shall mean the items specifically listed in the Swedish Military Equipment Act (*Lag (1992:1300) om krigsmateriel*).

1102. In this chapter 'Dual-Use Goods' shall mean the items specifically listed in the Swedish Act on Control of Dual – Use and of Technical Assistance (*Lag (2000:1064)*.

1103. EU Military List developed within the cooperation of GUSP updated as of 17 Mar. 2014, http://eur-lex.europa.eu/legal-content/SV/TXT/PDF/?uri=OJ:JOC_2014_107_R_0001&rid=1.

a binding offer/bid for the sale or provision of Defence Materials. Sweden has not implemented any regulation related to 'deemed' export connected to a person's citizenship.

Sweden imposes control on the export, not only on Defence Materials but also on other strategic or Dual-Use Goods which have both civilian and military use. In addition to their established civilian functions, these Dual-Use Goods can be used in the production or facilitation of weapons of mass destruction (WMD) and other Defence Material or for other military purposes. Efforts to prevent the distribution of WMD have been a significant focus of Sweden's foreign policy since the Second World War. For some time, Sweden has been an active participant in the international efforts for peace, détente and armaments control.

The Swedish export control regime of Dual-Use Goods presumes that export shall be allowed and only under certain circumstances should a licence be refused. An application for an Export Licence for the export of Dual-Use Goods should be refused if the goods are suspected to be used for a prohibited purpose.

Sweden applies the same view as many other EU Member States in relation to Dual-Use Services. Thus, at the present time, there is no specific regulatory framework which deals specifically with Dual-Use Services in Sweden. This issue is, however, closely linked to the matter of 'intangible transfers', and ISP will to a large extent apply a similar approach as for military services and technical assistance. Sweden does not apply any restriction on export purely via dual citizenships of a foreign national with respect to the export of Dual-Use Goods. The listed Dual-Use Goods can be found in the latest EC Regulation[1104] and its appendices. Sweden has not added any additional goods to the export control list of Dual-Use Goods.

Sweden only adheres to the international sanctions decided by the EU and the United Nation's (UN's) Security Council. Sweden has not imposed any further international sanctions toward any country or individual. This means that a company subject to Swedish jurisdiction is required to comply with the sanctions decided by the EU and the UN's Security Council. The applicable legal basis for Sweden's adherence to its international commitments can be found in the Swedish Act on International Sanctions (*lagen (1996:95) om vissa internationella sanktioner*).

SECTION 3 INTRODUCTION – ELEMENTS OF CONTEXT

Sub-Section 1 Regime Overall Philosophy

Par. 1 Export Control Regime for Military Goods

Sweden applies a strict legislative and regulatory framework to control export of products and services deemed sensitive. Sweden, as many other countries, applies the general rule 'prohibited unless and until authorized'. The export regime in Sweden is

1104. EC Regulation 388/2012, http://eur-lex.europa.eu/LexUriServ/LexUriServ.do?uri=OJ:L:2012:129:0012:0280:SV:PDF.

closely linked to the political agenda. Sweden, both historically and presently, has a successful industry focusing on the development and sale of Military Goods which has resulted in a pragmatic view when it comes to export control while ensuring political stability and non-proliferation. Export Licences will only be granted provided that the export:

- is considered to effectively fulfil Sweden's defence objectives;
- is deemed desirable in terms of Swedish security policy;
- does not constitute a breach of the principles and objectives of Swedish foreign policy related to, among other things, armed conflicts, human rights and multilateral agreements.

The responsible authority will make an overall assessment of all relevant circumstances, taking into account the above principles. Sweden has implemented the European list[1105] of Military Goods with only a couple of additional items. The items which are not included in the European list are divided into three entries: (1) nuclear charges and special components to such items, (2) fortification structures and technology for such structures, (3) saxitoxin and rincin.

Par. 2 Export Control Regime for Dual-Use Goods

The Swedish export control regime for Dual-Use Goods and Technology closely follows the European regime, which was established by Council Regulation (EC) no. 428/2009. The Swedish Government/Administration has thus refrained from establishing additional rules regarding Dual-Use export. Sweden has not included any additional products to the list of Dual-Use Goods included in the European regime.

Par. 3 Military Services

Sweden applies an export control of certain types of technical assistance which is similar to the concepts applied within the Dual-Use control. Technical assistance constitutes assistance in connection with any products included in the list of Military Goods. The export control of technical assistance includes any information that is required for the development, production or use of any listed product. The information can also consist of technical details or technical support.

Certain types of technical assistance are excluded from the export control regime:

- Technical assistance that is required for installation, operation, maintenance and/or repair or if an Export Licence has been granted.
- Technical assistance that falls within the definition of information that is publicly available or fundamental research and information required for a patent application.

1105. Please see EU Chapter for further details.

It is essential to differentiate between technical assistance and military training. Military training refers to the handling of Military Goods that can be used in connection to armed combat, both within Sweden and abroad. Regardless of whether the service is deemed as a technical assistance or military training it is necessary to apply for the relevant Export Licences.

Par. 4 Dual-Use Services

Sweden applies a similar view as many other EU Member States in relation to Dual-Use Services. Thus, at the present time, there is no regulatory framework in Sweden which deals specifically with Dual-Use Services. This topic is, however, closely linked to the issue of 'intangible transfers', and the rules would to a large extent be applied similarly as for military services describe under Par. 3 above. Services that are or maybe intended, in their entirety or in part, for use in connection with the development, production, handling or operation of a controlled product could constitute an 'intangible transfers' and thus be subject to export control.

Par. 5 Process to Be Followed by Exporters According to the Swedish Control Regime

Prior to considering an export of goods, technology or service, exporters need to consider if the regulations relating to Military Goods or Dual-Use Goods apply. In order to assess whether a product, technology or service constitute a controlled item, the exporters need to assess the item as a whole but also its components and scope of application. Even though the primary responsibility lies on the exporters, guidance can be retrieved from ISP. Furthermore, the exporters should collect as precise information as possible about the end-use, the end-user and to which country the goods are exported. The exporter needs to consider whether the goods or the exporter itself could be subject to any other export control regime such as the US, Canadian, Australian etc., both in relation to export control and sanctions. Finally, the exporters need to consider whether there are any practical issues that could constitute problems in the contemplated export, such as not being able to receive payment for the goods due to decisions made by financial service providers as well as the risk for new sanctions being imposed. If a product, technology or service is export controlled, the exporter should proceed and apply for any relevant applicable Export Licence. As regards Military Goods, it is also necessary to consider to what extent and under which circumstances the exporter can market its products as well as participate in procurements.

Sub-Section 2 Historical Outlook

Par. 1 Military Goods

Until 1993, the Swedish export regime on Military Goods consisted of the Swedish Act on Control of the Production of Military Equipment etc. *(lagen (1983:1034) om kontroll över tillverkningen av krigsmateriel, m.m.)* and the Swedish Act on the Prohibition to

Export Military Equipment etc. (*lagen (1988:558) om förbud mot utförsel av krigsmateriel, m.m.)*. The Swedish Government passed the current Swedish Military Equipment Act (*Lag (1992:1300) om krigsmateriel*) and the subordinate Regulation (1992:1303) on Military Equipment in 1992. The Swedish Government has recently decided to initiate an investigation with the assignment to present a motion for a new military act.[1106] The new act is intended to reinforce the Swedish export control against non-democratic nations.

Par. 2 Dual-Use Goods

Prior to the implementation of the current act dealing with export control of Dual-Use Goods such issues were dealt with in the Swedish Act on Strategic Products (*Lag (1991:341) om strategiska produkter*). Since the year 2000 export control of Dual-Use Goods is regulated through the Swedish Act on Control of Dual-Use Products and Technical Assistance (*lagen (2000:1064) om kontroll av produkter med dubbla användningsområden och av tekniskt bistånd*). The latest adjustments to the act were made in 2010. The act includes supplementary provisions to the EC Regulation no. 428/2009.

Sub-Section 3 Participation in International Regimes

In order to contribute to the strengthening of international security and stability, Sweden participates in the international struggle against the proliferation of WMD and their means of delivery, and has committed itself to a number of international treaties. Sweden is also an active member of the various multilateral export control regimes and suppliers groups which establish lists of sensitive materials whose export is subject to strict control, and provide for exchanges of information between participating states.

The following tables display Sweden's participation status in export control related international treaties and programmes. It is also stated, when relevant, if Sweden is party to a treaty either by signature and ratification or by accession.

Par. 1 Treaties and Regimes Dealing with Specific Items and Technologies

Table 15.1 Nuclear Weapons Treaties

Treaty Name	*Overall Status*	*Specific Status*	*Enforceable in Sweden*
Limited Test Ban Treaty[1107]	OS: 5 August 1963 EF: 10 October 1963	S: 12 August 1963 R: 9 December 1963	Yes

1106. Kommitté Direktiv 2012:50. The new investigation is also called the KEX-investigation.
1107. Treaty Banning Nuclear Weapon Tests in the Atmosphere, in Outer Space and Under Water, *U.N.T.S.*, vol. 480, p. 43.

Treaty Name	*Overall Status*	*Specific Status*	*Enforceable in Sweden*
Nuclear Non-Proliferation Treaty[1108]	OS: 1 July 1968 EF: 5 March 1970	S: 19 August 1968 R: 9 January 1970	Yes
Comprehensive Nuclear Test Ban Treaty[1109]	OS: 24 September 1996 EF: not in force	S: 24 September 1996 R: 2 December 1998	No

OS: Opened for signature; EF: Entry into force; S/R: Signature/Ratification; A: Accession

Table 15.2 Biological and Chemical Weapons Treaties

Treaty Name	*Overall Status*	*Specific Status*	*Enforceable in* Sweden
Geneva Protocol[1110]	OS: 17 June 1925 EF: 8 February 1928	S: 17 June 1925 R: 25 April 1930	Yes
Biological Convention[1111]	OS: 10 April 1972 EF: 26 March 1975	S: 27 February 1975 R: 5 February 1976	Yes
Chemical Convention[1112]	OS: 13 January 1993 EF: 29 April 1997	S: 13 January 1993 R: 17 June 1993	Yes

OS: Opened for signature; EF: Entry into force; S/R: Signature/Ratification; A: Accession

Table 15.3 Multilateral Export Control Regimes

Regime Name	*Formation*	*Participation*
Zangger Committee[1113]	1971	Yes
Nuclear Suppliers Group	1974	Yes
Australia Group	1985	Yes
Missile Technology Control Regime	1987	Yes
Wassenaar Arrangement[1114]	1994	Yes

1108. Treaty on the Non-Proliferation of Nuclear Weapons, *U.N.T.S.*, vol. 729, p. 161.
1109. U.N.G.A., resolution 50\245.
1110. Protocol for the Prohibition of the Use in War of Asphyxiating, Poisonous or Other Gases, and of Bacteriological Methods of Warfare, 94, *League of Nations Treaty Series*, No. 2138 (1929).
1111. Convention on the Prohibition of the Development, Production and Stockpiling of Bacteriological (Biological) and Toxin Weapons and On Their Destruction, *U.N.T.S.*, vol. 1015, p. 163.
1112. Convention on the Prohibition of the Development, Production, Stockpiling and Use of Chemical Weapons and on Their Destruction, Doc.CD/CW/WP.400/Rev.1.
1113. Non-Proliferation Treaty Exporters Committee (also called the Zangger Committee).
1114. Wassenaar Arrangement on Export Control for Conventional Arms and Dual-Use Goods and Technologies.

Table 15.4 Others

Name	Adoption	Participation
International Code of conduct[1115]	25 November 2002	Yes
The UN Arms Trade Treaty	S: 13 June 2014	Yes

OS: Opened for signature; EF: Entry into force; S/R: Signature/Ratification; A: Accession

Par. 2 Treaties Dealing with Specific Areas

Table 15.5 International Zones

Treaty Name	Overall Status	Specific Status	Enforceable in Sweden
Antarctic Treaty[1116]	OS: 1 December 1959 EF: 23 June 1961	A: 24 April 1984	Yes
Outer Space Treaty (OST)[1117]	OS: 27 January 1967 EF: 10 October 1967	S: 27 January 1967 R: 11 October 1967	Yes
Sea Bed Arms Control Treaty[1118]	OS: 11 February 1971 EF: 18 May 1972	S: 11 February 1971 R: 28 April 1972	Yes
Moon Agreement[1119]	OS: 18 December 1979 EF: 11 July 1984	–	No
Convention on the Law of the Sea[1120]	OS: 10 December 1982 EF: 16 November 1994	S: 10 December 1982 R: 26 June 1996	Yes

OS: Opened for signature; EF: Entry into force; S/R: Signature/Ratification; A: Accession

Table 15.6 Regional Nuclear Weapons-Free Zones

Treaty Name	Overall Status	Specific Status	Enforceable in Sweden
Treaty of Tlatelolco[1121]	OS: 14 February 1967 EF: 22 April 1967	–	No

1115. Hague Code of Conduct against Ballistic Missile Proliferation, not yet published.
1116. 402, *U.N.T.S.*, 7.
1117. Treaty on Principles Governing the Activities of States in the Exploration and Use of Outer Space, including the Moon and Other Celestial Bodies, *U.N.T.S.*, vol. 610, p. 205.
1118. Treaty on the Prohibition of the Emplacement of Nuclear Weapons and other Weapons of Mass Destruction on the Seabed and The Ocean Floor and in the subsoil thereof, *U.N.T.S.*, vol. 955, p. 115.
1119. Agreement governing the Activities of States on the Moon and Other Celestial Bodies, *I.L.M.*, vol. 18, p. 1434.
1120. Doc. A/CONF.62/122 and Corr.1-11.
1121. Treaty for the Prohibition of Nuclear Weapons in Latin America and the Caribbean, *U.N.T.S.*, vol. 634, p. 326.

Treaty Name	*Overall Status*	*Specific Status*	*Enforceable in Sweden*
Treaty of Rarotonga[1122]	OS: 6 August 1985 EF: 11 December 1986	–	No
Treaty of Bangkok[1123]	OS: 15 December 1995 EF: 27 March 1997	–	No
Treaty of Pelindaba[1124]	OS: 11 April 1996 EF: not in force	–	No

OS: Opened for signature; EF: Entry into force; S/R: Signature/Ratification; A: Accession

SECTION 4 CONTROL REGIME

Sub-Section 1 Military Goods and Services

Par. 1 Overall Presentation

The export control process for Military Goods is based on the Swedish Military Equipment Act. The Government's export guidelines direct the assessment on a case-by-case basis and include several conditions that should be met in order to permit export. The act applies to Defence Materials including both Military Goods used in combat and other Military Goods included in the appendix to the Military Equipment Act. The Swedish list on controlled goods consists mainly of the EU military list with only a few additional items. An Export Licence is required for all export of Defence Materials. Export is a broad concept that encompasses not only sales but also discontinuation, demonstrations, destructive testing, display purposes, returns, re-placements, temporary export, extensions of delivery time and transit. Thus, the export control regime for Defence Materials applies to all stages in the sales process starting from the manufacturing up to the confirmation of the receipt of the exported product. The Government's guidelines regarding follow-on deliveries, e.g., export of spare parts and ammunition related to previous approved export, is that such export should be approved unless international obligations require otherwise, such as an arms embargo imposed by the EU or UN.

Sub-Par. 1 Requirements Prior to Any Specific Import/Export (i.e., Construction Phase)

I Production Permit

In order to be allowed to produce or develop Defence Materials it is necessary for a company to apply for Production Permit. A licence is required for any material or

1122. South Pacific Nuclear Free Zone Treaty, *I.L.M.*, vol. 24, p. 1442.
1123. South East Asia Nuclear-Weapon-Free Zone Treaty, *I.L.M.*, vol. 35. p. 635.
1124. African Nuclear Weapon-Free Zone Treaty, *I.L.M.*, vol. 35, p. 698.

components listed as Defence Materials. The Production Permit also includes the right to provide the same materials to third parties. It is not necessary to apply for an Export Licence if the production consists of alterations or reconstruction of handheld firearms that are not fully automatic or concerns the construction of odd non-automatic weapons for personal use. Furthermore, it is not necessary to apply for a Production Permit to produce ammunition intended for personal use for someone authorized to possess hunting or similar activities. If the company intends to use reference weapons in its marketing efforts this should be stated when applying for the Production Permit. There are specific requirements associated with the production and sale of ammunition intended for third parties.

II Supply Permit

A company that only intends to sell and market Defence Material needs to apply for a Supply Permit. It is also necessary to apply for a Supply Permit if a Swedish company or person with a permanent residence or who has its habitual place of residence in Sweden sell or supply Defence Materials outside of Sweden. To sell and supply Defence Materials includes sales, granting a concession, leasing, gifts or brokering of such materials. It is not necessary to apply for a Supply Permit if the company has a Production Permit, when the recipient is a Swedish authority or when the recipient has a Production Permit.

Note that if the company acts as a broker for two or more parties established outside of Sweden the company should apply for a Separate Permit for each deal. Prior to applying for a Separate Permit it is necessary to apply for either a Production Permit or a Supply Permit. Finally, if a company is supplying Defence Materials to a party outside of Sweden it is necessary to apply for an Export Licence.

III Preliminary Ruling on Export of Defence Material

It is possible to submit a request for a preliminary ruling from ISP for a potential export of Defence Materials or services. It is especially important to use the possibility to get a preliminary ruling when exporting to new destinations which Sweden previously have not provided Defence Materials to or if the export is of a sensitive nature. After applying for a preliminary ruling the applicant receives a written statement from ISP. The ruling can be either positive or negative. ISP is also allowed to provide a statement which is conditional with specific requirements which needs to be met by the company. A preliminary ruling is valid approximately five years from its announcement. A preliminary ruling is not to be interpreted as an Export Licence as it is not a formal decision. ISP will always do a final assessment after receiving an application for an Export Licence. Even though a company applies for a preliminary ruling, it is still necessary to notify ISP in connection to the submission of an offer or a bid. Whether or not to submit an application for a preliminary ruling should be carefully considered. If the company decides to submit an application, the application should include information regarding:

- the company's competitive situation;
- the extent of the proposed business deal;
- timing of the proposed business deal as regards the buyers conclusion and delivery; and
- previous relations with the country in which the buyer is established.

Sub-Par. 2 Requirements at the Import and/or Export Stage

I Export and Licence

If a company wants to export Defence Material or services, it is necessary to apply for an Export Licence. It is necessary to assess a broad interpretation of what is included in the term 'export'. Export encompasses not only sales but also discontinuation, demonstrations, destructive testing, display purposes, returns, replacements, temporary export, extensions of delivery time and transit. Export to countries within and outside of the European Economic Area (EEA) is included in the Swedish export control regime. Export includes permanent as well as temporary export. There are three types of Export Licences available in Sweden: General, Individual and Global Export Licence. A company intending to export Defence Materials within the EEA can apply for either a General, an Individual or a Global Export Licence. For export to countries outside of the EEA, a company can apply for either an Individual or a Global Export Licence:

- A General Export Licence allows the exporting company to export Defence Materials and services to one or several categories of receivers in an EEA country in accordance with what has been approved in the licence. The licence will be limited to specific types of Defence Materials.
- There are two types of Global Export Licences available. The main licence grants the exporting company the right to export specific types of Defence Materials and services to one or several recipients in one or several countries regardless of whether such countries are located in the EEA or not. A Global Export Licence can be limited or unlimited in relation to volume of materials or services that are allowed to be exported under the licence. The other type of Global Export Licence is a Project Licence. The Project Licence is an alternative licence, adapted to meet the requirements stipulated under different framework agreements between Sweden and other countries.
- Individual Export Licence grants a specific company the right to supply specific Defence Materials or services to one or several named recipients in another country. The export can be made directly or indirectly through distributors and as one or several shipments.

It is always necessary to submit an end-user certificate when applying for an Export Licence. The end-user certificate will include details and requirements approved by the customer on the use and further dealings with the Defence Materials such as prohibiting the re-export of the items without the prior consent of the Swedish Government.

II Marketing, Bid/Offers

All companies that have been granted a Production Permit or a Supply Permit are obliged to report all marketing efforts outside of Sweden. The report should be in the form of a marketing report to ISP. The report is discussed by the company and ISP at periodical intervals in order to provide an overview of future business opportunities and in order for ISP to be able to provide feedback to the company at an early stage. ISP may grant a company an exception to the main rule of providing a marketing report.

Prior to submitting a binding offer or entering into an agreement with a customer, or signing a letter of intent with a potential customer, it is necessary to notify ISP of such action. The reason being that ISP should be able to prohibit the offer or agreement if necessary. Most often there is a close contact between ISP and the exporting company prior to an offer being submitted in order for the company to retrieve an approval on the proposed business opportunity. It is rare that ISP restricts a company from entering into an agreement or from providing an offer and those occasions are most often related to new developments in the receiving country. ISP will not formally address a notification regarding an offer or any other business opportunity and the company is free to proceed four weeks after submitting the notification unless ISP has provided a negative decision to the company. A notification is valid for twelve months after the four-week time limit has ended. After the twelve months period has ended ISP should be notified again if the business opportunity reoccurs.

III Goods in Transit and Other Issues

If a company needs to transit goods through Sweden it may be necessary to apply for either an Individual or Global Export Licence. It is not necessary to apply for a licence if the transit is from one EEA country to another and the exporting company has a valid Export Licence. If it is necessary to apply for a licence it is important that the material be accurately described in Swedish. Any available information on the classification of the materials should also be included in the application. Furthermore, it is necessary to state the value of the goods in transit. The addresses of the exporting and receiving parties should also be stated in the application.

In addition to the general rules included in the Swedish Military Equipment Act there are also specific rules on outsourcing of production, military training and certification of recipients of Defence Materials.

Sub-Par. 3 Military Services

Sweden applies export control of certain types of technical assistance which is similar to the concept applied within the Dual-Use control. Technical assistance constitutes assistance in connection with any Defence Materials. The export control of technical assistance includes any information that is required for the development, production or use of any Defence Materials. The information can also consist of technical details or technical support.

Certain types of technical assistance are excluded from the export control regime:

- technical assistance that is required for installation, operation, maintenance and/or repair or if an Export Licence has been granted; or
- technical assistance that falls within the definition of information that is publicly available or fundamental research and information required for a patent application.

It is essential to differentiate between technical assistance and military training. Military training refers to the handling of Military Goods that can be used in connection to armed combat both within Sweden and abroad.

Sub-Par. 4 Persons

Sweden has not implemented any regulation related to 'deemed' export. The restrictions that are included in the Swedish export control regime on Defence Materials are limited to the export of services and military training.

Par. 2 Control Lists

The export controlled Defence Material included in the Swedish export control regime can mainly be found in the annex to the subordinate Regulation (1992:1303) on Military equipment. The annex is divided into four separate sections A-D. The first section consists of a list with all export controlled Defence Materials. A subdivision in section A differentiate between Defence Materials included in the EU military list adopted 17 March 2014 and other materials not included in the EU military list. Sweden has incorporated the complete list set out in the EU military list and also uses the same terminology to define the different items (ML). The very limited list with materials not included in the EU military list can be found under section Ab. The other sections of the annex set out definitions (B), lists with products and substances for which a declaration obligation is imposed on the exporter due to Sweden's participation in the Organisation for the Prohibition of Chemical Weapons (OPCW) (C). The final section includes information on which Defence Material that are deemed as Military Goods intended for combat and which material that is not intended for combat (D).

In order to assess whether there are any export restrictions applicable to a company's business it is necessary to classify all products and compare the result of such classification to the export control list. A company that needs to classify a product, material or service can consider to either classify the products by itself or to submit a request for classification to ISP. Most often a combination of the two choices is used in which the company analyses the product and requests a confirmation from ISP. ISP also recommends companies to self classify its products. To submit a product for classification to ISP can take several months depending on the complexity and sensitivity of the product and the information available to ISP.

When classifying a product, it is necessary to decide whether it meets the requirements in the listed product entries. There are a couple of issues that especially need to be considered. It is necessary to assess whether it meets the requirements for an ML (included in the EU military list) or NL (national controlled products) item. Furthermore, the company needs to consider if the Military Goods are intended for combat or not. How an item should be assessed basically comes down to if the item has been developed or modified for military use and whether it can be used in a destructive way. If the product is intended to be used for or in combat the product will be defined as a KS product. If the product is not intended for combat it will be defined as an ÖK product.

Par. 3 Licensing and Enforcement Authorities

Sub-Par. 1 Requirements Prior to Any Specific Export (i.e., Manufacturing Stage)

The company needs to classify the items intended for export in order to assess whether any licence and permits are required. The company can either self classify the items or require assistance from ISP. Provided that the company comes to the conclusion that it will produce or market export controlled items it needs to apply for either a Production Permit or a Supply Permit from ISP.

Sub-Par. 2 Prior to the Export Stage

The company will need to have an ongoing communication with ISP regarding its marketing efforts and the company will need to submit marketing reports to ISP from time-to-time. When the company is presented with an interesting business opportunity to provide export controlled items to a customer outside the EEA, the company can submit a request for a preliminary ruling from ISP. The preliminary ruling will provide the company with guidance on whether it is likely that the company in the future will receive any necessary Export Licence in order to take advantage of the opportunity. After receiving a positive preliminary ruling the company will proceed and submit a notification of any bid submitted by the company to the end customer.

Sub-Par. 3 At the Export Stage

The company submits an application for an appropriate Export Licence to ISP. Whether ISP will grant the company the necessary Export Licence will depend on several different factors. Though, if the company has gone through all the different stages there should not be any problems for the company, as any issues should already have been identified and dealt with in the company's previous contacts with ISP. The company shall inform the customs of the granted Export Licence in connection to the export and finally submit a declaration of delivery to ISP showing that the exported goods have been delivered to the end customer every six or twelve months, depending on which licence the company has been granted.

Sub-Par. 4 Control Regime Procedure Chart

Figure 15.1

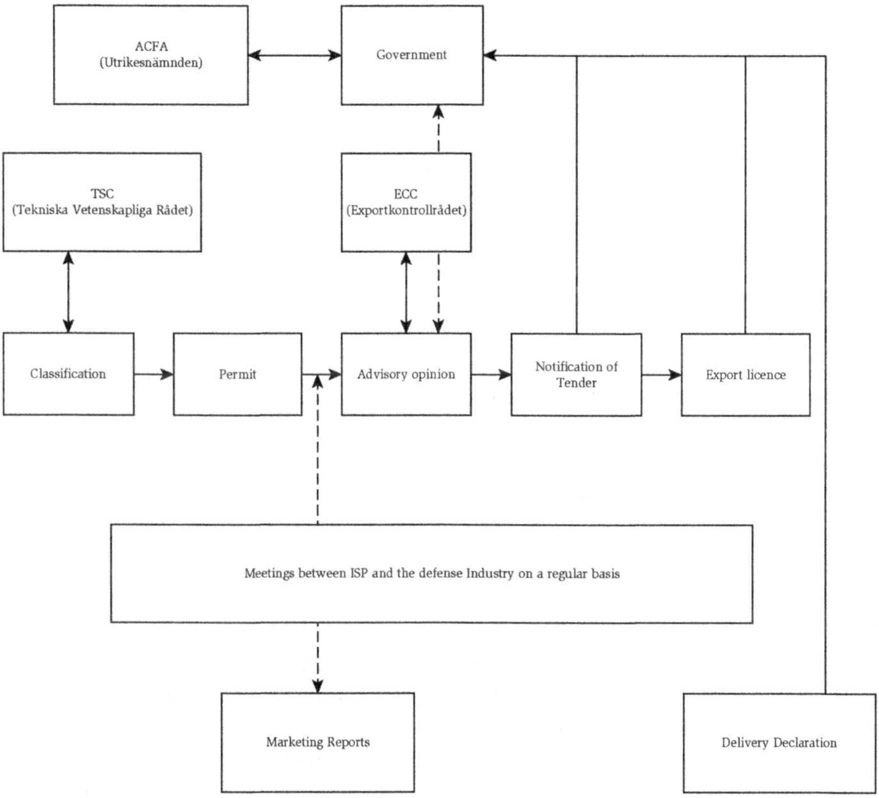

Par. 4 Sanctions and the Recourses of The Importer/Exporter

Should the company or any of its employees not comply with applicable regulation they could face a number of different civil and criminal sanctions. The sanctions can mainly be found in the Swedish Military Equipment Act but there are also sanction provisions in the Swedish Act on Penalties for Smuggling (2000:1225) and the Swedish Penal Code. The potential sanctions span between fines up to a maximum sanction of six years imprisonment. Sanctions can be imposed both for import and export in violation of applicable legislation. The available sanctions are mainly criminal, and in relation to some violations it is a requirement that the responsible person has acted with gross negligence, and in some cases intent, in order for liability to be imposed. In some cases, ISP needs to provide its consent prior to public prosecution can be initiated. Further, the company can be charged a penalty for not ensuring that it has sufficient procedures in place in order to avoid violating the applicable legislation. The maximum company penalty amounts to SEK 10,000,000 (approximately Euro 110,000-120,000). Furthermore, goods involved in a violation can be confiscated and forfeited.

Sub-Section 2 Dual-Use Goods and Services

Par. 1 Overall Presentation

Sweden imposes control on the export, not only of Defence Material but also on other strategic or Dual-Use Goods which have both civilian and military uses. In addition to their established civilian functions, these Dual-Use Goods can also be used in the production or facilitation of WMD and other Defence Material or for other military purposes. Efforts to prevent the distribution of WMD have been a significant focus of Sweden's foreign policy since the Second World War. For some time, Sweden has been an active participant in the international efforts for peace, détente and armaments control.

From Sweden's point of view, control originally related to nuclear weapons was laid down in Non-Proliferation Treaty (NPT) which came into force in 1970. This Treaty was then complemented by the Nuclear Suppliers Group (NSG) in 1974, an export control arrangement in the field of nuclear technology of which Sweden has been a member since the mid 1970s. In 1991, Sweden joined the MTCR, an international confederation which exercises control on the export of equipment and technology in the field of missiles.

In 1985 an international cooperation was initiated, in what is known as the Australia Group, for coordinating the control imposed by the various participating countries on the export of chemical precursors, biological agents and production equipment. This cooperation was initiated to prevent the development and production of biological and chemical weapons. Sweden became a member of this group in 1991.

Sweden ratified the UN Convention against Biological Weapons from 1972 in 1975. The UN Convention prohibits all development, production and storage of biological weapons and organic toxins for military purposes. The UN Chemical Weapons Convention (CWC) which came into force in April 1997, prohibits all possession, development, production and use of chemical weapons and orders the destruction of all existing stocks of chemical weapons. Sweden ratified this convention in 1993.

Since the end of the 1940s, there has been control on the export of advanced technology to the state-trading countries of that time within the framework for what is known as the COCOM cooperation associated with North Atlantic Treaty Organization (NATO). COCOM was abolished in 1994 and negotiations to formulate a new export control arrangement began, focusing on preventing the export of products which might contribute to destabilizing Defence Materials in different parts of the world. In 1995 the Wassenaar Arrangement was established for this purpose and was signed by Sweden the same year. Sweden held the chair in this arrangement during 1996-1999.

The Swedish export control regime of Dual-Use Goods presumes, as a matter of principle, that export shall be allowed. It is only under certain circumstances that a licence will be refused. An application for an Export Licence should, for example, be refused if the goods are suspected to be used for a prohibited purpose.

Sub-Par. 1 Requirements Prior to Any Specific Import/Export (i.e., Construction Phase)

Dual-Use Goods are products that can be used in the production of WMD or high-tech weapons. At the same time Dual-Use Goods can be used in the production of common civilian products. This is why they are known as Dual-Use Goods. Examples of Dual-Use Goods include various types of chemicals, advanced technology tool, machines or encryption software. The definition of Dual-Use Goods also includes information and services that fulfil the same purpose as a Dual-Use Good, such as blueprints and similar transfer of information.

Dual-Use Goods are not subject to export control because they are dangerous themselves, but because they can be used in the production of weapons or other destructive items. The legislation is basically intended and structured to allow trade in the majority of cases. A prohibition is only issued in exceptional cases. This occurs when there are reasonable grounds to suspect that the product may be intended for a prohibited end-use.

Prior to an export the exporting company needs to classify its products in order to assess whether it is necessary to apply for an Export Licence or not. The exporting company classifies its products and other transfers of information in accordance with the Dual-Use regulation. If the company is uncertain of a specific classification it may seek guidance from ISP.

Sub-Par. 2 Requirements at the Import and/or Export Stage

I Preliminary Ruling on Export of Dual-Use Goods

If a company is uncertain whether an Export Licence will be granted by ISP, it may apply for a preliminary ruling from ISP. A preliminary ruling is given subject to the final decision after the export application has been assessed by ISP. Preliminary ruling may also involve conditions which aim to call on the company's attention, or to factors that will have significant bearing on the final decision. ISP's assessment only takes into account the relevant, prevailing conditions. If conditions change at a later stage, this may affect the outcome of the final assessment. A positive advanced notification is not an Export Licence decision. It does not free the company from the obligation to apply to ISP for an Export Licence.

II Types of Export Licences

All export of Dual-Use Goods requires an Export Licence. The term ‘export’ refers to:

- community goods leaving the customs territory of the Community;
- the re-export of non-Community goods; or
- the transmission of software or technology by electronic media, fax or telephone to a destination outside the Community.

In principle, the transfer of Dual-Use Goods to other EU Member States does not require a licence. Particularly sensitive products are, however, the exception to that rule. A list of such products is given in Annex IV of the Council Regulation.

The following rules apply in general in relation to the transfer of Dual-Use Goods to another EU Member State:

- The relevant commercial documents must state that the products are subject to control if exported. Relevant commercial documents include all sales contracts, order confirmations, invoices or dispatch notes. The following wording may be used: ‘This product is subject to export control if exported out of the European Union’.
- Documents are to be kept on file for at least five years.

The different types of export licences available are:

A. Community General Export Authorizations EU001-006

Under the Council Regulation, a set of Community General Export Authorizations have been developed. These Export Licences cover certain export to specific non-EU countries which fulfil requirements specified by the EU. The Community General Export Authorizations are ‘open’, i.e., application to ISP is not required, but a notification should be sent to ISP when using this authorization the first time. The authorization number EU001-006 must be stated, however, when notifying the Swedish Customs of the export.

The authorizations may not be used if the exporter has been informed by ISP that the products in question are, or may be, intended for use in connection with WMD or for military end-use in a country that is subject to an arms embargo decreed by the EU, Organization for Security and Co-operation in Europe (OSCE) or the UN (this in accordance with the *‘catch-all’* clause). Neither may the authorizations be used if the exporter is aware of any intention to use the products in question in connection with any of the uses specified above.

B. National Export Licences

For all other export that requires Export Licences under the Council Regulation, licences are granted by ISP (with the exception of products classified under category 0 for which applications should be submitted to the Swedish Radiation Safety Authority), if the exporter is established in Sweden. There are two types of licences: individual and global. These types of licences may be issued throughout the whole world. When considering whether to grant an Export Licence or not, ISP is required to consider all relevant aspects of the case at hand, including:

- the international commitments agreed by Sweden as a member of the international non-proliferation systems and common understandings regarding export control;
- the requirements imposed due to the implemented international sanctions agreed by the EC Council or the UN Security Council;
- Swedish foreign and safety aspects including what is covered by the EU's Code of Conduct regarding export of arms; and
- the intended end-use and the risk for diversion.

Individual Licence

This licence is issued to a specific exporter for the export of a specified product to a recipient in a specified destination. An individual licence can include a series of exports or a specific quantity of products to a customer during a predetermined time period. Prior to applying for a global Export Licence companies are often required to use individual licences in order for ISP to closely monitor the level of knowledge and experience of the company in relation to export control issues.

Global Licence

A Global Export Licence is issued to a specific company. It may cover products listed in Annex I of the Council Regulation belonging to categories 1-9. The licence allows unlimited export until it expires or is revoked and is valid for export to one or several countries, as further stated in the licence. The licence may not be used to re-export products to a country that is not covered by the licence, i.e., a country which requires an individual licence application.

To be granted a global licence, the exporter must fulfil certain requirements. These are as follows:

- knowledge of the relevant legislation;
- well-functioning internal export control routines; and
- export documents kept on file for at least five years.

Internal export control routines can take many different forms depending on the type of company concerned. The following elements must, however, be part of the company's routines:

- a company policy of which the relevant personnel is aware;
- an export control organization staffed by people who can be held responsible;
- a process for product classification;

- end-use control;
- application routines for Export Licences; and
- efficient handling of suspicious enquiries.

Before such a licence application is processed, ISP will visit the company to go through the above-mentioned requirements.

III Export Licence Application

An application for an Export Licence should be submitted to ISP on a special form in accordance with regulation TFS 2000:25. Applications for the export of nuclear technology products should be sent to the Swedish Radiation Safety Authority.

IV End-User Certificate

When an application for an individual Export Licence is processed, ISP requires an end-user certificate. Ordinary, the end-user confirms the relevant circumstances, i.e., who the end-user is, what the product is, what the product will be used for (end-use), any order or contract numbers, the quantities and an undertaking not to re-export the product without the approval of the Swedish authorities.

In exceptional cases, certification of the above by a representative of the Swedish exporter in the recipient country or the distributor may suffice. If there is any uncertainty about the circumstances, ISP may be consulted in order to agree on an appropriate procedure toward the specific end-user. In other cases, it may be necessary for the authorities in the recipient country to confirm a certain end-use. This applies in relation to especially sensitive products. In such cases, ISP contacts the Swedish Embassy or Consulate in the recipient country and asks them to obtain an assurance from the relevant party. Such an assurance may also be associated with the requirement that an inspection is conducted to ensure that the product has been installed at the place stipulated and is used for the given purpose.

There are three different types of end-user certificates:

- The 'Commitment concerning re-export and peaceful use' certificate is used for civilian end-use. This certificate provides an assurance that forthcoming deliveries will only be used for peaceful purposes and that the product will not be re-exported.
- There are two types of 'Declaration of End-Use' certificates applicable for military end-use. One intended to be used when delivering directly to the military in a specific country and the second when delivering products to other companies which will deliver the products to the military that is the end-user.

A certificate should be drawn up on the consignee's letter headed document. It should be written in a Scandinavian, English, French or German language. Otherwise, an authorized translation must be attached. The certificate should be signed by an authorized representative of the consignee and should be sent in original to ISP along with the application.

Sub-Par. 3 Services

Sweden applies the same view as many other EU Member States in relation to Dual-Use Services. Thus, at the present time, there is no regulatory framework which deals specifically with Dual-Use Services in Sweden. This topic is, however, closely linked to the issue of 'intangible transfers', and the rules would to a large extent be applied similarly as for military services describe above. Services that are or maybe intended, in their entirety or in part, for use in connection with the development, production, handling or operation of a controlled product could constitute an 'intangible transfer'. Thus, a company would need an Export Licence if the provision of services would constitute an intangible transfer of information related to a controlled product.

Sub-Par. 4 Persons

There are no specific requirements under Swedish law on transfer or access to Swedish controlled technology similar to the US concept of deemed export and re-export.

Par. 2 Control Lists

The listed Dual-Use Goods, relevant for Sweden, can be found in the latest EC Regulation[1125] and its appendices. Sweden has not added any additional products to the export control list of Dual-Use Products. It is the exporting company that is responsible for classifying its products and other transfers of information in relation to the Dual-Use regulation. If the company is uncertain of a specific classification it may seek guidance from ISP. The company can also apply for a preliminary ruling from ISP. A preliminary ruling is given subject to the final decision after the export application has been assessed by ISP. Preliminary ruling may also involve conditions which aim to call the company's attention to the factors that will have significant bearing on the final decision. The assessment only takes into account the relevant, prevailing conditions. If conditions change at a later date, this may affect the outcome of the final assessment. A positive advanced notification is not an Export Licence decision. It does not free the company from the obligation to apply to ISP for an Export Licence. Classifications made

1125. EC Regulation 2420/2015.

by the company or any preliminary rulings from ISP are not disclosed or published in any way.

Par. 3 Licensing and Enforcement Authorities

Sub-Par. 1 Requirements Preliminary to Any Specific Export (i.e., Manufacturing Stage)

There are no requirements that need to be considered prior to the production or development of Dual-Use Goods in Sweden. Thus, it is not necessary to apply for any specific permit during the manufacturing stage.

Sub-Par. 2 Prior to the Export Stage

The first issue to address is whether the product or information that is to be exported is controlled. While carrying out the classification against the applicable Dual-Use regulation, it is also necessary to consider if any sanctions regulation is applicable and if such regulation impose further export control restrictions. Furthermore, it is necessary to consider whether the catch-all clause in paragraph 4 in the EC Regulation 428/2009 could be applicable.

Sub-Par. 3 At the Export Stage

If the product that is to be exported is a controlled product, the company needs to assess whether there are any available Export Licences. The first step is to assess whether there are any general Export Licences available as these do not require any examination by ISP. If there is no general Export Licence available, the company needs to apply for either an individual or a global Export Licence. The company can consider whether to request a preliminary ruling from ISP of the feasibility of the proposed export.

If the company is granted the necessary Export Licence the product may be exported. The company needs to include information on any relevant contract documentation that the products are Dual-Use Goods and export controlled. Furthermore, it is necessary to inform the Swedish Customs of any Export Licence that is used in connection to the export.

All companies established in Sweden that produce or provide Dual-Use Goods are required to file a declaration to ISP on the sale and transfer of Dual-Use Goods during the preceding year. The company will be charged a pro-rata share of the total export value of all Dual-Use Goods sold by companies established in Sweden each year. If the value of the exported products does not exceed SEK 2.5 million the company will be charged a minimum fixed fee amounting to SEK 2000 (approximately EUR 200–220).

ISP is entitled to carry out audits at any company that produce or provide export controlled Dual-Use Goods or technical assistance.

Sub-Par. 4 General Dual-Use Control Regime Procedure Chart

Figure 15.2

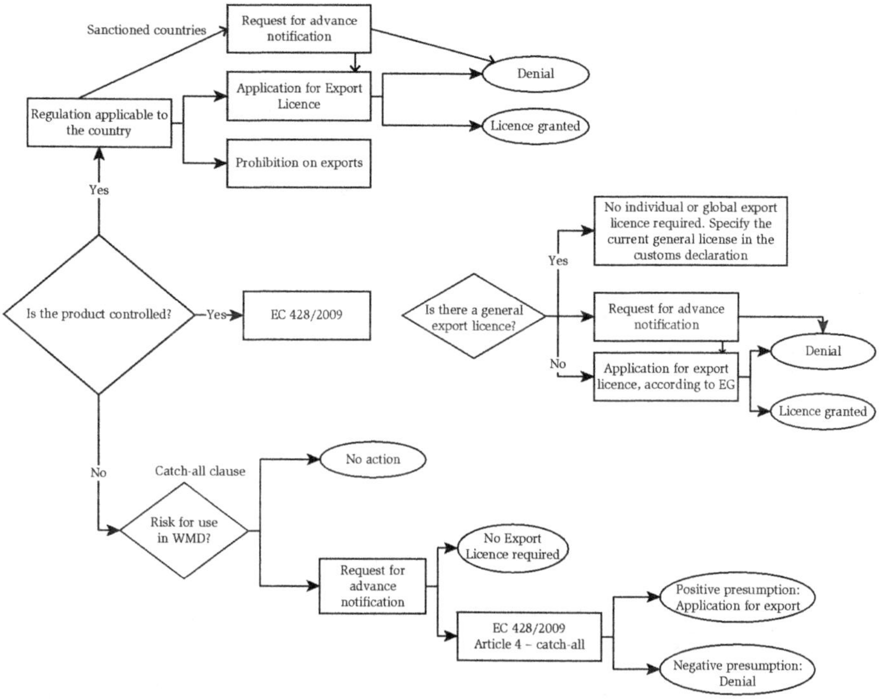

(a) Dual-Use licences Procedure Chart

Figure 15.3

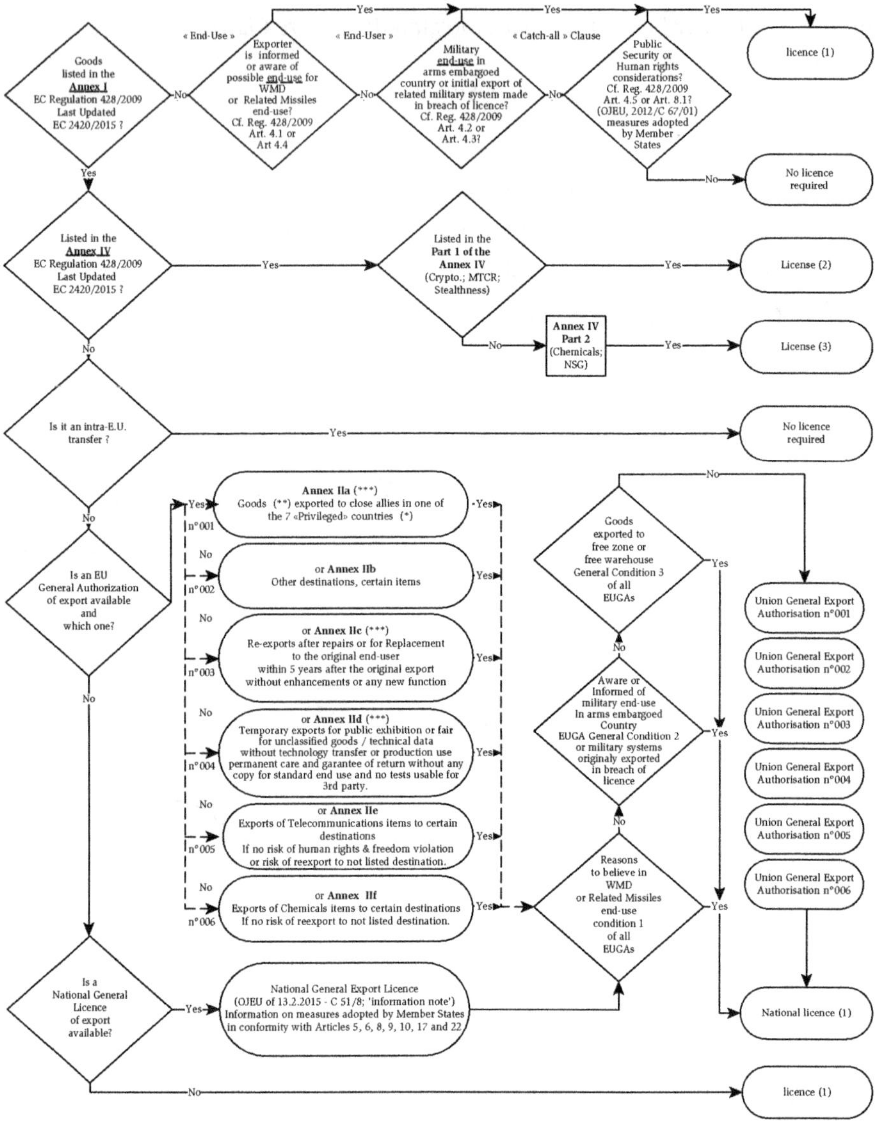

(1) Each EU Members states determines which type of EU licence (Individual or Global) is applicable.
(2) For goods and related technologies listed in Annex IV Part 1, Individual or Global EU licences are available.
(3) For goods and related technologies listed in Annex IV Part 2, only Individual licences are permitted.

(*) Seven countries listed in Annex IIa (EC) Regulation n° 428/2009 are the following: Australia, Canada, Japan, New-Zealand, Norway, Switzerland and US.
(**) Nearly all goods listed in Annex I excepted those listed in Annex IV and few others deemed very sensitive (cf. Annex g).
(***) cf. Annex 1Ig for possible other not authorized items.

Par. 4 Sanctions and the Recourses of the Importer/Exporter

Should the company or any of its employees not comply with applicable regulation they could face a number of different civil and criminal sanctions. The sanctions can mainly be found in the Swedish Act on Control of Dual-Use and of Technical Assistance. The available sanctions span between fines up to a maximum sanction of six years imprisonment. Sanctions can be imposed both for import and export in violation of applicable legislation. The available sanctions are mainly criminal, and in relation to some violations it is a requirement that the responsible person has acted with gross negligence, and in some cases it is a requirement that the violating party has acted with intent in order for liability to be imposed. Further, the company can be charged with a fine for not ensuring that it has sufficient procedures in place in order to avoid violating the applicable legislation. The maximum company penalty amounts to SEK 10,000,000 (approximately EUR 110,000-120,000). Furthermore, goods involved in a violation can be confiscated and forfeit.

SECTION 5 SPECIFICITIES/SPACE-RELATED PROVISIONS

There are no specificities in the Swedish export control or sanctions regimes for space-related equipment, technology or services. Sweden closely follows the EU in its application of international undertakings. Accordingly, we will not provide any further information to this section but refer the reader to the EU Chapter of this Handbook.

SECTION 6 SANCTIONS AND EMBARGOES

Sub-Section 1 Participation of Sweden in Embargoes or Other Related Sanctions

Sweden only adheres to the international sanctions decided and imposed by the EU and UN's Security Council. Sweden has not imposed any further international sanctions toward any country or individual. This means that a company subject to Swedish jurisdiction is required to comply with the sanctions decided by the EU and UN's Security Council. The applicable legal foundation for Sweden's adherence to its international commitments can be found in the Swedish Act on International Sanctions (*lagen (1996:95) om vissa internationella sanktioner*). The authorities with the main responsibility for ensuring that Sweden's international commitments are respected are the ISP and the Swedish Financial Supervisory Authority (*Finansinspektionen*) ('FI').

On the political arena Sweden takes an active role through different bi- and multi-lateral agreements and understandings in trying to enhance the legal security of the countries and individuals on which international sanctions are imposed. Should a company or any of its employees not comply with applicable regulation they could face a number of different civil and criminal sanctions. The sanctions can mainly be found in the Swedish Act on International Sanctions. The available penalties span between fines up to a maximum sanction of four years imprisonment. Sanctions can be imposed for both import and export in violation of applicable legislation. The available sanctions are mainly criminal and in relation to some violations it is a requirement that the responsible person has acted with gross negligence and in some cases intent is required in order for liability to be imposed. Further, the company can be charged a penalty for not ensuring that it has sufficient procedures in place in order to avoid violating the applicable legislation. The maximum company penalty amounts to SEK 10,000,000 (approximately EUR 110,000-120,000). Furthermore, goods involved in a violation can be confiscated and forfeited.

Sub-Section 2 Regime of the Embargoes or Related Sanctions in Sweden

Sweden only adheres to the sanctions decided by the EU and the UN's Security Council. Sweden has not imposed any further international sanctions toward any country or individual. This means that a company subject to Swedish jurisdiction is required to comply with the sanctions decided by the EU and the Security Council of the UN.

SECTION 7 LIST OF ACRONYMS

CWC	Chemical Weapons Convention
COCOM	Coordinating Committee for Multilateral Export Controls
EC	European Community/European Communities
EEA	European Economic Area
EU	European Union
EU OJ	Official Journal of the European Union
FI	The Swedish Financial Supervisory Authority/ (*Finansinspektionen*)
ISP	Swedish authority, the Swedish Agency for Non-Proliferation and Export Control / (*Inspektionen för Strategiska Produkter*)
KS	Export controlled military items intended for combat
ML	Export controlled military items subject to international regime agreement on controls
MTCR	Missile Technology Control Regime
NATO	North Atlantic Treaty Organization
NL	Export controlled military items subject to national control
NPT	Nuclear Non-Proliferation Treaty
NSG	Nuclear Suppliers Group
OPCW	Organization for the Prohibition of Chemical Weapons
OSCE	Organization for Security and Co-operation in Europe
SEK	Swedish krona
TFS	Tullverkets författningssamling

CWC	Chemical Weapons Convention
COCOM	Coordinating Committee for Multilateral Export Controls
EC	European Community/European Communities
EEA	European Economic Area
EU	European Union
EU OJ	Official Journal of the European Union
FI	The Swedish Financial Supervisory Authority/ (*Finansinspektionen*)
WMD	Weapons of mass destruction
ÖK	Export controlled military items not intended for combat

SECTION 8 REFERENCES

Sub-Section 1 Primary Documentation

Par. 1 Statutory Legislation

I. Military Goods

The Swedish Military Equipment Act (*Lag (1992:1300) om krigsmateriel*):

- http://www.riksdagen.se/sv/Dokument-Lagar/Lagar/Svenskforfattningssamling/Lag-19921300-om-krigsmateri_sfs-1992-1300/?bet=1992:1300
  Subordinate Regulation (1992:1303) on Military equipment (*Förordning (1992:1303) om krigsmateriel*))
- http://www.riksdagen.se/sv/Dokument-Lagar/Lagar/Svenskforfattningssamling/Forordning-19921303-om-krig_sfs-1992-1303/?bet=1992:1303

The Swedish Weapons Act (*Vapenlag* (1996:67)):

- http://www.riksdagen.se/sv/Dokument-Lagar/Lagar/Svenskforfattningssamling/Vapenlag-199667_sfs-1996-67/?bet=1996:67

The Swedish Act on Flammable and Explosive Products (*Lag (2010:1011) om brandfarliga och explosiva varor*) and associated regulation (2010:1075):

- http://www.riksdagen.se/sv/Dokument-Lagar/Lagar/Svenskforfattningssamling/Lag-20101011-om-brandfarlig_sfs-2010-1011/
- http://www.riksdagen.se/sv/Dokument-Lagar/Lagar/Svenskforfattningssamling/Forordning-20101075-om-bran_sfs-2010-1075/

II. Dual-Use Goods

The Swedish Act on Control of Dual-Use and of Technical Assistance (*Lag (2000:1064) om kontroll av produkter med dubbla användningsområden och av tekniskt bistånd*):

- http://www.riksdagen.se/sv/Dokument-Lagar/Lagar/Svenskforfattningssamling/Lag-20001064-om-kontroll-av_sfs-2000-1064/?bet=2000:1064

Subordinate Regulation (2000:1217) (*Förordning (2000:1217) om kontroll av produkter med dubbla användningsområden och av tekniskt bistånd*):

- http://www.riksdagen.se/sv/Dokument-Lagar/Lagar/Svenskforfattningssamling/Forordning-20001217-om-kont_sfs-2000-1217/?bet=2000:1217

III. Sanctions

The Swedish Act on Certain International Sanctions (*Lag (1996:95) om vissa internationella sanktioner*):

http://www.notisum.se/rnp/sls/lag/19960095.htm

Par. 2 Subordinate Legislation

I. Military Goods

- The Swedish Agency for Non-Proliferation and Export Control (TFS 2012:7) regulation concerning a general licence applicable to the export of Military Goods and the provision of technical assistance to a recipient that is part of the armed forces or a contracting authority in a Member State of EEA.
- The Swedish Agency for Non-Proliferation and Export Control (TFS 2012:8) regulation concerning a general licence applicable to the export of Military Goods and the provision of technical assistance to a certified recipient in a Member State of the EEA.
- The Swedish Agency for Non-Proliferation and Export Control (TFS 2012:9) regulation concerning a general licence applicable to the transfer of Military Goods and the provision of technical assistance to a Member State of the EEA for demonstration, evaluation and exhibition.
- The Swedish Agency for Non-Proliferation and Export Control (TFS 2012:10) regulation concerning a general licence applicable to the transfer of Military Goods and the provision of technical assistance to a specific recipient in a Member State of the EEA for maintenance or repair.
- The Swedish Agency for Non-Proliferation and Export Control (TFS 2012:11) regulation concerning a general licence applicable to the transfer of Military Goods and the provision of technical assistance to a specific recipient in a Member State of the EEA after maintenance, repair or demonstration.

II. Dual-Use Goods

ISP's regulation on application for Export Licence (*Inspektionens för strategiska produkter föreskrifter (TFS 2000:25) om ansökan om exporttillstånd*).

ISP's regulation on control of chemical substances (*Inspektionens för strategiska produkter föreskrifter (TFS 2000:26) om kontroll av kemiska prekursorer (utgångsämnen)*)

Par. 3 Annexes – Copies of Documents of Practical Use to the Importer/Exporter

A number of standard documents relevant for the import or export process in Sweden (e.g., most current official application forms for import or export licences, templates of contractual undertaking, or regulation extracts) as well as other non-official documents are available on a dedicated DropBox folder which can be accessed by following the link below: www.kluwerlawonline.com/eclrh-annexes.

Sub-Section 2 Secondary Documentation

Par. 1 Internet Sites

I. Military Goods and Dual-Use Goods

ISP's website contains various guidance on the Swedish export control regulation. The website also provides some information in relation to Sweden's application of international sanctions.

http://www.isp.se/sa/node.asp?node = 401

EU Military list:

http://eur-lex.europa.eu/legal-content/SV/TXT/PDF/?uri = OJ:JOC_2014_107_R_0001&rid = 1

II. Sanctions

Sweden's official website on international sanctions from which various information can be accessed on Sweden's participation in applicable international sanctions.

http://www.government.se/sb/d/9279/a/84519

The Swedish Financial Supervisory Authority (*Finansinspektionen*) official website regarding EU-sanctions.

http://www.fi.se/Tillsyn/Sanktioner/EU-sanktioner/

SECTION 9 USEFUL INFORMATION

Sub-Section 1 Enforcement Authorities Contact Details

Name of Organization	*The Swedish Agency for Non-Proliferation and Export Control, ISP (Sw. Inspektionen för strategiska produkter)*
Postal Address	Box 70252, S-107 22 Stockholm, Sweden
Telephone	+46 (0)8 406 31 00 (Office hours: 8.30-12.00, 13.00- 16.30 CET)

Name of Organization	*The Swedish Agency for Non-Proliferation and Export Control, ISP (Sw. Inspektionen för strategiska produkter)*
Fax	+46 (0)8 20 31 00
Email address	registrator@isp.se
Website	www.isp.se

Sub-Section 2 Other

Name of Organization	*The Swedish Financial Supervisory Board, FI (Sw. Finansinspektionen)*
Postal Address	Box 7821, 103 97 Stockholm, Sweden
Telephone	+46 (0)8 787 80 00
Fax	+46 (0)8 24 13 35
Email address	finansinspektionen@fi.se
Website	www.fi.se

Name of Organization	*The Swedish Radiation Safety Authority, SMM (Sw. Strålsäkerhetsmyndigheten)*
Postal Address	171 16 Stockholm, Sweden
Telephone	+46 (0)8 799 40 00
Fax	+46 (0)8 799 40 10
Email address	registrator@ssm.se
Website	www.stralsakerhetsmyndigheten.se

Name of Organization	*The Swedish Social Insurance Agency (Sw. Försäkringskassan)*
Postal Address	103 51 Stockholm, Sweden
Telephone	+46 (0)8 786 90 00
Fax	+46 (0)8 411 27 89
Email address	huvudkontoret@forsakringskassan.se
Website	www.forsakringskassan.se

CHAPTER 16
United Kingdom

David Lorello

SECTION 1 TABLE OF CONTENTS

SECTION 2 EXECUTIVE SUMMARY

The principal source of legislation in the United Kingdom (UK) governing the export of military, dual-use, and other controlled goods, software, and technology is the Export Control Act 2002 (hereinafter, the '2002 Act'). However, specific export controls restrictions are implemented pursuant to a range of other acts, regulations and orders. This chapter provides an overview of the history of the UK's approach to export controls, the key legislation currently in place, and the UK's current export controls licensing and enforcement policy.

SECTION 3 INTRODUCTION – ELEMENTS OF CONTEXT

Sub-Section 1 Regime Overall Philosophy

Over the past thirteen years, the UK Government has enacted a number of orders and regulations, under the authority of the 2002 Act, to control the export of sensitive goods, software, and technology. Principal among those measures is the Export Control Order 2008 (hereinafter, the '2008 Order'), which implements most of the EU and UK domestic dual-use and military export controls. The range of UK legislative measures focusing on export controls reflects the UK regime's continuing need to adapt to developments driven by domestic and EU politics, and the UK's long-standing engagement in numerous international export control initiatives, such as the Nuclear Suppliers Group, the Australia Group, the Missile Technology Control Regime, the Wassenaar Arrangement, and bi-lateral export controls arrangements that the UK has pursued in recent years (such as, for example, the US-UK Defence Trade Cooperation Treaty). Furthermore, the increasing use in Europe of economic sanctions legislation as a tool for addressing human rights abuses and threats to international peace and security has introduced new, and increasingly prominent, sanctions elements in the UK's general export control regime.

As a consequence of the multi-faceted nature of the UK's export controls regime, a variety of export controls 'lists' have been developed in the UK that exporters must be familiar with, including the following:

- the UK Military List (Schedule 2 of the 2008 Order);
- the UK Dual-Use List (Schedule 3 of the 2008 Order);
- the European Union (EU) Human Rights List (Annexes II and III of 2005 EC Regulation No. 1236/2005);
- the UK National Security and Paramilitary List (Article 9 of the 2008 Order);
- the UK National Radioactive Sources List (Schedule referred to in Article 2 of Export of Radioactive Sources (Control) Order 2006);
- the EU Dual-Use List (Annexes I and IV to EC Regulation No. 428/2009); and
- the several export controls lists implemented pursuant to European Council economic sanctions regulations, including the EU sanctions concerning

Crimea (EC Regulation No. 692/2014), Iran (EC Regulation No. 267/2012), Russia (EC Regulation No. 833/2014, and Syria (EC Regulation No. 36/2012).[1126]

As with other EU Member States, the UK also maintains 'catch-all' end-use controls that impose export prohibitions for any products, irrespective of whether they are captured in the above referenced lists, if they are intended for certain military or weapons of mass destruction (WMD) end uses. The UK also imposes controls associated with the 'brokering' or 'trade' in certain restricted products.

Given the high volume of controlled military and dual-use exports that originate in the UK, the UK's export controls framework has evolved over the years to allow for more permissive licensing frameworks – such as through open general licences – for controlled exports where the UK does not perceive a policy imperative to issue licences on a transaction-by-transaction basis, while maintaining more stringent controls concerning exports of more sensitive goods, software, and technology, or exports to destinations of concern. In considering whether to licence transactions covered under UK export controls, the UK Government considers a variety of factors, which are set forth in its Consolidated EU and National Arms Export Licensing Criteria (hereinafter, the 'Consolidated Criteria'). The Consolidated Criteria, which are published and periodically updated by the UK's Department for Business, Innovation, and Skills (BIS), contemplate the consideration of issues such as (1) the UK's international law commitments; (2) risks that exports will be used in furtherance of internal repression or will contribute to national or regional instability; (3) domestic UK national security considerations, and those of allied countries; (4) the risk of product diversion to undesirable end-users or for prohibited end-uses; and (5) compatibility of the exports in question with the recipient country's technical and economic capacity.

The application of those criteria results, in practice, in a flexible export controls regime, founded on considerations of the relative sensitivity of the goods, software, and technology at issue. More stringent controls are applied to more sensitive items – such as those listed in Annex IV to the EC Regulation No. 428/2009 (the Dual-Use Regulation), or those set forth in Categories A and B to the 2008 Order – and based on any unique foreign policy or security concerns that may relate to the destination, end-user, or project / end-use in question. Reviewing the UK's application of those standards over the years reveals a general consistency in approach with other EU Member States and major trading partners on export licensing matters, but also some areas where the UK's approach has been driven by domestic foreign policy considerations in a manner that places it in a somewhat unique position. (As an illustrative example, the UK Government has in recent years denied certain licence requests for exports of military and dual-use items to Israel, given concerns that the items may have

1126. The UK publishes a consolidated list of controlled dual use and military items, which is available for download at https://www.gov.uk/uk-strategic-export-control-lists-the-consolidated-list-of-strategic-military-and-dual use items. The consolidated list does not, however, incorporate products controlled for export under EU sanctions legislation.

been intended for use by the Israel Defence Forces in Gaza. That policy is not universally shared by other EU Member States or by other major trading partners, such as the United States.)

The UK export controls framework is implemented principally by the Export Controls Organisation (ECO), which operates under BIS. The ECO consults regularly, however, with other UK agencies on export controls policy and licensing matters. Those agencies include (1) the Foreign and Commonwealth Office (FCO), the Ministry of Defence (MoD), and the Department for International Development (DfID), who advise the ECO on foreign policy and defence trade matters; (2) the Communication-Electronics Security Group, which is responsible for assessing export controls matters involving sensitive communications and computer technology; and (3) the Department of Energy and Climate Change, which provides advice concerning the UK's biological, chemical, and nuclear non-proliferation policies. The ECO is also supported on enforcement-related matters by HM Treasury, through the newly created Office of Financial Sanctions Implementation (OFSI),[1127] HM Revenue & Customs (HMRC), the UK Border Force, and the Crown Prosecution Service (CPS). Finally, the UK export controls regime is subject to regular Parliamentary oversight, including through the work of the Parliamentary Committees on Arms Export Control, which receives periodic reports concerning export controls licensing and policy matters.[1128]

Sub-Section 2 Historical Outlook

In November 1992, the UK Government failed to successfully prosecute three executives of Matrix Churchill, a UK weapons manufacturing company, who were charged with illegally selling sensitive military equipment to Iraq. That failure was attributed, in part, to what were perceived to be significant deficiencies in the UK export controls laws in effect at the time. The event generated a political scandal and led to discussions concerning the need to modernize what was, at that time, an antiquated UK export controls regime – operating under legislation implemented at the outset of the Second World War.[1129]

In response to the Matrix Churchill matter, the Government established an inquiry into the export of defence, military, and dual-use equipment to Iraq, which was chaired by Sir Richard Scott. The inquiry's report, which extended to more than 2000 pages, was published in 1996.[1130] The report detailed a lack of political oversight and transparency in the UK's strategic export control regime, and called for major revisions to the underlying laws and regulations. One year later, the New Labour Government

1127. The OFSI was created on 31 Mar. 2016. The announcement made by HM Treasury is available here: https://www.gov.uk/government/news/new-body-to-support-financial-sanctions-implementation-launched.

1128. See, e.g., Scrutiny of Arms Exports and Arms Controls (2015). Committees on Arms Export Controls. House of Commons. 2015. (U.K.), available at http://www.publications.parliament.uk/pa/cm201415/cmselect/cmquad/608/60802.htm.

1129. Import Export and Customs Power Act, 1939, c 69. (U.K.).

1130. Report of the inquiry into the export of defence equipment and dual use goods to Iraq and related prosecutions. Scott, R., 1996, (U.K.).

released a white paper defining its vision for new export controls legislation, and calling for consultations.[1131] The result of those consultations, the Export Control Bill, was laid before Parliament in mid-2001. Following extensive dialogue with non-governmental organizations, defence industry manufacturers and practitioners, the 2002 Act received Royal Assent on 24 July 2002.[1132]

In the following years, the Government strengthened reforms initiated by the 2002 Act and gave effect to the Act through numerous statutory instruments. First, the Export of Goods, Transfer of Technology and Provision of Technical Assistance (Control) Order 2003[1133] consolidated the existing controls on military and dual-use goods, software and technology, and WMD-related restrictions. The Order also introduced WMD end-use controls on 'any relevant use' in connection with WMD-related activities, which the Order defined as any use in connection with the development, production, handling, operation, maintenance, storage, detection, identification or dissemination of chemical, biological or nuclear weapons or other nuclear explosive devices, or the development, production, maintenance or storage of missiles capable of delivering such weapons.[1134]

The second phase of enactments, under the Trade in Goods (Control) Order 2003[1135] and the Trade in Controlled Goods (Embargoed Destinations) Order 2004,[1136] strengthened the anti-trafficking provision of the Export Control Act. Those Orders imposed controls on trade of military and para-military goods, and prohibited the shipment of listed goods to embargoed countries.

A third round of legislation, the Technical Assistance Control Regulations of 2006,[1137] was enacted to give effect to the EU Anti-Torture Regulation.[1138] The Anti-Torture Regulation represented the culmination of a four-year process to regulate the trade of goods that have been deemed to have no practical use other than that of carrying out capital punishment or inflicting torture and other cruel, inhuman or

1131. Strategic Export Controls (Cm 3989). Department of Trade and Industry, 1998. (U.K.).
1132. Export Control Act, 2002, c 28. (U.K.).
1133. Export of Goods, Transfer of Technology and Provision of Technical Assistance (Control) Order 2003/2764, available at http://www.legislation.gov.uk/uksi/2003/2764/pdfs/uksi_20032764_en.pdf.
1134. Export of Goods, Transfer of Technology and Provision of Technical Assistance (Control) Order 2003/2764. (Article 2), available at http://www.legislation.gov.uk/uksi/2003/2764/pdfs/uksi_20032764_en.pdf.
1135. Trade in Goods (Control) Order 2003/2765, available at http://www.legislation.gov.uk/uksi/2003/2765/pdfs/uksi_20032765_en.pdf.
1136. Trade in Controlled Goods (Embargoed Destinations) Order 2004/318, available at http://www.legislation.gov.uk/uksi/2004/318/pdfs/uksi_20040318_en.pdf.
1137. Technical Assistance Control Regulations 2006/1719, available at http://www.legislation.gov.uk/uksi/2006/1719/pdfs/uksi_20061719_en.pdf.
1138. Council Regulation (EC) No. 1236/2005 of 27 Jun. 2005, concerning trade in certain goods which could be used for capital punishment, torture or other cruel, inhuman or degrading treatment or punishment, available at http://eur-lex.europa.eu/LexUriServ/LexUriServ.do?uri=OJ:L:2005:200:0001:0019:EN:PDF.

degrading treatment. Finally, the Export of Radioactive Sources (Control) Order 2006[1139] imposed restrictions on trade in certain high-activity radioactive source materials.

The Government's efforts to control sensitive goods, software, and technology resulted in a plurality of statutory instruments. To simplify the regime (thus promoting awareness and compliance) and close certain gaps, the Government enacted the 2008 Order.[1140] The 2008 Order consolidates the above-mentioned statutory instruments, with the exception of the Export of Radioactive Sources (Control) Order 2006, into one legislative source. The provisions of the Export of Radioactive Sources (Control) Order 2006 were excluded from the 2008 Order, as they were perceived as a distinct set of controls that did not necessarily relate to the UK's broader export controls policies on military and dual-use goods, software, and technology.[1141]

Since its entry into force on 6 April 2009, the 2008 Order is the main secondary instrument giving effect to the 2002 Act and implementing the licensing provisions and penalties of the EU Dual-Use Regulation[1142] and Anti-Torture Regulation. The Government has amended the 2008 Order numerous times since its enactment, typically in response to developments in EU export controls regimes (such as, for example, to reflect amendments to the EU Common Military List and emerging EU sanctions legislation) or to bring the UK into compliance with its broader treaty obligations. In 2014, for example, the Government amended the Order in preparation for the imminent ratification by the UK of the Arms Trade Treaty, to subject certain items to more stringent transit and trade controls.[1143] (The Arms Trade Treaty seeks, among other measures, to establish and strengthen common international standards for regulating the international trade in conventional arms.[1144]) The UK Government has also used the 2008 Order as a short-term measure to respond to geopolitical developments. For example, the Government suspended certain licences involving military and dual-use exports to Russia in March 2014 under the authority of the 2008 Order, four months in

1139. Export of Radioactive Sources (Control) Order 2006/1846, available at http://www.legislation.gov.uk/uksi/2006/1846/pdfs/uksi_20061846_en.pdf.
1140. Export Control Act 2002 – Review of Export Control Legislation (2007): Impact Assessment Department for Business Enterprise & Regulatory Reform, 2008. (July 2008). Available at http://webarchive.nationalarchives.gov.uk/20090504163027/http:/www.berr.gov.uk/files/file47075.pdf, and Department for Business, Innovation & Skills et al. 2008. United Kingdom Strategic Export Controls Annual Report 2008 (Cm 7662). Norwich: TSO.
1141. Controls on radioactive sources. Department for Business, Innovation & Skills and Export Control Organisation. 2012, available at https://www.gov.uk/controls-on-radioactive-sources.
1142. Council Regulation (EC) No. 1334/2000 of 22 Jun. 2000 setting up a Community regime for the control of exports of dual use items and technology as recast by Council Regulation (EC) No. 428/2009 of 5 May 2009 setting up a Community regime for the control of exports, transfer, brokering and transit of dual use items as amended, available http://www.sussex.ac.uk/Units/spru/hsp/documents/2000-0622%201334-2000.pdf.
1143. Export Control (Amendment) Order 2014/702, available at http://www.legislation.gov.uk/uksi/2014/702/pdfs/uksi_20140702_en.pdf.
1144. The Arms Trade Treaty. United Nations Office for Disarmament Affairs. December 2014, available at http://www.un.org/disarmament/ATT/.

advance of the implementation by the European Council of heightened arms export controls in respect of Russia and Crimea.[1145]

In terms of its forward-looking approach, the UK Government is among the more active EU Member States in assessing and pursuing revisions to international controls frameworks in response to geopolitical and technological developments. To take one example, the UK Government is considering, as of this writing, heightened export controls on certain types of cyber technologies, including 'surveillance' equipment and software, that are not captured in existing UK or EU export controls.[1146] In this regard, in November 2014 TechUK – the UK trade association for the information technology, telecommunications and electronic sectors – published guidance in cooperation with the Government to assess cyber security export risks associated with those and other items.[1147] Although not legally binding, the TechUK guidance aims to assist exporters in developing their due diligence processes and to enable them to identify and manage human rights and national security risks associated with the export of cyber security products and services. Similarly, in August 2015, the UK government published detailed guidance on intrusion software tools that were agreed by the Wassenaar Arrangement in December 2013 and implemented across the EU in December 2014.[1148]

Sub-Section 3 Participation to International Regimes

The following tables displays the UK's participation status to export control related international treaties and programmes. It is also stated, when relevant, that the UK is party to a treaty either by signature and ratification or by accession.

Par. 1 Treaties and Regimes Dealing with Specific Items and Technologies

Table 16.1 Nuclear Weapons Treaties

Treaty Name	*Overall Status*	*Specific Status*	*Enforceable in the UK*
Limited Test Ban Treaty[1149]	OS: 5 August 1963 EF: 10 October 1963	S: 5 August 1963 R: 10 October 1963	Yes

1145. Export Control Organisation, Notice to Exporters 2014/06: UK suspends all licences and licence applications for export to Russian military that could be used against Ukraine. Export Control Organisation, 18 Mar. 2014.

1146. Foreign & Commonwealth Office et al. 2012. United Kingdom Strategic Export Controls Annual Report 2012 (HC 561). London: TSO. p. 4; United Kingdom Strategic Export Controls Annual Report 2013. Foreign & Commonwealth Office et al. 2013. (HC 480). London: TSO. p. 7.

1147. TechUK. November 2014. Assessing Cyber Security Export Risks.

1148. The guidance is accessible here : http://blogs.bis.gov.uk/exportcontrol/uncategorized/eco-issues-guidance-on-intrusion-software-controls/.

1149. Treaty Banning Nuclear Weapon Tests in the Atmosphere, in Outer Space and Under Water, *U.N.T.S.*, 10 Oct. 1963, vol. 480, p. 43.

Treaty Name	Overall Status	Specific Status	Enforceable in the UK
Nuclear Non-Proliferation Treaty[1150]	OS: 1 July 1968 EF: 5 March 1970	S: 1 July 1968 R: 27 November 1968	Yes
Comprehensive Nuclear Test Ban Treaty[1151]	OS: 24 September 1996 EF: not in force	S: 24 September 1996 R: 6 April 1998	No

OS: Opened for signature; EF: Entry into force; S/R: Signature/Ratification; A: Accession

Table 16.2 Biological and Chemical Weapons Treaties

Treaty Name	Overall Status	Specific Status	Enforceable in the UK
Geneva Protocol[1152]	OS: 17 June 1925 EF: 9 May 1926	S: 17 June 1925 R: 9 April 1930	Yes
Biological Convention[1153]	OS: 10 April 1972 EF: 26 March 1975	S: 10 April 1972 R: 26 March 1975	Yes
Chemical Convention[1154]	OS: 13 January 1993 EF: 29 April 1997	S: 13 January 1993 R: 13 May 1996	Yes

OS: Opened for signature; EF: Entry into force; S/R: Signature/Ratification; A: Accession

Table 16.3 Multilateral Export Control Regimes

Regime Name	Formation	Participation
Zangger Committee[1155]	1971	Yes
Nuclear Suppliers Group	1974	Yes
Australia Group	1985	Yes
Missile Technology Control Regime	1987	Yes
Wassenaar Arrangement[1156]	1994	Yes

1150. Treaty on the Non-Proliferation of Nuclear Weapons, *U.N.T.S.*, 5 Mar. 1970, vol. 729, p. 161.
1151. U.N.G.A., resolution 50\245.
1152. Protocol for the Prohibition of the Use in War of Asphyxiating, Poisonous or Other Gases, and of Bacteriological Methods of Warfare, 94, League of Nations Treaty Series, No. 2138 (1929).
1153. Convention on the Prohibition of the Development, Production and Stockpiling of Bacteriological (Biological) and Toxin Weapons and On Their Destruction, *U.N.T.S.*, 26 Mar. 1975, vol. 1015, p. 163.
1154. Convention on the Prohibition of the Development, Production, Stockpiling and Use of Chemical Weapons and on Their Destruction, Doc.CD/CW/WP.400/Rev.1.
1155. Non-Proliferation Treaty Exporters Committee (also called the Zangger Committee), 29 Apr. 1997.
1156. Wassenaar Arrangement on export controls for conventional arms and dual use goods and technologies.

Table 16.4 Other

Name	*Adoption*	*Participation*
International Code of Conduct[1157]	25 November 2002	Yes

Par. 2 Treaties Dealing with Specific Areas

Table 16.5 International Zones

Treaty Name	*Overall Status*	*Specific Status*	*Enforceable in the UK*
Antarctic Treaty[1158]	OS: 1 December 1959 EF: 23 June 1961	S: 1 December 1959 R: 31 May 1960	Yes
Outer Space Treaty (OST)[1159]	OS: 27 January 1967 EF: 10 October 1967	S: 27 January 1967 R: 10 October 1967	Yes
Sea Bed Arms Control Treaty[1160]	OS: 11 February 1971 EF: 23 June 1961	S: 18 February 1971 R: 18 May 1972	Yes
Moon Agreement[1161]	OS: 18 December 1979 EF: 11 July 1984	-	No
Convention on the Law of the Sea[1162]	OS: 10 December 1982 EF: 16 November 1994	A: 25 July 1997	Yes

OS: Opened for signature; EF: Entry into force; S/R: Signature/Ratification; A: Accession

Table 16.6 Regional Nuclear Weapons-Free Zones

Treaty Name	*Overall Status*	*Specific Status*	*Enforceable in the UK*
Treaty of Tlatelolco[1163]	OS: 14 February 1967 EF: 22 April 1967	-	No[1164]

1157. Hague Code of Conduct against Ballistic Missile Proliferation. November 2002.
1158. 402, *U.N.T.S.*, 7.
1159. Treaty on Principles Governing the Activities of States in the Exploration and Use of Outer Space, including the Moon and Other Celestial Bodies, *U.N.T.S.*, 27 Jan. 1967, vol. 610, p. 205.
1160. Treaty on the Prohibition of the Emplacement of Nuclear Weapons and other Weapons of Mass Destruction on the Seabed and The Ocean Floor and in the subsoil thereof, *U.N.T.S.*, vol. 955, p. 115.
1161. Agreement governing the Activities of States on the Moon and Other Celestial Bodies, *I.L.M.*, 11 Jul. 1984, vol. 18, p. 1434.
1162. Doc. A/CONF.62/122 and Corr.1-11.
1163. Treaty for the Prohibition of Nuclear Weapons in Latin America and the Caribbean, *U.N.T.S.*, 14 Feb. 1967, vol. 634, p. 326.
1164. The UK signed and ratified the Protocols I and II (S: 20 Dec. 1967; R: 11 Dec. 1969).

Treaty Name	*Overall Status*	*Specific Status*	*Enforceable in the UK*
Treaty of Rarotonga[1165]	OS: 6 August 1985 EF: 11 December 1986	-	No[1166]
Treaty of Bangkok[1167]	OS: 15 December 1995 EF: 27 March 1997	-	No
Treaty of Pelindaba[1168]	OS: 11 April 1996 EF: not in force	-	No[1169]

OS: Opened for signature; EF: Entry into force; S/R: Signature/Ratification; A: Accession

SECTION 4 CONTROL REGIMES

As noted, the UK export controls regime is derived from various international commitments, as well as domestic foreign policy, defence and security objectives. This section provides an overview of the key UK military and dual-use measures.

Sub-Section 1 Military Goods and Services

Par. 1 Overall Presentation

The UK military export controls list is set forth in Schedule 2 to the 2008 Order. Schedule 2 is based on the EU Common Military List although it contains a number of supplemental provisions. It also includes definitions of key terms, most of which are drawn from EU legislation and/or the standards developed at the Wassenaar Arrangement. The 2008 Order also implements export controls associated with torture-related items controlled under the EU Anti-Torture Regulation, and it imposes similar controls (set forth in Article 9 of the 2008 Order) on additional torture-related instruments.

In addition to its export controls provisions, the UK also restricts the unlicensed import into the UK of certain military items, including certain firearms,[1170] ammunition, anti-personnel and land mines, nuclear materials, and chemical weapons precursors, as well as import controls mandated pursuant to EU sanctions legislation.[1171] Those import controls are administered by the BIS Import Licensing Branch.[1172]

1165. South Pacific Nuclear Free Zone Treaty, *I.L.M.*, vol. 24, p. 1442.
1166. The UK signed and ratified the Protocols I, II, and III (S: 25 Mar. 1996; R: 19 Sep. 1997).
1167. South East Asia Nuclear-Weapon-Free Zone Treaty, *I.L.M.*, 15 Dec. 1995, vol. 35. p. 635.
1168. African Nuclear Weapon-Free Zone Treaty, *I.L.M.*, 11 Apr. 1996, vol. 35, p. 698.
1169. The UK signed and ratified the Protocols I and II (S: 11 Apr. 1996; R: 19 Mar. 2001).
1170. A list of restricted firearms is set forth in Section 5 of the Firearms Act 1968, See Firearms Act 1968. c. 27. (U.K.).
1171. For example, in 2014 the EU implemented a broad-based embargo against the import of products originating in Crimea or Sevastopol. See EC Regulation No. 692/2014. Other EU sanctions measures including those relating to Iran, North Korea, Russia, Syria, and Somalia impose more targeted import-related restrictions.
1172. An overview of the UK's import licensing regime can be viewed on the BIS website at http://www.gov.uk/import-controls.

Finally, as with other EU Member States, the UK imposes controls in the transit of certain military items through the UK, and on brokering activities in respect of military items. Those measures are summarized, below.

Although the UK military export and import controls regimes derive principally from national legislation, the UK has revised its military controls regulations over the years to account for developments at the international level. For example, in 2012 the UK introduced amendments to the 2008 Order, and the creation of special licensing frameworks, to implement intra-EU military trade standards contemplated under the Inter-Community Transfer Directive.[1173] The UK likewise has implemented licensing frameworks to ease specific licensing requirements for exports of certain military items to the United States, as contemplated under the US-UK Defence Trade Cooperation Treaty.[1174] As noted above, the UK has also amended the 2008 Order in 2014 to account for requirements under the Arms Trade Treaty (including, in particular, to tighten transit and trade/brokering controls with regard to certain types of combat aircraft, battle tanks, armoured fighting vehicles, and other military equipment).[1175]

Sub-Par. 1 Requirements Prior to Any Specific Import/Export (i.e., Construction Phase)

The UK does not impose licensing or registration requirements with regard to the manufacturing of military items, and as a general matter there are no prior regulatory requirements from an export controls standpoint for activities prior to the actual export from the UK. An important exception to that general observation, however, is that all companies must receive MoD approval before they may release equipment, or even information about such equipment, where the item in question is classified as 'official-sensitive' or a higher grading.[1176] MoD approval is also required before the ECO will permit a company to use certain open general licences associated with military items, or to receive individual licensing for certain goods, software, and technology.

MoD approval can be obtained by completing MoD Form 680.[1177] Applications must be made to the Arms Control & Counter-Proliferation Policy (ACP), in the MoD

1173. Directive 2009/43/EC of the European Parliament and of the Council of 6 May 2009 simplifying terms and conditions of transfers of defence-related products within the Community, available at http://eur-lex.europa.eu/LexUriServ/LexUriServ.do?uri=OJ:L:2009:146:0001:0036:en:PDF.
1174. These measures are reflected in the Military Open General Export Licence (Exports under the US-UK Defence Trade Cooperation Treaty).
1175. See Export Control (Amendment) Order 2014/702, available at http://www.legislation.gov.uk/uksi/2014/702/pdfs/uksi_20140702_en.pdf.
1176. See MOD Form 680 Procedure Guidance For Government and Industry. Arms Control & Counter-Proliferation Policy Export Licensing Policy, Ministry of Defence, available at https://www.gov.uk/government/uploads/system/uploads/attachment_data/file/318813/10062014_MOD_680_guidance_Screen.pdf.
1177. Last time amended in December 2015. Please see the Notice to Exporters 2015/32: changes to MOD Form 680 – effective 13 Jan. 2016, available here: http://blogs.bis.gov.uk/exportcontrol/uncategorized/notice-to-exporters-201532-changes-to-mod-form-680-effective-13-jan-2016/.

via the SPIRE online export licensing portal.[1178] The forms can be used to cover the following activities: market surveys, initial discussion, promotion, demonstrations overseas, demonstrations within the UK, local assembly, and local manufacture. Applications are assessed by specialist advisers in the MoD, the FCO and, where sustainable development is an issue, the DfID.

Once the ACP has had the opportunity to consider the Form 680 application, it will issue an electronic outcome letter to the applicant via SPIRE. The letter will describe the goods or technology covered under the letter, and give the destination to which approval has been granted. The approvals may be outright, or they may (and typically do) include provisions and conditions limiting their applicability.

The MoD aims to respond to applications within thirty days. If the approval is granted, the approval is typically valid for forty-eight months.[1179] In the case of a refusal, the applicant is advised of the criteria against which the adverse decision was made. The decision by the MoD in relation to Form 680 is not subject to appeal.

It is important to bear in mind that the MoD approval does not constitute a licence to export or transfer restricted military items. The exporter must still apply for a licence from the ECO and the ECO may still deny the application.

Sub-Par. 2 Requirements at the Import and/or Export Stages

I Goods

Licences are required for the export of goods, software, or technology set forth in Schedule 2 and Article 9 to the 2008 Order, as well as the EU Anti-Torture Regulation, to any non-UK destination.

Consistent with standards set forth at the Wassenaar Arrangement, the UK military controls define the term ‘export’ to include both physical exports as well as intangible exports of ‘software’ and ‘technology’ (including, for example, electronic transfers). Those terms are specifically defined and elaborated on in Article 2 and Schedule 3 of the 2008 Order.

In addition to exports from the UK, controls apply on the mere transit through the UK of military or torture-related items in certain cases. Specifically, transit controls apply for transits to *any destination* for certain military items set forth in Article 17 of the 2008 Order, as well as designated torture-related items. Transit controls also apply for a broader range of military items to destinations set forth in Schedule 4 to the 2008 Order. The Schedule 4 list is periodically updated to account for new United Nations (UN) and EU control regimes.

1178. SPIRE can be accessed online, at https://www.spire.bis.gov.uk/eng/fox/espire/LOGIN/login.

1179. MOD Form 680 approvals for the release of defence-related material up to Official Sensitive (including UK material classified Restricted, graded prior to 2 Apr. 2014, and internationally security classified material) are valid for forty-eight months and for Secret and above (including Confidential for material classified by the UK prior to 2 Apr. 2014 or internationally security classified Confidential or above equivalent material) are valid for twenty-four months.

All UK military export licensing is handled through the SPIRE system. The ECO advises a company to register on SPIRE before applying for a licence, as the registration process can take weeks to complete. Once a user is registered, each of the military-related licences may be applied for through SPIRE, the ECO's online licensing platform.[1180] The ECO operates a helpline which is open on weekdays between the hours of 9.00 a.m. to 12.00 p.m. and 2.00 p.m. to 4.00 p.m. to assist with online licence applications.[1181]

There are three types of licences that are available for the export and transit of military items, as described below.

(i) Open General Licences

An OGEL is a pre-published export controls licence, which is available to all exporters. OGELs are issued by ECO, and the current versions of all OGELs are available on the ECO website.[1182] OGELs are, as a general matter, designed to authorize the export of controlled military goods, software, and technology that are of a less sensitive nature and are being provided to destinations that the UK has deemed to pose less significant export controls risks. Provided that the exporter meets the terms and conditions of the OGEL,[1183] and has registered to use it on SPIRE, they may use an OGEL without having to apply for an individual licence.

OGELs remain valid until they are amended or revoked by the ECO. The terms and conditions of the OGEL will vary depending on which licence is used. As noted above, several of the available OGELs require Form 680 approval before use. Further, the ECO advises exporters to know the control list classification or 'rating' of the item being exported before using an OGEL.

There are currently twenty-five different military export OGELs in place,[1184] including OGELs focused on certain types of items and/or destinations (e.g., exports to the United States, exports of technology for military items, exports of historic military goods), certain types of joint bi-lateral and multilateral defence projects (e.g., collaboration for Project Typhoon and the Joint Strike Fighter programme), and exports for specified purposes (e.g., repair/replacement, exhibition activities).[1185] By registering to

1180. SPIRE can be accessed online, at https://www.spire.bis.gov.uk/spire/fox/espire/LOGIN/login.
1181. General enquiries can be made to eco.help@bis.gsi.gov.uk or by telephone 020 7215 4594.
1182. See Open general export licences (OGELs). Department for Business, Innovations & Skill. September 2013, available at https://www.gov.uk/government/collections/open-general-export-licences-ogels.
1183. Exporters are able to check whether they meet all of the defined terms and conditions of open licences by using the ECO's OGEL checker database, which is available on the ECO SPIRE website at https://www.spire.bis.gov.uk/spirefox5live.
1184. The Open general export licence (international non-proliferation regime decontrols: military items) was revoked on 8 Oct. 2015. Please see the Notice to Exporters 2015/25: 23 open licences updated and 1 revoked, available here: http://blogs.bis.gov.uk/exportcontrol/uncategorized/notice-to-exporters-201525-23-open-licences-updated-and-1-revoked/. The most recent military OGEL was adopted on 14 Apr. 2016, Open general export licence (PCBs and components for military goods), and is available here: https://www.gov.uk/government/uploads/system/uploads/attachment_data/file/515105/16-153-ogel-pcb-military.pdf.
1185. The full list of military OGELs is available at https://www.gov.uk/guidance/military-goods-ogels.

use an OGEL, exporters should be aware that the registration would subject the exporter to compliance audits by the ECO's Compliance Unit (as discussed in further detail below). The exporter should, therefore, ensure that it understands all of the conditions of the use of the OGEL and is prepared to maintain appropriate records of shipments under the OGEL.

(ii) Standard Individual Export Licences

A Standard Individual Export Licence (SIEL) is the most common type of licence for the export of controlled military items, and represents a more targeted licensing approach than ECO's open licences.

SIELs can either be 'permanent' or 'temporary'. A permanent SIEL is issued for the general transfer of goods by an exporter, and permits the export of specific goods to the company and location specified in the application. The ECO may also issue a form of SIEL to cover long-term contracts, projects and repeat business.

Due to the specific nature of the information required in the SIEL licensing process – such as the exact quantities and value of each item being exported, details of the item's end-use, the destination and person to which they are being transferred, as well as supporting documents, including technical specifications and an end-user statement – SIELs can be time-consuming for exporters to complete, file, and track once the licences are issued, and they are less flexible in application. If, for instance, a new end-user emerges in a given country, or if unanticipated volumes of items are required to be exported, a new SIEL may be required. Items covered by SIELs are, however, not required to be sent in a single shipment as long as the quantities and values have not been exhausted across the aggregate shipments made under the licence.

Once an SIEL application is submitted (which should again be done through SPIRE), the ECO aims to process the applications quickly, with 70% of licence applications being processed within the first twenty days. Once issued, military SIELs typically are valid for a two-year period.

Temporary SIELs are similar to permanent SIELs, except that they mandate the return of the goods to the UK after some specified period (typically, one year). Temporary SIELs may be required, for example, if an exporter intends to ship goods for demonstrations, exhibitions or for repair or maintenance purposes.

Once a SIEL expires, the exporter should either advise the ECO of the licence expiration or send the expired licence to the ECO Licence Reception Unit.[1186] If an exporter does not ultimately utilize the SIEL, it should still return the licence to the Unit, attaching a covering letter to explain why the licence was not used.

As part of the SIEL licensing process, it is necessary to obtain from the end-user, and include in the licence application, a signed end-user undertaking where the end-user agrees to comply with certain conditions. The conditions, which are generally consistent with those implemented in end-user undertaking by other EU Member States in the military export context, include that (1) the goods, software, or technology covered under the licence will not be used for any purpose connected with chemical,

1186. Expired licences should be sent by post to: Licence Reception Unit, Export Control Organisation, 3rd Floor, 1 Victoria Street, London SW1H 0ET.

biological or nuclear weapons, or missiles capable of delivering such weapons; (2) the goods will not be re-exported or otherwise resold or transferred if it is known or suspected that they are intended or likely to be used for such purposes; (3) the goods will not be re-exported or otherwise resold or transferred to a destination in breach of arms embargoes; and (4) the goods, or any replica of them, will not be used in any nuclear explosive activity or unsafeguarded nuclear fuel cycle.

(iii) Open Individual Export Licences

An Open Individual Export Licence (OIEL) is broader in scope than a SIEL, allowing a named exporter to export multiple shipments of specific goods to specific countries, subject to meeting certain terms and conditions. Unlike SIELs, OIELs do not normally require consignees or end-users to be named in the licence request. However, exporters must demonstrate a 'clear business justification' to receive an OIEL.[1187] The justifications – which are set out in the OIEL licensing form – include but are not limited to: a record of the exporter having made at least five SIEL applications to different countries in the previous year, or a contract that demands delivery of goods within twenty working days. In practice, the ECO will also consider OIELs in circumstances where an individual contract or series of contracts will require a large number of SIELs, and where the key parameters of the contract (e.g., parties, items) can be ascertained with some degree of clarity.

The ECO operates a longer processing time for OIELs as compared to SIELs, with a target of 60% of applications being processed within sixty working days; and more complex cases taking up to 120 working days.

Military OIELs are usually valid for five years. As of February 2015, the ECO has also introduced a specific OIEL, known as the 'Through Life Support' OIEL, which can be used following an initial export of a military platform or major military equipment. This licence permits the subsequent export of systems, sub-systems and components for the platform or major system and the export from the UK to a government or other person outside the EU. This type of OIEL is generally valid for fifteen years.

As part of making a successful application for a Military OIEL, the ECO advise that applicants should avoid applying to export to a long list of possible future destinations, and they should limit the destinations to those that are known or form part of an organization's business plans. Second, the goods list should only include items which are realistically intended for export. Further, care should be taken when applying for 'sensitive' destinations, as the OIEL is more likely to be refused by the ECO in those circumstances.[1188] While consignee and end-user information does not need to be provided in the application, the exporter must obtain undertakings before the goods are shipped and ensure that these remain valid once the shipment is made. This includes an undertaking that the goods are not intended for re-export to a destination not

1187. Exporters that are in doubt as to whether or not they can demonstrate a clear business need should contact the ECO's OIELs team via the OIELs option on the ECO Helpline 020 7215 4594, or email eco.help@bis.gsi.gov.uk with 'OIELs' in the subject line.
1188. Sensitive destinations will include those listed at Schedule 4 to the Export Control Order 2008.

permitted in the licence. Finally, records should be stored by the exporter to ensure compliance. As with the other licences, OIELs are subject to periodic compliance reviews by the ECO.

Finally, with regard to import licensing, items that require import licences under UK law (as noted above) are subject to licensing by the Import Licensing Branch. Open individual licences are available for imports from outside of the EU, which are subject to a requirement that the importer certify as a registered firearms dealer. Imports of controlled items from within the EU can be handled in a more streamlined manner pursuant to transfer licences.

II Services

A. Overview

In addition to the export of military items, the UK Government also controls the 'trading' or 'brokering' of military goods.[1189] (For ease of reference, we refer to this activity herein as 'brokering.') The concept of 'brokering' is defined broadly to include supplying or delivering, agreeing to supply or deliver, or undertaking any act 'calculated to promote' the supply or delivery of military items from one third country to another. Brokering can occur even if the party engaged in the brokering does not serve as the exporter and is not involved in the actual export transaction. Notably, however, the UK military brokering controls do not apply to brokering activities involving the export of military goods, software, or technology from the UK itself (those activities are, rather, regulated as traditional export licensing matters pursuant to the framework described above).

The UK brokering framework operates as a tiered structure, with broader prohibitions and licensing requirements applicable for brokering activities in respect of embargoed destinations and/or more tightly controlled products as set forth in 'Category A' to Schedule 1 of the 2008 Order. Fewer restrictions, and broader licensing options (including the availability of open general licences), apply with regard to brokering activities involving shipments to less sensitive destinations, and/or involving less sensitive military items as set forth in 'Category B' and 'Category C' to Schedule 1 of the 2008 Order.

By way of background, Category A includes goods of the greatest concern, where trade is inherently undesirable, such as torture equipment and cluster munitions. Category B also includes goods of heightened concern, but in which there is legitimate trade, such as small arms and light weapons, long range missiles (including unmanned aerial vehicles or UAVs) and Man-Portable Air Defence Systems (MANPADS). Category C includes all other items contained in Schedule 1 that do not fall under categories A or B, as well as certain additional listed items.

The definition of 'brokering' is conceptually broad. With regard to Category A items, and brokering activities in respect of embargoed destinations (as defined in

1189. Export Control Order 2008, Part 4.

Schedule 4 of the 2008 Order), it could include contract promotional activities as well as arranging for the transport or financing of transfers of restricted items. The restrictions applicable to Category B items contain an exemption for brokering activities where the sole involvement of the UK party is to provide financing or financial services, insurance or reinsurance services, certain transportation services, or general advertising or promotional services, as well as for contract promotional activity that is not for payment (the latter standard could cover, for example, acts of an employee who incidentally performs brokering activities as part of a wider role, and is compensated only pursuant to a general wage or salary – receiving no bonus or supplemental income for the brokering activity). The controls applicable to Category C items are subject to the same exemptions as in respect of Category B, while also including a broader exemption for transportation-related services.

The UK brokering controls carry a broad jurisdictional reach – brokering restrictions with regard to Categories A and B goods, and transactions involving embargoed destinations, extend to the conduct of UK persons or entities anywhere in the world, as well as the activities of persons or entities of any nationality that occur within the territory of the UK. Extraterritorial controls also apply with regard to Category C brokering activities, but only where the items in question are intended for an embargoed destination. The term 'UK person' is defined to include British citizens, British overseas territories citizens, British National (Overseas) or British Overseas Citizens, or persons who qualify as British subjects or British protected persons under the British Nationality Act 1981.[1190]

In addition to the UK's brokering controls, Part 3 of the 2008 Order also prohibits the unlicensed provision of 'technical assistance' in relation to the supply, delivery, manufacture, maintenance, or use of any item that the person or entity is aware, or has been informed by the UK government, relates entirely or in part to WMD end-uses.

III Licensing

As with the export of military items, there are several types of licences available for brokering-related activities. Applications for UK brokering licences are available on and processed through the ECO's online platform, SPIRE. The available licences include the Open General Trade Control Licence (Category C Goods), which authorizes brokering activities for Category C goods with regard to a broad range of countries set forth in the licence, as well as narrower open general licences focusing on certain insurance and reinsurance activities, maritime anti-piracy efforts, and trading in certain small arms and light weapons.[1191] All of the brokering OGELs contain various conditions and recordkeeping requirements, and may subject the licence registrant to ECO auditing.

Separately, the Standard Individual Trade Control Licence (SITCL) is a licence specific to the exporter and may be used for a one-off transfer. A SITCL is usually valid

1190. British Nationality Act 1981. c. 61. (U.K.).
1191. See https://www.gov.uk/open-general-trade-control-licences.

for two years or until the trade occurs. Once this licence expires, the exporter must apply via a new application to carry out additional trades.

Finally, an Open Individual Trade Control Licence (OITCL) is a general licence which permits a range of activities. Both the SITCL and the OITCL require specific information from the exporter, such as end-user details, the origin and destination of the goods, as well as the country of destination. The ECO will usually require detailed technical specifications of the goods and an executed end-user certificate, and the OITCL may subject the licence holder to ECO auditing.

The ECO typically responds to brokering-related licence requests (as in the case of export licence applications) in a three to four week window.

IV Persons

The UK military export controls framework does not impose licensing requirements merely on the basis of the *nationality* of the recipient. Hence, the UK does not adopt the approach of the United States, in controlling the 'deemed' export or re-export of technical information that is shared within a given country, with a national of some other country, on the basis of licensing requirements applicable to the country of that person's nationality. However, the definition of 'export' in the UK military framework could encompass the sharing of information in the UK with some person, where the party providing the information is aware that the recipient will transfer or utilize that information overseas. In that case, the sharing of the information would not be controlled on the basis of the nationality of the recipient, but it may trigger controls on the basis that the recipient will remove the technical information from the UK or apply it outside of the UK.

Par. 2 Control Lists

The Export Control Order 2008 contains, in its schedules, the UK national list of items that require export authorization. Schedule 1 contains the list of category A, B and C goods that are subject to stricter export and trade controls.[1192] Schedule 2, most recently amended (as of this writing) by the Export Control (Amendment) Order 2015,[1193] is the UK National Military List.

The UK Strategic Export Control List consolidates various UK control lists, including Schedule 2 of the Export Control Order; the UK Dual-Use List at Schedule 3; the EU Human Rights List at Annexes II and III of Council Regulation (EC)

1192. Export Control Order 2008/3231 (schedule 1. pt. 1 and 2 last amended by Export Control (Amendment) Order 2015), available at https://www.gov.uk/export-control-order-2008.
1193. Export Control Order 2008/3231 (schedule 2. last amended by Export Control (Amendment) Order 2015), available at https://www.gov.uk/export-control-order-2008.

No. 1236/2005; UK Security and Human Rights List at Articles 4A and 9 to the Export Control Order 2008; the UK Radioactive Source List at Schedule to the Export of Radioactive Sources (Control) Order 2006; and the EU Dual-Use Lists at Annex I and Annex IV of Council Regulation (EC) No. 428/2009. The current list was last updated in December 2015.[1194]

The online Goods Checker tool, available on the ECO's website, can be used by UK exporters to assist in determining whether their goods, software or technology are controlled by UK or EU strategic export control legislation. Exporters may also seek formal export controls classification determinations, or 'ratings,' from the ECO's Technical Assessment Unit (TAU) pursuant to a formal process available through the SPIRE system. Classification determinations are subject to appeal. Determinations are not generally published by the ECO, although it is possible that they might be disclosed to interested third parties pursuant to requests made under the UK Freedom of Information Act 2000 (FOIA).

Par. 3 Licensing and Enforcement Authorities

The ECO is responsible for all licensing of military goods, software, and technology, as well as all brokering-related licences. The ECO is also, as noted above, responsible for responding to classification enquiries from UK exporters. The ECO accepts licences request and classification requests relating to military items only pursuant to the SPIRE online system. The ECO consults regularly with other agencies, including the DfID, the MoD, and the FCO, on policy issues with regard to individual licence requests. Import licensing matters are handled separately by the Import Licensing Branch.

As described below, enforcement of the UK military export and import controls is shared among different agencies. The ECO is responsible for supervising export controls compliance by UK exporters, including through its regular practice of auditing exporters that export under open licences. The ECO has limited administrative enforcement powers (including, in particular, the ability to dictate and limit exporters' eligibility to use licences). Civil and criminal enforcement matters are pursued in the first instance by HMRC, with the involvement of the CPS and/or the Serious Fraud Office (SFO) in significant cases.

The following flow chart (Figure 16.1) provides a brief overview and summary of the UK military *brokering* licensing process (we separately provide, in Sub-Section 2 in Section 4, a flow chart (Figure 16.2) describing the military and dual-use export licensing process in the UK):

1194. UK Strategic Export Control Lists. Department for Business, Innovation & Skills. December 2015, available at https://www.gov.uk/government/uploads/system/uploads/attachment_data/file/488993/controllist0151225.pdf.

Figure 16.1 UK Military Brokering – Licensing

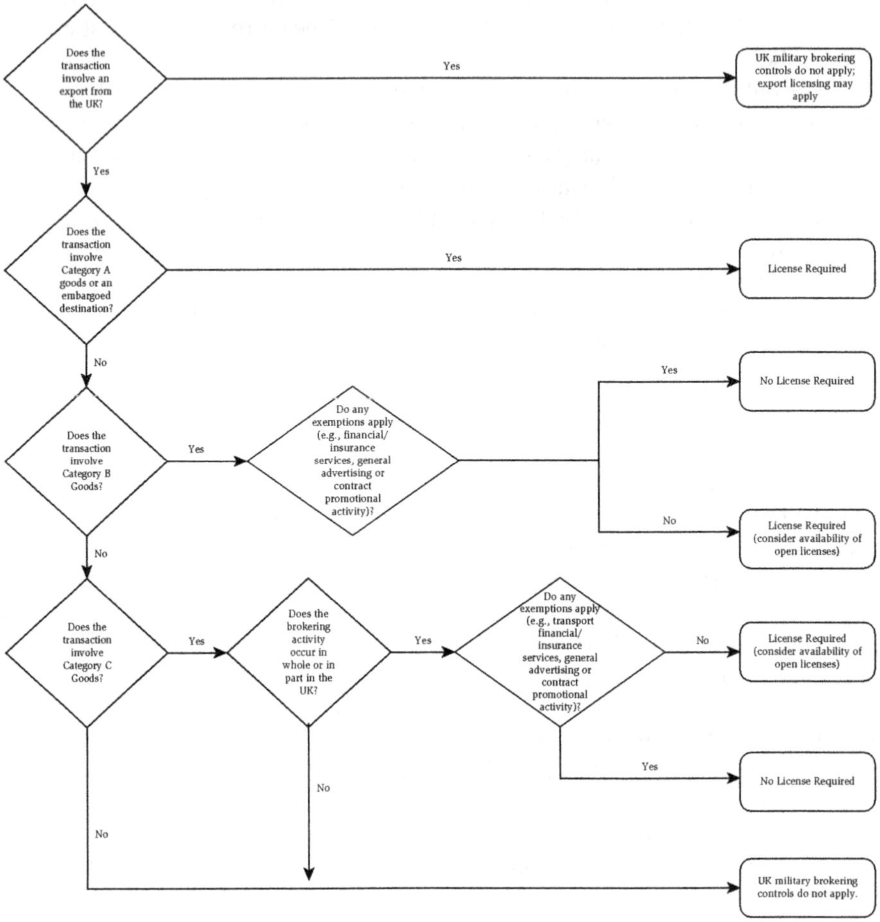

Par. 4 Sanctions and Recourses of the Importer/Exporter

The import or export of a controlled item without the proper licence or in violation of the licence terms, or the unlicensed provision of restricted technical assistance or brokering services, is a strict liability offence. The range of penalties will depend, however, on the nature of the offence.

First, the ECO Compliance Unit conducts regular audits (typically every twelve to twenty-four months) of UK parties that export under open licences, or that utilize open brokering licences, to evaluate their compliance with UK export controls. The ECO audits include reviews of export records, evaluation of the company's compliance policies and procedures, and interviews with relevant company personnel. The ECO audit will seek to ascertain whether unlicensed exports or services have occurred, and it will also conduct checks to ensure that licensing conditions have been followed and that relevant records have been maintained.[1195]

If the ECO determines that an exporter has failed to comply with export controls requirements, the ECO has administrative authority to suspend the exporter's eligibility to use existing licences (including open general, open individual, and specific licences), and to refuse applications for licences. Often, where breaches are identified the ECO will issue a warning letter and schedule a follow-up audit for several months following the initial visit. If, through the follow-up audit, the ECO determines that the underlying compliance issues have not been addressed, it will give more serious consideration to suspending, revoking, or refusing licences.

The ECO does not itself hold criminal or civil monetary enforcement powers. Where breaches are identified in the course of an audit, the ECO will routinely refer the matter to HMRC – it will typically make that referral shortly following the audit, even if the breaches are not substantial and if the exporter has committed to take internal remedial action. HMRC has the principal responsibility in the UK of investigating export controls breaches. It also has the power to seize goods that are the subject of export controls breaches, or to issue 'compound penalties' (a power granted to HMRC under Section 152 of the Customs and Excise Management Act 1979) against exporters who have committed violations. Compound penalties represent a flexible tool to enable HMRC to obtain monetary settlements with exporters, without having to refer the matter for prosecution. There are no specific thresholds as to the amounts of compound penalties that may be available in individual cases. Often, HMRC will use the value of the goods in question as a baseline, but typically the ultimate quantum of the compound penalty represents a negotiated settlement between HMRC and the exporter.

Similar to the ECO, HMRC also may issue warning letters to exporters, without taking the formal enforcement measures noted above. Warning letters are, as a matter of practice, issued in most cases where non-substantial or non-systemic breaches have been identified. The warning letters will remain on the exporter's HMRC file and may be factored into HMRC's enforcement analysis if new export controls breaches are identified in the future.

In serious cases, such as where there is evidence of intent to violate the law, HMRC may refer the matter to the UK CPS for formal investigation and potential prosecution. The UK SFO may also become involved in cases involving major export controls violations. Both imprisonment and monetary penalties (with unlimited fines in egregious cases) are available for breaches of the military export controls and brokering standards.

1195. See Compliance and enforcement of export controls Guidance. Department for Business, Innovation & Skills. October 2012, available at https://www.gov.uk/compliance-checks-and-enforcement-of-export-controls-on-strategic-goods-and-technology.

Finally, we note that in the export control context, there is no specific law in the UK allowing a director or officer to pass onto another person within the company their liability as a director or officer. As with any employee of a UK company, a director or officer could be exposed to personal liability if she or he were to individually and intentionally support export controls breaches (with the company also potentially exposed to an enforcement risk).

Sub-Section 2 Dual-Use Goods and Services

Par. 1 Overall Presentation

'Dual use' items are goods, software, and technology that may be used for both civil and military purposes. The UK implements the EU dual-use regime set forth in the Dual-Use Regulation, pursuant to the 2002 Act and 2008 Order.[1196] The UK incorporates the EU list of dual-use items (contained in Annex I of the EC Regulation) into the UK's consolidated list of controlled items, which (as with the relevant military lists) are published as the UK Strategic Export Control List. The UK has also implemented a small list of additional dual-use items which are subject to unilateral national export controls with regard to certain destinations (as set forth in Schedule 3 to the 2008 Order). Those items are listed in the UK Dual-Use List, which also forms part of the UK Strategic Export Controls List.[1197]

The UK also imposes transit controls on exports of dual-use items to certain destinations, or if the exporter is aware the export is intended to facilitate WMD-related activities.[1198]

The UK does not impose a specific import controls regime with regard to dual-use goods, software, or technology. In addition to the military import controls noted above, the UK implements certain targeted import controls under the EU Common Agricultural Policy, as well as controls relating to imports of certain animals and animal products, and certain types of chemical compounds. Those controls are implemented under a range of different regulations and licensing procedures.[1199]

Sub-Par. 1 Requirements Prior to Any Specific Import/Export

A licence must be secured before a transfer of dual-use goods, software, or technology is made. As per the structure of the Dual-Use Regulation, the UK does not control the

1196. Council Regulation (EC) No. 428/2009 of 5 May 2009 setting up a Community regime for the control of exports, transfer, brokering and transit of dual use items. This Regulation was last updated by Commission Delegated Regulation (EU) No. 1382/2014 of 22 Oct. 2014.
1197. This can be found in the Schedule to SI 2010/2007, which replaced Schedule 3 of the Export Control Order 2008.
1198. 2008 Order, Article 17.
1199. Further information concerning these special import controls can be found at https://www.gov.uk/government/collections/import-and-export-controls.

export of items set forth in Annex I to the Dual-Use Regulation where the end destination is another member of the EU, unless (1) the item in question is listed in Annex IV to the Dual-Use Regulation, (2) the item will merely transit through another Member State before being exported to a third country, or (3) the export triggers any of the 'catch all' provisions of the Dual-Use Regulation (discussed below).

As in the case of the UK military export controls, the method of transport outside of the EU is not dispositive in determining whether an 'export' has taken place. For example, physical shipment, regular mail, delivery by hand, downloading software from an internet site, and transmission of software or technology via e-mail can all constitute an export from the UK. Likewise, controls generally apply regardless of the purpose for export - temporary exports (i.e., of items that will return to the UK), gifts, contributions to research projects, shipments to a subsidiary outside the UK - all may constitute exports requiring prior licensing if the goods, software, or technology in question are controlled.

Aside from items specifically listed in the UK legislation, an exporter may require a licence to export items not included on the UK dual-use lists and the military lists, as per the 'catch all provisions' in the Dual-Use Regulation, if:

(i) the exporter knows, has reason to know, or is informed by the competent authority (i.e., the UK ECO) that the items may be intended for use in connection with the development, production and dissemination of WMD;
(ii) the exporter knows or is informed by the competent authority of: (a) military end-use of the exported item in a purchasing country or country of destination subject to an arms embargo imposed through an EU common position or joint action, or an Organisation for Security and Co-operation in Europe decision, or a UN Security Council resolution; or (b) use of the exported items as parts or components of military items exported from an EU Member State without authorisation or in violation of the national export controls of that state; or
(iii) the exporter knows, has reason to know or is informed by the competent authority that the item due for export will be incorporated into a military item and does not have a valid licence.

As discussed in further detail below, an exporter should also be aware of exporting an item to a country subject to targeted sanctions and embargoes, as additional controls may apply for exports to those destinations, including exports of a wider range of goods, software, and technology than those listed in the UK Strategic Export Controls List.

Apart from the obtaining of an export licence, UK exporters are required to register in advance with the ECO to utilize certain dual-use OGELs, as well as certain European Community General Export Authorisations (GEAs) issued by the European Council under the Dual-Use Regulation. Apart from those measures, however, there are no other prior registration requirements associated with dual-use exports.

Sub-Par. 2 Requirements at the Import and/or Export Stages

I Goods

As with the case of military items, the ECO is the responsible body for licensing dual-use exports. Broadly speaking, licences available for dual-use items are the same as those available for military goods, although the OGELs available in the dual-use context (which are sixteen in number as of this writing[1200]) cover different categories of exports as compared to the Military OGELs. For example, the UK has published OGELs specific to dual-use exports that focus on cryptography exports, exports in support of oil and gas projects, exports focusing on certain dual-use products intended for use in Turkey and Hong Kong, and low value shipments. As in the case of military exports, end-user undertakings are required for dual-use individual licences.

In addition to the available dual-use SIELs, OIELs and OGELs, UK exporters are able to utilize European Union General Export Authorisations (EU GEAs), which operate in a similar manner as the UK OGELs and include various conditions (including certain ECO registration and reporting requirements). Pursuant to EC Regulation No. 1232/2011 (amending the EU Dual-use Regulation), there are six types of EU GEAs, which came into force on 7 January 2012 (prior to that date, there was only one EU GEA). The available EU GEAs are as follows: EU001 which covers exports to Australia, Canada, Japan, New Zealand, Norway, Switzerland (including Liechtenstein) and the United States;[1201] EU002, which covers export of certain Dual-Use Items to certain destinations; EU003, which relates to the export after repair/replacement of an item; EU004, which is for the temporary export related to an exhibition or fair; EU005, which relates to telecommunications; and EU006, which relates to the export of certain chemicals.[1202]

To the extent SIELs are required, the ECO aims to process applications within twenty working days from its submission. Exporters will be informed through SPIRE once the application is granted or refused. If the application is refused, the ECO will provide the applicant with the reasons for refusal and the applicant will be offered the opportunity to appeal the decision.

1200. See Dual-use open general export licences. Department for Business, Innovation & Skills., available at https://www.gov.uk/government/collections/open-general-export-licences-ogels. The most recent dual-use OGEL was adopted on 14 April 2016, Open general export licence (PCBs and components for dual-use items), and is available here: https://www.gov.uk/government/uploads/system/uploads/attachment_data/file/515119/16-152-ogel-pcb-dual-use.pdf.
1201. This was previously known as the Community General Export Authorisation or CGEA.
1202. See Fact sheet on new EU General Export Authorisations. European Commission. Doc no.: CG/2011/Nov/02 rev 1. 2011, available at http://trade.ec.europa.eu/doclib/docs/2011/december/tradoc_148466.pdf.

The ECO is also available to provide classification or 'rating' decisions concerning potential dual-use items, consistent with the process noted above in connection with military classifications.

II Services

EC Regulation 428/2009 imposes controls on the brokering of dual-use goods, software, and technology, although those controls apply only in limited contexts. Specifically, the controls on 'brokering' were introduced to meet EU Member States obligations set out under UNSCR 1540[1203] in respect of WMD-related activities, and they apply to any items listed in Annex I to the Dual-Use Regulation where the broker has been informed or is aware that the listed items are or may be intended for a WMD end-use.[1204] The 2008 Order also extends those brokering controls to exports or transfers of any other items, even if they are not designated under the Dual-Use Regulation.[1205] As in the case of the military trade controls, 'brokering' has a wide definition and includes services such as buying or selling, or arranging or negotiating transactions for the purchase, sale, or supply, of dual-use items located in one third country for transfer to another.

Exporters engaging in dual-use brokering services will need to apply for a dual-use SITCL via SPIRE, since OGTCLs and OITCLs are not available for dual-use brokering services. Applications are considered by the ECO on a case-by-case basis, and they are scrutinized closely given the WMD nature of the end-use.

III Persons

As in the case of the UK military trade controls, the UK does not impose 'deemed' export or re-export controls (as that term is understood in the context of the U.S. export controls framework) with regard to dual-use software or technology.

Par. 2 Control Lists

The lists of controlled Dual-use goods and technologies are common to all EU Member States and have been established by the Regulation (EC) No. 428/2009.[1206] Schedule 3 of the Export Control Order 2008 adds items to the EU list (e.g., materials, chemicals, micro-organisms and toxins; telecommunications and related technology; vessels and related software and technology; and aircraft and related technology). The UK

1203. S.C. Res 1540 (28 Apr. 2004).
1204. Export Control (Amendment) (No. 3) Order 2009 (SI 2009/2151), available at http://www.legislation.gov.uk/uksi/2009/2151/pdfs/uksi_20092151_en.pdf.
1205. 2008 Order, Article 6.
1206. Council Regulation (EC) No. 428/2009 of 5 May 2009 setting up a Community regime for the control of exports, transfer, brokering and transit of dual use items as amended.

Strategic Export Control List consolidates all of the export control lists, including the UK Military List at Schedule 2 of the Export Control Order; the UK Dual-Use List at Schedule 3; the EU Human Rights List at Annexes II and III of Council Regulation (EC) No. 1236/2005; UK Security and Human Rights List at Articles 4A and 9 to the Export Control Order 2008; the UK Radioactive Source List at Schedule to the Export of Radioactive Sources (Control) Order 2006; and the EU Dual-Use Lists at Annex I and Annex IV of Council Regulation (EC) No. 428/2009. The current list was last updated in December 2015.[1207]

Par. 3 Licensing and Enforcement Authorities

As noted, the ECO is responsible for the dual-use licensing matters, and it consults regularly with the MoD, DfID, and the FCO. As in the case of the military export controls framework, dual-use export controls compliance is supervised by the ECO, which regularly audits holders of dual-use OIELs and dual-use OGEL registrants. Civil and criminal penalties for dual-use violations may also be pursued by HMRC, the CPS, and/or the SFO (the enforcement framework for dual-use exports is the same as in the military context).

The following flow chart (Figure 16.2) provides a general summary of export licensing considerations under UK law, with regard to both dual-use and military exports:

1207. UK Strategic Export Control Lists. Department for Business, Innovation & Skills. December 2015, available at https://www.gov.uk/government/uploads/system/uploads/attachment_data/file/488993/controllist0151225.pdf.

Figure 16.2

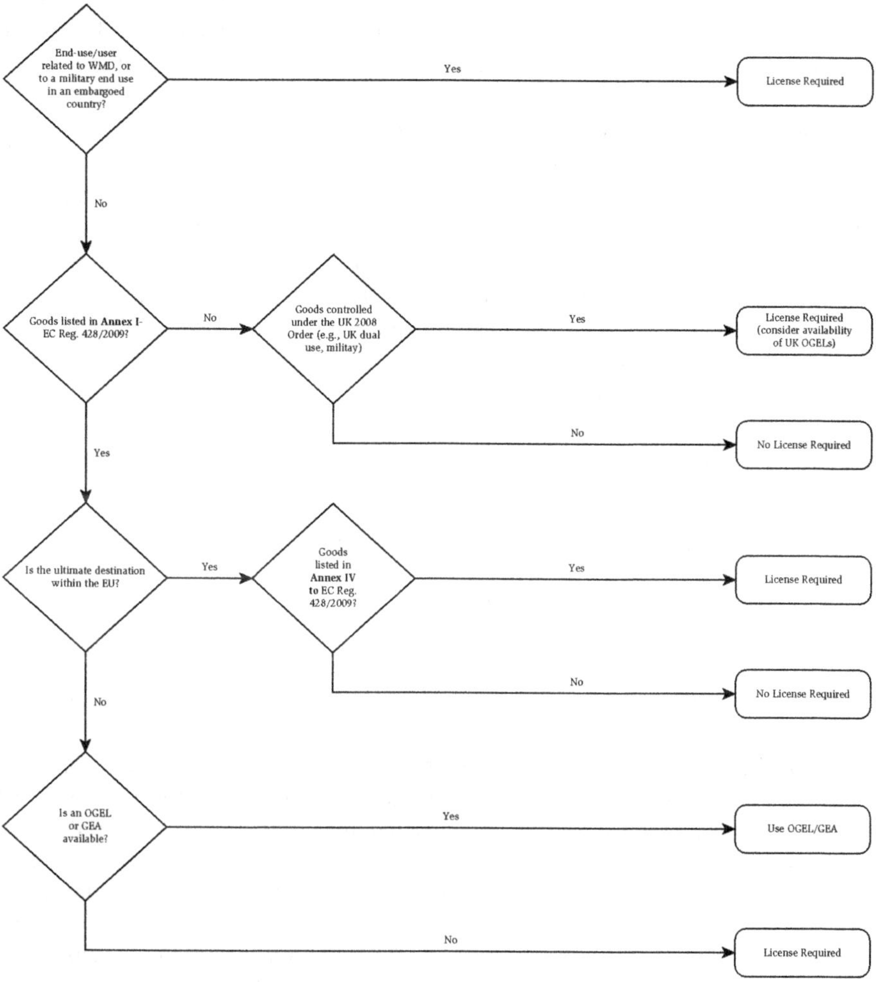

Par. 4 Sanctions and the Recourses of the Importer/Exporter

Non-compliance with the dual-use controls results in the same sanctions and penalties described in relation to the UK military controls.

Sub-Section 3 Radioactive Sources

The Export of Radioactive Sources (Control) Order 2006[1208] was introduced as part of the Government's commitment to minimize the risk of radioactive sources falling into the hands of terrorists or criminal groups who may seek radioactive material for the purposes of terrorist activities. The Order broadly implements the suggested controls and restrictions contained in the International Atomic Energy Agency's Code of Conduct on the Safety and Security of Radioactive Sources.[1209]

The Order prohibits the export from the UK of listed radioactive sources at defined radioactivity levels - Category 1 and Category 2 - without a valid export licence. The categories of radioactivity are derived from Annex 1 of the International Atomic Energy Agency (IAEA) Code of Conduct. The regime instituted by the Order is much narrower in scope than the general export controls under the Export Control Order 2008, as it relates only to the export of radioactive sources[1210] and certain transhipment activities in the UK.[1211]

SECTION 5 SPECIFICITIES/SPACE-RELATED PROVISIONS

Sub-Section 1 Specificities of the Control Regime

Par. 1 Extraterritorial Application

The UK brokering controls carry a broad extraterritorial reach. Due to the emphasis placed by the regime on discouraging and penalizing trafficking and brokering of sensitive goods from one third country to another, the UK brokering controls extend to brokering activities with regard to Category A and B goods on the part of any UK national anywhere in the world, even if the transaction has no connection to the UK apart from the nationality of the person engaging in brokering. Extraterritorial control also apply with regard to Category C goods, if the transaction involves transfers of restricted products to an embargoed destination. The ECO has noted in guidance that the UK brokering standards apply regardless of whether the UK person is working overseas for a UK company, for a foreign company, or acting on her or his own behalf.

The UK Government has received pressure from NGOs (Non-Governmental Organizations) and certain Members of Parliament to implement general extraterritorial trade controls on brokering with respect to Category C goods. The Government is

1208. Export of Radioactive Sources (Control) Order 2006/1846 (as amended by Export of Radioactive Sources (Control) (Amendment) Order 2009/585), available at http://www.legislation.gov.uk/uksi/2006/1846/pdfs/uksi_20061846_en.pdf.
1209. International Atomic Energy Agency, (2014). Code of Conduct on the Safety and Security of Radioactive Sources, and supplementary Guidance on the Import and Export of Radioactive Sources. (IAEA/CODEOC/2004) Vienna: IAEA.
1210. Export of Radioactive Sources (Control) Order 2006/1846 (as amended by Export of Radioactive Sources (Control) (Amendment) Order 2009/585. Article 3).
1211. Export of Radioactive Sources (Control) Order 2006/1846 (as amended by Export of Radioactive Sources (Control) (Amendment) Order 2009/585. Article 4).

reluctant to do so, however, as it views the enforcement of extraterritorial measures to be inherently cumbersome due to, among other considerations, reliance placed on extradition mechanisms and the difficulty of gathering evidence to build a successful prosecution case. The emphasis, therefore, is to reserve extraterritorial jurisdiction for situations where sufficient international consensus permitting this exists.

Apart from brokering controls, UK export controls generally have not been applied by the UK Government on an extraterritorial basis. As noted above, most UK export controls licensing regimes require the end-user to agree to certain undertakings as a precondition to receiving goods, software, or technology under a UK licence. However, the UK Government has not taken the position that the end-user undertaking itself confers jurisdiction over the foreign end-user. The UK authorities also, often, impose licensing conditions on the use of goods overseas that have been exported under a UK licence. However, those conditions would typically apply only against the UK exporter, rather than the foreign end-user.

Criticisms have been expressed from certain stakeholders that the UK export control regime does not apply to foreign subsidiaries of UK companies. The Government has, however, continued to hold to the view that it does not believe it appropriate to extend export controls restrictions to export activities by non-UK companies, even for entities that are owned or controlled by UK parties.[1212]

Par. 2 Confidentiality of Licensing Decisions

The ECO does not provide a publicly accessible database of licences due to commercial confidentiality reasons. However, the ECO launched a publicly searchable database of licence statistics in 2008. That system is the Strategic Export Controls: Reports and Statistics website. This website contains data on export licensing decisions which was historically published as read only in the quarterly and annual reports.[1213]

Interested parties in the UK have, on occasion, sought to obtain information from the ECO concerning licensing matters under the UK FOIA. The UK Government has, however, tended to resist those efforts, including through the application of exemptions in the FOIA that protect confidential commercial information from disclosure, as well as information obtained for national security, government policy, or law enforcement purposes.

1212. See House of Commons, Committees on Arms Exports Control, *Scrutiny of Arms Exports and Arms Controls (2015): Scrutiny of the Government's Strategic Export Controls Annual Report 2013, the Government's Quarterly Reports from October 2013 to June 2014, and the Government's policies on arms exports and international arms control issue, Second Joint Report of the Business, Innovation and Skills, Defence, Foreign Affairs and International Development Committees of Session 2014–15* (HC 608), 20 Mar. 2015, Vol. II, at 29.

1213. Frequently Asked Questions About Using SPIRE. Department for Business Innovation & Skills. March 2010, available at https://www.spire.bis.gov.uk/docs/FAQsSPIRE.pdf.

Sub-Section 2 Space-Related Provisions in the Control Regime

The Outer Space Act was introduced in 1986 to manage the UK's obligations under various UN space treaties and principles.[1214] In essence, these international agreements make the UK government responsible for ensuring that space activities carried out by UK individuals or organizations do not jeopardize public health or the safety of persons or property; and are consistent with the international obligations of the UK.

The Outer Space Act 1986 confers licensing and other powers on the Secretary of State to secure compliance with the international obligations of the UK with respect to the launching and operation of space objects[1215] and the carrying on of other activities in outer space by persons connected with the UK.[1216] The Act includes controls surrounding the use of outer space, including liability for damage caused by space objects, the registration of objects launched into outer space and the principles for the remote sensing of the earth.

Pursuant to those standards, 'UK nationals'[1217] and UK companies intending to launch or procure the launch of a space object, operate a space object or carry on any other activity in outer space must apply for a licence to carry out such activities. This must be done at least six months prior to the space-related activity. A template application form is available online and must be sent, by post or email to the UK Space Agency.[1218] The UK Space Agency was launched officially on 23 March 2010 and became an executive agency of BIS from 1 April 2011. The Agency is responsible for all strategic decisions on the UK civil space programme, and for outreach efforts to industry concerning space-related export controls issues.

SECTION 6 SANCTIONS AND EMBARGOES

Sub-Section 1 Participation of UK to Embargoes or Other Related Sanctions

Broadly speaking, sanctions and embargoes are political trade restrictions put in place against target countries with the aim of maintaining or restoring international peace and security. As described below, the UK implements sanctions that are issued at the EU and UN, and it also implements its own unilateral sanctions measures.

1214. Outer Space Act 1986, c. 38. (U.K.).
1215. Pursuant to section 7 of the Act, the Secretary of State maintains a register of space objects, available at https://www.gov.uk/government/uploads/system/uploads/attachment_data/file/431425/UK_Registry_of_Space_Objects_v4.pdf. A Supplementary version of the register is available at https://www.gov.uk/government/uploads/system/uploads/attachment_data/file/431497/Supplementary_Registry_of_Space_ObjectsV4.pdf.
1216. Outer Space Act 1986, c. 38. (U.K.).
1217. The Outer Space Act 1986 defines this to include an a British citizen, a British Dependent Territories citizen, a British National (Overseas), or a British Overseas citizen, a person who under the British Nationality Act 1981 is a British subject, or a British protected person within the meaning of that Act.
1218. Applications should be sent to Louise Hughes, Outer Space Act Licensing Manager, UK Space Agency, SFS Polaris House, North Star Avenue, Swindon, Wiltshire SN2 1SZ. Email: louise.hughes@spaceagency.bis.gsi.gov.uk.

Sub-Section 2 Regime of the Embargoes or Related Sanctions in the UK

Par. 1 UK Sanctions Legislation

In the EU, sanctions programmes typically are implemented pursuant to European Council Decisions and Regulations, which are directly applicable in the UK as in the other twenty-seven EU Member States. The EU sanctions measures include decisions and regulations that implement international sanctions imposed pursuant to United Nations Security Council Resolutions (UNSCRs), as well as sanctions imposed unilaterally at the EU level (such as the current EU sanctions pertaining to Russia and Crimea, and features of the EU-Iran sanctions).

Although the substantive prohibitions set forth in the EU sanctions regulations are directly applicable in the Member States, they require national implementing legislation to facilitate administration and enforcement. In the UK, each EU sanctions regime is implemented pursuant to an individual UK regulation or order, and in some cases several such measures. For example, for some sanctions programmes the UK issues separate implementing regulations or orders to cover the financial sanctions and export controls components of EU sanctions programmes.[1219] Most of the UK implementing measures contain common features, however. Although they typically adopt and cross-reference the EU sanctions, it is still important to carefully review the details of the UK implementing measures as they sometimes include language elaborating on definitional concepts, or including reporting and recordkeeping requirements, that extend beyond what is set forth in the EU sanctions regulation itself.

In addition to the EU sanctions, the UK also imposes certain unilateral, national sanctions measures. In particular, the UK imposes unilateral sanctions against certain designated parties pursuant to two principal measures: the Terrorist Asset Freezing etc. Act 2010 (the Terrorism Act)[1220] and the Counter-Terrorism Act 2008 (CTA).[1221] The Terrorism Act empowers HM Treasury to unilaterally designate parties for asset freezing measures if they are determined by the UK Government to have supported acts of terrorism.

Separately, Schedule 7 of the CTA authorizes HM Treasury to issue 'directions' to financial institutions to take certain actions deemed appropriate to facilitate anti-terrorist activities. Schedule 7 measures have been applied in sanctions contexts in the past; they are, however, typically narrow in scope and issued for limited durations. For

1219. This is reflected, for example, in the current UK sanctions relating to Iran. See: The Iran (European Union Financial Sanctions) Regulations 2012 (implementing financial sanctions elements of EC Regulation No. 267/2012); The Export Control (Iran Sanctions) Order 2012 (implementing export controls restrictions under EC Regulation No. 267/2012).
1220. The Terrorist Asset-Freezing Act 2010 replaced the Terrorism (United Nations Measures) Orders of 2001, 2006 and 2009). The 2001 and 2006 Orders have been replaced and revoked by the 2009 Order save that directions designating persons under Article 4 of the 2001 and 2006 Orders which remained in force on the date of the 2009 Order came into force continued to apply and the provisions of the 2001 and 2006 Orders continued to apply to such directions.
1221. Counter-Terrorism Act, 2008, c. 28. (U.K.).

example, in 2011/2012, the CTA was used to impose a range of restrictions against dealings with the Iranian financial sector that extended beyond those in place under EU regulations at the time.

For the consolidated list of the parties subject to UK financial sanctions, see the UK Government's financial sanctions webpage.[1222]

Finally, the UK Government can utilize the 2008 Order to impose heightened export controls against target countries as part of broader sanctions efforts. As discussed above, the UK adopted that approach in 2014 when it suspended and refused certain licences for exports to Russia and Crimea, in advance of the EU sanctions, in light of the Russia-Ukraine crisis.

Par. 2 Jurisdictional Reach of the UK Sanctions

The UK sanctions measures contain similar jurisdictional clauses. Generally speaking, all individuals and entities who are within UK territory must comply with the EU and UK sanctions, including persons who do not hold UK nationality and entities established outside of the UK. The UK also retains jurisdiction over the conduct of UK nationals or entities that occurs overseas.[1223]

Par. 3 Application of UK Financial Services Legislation to UK Sanctions

The UK Financial Conduct Authority (FCA) has jurisdiction concerning matters arising under the UK Financial Services and Markets Act 2000 (FSMA), the UK Money Laundering Regulations 2007, and several other UK financial services regulations. Those measures generally apply to firms that qualify as financial institutions or carry out certain types of financial services activities.

Although the FCA is not a sanctions regulator as such, it has the authority to issue penalties to firms operating in the financial sector who fail to implement adequate financial crime compliance procedures, including procedures relating to economic sanctions compliance, or who fail to comply with certain disclosure obligations set forth in the FSMA and associated regulations.[1224] The FCA has, as a matter of practice,

1222. https://www.gov.uk/government/publications/financial-sanctions-consolidated-list-of-targets/consolidated-list-of-targets.

1223. See Financial Sanction: Frequently Asked Questions (FAQs). HM Treasury. August 2013, at 7.3, available at https://www.gov.uk/government/uploads/system/uploads/attachment_data/file/302397/August_2013_version_-_amended.pdf.

1224. Principle 11 of the FCA *Principles for Business* include a general requirement on regulated firms to keep the FCA advised concerning matters that the FCA would normally expect notice. Although that standard has not been construed to impose a categorical obligation to report sanctions breaches to the FCA, it could warrant disclosures to the FCA in certain cases (such as egregious breaches that bring into question the adequacy of the firm's systems and controls). More broadly, many UK sanctions regulations include provisions requiring UK financial institutions to report information concerning sanctions breaches that the firms become aware of in the course of carrying on their business. See, e.g., The Iran (European Union Financial Sanctions) Regulations 2012, at Schedule 1. We stress, however, that any analysis of whether a firm should or must disclose sanctions breaches must be undertaken

been focused on sanctions compliance in recent years. The largest UK sanctions enforcement action, to date, has been issued by the FCA (against a UK bank for failing to maintain adequate sanctions systems and controls[1225]), and the FCA has issued a variety of reports and guidelines that focus on sanctions compliance in the financial services sector.[1226] However, the FCA is strictly a financial services regulator – it possesses no authority to restrict the export of goods to sanctioned countries or parties.

Par. 4 Administration and Enforcement of the UK Sanctions

As with the case of export controls, responsibilities for administering and enforcing the UK sanctions are divided among several agencies. For most sanctions programmes, restrictions focusing on financial transactions (such as, for instance, asset freezing measures) are administered by HM Treasury through its recently established[1227] Office of Financial Sanctions Implementation (the OFSI).[1228] The OFSI is responsible for administering and monitoring compliance with financial sanctions and receiving the notifications of suspected breaches or circumvention of them. It works with the relevant agencies and regulators to consider all suspected breaches reported to it.

Aspects of sanctions measures that focus on broader export controls and embargoes are typically administered by the ECO. Both HM Treasury and the ECO are responsible, within their respective areas, for issuing licences for transactions that are eligible for licensing under the relevant sanctions legislation.

The Joint Money Laundering Steering Committee (JMLSC), a group of financial services trade bodies, publishes detailed guidance on anti-money laundering guidance, which also addresses compliance with the UK financial sanctions regime. Although the JMLSC does not have any power or oversight when it comes to implementing or enforcing sanctions, the guidance may be used by other regulatory bodies when considering whether to bring a criminal prosecution against a person who has breached sanctions laws.[1229] As noted above, the FCA has also issued guidance to regulated firms concerning standards and best practices for complying with UK and EU sanctions requirements.

---

based on a careful assessment of the factual background concerning the underlying breaches, together with the aforementioned FCA and sanctions reporting standards.

1225. See FCA Press Release, *FSA fines Royal Bank of Scotland Group £5.6m for UK sanctions control failings*, FSA/PN/130/2010, 3 Aug. 2010.

1226. See, e.g., *Financial Crime: a guide for firms* (April 2015), at Chapter 7; FCA Thematic Review TR 14/16, *How small banks manage money laundering and sanctions risk* (November 2014). FCA Thematic Review TR 13/3, *Banks' control of financial crime risks in trade finance* (July 2013); *Financial services firms' approach to UK financial sanctions* (Financial Services Authority, April 2009).

1227. The announcement made by HM Treasury in relation to the formation of the OFSI was made on 31 Mar. 2016.

1228. https://www.gov.uk/government/organisations/office-of-financial-sanctions-implementation.

1229. Section 4 of Part III of the JMLSG Guidance published. Editor: David Swanney. November 2013, available at http://www.jmlsg.org.uk/industry-guidance/article/jmlsg-guidance-current.

Finally, the FCO has broad authority over the UK Government's policy concerning economic sanctions. The FCO does not have a direct role in administering or enforcing sanctions regulations, but it is frequently consulted on questions concerning the application or interpretation of sanctions measures.

Failure to comply with UK sanctions where that person does not have a valid authorization is a criminal offence.[1230] Specific penalties are set out in each UK regulation or order. Broadly speaking, a person who commits an offence under the financial sanctions is liable on conviction to imprisonment, a fine, or both. Certain UK sanctions regulations (including those implementing EU sanctions) include safeguards providing that a person or entity does not commit an offence if they did not know and had no reasonable cause to suspect that funds, economic resources or financial services were being made available, directly or indirectly, to or for the benefit of a sanctioned person.

HM Treasury and the ECO hold limited authority to take administrative enforcement measures, while HMRC has broader authority to impose fines for sanctions-related trade control breaches. As with the case of the UK's export controls regime, criminal cases may also be pursued by the CPS and, in significant matters, the SFO. As noted above, the FCA has jurisdiction to impose civil penalties against regulated firms that fail to implement adequate sanctions-related systems and controls, as does the OFSI for non-regulated firms.

Sub-Section 3 Participation of Overseas Territories

Finally, we note that the UK Government will often legislate to extend its sanctions, trade and export controls to the British Overseas territories. Those territories include: Anguilla, Bermuda, British Antarctic Territory, British Indian Ocean Territory, Cayman Islands, Falkland Islands, Montserrat, Pitcairn, St Helena, Ascension and Tristan da Cunha, South Georgia and the South Sandwich Islands, Akrotiri and Dhekelia, the Turks and Caicos Islands, and the British Virgin Islands.[1231] Equivalent sanctions are also often implemented by the governments of the Channel Islands and the Isle of Man, which constitute British Crown Dependencies. Licensing and enforcement matters under those measures are left to the cognizance of the local authorities.

1230. The announcement of the OFSI follows recent government efforts at adopting new legislation on penalties for breaches of financial sanctions. The Policing and Crime Bill 2015-16, introduced in February 2016, would introduce a range of new administrative penalties, including monetary penalties, and an increase in the maximum custodial sentence for breaching financial sanctions to seven years on conviction on indictment (or six months imprisonment on summary conviction).

1231. By way of recent example, the Ukraine (Sanctions) (Overseas Territories) Order 2014, SI 2014 No. 497, available at http://www.legislation.gov.uk/uksi/2014/497/pdfs/uksi_20140497_en .pdf extended the Order to the territories listed in Schedule 1. Notably, the overseas legislation enacted by the UK Government does not extend to Bermuda. Pursuant to powers conferred by Section 2 of the International Sanctions Act 2003, the Bermudan Minister of Legal Affairs implements the various UK overseas sanctions and trade controls legislation through the International Sanctions Regulation 2013. See International Sanctions Regulations 2013 BR14 /2013.

SECTION 7 LIST OF ACRONYMS

ACP	Arms Control & Counter-Proliferation Policy
BIS	Department for Business Innovation & Skills
CGEA	Community General Export Authorisation
CPS	Crown Prosecution Service
CTA	Counter-Terrorism Act
DfID	Department for International Development
ECO	Export Controls Organization
EU	European Union
EU GEA	European Union General Export Authorisations
FCA	UK Financial Conduct Authority
FCO	Foreign and Commonwealth Office
FOIA	UK Freedom of Information Act 2000
FSMA	UK Financial Services and Markets Act
HMRC	Her Majesty's Revenue and Customs
IAEA	International Atomic Energy Agency
JMLSC	Joint Money Laundering Steering Committee
MANPADS	Man-Portable Air Defence Systems
MoD	Ministry (or Minister) of Defence
NCA	UK National Crime Agency
NGO	Non-Governmental Organizations
OFSI	Office of Financial Sanctions Implementation
OGEL	Open General Export Licence
OGTCL	Open General Trade Control Licence
OIEL	Open Individual Export Licence
OITCL	Open Individual Trade Control Licence
OST	Outer Space Treaty
SFO	UK Serious Fraud Office
SIEL	Standard Individual Export Licence
SITCL	Standard Individual Trade Control Export Licence
SPIRE	The Export Control Organization's online export licensing system
TAU	Technical Assessment Unit
UAV	Unmanned Arial Vehicle
UK	United Kingdom
UN	United Nations
UNSCR	United Nations Security Council Resolution
WMD	Weapons of Mass Destruction

SECTION 8 REFERENCES

Sub-Section 1 Primary Documentation

Par. 1 Statutory Legislation

- CTA, 2008, Chapter 28. An Act to confer further powers to gather and share information for counter-terrorism and other purposes: http://www.legislation.gov.uk/ukpga/2008/28/introduction.
- European Communities Act 1972, Section 2. The Act enables the UK Government to issue regulations and orders implementing sanctions measures issued at the EU level.
- Export Control Act, 2002, Chapter 28. An Act to make provision enabling controls to be imposed on the exportation of goods, the transfer of technology, the provision of technical assistance overseas and activities connected with trade in controlled goods; and for connected purposes, 24 July 2002: http://www.legislation.gov.uk/ukpga/2002/28/contents.
- Outer Space Act, 1986, Chapter 38. An Act to confer licensing and other powers on the Secretary of State to secure compliance with the international obligations of the UK with respect to the launching and operation of space objects and the carrying on of other activities in outer space by persons connected with this country, 18 July 1986: https://www.gov.uk/government/uploads/system/uploads/attachment_data/file/295760/outer-space-act-1986.pdf.
- The Terrorist Asset-Freezing Act, 2010, Chapter 38. An Act to make provision for imposing financial restrictions on, and in relation to, certain persons believed or suspected to be, or to have been, involved in terrorist activities; to amend Schedule 7 to the CTA 2008; and for connected purposes: http://www.legislation.gov.uk/ukpga/2010/38/introduction.
- Anti-Terrorism, Crime and Security Act 2001: http://www.legislation.gov.uk/ukpga/2001/24/contents.

Par. 2 Regulations

Control Order 2008/3231, as amended: http://www.legislation.gov.uk/uksi/2008/3231/contents/made.

Export of Radioactive Sources (Control) Order 2006/1846, as amended: http://www.legislation.gov.uk/uksi/2006/1846/pdfs/uksi_20061846_en.pdf

(As described above, the UK has issued numerous sanctions-related regulations implementing specific measures under the UN, EU, and UK sanctions legislation. We have not specifically listed those measures here.)

Sub-Section 2 Secondary Documentation

Par. 1 Internet Sites

- http://www.bis.gov.uk (BIS)
- http://www.fco.gov.uk (FCO)
- http://www.parliament.the-stationery-office.co.uk (UK Parliament)
- http://www.the-dma.org.uk (The Defence Manufacturers Association)
- http://www.mod.uk (MoD)
- http://www.csis.org (Centre for Strategic and International Studies)
- http://www.spire.bis.gov.uk (SPIRE)
- http://www.businesslink.gov.uk (Business Link)
- http://www.opsi.gov.uk (The Office of Public Sector Information)
- http://www.fca.org.uk (The FCA)
- http://www.gov.uk/government/organisations/hm-revenue-customs (HM Revenue and Customs)
- http://www.gov.uk/guidance/sanctions-embargoes-and-restrictions (HM Treasury Financial Sanctions Unit)
- https://www.gov.uk/government/organisations/office-of-financial-sanctions-implementation
- https://www.gov.uk/government/publications/financial-sanctions-faqs
- https://www.gov.uk/government/uploads/system/uploads/attachment_data/file/488993/controllist0151225.pdf
- https://www.gov.uk/government/collections/open-general-export-licences-ogels
- https://www.gov.uk/government/uploads/system/uploads/attachment_data/file/515119/16-152-ogel-pcb-dual-use.pdf
- http://blogs.bis.gov.uk/exportcontrol/uncategorized/notice-to-exporters-201525-23-open-licences-updated-and-1-revoked/
- https://www.gov.uk/government/uploads/system/uploads/attachment_data/file/515105/16-153-ogel-pcb-military.pdf
- http://blogs.bis.gov.uk/exportcontrol/uncategorized/notice-to-exporters-201532-changes-to-mod-form-680-effective-13-jan-2016/
- http://blogs.bis.gov.uk/exportcontrol/uncategorized/eco-issues-guidance-on-intrusion-software-controls/
- https://www.gov.uk/government/news/new-body-to-support-financial-sanctions-implementation-launched

Par. 2 Paper Publications

Foreign & Commonwealth Office et al. *United Kingdom Strategic Export Controls Annual Report 2012 (HC 561)*. London: TSO, 2014.

The Committees on Arms Export Controls. *Second Joint Report of Session 2014-2015 (HC 608)*. London: HMSO, 2015.
Scott, R. *Report of the Inquiry into the Export of Defence Equipment and Dual Use Goods to Iraq and Related Prosecutions*. London: HMSO, 1996.

Par. 3 Annexes – Copies of Documents of Practical Use to the Importer/Exporter

The following documents are available on a dedicated DropBox folder which can be accessed by following the link: www.kluwerlawonline.com/eclrh-annexes:

- Annex I Compliance and enforcement of export controls. Department for Business, Innovation & Skills. September 2012.
- Annex II Financial Sanctions: Frequently Asked Questions (FAQs). HM Treasury. August 2013.
- Annex III Disclosure of suspected breach of financial sanctions in contravention of EU regulations. HM Treasury.
- Annex IV Trade controls (trafficking and brokering). Department for Business, Innovation & Skills. August 2012.
- Annex V Brokering (trade) of dual-use items. Department for Business, Innovation & Skills. September 2012.
- Annex VI Export of technology. Department for Business, Innovation & Skills. August 2012.

SECTION 9 USEFUL INFORMATION

Sub-Section 1 Enforcement Authorities Contact Details

Main point of contact for all export control matters including SPIRE

Name of Organization	*Export Control Organization*
Postal Address	3rd Floor, 1 Victoria Street, London SW1H 0ET
Telephone	020 7215 4594
Fax	020 7215 2635
Email	eco.help@bis.gsi.gov.uk

Contact Details for Licence Applications and Rating Enquiries
Details of licensing officers are provided below (June 2015)

Name	*Telephone Number*	*Email*
Control List	ECO Helpline	Eco.help@bis.gsi.gov.uk
Classification Enquiries	020 7215 4594	
Charles (Adetunji) Alabi	020 7215 8560	Charles.alabi@bis.gsi.gov.uk
Keith Bernard	020 7215 8012	Keith.Bernard@bis.gsi.gov.uk
Simon Copeland	020 7215 8400	Simon.Copeland@bis.gsi.gov.uk
Margaret Duncan	020 7215 0127	Margaret.Duncan@bis.gsi.gov.uk
Joyce Easmon-Nyamador	020 7215 8280	Joyce.Easmon-Nyamador@bis.gsi.gov.uk
Pam Elliott	020 7215 8401	Pam.Elliott@bis.gsi.gov.uk
Mimi Johnson	020 7215 8177	Mimi.Johnson@bis.gsi.gov.uk
Ann Marshall	020 7215 8388	Ann.Marshall@bis.gsi.gov.uk
Graham Miller	020 7215 8304	Graham.Miller@bis.gsi.gov.uk
Anthony Okine	020 7215 8301	Anthony.Okine@bis.gsi.gov.uk
Roli Omomedia	020 7215 5344	Roli.Omomedia@bis.gsi.gov.uk
Vikura Parmar	020 7215 0568	Vikura.Parmar@bis.gsi.gov.uk
Gillian Purkis	020 7215 8341	Gillian.Purkis@bis.gsi.gov.uk
Mervyn Salole	020 7215 5293	Mervyn.Salole@bis.gsi.gov.uk
Janet Springer	020 7215 4458	Janet.Springer@bis.gsi.gov.uk
Michelle Sullivan	020 7215 3502	Michelle.Sullivan@bis.gsi.gov.uk
Colin Wray	020 7215 5059	Colin.Wray@bis.gsi.gov.uk

Name of Organization	*HM Treasury*
Postal Address	Financial Sanctions HM Treasury 1 Horse Guards Road London SW1A 2HQ
Telephone	+44 (0) 20 7270 5454
Email	financialsanctions@hmtreasury.gsi.gov.uk

Name of Organization	*Office of Financial Sanctions Implementation HM Treasury*
Postal Address	Financial Sanctions HM Treasury 1 Horse Guards Road London SW1A 2HQ
Email	ofsi@hmtreasury.gsi.gov.uk

Name of Organization	*HM Revenue & Customs Local Compliance S0000*
Postal Address	Newcastle NE98 1ZZ
Telephone	+44 (0) 300 200 3700

Sub-Section 2 Other

Code for Crown Prosecutors: www.cps.gov.uk/publications/docs/code2004english.pdf

Home Office: www.homeoffice.gov.uk/security/terrorism-and-the-law

European Commission: http://ec.europa.eu/external_relations/cfsp/sanctions/list/consol-list.htm.

CHAPTER 17
United States

Corinne Kaplan, Candace Goforth & Julia Mason

SECTION 1 TABLE OF CONTENTS

SECTION 2 EXECUTIVE SUMMARY

The United States of America (U.S.) controls the export and import of goods (hardware, software, technology and services) as a means to protect national security interests and promote foreign policy objectives.

Under the Constitution of the U.S.,[1232] the power to regulate commerce lays with the U.S. Congress who has enacted a broad set of laws to regulate international commerce. The responsibilities for execution of those laws and the promulgation of implementing regulations are distributed between seven primary executive branch departments: Departments of Commerce, State and Justice, Treasury, Defense, Energy, and Homeland Security. The first three having authority to issue export/import authorizations and Treasury having authority over financial transactions and sanctions.

As a result, the U.S. export control system was overly complicated, contained too many redundancies, and tried to protect too much. This made it hard to administer and enforce the controls, and harder for exporters and re-exporters to comply. After forty years of incremental changes and several unfruitful attempts to engage into more fundamental reform, the U.S. Government has engaged in 2011 into an effective several phase comprehensive Export Control Reform (ECR)[1233] effort.

The goal of ECR is not to deregulate, but to implement a more effective export control system, advancing U.S. National Security by imposing more effective controls on the most sensitive items, while enabling U.S. industry to be competitive in the worldwide market place.

The first two phases of this reform, while maintaining the interagency (and multi-agency) structure, create consistent and coherent controlled good lists, supported by a more unified interagency Information Technology (IT) system and centralized enforcement apparatus. As of December 2015, these first two phases are well under way and implemented across the agencies, with fifteen out of twenty-one Munitions List categories revised and in effect with the less sensitive Space and Military goods transferred from the controls of the International Traffic in Arms Regulations (ITAR) administered by the Department of State (DoS) to the more flexible controls of the Export Administration Regulation (EAR) administered by Department of Commerce (DoC).

The third phase of this reform, which is still to be initiated, would establish a single export control agency bringing together all export control functions under one agency.

1232. US Constitution Section 8 Article 1 'The Congress shall have Power "To regulate Commerce with foreign Nations, and among the several States, and with the Indian Tribes"'.

1233. See 27 Nov. 2013 ECR fact sheet and other ECR documentation at http://export.gov/%5C/ecr/index.asp.

The ITAR[1234] controls the export and temporary import of tangible and intangible defence items as identified on the US Munitions List (USML). The DoS, Directorate of Defense Trade Controls (DDTC), administers these controls. No transactions related to items controlled under the ITAR, including brokering activities, may be conducted without an ITAR authorization or claiming an exemption from the licensing requirements of the ITAR. These controls extend to US-origin equipment and technology wherever located.

The EAR,[1235] administered by the DoC, Bureau of Industry Security (BIS), controls military and dual-use goods which are not subject to the exclusive jurisdiction of other agencies. Like the ITAR, these controls extend to US-origin equipment and technology wherever located. The controls are Classification based, End-Use based, End-User based and Country based. Many exports may be carried out as 'No License Required (NLR)' or if a licence is required, may benefit from an exception. In contrast with the ITAR, the EAR does not control transaction of foreign-manufactured product when the U.S.-content is below a given threshold (*De Minimis* rule).

The numerous situations where a BIS licence is not required, or if required, an exception is available, renders this regulation complex and puts more responsibility on the exporter/re-exporter who must make and take responsibility for their determination.

The other Jurisdictions that must be considered are:

- Department of Treasury, Office of Foreign Assets Control (OFAC), which regulates economic sanctions, whether these sanctions are imposed by the US unilaterally or international regimes including the United Nations (UN).
- Department of Justice (DoJ), Bureau of Alcohol, Tobacco, Firearms and Explosives (ATF), which regulates the permanent import into the US of Defense Articles listed in the US Munitions Import List (USMIL).
- Department of Energy (DoE) and the Nuclear Regulatory Commission (NRC), which regulate the export and import of nuclear material and nuclear technology. The DoE has the responsibility of licensing the export of nuclear technology, but some nuclear weapon related articles are under the responsibility of DoS.

While export/re-export under the ITAR is largely administered through positive U.S. Government authorizations with very few exemptions, the EAR is a complex system, under which the controls and thus the determination of the licence requirement is based on the classification, the country of destination and the end-use and end-user for each transaction. The large majority of the exports/re-exports will be either 'NLR' or, if requiring a licence, may benefit from an exception. Positive licences

1234. The ITAR implements the Arms Export Control Act (AECA). The complete text of the ITAR can be found at 22 CFR 120-130 http://pmddtc.state.gov.
1235. The EAR implements the Export Administration Act (EAA). The complete text of the EAR can be found at www.bis.doc.gov/index.php/regulations/export-administration-regulations-ear.

issued by the U.S. Government will not be systematic, giving the exporter/re-exporter more responsibility to make and document licensing determination, with more room for errors.

U.S. export/import laws and regulations apply to U.S. persons and to U.S. goods (U.S.-origin or derived from U.S.-origin) wherever located (extraterritoriality), i.e., the controls extend for the life of the product, material or technology, wherever located and may apply to non-U.S. persons if they handle, control or are in the possession of U.S.-controlled product or information.

Taking into account that, as the result of ECR, U.S.-origin military goods are either classified as Defense Articles under the USML or are controlled under the Commerce Control List (CCL), or may be under another jurisdiction, depending on their characteristics and end-use, it is fundamental to understand how to determine the proper Jurisdiction and Classification in order to identify correctly which regulation applies and how it applies.

The Jurisdiction and Classification are determined by following an 'order of review' including a 'specially designed' analysis, first under the ITAR, then under the EAR:

- An end-item, system, or part or component is considered a Defense Article (i.e., ITAR) if it is positively listed/enumerated in a USML category sub-paragraph, or if it is captured by a USML category / sub-paragraph 'catch-all' or 'specially designed' control.
- Conversely, if a part or component is not positively listed in the USML and is not captured by a "catch-all" or 'specially designed' entry on the USML, then it is not a Defense Article, and unless it is controlled under another jurisdiction (such as DoE or NRC), this item will be controlled under the EAR.
- Under the EAR, the item is subject to one of the foreign policy / military Export Control Classification Number (ECCN) 500 or 600 series if it is positively listed under these ECCNs or captured by a 'specially designed' entry of the EAR.
- Conversely, if it is not positively listed in 500 or 600 series or captured by a 'specially designed' clause, it will fall into another ECCN or under EAR99.

In order to implement the proper controls for these Space and Military goods transferred from the ITAR, DoC has created new ECCN series (500 series, 600 series) and new sub-categories in existing ECCNs. While the EAR offers more flexibility, in particular as it relates to the export to US allied countries, in order to satisfy the National Security and Foreign Policy requirements, DoC has also implemented new controls which results in limitations similar to the ITAR and in particular has limited the use of *De Minimis* and of some of the EAR exceptions, such as Strategic Trade Authorization (STA), for these new categories.

DoS and DoC have made remarkable efforts to coordinate and to define and implement a three-year transition period to smooth out the transition. The agencies have synchronized content, publication and effective implementation of the new lists and controls, harmonizing their approach and reaching out to non-U.S. Governments and to U.S. and non-U.S. industry.

Despite these efforts:

- The ECR presents a steep learning curve for the US and non-US Space and defence industry, which may not have been familiar with the complex and effort-intense usage of the EAR.
- The six-month period between the publication of each of the new rules and their effective implementation has not been sufficient for US industry to determine the proper reclassification of their goods, and most are 'behind the curve', generating either stop work situations or driving non-US industry to reclassify by themselves.
- While ECR facilitates the export of less sensitive Space and military goods to allies, it has also shifted a large part of the liability and of the record keeping requirements beyond the borders of the US to those allies.

Overall, and despite considerable efforts for simplification, the US export control laws and regulations remain a complex system, based on multiple rules and regulations, implementing evolving and nuanced national security and foreign policies, and controlling U.S.-origin technologies from cradle to grave. This system can be daunting to navigate. Help from U.S. export control professionals should be sought to address compliance issues, obtain U.S. Government authorizations or to determine whether an exemption or exception can be used.

SECTION 3 INTRODUCTION – ELEMENTS OF CONTEXT

This section describes the philosophy and the legal foundations of the US export control laws and regulations.

Sub-Section 1 Regime Overall Philosophy

Participation by U.S. persons in international commerce is not a right, but a privilege. Article I, Section 8 of the Constitution provides for the U.S. Congress to 'regulate commerce with foreign nations' through laws.[1236]

The responsibilities for execution of those laws and the promulgation of implementing regulations are distributed among seven primary executive branch departments: Departments of Commerce, Defense, Energy, Homeland Security, Justice, State, and Treasury, with three Departments having authority to issue authorizations (Commerce, State and Justice) and Treasury having authority over financial transactions.

The purpose of the US export control laws and regulations governing international commerce is to:[1237]

1236. US Constitution Section 8 Article 1 'The Congress shall have Power to regulate Commerce with foreign Nations, and among the several States, and with the Indian Tribes'.
1237. See for more details http://www.state.gov/strategictrade/overview/

- Provide for US and allies national security by limiting access to the most sensitive US technology and weapons.
- Enhance regional stability.
- Take into account hûman rights considerations.
- Prevent proliferation of weapons and technologies, including weapons of mass destruction (WMD), to problem end-users and supporters of international terrorism.
- Comply with international commitments, i.e., international non-proliferation regimes and the UN Security Council sanctions and resolutions.

The pursuit of these goals through the definition and implementation of export control laws and regulations has historically been an exercise in finding the correct balance between national security and foreign policy interests versus commercial and industrial interests.

Since the end of the Cold War and particularly since the 2001 attacks on the World Trade Center and on the Pentagon, and more recently since the renewed tension with Russia, finding the right balance has required complex analysis and implementation with built-in flexibility.

The underlying policy goals are to establish and maintain war-fighter superiority (including information superiority) while achieving interoperability with allies. At the same time that it protects the superiority of the US, the policy also needs to support the manufacturing and exporting industries so that they can benefit from outsourcing and globalization of supply chains, which in turn strengthens the national defence industrial base.[1238]

Therefore, a balance is sought between:

- The interests of the manufacturing and exporting industries who desire an orderly administrative process, certainty and predictability in the application of export controls.
- The interests of the US government agencies responsible for national security and foreign policy, who desire flexibility and ability to evaluate situations case-by-case without being bound by requirement to change the laws and regulations or by precedents.

1238. Numerous studies and publications have preceded and accompanied the US Export Control Reform effort, see for instance:

- 'Export Controls and the U.S. Defense Industrial Base' – Institute for Defense Analysis, January 2007 www.dtic.mil/cgi-bin/GetTRDoc?AD=ADA465592.
- 'Impact of U.S. Export Control on the Space Industrial Base', BIS February 2014 http://www.bis.doc.gov/index.php/forms-documents/doc_view/898-space-export-control-report.
- 'Impact of Export Controls on the Domestic Aerospace Industry' AIAA https://www.aiaa.org/.
- Center for Strategic International Studies, 'U.S. Defense Export Control Regulations' multiple papers available at http://csis.org/program/us-defense-export-control-regulations.

Thus, there is a trade-off between the degree of precision of language in the regulations and the flexibility that needs to be provided to the U.S. Government in using export control as a tool of national security and foreign policy. For this purpose, in addition to the export laws enacted by Congress, each implementing agency can edict changes to the implementation regulations which do not require approval from Congress. These changes are made through publication in the *Federal Register* or by setting published or unpublished rules and guidance.[1239]

In all circumstances, knowing the law and regulations is necessary but may not be sufficient. The regulations are only a road map, translated into processes, rules and case-by-case reviews by the agencies. The policies behind those rules and processes necessary to obtain export approval are not always expressed explicitly and continuously evolve as the political, economic and technological environments changes.

The Arms Export Control Act (AECA) is the cornerstone of US munitions export control law. The DoS implements this statute through the ITAR. All persons or entities that engage in the manufacture, export, or brokering of Defense Articles and Defense Services must be registered with the US government. The ITAR sets out the requirements for licences or other authorizations for specific exports of Defense Articles and Defense Services. The AECA requires DoS to provide an annual and quarterly report of export authorizations to Congress. Some proposed export approvals and 'substantial violations' also require congressional notification.[1240]

The Export Administration Act of 1979 (EAA), as amended, authorizes the DoC, in consultation with other appropriate agencies, to regulate the export or re-export of US-origin dual-use goods, software, and technology. Even before ECR, less sensitive Military goods have been regulated by the DoC.

The DoC implements this authority through the EAR. In addition to export controls agreed in multilateral regimes, the DoC also imposes certain unilateral export and re-export controls for foreign policy reasons, most notably against countries designated by the US Secretary of State as state sponsors of international terrorism, as well as countries, entities and individuals subject to U.S. unilateral or UN sanctions.

Additionally, the DoC administers and enforces regulations that prohibit certain trade and transactions with certain countries, entities, and individuals by US persons or from the US under the Trading with the Enemy Act (TWEA) and the International Emergency Economic Powers Act (IEEPA).

Sub-Section 2 Historical Overview

The scope of U.S. export controls and the structure for the implementation of such controls have evolved over time to meet the challenges of ever-changing national security and foreign policy requirements.

1239. For example, in April 2015, DDTC and BIS published expansion of export restriction on Russia as a result of the Crimea crisis http://www.state.gov/r/pa/prs/ps/2014/04/225241.htm
1240. For examples of such situation, see Congressional Research Services, Arms Sales: Congressional Review Process at https://www.fas.org/sgp/crs/weapons/RL31675.pdf.

Early U.S. policy, through various neutrality measures, initially attempted to avoid being drawn into disputes between other countries and advantaging one country over another by trade. The first U.S. measure enacted to control U.S. participation in foreign commerce for reasons of national security was the boycott of trade with Great Britain enacted during the Revolutionary War by the First Continental Congress in 1775.[1241]

The U.S. export control regime started to develop between the early days of World War I and the close of World War II: (1) economic sanctions; (2) controls on the import of munitions; and (3) munitions control (including regulations of munitions manufacturers).

After World War II, controls were added for dual-use materials and equipment. Multilateral controls were also adopted, first during the Cold War and then later, for specific threats.

The legislative foundation of the current U.S. Export Control laws can be traced back to legislative actions taken during the cold war years:

- 1954 Mutual Security Act sought to regulate U.S. military assistance, promoting national security interests, preventing WMD proliferation and reducing conventional arms sales, which later morphed in 1961 into separating Military Assistance from Non-Military assistance with the creation of the US Agency for International Development (USAID).
- 1961 Foreign Assistance Act initiated the Cuban Trade Embargo (which is in the process of being revised as part of the 2015 efforts to evolve the US-Cuba relationship and lift the corresponding sanctions).
- 1976 AECA, which regulated arms sales and increase US leverage over weapon recipients and which is still today the foundation of the ITAR.
- 1977 International Emergency Economics Powers Act (IEEPA), which granted presidential authority to regulate commerce after declaring a national emergency in response to any unusual and extraordinary threat to the U.S. which has a foreign source. The IEEPA is still today the foundation for US economic sanctions (and case-by-case policies).
- 1979 EAA, which granted presidential authority to control exports for reasons of national security, foreign policy or short supply. The EAA is the foundation of the EAR. The EAA expired in 1994, and was reauthorized in 2000, and lapsed again in 2001, but was maintained in effect through executive order under the IEEPA.
- 1977 Foreign Corrupt Practice Act (FCPA), which prohibits U.S. companies from accepting bribes or other corrupt compensation in soliciting business with foreign countries.

1241. For more information, see US Department of State, Office of the Historian at https://history.state.gov/milestones/1750-1775/parliamentary-taxation.

In 1990, President George H.W. Bush ordered the removal of certain items, including commercial communications satellites, from the USML and transferred those items to the CCL. This decision was not implemented until 1996.

In the late 1990s, following a series of launch failures involving U.S. satellites that were being launched by Chinese launch vehicles, an investigation and subsequent report ('Cox Report') by a Select Committee of the House of Representatives highlighted national security concerns about the licensing of satellite exports.

As a result of the Cox Report, Congress passed *The Fiscal Year 1999 National Defence Authorization Act* (Strom Thurmond Act)[1242] that transferred satellites licensing jurisdiction back to the DoS. This transfer of satellites back to the DoS is one example of the ITAR controlling items that did not meet the definition of a Defense Article.

Various aspects of the U.S. export control system have long been criticized by exporters, non-proliferation advocates, allies, and other stakeholders as being too rigorous, insufficiently rigorous, cumbersome, obsolete, inefficient, or any combination of these descriptions. Some contend that U.S. export controls overly restrict U.S. exports and make firms less competitive. Others argue that U.S. defence and foreign policy considerations should trump commercial concerns.

In January 2007, the Government Accountability Office (GAO) designated government programmes designed to protect critical technologies, including the U.S. export control system, as a 'high-risk' area 'that warrants a strategic re-examination of existing programs to identify needed changes. The GAO report cited poor coordination among export control agencies, disagreements over commodity jurisdiction (CJ) between DoS and DoC, unnecessary delays and inefficiencies in the licence application process, and a lack of systematic evaluation mechanisms to determine the effectiveness of export controls.[1243]

In 2009, the White House ordered a wide review of the Export Control Regulations (the ECR initiative) to overhaul the U.S. export control system.

After forty years of incremental changes and several unfruitful attempts to engage into more fundamental reform, the U.S. Government has engaged in 2011 into an effective several phase comprehensive reform effort.[1244]

As a result of the Strom Thurmond Act, USML Category XV (Satellites) was the only category of the USML that had to be changed by an act of law voted by the US Congress. Under Section 38(f) of the AECA (P.L. 90-629),[1245] the other USML categories

1242. *FY 1999 National Defense Authorization Act*, P.L. 105-261, 112 Stat 2174 (1999).

1243. Congressional Research Service The US Export Control System and the President's Reform Initiative https://www.fas.org/sgp/crs/natsec/R41916.pdf.

1244. See 27 Nov. 2013 ECR fact sheet and other ECR documentation at http://export.gov/%5C/ecr/index.asp.

1245. See http://fas.org/asmp/resources/govern/aeca00.pdf:

> The President shall periodically review the items on the United States Munitions List to determine what items, if any, no longer warrant export controls under this section. The results of such reviews shall be reported to the Speaker of the House of Representatives and to the Committee on Foreign Relations and the Committee on Banking, Housing, and Urban Affairs of the Senate. Such a report shall be submitted at least 30 days before any item is removed from the Munitions List and shall describe the nature of any controls to be imposed on that item under the Export Administration Act of 1979.

could be revised, thereby moving articles from the USML to the CCL, only after providing a prior thirty-day notice to the U.S. Congress including a description of the nature of any subsequent controls on the item.

The ECR effort came at a time of increased pressure due to the dynamics of fast evolving technology and globalization of the Space and Defence markets. Success was due to a combination of strong presidential backing, multiple cabinet-level endorsements (Departments of State, Defense and Commerce) and a deliberate effort to ensure concurrence of the U.S. Congress by addressing meticulously political concerns, in particular those related to Space Technologies.[1246]

Sub-Section 3 The US Export Control Reform

On 13 August 2009, President Obama announced the launch of a comprehensive review of the US export control system, and this was followed in April 2010 with a speech by Secretary of Defense Robert M. Gates announcing key elements of the Administration's agenda for reform, with further elaboration in subsequent months. The proposed four-pronged approach intended to establish:

- a single export control licensing agency for both dual-use, munitions and exports licensed to embargoed destinations;
- a unified control list;
- a single enforcement coordination agency; and
- a single integrated U.S. Government IT system, which would include a single database of sanctioned and denied parties.

The Administration's blueprint envisioned that these changes would be implemented in three phases, with the final phase – a single export control licensing agency – requiring legislative action.

In Phase I, starting mid-2010, preparatory work was undertaken to harmonize the CCL with the USML as well as the philosophy and key concepts of the ITAR and EAR. Standardized licensing processes among the control agencies would be developed, and an 'Enforcement Fusion Center' to synchronize enforcement would be created along with a single US government IT system to allow all agencies to be on the same page.

Phase II, starting mid-2012, began the implementation of a harmonized licensing system with two similarly structured control lists, potentially allowing for a reduction in the amount of licences required by the system. Many items were moved from the USML to the CCL, for which congressional notification was required; unilateral controls on certain items have been examined; and consultations took place with multilateral control regime partners to add or remove multilateral controls on certain items. A single IT system for licensing and enforcement also became operational, with the majority of the interagency on-board.

1246. See Center for Strategic and International Studies (CSIS) 'the Time is Right for Export Control Reform' (May 2010) http://csis.org/files/publication/100517_DIIG_Current_Issues_n21.pdf.

In Phase III, a single licensing agency would be established; the two harmonized, control lists would be merged with mechanisms for review and updating; the two primary export control enforcement agencies, the DoC's Office of Export Enforcement (OEE) and the Department of Homeland Security's (DHS's) Homeland Security Investigations (HSI) would be merged.

As of December 2015, the U.S. administration has successfully completed to a great extent the first two phases. It is unknown whether and how Phase III will be implemented.

The Export Enforcement Coordination Center (EECC), also known as the 'fusion center,' was created by Executive Order on 9 November 2010, and is being housed and funded by the DHS. The EECC was formally stood up in March 2013 and has successfully de-conflicted hundreds of U.S. Government investigations.

The Administration made its first Section 38(f) notifications to Congress for Category VIII (Aircraft and Related Articles) and Category XIX (Gas Turbine Engines) on 8 March 2013, and other notifications subsequently have been made prior to the rulemaking process.

The road to this point was quite gruelling and was new ground for most everyone involved. There were weekly interagency briefings to the effected U.S. Congressional committees and daily interaction within the interagency to make these briefings a success. The U.S. Congressional committees were kept abreast of all proposed changes and many of their comments and concerns have been integrated into the final ECR framework. One such concern was that the ECR effort only effect Direct Commercial Sales (DCS) and not the Foreign Military Sales (FMS) programme. This has caused a lot of issues for recipients of FMS-procured articles as it greys the line of services and spares as they remain subject to the ITAR.

Each category of the USML and of the CCL has been screened by an interagency team led by the Department of Defense (DoD), in order to ensure that the USML contains 'only those items that provide at least significant military and intelligence applicability that warrant the controls of the AECA', while moving the other items to the CCL. As of December 2015, rewrites to eighteen of the twenty-one USML and corresponding EAR categories, have being published as proposed and effective rulemakings or have been published for public comments (see Table 17.1).

Table 17.1 ECR Implementation Status

USML Category		*Key Milestones*		*ITAR Federal Register Notice(s)*		*EAR Federal Register Notice(s)*	
No.	Description	Effective Date	Transition End Date[1247]	Final Rule	Correction Rule	Final Rule	Correction Rule
I	Firearms	TBD	TBD	TBD	TBD	TBD	TBD

1247. The transition period, initially of two years for all categories, was extended to three years in October 2015, amid unpreparedness of industry to manage the end of the two-year transition period for Cat VIII and XIX.

USML Category		*Key Milestones*		*ITAR Federal Register Notice(s)*		*EAR Federal Register Notice(s)*	
No.	Description	Effective Date	Transition End Date[1247]	Final Rule	Correction Rule	Final Rule	Correction Rule
II	Artillery	TBD	TBD	TBD	TBD	TBD	TBD
III	Ammunition	TBD	TBD	TBD	TBD	TBD	TBD
IV	Launch Vehicles, Guided Missiles, Ballistic Missiles, Rockets, Torpedoes, Bombs, and Mines	1 July 2014	30 June 2017	*79 FR 34*	*79 FR 36393*	79 FR 264	79 FR 32611
V	Explosives and Energetic Materials, Propellants, Incendiary Agents, and Their Constituents	1 July 2014	30 June 2017	*79 FR 34*	*79 FR 36393*	79 FR 264	79 FR 32611
VI	Surface Vessels of War and Special Naval Equipment	6 January 2014	5 January 2017	*78 FR 40922*	*79 FR 26*	78 FR 40892	79 FR 22
VII	Ground Vehicles	6 January 2015	5 May 2018	*78 FR 40922*	*79 FR 26*	78 FR 40892	79 FR 22
VIII	Aircraft and Related Articles	15 October 2013	14 October 2016	*78 FR 22740*	*78 FR 61750*	78 FR 22660	79 FR 61874
IX	Military Training Equipment	1 July 2014	30 June 2017	*79 FR 34*	*79 FR 36393*	79 FR 264	79 FR 32611
X	Personal Protective Equipment	1 July 2014	30 June 2017	*79 FR 34*	*79 FR 36393*	79 FR 264	79 FR 32611
XI	Military Electronics	30 December 2014	29 December 2017	*79 FR 37536*	*79 FR 77884*	79 FR 37551	79 FR 126
XII	Fire Control/Sensors/ Night Vision (Proposed rule 5/6/2015 & 2/19/2016))	TBD	TBD	TBD	TBD	TBD	TBD

USML Category		*Key Milestones*		*ITAR Federal Register Notice(s)*		*EAR Federal Register Notice(s)*	
No.	Description	Effective Date	Transition End Date[1247]	Final Rule	Correction Rule	Final Rule	Correction Rule
XIII	Materials and Miscellaneous Articles	6 January 2014	5 January 2017	*78 FR 40922*	*79 FR 26*	78 FR 40892	79 FR 22
XIV	Toxicological Agents (Proposed rule 6/17/2015)	TBD	TBD	TBD	TBD	TBD	TBD
XV	Spacecraft and Related Articles	27 June 2014 and 10 November 2014	26 June 2017 and 9 November 2017	*79 FR 27180*	*79 FR 66608*	79 FR 27417	79 FR 67055
XVI	Nuclear Weapons Related Articles	1 July 2014	30 June 2017	*79 FR 34*	*79 FR 36393*		
XVII	Classified Articles, Technical Data, and Defense Services	15 October 2013	14 October 2016	*78 FR 22740*	*78 FR 61750*		78 FR 61744
XVIII	Directed Energy Weapons (Proposed rule 6/17/2015)	TBD	TBD	TBD	TBD	TBD	TBD
XIX	Gas Turbine Engines and Associated Equipment	15 October 2013	14 October 2017	*78 FR 22740*	*78 FR 61750*	78 FR 22660	79 FR 61874
XX	Submersible Vessels and Related Articles	6 January 2014	2 January 2017	*78 FR 40922*	*79 FR 26*	78 FR 40892	79 FR 22
XXI	Articles, Technical Data, and Defense Services Otherwise Not Enumerated	15 October 2013	14 October 2016	*78 FR 22740*	*78 FR 61750*		78 FR 61744

Some of the most controversial elements (such as the definition of Defense Services) are still open, for which work is ongoing, with an expected completion of end of 2016.

The manner in which USML items transferred to the CCL involves the creation of 600 Series and 500 Series. These new series are populated by items that are judged to not require the stricter controls mandated under the ITAR.

Items moved to the CCL in this manner require a licence to all destinations except Canada.[1248] All items controlled pursuant to multilateral control regimes retain their existing controls. In addition, 600 Series and 500 Series items are subject to a general policy of denial to countries subject to a U.S. or UN arms embargo.

With the addition of the 600 and 500 series, it was necessary to add, within each USML category of the ITAR, a paragraph (x), to cover the EAR items which are used in and within a Defense Article. This addition of USML paragraph (x) avoids double ITAR and EAR licensing for the same transaction.

The transfer of the less sensitive Space goods from the ITAR to the EAR was of specific concern to Congress, who mandated additional assurances as follows:[1249]

- The National Defense Authorization Act (NDAA) for Fiscal Year 2010 mandated that DoS and DoD present a report to Congress to document that the transfer of Commercial Telecommunications satellites would not represent a risk to US national security (1248 report).
- The NDAA for Fiscal Year 2011 mandated that DoD present a report to Congress to document the impact of the reform on the protection and monitoring of militarily critical technologies (1237 report).
- The NDAA for Fiscal year 2013 further mandated that DoC to present a report to Congress demonstrating the implementation of the compliance and enforcement measures related to satellite technologies. (1263 report).

The interagency provided these assurances and the transfer of less sensitive Space goods to the EAR became effective on 10 November 2014.

Sub-Section 4 Participation in International Regimes

The U.S. participates in multilateral controls and cooperation with allied nations.[1250]

1248. Licence Exception STA (Strategic Trade Authorization), initially established in 2011 for a group of thirty-six countries made of NATO partners and members of the four multilateral control regimes is available for most transfer of items subject to licensing requirements under 600 and 500 series. Dual-use items controlled for missile technology (MT), chemical weapons (CW), short supply (SS), or surreptitiously listening (SL) are not be eligible for export under STA. Certain implements of execution and torture, pathogens and toxins, software and technology for 'hot sections' of aero gas turbine engines, and encryption have also been excluded from the STA.

1249. These reports can be found at http://www.export.gov/ecr/eg_main_023180.asp.
The 1248 report in particular contains an expansive analysis on China Space-related goals, capabilities and methods for acquiring Space technologies.

1250. The Export Administration Act of 1979 carries the following provision:

> It is the policy of the United States (A) to apply any necessary controls to the maximum extent possible in cooperation with all nations, and (B) to encourage observance of a uniform export control policy by all nations with which the United States has defence treaty commitments or common strategic objectives.

Currently the US is a member of several multilateral non-proliferation regimes, including:

- Nuclear Suppliers Group (NSG) - With thirty-nine Member States, the NSG is a widely accepted, mature and effective export control arrangement which contributes to the non-proliferation of nuclear weapons through implementation of guidelines for control of nuclear and nuclear-related exports.
- Zangger Committee - The purpose of the thirty-five-nation Nuclear Non-proliferation Treaty (NPT) Exporters (Zangger) Committee is to harmonize implementation of the NPT requirements to apply International Atomic Energy Agency (IAEA) safeguards to nuclear exports. The Committee maintains and updates a list of equipment and materials that may only be exported if safeguards are applied to the recipient facility (called the 'Trigger List' because such exports trigger the requirement for safeguards).
- Missile Technology Control Regime (MTCR) - The thirty-four MTCR partners have committed to apply a common export policy (MTCR Guidelines) to a common list of controlled items, including all key equipment and technology needed for missile development, production, and operation. MTCR guidelines restrict transfers of missiles - and technology related to missiles - for the delivery of WMD. The regime places particular focus on missiles capable of delivering a payload of at least 500 kg with a range of at least 300 km - so-called Category I or MTCR-class missiles. The MTCR also covers other platforms such as rockets, Unmanned Aerial Systems (UASs), space launch vehicles, and drones with the same capability for delivering WMD.
- Australia Group (AG) - Objective is to ensure that the industries of the thirty-eight participating countries do not assist, either purposefully or inadvertently, states or terrorists seeking to acquire a chemical and/or biological weapons (CBW) capability.
- Wassenaar Arrangement (WA) - The regime with the most extensive set of control lists; it seeks to prevent destabilizing accumulations of arms and dual-use equipment and technologies that may contribute to the development or enhancement of military capabilities that would undermine regional security and stability, and to develop mechanisms for information sharing among the thirty-four partners as a way to harmonize export control practices and policies.

In addition to International Treaties, it is the policy of the US to enter into specific bilateral and multilateral Agreements or Treaties as required by its national security and foreign policies.

Par. 1 Treaties and Regimes Dealing with Specific Items and Technologies

The following tables display the U.S.' participation status in export control related international treaties and programmes. It is also stated, when relevant, whether the U.S. is party to a treaty by signature and ratification or by accession.

Table 17.2 Nuclear Weapons Treaties

Treaty Name	*Overall Status*	*Specific Status*	*Enforceable in the U.S.*
Limited Test Ban Treaty[1251]	OS: 5 August 1963 EF: 10 October 1963	S/R: 5 August 1963 A: 10 October 1963	Yes
Nuclear Non-Proliferation Treaty[1252]	OS: 1 July 1968 EF: 5 March 1970	S: 1 July 1968 R: 5 March 1970 A: 5 March 1970	Yes
Comprehensive Nuclear Test Ban Treaty[1253]	OS: 24 September 1996 EF: not in force		No

OS: Opened for signature; EF: Entry into force; S/R: Signature/Ratification; A: Accession

Table 17.3 Biological and Chemical Weapons Treaties

Treaty Name	*Overall Status*	*Specific Status*	*Enforceable in the US*
Geneva Protocol[1254]	OS: 17 June 1925 EF: 8 February 1928	S/R: 17 June 1925 A: 8 February 1928	Yes
Biological Convention[1255]	OS: 10 April 1972 EF: 26 March 1975	S/R: 10 April 1972 A: 26 March 1975	Yes
Chemical Convention[1256]	OS: 13 January 1993 EF: 29 April 1997	S/R: 13 January 1993 A: 29 April 1997	Yes

OS: Opened for signature; EF: Entry into force; S/R: Signature/Ratification; A: Accession

1251. Treaty Banning Nuclear Weapon Tests in the Atmosphere, in Outer Space and Under Water, *U.N.T.S.*, vol. 480, p. 43. – see also http://www.state.gov/t/isn/4797.htm.
1252. Treaty on the Non-Proliferation of Nuclear Weapons, *U.N.T.S.*, vol. 729, p. 161. – see also http://www.state.gov/t/isn/npt/index.htm.
1253. U.N.G.A., resolution 50\245 – see also http://www.state.gov/t/avc/c42328.htm. Since 1992, the United States has observed a unilateral moratorium on nuclear explosive testing. This moratorium is based on the national security assessment that the United States does not need to conduct nuclear explosive tests in order to ensure the safety, security and effectiveness of its nuclear force; however, the US Congress never ratified this treaty.
1254. Protocol for the Prohibition of the Use in War of Asphyxiating, Poisonous or Other Gases, and of Bacteriological Methods of Warfare, 94, *League of Nations Treaty Series*, No. 2138 (1929). See also http://www.state.gov/t/isn/4784.htm.
1255. Convention on the Prohibition of the Development, Production and Stockpiling of Bacteriological (Biological) and Toxin Weapons and On Their Destruction, *U.N.T.S.*, vol. 1015, p. 163. – see also http://www.state.gov/t/isn/bw/.
1256. Convention on the Prohibition of the Development, Production, Stockpiling and Use of Chemical Weapons and on Their Destruction, Doc.CD/CW/WP.400/Rev.1. – see also http://www.state.gov/r/pa/pl/176872.htm.

Table 17.4 Multilateral Export Control Regimes

Regime Name	*Formation*	*Participation*
Zangger Committee[1257]	1971	Yes
Nuclear Suppliers Group	1974	Yes
Australia Group	1985	Yes
Missile Technology Control Regime	1987	Yes
Wassenaar Arrangement[1258]	1994	Yes

Table 17.5 Other

Name	*Adoption*	*Participation*
International Code of Conduct[1259]	25 November 2002	Yes

Par. 2 Treaties Dealing with Specific Areas

Table 17.6 International Zones

Treaty Name	*Overall Status*	*Specific Status*	*Enforceable in [Country]*
Antarctic Treaty[1260]	OS: 1 December 1959 EF: 23 June 1961	S: 1 December 1959 A: 23 June 1961	Yes
Outer Space Treaty (OST)[1261]	OS: 27 January 1967 EF: 10 October 1967	S: 27 January 1967 A: 10 October 1967	Yes

1257. Non Proliferation Treaty Exporters Committee (also called the Zangger Committee).- see also http://www.state.gov/p/wha/rls/71518.htm.
1258. Wassenaar Arrangement on export controls for conventional arms and dual-use goods and technologies.
1259. Hague Code of Conduct against Ballistic Missile Proliferation. See text from 30 Nov. 2012 at http://www.hcoc.at/?tab=background_documents&page=text_of_the_hcoc – see also http://www.state.gov/t/isn/trty/101466.htm, As of July 2014, 137 countries have subscribed to the HCOC, including the US The HCOC is aimed at bolstering efforts to curb ballistic missile proliferation worldwide and to further delegitimize such proliferation. The HCOC consists of a set of general principles, modest commitments, and limited confidence-building measures. It is intended to supplement, not supplant, the Missile Technology Control Regime (MTCR), and is administered collectively by all subscribing states.
1260. 402, *U.N.T.S.*, 7. – see also the US National Science Foundation information at: http://www.nsf.gov/geo/plr/antarct/anttrty.jsp.
1261. Treaty on Principles Governing the Activities of States in the Exploration and Use of Outer Space, including the Moon and Other Celestial Bodies, *U.N.T.S*, vol. 610, p. 205. – see also http://www.unoosa.org/oosa/SpaceLaw/outerspt.html.

Treaty Name	*Overall Status*	*Specific Status*	*Enforceable in [Country]*
Sea Bed Arms Control Treaty[1262]	OS: 11 February 1971 EF: 23 June 1961	S: 11 February 1971 A: 18 May 1972	Yes
Moon Agreement[1263]	OS: 18 December 1979 EF: 11 July 1984		No
Convention on the Law of the Sea[1264]	OS: 10 December 1982 EF: 16 November 1994		No

OS: Opened for signature; EF: Entry into force; S/R: Signature/Ratification; A: Accession

Table 17.7 Regional Nuclear Weapons-Free Zones

Treaty Name	*Overall Status*	*Specific Status*	*Enforceable in [Country]*
Treaty of Tlatelolco[1265]	OS: 14 February 1967 EF: 22 April 1967		No
Treaty of Rarotonga[1266]	OS: 6 August 1985 EF: 11 December 1986		No
Treaty of Bangkok[1267]	OS: 15 December 1995 EF: 27 March 1997		No
Treaty of Pelindaba[1268]	OS: 11 April 1996 EF: not in force		No

OS: Opened for signature; EF: Entry into force; S/R: Signature/Ratification; A: Accession

1262. Treaty on the Prohibition of the Emplacement of Nuclear Weapons and other Weapons of Mass Destruction on the Seabed and The Ocean Floor and in the subsoil thereof, *U.N.T.S.*, vol. 955, p. 115. – see also http://www.state.gov/t/isn/5187.htm.
1263. Agreement governing the Activities of States on the Moon and Other Celestial Bodies, *I.L.M* vol. 18, p. 1434. – see http://www.unoosa.org/pdf/limited/c2/AC105_C2_2015_CRP08E.pdf.
1264. Doc. A/CONF.62/122 and Corr.1-11. Not signed by the US though the signature of this treaty is well supported by the US Armed Forces and by the Administration, US Congress has not ratified the UN convention on the Law of the Sea.
1265. Treaty for the Prohibition of Nuclear Weapons in Latin America and the Caribbean, *U.N.T.S.*, vol. 634, p. 326.
1266. South Pacific Nuclear Free Zone Treaty, *I.L.M.*, vol. 24, p. 1442.
1267. South East Asia Nuclear-Weapon-Free Zone Treaty, *I.L.M.*, vol. 35. p. 635.
1268. African Nuclear Weapon-Free Zone Treaty, *I.L.M.*, vol. 35, p. 698.

SECTION 4 CONTROL REGIMES

Defense items and Munitions are regulated by the ITAR and licensed by the DoS. Exports of dual-use goods and technologies - as well as of some military items, are regulated by the EAR and licensed by the DoC - and restrictions on exports based on US sanctions are administered by the Department of the Treasury.

The US Government has engaged in 2011 into an effective several phase comprehensive ECR effort.[1269] The goal of ECR is not to deregulate, but to implement a more effective export control system, advancing US National Security by imposing more effective controls on the most sensitive items, while enabling U.S. industry to be competitive in the worldwide market place.

As the outcome of the first two phases of ECR, the ITAR and the EAR co-exist; the control lists of the two regimes have been revised and streamlined in order to provide the control of the ITAR on those items that are considered critical military capabilities, while the EAR controls the less sensitive military items and the dual-use items.

Administrative enforcement of export controls is conducted by these agencies, while criminal enforcement is carried out by the DoC, the DHS and by the DoJ.

Sub-Section 1 Military Goods and Services - ITAR

Par. 1 Overall Presentation

The ITAR controls the export and temporary import of Defense Articles as identified on the USML. The DoS, DDTC, administers the controls defined by the ITAR. No Defense Article or related technical data may be exported from the US or temporarily imported into the US, no Defense Services may be provided to non-U.S. persons and no brokering activities may be conducted by persons subject to the U.S. Jurisdiction without an ITAR licence or claiming an exemption from the licensing requirements of the ITAR.

The ITAR (22 CFR 120-130)[1270] includes a number of definitions (Part 120), the USML (Part 121) and the applicable licensing requirements and regulations (Part 122-130), as follows:

- *ITAR Part 120 – Purpose and Definitions.*
- *ITAR Part 121 – The United States Munitions List.*
- *ITAR Part 122 – Registration of Manufacturers and Exporters.*
- *ITAR Part 123 – Licenses for the Export of Defence Articles.*
- *ITAR Part 124 – Agreements, Off-Shore Procurement and Other Defence Services.*
- *ITAR Part 125 – Licenses for the Export of Technical Data and Classified Defense Articles.*

1269. See 27 Nov. 2013 ECR fact sheet at http://www.export.gov/static/ECR%20Factsheet%201%20-%20The%20Basics%20v%205_Latest_eg_main_047472.pdf.
1270. 22CFR120-130 can be found at http://www.ecfr.gov/; the DDTC site http://www.pmddtc.state.gov/ should be consulted to identify changes in regulations or guidance.

- *ITAR Part 126 – General Policies and Provisions.*
- *ITAR Part 127 – Violations and Penalties.*
- *ITAR Part 128 – Administrative Procedures.*
- *ITAR Part 129 – Registration and Licensing of Brokers.*
- *ITAR Part 130 – Political Contributions, Fees and Commissions.*

The export, re-export (including in country retransfer and transfer to a dual or third country national (DN/TCN)) or temporary import of Defense Articles requires a positive authorization from the DoS in the form of an Agreement (Technical Assistance Agreements (TAA), Manufacturing Licensing Agreement (MLA) or Warehouse Distribution Agreement (WDA)) or a licence (DSP-5, DSP-73, DSP-61, DSP-85).

A few exemptions are available but these exemptions are generally very limited. (Refer to Sub-section 3, Par. 5 – Exemptions and Exceptions)

Registration: All U.S. persons (including U.S. person residing outside of the U.S.), who are involved in the manufacture of Defense Articles, or the provision of Defense Services, must register with DDTC. This registration does not provide any authorization, but is a pre-requisite to applying for an authorization. Registration carries an annual fee, plus a fee per licence. A non-U.S. person cannot register with DDTC as a US exporter.

Defense Article: A Defense Article is any item (hardware, software or technical data) which is controlled on the USML. To be noted that with the implementation of ECR, this is not anymore 'any item specially designed or modified for Military applications', but any item positively listed in the USML. (Refer to further discussion in Par. 2 on the Control List)

Technical Data and Defense Services: Technical Data and Defense Services each have a wide definition. Technical Data captures information which is required for the design, development, production, manufacture, assembly, operation, repair, testing, maintenance or modification of Defense Articles. Defense Services includes assistance related to the design, development, engineering, manufacture, production, assembly, testing, repair, maintenance, modification, operation, demilitarization, destruction, processing or use of defence articles. Note that the verbs of the two definitions are similar but not identical.

Technical Data excludes public domain information and basic marketing information. Provision of a Defense Service can be performed without transfer of technical data.

Brokering: Brokering is the act of facilitating, on behalf of others, the manufacture, export, permanent import, transfer, re-export, or retransfer of a U.S. or foreign Defense Article or Defence Service, regardless of its origin. Note that the regulation changed in October 2013,[1271] brokering now only applies to U.S. persons, or foreign persons located in the US or foreign person owned or controlled by a U.S. person. Therefore, unless a non-U.S. person or company is owned by a U.S. person or

1271. Refer to 78 FR 52690, 26 Aug. 2013 https://www.pmddtc.state.gov/FR/2013/78FR52680.pdf, effective 25 Oct. 2013.

company, or performs its activity in the U.S., it will not be subject to ITAR brokering requirements (contrary to the regulation prior to October 2013).

Compliance: The U.S. Government encourages U.S. exporters (and non-US re-exporters) to implement an internal export compliance programme, supported by a Technology Transfer Control Plan (either generic or specific to a programme or to an authorization).

Violations: A violation of U.S. export control laws can lead to both civil fines and criminal penalties. U.S. exporters (and non-US re-exporters) are encouraged to disclose voluntarily and implement mitigation measures. The process for Voluntary Disclosures is outlined in the regulation (22 CFR 127.12). Failure to disclose voluntarily may lead to much higher fines and far more stringent administrative and legal actions.

Embargoes: The ITAR implements international arms embargoes and US country policies.[1272] In particular, 22 CFR 126.1 defines the prohibited exports, imports, and sales to and from certain countries.

Information Required for Export Licence, Re-Export Licences: The same information is required for export licences and re-export licences, i.e.:

- What is it: Technical description, brochures, quantities, financial values.
- Why: Purchase order or letter of intent and programme description.
- Who: End-User Certificate describing the end-use and if necessary a DSP-83 (Non-transfer and Use Certificate) – list of all end-users, consignees, intermediate consignees and nationalities.
- Where: Name, location and addressed of all parties.
- When: Period of performance.
- 22 CFR 126.13 certification: Certification that none of the principals (board of director, CEO, comptroller, general counsel,...) are subject to indictment or otherwise charges or convicted of violation of any of the US criminal statutes enumerated under the ITAR or ineligible to receive a licence. This certification is now compulsory not only for export licences but also for non-US companies applying for re-export requests submitted via General Correspondence.
- If applicable Part 130 statement: This statement is related to payment/non-payment by the applicant or its vendors of fees and commission for a transaction in excess of USD 500,000 for the benefit of non-U.S. armed forces.

Technical Assistance Agreements: A TAA[1273] is an authorization for U.S. parties to provide Defense Services (as well as Technical Data and Hardware) to non-U.S. parties. Each TAA authorization will have a defined scope in terms of: who (U.S. and non-U.S. parties, including nationalities), what (Statement of Work including Defense Services), where (entities and countries), when (period of performance) and why (what is it going to be used for).

1272. For further details, see http://www.pmddtc.state.gov/embargoed_countries/.
1273. See the DDTC Agreement guidelines at http://www.pmddtc.state.gov/licensing/agreement.html.

When discussing the scope of a TAA with a U.S. applicant, it is critical for non-US companies to identify the full scope of what will be needed to execute the programme (including such as software models, hardware loans, sub-contractors and test houses, ...). Only what is positively authorized under the TAA can be performed by the parties, additional scope requires a formal amendment to be authorized by DDTC.

Manufacturing Licensing Agreements: A MLA is an authorization for U.S. parties to provide Defense Services (as well as Technical Data and Hardware) to non-U.S. parties, in order for these non-US parties to manufacture Defense Articles outside of the US.

Warehouse Distribution Agreements: A WDA is an authorization for US parties to provide to non-US parties Defense Articles for the purpose of redistributing. A WDA will have a defined territory and purpose (where and for what).

Par. 2 Control List

Military and Space items controlled under the ITAR are listed in the USML (ITAR Part 121).

As a result of the US ECR, the USML has become a positive list, where items controlled under the ITAR are described in positive technical terms. Not all items 'specifically designed or modified' for military applications are captured under the USML anymore. Only those items which are positively described by functionalities and performance or which are captured by a 'specially designed' clause are positively listed in the USML and thus controlled under the ITAR.

The USML is composed of twenty-one categories (each designated by a Roman numeral) and one MTCR annex. With each revised USML Category, the parameters of the MTCR Annex are being included in the USML using the designation of MT (Missile Technology).

Each category includes sub-categories (identified by Latin letters and numerals). Articles designated as Significant Military Equipment (SME) are preceded by an asterisk (*):

Category I – Firearms, Close Assault Weapons and Combat Shotguns.
Category II – Guns and Armament.
Category III – Ammunition/ Ordnance.
Category IV – Launch Vehicles, Guided Missiles, Ballistic Missiles, Rockets, Torpedoes, Bombs and Mines.
Category V – Explosives and Energetic Materials, Propellants, Incendiary Agents and Their Constituents.
Category VI – Surface Vessels of War and Special Naval Equipment.
Category VII – Ground Vehicles.
Category VIII – Aircraft and Related Articles.
Category IX – Military Training Equipment and Training.
Category X – Personal Protective Equipment.
Category XI – Military Electronics.

Category XII – Fire Controls, Range Finder, Optical and Guidance and Control Equipment.
Category XIII – Materials and Miscellaneous Articles.
Category XIV – Toxicological Agents, including Chemical Agents, Biological Agents and Associated Equipment.
Category XV – Spacecraft and Related Articles.
Category XVI – Nuclear Weapons Related Articles.
Category XVII – Classified Articles, Technical Data and Defense Services not otherwise enumerated.
Category XVIII – Directed Energy Weapons.
Category XIX – Gas Turbine Engines and Associated Equipment.
Category XX – Submersible Vessels and Related Articles.
Category XXI – Articles, Technical Data and Defence Services not otherwise enumerated.

An item may be designated by DDTC as a Defense Article, and thus within the jurisdiction of the ITAR, if it either:

(1) meets the criteria of a defence article or defence service of the USML (positively listed / described in the above categories); or
(2) provides the equivalent performance capabilities of a Defense Article on the USML.

In addition, an item may be designated in the future as a Defense Article or Defense service (and added to the USML), if it provides a critical military or intelligence advantage such that it warrants control under the ITAR.

If an item is not controlled under the ITAR, then it is controlled under another Jurisdiction. This classification analysis follows what is known as 'order of review', which includes a 'catch and release' for items which are 'specially designed'.

Some USML sub-categories refer to 'components, parts, accessories, attachments, and associated equipment specifically designed, modified, configured, or adapted for use' with the articles listed in the category. These items follow the pre-ECR rule that any modification to form, fit and function to an item for military application makes that item ITAR controlled. These entries are being retired with each revision to that USML Category per ECR.

'Specially designed' has a specific definition: A commodity or software is specially designed only if:

(1) It has properties peculiarly responsible for meeting or exceeding the characteristics identified in the USML.
(2) Is a component, part, accessory, attachment used with or within a Defense Article.

Conversely, a part, component, accessory, attachment, or software is not specially designed if:

(1) It has been determined to be controlled under the EAR by a CJ.
(2) It is a fastener (screw, bolt, nuts, nut plates, studs, inserts, clips, rivets, pins), washer, spacer, insulator, grommet, bushing, spring, wire, or solder (these are EAR 99).
(3) Has the same function, performances capabilities, form and fit as a commodity with is or was in production and is not enumerated in the USML.
(4) Was or is being developed that it would be used in or with both a Defense Article and an article which is not in the USML.
(5) Was or is developed for general purpose with no knowledge for use for a particular commodity.

This definition of 'specially designed' enables the 'release' for the USML of parts and components which meet one or several of the criteria above.

Those military items that are not positively listed in the USML and are not caught as 'specially designed' are controlled under the EAR. (600 Series for Military items and 500 Series for Space items).

(Further discussion on Jurisdiction and Classification can be found in Sub-section 3 - Par. 1)

Sub-Section 2 Dual-Use Goods and Services – EAR

Those articles which are not controlled on the USML and are not controlled by another agency (such as DoE or NRC), are controlled by the EAR. This includes less sensitive military and Space items, as well as dual-use items.

Par. 1 Overall Presentation

The EAR regulates exports (including re-exports and 'deemed exports') of certain military and 'dual-use' goods, software and technology. These regulations are administered by the DoC's Bureau of Industry and Security (BIS). All goods which are not subject to another jurisdiction (ITAR, NRC, etc.), are subject to the jurisdiction of the EAR.

Contrary to the ITAR which always requires an authorization, under the EAR, many items require a licence only for a limited number of countries and licensing requirement will depend on several factors:

- Product based: The CCL will identify for each ECCN and sub-number, the reason for control for the specific item.
- Country based: the CCL will identify for each country what are the applicable reason for control for this county (Part 738, Part 2 - Country Chart). In addition, certain rules or exceptions only apply to certain country groups; (see supplement 1 - Part 740 country group).[1274]

1274. http://www.bis.doc.gov/index.php/regulations/export-administration-regulations-ear.

- End-Use and End-User based: A licence may be required due to the nature of the end-use or of the end-user; (see Part 736 General Prohibitions and Part 744 End-Use and End-User based controls including screening lists).
- Retransfer of US-origin items integrated into non-US-made products is not subject to the EAR if the value of the US-origin content is below the *De Minimis* level (refer to Sub-section 3, Par. 9).

In order to satisfy the control requirements for military goods, numerous paragraphs of the EAR have been updated to implement restrictions similar to the ITAR. For instance, a licence is required and no *De Minimis* can be used for export of 500 and 600 series to D:5 countries (which is similar to ITAR §126.1)

In order to determine if a BIS licence is required, the US exporter or non-US re-exporter will have to follow the process described in Part 732, which details this analysis in twenty-nine steps and two decision trees which are not reproduced here but can be found at: http://www.bis.doc.gov/index.php/forms-documents/doc_view/411-part-732-steps-for-using-the-ear, as summarized below:

- Is the item subject to the EAR and if yes under which ECCN (including sub-number)? (This includes *De Minimis* analysis for retransfers and re-exports).
- What is the transaction (in terms of destination, end-user, end-use and conduct)?
- Does the transaction trigger any of the prohibitions identified in part 736 and 744 (including end-use and end-user based prohibitions), such as is the transaction in support of financing, contracting or otherwise facilitating a proliferation undertaking as prohibited by Part 744?
- What are the reasons for control? Are they applicable for the destinations considered?

Once a determination has been made that a BIS licence is required, there might be several available exceptions. (Refer to Sub-section 3, Par. 5). If several exceptions are available (such as STA and GOV, or Servicing and Replacement (RPL) and Temporary Imports, Exports and Re-exports (TMP)), choose the less constraining and document that all the conditions of the use of the exception have been met. Part 740 describes these exceptions, note that prior to using an exception, it must be verified that the exception is available (see in particular EAR 740.2 which list the circumstances under which an exception cannot be used).

Par. 2 Control List

Military and Space items which are not controlled on the USML and dual-use items are controlled under the EAR and listed in the CCL.

Commerce Control List

The CCL[1275] is divided in ten categories:

Category 0 – Nuclear Materials, Facilities and Equipment and Miscellaneous.
Category 1 – Material, Chemicals Micro-organisms and Toxins.
Category 2 – Material processing.
Category 3 – Electronics.
Category 4 – Computers.
Category 5 – Part 1 – Telecommunications.
Category 5 – Part 2 – Information Security.
Category 6 – Sensors and Lasers.
Category 7 – Navigation and Avionics.
Category 8 – Marine.
Category 9 – Aerospace and Propulsion.

Any item which is not under the jurisdiction of another agency, and is not positively listed in these categories is EAR 99.

Within each of these categories, items are organized by groups:

A for Equipment, Assembly and Components (Hardware).
B for Test, Inspection and Production Equipment.
C for Materials.
D for Software.
E for Technology.

Within these groups, each entry will be described in detail (technical description and performance) and bear three digits (such as 3A001), the first digit after the group letter is associated with the reasons for control.

As a general rule, the categories of the CCL correspond to those of the Wassenaar Agreement.

In order to control specifically items which have transitioned from the ITAR, the CCL has created 500 and 600 series (500 for Space and 600 for military). For these series, the first digit after the group letter will be a '5' or a '6' for 500 or 600 series and the two following digits will represent the associated Wassenaar Agreement Munitions List Category (for instance 3A611 is 3 for Electronics, A for Hardware, 6 for 600 series and 11 for ML11 of the Wassenaar Agreement Munitions List).

Refer to Figure 17.1 – Aircraft 600 Series; Figure 17.2 – Electronics 600 Series and Figure 17.3 – Space 500 Series.

1275. Part 774 – http://www.bis.doc.gov/index.php/regulations/commerce-control-list-ccl.

Figure 17.1 Aircraft 600 Series

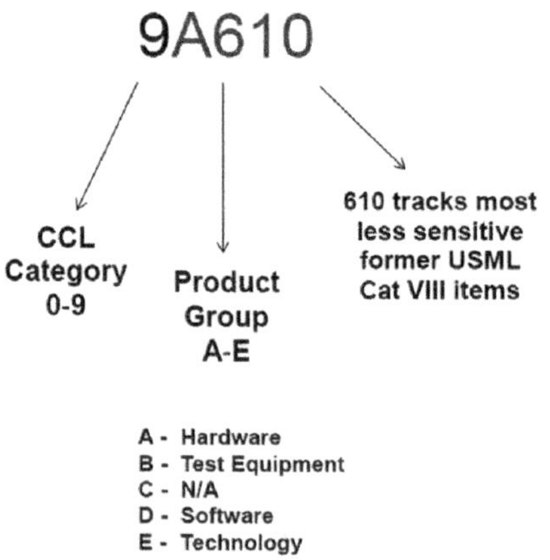

Paragraphs:

- .a: aircraft
- .b - .e: RESERVED
- .f: Ground Equipment "specially designed for aircraft under paragraph a.
- .g: Aircrew life support equipment
- .h: Parachutes, paragliders, complete parachute canopies, etc.
- .i: controlled opening equipment or automatic piloting systems designed for parachuted loads.
- .j: Ground effect machines (GEMS)
- .h: Parachutes, paragliders, complete parachute canopies, etc.
- .k - .t: RESERVED
- .u: Apparatus and devices "specially designed" for the handling, control, activation and non-ship-based launching of UAVs or drones controlled by either USML paragraph VIII(a) or ECCN 9A610.a, and capable of a range equal to or greater than 300 km.
- .v: Radar altimeters designed or modified for use in UAVs or drones controlled by either USML paragraph VIII(a) or ECCN 9A610.a., and capable of delivering at least 500 kilograms payload to a range of at least 300 km
- .w: Hydraulic, mechanical, electro-optical, or electromechanical flight control systems (including fly-by-wire systems) and attitude control equipment designed or modified for UAVs or drones.
- . x: "Parts," "components," "accessories," and "attachments" that are "specially designed" for a commodity subject to control in this ECCN or a defense article in USML Category VIII and not elsewhere specified on the USML or in ECCN 9A610.y.
- .y: Specific "parts," "components," "accessories," and "attachments" (see list in CCL)

Figure 17.2 Electronics 600 Series

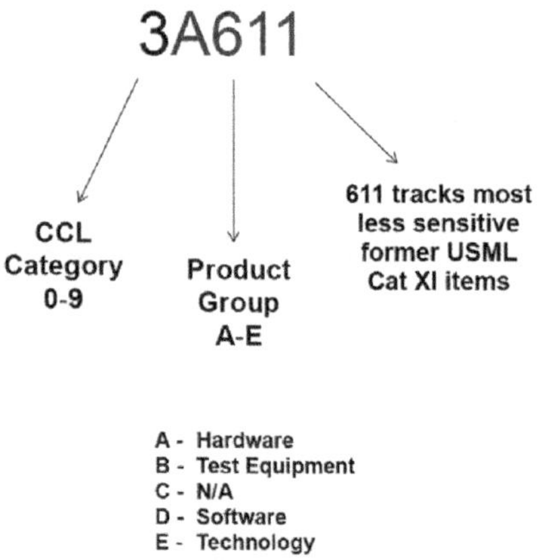

Paragraphs:

- .a: equipment and end items specially designed for military applications
- .b - .d: reserved
- .e: high frequency surface wave radar
- .f: Asic and PLD programmed for 600 series
- .g: PCB and boards specially designed for 600 series
- .h: MCM specially designed for 600 series
- .i – w: reserved
- . x: "Parts," "components," "accessories," and "attachments" that are "specially designed" for a commodity subject to control in this ECCN or a defense article
- .y: Specific "parts," "components," "accessories," and "attachments" (see list in CCL)

Figure 17.3 Space 500 Series

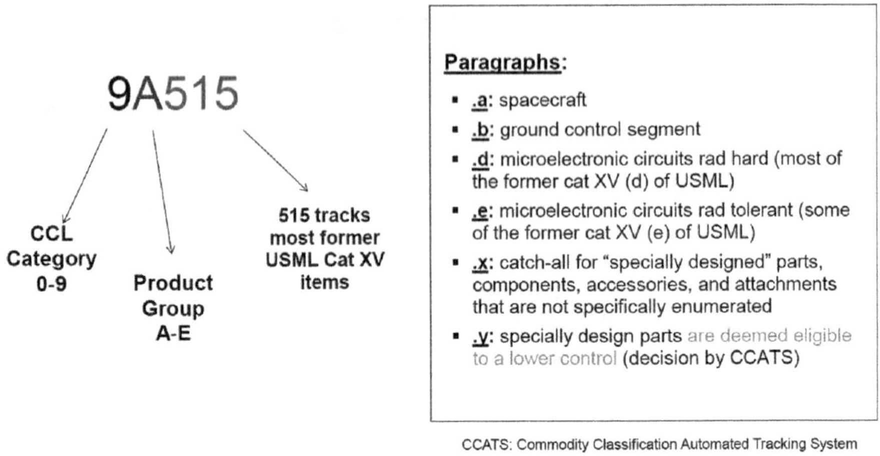

9A515
CCL Category 0-9
Product Group A-E
515 tracks most former USML Cat XV items
Paragraphs:
.a: spacecraft
.b: ground control segment
.d: microelectronic circuits rad hard (most of the former cat XV (d) of USML)
.e: microelectronic circuits rad tolerant (some of the former cat XV (e) of USML)
.x: catch-all for "specially designed" parts, components, accessories, and attachments that are not specifically enumerated
.y: specially design parts are deemed eligible to a lower control (decision by CCATS)
CCATS: Commodity Classification Automated Tracking System

Commerce Country Chart

The Commerce Country Chart[1276] identifies the reasons for control for each country The reasons for control are as follows:

- Chemical and Biological Weapons – with three levels CB1, CB2 and CB3.
- Nuclear Non-Proliferation – with two levels NP1 and NP2.
- National Security – with two levels NS1 and NS2.
- Missile Technology – MT.
- Regional Stability – with two levels RS1 and RS2.
- Firearms Control – FC.
- Crime Control – with three levels CC1, CC2 and CC3.
- Anti-terrorism – with two levels AT1 and AT2.

For each country, the Commerce Country Chart shows an 'x' if the reason for control applies.

Screening List

The ITAR, EAR and OFAC regulations separately maintain several lists. The US Government is now offering a consolidated screening tool at: http://export.gov/ecr/eg_main_023148.asp.

1276. http://www.bis.doc.gov/index.php/forms-documents/doc_view/14-commerce-country-chart.

The Lists are as follows:

(1) *Denied Party List:*
The denied party list identifies the US individuals and entities that have been denied export privileges. Any dealings with a party on this list that would violate the terms of its denial order are prohibited.

(2) *Entity List*:
The EAR contains a list of names of certain non-US persons - including businesses, research institutions, government and private organizations, individuals, and other types of legal persons - that are subject to specific licence requirements for the export, re-export and/or transfer (in country) of specified items. These persons comprise the Entity List, which is found in Supplement No. 4 to Part 744 of the EAR. On an individual basis, the persons on the Entity List are subject to licensing requirements and policies supplemental to those found elsewhere in the EAR.

(3) *Unverified List*:
Parties listed on the Unverified List (UVL) are ineligible to receive items subject to the EAR by means of a licence exception. In addition, exporters must file an Automated Export System record for all exports to parties listed on the UVL and obtain a statement from such parties prior to exporting, re-exporting, or transferring to such parties any item subject to the EAR which is not subject to a licence requirement. Restrictions on exports, re-exports and transfers (in-country) to persons listed on the UVL are set forth in Part *744.15* of the EAR. The Unverified List is set forth in *Supplement No. 6* to Part 744 of the EAR.

(4) *Specially Designated Nationals*:
OFAC publishes a list of individuals and companies owned or controlled by, or acting for or on behalf of, targeted countries. It also lists individuals, groups, and entities, such as terrorists and narcotics traffickers designated under programmes that are not country-specific. Collectively, such individuals and companies are called 'Specially Designated Nationals' or 'SDNs.' Their assets are blocked and US persons are generally prohibited from dealing with them.

(5) *Statutorily Debarred Parties:*
DoS publishes a list of the persons subject to statutory debarment pursuant to §127.7(c) of the ITAR on persons convicted of violating, attempting to violate or conspiring to violate Section 38 of the AECA, as amended, Persons on this list are debarred from export privileges.

(6) *Non-Proliferation sanctions:*
DoS publishes the list of the sanctions under various legal authorities against foreign individuals, private entities, and governments that engage in proliferation activities.

Sub-Section 3 Implementation

As a result of the US ECR, this chapter is common to the ITAR and to the EAR. It addresses the main concepts and their implementation throughout the ITAR and the EAR.

Par. 1 Jurisdiction and Classification

To determine the licences or other US government approval required to export or re-export or retransfer a Space or defence related item, an exporter or re-exporter must first determine which agency, DoS or DoC or other agencies, has jurisdiction over the item and what are the controls applicable under this jurisdiction, i.e., determine the proper classification of the item under the US Export Regulations.

The analysis to be conducted to determine the jurisdiction and classification under the ITAR or the EAR follows an 'order of review'. It is important to keep in mind that, contrary to the 'pre- ECR' era, not all military items are controlled under the ITAR, but military items are controlled either under the ITAR or under the EAR, based on their performance characteristics and function.

To correctly conduct the analysis, one should not only understand the characteristics of the item to be classified but also, in order to conduct certain aspects of the 'specially designed' analysis, have knowledge of its design and/or development intent and of its end-use.

While the first resource is to turn to the original US manufacturer to obtain a classification / reclassification under ECR of the US-origin item, it is the responsibility of each exporter and of each re-exporter to handle items under their proper jurisdiction and classification. This means that non-US companies must know how to classify under US regulation not only the US-origin products in their possession, but also identify the US classification of the non-US higher assemblies, as the classification of this higher assembly is a factor in the classification of the US-origin part.

If the original US manufacturer or exporter is unresponsive or provides a response which is not consistent with the regulations (such as quoting a pre-ECR classification or quoting a classification which is not credible); then it is the responsibility of the non-US party to determine the proper classification under the applicable US regulations.[1277]

1277. In a joint DDTC and BIS response to a question from the UK Export Group for Aerospace and Defence dated 22 Aug. 2014, the US Government stated:

> *The Departments of Commerce and State confirm that this is the case for both the ITAR and the EAR. Not only is a foreign person permitted to make such self-determinations, a foreign person indeed must know whether an article or item is subject to the jurisdiction of the ITAR or the EAR and how it is classified under the applicable set of regulations to know what, if any, licensing or other obligations the ITAR or the EAR impose on that party's re-export or retransfer of the article or the item. This is because a core element of the ITAR and the EAR is that the person, whether U.S. or foreign, conducting a controlled transaction is the person primarily responsible for determining how to comply with such controls. Because the regulations do not control all articles and items equally, a person*

Section 11 – Sub-section 1 in annex provides the definitions of the terms relevant to this analysis.

An item may be designated by DDTC as a defence article, and thus within the jurisdiction of the ITAR, if it either:

(1) meets the criteria of a defence article or defence service on the USML (positively listed); or
(2) provides the equivalent performance capabilities of a defence article on the USML.

In addition, an item may be designated in the future as a Defense Article or Defense Service (and added to the USML) if it provides a critical military or intelligence advantage such that it warrants control under the ITAR.

Under the ECR, the ITAR has enumerated the items that are controlled (positively listed). Those military items that are not positively listed in the USML are the ones that have moved to the EAR and comprise the 600 series, the Space items that are not positively listed in the USML are the ones that have moved to the EAR and comprise the 500 series.

Some USML sub-categories refer to 'components, parts, accessories, attachments, and associated equipment specifically designed, modified, configured, or adapted for use' with the articles listed in the category'. These items follow the pre-ECR rule of any modification to form, fit and function to an item for a military application makes that item ITAR controlled. These entries are being retired with each revision to that USML Category per ECR.

'Specially designed' has a specific definition.[1278] This 'specially designed' definition enables the 'release' from the USML of parts and components which meet one or several of the criteria below:

A commodity or software is specially designed only if:

(1) It has properties peculiarly responsible for meeting or exceeding the characteristics identified in the USML.
(2) Is a component, part, accessory, attachment used with or within a Defense Article.

about to export, re-export, or retransfer an article or item subject to the ITAR or the EAR must first determine which set of regulations governs and how the applicable regulation classifies the article or item. Only then can the person conduct the additional steps necessary to determine whether the ITAR or the EAR impose a licensing or other obligation on the proposed transaction. Because the ITAR and the EAR are extraterritorial, a foreign person's failure to take the steps necessary to ensuring compliance with the ITAR or the EAR can result in its being subject to fines or other punishment if its re-export or retransfer violated the ITAR or the EAR.

1278. For the definition of 'specially designed,' under the ITAR, see section 120.41.

Conversely, a part, component, accessory, attachment, or software is not specially designed if:

(1) It has been determined to be controlled under the EAR by a CJ.
(2) It is a fastener (screw, bolt, nuts, nut plates, studs, inserts, clips, rivets, pins), washer, spacer, insulator, grommet, bushing, spring, wire, or solder (these are generally EAR 99).
(3) Has the same function, performances capabilities, and equivalent form and fit as a commodity with is or was in production and is not enumerated in the USML.
(4) Was or is being developed that it would be used in or with both a Defense Article and an article which is not in the USML.
(5) Was or is developed for general purpose with no knowledge for use for a particular commodity.

If an item is not positively listed in the USML and is not a 'components, parts, accessories, attachments, and associated equipment specifically designed' caught into a 'specially designed' clause, then the item is released from the USML and is controlled under the EAR. (600 series for military items and 500 series for Space items).

Under the EAR, a similar 'catch and release' analysis needs to be conducted: Is the item positively listed under 600 or 500 series, or is the item caught in a 'specially designed' clause of the EAR. If not, the item may be included in another category of the CCL, or EAR99. See specific EAR definition in Section 11 – Sub-section 1)

Note that in order to conduct this analysis, it is important not only to understand the characteristics of the item being analysed, but also to understand in which higher assemblies this item is being used into or has been designed for and the classification and controls associated with these higher assemblies.

The decision tree may seem complex, but may be broken down in – sub-steps described below and further detailed in each sub-chart (Refer to Figure 17.4 – Order of Review and Figure 17.5 – Classification Overview):

- Is the item positively listed in the USML? (Refer to Figure 17.6- Is the item caught under the USML?)
- Is the item released from the UMSL? (Refer to Figure 17.7 – Is the item released from the USML?)
- Is the item positively listed in 600 or 500 series? (Refer to Figure 17.8 – Is the item caught under 600 / 500 series?)

Figure 17.4 Order of Review

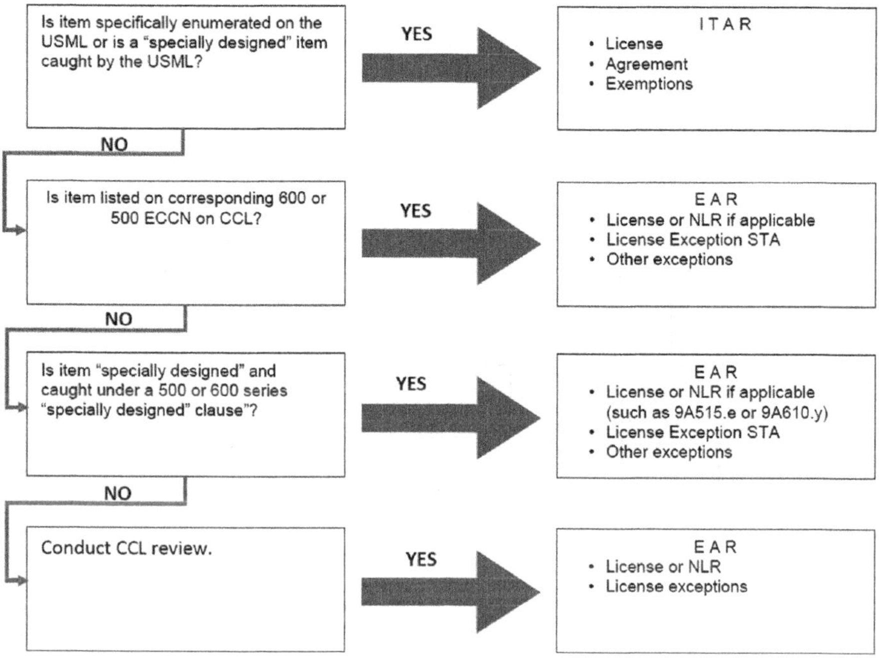

Where it may still be unclear whether an item is under the jurisdiction of DoS, an entity (U.S. or non-U.S.) may submit to DDTC a CJ request. The purpose of the CJ is to eliminate doubt as to whether the ITAR has jurisdiction over a particular item, or to request that the agency considers removing an article from the USML. A determination that an article is not covered by the ITAR does not necessarily mean that it can be exported without a licence because it may require a licence under the EAR. All CJs are coordinated between the Departments of State, Defense and Commerce. In the response, DDTC will provide either the jurisdiction of the item (ITAR or EAR), and if EAR the appropriate classification of the item or will direct the applicant to further seek classification from BIS through a Commodity Classification (CCATS) request.

Figure 17.5 Classification of Overview

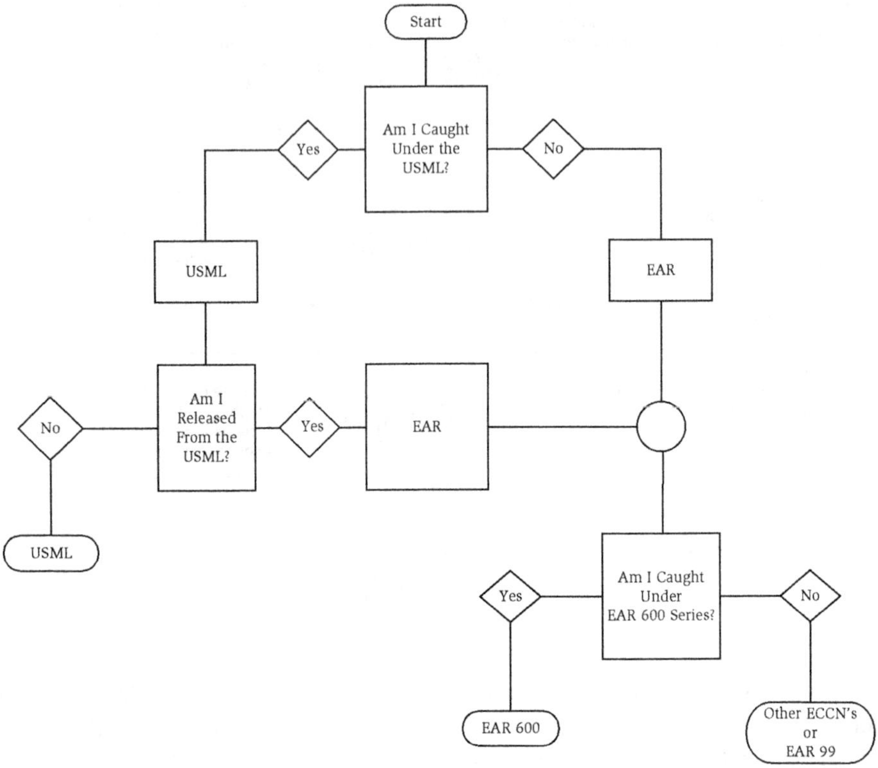

Figure 17.6 Is the Items Caught under USML

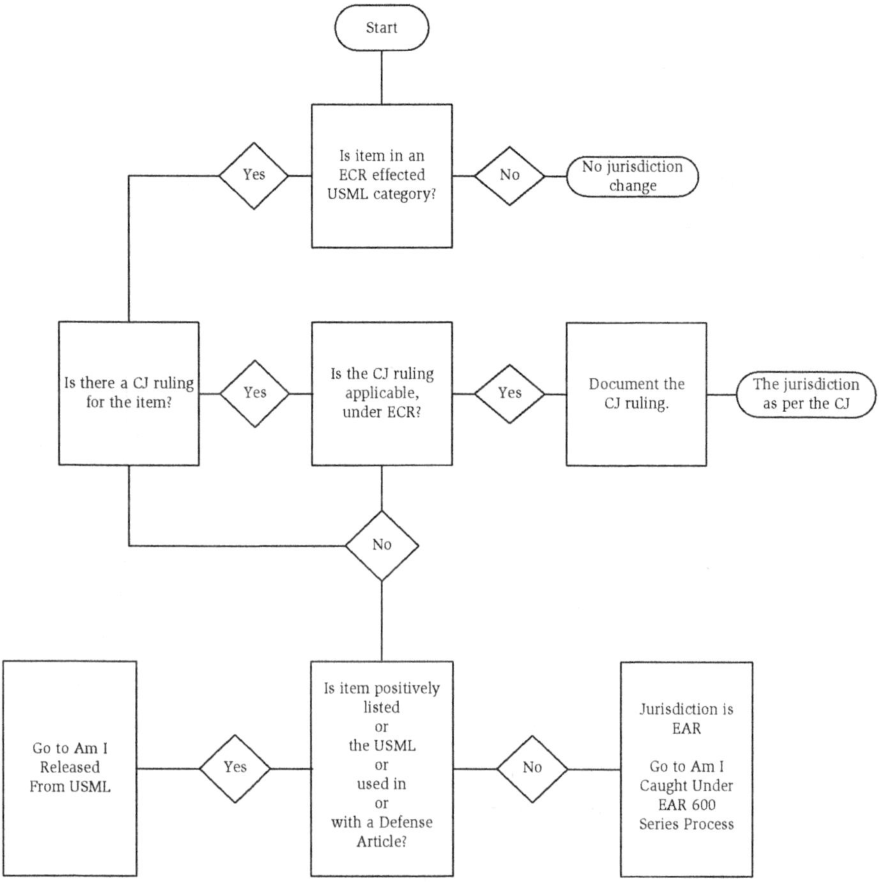

Figure 17.7 Is the Item Released from USML

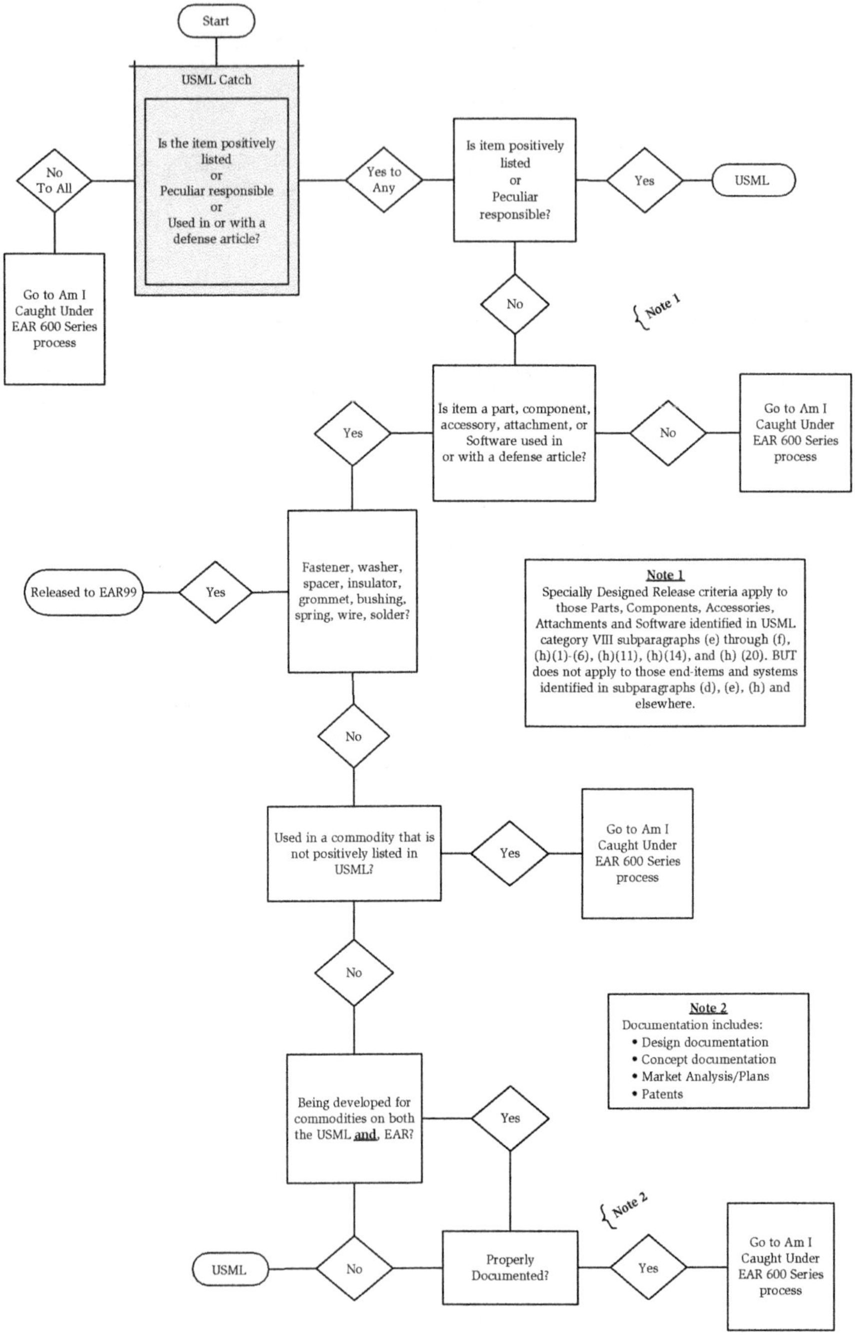

Figure 17.8 Is the Items Caught under EAR 600 Series

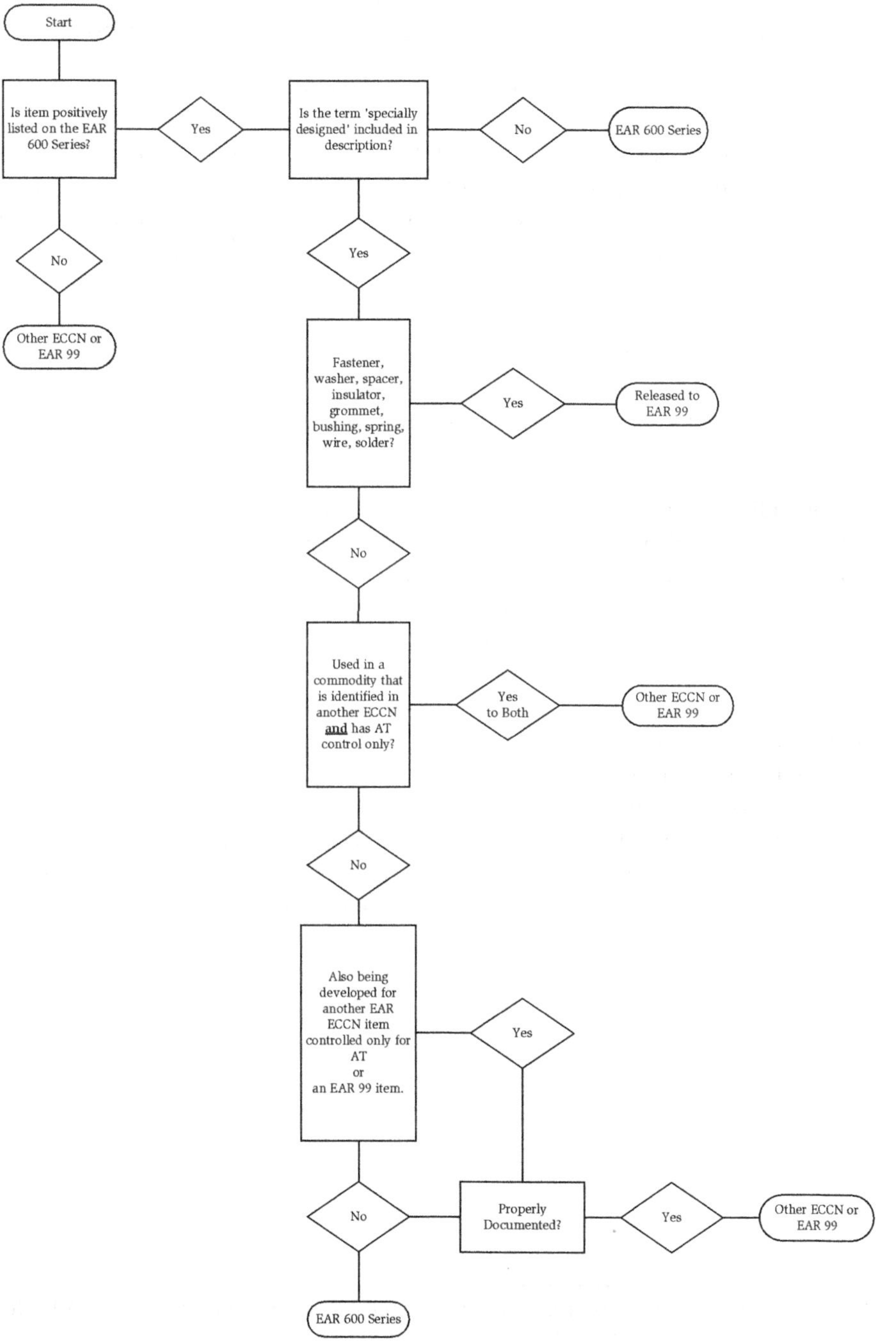

Par. 2 ECR Transition Period

In an attempt to smooth the transition and facilitate the implementation effort of the ECR, the U.S. Government has implemented several 'transition mechanisms':

- Rules are first published in draft form for public comments. Typically, the period for public comments is forty-five days. Some of these comments have led to significant changes prior to the publication of the interim or final rules. When publishing the corresponding updates, both BIS and DDTC have made extensive effort to address the comments and justify their positions with regards to each of the points raised through these comments.
- For each rule change, there is a period of six months between the final publication of the rule and its effective date. The objective is to enable industry to take the appropriate measures in terms of reclassification and also enable to identify any remaining implementation issues.
- Publications of corrections are also made as needed prior to the rule becoming effective.

In addition to these efforts, in order to avoid a gap in authorizations, BIS and DDTC have also implemented a two[1279] year transition period, starting from the time of the effective date of the applicable rule, during which time prior ITAR authorizations can continue to be used for items which have transitioned. Prior ITAR authorizations covering both transitioning and non-transitioning items remain valid for their full validity. In particular for each revised category of the ITAR, there is a sub-paragraph (x), to cover the EAR items which are used in and within a Defense Article. Use of USML paragraph (x) avoids double ITAR and EAR licensing for the same transaction. Note that in order to use paragraph (x) to cover EAR items on a ITAR licence, the EAR items have to be used 'in or with' the ITAR items under the same licence, and that in order to use paragraph (x) for items exported or re-exported in furtherance of an Agreement (TAA), the Agreement must have been amended (minor amendment) to reflect the ECR. (Refer to Table 17.8 – ECR Transition Guidance).

1279. The initial FRN states the transition is a two-year period, however, in October 2015, DDTC has provided extension to allow for a three-year transition period.

Table 17.8 Re-Export / Re-Transfer of US Items Transitioned from the ITAR to the EAR

Initial Export from the US	*Re-Export within Transition Period (Two Years)*	*Re-Export after Transition Period*
Stand-alone DSP-5	- **Handle as 'ITAR'**** within the scope of DSP 5, but no GC can be obtained - **Handle as EAR**: Reclassify and handle per the new ECCN (e.g., 500 or 600 series)	**ITAR**: Not applicable any longer **EAR**: as per ECCN
DSP-5 in furtherance of a WDA/TAA that has transitioning and non-transitioning USML items	- As long as WDA/TAA remain valid, **Handle as 'ITAR'** within scope of WDA/TAA For re-exports outside the scope, amend WDA/TAA to expand the territory and include transitioned (USML (x)* items - **Handle as EAR:** Reclassify and handle per the new ECCN (e.g., 500 or 600 series)	**ITAR**: as per WDA/TAA as long as valid **EAR**: as per ECCN
DSP-5 in furtherance of a WDA/TAA that has transitioning items only and end-item is a (foreign) Defence Article	- As long as WDA/TAA remain valid, **Handle as 'ITAR'** within scope of WDA/TAA - TAA can be amended to expand Defence Services only - **Handle as EAR**: Reclassify and handle per the new ECCN (e.g., 600 series)	**ITAR**: WDA/TAA, needs to be maintained to cover Defence Services if relevant **EAR**: as per ECCN
DSP-5 in furtherance of a WDA/TAA that has transitioning items only and end-item is not a (foreign) Defense Article	- As long as WDA/TAA remains valid, **Handle as 'ITAR'** within scope of WDA/TAA. For re-exports outside the scope, items must be reclassified and handled as EAR - **Handle as EAR**: Reclassify and handle per the new ECCN (e.g., 500 or 600 series)	**ITAR: Not applicable any longer,** WDA/TAA cannot be amended and has to be terminated **EAR**: as per ECCN
Valid WDA/TAA: Item was delivered under BIS licence, no Defense Services	- **Handle as EAR**: Use BIS licence **-OR-** Use EAR exceptions	**ITAR: Not applicable any longer,** WDA/TAA has to be terminated **EAR**: See left column
Valid WDA/TAA: Item was delivered under STA, no Defense Services	- **Handle as EAR**: Apply for BIS re-export licence **-OR-** Use EAR exceptions	**ITAR: Not applicable any longer,** WDA/TAA has to be terminated **EAR**: See left column

Initial Export from the US	*Re-Export within Transition Period (Two Years)*	*Re-Export after Transition Period*
No TAA or WDA: Item was delivered under BIS licence, no Defense Services	- **Handle as EAR:** Use BIS licence **-OR-** Use EAR exceptions	**EAR**: See left column
No TAA or WDA: Item was delivered under EAR, no Defense Services	- **Handle as EAR:** Apply for BIS re-export licence **-OR-** Use EAR exceptions	**EAR**: See left column

*Legally, these items have to be considered as being subject to the EAR. However, within the transition period you may continue to handle them as if they were controlled by the ITAR. USML (x) items are subject to the EAR, thus classified by an ECCN, but enumerated together with USML items on an ITAR authorization to avoid double licensing by DDTC and BIS.

Despite these measures, both US and non-US industry may be caught short and un-prepared at the end of each transition period, the first one for Aircraft and Gas Turbine Engines was initially set to 15 October 2015. A few days before the deadline, in light of the industry lack of preparedness, the transition period for these categories and for all others was extended to three years.

Par. 3 Requirements Prior to Any Specific Import/Export

It is important to understand which elements of a transaction need to be analysed to determine if the transaction is permissible and which US Government authorizations are required, as this will inform the elements that need to be provided by the non-US buyer to its US supplier, as well as the elements that need to be analysed prior to re-exports or retransfers. These are commonly summarized as the five ‘W’s (What, Why, When, Who, Where)

In order for the US exporter to determine their obligations under the ITAR or under the EAR and to determine if an export from the US requires prior written authorization from DDTC or from BIS in the form of a licence or other authorization, the US exporter must first determine the jurisdiction of the transaction (ITAR or EAR), i.e., the classification of the item (service and hardware) to be exported.[1280]

If the transaction is subject to the ITAR, the exporter must determine if the transaction triggers any of the ITAR prohibitions, if an exemption is available and which authorization is required (TAA, MLA, DSP-5, DSP-61, or DSP-73). Generally, under the ITAR, a positive authorization will be required.

1280. Note that when making this determination, the U.S. exporter will have to determine not only the classification of any hardware exported, but also the classification of any Services and Technical Data. If there is any assistance provided to the foreign parties as it relates to a foreign Defense Article (as defined by the ITAR), then a Defense Service will be provided and an ITAR authorization will be required. In other words, the US exporter may be exporting Hardware and Technology subject to the EAR.

If the transaction is subject to the EAR, the US exporter must determine the reasons for control of the item and whether a licence is required for the transaction and if an exception available. In order to make this determination, the US exporter will need to determine of any of the aspects of the transaction trigger any of the ten General Prohibitions under Part 736 or End-User Controls under Part 744.

Therefore, the following five elements must be identified (also known as the five W's: What, Where, Who, When, Why:

(1) *What is it?* The classification of the product determines how the item is controlled and if a licence exception is available under the EAR (Part 774 of the EAR).

(2). *Where is it going?* The *country of ultimate destination* is another factor in determining how the item is controlled for a given transaction (Parts 738 and 774 of the EAR).

(3) *Who will receive it?* The *ultimate end-user* cannot be on any denied or restricted party list, to include the Entity List in Supplement No. 4 to Part 744 (Parts 736.2(b)(4), and parts 744 and 764 of the EAR). Who are the parties (legal entities and locations), which nationalities? *Conduct* such as contracting, financing or freight forwarding in support of a proliferation project will prevent the U.S. exporter from being able to participate in the transaction (Part 744.6 of the EAR).

(4) *When?* When delivered, Duration of the programme, schedule of the different phases of the programme (if relevant).

(5) *Why?* For which ultimate end-use? The *ultimate end-use* of the item cannot be for the benefit of a prohibited end-use as defined in Part 744 of the EAR (Parts 736.2(b)(5) and 744 of the EAR).

The U.S. exporter must be able to verify whether the transaction (export) requires prior written authorization in the form of a licence from BIS prior to exporting.

A BIS export licence has to be applied for and licence exception (to include NLR) cannot be used if an export from the U.S. is related to a transaction that meets any of the ten General Prohibitions (Part 736) or End-Use Controls (Part 744).

For instance, the US exporter must be able to determine, based on the information provided by the non-US parties, if the transaction is for:

- nuclear end-use; (744.2);
- rocket systems; (744.3);
- chemical and biological; (744.4);
- Russian sanctions; (744.10);
- China, Russia and Venezuela Military end-use (744.17 and 744.21);
- sanctioned entities, blocked persons, SDNs and entity list.[1281]

1281. Such as denial order (736 b) 4) or SDGT (744.12) or SDT (744.13) or FTO (744 14), unverified list (744.15), Iraq (744.18), entity list (744.20) or OFAC SDN (744.22).

For many EAR controlled items, to include certain 500 and 600 series items (i.e., 9A515.e or 9A610.y), No Licence is Required for exports to most European Union (EU) and NATO member countries. However, if the EU or NATO entity is not the *ultimate end-user* of the item, then as per Part 736 and 744, the US exporter should know the *ultimate end-use* to determine if a licence is required.

If the non-US entity procuring the EAR items is unsure of the ultimate end-user/use at the time of the procurement, the compliance requirements and liability under the EAR associated with the eventual re-export lies entirely with the non-US entity.

Due to additional restrictions on 500 and 600 Series items (e.g., *De Minimis* restrictions), the EAR requires that all 500 or 600 Series items be identified as part of the Destination Control Statement (DCS) (see Part 758.6(b)).

Therefore, to efficiently and expeditiously respond to orders, the US exporter should be provided with the following information:

- If known, what and who the ultimate end-use/end-user is, to include:
  - List of countries in which loose parts will be distributed.
  - List of consignees/end-users to enable denied party check.
- Certification of *De Minimis* and list of countries in which the parts will be subject to *De Minimis*; to include *De Minimis* restrictions for 500 and 600 series for D:5 countries.
- If unsure of the ultimate end-user/end-use, a certification that the transaction will be compliant to the EAR and in particular does not meet any of the prohibitions of Part 736 and 744 of the EAR.
- For 500 or 600 series items and if licence exemption STA is available, a Prior Consignee Statement.

Prior to re-export or retransfer, the same analysis needs to be done by non-US re-exporter and thus the non-US re-exporter should seek the same type of information.

Par. 4 Control of Technical Data and Technology

Technical Data (ITAR) is generally controlled at the same level as the related Hardware and Services. Technology (EAR) is generally controlled at the same or higher level than the related Hardware.

In the frame of ECR, BIS and DDTC are attempting to harmonize the definition of Technical Data and Technology; but this task is still under way, thus both definitions need to be taken into account.

Technical Data[1282] is defined by the ITAR (22 CFR 120.10) as Information:

- required for the design, development, production, manufacture, assembly, operation, repair, testing, maintenance or modification of a Defense Article;

1282. In addition to marking identifying jurisdiction and classification, US companies may also characterize Technical Information as being either '*CUI*' Controlled Unclassified Information or '*UUI*' Uncontrolled Unclassified Information.

- Classified Information related to a Defense Article, Defence Services and 500-600 series items controlled by the CCL;
- Information covered by an invention secrecy order;
- Software related to a Defense Article.

The EAR defines export controlled Technology as that which is required for 'production,' 'development' and/or 'use' (see 'General Technology Note' -Supplement No. 2 to Part 774).[1283] The EAR also defines 'required' (EAR Part 722) to only include that 'portion of technology which is peculiarly responsible for achieving or exceeding the controlled performance levels, characteristics or functions.'

Additionally, there are differences in the control language. The CCL only controls key technologies as specifically enumerated under a Product Group E (Technology) ECCN while the ITAR controls all data directly related to a Defense Article enumerated in a specific USML category. The 600 Series and 500 Series Technology ECCNs do not always include the term 'for use' in the description of the scope of the controls, but rather breaks down this scope into its individual verbs.

The obligation to obtain an export licence from BIS before releasing controlled technology to a non-US-person is informally referred to as a deemed export or deemed re-export licence requirement. Release of controlled technology to a non-US person is 'deemed' to be an export/ re-export to the person's country or countries of nationality as defined in Part 734.2(b) of the EAR. Note that as part of the ECR, BIS has published guidance related to deemed exports to Dual and Third Country Nationals employed by non-U.S. entities, which are similar and reference those previously implemented under the ITAR, while maintaining its legacy BIS definition of 'nationality' as being the latest country of nationality/residence.

If a U.S. munitions item has transitioned to the DoC, the related Technical Data (if it is not a Defense Service) will be generally reclassified under the Product Group E (Technology) ECCN which corresponds to the ECCN of the Hardware.

Derived Controlled Data[1284] is technical data developed from U.S.-origin Controlled Data (ITAR or EAR) and which includes either directly or indirectly[1285] US-origin Controlled Information, regardless of how much.

There is no *De Minimis for* ITAR controlled Technical Data. While available, it is difficult to apply the *De Minimis* rule to EAR 'Technology'.[1286]

1283. See http://www.bis.doc.gov/index.php/regulations/export-administration-regulations-ear – Part 774 Supplement 2.
1284. Examples of Derived Data include specifications developed from, or incorporating, U.S.-origin ICDs, system analysis incorporating performance parameters of US-origin.
1285. Example of Indirect incorporation includes incorporation of technical information such as performance calculations or tests results which are dependent on US-origin underlying figure, even though they are not directly shown in the document.
1286. In order to De Minimize EAR technology, the demonstration has to be made that the technology is 'commingled' (734.3.3) and the corresponding *De Minimis* calculation needs to be reviewed by BIS (734.4 c) 3 and d) 3).)

Marking of Technical Data

Both the ITAR (22 CFR 123.9(b)(1)) and the EAR (Part 758.6) require that the exporter and re-exporter inform all recipients that the Controlled Technical Data (see Defense Article under 22 CFR 120.6, and 'Technology' under the EAR Part 772) are subject to US Export control laws as identified by a DCS. This DCS is required on all bills of lading, airway bills and other shipping documents.

In order to fulfil the requirements related to informing the recipients and prevent any unauthorized transfer, as a Best Practice, export control markings should be attached and maintained on all export controlled documents for all U.S.-origin and Derived controlled Technical Data under the ITAR or the EAR, that are not classified as EAR99 as follows:

> EAR Destination Control Statement (Part 758.6):
> *'These commodities, technology, or software were exported from the United State in accordance with the Export Administration Regulations. Diversion contrary to U.S. law is prohibited'*
> *Add (compulsory for 500/600 series) – 'These commodities, technology or software are controlled under ECCN (ECCN as applicable)';*
> ITAR Destination Control Statement (22 CFR 123.9(b)(1)):
> *'This Controlled Information is authorized by the U.S. Government for export only to (country of ultimate destination) for use by (end –user) under (license or other approval number or exemption citation). They may not be resold, diverted, transferred or otherwise be disposed of, to any other country or to any person other than the authorized end-user or consignee(s), either in their original form or after being incorporated into other end items without first obtaining approval from the U.S. Department of State or use of an applicable exemption'.*

In addition, a DCS can also be used for Technical Data that is not of U.S.-origin or which does not contain U.S.-origin Controlled Information as follows:

> *'This Information is of (company / country) origin and does not contain U.S.-origin ITAR or EAR controlled Information.' Add control statement as required by national law.*

Derived Controlled Data needs to be handled and marked with the same controls and DCS than the U.S.-origin Controlled information from which it is derived.

Legacy documents, that may not have been marked at the time of their creation, should be either fully marked, or a cover page added, to include the appropriate DCS prior to any transfer outside of the company or to an employee whose nationality is not the nationality of their employer.

Cloud Computing

Cloud Computing can be described as a technology to remotely safeguard, manage and access large amount of data.

For the purpose of U.S. export control, Cloud Computing, whether self-hosted or provided as a service, should be analysed as any other storage and accessed controlled venue:

- Where are these servers, through where is the information routed?
- How is the information encrypted?
- How is the access protected and how is it administered?
- Who has access, administers, services, maintains, etc. those servers (including who hires, what is the nationality of the employees, etc.)?
- Who has the ability to make changes in control and configuration, take mitigation actions?

The same compliance considerations applicable to any access, transfer or deemed export of Controlled Technical Data (ITAR) or Controlled Technology (EAR) should be applied when storing U.S.-origin or U.S. derived information in a Cloud Computing environment.

Par. 5 Exemptions and Exceptions

There are numerous exemptions (term used by the ITAR) and exceptions (term used by the EAR). There are general conditions for their use, in addition, each exemption and exception may carry its own particular requirements.

It is important when considering the use of an exemption or an exception to verify that all the conditions of their use are met and to document the analysis accordingly.

Though there are more ITAR exemptions than EAR exceptions, in practical terms, there are limited circumstances where the ITAR exemptions will be available, whereas there will be numerous circumstances where EAR exceptions will be available, increasing the risk of errors in the appreciation of whether and how a transaction can be conducted under an EAR exception.

Subject to specific conditions, the ITAR licence exemptions allow exports or temporary imports of Defense Articles, including technical data, or the performance of Defense Services, without prior authorization (or pursuant to reduced requirements for authorization). The exemptions may not be used with respect to articles originating in or for export to any proscribed countries, areas, or persons listed in Section 126.1 of the ITAR.

The intent of ECR was not to remove the exporter's capability to export items. Therefore, if an exporter was using an ITAR exemption before ECR, and if a BIS licence is required, there is most likely an EAR exception also available to export these items, but every situation is unique, and these exemptions/exceptions may not match up exactly.

The use of EAR exceptions is limited by end-use, end-user and country, by the general prohibitions or by controls (see part 736 and part 740.2 - for instance no exception can be used for items controlled for MT, or no exception, except GOV, can be used for 600 and 500 series for D:5 countries).

EAR Part 740 describes the restrictions on licence exceptions and each exception together with its specific limitations. Use of an exception may also be limited for a given ECCN / ECCN sub-categories as identified in each ECCN description.

Some EAR exceptions (such as Technology and Software under Restriction (TSR) or STA) carry specific documentation requirements; therefore the use of an EAR exception must be scrutinized and documented appropriately.

Due to ECCN specific limitations, it is critical, before considering the use of any EAR exception, to ensure that the classification of the item subject to the transaction has been properly determined and documented.

Note that an exception is only necessary if there is an initial licence requirement, so an exception does not apply to a transaction which is 'NLR'.

A complete list is provided in annex Section 11, Sub-section 2. This list is intended only as a reference and should not be relied upon in conducting exports under any of the exemptions/ exceptions. Exclusions, conditions and specific requirements or processes for use of ITAR exemptions or EAR exceptions apply which are not described in this list.

Persons wishing to conduct a transaction under any ITAR exemption or EAR exception should consult the relevant provisions and seek professional guidance to determine eligibility and procedures for use.

Strategic Trade Authorization

The EAR 'STA' licence exception was first implemented in 2011, to enable the export, re-export, and transfer (in country) of specified items to destinations that pose relatively low risk. With the transfer of ITAR items to 500 and 600 series, this exception has become a very important vehicle for the transfer of 500 and 600 series items to European countries.

This exception is applicable to:

- Per 740.20(c)(1): Country Group A:5 (thirty-six countries) – commonly referred to as 'STA 36'.
- Per 740.20(c)(2): Country Group A:5 and A:6 (thirty-six + eight countries).

Table 17.9

	Country Group A:5		*Country Group A:6*
Argentina	Germany	Norway	Albania
Australia	Greece	Poland	Hong Kong
Austria	Hungary	Portugal	India
Belgium	Iceland	Romania	Israel
Bulgaria	Ireland	Slovakia	Malta
Canada	Italy	Slovenia	Singapore
Croatia	Japan	South Korea	South Africa
Czech Republic	Latvia	Spain	Taiwan
Denmark	Lithuania	Sweden	
Estonia	Luxembourg	Switzerland	

	Country Group A:5		Country Group A:6
Finland	Netherlands	Turkey	
France	New Zealand	United Kingdom	

Use of the exception is conditioned upon the creation and exchange by the parties to the transaction of notifications and statements designed to provide assurance against diversion of such items to other destinations. The exception is only relevant to exports, re-exports, and transfers for which a licence is required under the EAR. Thus, if the EAR does not impose an obligation to obtain a licence before exporting, re-exporting, or transferring an item subject to the EAR, then STA is not relevant to the transaction.

This exception is particularly relevant in the frame of ECR, as the export, re-export, and transfer of the very large majority of the items transitioning from the ITAR, to the new 600 and 500 series, require an EAR licence for all destinations except Canada.

Conditions for Use of STA:

- The transaction is not impacted by any of the General Prohibitions.
- The item is not controlled for missile technology (MT).
- The item's ECCN designates STA as eligible for the controlled items.
- For non-500 and non-600 series items, consignee is in country group A:5 or A:6.
- For 500 and 600 series items, consignee is in country group A:5, and for 600 series, the ultimate end-user is a government of country group A:5. Both the consignees and ultimate end-user was previously approved to receive the item under a valid US government authorization (i.e., TAA, MLA, WDA, DSP-5 or BIS licence).
- Prior to the export/re-export/transfer the recipient was notified in writing of the items export control classification. (ECCN Notification[1287]).
- Prior to export/re-export/transfer recipient provided a *Prior Consignee Statement*.
- Export documentation stipulates the export/re-export/transfer is conducted pursuant to STA and the appropriate *DCS* is included.

Once a non-US company has signed a Prior Consignee Statement for a given part type, this part type can be supplied under STA for any subsequent delivery.

While for purchasing purposes only one 'paper trail' is necessary, for subsequent re-exports of items subject to STA – as they generally occur in after-sales business or with regard to technology transfers – the number of notifications, signatures, etc. multiplies by the number of consignees and/or partners to be supplied under STA.

1287. The terms ECCN Notification, Prior Consignee Statement and Destination Control Statement are defined in the regulation and wording is provided at http://www.ecfr.gov/cgibin/retrieveECFR?gp=&SID=ec168ba4987b7271f6f3b98780c0bf62&mc=true&n=pt15.2.740&r=PART&ty=HTML#se15.2.740_120.

In order to mitigate the burden of the 'paper trail' of ECCN Notification and subsequent Prior Consignee Statements, both documents can be implemented 'end-to-end' of the industrial chain; i.e., there can be one Prior Consignee Statement, signed by all parties involved, rather than each entity providing individual statements. However, this does not relieve the requirement of getting signatures of all parties involved.

If an item has been received under STA, *De Minimis* cannot be applied until all the conditions of the Prior Consignee Statement are met (including for 600 series, end-use by an A:5 Government), which may require the non-US recipient to segregate the items received under STA from the items received under a BIS licence.

While use of licence exception STA does enable U.S. suppliers to export quickly without applying for a prior U.S. Government authorization, it also shifts traceability and documentation burdens from the U.S. exporter to the non-U.S. re-exporter and generates additional constraints.

Therefore, the decision of whether or not to rely on use of the exception should not be left to a supplier but made pro-actively; either in general or on a case-by-case basis (e.g., only for certain projects). Furthermore, it is recommended that all respective processes and procedures (who is authorized to sign Prior Consignee Statements, what is the impact for logistic and technology flows, etc.) are reviewed carefully to ensure compliance with the EAR prior to authorizing U.S. suppliers or non-U.S. industrial partners to ship under STA.

Even if exception STA is available, it might be simpler from an administrative and compliance point of view, to put in place end-to-end EAR licences, which will identify all the required 'end users'.

Par. 6 Dual and Third Country Nationals – Deemed Export

Transfer of Controlled Information to a non-U.S. person, whether in the U.S. or outside of the U.S. is an export which requires authorization under one form or another. In order to facilitate transfer to employees who may not be of the same nationality as their employers, both the ITAR and the EAR have implemented rules related to the transfer of Controlled Information to these employees.

There are several forms of authorizations available under the ITAR and under the EAR, depending on how the information is controlled, the nationalities of the recipient and the circumstances of the transfers.

Definitions – A U.S. person is an individual who is a U.S. permanent resident alien (commonly called 'green card holder') or a U.S. citizen, or has status of protected persons,[1288] whatever their country of birth, nationality, country of residence or country and location of employment.

1288. ITAR 120.15 definition: *U.S. person* means a person (as defined in §120.14 of this part) who is a lawful permanent resident as defined by 8 U.S.C. 1101(a)(20) or who is a protected individual as defined by 8 U.S.C. 1324b(a)(3). It also means any corporation, business association, partnership, society, trust, or any other entity, organization or group that is incorporated to do business in the United States. It also includes any governmental (federal, state or local) entity. It does not include any foreign person as defined in §120.16 of this part.

A TCN is an employee who holds a nationality from a country other than the country of incorporation of his/her employer. In the U.S., the term used to designate a person who is not a U.S. person is Foreign National.

A Dual National (DN) is an employee who holds dual nationalities, one of them being the country of incorporation of its employer, and also holds nationality from one or more additional countries. For export control purpose, a U.S. person is not considered a DN of the US and of another county as U.S. person status will trump for export control purposes, even if they hold dual citizenship of the U.S. and another country.

Requirements – Release or transfer of Controlled Technology to a non-US person is informally referred to as a deemed export or deemed re-export. Release of controlled technology to non-US persons are 'deemed' to be an export/ re-export to the person's country or countries of nationality and needs to be authorized as such.

As a result of the harmonization effort within the ECR, on 1 November 2013, BIS published guidance related to deemed exports of EAR controlled technology to Dual and Third Country Nationals employed by non-US entities, which are similar and reference those previously implemented by DDTC under the ITAR, while maintaining its legacy definition of 'nationality' as being the most recent country of citizenship or the country of permanent residence[1289]

When assessing nationality, the ITAR takes into consideration the country of birth and all countries of citizenship which means individuals can be a dual or third country national while these same individuals may not be dual or third country national under the EAR.

Persons Employed by US Companies – Any transfer or release (including inadvertent access) of US Controlled Information to a non-U.S. person employed by a U.S. company needs to be authorized, and, if there is a licence requirement, a licence obtained from DDTC or BIS:

- Under the ITAR, employment DSP-5.
- Under the EAR, deemed export technology licence (if the information is controlled for the country of nationality of the employee).

Dual and Third Country Nationals Employed by non-U.S. Companies – The following provisions of the ITAR related to Dual and Third country nationals have also been adopted by BIS, with the exception of the definition of nationalities, for which BIS has kept its legacy definition:

(1) 22 CFR 124.8(5) authorizes transfer of controlled classified and unclassified information to all nationalities specifically approved by country in the Agreement (TAA or MLA). Employees authorized under 22 CFR 124.8(5) must sign a Non-disclosure Agreement (NDA).

1289. See BIS guidance on retransfer to dual and third country nationals at: http://www.bis.doc.gov/index.php/policy-guidance/deemed-exports/deemed-reexport-guidance1.

(2) 22 CFR 124.16 authorizes the transfer of Controlled Unclassified Information (CUI) to nationals of EU member countries, NATO member countries, Australia, Japan, New Zealand and Switzerland. The Agreement must specify the use of this provision and employees authorized under 22 CFR 124.16 do not need to execute an NDA. 22 CFR 124.16 applies only to 'bona fide employees', directly employed by the parties (to include end-user signatories or the authorized sub-licensees). All transfers must take place within the 22 CFR 124.16 territory.

(3) 22 CFR 126.18 is an exemption taken by the non-US company and it authorizes transfers of CUI to certain dual and third country national employees. (Note that 22 CFR 126.18 does not cover Classified Information, for which authorization has to be obtained through 22 CFR 124.8.5).

The requirements of 22 CFR 126.18 can be met through two processes:

- Under 22 CFR 126.18(c)(1) by the employee holding a national security clearance, i.e., a security clearance of the employer's country. Employees authorized under 22 CFR 126.18(c)(1) do not need to sign an NDA.
- Under 22 CFR 126.18(c)(2) by the implementation of an internal vetting process of the non-US employer, i.e., the individual is screened by the employer against substantive contacts with embargoed destinations of 22 CFR 126.1 (EAR Country Group D:5) and a NDA is executed.

(As this process may not be compatible with European Privacy laws, it is recommended to consider any national issues prior to implementing internal vetting process.)

Several countries (Canada, Australia, United Kingdom, the Netherlands,[1290]...) have entered into agreements or exchange of letters with the US Government, per which the employment screening performed by this country is considered as meeting the requirements of ITAR 126.18. BIS has referenced the same Government-to-Government agreements in terms of acceptable national screening for transfers of EAR controlled technology to non-U.S. nationals.

Contract Labour and Consultants are eligible for the same treatment, provided that, as per the requirement related to contract labour, the employer has certified that each employee is individually aware of their responsibility with regard to proper handling of ITAR controlled defence articles, technical data and defence services. Retransfer to the parent company is not authorized.

The table 17.10 is a high level summary of the applicability and of the NDA requirements under both the ITAR and EAR:

1290. France and New Zealand are in process.

Table 17.10 Dual and Third Country Nationals Regulations and NDA Requirements

	124.8(5) (nationalities approved by the US Government)	124.16 (EU, NATO, Australia, Japan, New Zealand and Switzerland)	126.18(c)(1) (National clearance)	126.18(c)(2) (self-vetting)
Applicability	Applicable only if language included in the TAA / MLA / BIS licence and nationality listed	For ITAR, Applicable only if language included in the TAA or MLA	Applicable by law	Applicable by law
Unclassified Information	NDA to be returned to the US applicant	No NDA	No NDA	NDA on file
Classified Information	Applicable only to the nationalities approved under the TAA or MLA; NDA to be returned to the US applicant	Not Applicable	Not Applicable	Not Applicable

Implementation Recommendations – Due to the difference of guidance between the ITAR and the EAR as it relates to the definition of 'nationality', a given employee could be authorized to have access to EAR Controlled Information without vetting under her / his 'nationality', while requiring authorization through 22 CFR 126.18 or other vehicle under the ITAR because of her / his place of birth.

In some countries (Europe in particular), self-vetting by the employer under 22 CFR 126.18(c)(2) may be conflicting with national employment and privacy laws, in which case the employer can either rely on 22 CFR 124.16, 22 CFR 126.18(c)(1) or require positive authorization under 22 CFR 124.8(5).

Note that 22 CFR 124.16 is not an exemption, and thus needs to be positively identified in the TAA or MLA to be applicable.

Note also that a 22 CFR 126.1(a) national not covered by 22 CFR 126.18(c)(1), needs to be approved individually (since the nationality cannot be approved per 22 CFR 126.18(c)(2)). For the purpose of this approval, information must be provided to the US Government under the format of a General Correspondence addressed to DDTC Policy, including resume, education, job description, residence and nature and details of the links to the country of origin.

Par. 7 Contract Labour

It is very common in the industry to hire through staffing agencies or specialized service providers. Specific rules apply in this case.

This paragraph only addresses the implications of the U.S. export control regulations and does not address host nation legal or employment laws which may vary from one country to another. The terms 'Regular Employee' and 'Contract

Employee' or 'Contract Labor' used in this paragraph are as defined in the ITAR, DDTC Agreement Guidelines and BIS Advisory Opinion.

As there might be labour law and regulation impact in addition to (and sometimes in contradiction with) the U.S. regulations, it is good practice to consult with Human Resources, Contracts or Legal specialists to ensure that there is no conflict with national laws.

An individual in a contractual relationship with a Company, or seconded by a third party (i.e., staffing agency, or technician from an IT provider) may be considered as a 'Regular Employee' under the definition of the ITAR at 22 CFR 120.39 and be eligible to access EAR controlled technology or ITAR controlled technical data under the US export authorizations of the Company. In such cases there would be no need to obtain authorization for the individual's specific employing company.

Per 22 CFR 120.39 of the ITAR, Companies may consider and treat individual 'Contract Employee(s)' as their own 'Regular Employee(s)' for the purpose of handling ITAR controlled technical data and information provided that:

- There is a long-term relationship and the individual works full time, exclusively and on site at a Company facility.
- The individual takes direction from the Company (either direct management or through definition of task).[1291]
- The individual has been trained and certified by the Company as being considered as 'Contract Employee'.
- If the individual is seconded from a staffing agency/personnel provider,[1292] the individual does not share any US-controlled information with the staffing agency/personnel provider and the staffing agency/ personnel provider is not in the business of providing Defence Services in the same area of expertise independent of the contract entered into by the Company.

Common examples of 'Contract Employee(s)':

- An Engineer / Project Manager / Commercial Officer seconded by a staffing agency.
- IT support personnel of a third party working at the Company under Company direction.

Once an individual has been certified as 'Contract Employee', all the obligation applicable to 'Regular Employees' apply, including assessing nationality and national clearance for eligibility under 22 CFR 124.16 and 126.18 or 124.8 5) as applicable by the authorizations that govern the related US-controlled information.

1291. The Definition of task can be a statement of work agreed upon with the Labour Provider.

1292. We are using both terms 'staffing agency' and 'personnel provider' to reflect the practice that providers of personnel with specific expertise, such as engineering or IT, often do not qualify themselves as 'staffing agencies', but as 'service providers'.

For US-origin controlled information governed by an ITAR DSP-5, no specific language is required, but TAAs and MLAs *must* contain the following paragraph:

> *Contract employees to any party to the agreement hired through a staffing agency or other contract employee provider shall be treated as employees of the party, and that party is legally responsible for the employees' actions with regard to transfer of ITAR controlled Defense Articles to include technical data, and defense services. Transfers to the parent company by any contract employees are not authorized. The party is further responsible for certifying that each employee is individually aware of their responsibility with regard to the proper handling of ITAR controlled defense articles, technical data, and defense services.*

EAR: Concerning the transfer of technology controlled under the EAR, including 500 and 600 series, there is no requirement to include specific wording.

In order to utilize the concept of 'Contract Employees' as described above, it is mandatory to meet and document the requirements of 22 CFR 120.39 as well as the conditions defined in the DDTC Agreement Guidelines[1293] related to issuing a certification.

In addition to the certification which is required by US Government, it is also recommended to have the Contract Employee sign an NDA.

This may either be done by:

(1) Obtaining signature on an individual certification letter and individual NDA.
(2) Modifying existing agreements or certifications accordingly (such as non-disclosure statements that need to be signed by 'Contract Employees' for being granted access on site).
(3) Other processes and procedures (internal guidelines, contractual obligations, etc.).

1293. DDTC Agreement Guidelines, Section 3.9 (b)Foreign Company Contract Employees:

(1) When a foreign company (foreign licensee/foreign sublicensee) hires contract employees, including Information Technology (IT) support personnel, through foreign staffing agencies or other contract employee providers, there is no requirement for the foreign staffing agency or other contract employee provider to be identified as signatories or sub-licensees to the agreement, so long as:
   (a) The transfer of defence articles to include technical data and the provision of defence services are limited only to the specific contract employees and NOT to the staffing agency or contract employee provider itself. Transfer/retransfer of defence articles to include technical data to the parent staffing agency or contract employee provider, either directly from the parties to the agreement, or indirectly from the contract employees, IS NOT authorized.
   (b) The foreign staffing agency or contract employee provider is not in the business of providing defence services independently of the contract entered into as related to the specific agreement.
   (c) The employing party (foreign licensee/foreign sublicensee) assumes full responsibility for the employees' actions with regard to transfer of ITAR controlled defense articles to include technical data, and defense services.

Par. 8 Re-Export

A re-export (to another country) or retransfer (within the same country) is the transfer by a non-US person to another non-US person not previously authorized or a change of end-use of controlled items in the form of Technical data, Hardware or Software, including Derived Data.[1294]

Derived Data is technical data developed by a non-US person and which includes US-origin Controlled Information, whether in its original form or resulting from US-origin Controlled Information. Derived Data must be handled and controlled in the same manner than the original US-origin data.

In multiple circumstances, a non-US entity will be in the possession of a US-origin controlled item (ITAR or EAR) and will have a need to use the item outside of its original US Government authorization. This will generate a situation where the non-US entity will have to engage into a re-export and determine whether a new authorization is needed and obtain such authorization.

The first step in determining how to re-export / retransfer is to identify the US controls of the original item (ITAR or BIS licence or exemption/ exception) and to determine the proper classification of the item and the jurisdiction of the new transaction.

If the item to be retransferred or re-exported has transitioned to the EAR, during the ECR transition period (i.e., two years from the change of classification having become effective) the parties can chose to conduct the re-transfer / re-export either under the previous jurisdiction (but in this case the prior ITAR authorization cannot be modified) or to reclassify and conduct the retransfer/ re-export under the EAR.

If the new transaction is subject to the ITAR:

- if the controls are a valid Agreement, then the Agreement needs to be amended to reflect the new transaction (additional end-use / end-users/ sub-licensees). Amendment to an Agreement can only be obtained by the original US applicant.
- if the controls are a DSP-5 which is not in furtherance of an Agreement, then authorization can be obtained by a General Correspondence (GC) applied for either by the original US applicant or a non-US party.

General Correspondence – A General Correspondence (GC) is the process per which a US or non-US entity requests authorization from DDTC to do a re-export or retransfer (temporary or permanent change of end-use, end-user, or additional of consignees) for items subject to the ITAR (and for which the licence was not in furtherance of a valid TAA or MLA).

1294. Derived Data is technical data developed by a foreign person and which includes US-origin Controlled information, whether in its original form or resulting from US-origin Controlled information. Derived Data must be handled and controlled in the same manner than the original US-origin data.

This request takes the form of a letter addressed to DDTC and which must contain the same information as would be required in a licence application, i.e.:[1295]

- Name and full address of the applicant.
- Description and value of the articles to be retransferred (including prior authorizations).
- End-use/ end-users and consignees, with descriptions (description of the end-use/ end-user and role of the consignees).
- 22 CFR 126.13 certification.[1296]
- If applicable, Part 130 statement.[1297]

The letter must include a Point of Contact designated to respond to questions from the US Government and include their contact information. Non-US entities may designate a US Point of contact (such as law firm or US branch or affiliate).

The GC is sent by the applicant to DDTC. Upon receiving the request, DDTC will assign a 'GC number' which enables the applicant to track the status of the request. Non-US companies do not need to be registered with DDTC to apply for a GC.

In a similar way to a DSP-5, a GC will be staffed to various agencies, depending on the nature of the request. If the request is adjudicated favourably, DDTC will issue an approval letter outlining any provisos (i.e., limitations). DDTC will not restate the scope of the request, but will attach to the approval part of the request which represent the scope approved.

Note that if a hardware DSP-5 has been issued in furtherance of a TAA or MLA, and if the TAA or MLA is still active, this TAA/MLA is the re-export/retransfer authority for the hardware. Therefore, if additional consignees or a change of end-use need to be authorized, the TAA or MLA will have to be amended (in lieu of a GC).

BIS Re-Export Licences – If the re-export is subject to the EAR, the re-exporter will have to conduct an analysis of whether a licence is required for the transaction considered.

If a licence is required, the re-exporter can then determine whether an EAR exception is available and either use this exception, or request a BIS re-export licence.

A BIS re-export licence is requested by a U.S. or non-U.S. applicant through SNAP-R.[1298] In order to open a SNAP-R account, the company must first apply for a Company Identification Number (CIN) and designate one or several users and their level of authority (view, review, edit, submit or administrator). There is no fee associated with obtaining a CIN.

Once the CIN is obtained and the user authorized on the account, the user will apply for a BIS re-export licence, selecting 're-export' at the type of the application.

1295. 22 CFR 123.9(c).
1296. See DDTC guidance requiring 126.13 certification for General Correspondence at http://www.pmddtc.state.gov/licensing/guidelines_instructions.html.
1297. A statement of compliance to ITAR Part 130 must be made for any transaction over USD 500,000 for end-use by armed forces or an international organization.
1298. See https://snapr.bis.doc.gov/snapr/docs/snaprFAQ.htm for tutorial on SNAPR.

Application for a BIS re-export licence requires the same information than for a BIS export licence, i.e.:

- Part number, ECCN, technical description, quantities and values of each item to be re-exported or retransferred.
- Name and address of each end-user.
- Description of the end-use.
- Supporting technical documentation.
- If the re-export is related to Technology, a letter of explanation (LoE) identifying the scope and nature of the technology, in addition to explanation addressing the five 'W's' (Why, What, Where, Who, When).

For BIS re-export licence requests, similar to BIS licence requests, any questions from the US Government will be communicated to the applicant through the SNAP-R account.

Destruction of Controlled Items – If a controlled item is governed under the ITAR by a DSP-5 or Agreement or by an exemption or under the EAR by a BIS licence or an exception, the terms of these authorizations must be abided by. If the authorization specifies a given end-use and end-user, and destruction or disposition is not in line with the authorized end-use or end-user, then an authorization from the US government may be required (through a GC under the ITAR or a BIS re-export licence under the EAR, or an EAR licence exception if available).

In some cases, the destruction or disposition will be a change of authorized end-use, and may also be a change of authorized end-user.

Note that if the authorization covers normal 'manufacturing and testing attritions', no additional authorization would be required, but the 'disposition or destruction' and the method of disposition or destruction should be documented (to include how, who, what and where).[1299]

If the articles to be destroyed are eligible to be reclassified as a result of ECR, the articles should be first reclassified, and if the article is under the jurisdiction of the EAR, then an analysis should be conducted as to whether a BIS licence is required. If a BIS licence is not required for the export to the entity/country in which the disposition or destruction takes place, a BIS re-export licence will not be necessary.

In the specific case where the parts have been previously received under exemption STA, particular attention should be paid to the conditions of the Prior Consignee Statement.

In all cases, the destruction or disposition should be documented, to include quantities and method of destruction or disposition, including documentation that the method of destruction or disposition effectively prevents any further transfer of controlled technology to unauthorized third parties. If required (by the US supplier or the provisos of the licences), written notification to the original manufacturer should be made regarding the destruction or disposition.

1299. Unless there is a specific proviso in the original licence, there is no obligation to notify the original exporter, but this may be done by courtesy.

Par. 9 De Minimis

Under the EAR (and only under the EAR), re-export of a non-US/ made item that has less than '*De Minimis*' content is not subject to the EAR.

De Minimis is a calculation to determine if the percentage of the value of US-origin controlled items compared to the non-US[1300] product's fair market value is low enough to deem the US-origin controlled content as no longer 'Subject to the EAR'. US-Origin Controlled Content is defined as, any US-origin items that require a licence to the ultimate destination of the non-US product. This includes EAR99 items when the end-item is destined to Cuba, North Korea and Syria.

De Minimis may not be applied to any item, technical data or service which is controlled under the ITAR.

Concepts – 'Subject to the EAR' is a term used in the EAR to describe those items and activities over which the U.S. exercises regulatory jurisdiction under the EAR:

- Non-US-made items that do not exceed a '*De Minimis*' amount of US-controlled content are not subject to the EAR.[1301]
- *De Minimis* is based on the financial ratio of the value of the US-controlled content to the total 'fair market value' of the non-US item.[1302]
- *De Minimis* can only be applied to a re-export or re-transfer, it cannot be used for export from the US, even for the export of non-US-origin goods.
- Items received under a BIS licence can be eligible for *De Minimis*.
- Items received under STA may only be eligible for *De Minimis* after all the conditions of the Prior Consignee Statement have been met. For 600 series, after the item has been transferred to the final government end-user, or for 500 series after the item has been transferred to an A:5 country 'end user' (such as the satellite integrator).
- Use of *De Minimis* for the re-export of 500 or 600 series items to D:5 countries is prohibited.
- If a non-US-made item contains US-controlled content that exceeds the '*De Minimis*' threshold, then the end-item is 'subject to the EAR' and the re-export must be conducted in compliance with the EAR, through the use of a specific BIS licence, use of a licence exception, or as NLR (No Licence Required).
- ITAR items embedded into a non-US item are not eligible for *De Minimis* and have to be re-exported or retransferred in accordance with the ITAR. This does not prevent the use of *De Minimis*, if applicable, for the EAR content of the same non-US item.

1300. The EAR uses the term 'foreign' to designate 'non-US'.

1301. Note, once an assembly has been determined as '*not subject to the EAR*' as a result of *De Minimis*, the transaction does not need to be tested against the general prohibitions defined in Part 744.

1302. That is, all items that would require a licence for export as loose items to the country of destination; this may include EAR 99 for Cuba, North Korea and Syria.

De Minimis Levels - There are different levels of *De Minimis* depending on the country of destination of the foreign made item as well as the ECCN, of the incorporated US origin items. The following table 17.11 delineates the varying *De Minimis* percentages by ECCN and country:

Table 17.11 De Minimis Levels

	500 Series (a - x)	*600.a -.x Series*	*500 & 600.y Series*	*All Other ECCNs*
Cuba	0%	0%	0%	25% (includes EAR99)
Iran	0%	0%	0%	10%
North Korea	0%	0%	0%	10% (includes EAR99)
Sudan	0%	0%	0%	10%
Syria	0%	0%	0%	10% (includes EAR99)
China (PRC)	0%	0%	0%	25%
Country Group D5	0%	0%	25%	25%
All Other Countries	25%	25%	25%	25%

Note that there is no *De Minimis* level for non-US made items incorporating certain computers, encryption items, military aircraft embedding QRS11, etc.[1303]

Country Group D:5: Afghanistan, Belarus, Burma, China, Congo, Cote d'Ivoire, Cuba, Cyprus, Eritrea, Fiji, Haiti, Iran, Iraq, North Korea, Lebanon, Liberia, Libya, Somalia, Sri Lanka, Sudan, Syria, Venezuela, Vietnam, Zimbabwe.

De Minimis *Calculation Method* - Include all EAR US-origin items that would require a licence if exported as loose parts to the country of destination (per the Commerce Country Chart) unless they qualify for licence exception GBS:[1304]

- Compare separately hardware with hardware, software with software and technology with technology.[1305]
- The regulation requires that the total value be 'fair market price' (purchase price without deductions, selling price without customs, taxes and freight forwarding expenses).

1303. See 734.4 and in particular (a) (1): no *De Minimis* for certain computers exceeding 8 WT to computer Tier three countries, or exceeding 0.002WT for Cuba, Iran, North Korea, Sudan, and Syria. (a) (2) no *De Minimis* for encryption (5D002); (a) (3) no *De Minimis* for QSR11; (a) (6) no *De Minimis* for 500 and 600 series, except for ".y" items for D5 countries, no *De Minimis* for 500 and 600 series ".y" items for E:1 countries.

1304. In order to determine the *De Minimis* level, there is no regulatory requirement to consider whether the recipient is subject to an EAR sanctioned party list. However, this may determine the political consideration of such business.

1305. Each of the *De Minimis* calculations (i.e., for Hardware, Software and Technology) should be below the prescribed '*De Minimis*' level.

- If there is no documented 'fair market' value, for example when the sales price is based on customer negotiations or is specific to a programme, value should be documented conservatively, for instance manufacturing cost without non-recurring nor profit.

$$\frac{\textbf{Fair market value of U.S. controlled content}}{\textbf{Fair market value of foreign end item}} \textbf{ X 100} = \textbf{U.S. content value in \%}$$

If certain EAR items cannot benefit from the *De Minimis* (for instance 500 and 600 series items destined to a D:5 country), then obtain re-export authorization for those items that cannot benefit from *De Minimis*, and assess *De Minimis* for the other ECCN items that can benefit from *De Minimis*.[1306]

Documentation Requirements – All *De Minimis* calculations should be recorded and stored for a minimum of five years after the re-export. *De Minimis* method and calculations can be subject to audit by the US Government.

If the *De Minimis* calculation includes commingled Software or Technology, the use of *De Minimis* requires a prior one-time report to BIS including calculation method.[1307] Calculation documentation should include:

- The rational of the calculation (licensing requirements for the destination).
- Classification of the items included, quantity and value of each item included in the calculation.
- Value of the assembly and justification of the value.
- Calculation of the ratio.

DCS – There is no US legal regulatory requirement to include a DCS for non-US end-items which include *De Minimis* 500 and 600 series. However to ensure that the D:5 country prohibition is addressed, it is recommended to include the following DCS:

'This item contains De Minimis EAR 500/ 600 series content and may not be resold, diverted, transferred or otherwise disposed contrary to U.S. law.'

If the *De Minimis* level is exceeded, then the licensing requirement needs to be analysed for each item based on its ECCN, the sub-category of this ECCN and the country of destination.

If a licence is required for the export/re-export to the final destination, a BIS re-export licence should be requested. This BIS re-export licence should be limited to the items for which there is a licensing requirement. If a licence exception is available for some or all of the items, then the exception can be used provided that it is

1306. If some items benefit from exemption GBS, their value does not need to be included in the numerator. In this case, the value of the numerator is the value of those ECCN items that would require a licence if loose, but do not benefit from GBS, plus the value of those 500 and 600 series items that are subject to a re-export licence.
1307. For further details refer to EAR 734, Supplement No. 2 (b) (1).

documented that the transaction meets all the conditions required for the use of the exception. In some cases, it might be easier to require a BIS re-export licence.

Par. 10 Licensing Authorities

Each administration has full authority to deliver licences: Most licence applications are done through electronic transactions. This paragraph summarizes the licensing authorities.

As part of the process of examining and making a decision on a licence application, the agency in charge will 'staff' the request for advice and review to several other relevant agencies. One agency almost always involved in these reviews is DoD, Defense Technology Security Administration (DTSA) who conducts DoD technical and policy reviews.

In addition to DTSA, applications can be staffed as needed to other agencies or departments such as: DoS country, regional or policy desks; Navy, Air Force or Army international and cooperation offices; DoE for MTCR and Nuclear non-proliferation reviews, National Aeronautical and Space Administration (NASA) for Space, etc.

DTRADE is the electronic application system of DoS, DDTC, and SNAP-R is the electronic system of DoC, BIS.

DTRADE can only be used by US companies and requires a fee-based registration. SNAP-R can be used by US and non-US companies and is free of charge, but requires each legal entity to obtain a CIN delivered by BIS.

Table 17.12 Type and Validity of U.S. Export Licences

Agency	*Name of Authorization*	*Application Vehicle*	*Validity*
DDTC	Technical Assistance Agreement / Manufacturing Licensing Agreement / Warehouse and Distribution Agreement	DSP-5 under DTRADE	Usually ten years, unless shortened due to ECR
DDTC	Permanent Export Licence	DSP-5 under DTRADE	Four years
DDTC	Temporary Import Licence	DSP-61 under DTRADE	Four years
DDTC	Temporary Export Licence	DSP-73 under DTRADE	Four years
DDTC	Re-export Licence	General Correspondence	N/A
DDTC	Advisory Opinion and Proviso Reconsiderations	General Correspondence	N/A
DDTC	Commodity Jurisdiction	CJ through EFS	N/A
BIS	Export licence	748 under SNAP-R	Four years
BIS	Re-export licence	748 under SNAP-R	Four years

Agency	*Name of Authorization*	*Application Vehicle*	*Validity*
BIS	Classification Request (CCATS)	748 under SNAP-R	N/A
Treasury	OFAC Licence	OFAC Web Site	As Approved, usually less than two years
Justice	ATF Licence	ATF Web Site (Form 6)	As Approved

Par. 11 Enforcement Authorities

Enforcement of the US export control system is undertaken by the agencies responsible for export licensing (DDTC or BIS) and also by the DHS, the DoJ (National Security Division and the Federal Bureau of Investigation (FBI)), and the Defense Criminal Investigative Service (DCIS):

Though these enforcement agencies each have their own attributes, as a result of ECR and of the creation in 2010 of the EECC, these enforcement entities overlap and cooperate:

- *OEE*, at the BIS. OEE investigates criminal and administrative violations of the dual-use export control regime. OEE is authorized to conduct domestic investigations and works with HSI (formerly Immigration and Customs Enforcement Agency) (HIS-ICE) of DHS on investigations of export control violations overseas. OEE refers civil violations to the Office of Chief Counsel at BIS and criminal violations to DoJ.
- *Office of Defense Trade Controls Compliance (DTCC)*, at the DDTC. DTCC primarily administers civil enforcement actions, including charging letters and consent agreements, policies of denial, debarments, transaction exceptions, and reinstatements. DTCC provides agency support to investigations and criminal enforcement actions primarily conducted by ICE and the FBI.
- *Office of Enforcement, NRC*, investigates export control violations of nuclear facilities and material licensed by the NRC's Office of International Programmes. The Office of Enforcement refers criminal violations to DoJ.
- *HSI (HSS- ICE)*, part of DHS. As with its predecessor at the US Customs Service, ICE has been the lead agency for criminal export enforcement activities. The Counter-Proliferation Investigations (CPI) Unit investigates violations of dual-use and munitions export controls, exports to sanctioned countries, and violations of economic embargoes. ICE supplements and provides enforcement capacity to the export licensing agencies (BIS and DDTC) and undertakes investigations based on its own and other agency intelligence. In addition, export controls are enforced at the port of departure by DHS Customs and Border Protection.

- *National Security Division of DoJ.* The counter-espionage section of this division undertakes criminal prosecutions resulting from investigations conducted by the licensing agencies, ICE, and the FBI. An October 2007 DoJ National Export Enforcement Initiative established task forces between the licensing and enforcement agencies and US Attorney's Offices in twenty cities to coordinate export control prosecutions and has facilitated new counter-proliferation coordination among law enforcement agencies, export licensing agencies, and the intelligence community.
- *FBI.* The FBI's WMD Directorate receives and analyses intelligence regarding proliferation networks, provides specialized training on counter-proliferation for the National Export Enforcement Initiative, and cooperates with above-mentioned investigative partners and export licensing agencies.
- *DCIS.* DCIS is the criminal investigative arm of the Inspector General of DoD. Among its varied activities, DCIS investigates the transfer of sensitive defence technologies to proscribed nations and criminal elements.

Par. 12 Sanctions and the Recourses of the Importer/Exporter

Failure to comply with the US Export Control laws and regulations can lead to civil and criminal charges.

Both BIS and DDTC encourage the US exporters and the non-US re-exporters to implement sturdy compliance programmes and to voluntarily disclose non-compliances. Both regulators have compliance guidelines for US and non-US companies to use when developing their compliance programmes.

The processes and requirements are similar for Voluntary Disclosures (DDTC) and Voluntary Self Disclosures (BIS). In both cases, an Initial Notification can be submitted to notify the agency of a potential issue while the company completes its internal investigation and drafts its final disclosure. Unless otherwise stated, DDTC provides sixty days to file a complete disclosure (with the possibility of extension, if requested), while BIS provides by regulation 180 days.

Failure to voluntarily disclose may lead to a 'directed disclosure' with a much higher probability of penalties.[1308]

DDTC may determine that a company has not put into place actions to mitigate further violations and it could be determined that a 'Consent Agreement' is in order. When DDTC settles under a 'Consent Agreement', the Company agrees to spend part of the fine in mitigation and remedial measures and to be monitored for a period of usually three to four years, by an outside monitor appointed in concurrence with the U.S. Government.[1309]

1308. One can read with interest the criminal charges brought by BIS and DDTC at: http://www.pmddtc.state.gov/compliance/documents/OngoingExportCaseFactSheet.pdf.
1309. See the most recent charging letters and consent agreements at: http://www.pmddtc.state.gov/compliance/consent_agreements.html.

If BIS determines that a Company has not put in place actions and polices to mitigate further violations, it will generally impose fines and/or debarment which are determined when BIS levies administrative and or criminal charges against a Company.

In conclusion, while most cases disclosed voluntarily will close without penalties; repetitive violations, without fulsome and measureable corrective actions, may lead to administrative and criminal charges. This type of procedure applies at both US and non-US companies with some changes in nomenclature to determine charges.

SECTION 5 SPECIFICITIES/SPACE-RELATED PROVISIONS

The US and Europe have traditionally handled Space technologies differently, the US as military items and Europe as dual-use. With ECR, the control regimes are now similar, this paragraph identified the specificities and the history of the US controls of Space technologies.

Sub-Section 1 Specificities of the Space Control Regime

From the very beginning of the Space era, the US has historically treated satellites, including commercial communication satellites and launch vehicles (i.e., rockets) as munitions or defence items and has controlled those items accordingly. The US has specific space-related provisions in both the EAR and, in the ITAR. However, European countries have treated commercial communication satellites as dual-use items and commercial communications satellites were treated as civil items on the Coordinating Committee for Multilateral Export (COCOM) industrial list.

The issue of whether communications satellites should be regarded as military items or dual-use items has been addressed back and forth several times, and took on a new importance as China developed into a major supplier of launch services on the international market. Implementing a satisfying solution to prevent the export of US Space technologies to China was one of the political conditions of the recent ECR.

In 1990, President George H.W. Bush ordered the removal of certain items, including commercial communications satellites, from the USML and transferred those items to the CCL (i.e., transferred jurisdiction from DoS to DoC).[1310] That decision was not implemented until 1996 when President Clinton transferred all commercial communications satellites to the CCL and implementing regulations were published by DoS and DoC.[1311]

In the late 1990s, there were a series of launch failures involving US satellites that were being launched by Chinese launch vehicles. In the subsequent launch failure investigations, a number of unauthorized transfers of technical data related to both satellites and launch vehicles occurred. An investigation and subsequent report ('Cox

1310. *Memorandum of Disapproval for the Omnibus Export Amendments Act of 1990 (H.R. 4653), November 16, 1990*, 26 Weekly Comp. Pres. Doc 1839.

1311. 'Removal of Commercial Communications satellites and Hot Section Technology from State's USML for Transfer to Commerce's CCL,' 61 F.R. 215 (5 Nov. 1996).

Report') by a Select Committee of the House of Representatives detailed those transfers and highlighted national security concerns about the licensing of satellite exports by DoC instead of DoS.[1312]

As a result of the Cox Report, Congress passed *The Fiscal Year 1999 National Defence Authorization Act* (Strom Thurmond Act)[1313] that transferred all satellites and related items back from the CCL to the USML; i.e., transferred licensing jurisdiction from BIS back to DDTC. The effect of this transfer was that exports of all US-origin satellites and all foreign-manufactured satellites containing USML parts or components were prohibited to any country that was subject to a US arms embargo. Because China was subjected to such an embargo, all exports to China for either use in China or launch from China of US-origin technologies were prohibited.

The Strom Thurmond Act also tightened the requirements for any 'national interest' determination by the President to allow an exemption for exports of satellites for launch from China. These requirements resulted in a total embargo of export of satellites and satellite parts to China because of the near impossibility of obtaining the necessary national interest determination.

In 2009, the White House ordered a wide review of the Export Control Regulations (the ECR Initiative) to overhaul the US export control system. As a result of the Strom Thurmond Act, Cat XV was the only category of the ITAR that could only be changed with the consent of the US Congress. Section 1248 of the NDAA of Fiscal Year 2010 (Public Law 111-84) provided that the Secretaries of Defence and State carry out an assessment of the risks associated with removing satellites and related components from the USML. The initial report was due in April 2010, but was only published on 18 April 2012[1314] (late by two years, which demonstrates how difficult it had been to reach a consensus).

The report concluded that most communication and lower performing remote sensing satellites and related components could be moved from the USML to the CCL without harm to national security, and that this change would facilitate cooperation with US allies and export control regime partners, strengthen the competitiveness of sectors key to US national security, and increase US exports – while maintaining robust controls where needed to enhance US national security.

The report recommended that Congress return to the President authority to determine the export control jurisdictional status of satellites and related items. It further recommended that DoD be provided authority to apply appropriate monitoring and other export control measures to individual cases, in order to most effectively reduce risks to national security.

In order to prevent transfer of dual-use satellites and related items to China, including for the purpose of launch, the report recommended that CCL licensing

1312. *U.S. National Security and Military/Commercial Concerns with the Peoples Republic of China* (also known as the 'Cox Report'), Select Committee, United States House of Representatives (1999).
1313. *FY 1999 National Defense Authorization Act*, P.L. 105-261, 112 Stat 2174 (1999).
1314. http://www.defense.gov/home/features/2011/0111_nsss/docs/1248_Report_Space_Export_Control.pdf.

policies prohibit transfers to any embargoed country. This was implemented in many ways throughout the CCL, in particular by imposing a 'zero' *De Minimis* level for 500 and 600 series for D:5 countries.

Once Congress was satisfied that all the national security issues had been addressed, the draft rules were issued in May 2014, for applicability in June 2014 for the integrated circuits and October 2014 for the rest of the of the Space items. The 'rush' on the integrated circuits resulted from pressures from the microelectronics industry, who were concerned to see more and more dual-use radiation tolerant integrated circuits captured inadvertently under the ITAR.

The new regulation greatly facilitates the interaction between non-U.S. industry and U.S. customers and US suppliers and also facilitates the handling of items which are being transferred to the EAR and which for most benefit from the exception STA countries (STA 36).

Nevertheless, the implementation of these new regulations is putting an increased documentation and compliance burden on the non-US industry. The non-US industry, and in particular the European industry, needs to become familiar with the complexity of the Commerce regulations as well as being responsible for reclassifying stocks previously received under the ITAR, implementing end-to-end controls and processes required for the use of Commerce exceptions and of *De Minimis* and eventually seek BIS re-export authorizations.

Sub-Section 2 Space-Related Provisions in the Control Regime

As a result of the ECR, the rules applicable to Space have lost their 'Space' specificities.

Just as any other military goods, the most sensitive space items are positively listed in the USML (launchers in Cat IV, propellant in Cat V and satellites in Cat XV), while less sensitive items are controlled under the EAR.

Telecom, scientific and medium-resolution optical satellites have been transferred to the EAR and there is no wide-open 'modified for Space applications' catch-all clause under the ITAR anymore. A very large majority of the parts, components, equipment and services procured by non-US customers from the US have moved to the EAR. (Refer to Table 17.13 - Space ECR).

Only those satellites which are positively defined by their sensitive performance and functionality, and not by the type of application (military, civil or commercial), are still regulated by the ITAR. The parts and components that stay under the ITAR are also positively listed and characterized by their performance.

In order to satisfy the Space-proliferation concerns related to China, the ECR has imposed on 500 series the same restrictions that on 600 series, i.e., 500 series parts are not eligible for *De Minimis* for re-export to a D:5 Country, including for the purpose of launch.

Table 17.13 Space ECR

Item Classification 1	*Controls and Licence Requirements of Item MIN*	*Classification Associated Technology*	*Controls and Licence Requirements of Technology*	*Sta [1] Available Item*	*Sta [1] Available Technology*
9A515.a (satellites)	RS1 and AT1 - licence required for all countries except Canada	9E515.2	NS1, RS1 and AT1 - licence required for all countries except Canada	Yes	Yes
9A515.b (ground control segment)	RS1 and AT1 - licence required for all countries except Canada			Yes	
9A515.e (microcircuits rad tolerant)	RS2 and AT1 - licence required only for countries controlled under RS2 - STA not available	9E515.e	NS1, RS1 and All - licence required for all countries except Canada	N/A	No
9A515.d (microcircuits rad hard)	RS1 and AT1 - licence required for all countries except Canada	9E515.d	NS1, RS1 and All- licence required for all countries except Canada	Yes	No
9A515.x (specially designed items except a, d, e)	RS1 and All - licence required for all countries except Canada	9E515.a	NS1, RS1 and All - licence required for all countries except Canada	Yes	Yes
9A515.y (specially designed items, lower control by CCATS)	AT1 - no licence required for most countries	9E515.a	NS1, RS1 and All - licence required for all countries except Canada	N/A	Yes
99515 (tests equipment)	NS1 - RS1 - AT1 licence required for all countries except Canada	9E515.a	NS1, RS1 **and** All - licence required for all countries except Canada	Yes	Yes

Item Classification 1	*Controls and Licence Requirements of Item MIN*	*Classification Associated Technology*	*Controls and Licence Requirements of Technology*	*Sta [1] Available Item*	*Sta [1] Available Technology*
9D515 a. (software for 9A515 .a, .b, .x, .y)	NS1 - RS1 - AT1 licence required for all countries except Canada	9E515.a	NS1, RS1 **and All** - licence required for all countries except Canada	Yes	Yes
9D515 b. (source code)	NS1 - RS1 - AT1 licence required for all countries except Canada	9E515.b	NS1, RS1 **and AT1 - licence** required for all countries except Canada	**No**	**No**
9D515 .d or .e (software for microcircuits)	NS1 - RS1 - AT1 licence required for all countries except Canada	9E515.d, .e	NS1, RS1 and All - licence required for all countries except Canada	**No**	**No**

[1] STA 740.20 cl (thirty-six countries only)

Remains under the ITAR

(1) Launchers and launch services provided by US launch providers remain ITAR controlled whatever the classification of the satellite USML (Cat IV).

(2) Satellites identified by their performance (and not by the end-use commercial, scientific, military, etc.):
- Radiation hardened (flash), ability to mitigate or detect nuclear detonations satellites.
- Remote sensing radar and optical satellites beyond a given performance.
- ELINT, SIGINT and other intelligence gathering satellites.
- Navigation satellites.
- Servicing, refuelling, human rated, propulsion other than to reach or maintain orbit.
- Weaponized.
- Ability to fly in formations, use with UAVs.
- Items that include classified information (including classified encryption).

(3) Certain Spacecraft parts and components identified by their functionality and performances such as:
- Large Antennas, optics, Focal Plane Arrays (FPA), Cryo-coolers, kinetic and directed energy systems, atomic clocks, GPS above certain

performance or with US military code, engines, gyroscopes and CMGs, certain MMICs, certain star-trackers, DoD payloads, re-entry, etc.

The classification of a Space item will follow the same 'order of review' than other military goods:

- Is the item positively listed in the USML? (Cat IV, Cat V or CAT XV or other category)?
- Is the item caught by a 'specially designed' clause of the USML? (note that there is no 'specially designed' catch-all clause in Cat XV).
- If not, the item is controlled under the EAR, either in a 600 series (9X604 for launchers), or a 500 series (9X515 for satellites)?
- If not, is released to an alternate control, either as not positively listed in a 500 or 600 ECCN or as a result of the EAR 'specially designed' analysis.

Note that prior to ECR, any microcircuit that had any radiation tolerance properties (even if those were only compatible with very short missions or required mitigating SEU and total dose such as shielding or gate-upset tolerant design), were captured as Cat XV(e) as 'specially designed for Space applications'

As a result of the reform, microcircuits are not positively listed under the USML (with the exception of circuits that would embed classified firmware or ASICs specially designed to provide functionalities described in the USML).

Integrated circuits are captured under 9A515.e or 9A515.d based on their radiation total dose and SEU tolerance.

If an Integrated circuit does not meet the criteria of 9A515.d and does not meet both the criteria of total dose (100 Krads) and SEU immunity (80 MeV-cm^2/mg) of 9A515.e, then it is released from 500 series, and will be controlled by an ECCN of lesser control (such as ECCN 3A001) or under EAR99.

It is customary in the Space industry to provide access to the customer / operator and its consultants to work in progress and to extended detailed technical information. If this entails US controlled information:

- Under the ITAR, the customer and its non-U.S. consultants will have to be parties or sub-licensees to Technical Assistance Agreement or consignees/ end-users on DSP-5.
- Under the EAR, the customer and its non US consultants will have to be authorized either through a transaction under exception STA (if applicable and limited to authorized countries (STA 36), or identified as 'end users' on a BIS licence.

If insurance is provided through a U.S. insurance broker, this U.S. insurance broker will have to obtain from DDTC or from BIS the authorization to share controlled information with the rest of the non-U.S. insurance community.

If there is no U.S. insurance broker (or this insurance broker is not willing to get an authorizations), then this authorization can be obtained by the satellite manufacturer or the satellite operator.

The retransfer of a non-U.S. manufactured satellite, which has no ITAR content and has less than *De Minimis* content of EAR content, will not be subject to the EAR, whether it is for its transfer to the launch site (except of D:5 countries, i.e., for launch from China) or for its transfer of title (again except for D:5 countries).

This has been a profound change in the US extraterritoriality controls of non-US commercial satellite and has significantly lessen the impact of this extraterritoriality on other Space faring nation, except China, including on such sensitive matters such as high resolution remote sensing.

SECTION 6 SANCTIONS AND EMBARGOES

The U.S. implements sanctions and embargoes of the International Organizations and Treaties that they participate in (in particular the UN) and also implement temporary or permanent embargoes or sanctions in support of specific US national security or policy interests.

The US also participates into several Multilateral export control regimes which limit the export of certain technologies to certain countries for identified end-use: The Wassenaar Agreement (WA), the NSG, the AG and the MTCR, as detailed in Section 3, Sub-section 4.

Sub-Section 1 Participation of U.S. to Embargoes or Other Related Sanctions

The US complies with all arms embargoes imposed by the UN Security Council, such as: Cote d'Ivoire, Democratic Republic of Congo, Eritrea, Iraq, Iran, Lebanon, Liberia, Libya, North Korea, Somalia, Republic of Sudan.

These sanctions are reflected in the ITAR (22 CFR 126.1) and in the EAR (Part 746)

Sub-Section 2 Regime of the Embargoes or Related Sanctions in the US

The US also implements its own embargoes and sanctions as deemed necessary for national security and policy reasons.

These embargoes and sanctions can take the form of complete embargoes or selective embargoes for certain countries, economic and targeted sanctions, or sanctions on selected categories of items to specific destinations.

Most of the sanctions will have both an economic implementation through OFAC and an export control implementation through DDTC and BIS with very similar criteria.

Under both the ITAR and the EAR, complete or partial embargo are imposed on countries which the Secretary of State has determined support act of International

Terrorism. These countries are Cuba, Iran, The Republic of Sudan and Syria. These countries are designated in the ITAR in 22 CFR 126.1(d) and in the EAR as Country Group E.

In April 2015, the President of the U.S. recommended to Congress to remove Cuba from the list of countries supporting International Terrorism, but as of December 2015, corresponding changes to the ITAR or EAR have yet to be made.

The ITAR[1315] and the EAR[1316] implement also US specific policies limiting the export of military goods. These policies may change as the geo-political situation evolves, such as:

- Afghanistan (export of military items limited to the Government and the coalition forces).
- Russian industry sectorial sanctions (oil and gas and military end-users).
- Iraq (special Iraq reconstruction provisions).
- Somalia (except in support of the African Union AMISOM).
- Vietnam (except for non-lethal).
- Sri Lanka (except for humanitarian demining).
- Cyprus (except for UN) and civilian end-users.
- Zimbabwe (firearms).
- Lebanon (except UNIFIL).
- Central African Republic (except for UN, and other peacekeeping forces).
- Sudan (South Sudan on a case-by-case basis).

The economic sanctions are implemented by OFAC and can be found at http://www.treasury.gov/resource-center/sanctions/Programs/Pages/Programs.aspx and are listed also in Section 9.

The DDTC country policies and sanctions can be found at http://www.pmddtc.state.gov/embargoed_countries/,

As these sanctions and policies vary, the web site of OFAC, DDTC and BIS should be consulted to determine the applicable rules.

SECTION 7 CONCLUSION

The objective of the US ECR was to implement more efficient controls providing 'higher walls around a smaller garden', strengthening the US industry; and facilitating trade with allies, while ensuring US national security and foreign policies.

While this reform is providing more predictable and clear rules, despite considerable efforts for simplification, the US export control laws and regulations remain an ambiguous and complex system, which captures and implements evolving and nuanced national security and foreign policies in an ever-changing environment.

1315. The DDTC country policies and sanctions can be found at http://www.pmddtc.state.gov/embargoed_countries/.

1316. EAR sanctions can be found in Part 746, Iraq reconstruction provisions in Part 747.

The US export control laws and regulations, under both the ITAR and the EAR, control Military, Space and Dual-Use US-origin technologies from cradle to grave with high compliance risks for both the US exporter and the non-US re-exporter and requires extended expertise to navigate.

SECTION 8 LIST OF ACRONYMS

ATS	Australian Treaty Series
AEC	Atomic Energy Commission
AECA	Arms Export Control Act
AG	Agreement or Australia Group
ATF	Alcohol, Tobacco, Firearms and Explosives, Department of Justice
BIS	Bureau of Industry and Security, Department of Commerce
CBP	Customs and Border Protection, Department of Homeland Security
CCATS	Commodity Classification Automated Tracking System (EAR)
CCL	Commerce Control List
CFR	Code of Federal Regulations
CIN	Company Identification Number (SNAP-R)
CJ	Commodity Jurisdiction
COCOM	Coordinating Committee for Multilateral Export Controls
CPI	Counter-Proliferation Investigations
DDTC	Directorate of Defense Trade Controls, Department of State
DTCC	Defense Trade Controls Compliance, DDTC, Department of State
DHS	Department of Homeland Security
DCIS	Defense Criminal Investigation Services
DN	Dual National
DoC	Department of Commerce
DoD	Department of Defense
DoE	Department of Energy
DoJ	Department of Justice
DoS	Department of State
DCS	Destination Control Statement (DCS is also used for Direct Commercial Sale)
DTSA	Defense Technology Security Administration
EAA	Export Administration Act
EAR	Export Administration Regulations
ECA	Export Control Act
ECCN	Export Control Classification Number
EECC	Export Enforcement Coordination Center
ECR	Export Control Reform
FBI	Federal Bureau of Investigation

FCPA	Foreign Corrupt Practice Act
FRN	Federal Register Notice
GBS	Group B Shipment (EAR Exception)
GC	General Correspondence
HSI	Homeland Security Investigation
ICE	Immigration and Customs Enforcement
IEEPA	International Emergency Economic Powers Act (EAR & OFAC)
IAEA	International Atomic Energy Agency
IT	Information Technology
ITAR	International Traffic in Arms Regulations
Krads	Kilo Rad (1000 Rad or 10 Gy)
LoE	Letter of Explanation
LVS	Limited Value Shipment (EAR Exception)
MLA	Manufacturing License Agreement
MT	Missile Technology
MTCR	Missile Technology Control Regime
NDAA	National Defense Authorization Act
NLR	No License Required
NPT	Nuclear Non-Proliferation Treaty
NRC	Nuclear Regulatory Commission
NSA	National Security Agency
NSG	Nuclear Suppliers Group
OEE	Office of Export Enforcement
OFAC	Office of Foreign Assets Controls, Department of Treasury
RPL	Servicing and Replacement (EAR Exception)
SDN	Specially Designated National
SME	Significant Military Equipment
SNAP-R	Simplified Network Application Process-Redesign (EAR)
STA	Strategic Trade Authorization (EAR Exception)
TAA	Technical Assistance Agreement
TCN	Third Country National
TMP	Temporary Imports, Exports and Re-exports (EAR Exception)
TSCP	Transatlantic Secure Collaboration Program
TWEA	Trading With the Enemy Act
UAS	Unmanned Aerial Systems
UAV	Unmanned Aerial Vehicles
UN	United Nations
US	United States of America
USAID	US Agency for International Development
USMIL	US Munitions Import List

USML	US Munitions List
VD	Voluntary Disclosure
VSD	Voluntary Self-Disclosure
WA	Wassenaar Agreement
WDA	Warehouse and Distribution Agreement
WMD	Weapons of Mass Destruction

SECTION 9 REFERENCES

Sub-Section 1 Primary Documentation

Par. 1 Statutory Legislation

These legislations provide authority for the President to promulgate regulations either through Executive Orders or by delegation to the Administration:

- EAA of 1979, and Administration of the EAA of 1969, as amended.
- IEEPA, as amended.
- Nuclear Non-Proliferation Act, 309(c).
- AECA as amended (22 USC 2778).

Due to the Strom Thurmond NDAA of 1999, Congress had to pass specific legislation to return to the President authority to determine the export control jurisdictional status of satellites and related items, and thus authorize the US ECR to progress.

Congress required assurances as follows:[1317]

- The NDAA for Fiscal Year 2010 (NDAA) mandated that DoS and DoD present a report to Congress to document that the transfer of Commercial Telecommunications satellites would not represent a risk to US national security. (1248 report)
- The NDAA for Fiscal Year 2011 (NDAA) mandated that DoD present a report to Congress to document the impact of the reform on the protection and monitoring of militarily critical technologies. (1237 report)
- The NDAA for Fiscal year 2013 (NDAA) further mandated that DoC to present a report to Congress demonstrating the implementation of the compliance and enforcement measures related to satellite technologies. (1263 report)

1317. These reports can be found at http://www.export.gov/ecr/eg_main_023180.asp.
The 1248 report in particular contains an expensive analysis on China Space-related goals, capabilities and methods for acquiring Space technologies.

Par. 2 Regulations

All regulations are available online and should be checked regularly to ensure up to date content.

See the US Government printing office at www.gpo.gov or *http://www.ecfr.gov/* or on the site of the implementing agencies.

- *Export Administration Regulations* (EAR), 15 CFR Parts 730-774.
- *International Traffic in Arms Regulations* (ITAR), 22 CFR Parts 120-130.
- *Burmese Sanctions Regulations*, 31 CFR Part 537.
- *Cuban Assets Control Regulations*, 31 CFR Part 515.
- *Foreign Assets Control Regulations* (FACR), 31 CFR Part 500.
- *Foreign Narcotics Kingpin Sanctions Regulations*, 31 CFR Part 598.
- *Foreign Terrorist Organizations Sanctions Regulations*, 31 CFR Part 597.
- *Global Terrorism Sanctions Regulations*, 31 CFR Part 594.
- *Highly Enriched Uranium Assets Control Regulations*, 31 CFR Part 540.
- *Iranian Assets Control Regulations*, 31 CFR Part 535.
- *Iranian Transactions Regulations*, 31 CFR Part 560.
- *Iraqi Sanctions Regulations*, 31 CFR Part 575.
- *Narcotics Trafficking Sanctions Regulations*, 31 CFR Part 536.
- *Rough Diamonds Control Regulations*, 31 CFR Part 592.
- *Sudanese Sanctions Regulations*, 31 CFR Part 538.
- *Syrian Sanctions Regulations*, 31 CFR Part 542.
- *Terrorism Sanctions Regulations*, 31 CFR Part 595.
- *Terrorism List Governments Sanctions Regulations*, 31 CFR Part 596.
- *Weapons of Mass Destruction Trade Control Regulations*, 31 CFR Part 539.
- *Western Balkans Stabilization Regulations*, 31 CFR Part 588.
- *Zimbabwe Sanctions Regulations*, 31 CFR Part 541.
- OFAC Sanctions:

Balkans-Related Sanctions	*7 February 2014*
Belarus Sanctions	*11 August 2011*
Burma Sanctions	*23 April 2015*
Central African Republic Sanctions	*7 July 2014*
Cote d'Ivoire (Ivory Coast)-Related Sanctions	*6 January 2011*
Counter Narcotics Trafficking Sanctions	*28 April 2015*
Counter Terrorism Sanctions	*28 April 2015*
Cuba Sanctions	*16 April 2015, updated 15 March 2016*
Cyber-related Sanctions	*1 April 2015*

Democratic Republic of the Congo-Related Sanctions	*8 July 2014*
Iran Sanctions	*3 April 2015 updated 16 January 2016*
Iraq-Related Sanctions	*27 May 2014*
Lebanon-Related Sanctions	*30 July 2010*
Former Liberian Regime of Charles Taylor Sanctions	*2 April 2013*
Libya Sanctions	*11 September 2014*
Magnitsky Sanctions	*29 December 2014*
Non-Proliferation Sanctions	*3 April 2015*
North Korea Sanctions	*2 January 2015*
Rough Diamond Trade Controls	*21 May 2008*
Somalia Sanctions	*5 July 2012*
Sudan Sanctions	*17 February 2015*
South Sudan-related Sanctions	*18 September 2014*
Syria Sanctions	*13 April 2015*
Transnational Criminal Organizations	*21 April 2015*
Ukraine-/Russia-Related Sanctions	*11 March 2015*
Venezuela-Related Sanctions	*9 March 2015*
Yemen-Related Sanctions	*14 April 2015*
Zimbabwe Sanctions	*10 July 2014*

Par. 3 Annexes – Copies of Documents of Practical Use to the Importer/Exporter

A number of standard documents relevant for the import or export process in China (e.g., most current official application forms for import or export licences, templates of contractual undertaking, or regulation extracts) as well as other non-official documents are available on a dedicated DropBox folder which can be accessed by following the link below: www.kluwerlawonline.com/eclrh-annexes.

Sub-Section 2 Secondary Documentation

The U.S., administration hosts on their web sites applicable laws, regulations, guidance and user tools which are listed below

Par. 1 Internet Sites

U.S. ECR Policies, publications, news, tools and decision trees, all about the ECR	http://export.gov/%5C/ecr/index.asp
BIS Regulations, licensing, policy guidance, training, decision trees, news	http://www.bis.doc.gov/
BIS SNAP-R Export and re-export applications	https://snapr.bis.doc.gov/snapr/
Directorate of Defense Trade Controls Regulations, laws and licensing guidance, licence application, registration, announcements	http://www.pmddtc.state.gov/index.html
Directorate of Defense Trade Controls DTRADE Electronic Licensing System, login, forms and status	http://pmddtc.state.gov/DTRADE/index.html
DoS ELISA DoS/Defense licence status	http://elisa.dtsa.mil/
DoC STELA DoC licence status	https://snapr.bis.doc.gov/stela/
Bureau of Alcohol, Tobacco, Firearms and Explosives Regulations, licensing and agency news	http://www.atf.gov/
DoS, Bureau of Political and Military Affairs Policies in International security, military assistance and defense trade	http://www.state.gov/t/pm/
DTSA DoD, DTSA, policies and news of the agency	http://www.dtsa.mil/
Defense Threat Reduction Agency DoD, Defense Threat Reduction Agency, policies and news of the agency with emphasis on managing prevention against WMD and Nuclear Threat	http://www.dtra.mil/
DoS U.S. Foreign affairs, policies, events, countries and regions analysis	http://www.state.gov/
DHS Homeland Security policies, regulations and news	http://www.dhs.gov/

U.S. ECR Policies, publications, news, tools and decision trees, all about the ECR	http://export.gov/%5C/ecr/index.asp
Export Control and Related Border Security Assistance Export Control border security, international cooperation	http://www.state.gov/strategictrade/
Homeland Investigation Services - ICE Through its custom enforcement role, ICE plays a major role in export violation investigations	http://www.ice.gov/
Customs and Border Protection (CBP)	http://www.cbp.gov/
MTCR	http://www.mtcr.info/
Society of International Affairs Association of Export Control Professionals, educating the international trade community on Export and import process, organizes conferences several times a year (basic and advanced), key vehicle of dialog between Government officials and industry on export control matters	http://www.siaed.org/
Department of the Treasury, OFACs	http://www.treasury.gov/about/organizational-structure/offices/Pages/Office-of-Foreign-Assets-Control.aspx
DoE, Nuclear Security Administration	http://www.nnsa.energy.gov/

SECTION 10 USEFUL INFORMATION

Sub-Section 1 Authorities Contact Details

Phone numbers are generally per person/department, and thus are not provided.

Name of Organization	*United States Department of State*
Postal address	2201 C Street NW, Washington DC 20520

Name of Organization	*United States Department of State, Directorate of Defense Trade Controls*
Postal address	2401 E Street NW, Washington DC 20522

Name of Organization	*United States Department of Commerce*
Postal address	1401 Constitution Avenue NW, Washington DC 20230

See also local offices throughout the US

Name of Organization	*United States Department of Defense, Defense Technology Security Administration*
Postal address	4800 Mark Center Drive, Alexandria VA 22350

Name of Organization	*United States Department of Defense, Navy International Programs (Navy/IPO)*
Postal address	Washington Navy Yard, 1250 10th Street SE, Washington DC 20374

Name of Organization	*United States Department of Defense, Air Force International Affairs (SAF/IAPD)*
Postal address	1080 Air Force Pentagon, Washington DC 20330

Name of Organization	*United States Department of Treasury, Office of Foreign Assets Control)*
Postal address	1500 Pennsylvania Avenue NW, Washington DC 20220

Name of Organization	*Bureau of Alcohol, Tobacco, Firearms and Explosives (ATF)*
Postal address	99 New York Avenue NE, Washington DC 20226

Name of Organization	*National Aeronautical and Space Administration (NASA)*
Postal address	300 E Street SW, Washington DC 20546

Sub-Section 2 Other Useful Information

All the forms referred in this chapter are available from the US government agencies, through their web sites:

DDTC – Department of State

Note that licence applications require the installation of specific viewer software which can be downloaded from the DDTC web site:

- Application/Licence for permanent export of unclassified Defense Articles and related technical data (Form DSP-5). See http://www.pmddtc.state.gov/DTRADE/index.html for forms and guidelines.
- Statement of Registration (Form DS-2032).

- Application/Licence for temporary import of unclassified Defense Articles (Form DSP-61). See http://www.pmddtc.state.gov/DTRADE/index.html for form and guidelines.
- Application/Licence for temporary export of unclassified Defense Articles (Form DSP-73). See http://www.pmddtc.state.gov/DTRADE/index.html for form and guidelines.
- Non-transfer and use certificate (Form DSP-83). See http://www.pmddtc.state.gov/licensing/forms.html for form and guidelines.
- Application/Licence for permanent/temporary export or temporary import of classified Defense Articles and related classified technical data (Form DSP-85). See http://www.pmddtc.state.gov/licensing/forms.html for form and guidelines.
- Authority to Export Defense Articles and Defense Services sold under the FMS programme (Form DSP-94). See http://www.pmddtc.state.gov/licensing/forms.html for form and guidelines.
- CJ Determination Form (Form DS-4076). See http://www.pmddtc.state.gov/commodity_jurisdiction/index.html for form and guidelines.

BIS – DoC, Bureau of Industry and Security

Under BIS, all export and re-export licences and CCATS are filed electronically under the SNAP-R system. Use of SNAP-R requires that the company obtains a CIN which can be obtained at no cost.

See http://www.bis.doc.gov/index.php/licensing for all information on how to obtain a CIN and export and re-export application guidance.

Guidelines and other useful information

DDTC, BIS and OFAC provide extensive guidelines, forms, regulation and tools on their web sites:

- DDTC: http://www.pmddtc.state.gov.
- BIS: http://www.bis.doc.gov.
- OFAC: http://www.treasury.gov/resource-center/sanctions/Pages/licensing.aspx.

Index

1. Emmanuel T. Laryea, *Paperless Trade: Opportunities, Challenges and Solutions*, 2002 (ISBN 90-411-9897-0).
2. Xiang Gao, *The Fraud Rule in the Law of Letters of Credit: A Comparative Study*, 2002 (ISBN 90-411-9898-9).
3. Yuwa Wei, *Comparative Corporate Governance: A Chinese Perspective*, 2003 (ISBN 90-411-9908-X).
4. Ross P. Buckley (ed.), *The WTO and the Doha Round: The Changing Face of World Trade*, 2003 (ISBN 90-411-9947-0).
5. Bradley J. Condon, Joyce C. Sadka & Tapen Sinha (eds), *Insurance Regulation in North America: Integrating American, Canadian and Mexican Markets*, 2003 (ISBN 90-411-2301-6).
6. Jan Hoogmartens, *EC Trade Law Following China's Accession to the WTO*, 2004 (ISBN 90-411-2301-6).
7. Yang Guohua, Bryan Mercurio & Li Yongjie, *WTO Dispute Settlement Understanding: A Detailed Interpretation*, 2005 (ISBN 90-411-2361-X).
8. Jan Job de Vries Robbé, Paul U. Ali, *Securitisation of Derivatives and Alternative Asset Classes, Yearbook*, 2005 (ISBN 90-411-2375-X).
9. Markus W. Gehring, Marie-Claire Cordonier Segger, *Sustainable Development in World Trade Law*, 2005 (ISBN 90-411-2366-0).
10. Yann Aubin & Arnaud Idiart, *Export Control Law and Regulations Handbook: A Practical Guide to Military and Dual-Use Goods Trade Restrictions and Compliance*, 2007 (ISBN 90-411-2601-5).
11. Henry Kibet Mutai, *Compliance with International Trade Obligations: The Common Market for Eastern and Southern Africa*, 2007 (ISBN 978-90-411-2664-1).
12. Yong-Shik Lee, *Economic Development through World Trade: A Developing World Perspective*, 2007 (ISBN 978-90-411-2681-8).
13. Yanning Yu, *Circumvention and Anti-Circumvention Measures: The Impact on Anti-Dumping Practice in International Trade*, 2007 (ISBN 978-90-411-2686-3).
14. Ross Buckley, Vai Io Lo & Laurence Boulle, *Challenges to Multilateral Trade: The Impact of Bilateral, Preferential and Regional Agreements*, 2008 (ISBN 978-90-411-2711-2).
15. K.D. Raju, *World Trade Organization Agreement on Anti-dumping: A GATT/ WTO and Indian Jurisprudence*, 2008 (ISBN 978-90-411-2780-8).
16. Xiaochen Wu, *Anti-dumping Law and Practice in China*, 2008 (ISBN 978-90-411-2790-7).
17. Amin Alavi, *Legalization of Development in the WTO: Between Law and Politics*, 2008 (ISBN 978-90-411-2795-2).
18. Henrik Andersen, *EU Dumping Determinations and WTO Law*, 2009 (ISBN 978-90-411-2827-0).

19. Sherzod Shadikhodjaev, *Retaliation in the WTO Dispute Settlement System*, 2009 (ISBN 978-90-411-2811-9).
20. Yi Shin Tang, *The International Trade Policy for Technology Transfers: Legal and Economic Dilemmas on Multilateralism versus Bilateralism*, 2009 (ISBN 978-90-411-2825-6).
21. Reem Anwar Ahmed Raslan, *Antidumping: A Developing Country Perspective*, 2009 (ISBN 978-90-411-3128-7).
22. Pietro Poretti, *The Regulation of Subsidies within the General Agreement on Trade in Services of the WTO: Problems and Prospects*, 2009 (ISBN 978-90-411-3162-1).
23. Esther Lam, *China and the WTO: A Long March towards the Rule of Law*, 2009 (ISBN 978-90-411-3144-7).
24. Jorge Alberto Huerta-Goldman, *Mexico in the WTO and NAFTA: Litigating International Trade Disputes*, 2009 (ISBN 978-90-411-3169-0).
25. Laurence Boulle, *The Law of Globalization: An Introduction*, 2009 (ISBN 978-90-411-2828-7).
26. Daniel Lovric, *Deference to the Legislature in WTO Challenges to Legislation*, 2010 (ISBN 978-90-411-3145-4).
27. Gregory W. Bowman, Nick Covelli, David A. Gantz & Ihn Ho Uhm, *Trade Remedies in North America*, 2010 (ISBN 978-90-411-2840-9).
28. Madalina Diaconu, *International Trade in Gambling Services*, 2010 (ISBN 978-90-411-3248-2).
29. Mohamed Ramadan Hassanien, *United States Bilateral Free Trade Agreements: Consistencies or Conflicts with Norms in the Middle East?*, 2010 (ISBN 978-90-411-3281-9).
30. Marie-Claire Cordonier Segger, Markus W Gehring & Andrew Newcombe, *Sustainable Development in World Investment Law*, 2011 (ISBN 978-90-411-3166-9).
31. Nellie Munin, *Legal Guide to GATS*, 2010 (ISBN 978-90-411-2824-9).
32. Thomas G. Kelch, *Globalization and Animal Law: Comparative Law, International Law and International Trade*, 2011 (ISBN 978-90-411-3338-0).
33. Yann Aubin & Arnaud Idiart (eds), *Export Control Law and Regulations Handbook: A Practical Guide to Military and Dual-Use Goods Trade Restrictions and Compliance*, Third Edition, 2016 ISBN (978-90-411-5443-9).
34. Yulia Selivanova (ed.), *Regulation of Energy in International Trade Law: WTO, NAFTA and Energy Charter*, 2011 (ISBN 978-90-411-3264-2).
35. Germano Franceschin & Francesco Misuraca, *India: Commercial Law, Customs and Taxation*, 2011 (ISBN 978-90-411-2836-2).
36. Humberto Zúñiga Schroder, *Harmonization, Equivalence and Mutual Recognition of Standards in WTO Law*, 2011 (ISBN 978-90-411-3657-2).

37. Kati Kulovesi, *The WTO Dispute Settlement System: Challenges of the Environment, Legitimacy and Fragmentation*, 2011 (ISBN 978-90-411-3406-6).
38. Martín Molinuevo, *Protecting Investment in Services: Investor-State Arbitration versus WTO Dispute Settlement*, 2012 (ISBN 978-90-411-3827-9).
39. Joachim Åhman, *Trade, Health, and the Burden of Proof in WTO Law*, 2012 (ISBN 978-90-411-3825-5).
40. Umair Hafeez Ghori, *Global Textiles and Clothing Trade: Trade Policy Perspectives*, 2012 (ISBN 978-90-411-3875-0).
41. Yenkong Ngangjoh Hodu, *Theories and Practices of Compliance with WTO Law*, 2012 (ISBN 978-90-411-3228-4).
42. Dan Wei & Fernando M. Furlan, *Brazil in World Trade: Contingent Protection Measures*, 2012 (ISBN 978-90-411-3335-9).
43. Jorge A. Huerta-Goldman, Antoine Romanetti & Franz X. Stirnimann (eds), *WTO Litigation, Investment Arbitration, and Commercial Arbitration*, 2013 (ISBN 978-90-411-4686-1).
44. Gilles Muller, *Liberalization of Trade in Legal Services*, 2013 (ISBN 978-90-411- 4853-7).
45. Christian Struck, *Product Regulations and Standards in WTO Law*, 2014 (ISBN 978-90-411-4950-3).
46. Gonzalo Villalta Puig, *Economic Relations between Australia and the European Union: Law and Policy*, 2014 (ISBN 978-90-411-3405-9).
47. Maurizio Gambardella, Davide Rovetta & Simon van Cutsem, *Remission and Repayment of Customs Duties in the EU*, 2014 (ISBN 978-90-411-4764-6).
48. Lisa Spagnolo, *CISG Exclusion and Legal Efficiency*, 2014 (ISBN 978-90-411-5407-1).
49. Dennis Ndonga, *Single Windows and Trade Facilitation: A Tool for Development*, 2015 (ISBN 978-90-411-5834-5).
50. Malebakeng Agnes Forere, *The Relationship of WTO Law and Regional Trade Agreements in Dispute Settlement: From Fragmentation to Coherence*, 2015 (ISNB 978-90-411-6274-8).